second edition

CoreMicroeconomics

Gerald W. Stone

Metropolitan State College, Denver

Worth Publishers

To Josephine and Sheila

Senior Publisher: Catherine Woods
Executive Editor: Charles Linsmeier
Development Editor: Bruce Kaplan
Media and Supplements Editor: Tom Acox
Executive Marketing Manager: Scott Guile
Associate Managing Editor: Tracey Kuehn
Project Editors: Vivien Weiss and TSI Graphics
Art Director: Babs Reingold
Senior Designer: Kevin Kall
Interior Designer: Lissi Sigillo
Photo Editor: Christine Buese
Photo Researcher: Deborah Anderson
Production Manager: Barbara Anne Seixas
Composition: TSI Graphics
Printing and Binding: RR Donnelley
Cover Photo Credits: Mike Kemp/Rubberball/Corbis

Library of Congress Cataloging in Publication Data: 2010940230

ISBN-13: 978-1-4292-4000-0
ISBN-10: 1-4292-4000-8

Printed in the United States of America

First printing 2011

Worth Publishers
41 Madison Avenue
New York, NY 10010
www.worthpublishers.com
www.wortheconomics.com

Gerald W. Stone was Emeritus Professor of Economics at Metropolitan State College of Denver. He taught principles of economics to over 10,0000 students throughout his career, and he also taught courses in labor economics and law and economics. He authored or coauthored over a half dozen books and numerous articles that have been published in economic journals, such as the *Southern Economic Journal* and the *Journal of Economics and Sociology.* He earned his Bachelor's and Master's degrees in economics at Arizona State University, his Ph.D. in economics at Rice University, and a J.D. in law at the University of Denver.

For many years I taught two classes that met only on Saturday for three hours each. Two problems arose. First, many of my students were business people who were more vocal than other students and were not afraid to voice any concerns they might have. Because I could effectively cover only maybe two-thirds of the standard principles of microeconomics text, these students continually complained that they were not getting full value with their textbooks. They thought their texts too expensive, too long, too encyclopedic, and they often resented paying for so much unused extra material. The *CoreMicroeconomics* text grew out of this experience.

Second, it soon became clear that students needed more feedback than what a once-a-week meeting could provide. I gave short quizzes on Saturday, analyzed each student's responses on Sunday, and sent each student a personalized set of study suggestions and additional exercises on Monday. The *CourseTutor* supplement evolved from this approach and is intended to help students who need something more than just a traditional study guide.

One thing more. My experience with my students at Metropolitan State College of Denver, who come from varied backgrounds in an urban setting, led me to produce a text that is interesting and usable for a broad group of instructors and students alike. My concern to give a broad range of students more help led me to produce a unique student supplement (*CourseTutor*) that is integrated with this text and that contains a wide variety of material, from tutorials and hints to practice problems and essay questions as well as standard assessment questions. Together, the *CoreMicroeconomics* textbook and *CourseTutor* supplement provide instructors and students with something that no one else provides.

What Does *Core* Mean?

CoreMicroeconomics is not an encyclopedic offering. It does not cover every topic, but is partly based on a survey of economics professors to determine what they actually covered in their courses. Two important points emerged from this survey:

- **One chapter per week.** Instructors typically cover one chapter per week, or 15 chapters in a 15-week semester.
- **The majority of instructors teach roughly the same two-thirds of a standard economics textbook**. The overwhelming majority of instructors covers the same chapters in their course and then spends minimal time covering additional chapters. Over 90% of professors cover roughly 15 chapters in their microeconomics or macroeconomics text, which typically includes 19–22 chapters.

In this sense, "core" does not mean brief or abridged. Rather, it means that the textbook contains the chapters that most instructors need with only a few additional chapters on special-interest topics.

The Core Text

Having a class meet only on Saturdays left my students more reliant on a text than usual. This text is written with these students in mind. I set out to provide a text that reduced student anxiety and made the material more accessible and interesting.

CoreMicroeconomics follows a traditional organization. Coverage is concise. Concepts are thoroughly explained and illustrated with contemporary examples and issues integrated into the text with the aim of enhancing the reading–learning experience. A conscious effort has been made to resist putting too much information—more than students need and unnecessarily detailed—to keep students honed in on the most important concepts. The goal has been to give students what is needed and no more.

A number of elements have been included to pique and sustain the interest of a broad range of students. Several of these are unique to this book.

By the Numbers

"By the Numbers" is a new feature of the second edition. It grew out of the fact that my students were bombarded with data and data graphs in the popular press and online, and they wanted some help dealing with them. The "By the Numbers" feature appears on the third page of select chapters and presents data, data graphs, and pictures focused around a theme, such as the possibility of creating a sustainable environment or how innovation, productivity, and costs rule business. The goal is to help students feel comfortable with data. The "By the Numbers" feature can be found in:

- Chapter 1: Economic Issues Are All Around Us (page 3)
- Chapter 2: Growth, Productivity, and Trade Are Key to Our Prosperity (page 27)
- Chapter 7: Innovation, Productivity, and Costs Rule Business (page 161)
- Chapter 13: The Environment and Sustainability (page 313)
- Chapter 15: International Trade (page 363)

Issues

The second edition contains a set of varied applications throughout, called Issues. Some are obviously related to economic theory, such as the value of brands. Other issues take the student further from normal pursuits, showing how economic theory can be applied in surprising ways. Here is a small sample of the issues that can be found in every chapter:

- In chapter 1 (page 8), the behavior of hummingbirds is looked at from the perspective of economic theory. Hummingbirds make good economists.
- In chapter 3 (page 49), census data from 1910 is used to show that supply and demand did matter in the marriage market in the old West.
- In chapter 5 (page 126), we look at Hubbert's Peak, the 1950s prediction by Marion King Hubbert that *U.S.* oil production would peak in the 1970s. This in fact happened. Hubbert's model predicts that *world* oil production will peak within the next decade. If true, what will happen? How will markets adjust?
- In chapter 11 (page 266), we examine the effects of cell phones, WiFi, and smart phones on the way we work and where we work.
- In chapter 13 (page 319), we look at Chilean sea bass and the tragedy of the commons.

End-of-Chapter Questions and Problems

The second edition has grouped the end-of-chapter questions and problems into four categories to help in student assessment of concept mastery. Check Your Understanding questions test understanding of basic concepts and definitions. Apply the Concepts check if students can apply chapter concepts. In the News questions take quotes on recent issues found in the popular press and ask students to analyze them, extending chapter concepts in unique ways. Finally, Solving Problems test analytical skills and often stretch student understanding.

History of Economics as a Discipline

The text incorporates the historical development of economics so students see how ideas and theories evolve with the times. Historical figures such as Adam Smith and Jeremy Bentham are highlighted in biographies and, in addition, the biographies of Nobel Prize winners are included when their contributions are of particular importance to the chapter.

Descriptive Art

Time series graphs can be visually boring so I have tried to make this book more visually appealing by including a photo or drawing with many of these graphs. Some of these can be whimsical. See, for example, union membership as a percentage of the employed workforce (page 301) and the figures on poverty rates (page 352). The photos and drawings help students see what is sitting behind the data.

What Is the *CourseTutor?*

As mentioned above, the *CourseTutor* evolved from the need to give my Saturday students more help than can be found in a traditional study guide.

Each chapter of the *CourseTutor* is divided into two basic sections: a six-step detailed walk through the material to help each student check his or her individual progress, followed by a section with standard study material such as fill-in, true/false, multiple-choice, and short essay questions. Both sections are designed for interactivity.

The first part of the *CourseTutor* is divided into six self-paced steps:

- **STEP ONE:** What You Need to Know
    - Lists the chapter objectives as they appear in the text.
- **STEP TWO:** Review the Key Terms
    - Outlines vocabulary words and definitions.
- **STEP THREE:** Work Through the Chapter Tutorials
    - This step includes solved problems, self quizzing, and a student-directed worked example that asks the student to draw graphs.
- **STEP FOUR** Consider These Hints, Tips, and Reminders
    - Studying tips
- **STEP FIVE** Do the Homework
    - Additional practice questions—the only section of the *CourseTutor* where students are not provided with the answers. Ideal for homework assignments.
- **STEP SIX** Use the ExamPrep to Get Ready for Exams
    - Boils down key concepts of the chapter to help students prepare for exams—a favorite for students.

The second part of the *CourseTutor* provides extensive questions and problems—standard study guide material—that students can use to test their mastery of concepts. Answers are provided for all questions and problems.

Students learn by many different methods. *CourseTutor* addresses this by providing a **buffet of learning choices**. Students select those methods that best help them learn. Students having problems with specific material can turn to that particular section in the *CourseTutor* for help. It is important to note that students are not expected to work through all of the material unless they absolutely need this level of additional help.

CourseTutor should save you time if students work through the tutorial before they come to see you; they should have fewer unfocused questions when they show up at your office for help. I believe you will find the *CourseTutor* a very worthwhile addition for your students.

Together, I think *CoreMicroeconomics* and *CourseTutor* provide something to you and your students that no one else in the market provides.

Outline of the Book

CoreMicroeconomics follows a traditional organizational sequence. Students are introduced to economics in the first five chapters that focus on the nature of economics, trade, markets, supply, demand, and elasticity. Chapters 1 and 2 provide a foundation for the study of economics along with a brief look at production and trade. Chapter 3 lays out supply, demand, and market equilibrium and details the efficiency of markets. Chapter 4 provides a balance to chapter 3 by introducing the requirements for efficient markets, what happens when markets fail and how they tend to fail, and what government can do, along with a brief economic history of the United States over the past 150 years. These two chapters give students a good grounding in the benefits of markets along with some of the caveats. Chapter 5 introduces elasticity with its ramifications for total revenue and tax policy.

Chapters 6 and 7 provide students with an understanding of what's behind supply and demand curves. Chapter 6 on consumer decision-making covers marginal utility analysis with an indifference curve appendix. Chapter 7 lays out production and cost analysis for both the short run and long run.

The next three chapters (8–10) take students through market structure analysis plus a discussion of antitrust issues and an expanded coverage of game theory. The ability to discern behavior from market structure data is a fundamental aspect of microeconomics and these three chapters cover that material in detail.

Chapters 11 and 12 discuss the theory and issues surrounding input markets, especially labor markets. Chapter 11 uses market structure analysis to examine input markets and chapter 12 goes into more detail on issues of human capital, economic discrimination, labor unions, and collective bargaining.

Market failures, public goods, and environmental economics are the issues in chapter 13, while poverty and income distribution are covered in Chapter 14. These two chapters provide the economic background to several of the most widely discussed issues in microeconomics today including poverty, growing income inequality, and global climate change.

The final chapter of the book is devoted to the international economy. Chapter 15 covers the classical issues of international trade including the gains from trade (the Ricardian perspective), the terms of trade, along with a discussion of the impacts of tariffs and quotas, and an expanded discussion and evaluation of the arguments against trade.

Supplements: *By* Educators, *For* Students.

A useful and seamless supplements package has been developed by instructors who actively teach the principles of economics course. Most of the supplements authors have taught for many years. The result: a supplements package crafted with instructors and students in mind.

For Instructors

Teaching Manual with Suggested Answers to Problems

The Teaching Manual prepared by Dr. Mary H. Lesser (Iona College) is an ideal resource for instructors trying to enliven their classroom lectures while teaching the CORE concepts. The Teaching Manual focuses on highlighting varied ways to bring real-world examples into the classroom by expanding on examples and real-world problem material within the text. Portions of the Teaching Manual have been designed for use as student handouts.

Every chapter of the Teaching Manual includes:

- *Chapter Overview:* A brief summary of the main topics covered in each chapter is provided.
- *Ideas for Capturing Your Classroom Audience:* Written with both the experienced and novice instructor in mind, this section provides ideas for introducing the chapter material. The suggestions provided can be used in a number of ways—they can be in-class demonstrations or enrichment assignments, and can be used in on-site, distance-learning, or hybrid course formats.
- *Chapter Check Points:* Each chapter of the text has Chapter Check Point sections that provide both bulleted review points and a question designed to assess whether students have mastered the main points of the section material. The TM provides the instructor with suggested answers to those questions, notations about points to emphasize, and suggestions about reinforcing the assessment of student learning.
- *Debate the Issues in the Chapter:* The TM reproduces the issues used in each chapter and provides a discussion of these examples. As with the Chapter Check Point material, teachers will find that these sections delineate points to emphasize and provide additional resources for spurring student debate.
- *Examples Used in the End-of-Chapter Questions:* A number of the end-of-chapter questions refer to specific articles in major newspapers or particular real-world examples. The TM provides the instructor with a succinct overview of those questions and cites additional resources that can be used to develop more in-depth analysis of the topics involved. Note that this is in addition to the sample answers that are also provided.
- *For Further Analysis:* Each TM chapter contains an additional extended example that can be used in a variety of ways. *Formatted as a one-page handout,* it can be duplicated and distributed in-class (or posted online), and is designed for use either as an in-class group exercise or as an individual assignment in both the on-site and on-line class format. Asking students to document research allows the instructor to use the example as a case study or group project as well. Learning objectives are specified and a one-page answer key is also available for reference or distribution.
- *Web-based Exercise:* Each TM chapter includes a Web-based example that requires students to obtain information from a web site and use it to answer a set of questions. This Web-based Exercise can be used in a variety of ways, as in-class group exercises or as individual assignments. Learning objectives are specified and suggested answers to questions are provided that can be used for reference or distribution.
- *Tips from a Colleague:* Each chapter of the TM concludes with a "tips" section which shares ideas about classroom presentation, use of other resources, and insights about topics that students typically find difficult to master.
- *New to this edition* are "Economics Is Everywhere" sections. These contain short synopses selected from the many vignettes in *Economics is Everywhere* by Daniel S. Hamermesh that correspond to the material covered in the chapter. The question that accompanies each vignette appears as an essay-type question in the Hamermesh book; for use with the Stone text those questions are adapted to a multiple-choice format and are assignable in EconPortal (see below for an explanation of Portal). The correct answers are indicated and feedback is provided.

Test Bank

Coordinator and Contributor: Richard Croxdale (Austin Community College). *Test bank contributors:* Emil Berendt (Siena Heights University), Dennis Debrecht (Carroll College), Fred W. May (Trident Technical College), Tina A. Carter (Flagler College and University of Phoenix), Thomas Rhoads (Towson University), TaMika Steward (Tarrant County College), and Michael Fenick (Broward College).

This Test Bank contains nearly 5,000 carefully constructed questions to help you assess your students' comprehension, interpretation, analysis, and synthesis skills. Questions have been checked for this continuity with the text content and reviewed extensively for accuracy.

The Test Bank features include the following:

- *New to this edition* are skill descriptors. To aid instructors in building tests, each question has been categorized according to their skill descriptor geared for economics and based upon Bloom's Taxonomy. The skill descriptor was designed in order to aid in the evaluation both of students' abilities to "think like an economist" and to apply knowledge to the real world desirable for accredited business programs.

- Each question has also been categorized according to their general *degree of difficulty*. The three levels are: easy, moderate, or difficult. *Easy* questions require students to recognize concepts and definitions. These are questions that can be answered by direct reference to the textbook. *Moderate* questions require some analysis on the student's part. These questions may require a student to distinguish between two or more related concepts, to apply a concept to a particular situation, or to use an economic model to determine an answer. *Difficult* questions will usually require more detailed analysis by the students.

- To further aid instructors in building tests, each question is referenced by the specific topic heading in the textbook. Questions are presented in the order in which concepts are presented in the text.

- Questions have been designed to correlate with the questions and problems within the text and *CourseTutor*. A beginning set of *Objectives Questions* are available within each chapter. These questions focus directly on the key concepts from the text that students should grasp after reading the chapter. These questions can easily be used for brief in-class quizzes.

- The test bank includes questions with tables that students must analyze to solve for numerical answers. It contains questions based on the graphs that appear in the book. These questions ask students to use the graphical models developed in the textbook and to interpret the information presented in the graph. Selected questions are paired with scenarios to reinforce comprehension.

Computerized Test Bank

Diploma was the first software for PCs that integrated a test-generation program with grade-book software and an on-line testing system. Diploma is now in its fifth generation. The printed Test Banks for *CoreMicroeconomics* are available in CD-ROM format for both Windows and Macintosh users.

With Diploma, you can easily create and print tests and write and edit questions. You can add an unlimited number of questions, scramble questions, and include figures. Tests can be printed in a wide range of formats. The software's unique synthesis of flexible word-processing and database features creates a program that is extremely intuitive and capable.

Instructor's Resource CD-ROM

Using the Instructor's Resource CD-ROM, instructors can easily build classroom presentations or enhance online courses. This CD-ROM contains two alternate sets of classroom presentation PowerPoints, all text figures (in JPEG and GIF formats), the Teaching Manual and detailed solutions to all End-of-the-Chapter Questions. You can choose from the various resources, edit, and save for use in your classroom.

Two Sets of PowerPoints

New to this edition is the **Dynamic PowerPoint Presention:** PowerPoint slides designed by Solina Lindahl (California Polytechnic State University) with front of the classroom presentation and visual learning experience in mind. This set of PowerPoints contains fully animated graphs, visual learning images, additional examples, links, and embedded questions suitable both for classroom discussion and assessment. These slides may be customized by instructors to suit individual needs. These files may be accessed on the instructor's side of the Web site or on the Instructor's Resource CD-ROM.

Lecture PowerPoint Presentation consist of PowerPoint slides designed by Debbie Evercloud (University of Colorado, Denver) that provide graphs from the textbook, data tables, and bulleted lists of key concepts suitable for lecture presentation. Key figures from the text are replicated and animated to demonstrate how they build. The *CheckPoints* from the text have been included to facilitate a quick review of key concepts. These slides may also be customized by instructors to suit individual needs. These files may be accessed on the instructor's side of the Web site or on the Instructor's Resource CD-ROM.

For Instructors and Students

Companion Web Site: bcs.worthpublishers.com/stonemicro2

The Companion site is a virtual study guide for students and an excellent resource for instructors. The tools on the site include:

Student Resources

- *Self-test Quizzes:* this quizzing engine provides a set of quiz questions per chapter with appropriate feedback and page references to the textbook. All student answers are saved in an online database that can be accessed by instructors.
- *Key Term Flashcards:* Students can test themselves on the key terms with these pop-up electronic flashcards.
- *Web Links:* Key Web sites, online data bases and online news articles selected and categorized by chapter to help students further access key concepts and principles.
- *Learning Objectives:* The Key concepts from each chapter listed out for easy access to students to evaluate whether they have grasped each objective after completing each chapter.

Instructor Resources

- *Quiz Gradebook:* The site gives you the ability to track students' work by accessing an online gradebook. Instructors have the option to have student results emailed directly to them.
- *Both Dynamic PowerPoint and Lecture Outline PowerPoint Presentations:* These two sets of PowerPoint slides are designed to assist instructors with lecture preparation and presentation by providing bulleted lecture outlines suitable for large lecture presentation. Instructors can customize these slides to suit their individual needs.
- *Textbook Illustrations:* A complete set of figures and tables from the textbook in JPEG and PowerPoint format.
- *Teaching Manual and Suggested Solutions to End-of-Chapter Questions:* The teaching manual and solutions are printed electronically for easy access.

EconPortal—*AVAILABLE FOR FALL 2011*

EconPortal is the digital gateway to *CoreMicroeconomics*, designed to enrich your course and improve your students' understanding of economics. EconPortal provides a powerful, easy-to-use, completely customizable teaching and learning management system complete with the following:

- *An Interactive eBook with Embedded Learning Resources:* The eBook's functionality will provide for highlighting, note-taking, graph and example enlargements, and a full text and glossary search. Embedded icons will link students directly to resources available to enhance their understanding of the key concepts.
- *A Personalized Study Plan for Students, Featuring Diagnostic Quizzing:* Students will be asked to take the PSP: Self-Assessment Quiz after they have read the chapter

and before they come to the lecture that discusses that chapter. Once they've taken the quiz, a personalized study plan (PSP) based on the quiz results is created for them. This PSP will provide a path to the appropriate eBook materials and resources for further study and exploration, helping students learn and retain the course material.

- *A Fully Integrated Learning Management System:* EconPortal is meant to be a fully customizable and highly interactive one-stop shop for all the resources tied to the book. The system will carefully integrate the teaching and learning resources for the book into an easy-to-use system. EconPortal will enable you to create assignments from a variety of question types to prepare self-graded homework, quizzes, or tests, saving many hours of preparation time.
- Instructors can assign and track any aspect of their students' EconPortal activities. The Gradebook will capture students' results and allow for easily exporting reports as well as importing grades from offline assignments.

This dynamic virtual homework and course management system enables students to gauge their comprehension of concepts and provides a variety of resources to help boost their performance within the course. This is an alternative to the pen and paper version of the *CourseTutor*. Instead, students can work through the *CourseTutor* content and additional resources online. In this online format, students can follow their own pace and complete any or all steps of the *CourseTutor*. All of this is possible with or without instructor involvement.

EconPortal includes the following *CourseTutor* **Interactive Resources**:

- *Solved Problems:* problems designed for this online environment using a graphing and assessment engine. Students may be asked to draw, interpret, or interact with a graph to provide an answer. Students will receive detailed feedback and guidance on where to go for further review.
- *Core Graphs:* animated versions of these key graphs *with assignable questions.*
- *Core Equations:* animated versions of the key equations *with assignable questions.*

STUDENTS: What can they do with the EconPortal?

- Test mastery of important concepts from the text.
- Access *The Economist* news feed within EconPortal.
- Improve understanding of difficult topics by working with interactive tutorials, graphing questions, flashcards, as well as the assets that make up the printed *CourseTutor*.
- Take notes on any of the resources.
- Browse by chapter or search by topic if they need quick information about a specific concept.

INSTRUCTORS: What can you do with the EconPortal?

- Interact with your students as little or as much as you like! You can assign the exercises as out-of-class activities, or allow your students to work independently.
- If you so desire, monitor your students' progress within the EconPortal using a sophisticated online gradebook.
- Export grades to your current Course Management System.

Additional Online Offerings

Aplia—Integrated Textbook Solution

Aplia is the leading homework management solution in principles of economics. Worth was the first publisher to partner with Aplia in 2004 and continues to offer full Aplia integration for all of our principles of economics texts.

aplia.com/worth

Our premium Aplia solution includes:

- **Full eBook integration**. The Stone Aplia course includes a full eBook.
- **Homework sets correlated to the text.** Online homework is easy to assign, and it grades automatically. The course gradebook quickly puts results at your fingertips.
- **Algorithmic problem sets**. All homework problem sets offer Grade It Now. Students can attempt any problem set up to three times with variables that randomize on each attempt.
- **Multiple purchase options.** Aplia access can be packaged with any version of the text, or purchased separately online as a less expensive alternative to the book because it includes an eBook. Students who purchase on-line access can also buy a physical textbook directly from Aplia at a significant discount.

Visit www.aplia.com/worth for demos and information on Worth Aplia. Contact your campus rep or support@aplia.com for access to a course for your class.

Blackboard and WebCT

The Stone WebCT & Blackboard e-Packs enable you to create a thorough, interactive, and pedagogically sound online course or course Web site. The e-Packs, provided free, give you cutting-edge online materials that facilitate critical thinking and learning, including Test Bank content, preprogrammed quizzes, links, activities, animated graphs, and a whole array of other materials. Best of all, this material is pre-programmed and fully functional in the WebCT or Blackboard environment. Pre-built materials eliminate hours of course-preparation work and offer significant support as you develop your online course. The result: an interactive, comprehensive online course that allow for effortless implementation, management, and use. The files can be easily downloaded from our Course Management System site directly onto your department server.

Further Resources Offered

i>clicker

Developed by a team of University of Illinois physicists, i>clicker is the most flexible and most reliable classroom response system available. It is the only solution created *for* educators, *by* educators—with continuous product improvements made through direct classroom testing and faculty feedback. You'll love i>clicker no matter your level of technical expertise, because the focus is on *your* teaching, *not the technology*. To learn more about packaging i>clicker with this textbook, please contact your local sales rep or visit www.iclicker.com.

Financial Times Edition

For adopters of the Stone textbook, Worth Publishers and the *Financial Times* are offering a 15-week subscription to students at a tremendous savings. Instructors also receive their own free *Financial Times* subscription for one year. Students and instructors may access research and archived information at www.ft.com.

Dismal Scientist

A high-powered business database and analysis service comes to the classroom! Dismal Scientist offers real-time monitoring of the global economy, produced locally by economists and professionals at Economy.com's London, Sydney, and West Chester offices. Dismal Scientist is *free* when packaged with the Stone textbook. Please contact your local sales rep for more information or go to www.economy.com.

The Economist

The Economist has partnered with Worth Publishers to create an exclusive offer that will enhance the classroom experience. Faculty receive a complimentary 15-week subscription when 10 or more students purchase a subscription. Students get 15 issues of *The Economist* at a huge savings. Inside and outside the classroom, *The Economist* provides a global perspective that helps students keep abreast of what's going on in the world, and gives insight into how the world views the United States. *The Economist* ignites dialogue, encourages debate, and enables readers to form well-reasoned opinions—while providing a deeper understanding of key political, social, and business issues. Supplement your textbook with the knowledge and insight that only *The Economist* can provide. To get 15 issues of *The Economist,* go to www.economistacademic.com/worth.

Acknowledgements

No project of this scope is accomplished alone. Many people have helped make this package a better resource for students, and I sincerely appreciate their efforts. These include reviewers of blocks of manuscript chapters, focus group participants, reviewers of the *CourseTutor* chapters, accuracy reviewers, and the production and editorial staff of Worth Publishing.

First, I want to thank those reviewers of the second edition who read through chapters in manuscript and offered many important suggestions that have been incorporated into this project. They include:

Innocentus Alhamis, Southern New Hampshire University

Scott Beaulier, Mercer University

Margot Biery, Tarrant County College, South Campus

Andrea Borchard, Hillsborough Community College

Stacey Brook, University of Iowa

Gary Campbell, Michigan Technological University

Kevin Coyne, Southern New Hampshire University

Michael Fenick, Broward College

Aaron Finkle, California State University, San Marcos

Michael Forney, Austin Community College

Adam Gifford, Lake-Sumter Community College

Jane Himarios, University of Texas at Arlington

Janis Y. F. Kea, West Valley College

Delores Linton, Tarrant County College

Fred May, Trident Technical College

Jaishankar Raman, Valparaiso University

Tom Rhoads, Towson University

Richard Rouch, Volunteer State Community College

Peter Schwarz, University of North Carolina, Charlotte

Lea Templer, College of the Canyons

Wesseh Wollo, Lincoln University

Reviewers of the first edition manuscript gave many useful suggestions. They include:

Dwight Adamson, South Dakota State University

Norman Aitken, University of Massachusetts, Amherst

Fatma Wahdan Antar, Manchester Community College

Anoop Bhargava, Finger Lakes Community College

Craig Blek, Imperial Valley College

Mike W. Cohick, Collin County Community College

Kathleen Davis, College of Lake County

Dennis Debrecht, Carroll College

Christopher Erickson, New Mexico State University

Shaikh M.Ghanzanfar, University of Idaho

Lowell Glenn, Utah Valley State College

Jack Hou, California State University, Long Beach

Charles Kroncke, College of Mt. St. Joseph

Laura Maghoney, Solano Community College

Pete Mavrokordatos, Tarrant County College

Philip Mayer, Three Rivers Community College

John McCollough, Penn State University, Lehigh

Pat Mizak, Canisius College

Jay Morris, Champlain College

Jennifer Offenberg, Loyola Marymount University

Joan Osborne, Palo Alto College

Diana Petersdorf, University of Wisconsin, Stout

Oscar Plaza, South Texas Community College

Mary Pranzo, California State University, Fresno

Mike Ryan, Gainesville State College

Supriya Sarnikar, Westfield State College

Lee Van Scyoc, University of Wisconsin, Oshkosh

Paul Seidenstat, Temple University

Ismail Shariff, University of Wisconsin, Green Bay

Garvin Smith, Daytona Beach Community College

Gokce Soydemir, University of Texas, Pan America

Martha Stuffler, Irvine Valley College

Ngoc-Bich Tran, San Jacinto College

Alan Trethewey, Cuyahoga Community College

Chad Turner, Nicholls College

Va Nee L. Van Vleck, California State University, Fresno

Dale Warnke, College of Lake County

Second, I would like to take this opportunity to thank those focus group participants who devoted a lot of time and effort to discussing the elements of this project before it was published in its first edition. Their thoughts and suggestions (and criticisms) contributed immensely to the development of this project. They include:

Emil Berendt, Friends University

Harmanna Bloemen, Houston Community College, Northeast

Mike Cohick, Collin County Community College

Rohini Divecha, San Jacinto College, South

Bob Francis, Shoreline Community College

John Kane, State University of New York, Oswego

Sukanya Kemp, University of Akron

Charlene Kinsey, Houston Community College, Northwest

Delores Linton, Tarrant Community College, Northwest

Fred May, Trident Tech

Saul Mekies, Kirkwood Community College

Diego Mendez-Carbajo, Illinois Wesleyan

Cyril Morong, San Antonio College

Oscar Plaza, South Texas Community College

Michael Polcen, Northern Virginia Community College

Jaishankar Raman, Valparaiso University

Belinda Roman, Palo Alto College

Greg Rose, Sacramento City College

Ted Scheinman, Mt. Hood Community College

Marianna Sidoryanskaya, Austin Community College, Cypress

Lea Templer, College of the Canyons

Bich Tran, San Jacinto College, South

Don Weimer, Milwaukee Area Technical College, Downtown

Third, my thanks go out to those who took the time to review single chapters of the first edition text and the *CourseTutor* together, and to those who class-tested single chapters. Thanks for the reviews and the suggestions. These reviewers included:

Shawn Abbott, College of the Siskiyous

Roger Adkins, Marshall University

Richard Agesa, Marshall University

Ali Akarca, University of Illinois—Chicago

Frank Albritton, Seminole Community College

Anca Alecsandru, Louisiana State University

Innocentus Alhamis, Southern New Hampshire University

Basil Al-Hashimi, Mesa Community College

Samuel Andoh, Southern Connecticut State University

William Ashley, Florida Community College at Jacksonville

Rose-Marie Avin, University of Wisconsin—Eau Claire

Sukhwinder Bagi, Bloomsburg University

Dean Baim, Pepperdine University

Joanne Bangs, College of St. Catherine

Abby Barker, University of Missouri—St. Louis

Perry Barrett, Chattahoochee Technical College

David Bartram, East Georgia College

Robert Beekman, University of Tampa

Emil Berendt, Siena Heights University

Gerald Bialka, University of North Florida

Paul Biederman, New York University

Richard Bieker, Delaware State University

Tom Birch, University of New Hampshire—Manchester

John Bockino, Suffolk Community College

Orn Bodvarsson, St. Cloud State University

Antonio Bos, Tusculum College

Laurette Brady, Norwich University

Bill Burrows, Lane Community College

Rob Burrus, University of North Carolina—Wilmington

Tim Burson, Queens University of Charlotte

Dean Calamaras, Hudson Valley Community College

Charles Callahan, State University of New York—Brockport

Colleen Callahan, American University

Dave Cauble, Western Nebraska Community College

Henrique Cezar, Johnson State College

Matthew Chambers, Towson University

Lisa Citron, Cascadia Community College

Ray Cohn, Illinois State University

Kevin Coyne, Southern New Hampshire University

Tom Creahan, Morehead State University

Richard Croxdale, Austin Community College

Rosa Lea Danielson, College of DuPage

Amlan Datta, Cisco Junior College

Helen Davis, Jefferson Community & Technical College

Susan Davis, Buffalo State College

Dennis Debrecht, Carroll College

Robert Derrell, Manhattanville College

Julia Derrick, Brevard Community College

Jeffrey Dorfman, University of Georgia

Justin Dubas, St. Norbert College

Harold Elder, University of Alabama

G. Rod Erfani, Transylvania University

William Feipel, Illinois Central College

Rick Fenner, Utica College

James Ford, San Joaquin Delta College

Marc Fox, Brooklyn College

Lawrence Fu, Illinois College

Mark Funk, University of Arkansas, Little Rock

Mary Gade, Oklahoma State University

Khusrav Gaibulloev, University of Texas—Dallas

Gary Galles, Pepperdine University

Lara Gardner, Florida Atlantic University

Kelly George, Florida Community College at Jacksonville

Lisa George, Hunter College

J. P. Gilbert, Mira Costa College

Chris Gingrich, Eastern Mennonite University

James Giordano, Villanova University

Susan Glanz, St. John's University

Devra Golbe, Hunter College

Michael Goode, Central Piedmont Community College

Gene Gotwalt, Sweet Briar College

Glenn Graham, State University of New York—Oswego

David Gribbin, East Georgia College

Phil Grossman, St. Cloud State University

Marie Guest, North Florida Community College

J. Guo, Pace University

N. E. Hampton, St. Cloud State University

Deborah Hanson, University of Great Falls

Virden Harrison, Modesto Junior College

Fuad Hasanov, Oakland University

Scott Hegerty, University of Wisconsin—Milwaukee

Debra Hepler, Seton Hill College

Jim Henderson, Baylor University

Jeffrey Higgins, Sierra College

Jannett Highfill, Bradley University

Harold Hotelling, Lawrence Technological University

Wanda Hudson, Alabama Southern Community College

Terence Hunady, Bowling Green University

Mitchell Inman II, Savannah Technical College

Anisul Islam, University of Houston—Downtown

Eric Jamelske, University of Wisconsin—Eau Claire

Russell Janis, University of Massachusetts, Amherst

Andres Jauregui, Columbus State University

Jonathan Jelen, The City College of New York

George Jouganatos, California State University—Sacramento

David Kalist, Shippensburg University

Jonathan Kaplan, California State University—Sacramento

Nicholas Karatjas, Indiana University of Pennsylvania

Janis Kea, West Valley College

Deborah Kelly, Palomar College

Kathy Kemper, University of Texas—Arlington

Brian Kench, University of Tampa

Mariam Khawar, Elmira College

Young Jun Kim, Henderson State University

T. C. Kinnaman, Bucknell University

Paul Koch, Olivet Nazarene College

Andy Kohen, James Madison University

Lea Kosnik, University of Missouri—St. Louis

Charles Kroncke, College of Mount Saint Joseph

Craig Laker, Tri-State University

Carsten Lange, California Polytechnic State University—Pomona

Gary Langer, Roosevelt University

Leonard Lardaro, University of Rhode Island

Daniel Lawson, Drew University

Bill Lee, St. Mary's College

Mary Jane Lenon, Providence College

Mary Lesser, Iona College

Bozena Leven, The College of New Jersey

Ralph Lim, Sacred Heart University

Anthony Liuzzo, Wilkes University

Jennifer Logan, Southern Arkansas University

Dening Lohez, Pace University

Ellen Magenheim, Swarthmore College

Y. Lal Mahajan, Monmouth University

Mary Ellen Mallia, Siena College

Don Mathews, Coastal Georgia Community College

Phil Mayer, Three Rivers Community College

Norman Maynard, University of Oklahoma

Kimberly Mencken, Baylor University

John Messier, University of Maine, Farmington

Randy Methenitis, Richland College

Charles Meyer, Cerritos College

David Mitchell, Missouri State University

Ilir Miteza, University of Michigan—Dearborn

Jay Morris, Champlain College

Charles Myrick, Dyersburg State Community College

Natalie Nazarenko, State University of New York—Fredonia

Tim Nischan, Kentucky Christian University

Tom Odegaard, Baylor University

Jennifer Offenberg, Loyola Marymount University

Jack Peeples, Washtenaw Community College

Don Peppard, Connecticut College

Elizabeth Perry, Randolph-Macon Women's College

Dean Peterson, Seattle University

John Pharr, Cedar Valley College

Chris Phillips, Somerset Community College

Mary Pranzo, California State University—Fresno

Joseph Radding, Folsom Lake College

Jaishankar Raman, Valparaiso University

Donald Richards, Indiana State University

Bill Ridley, University of Oklahoma

William Rieber, Butler University

Dave Ring, State University of New York—Oneonta

Paul Robillard, Bristol Community College

Denise Robson, University of Wisconsin—Oshkosh

Rose Rubin, University of Memphis

Chris Ruebeck, Lafayette University

Randy Russell, Yavapai College

Marty Sabo, Community College of Denver

Hedayeh Samavati, Indiana University-Purdue University—Fort Wayne

Julia Sampson, Malone College

Paul Schoofs, Ripon College

Peter Schwarz, University of North Carolina—Charlotte

Paul Seidenstat, Temple University

T. M. Sell, Highline Community College

Chad Settle, University of Tulsa

Bill Seyfried, Rollins College

Maurice Shalishali, Columbus State

R. Calvin Shipley, Henderson State University

William Simeone, Providence College

Geok Simpson, University of Texas—Pan American

Noel Smith, Palm Beach Community College

Phil Smith, Georgia Perimeter College, Lawrenceville

Dennis Spector, Naugatuck Valley Community College

Todd Steen, Hope College

Richard Stratton, University of Akron

Stuart Strother, Azusa Pacific University

Martha Stuffler, Irvine Valley College

Boo Chun Su, Santa Monica Community College

Della Lee Sue, Marist College

Abdulhamid Sukar, Cameron University

Thomas Swanke, Chadron State College

Thomas Sweeney, Des Moines Area Community College

Michael Tansey, Rockhurst University

Henry Terrell, University of Maryland

Thomas Tiemann, Elon College

Dosse Toulaboe, Fort Hays State University

Christine Trees, State University of New York—Cobbleskill

Andrew Tucker, Tallahassee Community College

David Tufte, Southern Utah University

Jennifer VanGilder, Ursinus College

Yoav Wachsman, Coastal Carolina University

Craig Walker, Oklahoma Baptist University

Elizabeth Wark, Springfield College

Jonathan Warner, Dordt College

Roger White, Franklin & Marshall College

Jim Wollscheid, Texas A&M University—Kingsville

John Yarber, NE Mississippi Community College

Haichun Ye, University of Oklahoma

Anne York, Meredith College

Nazma Zaman, Providence College

Madeline Zavodny, Agnes Scott College

Fourth, I owe a special debt and want to give a special thanks to Eric Chiang of Florida Atlantic University and Greg Rose of Sacramento City College for their tireless examination of the page proofs to ensure accuracy. Together, they caught errors that none of us want to see. Thanks again!

Fifth, a huge debt of gratitude is owed to Tom Acox and the supplements authors. Tom coordinated the development of the supplements and our online presence. He did a remarkable job and was able to get some great people to author the supplements. They include Mary H. Lesser from Iona College who authored the Teaching Manual. Among other things, she did a wonderful job of adding real-world examples designed for use as student handouts. My thanks to Richard Croxdale from Austin Community College who coordinated the development of the Test Bank along with creating questions. Emil Berendt (Siena Heights University), Dennis Debrecht (Carroll College), Fred W. May (Trident Technical College), Tina A. Carter (Flagler College and University of Phoenix), Thomas Rhoads (Towson University), TaMika Steward (Tarrant County College), and Michael Fenick (Broward College) all contributed questions. Thanks to all of you for creating a Test Bank with nearly 5,000 questions.

Sixth, the production team at Worth is outstanding. My thanks to the entire team including Kevin Kall, Senior Designer, for a great set of interior and cover designs; Babs Reingold, the Art Director; Tracey Kuehn, Associate Managing Editor, Vivien Weiss, Project Editor, Susie Bothwell, Project Supervisor, and Barbara Anne Seixas, the Project Manager—all who made sure each part of the production process went smoothly. Thanks for a job well done.

I want to thank Charles Linsmeier, executive editor of economics, for his help and guidance. Thanks to Paul Shensa for his support and ideas on editorial changes and marketing; he is a valuable resource for any author. There is no way that I can thank Bruce Kaplan enough for what he has meant to this project and me. He has kept me focused and has suggested so many good ideas that I could fill several pages with his contributions. Thanks Bruce, you are the best!

You couldn't ask for a better marketing manager than Scott Guile. His enthusiasm is infectious and I appreciate the huge effort he has put into this project. Steven Rigolosi created an extensive pre-launch marketing review program that was very helpful at an important juncture of the text's development. Also I want to thank Tom Kling for helping sales reps see many of the benefits of this project. He is an incredible personality and I appreciate his efforts.

Finally, I am grateful to my wife, Sheila, for putting up with the forgone vacations given the demands a project like this requires. I hope it lives up to her expectations.

Gerald W. Stone

Memorial

Worth Publishers regrets to inform you that Jerry Stone passed away after a difficult battle with cancer at the end of August 2010, as *Core Microeconomics* and its accompanying *CourseTutor* were finishing up in the production process. Jerry Stone had a remarkable career as a long-time teacher at Metropolitan State College of Denver and as an author of two successful principles of

economics textbooks. Those who knew Jerry will miss his steadfast commitment to the teaching of economics, a legacy that lives on in each new edition of *Core Microeconomics*.

Jerry Stone long-believed that the best principles of economics textbooks are authored by people invested in their students' classroom experience. The decisions made in the shaping of the second edition were educated by Jerry's thirty-plus years in the classroom and by the team of instructors that contributed to every aspect of the media and supplements package. The second edition is Jerry's accomplishment: a book envisioned, designed, and executed to be the principles of economics book that teaches better than any other textbook on the market.

A Look Ahead

In the months preceding his passing, Jerry was very conscious of ensuring a successful future for *CoreMicroeconomics* at Worth. Earlier this year, Jerry and the economics team at Worth worked to find the perfect candidate to lead *CoreMicroeconomics* in its subsequent editions. We found that person in Eric Chiang, associate professor of economics at Florida Atlantic University. Eric is a young, dynamic teacher, and a 2009 recipient of FAU's highest teach-

ing honor, the Distinguished Teacher of the Year. He also received the Stewart Distinguished Professorship awarded by the College of Business, and has been a recipient of numerous other teaching awards. Eric embodies Jerry's belief that *CoreMicroeconomics* should be a book written "by educators, for students." Eric is currently contributing two online chapters to the second edition—one on health care economics and another on the economics of network goods and services. He is also the lead academic on EconPortal, available with *CoreMicroeconomics*, 2e, and he will assume all authorial responsibilities on the third edition of the textbook.

Brief Contents

Contents

Production, Economic Growth, and Trade

2

Supply and Demand

3

Market Efficiency, Market Failure, and Government

4

Elasticity

5

Consumer Choice and Demand

6

7

Production and Cost

Competition   8

Monopoly   9

Monopolistic Competition, Oligopoly, and Game Theory

10

Theory of Input Markets   11

Labor Market Issues   12

Public Goods, Externalities, and Environmental Economics   13

Poverty and Income Distribution   14

International Trade

15

Exploring Economics

Jack Hollingsworth/Getty Images

Ideas are important. They change civilizations. Most of the world in the last half-century has renewed its interest in economic ideas. The two most recent U.S. presidential administrations (Bush and Obama) and the Federal Reserve have turned to ideas from the 1930s to provide policy guidance for the 2008–2009 financial crisis and subsequent recession. In 1936, British economist John Maynard Keynes created the field of macroeconomic analysis—analysis of the broad economy—and suggested the solution to the Great Depression. He argued that increased government spending and lower taxes were needed to replace falling consumer spending and declining business investment. Additional government spending was necessary to return the economy to its long-run trend of economic growth.

Why are governments so preoccupied with economic growth? Our level of economic growth today largely determines the standards of living for our children, and their children, and then their children.

How important is economic growth, really? To put this in perspective, let's conduct the following experiment. Today, our real gross domestic product (GDP; it represents all the goods and services produced annually) is roughly $15 trillion (that's a 15 with 12 zeros—a very big number). The United States has the largest economy in the world, with the European Union a close second. To see the importance of economic growth rates on our standard of living, let's assume that from 1930 to today our growth rate was just *1 percentage point less* every year. So, for example, if our economy grew at a 7% rate between 1953 and 1954, we will assume that it really only grew at a 6% rate.

Simply subtracting 1 percentage point from our growth rate every year over the last 80 years *would cut in half the size of our economy today.* Since we have removed the effects of inflation from our estimates, this small adjustment in economic growth rates each year would give us real (adjusted for inflation) aggregate income of roughly $7 trillion today—not the $15 trillion we actually have.

While real GDP for the total economy is not a perfect measure of our standard of living, real GDP per capita, a better measure, would also roughly be cut in half. So, toss out half your stuff and move to an apartment half the size you are in today. Note that we have *ignored* a bunch of complementary impacts like reduced education, as well as reduced research and development, that are closely associated with lower incomes. These impacts probably would have reduced these numbers and our standard of living even further. If we were to conduct this little experiment going back to the beginning of the century rather than from 1930, we would likely have the standard of living of Mexico today.

This calculation shows that economic growth makes the world a better place to live. This example leads to an obvious question: What causes economic growth? Why have some countries leaped ahead, while others have made little progress at all?

Economist John Kay[1] examined 19 highly productive countries with the highest living standards in the world. He found that they were distinguished from the other countries in the world by numerous complex relationships. Highly productive countries have the following characteristics:

- Most are democracies.
- Most have high environmental standards.
- Most have cool climates.
- Most enjoy freedom of expression.
- Women's rights and freedoms are better protected.
- Most enjoy better health.
- Population is taller.
- Government is less corrupt.
- Income inequality is lower.
- Inflation is lower.
- Population is more literate.
- Most have fewer restrictions on trade (more open).
- Population growth is lower.
- Property rights are more secure.

John Kay noted that "correlation does not imply causation." Some of these characteristics follow from a nation being more productive and rich; some, like literacy and health, help promote productivity. These are clearly complex relationships. As Jared Diamond[2] has argued, development in Europe and the United States benefited from immense luck with the weather and the types of flora and fauna native to those regions. Without all three, he argued, we would probably not have seen the high level of economic growth that has transpired.

This is why the structure of the society and the economy are so important, and why politicians and governments focus so much of their attention on economic issues. Economies do not develop overnight; it can take 50 years or more to produce modern living standards. For many countries of the world, even beginning today with the right economic programs and policies might mean it would not be until the end of this century before their living standards reach our standards of today. And by that time, much of the world will have moved on.

---

[1] John Kay, *The Truth About Markets: Their Genius, Their Limits, Their Follies* (London: Allen Lane), 2003, pp. 27–31. The highly productive countries are United States, Singapore, Switzerland, Norway, Canada, Denmark, Belgium, Japan, Austria, France, Hong Kong, Netherlands, Germany, United Kingdom, Finland, Italy, Australia, Sweden, and Ireland.

[2] Jared Diamond, *Guns, Germs, and Steel: The Fates of Human Societies* (New York: Norton), 1999.

By the *Numbers*

Economic Issues Are All Around Us

So much of what we do and the issues we face ultimately involve economics.

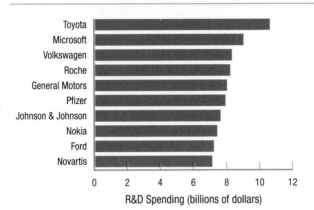

New products come from research and development (R&D)
and carmakers and drug and technology firms spend the most on
R&D. Half of the top 310 companies based on R&D spending are
in the United States.

25%	403,000
Percent of all U.S. companies in the last decade founded by immigrants.	Estimate of the number of ATM machines in the United States

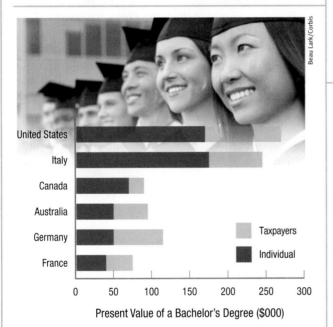

A college degree in the United States is worth over $250,000 on the
day you graduate. This takes into account the added funds you get
and what taxpayers receive in the form of higher tax payments over
your working life. Graduates in other countries do not fare as well.

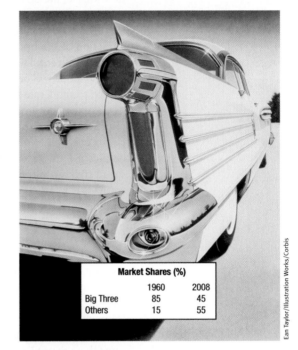

Market Shares (%)		
	1960	2008
Big Three	85	45
Others	15	55

The market share of America's Big Three automakers—
General Motors, Ford, and Chrysler—have fallen consistently and
dramatically since 1960. Asian automakers have gained substantial
ground, and Toyota now is the leading seller in America.

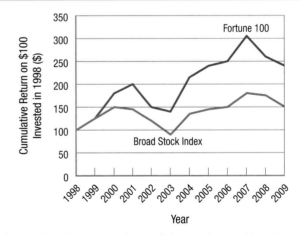

Companies that are good to work for are also good investments. Fortune magazine's top 100 firms to work for saw higher
returns than a broad stock market index of all firms on the Nasdaq,
New York Stock Exchange, and the American Stock Exchange.

Sources: Research and development spending: *The Economist*, 11-20-2009. Automobile market shares: *The Economist*, 4-30-2009. Companies founded by immigrants: *The Economist*, 3-13-2009. ATM machines: Business Week, 9-2009. Value of a college degree: *The Economist*, 9-8-2009. Companies that are good to work for: *The Economist*, 2-17-2009.

Today, many are concerned about outsourcing, globalization, and international trade. Look at this from an undeveloped country's point of view. These things can help them rise from abject poverty to attain modern living standards. After all, the United States was once underdeveloped, and trade with richer nations like France and Britain helped us develop.

Modern technologies and improvements in computing, transportation, and communications all are accelerating the development process. For example, cellular phone infrastructure is so much cheaper to install than the landline technology of the past. This has meant that developing nations can now get a state-of-the-art communications network at a fraction of the price that the United States paid to string telephone wires and lay cables over the last century. Future communications will undoubtedly be wireless, so many developing nations will be up to speed in a decade. We will see early in this book what countries can do to accelerate their economic growth.

This is the broad picture. Living standards are important, and economic growth improves living standards. Certain programs and policies can foster economic growth. So far, so good. But you are probably asking: What is in it for me? Why should I study economics if I am never going to be an economist? Probably the best reason is that you will spend roughly the next 40 years working in an economic environment. You will have a job; you will pay taxes; you will see the overall economy go from recession to a growth spurt and then maybe stagnate; you will have money to invest; and you will have to vote on economic issues affecting your locality, your region, and your country. It will benefit you to know how the economy works, what to expect in the future, and how to correct the economy's flaws.

But more than that—much more, in fact—economic analysis gives you a structure from which you can make decisions in a more rational manner. This course may well change the way you look at the world. It can open your eyes to how you make everyday decisions from what to buy to whom to marry. It may even make you reconsider your major.

Notice that we have just talked about economic analysis as a way of analyzing decisions that are not "economic" in the general sense of the term. This is the benefit of learning economic analysis. It can be applied all over the map. Sure, learning economic thinking may change your views on spending and saving, on how you feel about government deficits and public debt, and on your opinion of globalization and international trade. You may also reflect differently on environmental policies and what unions do. But you also may develop a different perspective on how much time to study each of your courses this term, or how much to eat at an all-you-can-eat buffet. Such is the broad scope of economic analysis.

In this introductory chapter, we look at what economics is about. We take a brief look at a key method of economic analysis: model building. Economists use stylized facts and the technique of holding some variables constant to develop testable theories about how consumers, businesses, and governments act. Second, we turn to a short discussion of some key principles of economics to give you a sense of the guiding concepts you will meet throughout this book.

The purpose of this introductory chapter is just that: an introduction. It seeks to give you a sense of what economics is, what concepts it uses, and what it finds to be important. Do not go into this chapter thinking you have to memorize these concepts. You will be given many opportunities to understand and use these concepts throughout this course. Rather, use this chapter to get a sense of the broad scope of economics. Then return to this chapter at the end of the course and see if everything has now become crystal clear.

What Is Economics About?

Economics is a very broad subject, and often it seems that economics has something important to say about almost everything.

For example, economics has some important things to say about crime and punishment. On first glance, you might think we are talking about the cost of a prison system when we apply economic analysis here. But if we categorize economics as a way of thinking about how people make rational decisions, we can broaden the discussion. Economics considers criminals and potential criminals as rational people who follow their incentives. Criminals are concerned with getting caught and being punished: That is their cost. Longer prison sentences potentially raise the cost of committing a crime. Possibly more important than longer prison sentences is the probability of being convicted for an offense: A long sentence is not an effective deterrent if it is rarely used. This is why wounding or killing police officers is prosecuted aggressively and publicized: Potential criminals know they will pay a high cost if a police officer is harmed. Thus, economics looks at all of those factors that raise the cost of crime to criminals. Economics is a way of thinking about an issue, not just a discipline that has money as its chief focus.

Economists tend to have a rational take on nearly everything. Now all of this "analysis/speculation" may bring only limited insight in some cases, but it gives you some idea of how economists think. We look for rational responses to incentives. We begin most questions by considering how rational people would respond to the incentives that specific situations provide. Sometimes (maybe even often) this analysis leads us down an unexpected path.

Microeconomics Versus Macroeconomics

Economics is split into two broad categories: microeconomics and macroeconomics. **Microeconomics** deals with decision making by individuals, business firms, industries, and governments. It is concerned with issues such as which orange juice you should buy, which job to take, and where to go on vacation; which products a business should produce and what price it should charge; and whether a market should be left on its own or be regulated.

Microeconomics: The decision making by individuals, businesses, industries, and governments.

We will see that markets—from flea markets to real estate markets to international currency markets—are usually efficient and promote competition. This is good for society. The opposite of competitive markets—monopoly, where one firm controls the market—leads to high prices, and it is bad for society. There is also a vast middle area between the extremes of competition and monopoly, and we will spend some time on those.

Microeconomics extends to such things as labor markets and environmental policy. Labor market analysis looks at both the supply (how much we as individuals are willing to work and at what wage) and demand (how much business is willing to hire and at what wage) of labor to determine market salaries. Designing policies to mitigate environmental damage uses the tools of microeconomics.

Macroeconomics, on the other hand, focuses on the broader issues we face as a nation. Most of us don't care whether an individual buys Nike or Merrell shoes. We *do* care whether prices of *all* goods and services rise. Inflation—a general increase in prices economy-wide—affects all of us. And as we have already seen, economic growth is a macroeconomic issue that affects everyone.

Macroeconomics: The broader issues in the economy such as inflation, unemployment, and national output of goods and services.

Macroeconomics uses microeconomic tools to answer some questions, but its main focus is on the broad aggregate variables of the economy. Macroeconomics has its own terms and topics: business cycles, recession, depression, unemployment, and job creation rates. Macroeconomics looks at policies that increase economic growth, the impact of government spending and taxation, the effect of monetary policy on the economy, and inflation. It also looks closely at theories of international trade and international finance. All of these topics have broad impacts on our economy and our standard of living.

Economics is a social science that uses many facts and figures to develop and express ideas. After all, economists try to explain the behavior of the economy and its participants. This inevitably involves facts and numbers. For macroeconomics, this means getting used to talking and thinking in huge numbers: billions (9 zeros) and trillions (12 zeros). Today we are talking about a federal government budget approaching $4 trillion. To wrap your mind around such a huge number, consider how long it would take to spend a trillion dollars if you spent a dollar every second, or $86,400 per day. To spend $1 trillion would require over 31,000 years. And the federal government now spends nearly 4 times that much in one year.

Although we break economics into microeconomics and macroeconomics, there is considerable overlap in the analysis. We use simple supply and demand analysis to understand both individual markets and the general economy as a whole. You will find yourself using concepts from microeconomics to understand fluctuations in the macroeconomy.

Economic Theories and Reality

If you are like me, the first thing you do when you buy a book is flip through the pages to see what's inside. If the number of charts and graphs in this book, along with the limited number of equations, started to freak you out, relax. All of the charts and graphs become relatively easy to understand since they all basically read the same way. The few equations in this book stem from elementary algebra. Once you get through one equation, the rest are similar.

Graphs, charts, and equations are often the simplest and most efficient ways to express data and ideas. Simple equations are used to express relationships between two variables. Complex and wordy discussions can often be reduced to a simple graph or figure. These are efficient techniques for expressing economic ideas.

Model Building

As you study economics this semester or quarter, you will encounter stylized approaches to a number of issues. By *stylized*, we mean that economists boil down facts to their basic relevant elements and use assumptions to develop a stylized (simple) model to analyze the issue. While there are always situations that lie outside these models, they are the exception. Economists generalize about economic behavior and reach generally applicable results.

We begin with relatively simple models, then gradually build in more difficult issues. For example, in the next chapter we introduce one of the simplest models in economics, the production possibilities frontier that illustrates the limits of economic activity. This simple model has profound implications for the issue of economic growth. We can add in more dimensions and make the model more complex, but often this complexity does not provide any greater insight than the simple model.

Ceteris Paribus: All Else Held Constant

Ceteris paribus: Assumption used in economics (and other disciplines as well), where other relevant factors or variables are held constant.

To aid in our model building, economists use the **ceteris paribus** assumption: "Holding all other things equal" means we will hold some important variables constant. For example, to determine how many songs you might be willing to download from iTunes in any given month, we would hold your monthly income constant. We then would change song prices to see the impact on the number purchased (again holding your monthly income constant).

Though model building can lead to surprising insights into how economic actors and economies behave, it is not the end of the story. Economic insights lead to economic theories, but these theories must then be tested. We will see many instances where economic predictions turned out to be false. One of the major errors was the classical notion that economy-wide contractions would be of short duration. The Great Depression that lasted a decade turned this notion on its head. New models were then developed to explain what had happened. So it may be best to think of model building as a *process* of understanding economic actors and the general economy: Models are created and then tested; if they fail to explain reality, new models are constructed. Some models have met the test of time. Others have had to be corrected or discarded. Progress, however, has been made.

Efficiency Versus Equity

Efficiency: How well resources are used and allocated. Do people get the goods and services they want at the lowest possible resource cost? This is the chief focus of efficiency.

Efficiency deals with how well resources are used and allocated. No one likes waste. Much of economic analysis is directed toward ensuring that the most efficient outcomes result from public policy. *Production efficiency* occurs when goods are produced at the lowest possible cost, and *allocative efficiency* occurs when individuals who desire a product the most (as measured by their willingness to pay) get those goods and services. It would not make sense for society to allocate to me a large amount of cranberry sauce—I would not eat the stuff. Efficient policies are generally good policies.

The other side of the coin is **equity,** or fairness. Is it fair that the CEOs of large companies make hundreds of times more money than rank-and-file workers? Many think not. Is it fair that some have so much and others have so little? Again, many think not. There are many divergent views about fairness until we get to extreme cases. When just a few people earn nearly all of the income and control nearly all of a society's wealth, most people agree that this is unfair.

Throughout this course you will see instances where efficiency and equity collide. You may agree that a specific policy is efficient, but think it is unfair to some group of people. This will be especially evident when you consider tax policy and its impact on income distribution. Fairness or equity is a subjective concept, and each of us has different ideas about what is just and fair. Economists generally stay out of discussions about fairness, leaving that issue to philosophers and politicians. When it comes to public policy issues, economics will help you see the tradeoffs between equity and efficiency, but you will ultimately have to make up your own mind about the wisdom of the policy given these tradeoffs.

Equity: The fairness of various issues and policies.

■ CHECKPOINT

WHAT IS ECONOMICS ABOUT?

- Economics is separated into two broad categories: microeconomics and macroeconomics.

- *Microeconomics* deals with individuals, firms, and industries and how they make decisions.

- *Macroeconomics* focuses on broader economic issues such as inflation, employment and unemployment, and economic growth.

- Economics uses a stylized approach, creating simple models that hold all other relevant factors constant (*ceteris paribus*).

- Economists and policymakers often face a tradeoff between efficiency and equity. Economists have much to say about efficiency.

QUESTION: In each of the following situations, determine whether it is a microeconomic or macroeconomic issue.

1. Hewlett-Packard announces that it is lowering the price of printers by 15%.

2. The president proposes a tax cut.

3. You decide to look for a new job.

4. The economy is in a recession, and the job market is bad.

5. The Federal Reserve announces that it is raising interest rates because it fears inflation.

6. You get a nice raise.

7. Average wages grew by 2% last year.

Answers to the Checkpoint questions can be found at the end of this chapter.

Key Ideas of Economics

Economics has a set of key principles that show up continually in economic analysis. Some are more restricted to specific issues, but most apply universally. As mentioned earlier, these principles should give you a sense of what you will learn in this course. Do not try to memorize these principles at this juncture. Rather, read through them now, and return to them later in the course to assess your progress. By the end of this course, these key principles should be crystal clear.

Choice and Scarcity Force Tradeoffs

Wouldn't it be grand if we all had the resources of Bill Gates or if nanotechnology developed to the point where any product could be made with sand and thus was virtually costless? But we don't, and it hasn't, so back to reality.

We all have limited resources. Some of us are more limited than others, but each of us has time limitations: There are only 24 hours in a day, and some of that must be spent in sleep. Our wants are always greater than our resources. Therefore, we face **scarcity.**

The fact that we have limited resources (scarcity) means that we must make tradeoffs in nearly everything we do. In fact, *economics is often defined as the study of the allocation of scarce resources to competing wants.* We have to decide between alternatives.

Such decisions as which car to buy, which school to attend (this may be constrained by factors other than money), and whether to study or party all involve tradeoffs. We cannot do everything we would like if for no other reason than our time on earth is limited.

Scarcity: Our unlimited wants clash with limited resources, leading to scarcity. Everyone faces scarcity (rich and poor) because, at a minimum, our time is limited on earth. Economics focuses on the allocation of scarce resources to satisfy unlimited wants.

Opportunity Costs Dominate Our Lives

Economics is often categorized as the discipline that always weighs benefits against costs. This is straightforward enough. What makes this task harder is that if we undertake to do one activity, some other highly valued activity must be given up, a special concept economists use called **opportunity costs.** For example, when you wait hours in line to buy a concert ticket and then attend the concert, your total costs are your time in line *plus* the price of the ticket *plus* your time at the concert. That time and money could have been spent on another highly valued activity. Economists refer to these total costs (hours in line plus ticket price plus time at concert) as opportunity costs.

We have limited resources. College students have limited budgets. Say we can purchase that new music CD we want or have ice cream for a week, but not both. Ice cream for a week is the opportunity cost of purchasing that music CD.

Every activity we do involves opportunity costs. Sleeping, eating, studying, partying, running, hiking, and so on, all require that we spend resources that could be used in another activity. This other activity represents the opportunity costs of the current activity chosen. Opportunity costs apply to us as individuals and to societies as a whole. The next chapter focuses on this issue in detail.

Opportunity costs: The next best alternative; what you give up to do something or purchase something. For example, to watch a movie at a theater, there is not just the monetary cost of the tickets and refreshments, but the time involved in watching the movie. You could have been doing something else (knitting, golfing, hiking, or studying economics).

Issue: Do Hummingbirds Make Good Economists?

Black-chinned hummingbirds found in the Sonoran desert of Arizona are models of economy when it comes to battling for territory and resources. Nectar feeders on flowers of the saguaro cactus, they defend a feeding territory against other hummingbirds by vocalizations and aerial combat against intruders. But as John Alcock has noted, "No knee-jerk aggressiveness for them; they want a payoff, and they somehow know when fighting is counterproductive."

Studies by researchers have shown that these hummingbirds are extremely sensitive to the cost and benefits of defending a nectar territory. They will fiercely defend a rich source and significantly reduce their efforts for a less ideal territory. Even juveniles who would normally be at a disadvantage against adults will be sufficiently aggressive to successfully defend a nectar-rich territory.

The birds use vocalization (chatter) to both defend and signal to others their willingness to defend their territories, and they conduct aerial duels with their dagger-like bills. Defending nectar-rich territories involves noisier and longer aerial combat than in less favorable territory. According to Alcock, "hummingbirds chat-

Arthur Morris/Corbis

ter and squeak in their hot-blooded struggle, fashioning an aerial ballet based on cold-blooded economics."

Source: John Alcock, *Sonoran Desert Summer* (Tucson: The University of Arizona Press), 1990.

Rational Behavior Requires Thinking at the Margin

Have you ever noticed that when you eat at an all-you-can-eat buffet, you always go away fuller than when you order and eat at a normal restaurant? Is this phenomenon unique to you, or is there something more fundamental? Remember, economists look at facts to find incentives to economic behavior.

In this case, people are just rationally responding to the price of *additional* food. They are thinking at the margin. In a restaurant, dessert costs extra, and you make a decision as to whether the dessert is worth the extra cost. At the buffet, dessert is free. So now you don't have to ask yourself if dessert is worth the extra money since it costs nothing. Where you might be nearly full and decline dessert in a restaurant, you will often have dessert in the buffet even if you are stuffed afterwards.

Throughout this book, we will see examples of thinking at the margin. Businesses use marginal analysis to determine how much of their products they are willing to supply to the market. People use marginal analysis to determine how many hours to work. And governments use marginal analysis to determine how much pollution should be permitted.

People Follow Incentives

Tax policy rests on the idea that people follow their incentives. Do we want to encourage people to save for their retirement? Then let them deduct a certain amount that they can put in an individual retirement account (IRA), and let this money compound tax free. Do we want businesses to spend more to stimulate the economy? Then give them tax credits for new investment. Do we want people to go to college? Then give them tax advantages for setting up education savings accounts when their children are young, and provide tuition tax credits.

Tax policy is an obvious example in which people follow incentives. But this principle can be seen in action wherever you look. Want to encourage people to use commuter trains during non-rush-hour times? Provide an off-peak discount. Want to spread out the dining time at restaurants? Give Early-Bird Special discounts for those willing to consider a 5:00 P.M. dinner time slot rather than the more popular 8:00 P.M. slot. Want to fill up airplanes during the slow travel days of Tuesday and Wednesday? Offer price discounts or additional frequent flyer miles for flying on those days.

Note that in saying that people follow incentives, economists do not claim that everyone follows each incentive at every time. You may not want to eat dinner at 4:30 P.M. But there might be a sufficient number of people who are willing to accept an earlier time slot in return for a cheaper meal.

If not properly constructed, incentives may not work to our economy's advantage. In the recent financial crisis, it became clear that the incentives for executives and traders set by Wall Street investment banks were perverse. Traders and executives were paid bonuses based on short-term (annual) profits. This encouraged them to take extreme risks to generate quick profits and high bonuses with little regard for the long-term viability of the bank. The bank may be gone tomorrow, but these people still have those huge (often seven-figure) bonuses.

Markets Are Efficient

Private markets and the incentives they provide are the best mechanisms known today for providing products and services. There is no government food board that makes sure that bread, cereal, coffee, and all the other food products you demand are on your plate during the day. The vast majority of products we consume are privately provided, assuming, of course, that we have the money to pay for them.

Markets bring buyers and sellers together. Competition for the consumer dollar forces firms to provide products at the lowest possible price, or some other firm will undercut their high price. New products enter the market and old products die out. Such is the dynamic characteristic of markets. Starbucks has made latte drinkers of us all, whereas just a short time ago, few of us could even spell the word.

What drives and disciplines markets? Prices and profits are the keys. Profits drive entrepreneurs to provide new products (think of pharmaceutical firms or Apple) or existing products at lower prices (think of Wal-Mart). When prices and profits get too high in any market, new firms jump in with lower prices to grab away customers. This competition, or sometimes even the threat of competition, keeps markets from exploiting consumers.

Government Must Deal With Market Failure

As efficient as markets usually are, there are some classes of products and services that markets fail to provide efficiently. Where consumers have no choice but to buy from one firm (local utility, telephone, or cable companies), the market will fail to provide the best solution, and government regulation is often used to protect consumers. Another example is pollution: Left on their own, companies will pollute the air and water—we will see why later in this book. Governments then intervene to deal with this market failure.

Information Is Important

Markets are efficient because people tend to make rational choices. To help make these choices, people rely on information. Each of us has to decide when we have enough information: Complete information may not be possible to obtain, and too much information can be debilitating. Some decisions require little information: What brand of table salt should you buy? Other decisions require more information: What type of automobile should you buy? Information is valuable.

Strange things happen to markets when one side of a transaction has a consistently superior information advantage. Martha Stewart was convicted of lying about selling stock based on inside information. The top officials of a business know much more quickly than anyone else if their company is developing business problems. These problems might lead to a fall in the price of the company's stock. If the officials act on this inside information while it is still secret, they can sell their stock before the price dips. This information gives them an unfair advantage over the other stockholders or people who may want to own the stock. This is why there are laws preventing insiders from taking undue advantage of their privileged position.

Markets work best when both sides of a transaction can weigh carefully the costs and benefits of goods and services. Superior information can provide significant advantages. We will see what markets can do to correct for information problems, and what government can do when the market cannot provide an acceptable solution.

Specialization and Trade Improve Our Lives

Trading with other countries leads to better products for consumers at lower prices. David Ricardo laid out the rationale for international trade almost two centuries ago, and it still holds true today. We will expand on this in the next chapter.

As you will learn, economies grow by producing those products where they have an advantage over other countries. This is why few of us grow our own food, sew our own clothes, make our own furniture, or write the books we read. We do those things we do best and let others do the same. In nearly all instances, they are able to do it cheaper than we can. The next time you come back from a shopping trip, look closely to discover where every product was made. More than likely, over half will have come from another country.

Productivity Determines Our Standard of Living

You can see the computer age everywhere but in the productivity statistics.

ROBERT SOLOW

If you want jobs for jobs' sake, trade in bulldozers for shovels. If that doesn't create enough jobs, replace shovels with spoons. Heresy! But there will always be more work to do than people to work. So instead of counting jobs, we should make every job count.

ROBERT McTEER, JR.[3]

---

[3] Past president of the Federal Reserve Bank of Dallas.

Adam Smith (1723–1790)

When Adam Smith was a four year-old boy, he was kidnapped by gypsies and held for ransom. Had the gypsies not taken fright and returned the boy unharmed, the history of economics might well have turned out differently.

Born in Kirkaldy, Scotland in 1723, Smith graduated from the University of Glasgow at age 17 and was awarded a scholarship to Oxford—time he considered to be largely wasted. As he so succinctly put it, "professors have, for these many years, given up altogether even the pretense of teaching". Returning to Scotland in 1751, Smith was named Professor of Moral Philosophy at the University of Glasgow. His health from an early age was never good. He suffered from a "shaking in the head", was notoriously absent-minded, had an unusual walk (wavy, worm-like). Rising early, he began his daily lectures at 7:30am and these lectures were well liked and well attended.

After twelve years at Glasgow, Smith, who never married, began tutoring the son of a wealthy Scottish nobleman. This job provided him with a life-long income, as well as the opportunity to spend several years touring the European continent with his young charge. In Paris, Smith met some of the leading French economists of the day, which helped stoke his own interest in political economy. While

there, he wrote a friend, "I have begun to write a book in order to pass the time."

Returning to Kirkaldy in 1766, Smith spent the next decade finishing *An Inquiry Into the Nature and Causes of the Wealth of Nations*. Before publication in 1776, he read sections of the text to Benjamin Franklin. Smith's genius was in taking the disparate forms of economic analysis his contemporaries were then developing and putting them together in systematic and comprehensive fashion, thereby making sense of the national economy as a whole. Smith further demonstrated numerous ways in which individuals left free to pursue their own economic interests end up acting in ways that enhance the welfare of all. This is Smith's famous "invisible hand." In Smith's words: "By directing that industry in such a manner as its produce may be of the greatest value, he intends only his own gain, and he is in this, as in many other cases, led by an invisible hand to promote an end which was no part of his intention."

How important was Adam Smith? He has been called the "father of political economy", but that is inadequate. As Wilhelm Roscher has argued, ". . . the whole of political economy might be divided into two parts—before and since Adam Smith; the first part being a prelude and the second a sequel (in the way either of continuation or opposition to him)."

Sources: Howard Marshall, *The Great Economists: A History of Economic Thought*, (New York: Pitman Publishing Corporation), 1967; Paul Strathern, *A brief History of Economic Genius*, (New York: Texere), 2002; Ian Ross, *The Life of Adam Smith*, (Oxford: Clarendon Press), 1995.

Imagine you need to hire someone in your own business (you've finished college and you are now an entrepreneur). You have narrowed the field down to two candidates who are equal in all respects except two. One person can do twice as much as the other (assume you can accurately measure these things), and this same person wants a salary that is 50% higher. Other than that they are equal. Whom should you hire?

The answer is obvious in this situation, because the more productive person is actually the best buy since she produces twice as much as the other candidate, but only wants half again as much pay. In this case, you would be willing to pay even more to get this person. Productivity and pay go together. Highly paid movie stars get high pay because they are worth it to the movie producer. The same is true of professional athletes, corporate executives, rocket scientists, and heart surgeons.

The same is true for nations. Those countries with the highest average per capita income are also the most productive. Their labor forces are highly skilled, and firms are willing to place huge amounts of capital with these workforces because this results in immense productivity. In turn, these workers earn high wages. So, high productivity growth results in solid economic growth, high wages and income, and large investments in education and research. All of this leads to higher standards of living.

Government Can Smooth the Fluctuations in the Overall Economy

All of us have heard of recessions and depressions. These terms refer to downturns in the general economy. The general movement of the economy from good times to bad and back again is called the business cycle.

Early economists viewed the overall economy as a self-correcting mechanism that would quickly adjust to disturbances in the business cycle if only it was left to itself. Along came the Great Depression of the 1930s, which showed that the overall economy could get stuck in a downturn. The solution was government intervention. Just as government can intervene successfully in individual markets when market failure occurs, so too can government intervene successfully when the overall economy gets stuck in a downturn. You can observe this principle at work when you hear discussions of using increased government spending or a tax cut to pull an economy out of a recession.

The intricacies of what government can do to smooth out the business cycle are a major part of your study of macroeconomics. Remember, saying the government *can* successfully intervene does not mean it *always* successfully intervenes. The macroeconomy is not a simple machine. Successful policymaking is a tough task.

You will learn more about these important ideas as the semester progresses. For now, realize that economics rests on the foundation of a limited number of important concepts.

■ CHECKPOINT

KEY IDEAS OF ECONOMICS

- Choice and scarcity force tradeoffs.
- Opportunity costs dominate our lives.
- Rational behavior requires thinking at the margin.
- People follow incentives.
- Markets are efficient.
- Government must deal with market failure.
- Information is important.
- Specialization and trade improve our lives.
- Productivity determines our standard of living.
- Government can smooth the fluctuations in the overall economy.

QUESTION: McDonald's introduced a premium blend of coffee that sells for more than its standard coffee. How does this represent thinking at the margin?

Answers to the Checkpoint question can be found at the end of this chapter.

Key Concepts

Microeconomics, p. 5
Macroeconomics, p. 5
Ceteris paribus, p. 6
Efficiency, p. 6

Equity, p. 7
Scarcity, p. 8
Opportunity costs, p. 8

Chapter Summary

What Is Economics About?

Economic analysis can be usefully applied to topics as diverse as how businesses make decisions, how college students allocate their time between studying and relaxing, and how government deals with electric utilities that pollute nearby rivers.

Economics is separated into two broad categories: microeconomics and macroeconomics. *Microeconomics* deals with individual, firm, industry, and public decision making.

Macroeconomics, on the other hand, focuses on the broader economic issues confronting the nation. Issues such as inflation (a general increase in prices economy-wide), employment and unemployment, and economic growth affect all of us.

Economics uses a *stylized* approach to a number of issues. Stylized models boil issues and facts down to their basic relevant elements. To build models means that we make use of the *ceteris paribus* assumption and hold some important variables constant. This useful device often provides surprising insights about economic behavior.

Economists and policymakers often confront the tradeoff between efficiency and equity. Efficiency reflects how well resources are used and allocated. Equity (or fairness) of an outcome is a subjective matter; there are differences of opinion about fairness except in extreme cases where people tend to come to a general agreement. Economics illuminates the tradeoffs between equity and efficiency.

Key Ideas of Economics

1. Choice and scarcity force tradeoffs because we face limited resources and limitless wants. We must make tradeoffs in nearly everything we do. Economics is often defined as the study of the allocation of scarce resources to competing wants.
2. Opportunity costs—resources (e.g., time and money) that could be used in another activity—dominate our lives. Everything we do involves opportunity costs.
3. Rational behavior requires thinking at the margin.
4. People follow incentives.
5. Markets are efficient. Markets bring buyers and sellers together. Competition forces firms to provide products at the lowest possible price, or some other firm will undercut the price. New products are introduced to the market and old products disappear. This dynamism makes markets efficient.
6. Government must deal with market failure. Though markets are usually efficient, there are recognized times when they are not. Pollution is an example.
7. Information is important. Superior information gives economic actors a decided advantage. Sometimes information advantages can result in dysfunctional markets.
8. Specialization and trade improve our lives. Trading leads to better products at lower prices. Economies grow by producing those products where they have an advantage over other countries.
9. Productivity determines our standard of living. Countries with the highest average per capita income are also the most productive.
10. Government can smooth the fluctuations in the overall economy.

Questions and Problems

Check Your Understanding

1. Does your going to college have anything to do with expanding choices or reducing scarcity? Explain.
2. You normally stay at home on Wednesday nights and study. Next Wednesday night, the college is having a free concert on the main campus. What is the opportunity cost of going to the free concert?

Apply the Concepts

3. Gregg Easterbrook, in his book *The Progress Paradox* (New York: Random House, 2003), noted that life in the United States is significantly better today than in the past and provided many statistical facts, including:
   a. Nearly a quarter of households (or 60+ million people) have incomes of at least $75,000 a year.
   b. Real (inflation adjusted) per capita income has more than doubled since 1960—people on average have twice the real purchasing power now as in 1960.
   c. In 1956, the typical American had to work 16 weeks for each 100 square feet of new housing. Today that number is 14 weeks, and new houses are considerably more luxurious.
   d. The United States accepts more legal immigrants than all other nations of the world combined.

e. The quality of health care improved substantially over the last half-century, and life spans have grown dramatically.

This is just a sampling of the improvements in living standards Easterbrook catalogued. However, his book is subtitled *How Life Gets Better While People Feel Worse*, and this is a paradox he set out to explain. What reasons might explain why even though our lives have improved, people feel that life was better in an earlier time?

4. In 2001 Nobel Prize winner Robert Solow noted that "the computer age is seen everywhere except in productivity data." More recent studies suggest that it takes roughly seven years for investment in computers to have an impact on productivity. Why do you think this is the case?

5. In contrasting equity and efficiency, why do high-tech firms seem to treat their employees better (better wages, benefits, working environments, vacations, etc.) compared to how landscaping or fast-food franchises treat their employees? Is this fair? Is it efficient?

6. People talk about a big fall in the housing market. Who specifically is hurt by this fall? Consider real-estate agents, current homeowners, home builders, banks or financing institutions, and newly married couples who want to buy a home. Now consider what happens if the economy is booming. What happens to these groups?

7. In 2006 the Nobel Peace Prize went to economist Muhammad Yunus and the Grameen Bank "for their efforts to create economic and social development from below." Yunus led the development of micro loans to poor people without financial security: loans of under $200 to people so poor they could not provide collateral, to use for purchasing basic tools or other basic implements of work. This helped to pull millions of people out of poverty. Discuss how economic prosperity and security for everyone can result in a more peaceful planet.

In the News

8. *The Wall Street Journal* recently noted that bachelor's degrees in economics were up 40% between 1999 and 2004: "There is a clear explosion in economics as a major," and "the number of students majoring in economics has been rising even faster at top colleges." What might be some reasons for this now? (Jessica E. Vascellaro, "The Hot Major for Undergrads Is Economics," *Wall Street Journal*, July 5, 2005, p. A11.)

Solving Problems

9. The black rhinoceros is extremely endangered. Its horn is considered a powerful aphrodisiac in many Asian countries, and a single horn fetches many thousands of dollars on the black market, creating a great incentive for poachers. Unlike other stories of endangered species, this one might have a simple solution. Conservationists could simply capture as many rhinos as possible and remove their horns, reducing the incentive to poach. Do you think this will help reduce poaching? Why or why not?

10. With higher gasoline prices, the U.S. government wants people to buy more hybrid cars that use much less gasoline. Unfortunately, hybrids are approximately $4,000 to $5,000 more expensive to purchase than comparable cars. If people follow incentives, what can the government do to encourage the purchase of hybrids?

11. The By the Numbers box suggests that the stocks of companies that are good to work for (such as Google, Cisco, Genentech, Goldman Sachs, and Adobe) also tend to outperform general stock market averages. What factors or characteristics of these companies might account for their stellar stock market performance?

Answers to Questions in CheckPoints

Check Point: What Is Economics About?

(1) microeconomics, (2) macroeconomics, (3) microeconomics, (4) macroeconomics, (5) macroeconomics, (6) microeconomics, (7) macroeconomics.

Check Point: Key Ideas of Economics

McDonald's is adding one more product (premium coffee) to its line. Thinking at the margin entails thinking about how you can improve an operation (or increase profits) by adding to your existing product line or reducing costs.

Appendix: Working With Graphs and Formulas

You can't watch the news on television or read the newspaper without looking at a graph of some sort. If you have flipped through this book, you have seen a large number of graphs, charts, and tables, and a few simple equations. This is the language of economics. Economists deal with data for all types of issues. Just looking at data in tables often doesn't help you discern the trends or relationships in the data.

Economists develop theories and models to explain economic behavior and levels of economic activity. These theories or models are simplified representations of real-world activity. Models are designed to distill the most important relationships between variables, and then these relationships are used to predict future behavior of individuals, firms, and industries, or to predict the future course of the overall economy.

In this short section, we will explore the different types of graphs you are likely to see in this course (and in the media) and then turn to an examination of how graphs are used to develop and illustrate models. This second topic leads us into a discussion of modeling relationships between data and how to represent these relationships with simple graphs and equations.

Graphs and Data

The main forms of graphs of data are time series, scatter plots, pie charts, and bar charts. Time series, as the name suggests, plots data over time. Most of the figures you will encounter in publications are time series graphs.

Time Series

Time series graphs involve plotting time (minutes, hours, days, months, quarters, or years) on the horizontal axis and the value of some variable on the vertical axis. Figure APX-1 on the next page illustrates a time series plot for civilian employment of those 16 years and older. Notice that since the early 1990s, employment has grown by almost 20 million for this group. The vertical strips in the figure designate the last two recessions. Notice that in both cases when the recession hit, employment fell, then rebounded after the recession ended.

Scatter Plots

Scatter plots are graphs where two variables (neither variable is time) are plotted against each other. Scatter plots often give us a hint if the two variables are related to each other in some consistent way. Figure APX-2 on the next page plots one variable, the number of strikes, against another variable, union membership as a percent of total employment.

Two things can be seen in this figure. First, these two variables appear to be related to each other in a positive way. A rising union membership as a percent of employment leads

> **After studying this appendix you should be able to:**
>
> ☐ Describe the four simple forms of data graphs.
>
> ☐ Make use of a straightforward approach to reading graphs.
>
> ☐ Read linear and nonlinear graphs and know how to compute their slopes.
>
> ☐ Use simple linear equations to describe a line and a shift in the line.
>
> ☐ Explain why correlation is not the same as causation.

FIGURE APX-1—
Civilian Employment,
16 Years and Older

This time series graph shows the number of civilians 16 years and older employed in the United States since 1990. Employment has grown steadily over this period, except in times of recession, indicated by the vertical strips. Note that employment fell during the recession, and then bounced back after each recession ended.

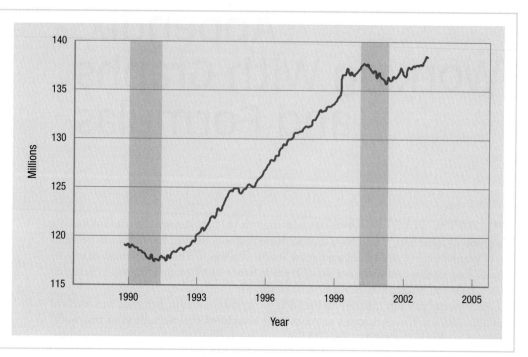

to a greater number of strikes. It is not surprising that greater union membership and more strikes are related, because greater union membership means more employees are covered by collective bargaining agreements, and thus we would expect more strikes. Also, greater union membership means that unions would be more powerful, and strikes represent a use of this power. Second, given that the years for the data are listed next to the dots, we can see that union representation as a percent of total employment has fallen significantly over the last half century. From this simple scatter plot, we get a lot of information and ideas about how the two variables are related.

FIGURE APX-2—The
Relationship Between the
Number of Strikes and Union
Membership as a Percent of
Total Employment

This scatter diagram plots the relationship between the number of strikes and union membership as a percent of total employment. The number of strikes increased as union membership became a larger percentage of those employed. Note that union membership as a percentage of those employed has fallen in the last half century.

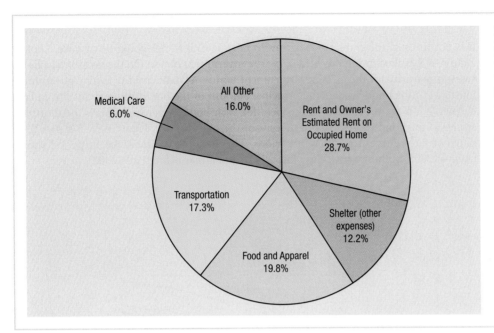

FIGURE APX-3—Relative Importance of Consumer Price Index (CPI) Components (2003)

This pie chart shows the relative importance of the components of the consumer price index, showing how typical urban households spend their income.

Pie Charts

Pie charts are simple graphs that show data that can be split into percentage parts that combined make up the whole. A simple pie chart for the relative importance of components in the consumer price index (CPI) is shown in Figure APX-3. It reveals how the typical urban household budget is allocated. By looking at each slice of the pie, we get a picture of how typical families spend their income.

Bar Charts

Bar charts use bars to show the value of specific data points. Figure APX-4 is a simple bar chart showing the annual changes in real (adjusted for inflation) gross domestic product (GDP). Notice that over the last 40+ years the United States has had only 5 years when GDP declined.

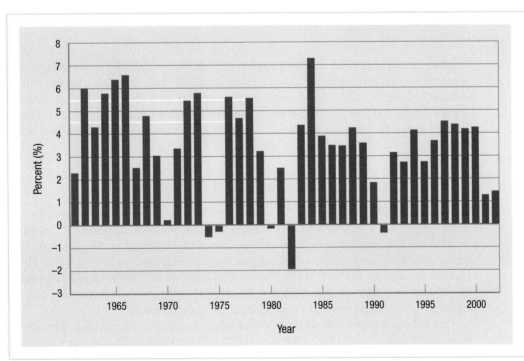

FIGURE APX-4—Percent Change in Real (Inflation Adjusted) GDP

This bar chart shows the annual percent change in real (adjusted for inflation) gross domestic product (GDP) over the last 40 years. Over this period, GDP has declined only five times.

Simple Graphs Can Pack In a Lot of Information

It is not unusual for graphs and figures to have several things going on at once. Look at Figure APX-5, illustrating the yield curve for government bonds. On the horizontal axis are years to maturity for the existing government bonds. At maturity, the federal government must pay to the bond holders the principal amount of the bond (more about this in later chapters). On the vertical axis is the yield for each bond in percent. This is the monetary return to the bond expressed as a percent of the bond's price. Figure APX-5 shows three different yield curves for different periods. They include the most recent period shown (August 2003), a month previous (July 2003), and a year before (July 2002).

FIGURE APX-5—Yield Curve

This yield curve for government bonds shows that interest rates fell between the middle of 2002 and the middle of 2003, shown by each point on the August 2003 curve being below the corresponding point on the July 2002 curve. Also, this figure shows that the yield (rate of return) for each bond grew as the time to maturity grew. This is due to higher risk associated with longer term bonds.

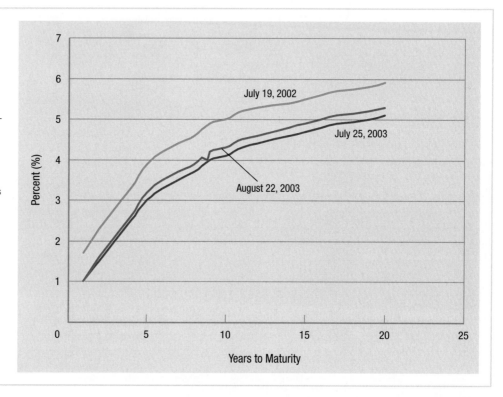

You should notice two things in this figure. First, at this time the yield curves sloped upward (they do not always do this). This meant that bonds that had a longer time to mature had higher yields; bonds with longer maturity periods are riskier and usually require a higher return. Second, interest rates fell over this period (July 2002 to August 2003) as shown by the position of the curves. Each point on the August 2003 curve is below the corresponding point on the July 2002 curve.

A Few Simple Rules for Reading Graphs

Looking at graphs of data is relatively easy if you follow a few simple rules. First, read the title of the figure to get a sense of what is being presented. Second, look at the label for the horizontal axis (*x* axis) to see how the data are being presented. Make sure you know how the data are being measured. Is it months or years, hours worked or hundreds of hours worked? Third, examine the label for the vertical axis (*y* axis). This is the value of the variable being plotted on that axis; make sure you know what it is. Fourth, look at the graph itself and see if it makes logical sense. Are the curves (bars, dots) going in the right direction?

Look the graph over and see if you notice something interesting going on. This is really the fun part of looking closely at figures both in this text and in other books, magazines, and newspapers. Often simple data graphs can reveal surprising relationships between variables. Keep this in mind as you examine graphs throughout this course.

One more thing. Graphs in this book are always accompanied by explanatory captions. Examine the graph first, making your preliminary assessment of what is going on. Then carefully read the caption, making sure it accurately reflects what is shown in the graph. If the caption refers to movement between points, follow this movement in the graph. If you think there is a discrepancy between the caption and the graph, reexamine the graph to make sure you have not missed something.

Graphs and Models

Let's now take a brief look at how economists use graphs and models, also looking at how they are constructed. Economists use what are called *stylized graphs* to represent relationships between variables. These graphs are a form of modeling to help us simplify our analysis and focus on those relationships that matter. Figure APX-6 is one such model.

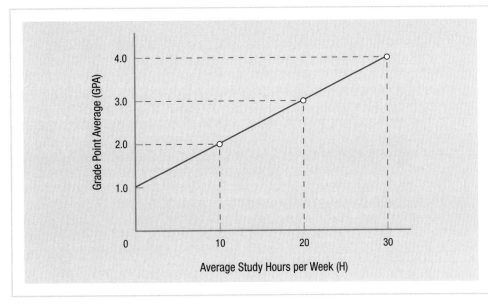

FIGURE APX-6—Studying and Your GPA

This figure shows a hypothetical linear relationship between average study hours and GPA. Without studying, a D average results, and with 10 hours of studying, a C average is obtained, and so on.

Linear Relationships

Figure APX-6 shows a linear relationship between average study hours and grade point average (GPA). The more you study, the higher your GPA (duh!). By a linear relationship, we mean that the "curve" is a straight line. In this case, if you don't study at all, we assume you are capable of making Ds and your GPA will equal 1.0, not enough to keep you in school for long. If you hit the books for an average of 10 hours a week, your GPA rises to 2.0, a C average. Studying for additional hours raises your GPA up to its maximum of 4.0.

The important point here is that the curve is linear; any hour of studying yields the same increase in your GPA. All hours of studying provide equal yields from beginning to end. This is what makes linear relationships unique.

Computing the Slope of a Linear Line

Looking at the line in Figure APX-6, we can see two things: The line is straight, so the slope is constant, and the slope is positive. As average hours of studying increase, GPA increases. Computing the slope of the line tells us how much GPA increases for every hour that studying is increased. Computing the slope of a linear line is relatively easy and is shown in Figure APX-7 on the next page.

FIGURE APX-7—Computing Slope for a Linear Line

Computing the slope is based on a simple rule: rise over run (rise divided by run). In the case of this straight line, the slope is equal to 0.1 because every 10 additional hours of studying yields a 1.0 increase in GPA.

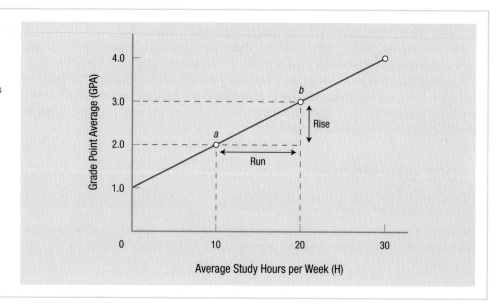

The simple rule for computing slope is: Slope is equal to rise over run (or rise ÷ run). Since the slope is constant along a linear line, we can select any two points and determine the slope for the entire curve. In Figure APX-7 we have selected points *a* and *b* where GPA moves from 2.0 to 3.0 when studying increases from 10 to 20 hours per week.

Your GPA increases (rises) by 1.0 for an additional 10 hours of study. This means that the slope is equal to 0.1 (1.0 ÷ 10 = 0.1). So for every additional hour of studying you add each week, your GPA will rise by 0.1. Thus, if you would like to improve your grade point average from 3.0 to 3.5, you would have to study five more hours per week.

Computing slope for negative relations that are linear is done exactly the same way, except that when you compute the changes from one point to another, one of the values will be negative, making the relationship negative.

Nonlinear Relationships

It would be nice for model builders if all relationships were linear, but that is not the case. It is probably not really the case with the amount of studying and your GPA either. Figure APX-8 depicts a more realistic nonlinear and positive relationship between studying and

FIGURE APX-8—Studying and Your GPA (nonlinear)

This nonlinear graph of study hours and GPA is probably more typical than the one shown in Figures APX-6 and APX-7. Like many other things, studying exhibits diminishing returns. The first hours of studying result in greater improvements to GPAs than further hours of studying.

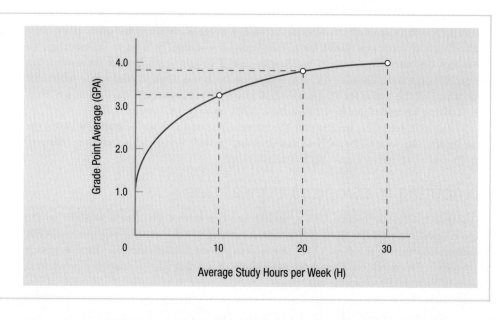

GPA. Again, we assume that you can get a D average (1.0) without studying and reach a maximum of straight As (4.0) with 30 hours per week.

Figure APX-8 suggests that your first few hours of study per week are more important to raising your GPA than are the others. Your first 10 hours of studying yields more than the last 10 hours: You go from 1.0 to 3.3 (a gain of 2.3), as opposed to going only from 3.8 to 4.0 (a gain of only 0.2). This curve exhibits what economists call diminishing returns. Just as the first bite of pizza tastes better than the one-hundredth, so the first 5 hours of studying brings a bigger jump in GPA than the 25th to 30th hours.

Computing the Slope of a Nonlinear Curve

As you might suspect, computing the slope of a nonlinear curve is a little more complex than for a linear line. But it is not that much more difficult. In fact, we use essentially the same rise over run approach that is used for lines.

Looking at the curve in Figure APX-8, it should be clear that the slope varies for each point on the curve. It starts out very steep, then begins to level out above 20 hours of studying. Figure APX-9 shows how to compute the slope at any point on the curve.

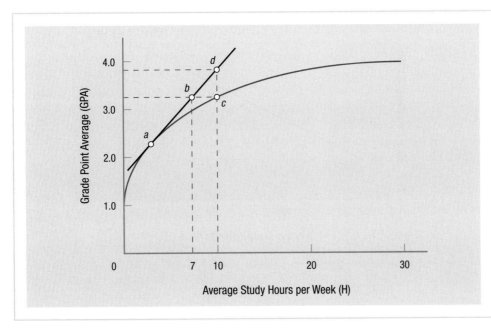

FIGURE APX-9—Computing Slope for a Nonlinear Curve

Computing the slope of a nonlinear curve requires that you compute the slope of each point on the curve. This is done by computing the slope of a tangent to each point.

Computing the slope at point *a* requires drawing a line tangent to that point, then computing the slope of that line. For point *a*, the slope of the line tangent to it is found by computing rise over run again. In this case, it is length *dc* ÷ *bc* or [(3.8 − 3.3) ÷ (10 − 7)] = 0.5 ÷ 3 = 0.167. Notice that this slope is significantly larger than the original linear relationship of 0.1. If we were to compute the slope near 30 hours of studying, it would approach zero (the slope of a horizontal line is zero).

Ceteris Paribus, Simple Equations, and Shifting Curves

Hold on while we beat this GPA and studying example into the ground. Inevitably, when we simplify analysis to develop a graph or model, important factors or influences must be controlled. We do not ignore them, we hold them constant. These are known as *ceteris paribus* assumptions.

Ceteris Paribus: All Else Equal

By *ceteris paribus* we mean other things being equal or all other relevant factors, elements, or influences are held constant. When economists define your demand for a product, they want to know how much or how many units you will buy at different prices. For example, to determine how many DVDs you will buy at various prices (your demand for DVDs), we hold your income and the price of movie tickets constant. If your income suddenly jumped, you would be willing to buy more DVDs at all prices, but this is a whole new demand curve. *Ceteris paribus* assumptions are a way to simplify analysis; then the analysis can be extended to include those factors held constant, as we will see next.

Simple Linear Equations

Simple linear equations can be expressed as: $Y = a + bX$. This is read as, Y equals a plus b times X, where Y is the variable plotted on the y axis and a is a constant (unchanging), and b is a different constant that is multiplied by X, the value on the x axis. The formula for our studying and GPA example introduced in Figure APX-6 is shown in Figure APX-10.

FIGURE APX-10—Studying and Your GPA: A Simple Equation

The formula for a linear relationship is $Y = a + bX$, where Y is the y axis variable, X is the x axis variable, and a and b are constants. For the original relationship between study hours and GPA, this equation is $Y = 1.0 + 0.1X$.

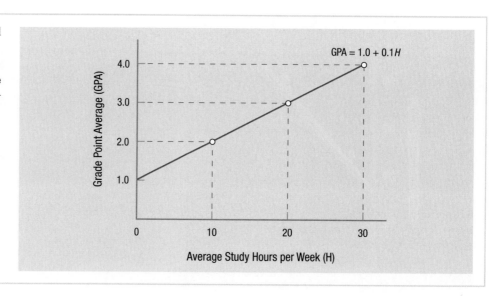

The constant a is known as the vertical intercept because it is the value of your GPA when study hours (X) is zero, and therefore when it cuts (intercepts) the vertical axis and is equal to 1.0 (D average). Now each time you study another hour on average, your GPA rises by 0.1, so the constant b (the slope of the line) is equal to 0.1. Letting H represent hours of studying, the final equation is: $GPA = 1.0 + 0.1H$. You start with a D average without studying and as your hours of studying increase, your GPA goes up by 0.1 times the hours of studying. If we plug in 20 hours of studying into the equation, the answer is a GPA of 3.0 $(1.0 + (0.1 \times 20) = 1.0 + 2.0 = 3.0)$.

Shifting Curves

Now let's introduce a couple of factors we have been holding constant (the *ceteris paribus* assumption). These two elements are tutoring and partying. So, our new equation now becomes $GPA = 1.0 + 0.1H + Z$, where Z is our variable indicating whether you have a tutor or whether you are excessively partying. When you have a tutor, $Z = 1$, and when you party too much, $Z = -1$. Tutoring adds to the productivity of your studying (hence $Z = 1$), while excessive late-night partying reduces the effectiveness of studying because

FIGURE APX-11—The Impact of Tutoring and Partying on Your GPA

The effect of tutoring and partying on our simple model of studying and GPA is shown. Partying harms your academic efforts and shifts the relationship to the right, making it harder to maintain your previous average (you now have to study more hours). Tutoring, on the other hand, improves the relationship (shifts the curve to the left).

you are always tired (hence $Z = -1$). Figure APX-11 shows the impact of adding these factors to the original relationship.

With tutoring, your GPA-studying curve has moved upward and to the left. Now, because $Z = 1$, you begin with a C average (2.0), and with just 20 hours of studying (because of tutoring) you can reach a 4.0 GPA (point *a*). Alternatively, when you don't have tutoring and you party every night, your GPA-studying relationship has worsened (shifted downward and to the right). Now you must study 40 hours (point *c*) to accomplish a 4.0 GPA. Note that you begin with failing grades.

The important point here is that we can simplify relationships between different variables and use a simple graph or equation to represent a model of behavior. In doing so, we often have to hold some things constant. When we allow those factors to change, the original relationship is now changed and often results in a shift in the curves. You will see this technique applied over and over as you study economics this semester.

Correlation Is Not Causation

Just because two variables seem related or appear related on a scatter plot does not mean that one causes another. Economists a hundred years ago correlated business cycles (the ups and downs of the entire economy) with sunspots. Because they appeared related, some suggested that sunspots caused business cycles. The only rational argument was that agriculture was the dominant industry and sunspots affected the weather; therefore, sunspots caused the economy to fluctuate.

Another example of erroneously assuming that correlation implies causality is the old Wall Street saw that related changes in the Dow Jones average to women's hem lines. Because two variables appear to be related does not mean that one causes the other to change.

Understanding graphs and using simple equations is a key part of learning economics. Practice helps.

Production, Economic Growth, and Trade

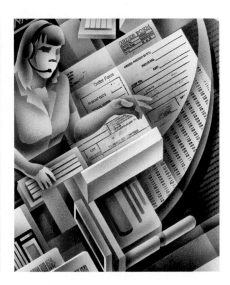

Boris Lyubner/Getty Images

We live in a consumer world. Everywhere you look, people are purchasing and consuming things. Everything from plastic wrap to baseballs, from artichokes to cellular phones, gets produced, traded, and consumed. Whether an economy is a capitalist market economy as in the United States, a capitalist marketplace with a strong touch of socialism as in many European countries, or a predominately communist economy as is true of many of China's markets, goods and services must change hands. Several centuries ago, individuals produced most of what they consumed. Today, most of us produce little of what we consume. Instead, we work at specialized jobs, then use our wages to purchase the goods we need. And purchase we do.

Though newspapers frequently report consumption excesses—and these excesses occur in rich *and* poor countries around the globe—we should not let these excesses obscure the fact that consumption is a great driver of economic growth. In many respects, consumption is simply a way for people to better themselves, to make their lives less of a drudgery, or to enrich their lives. Farmers in poor countries move from a precarious existence as subsistence farmers to producers of cash crops—keeping enough to live on but generating a surplus to sell—to obtain those consumption goods that better their lives.

Another great driver of economic growth is technological change. Technological advances have led to a telecommunications industry that simply was not dreamed of 50 years ago. In 1950, long distance phone calls were placed with the assistance of live operators, every minute costing the average consumer several hours' worth of pay. Today, fiber-optic cables allow thousands of calls to be made on one cable, thus drastically reducing the cost of telephone service. Cell phones, meanwhile, have become necessities because they are convenient and raise productivity. The globe is shrinking as communications bring us closer together.

After studying this chapter you should be able to:

□ Describe the three basic questions that must be answered for any economy.

□ Describe production and the factors that go into producing various goods and services.

□ Describe the opportunity cost an economy incurs to increase the production of one product.

□ Use a production possibilities frontier (PPF) or curve to analyze the limits of production.

□ Describe economic growth and the impacts of expanding resources through increasing human resources, capital accumulation, and technological improvements.

□ Describe the concepts of absolute and comparative advantage and explain what they tell us about the gains from trade when countries specialize in certain products.

□ Describe the practical constraints on free trade and how some industries might be affected.

Another driver of economic growth—trade—is less obvious. Yet its effect is clear. Nearly every country engages in commercial trade with other countries to expand the opportunities for consumption and production by its people. As products are consumed, new products must be produced, so increased consumption in one country can spur economic growth in another. Given the ability of global trade to open economic doors and raise incomes, it is vital for growth in developing nations. China's per person income has jumped dramatically in the decades since it opened its doors to trade.

This chapter gives you a framework for understanding economic growth. It provides a simple model for thinking about production, then applies this model to economies at large so you will know how to think about economic growth and its determinants. It then goes on to analyze international trade as a special case of economic growth. By the time you finish this chapter, you should understand the importance of economic growth and what drives it. To start, we turn to an examination of the three basic questions that every economy, no matter how it is organized, must solve.

Basic Economic Questions and Production

Regardless of the country, its circumstances, or its precise economic structure, every economy must answer three basic questions.

Basic Economic Questions

The three basic economic questions that each society must answer are:

- What goods and services are to be produced?
- How are these goods and services to be produced?
- Who will receive these goods and services?

The response an economy makes to the first question—What to produce?—depends on the goods and services a society wants. In a communist state, the government decides what a society wants, but in a capitalist economy, consumers signal what products they want by way of their demands for specific commodities. In the next chapter, we investigate how consumer demand for individual products is determined and how markets meet these demands. For now, we assume that consumers, individually and as a society, are able to decide on the mix of goods and services they most want, and that producers supply these items at acceptable prices.

Once we know what goods a society wants, the next question its economic system must answer is how these goods and services are to be produced. In the end, this problem comes down to the simple question of how labor, capital, and land should be combined to produce the desired products. If a society demands a huge amount of corn, say, we can expect its utilization of land, labor, and capital will be different from a society that demands digital equipment. But even an economy devoted to corn production could be organized in different ways, perhaps relying on extensive use of human labor, or perhaps relying on automated capital equipment.

Once an economy has determined what goods and services to produce and how to produce them, it is faced with the distribution question: Who will get the resulting products? *Distribution* refers to the way an economy allocates to consumers the goods and services it produces. How this is done depends on how the economy is organized.

Economic Systems

All economies have to answer the three basic economic questions. How that is done depends on who owns the factors of production (land, labor, capital, and entrepreneurship) and how decisions are made to coordinate production and distribution.

In *capitalist* or *market* economies, private individuals and firms own most of the resources. The what, how, and who decisions are determined by individual desires

By the *Numbers*

Growth, Productivity, and Trade Are Key to Our Prosperity

In the last half-century, average annual working hours fell by 13% but productivity has risen 200%, so real (adjusted for inflation) GDP per person and our standard of living have risen dramatically.

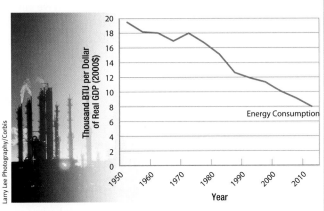

Energy in BTU per dollar of real (inflation adjusted) GDP has been steadily declining over the last 60 years. Today it is less than half of what it was in 1950.

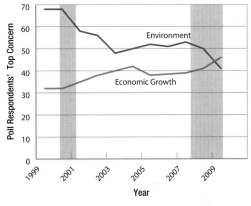

American attitudes about concerns for the environment or a preference for economic growth vary based on the state of the economy. As the economy enters a recession (shaded areas), the desire for economic growth grows while concern for the environment ebbs.

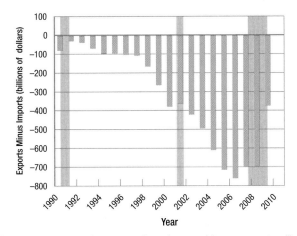

Our trade balance (exports minus imports) has grown steadily negative over the last 20 years. During the current recession, however, we cut our purchases of imported goods by 25% while exports held steady, balancing exports and imports.

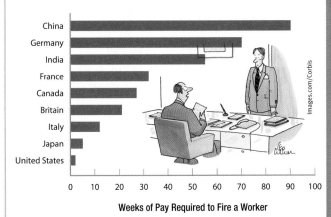

Weeks of Pay Required to Fire a Worker

Firing workers can be costly in some countries. Firing a full-time worker with 20 years at the company costs roughly 70 weeks pay in Germany, but it is even more costly in China.

Chapter 2 Hours worked, Productivity and GDP: The Conference Board, Total Economy Database, 1-2009. Energy use per dollar of GDP, *The Economist*, 5-8-2008. Exports and imports: U.S Department of Commerce. American attitudes on environment and economic growth, *The Economist*, 12-5-2009. Cost of firing workers, *The Economist*, 9-16-2008.

for products and profit-making decisions by firms. Product prices are the principal mechanism for communicating information in the system. Based on prices, consumers decide whether to buy or not, and firms decide how to employ their resources and what production technology to use. This competition between many buyers and sellers leads to highly efficient production of goods and services. Producers are free to survive or perish based on their efficiency and the quality of their products. The government's primary roles are protecting property rights, enforcing contracts between private parties, providing public goods such as national defense, and establishing and ensuring the appropriate operating environment for competitive markets. Today the U.S. economy is not a pure *laissez-faire* ("leave it alone," or minimal government role) market economy but more of a mixed economy with many regulations and an extended role for government.

In contrast, *planned* economies (socialist and communist) are systems where most of the productive resources are owned by the state and most economic decisions are made by central governments. Big sweeping decisions for the economy, often called "five-year plans," are centrally made and focus productive resources on these priorities. Both the former Soviet Union and China (until quite recently) were highly centrally planned, and virtually all resources were government owned. Although Russia and China have moved toward market economies, a large portion of each country's resources is owned by the communist state. Socialist countries (e.g., the Scandinavian countries of Europe) enjoy a high degree of freedom with a big role both for government services paid for by high taxes, and for highly regulated private businesses.

Resources, Production, and Efficiency

Having examined the three basic economic questions, let's take a look at the production process. **Production** involves turning **resources** into products and services that people want. Let's begin our discussion of this process by examining the scarce resources used to produce goods and services.

Land

For economists, the term **land** includes both land in the usual sense, but it also includes all other natural resources that are used in production. Natural resources like mineral deposits, oil and natural gas, and water are all included by economists in the definition of land. Economists refer to the payment to land as *rent*.

Labor

Labor as a factor of production includes both the mental and physical talents of people. Few goods and services can be produced without labor resources. Improvement to labor capabilities from training, education, and apprenticeship programs, typically called human capital, all add to labor's productivity and ultimately to a higher standard of living. Labor is paid *wages*.

Capital

Capital includes all manufactured products that are used to produce other goods and services. This includes equipment such as drill presses, blast furnaces for making steel, and other tools used in the production process. It also includes trucks and automobiles used by businesses, as well as office equipment such as copiers, computers, and telephones. Any manufactured product that is used to produce other products is included in the category of capital. Capital earns *interest*.

Note that the term *capital* as used by economists refers to real capital—actual manufactured products used in the production process—not money or financial capital. Money and financial capital are important in that they are used to purchase the real capital that is used to produce products.

Production: The process of converting resources (factors of production)—land, labor, capital, and entrepreneurial ability—into goods and services.

Resources: Productive resources include land (land and natural resources), labor (mental and physical talents of people), capital (manufactured products used to produce other products), and entrepreneurial ability (the combining of the other factors to produce products and assume the risk of the business).

Land: Includes natural resources such as mineral deposits, oil, natural gas, water, and land in the usual sense of the word. The payment to land as a resource is called rent.

Labor: Includes the mental and physical talents of individuals who produce products and services. The payment to labor is called wages.

Capital: Includes manufactured products such as welding machines, computers, and cellular phones that are used to produce other goods and services. The payment to capital is referred to as interest.

Entrepreneurial Ability

Entrepreneurs *combine* land, labor, and capital to produce goods and services, and they assume the *risks* associated with running a business. Entrepreneurs combine and manage the inputs of production, and manage the day-to-day marketing, finance, and production decisions. Today, the risks of running a business are huge, as the many bankruptcies and failures testify; and globalization has opened many opportunities as well as risks. For undertaking these activities and assuming the risks associated with business, entrepreneurs earn *profits*.

Entrepreneurs: Entrepreneurs combine land, labor, and capital to produce goods and services. They absorb the risk of being in business, including the risk of bankruptcy and other liabilities associated with doing business. Entrepreneurs receive profits for this effort.

Production and Efficiency

Production turns *resources*—land, labor, capital, and entrepreneurial ability—into products and services. The necessary production factors vary for different products. To produce corn, for instance, one needs arable land, seed, fertilizer, water, farm equipment, and the workers to operate that equipment. Farmers looking to produce corn would need to devote hundreds of acres of open land to this crop, plow the land, plant and nurture the corn, and finally harvest the crop. Producing digital equipment, in contrast, requires less land but more capital and highly skilled labor.

As we have seen, every country has to decide what to produce, how to produce it, and decide who receives the output. Countries desire to do the first two as efficiently as possible, but this leads to two different aspects of efficiency.

Production efficiency occurs when the mix of goods society decides to produce is produced at the lowest possible resource or opportunity cost. Alternatively, production efficiency occurs when as much output as possible is produced with a given amount of resources. Firms use the best technology available and combine the other resources to produce products at the lowest cost to society.

Production efficiency: Goods and services are produced at their lowest resource (opportunity) cost.

Allocative efficiency occurs when the mix of goods and services produced is the most desired by society. In capitalist countries this is determined by consumers and businesses and their interaction through markets. The next chapter explores this interaction in some detail. Needless to say, it would be inefficient (a waste of resources) to be producing vinyl records in the age of digital music players. Allocative efficiency requires that the right mix of goods be produced at the lowest cost.

Allocative efficiency: The mix of goods and services produced is just what the society desires.

Every economy faces constraints or limitations. Land, labor, capital, and entrepreneurship are all limited. No country has an infinite supply of available workers or the space and machinery that would be needed to put them all to work efficiently; no country can break free of these natural restraints. Such limits are known as production possibilities frontiers, and they are the focus of the next section.

■ CHECKPOINT

BASIC ECONOMIC QUESTIONS AND PRODUCTION

- Every economy must decide what to produce, how to produce it, and who will get what is produced.

- Production is the process of converting factors of production (resources)—land, labor, capital, and entrepreneurial ability—into goods and services.

- Land includes land and natural resources. Labor includes the mental and physical resources of humans. Capital includes all manufactured products used to produce other goods and services. Entrepreneurs combine resources to produce products, and they assume the risk of doing business.

- Production efficiency requires that products be produced at the lowest cost. Allocative efficiency occurs when the mix of goods and services produced is just what society wants.

QUESTION: The one element that really seems to differentiate entrepreneurship from the other resources is the fact that entrepreneurs shoulder the *risk* of failure of the enterprise. Is this important? Explain.

Answers to the Checkpoint question can be found at the end of this chapter.

Production Possibilities and Economic Growth

As we discovered in the previous section, all countries, and all economies, face constraints on their production capabilities. Production can be limited by the quantity of the various factors of production in the country and its current technology. Technology includes such considerations as the country's infrastructure, its transportation and education systems, and the economic freedom it allows. Though perhaps going beyond the everyday meaning of the word *technology,* for simplicity, we will assume all of these factors help determine the state of a country's technology.

To further simplify matters, production possibilities analysis assumes that the quantity of resources available and the technology of the economy remain constant. Moreover, all economic agents—workers and managers—are assumed to be technically efficient, meaning that no waste will occur in production. Finally, we will examine an economy that produces only two products. While keeping our analysis simple, altering these assumptions will not fundamentally change our general conclusions.

Production Possibilities

Assume our sample economy produces leather jackets and microcomputers. Figure 1 with its accompanying table shows the production possibilities frontier for this economy. The table shows seven possible production levels (*a–g*). These seven possibilities, which range from 12,000 leather jackets and zero microcomputers to zero jackets and 6,000 microcomputers, are graphed in Figure 1.

Production possibilities frontier (PPF): Shows the combinations of two goods that are possible for a society to produce at full employment. Points on or inside the PPF are feasible, and those outside of the frontier are unattainable.

When we connect the seven production possibilities, we delineate the **production possibilities frontier** (**PPF**) for this economy (some economists refer to this curve as the production possibilities curve). All points on the PPF curve are considered *attainable* by our economy. Everything to the left of the PPF curve is also attainable, but is an inefficient use of resources—the economy can always do better. Everything to the right of the

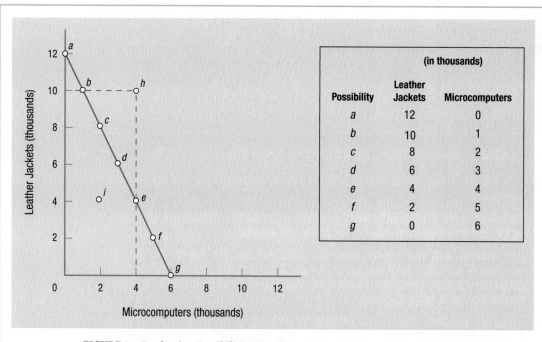

FIGURE 1—Production Possibilities Frontier

Using all of its resources, this stylized economy can produce many different mixes of leather jackets and microcomputers. Production levels on, or to the left of, the resulting PPF are attainable for this economy. Production levels to the right of the PPF curve are unattainable.

curve is considered *unattainable.* Therefore, the PPF maps out the economy's limits; it is impossible for the economy to produce at levels beyond the PPF. What the PPF in Figure 1 shows is that, given an efficient use of limited resources and taking technology into account, this economy can produce any of the seven combinations of microcomputers and leather jackets listed. Also, the economy can produce any combination of the two products on or within the PPF, but not any combinations beyond it.

Full Employment

As Figure 1 further suggests, all of the points along the PPF represent points of maximum output for our economy, that is, points at which all resources are being fully used. Therefore, if the society wants to produce 1,000 microcomputers, it will only be able to produce 10,000 leather jackets, as shown by point *b* on the PPF curve. Should the society decide Internet access is important, it might decide to produce 4,000 microcomputers, which would force it to cut leather jacket production down to 4,000, shown by point *e*.

Contrast points *c* and *e* with production at point *i*. At point *i* the economy is only producing 2,000 microcomputers and 4,000 jackets. Clearly, some resources are not being used and unemployment exists. When fully employed, the economy's resources could produce more of both goods (point *d*).

Because the PPF represents a maximum output, the economy could not produce 4,000 microcomputers and still produce 10,000 leather jackets. This situation, shown by point *h*, lies to the right of the PPF and hence outside the realm of possibility. Anything to the right of the PPF is impossible for our economy to attain; all points along the curve represent full employment.

Opportunity Cost

Whenever a country reallocates resources to change production patterns, it does so at a price. This price is called **opportunity cost.** Opportunity cost is the price an economy or an individual must pay, measured in units of one product, to increase its production (or consumption) of another product. In moving from point *b* to point *e* in Figure 1, microcomputer production increases by 3,000 units, from 1,000 units to 4,000 units. In contrast, our country must forgo producing 6,000 leather jackets because production falls from 10,000 jackets to 4,000 jackets. Giving up 6,000 jackets for 3,000 more computers represents an opportunity cost of 6,000 jackets, or two jackets for each microcomputer.

Opportunity cost thus represents the tradeoff required when an economy wants to increase its production of any single product. Governments must choose between guns and butter, or between military spending and social spending. Since there are limits to what taxpayers are willing to pay, spending choices are necessary. Think of opportunity costs as what you or the economy must give up to have more of a product or service.

Every day, everyone faces tradeoffs based on opportunity cost. A day has only 24 hours: You must decide how much time to spend eating, watching movies, going to class, sleeping, playing golf, partying, or studying—more time partying means less time for study. If you set aside a certain amount of time for studying, more time studying biology means less time studying history. But time is not the only constraint we face. Money restricts our choices as well. Should you buy a new computer, move to a nicer apartment, or save up for next semester's tuition? Indeed, virtually every choice in life involves tradeoffs or opportunity costs.

Increasing Opportunity Costs

In most cases, land, labor, and capital cannot easily be shifted from producing one good or service to another. You cannot take a semi truck and use it to plow a farm field, even though the semi and a top-notch tractor cost about the same. The fact is that some resources are suited to specific sorts of production, just as some people seem to be better suited to performing one activity over another. Some people have a talent for music or art, and they would be miserable—and inefficient—working as accountants or computer programmers. Some people find they are more comfortable working outside, while others require the amenities of an environmentally controlled, ergonomically designed office.

Opportunity cost: The cost paid for one product in terms of the output (or consumption) of another product that must be forgone.

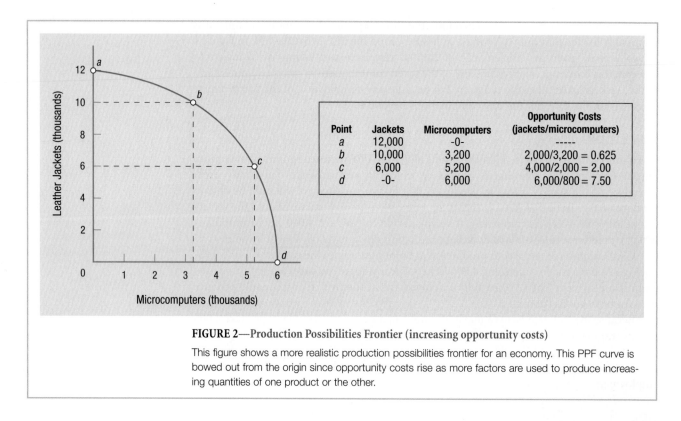

FIGURE 2—Production Possibilities Frontier (increasing opportunity costs)

This figure shows a more realistic production possibilities frontier for an economy. This PPF curve is bowed out from the origin since opportunity costs rise as more factors are used to produce increasing quantities of one product or the other.

Thus, a more realistic production possibilities frontier is shown in Figure 2. This PPF curve is bowed out from the origin, since opportunity costs rise as more factors are used to produce increasing quantities of one product. Let's consider why this is so.

Let's begin at a point where the economy's resources are strictly devoted to leather jacket production (point *a*). Now assume that society decides to produce 3,200 microcomputers. This will require a move from point *a* to point *b*. As we can see, 2,000 leather jackets must be given up to get the added 3,200 microcomputers. This means the opportunity cost of 1 microcomputer is 0.625 leather jackets (2,000 ÷ 3,200 = 0.625). This is a low opportunity cost, because those resources that are better suited to producing microcomputers will be the first ones shifted into this industry, resulting in rapidly increasing returns from specialization.

But what happens when this society decides to produce an additional 2,000 computers, or moves from point *b* to point *c* on the graph? As Figure 2 illustrates, each additional computer costs 2 leather jackets since producing 2,000 more computers requires the society to sacrifice 4,000 leather jackets. Thus, the opportunity cost of computers has more than tripled due to diminishing returns on the computer side, which arise from the unsuitability of these new resources as more resources are shifted to microcomputers.

To describe what has happened in plain terms, when the economy was producing 12,000 leather jackets, all its resources went into jacket production. Those members of the labor force who are engineers and electronic assemblers were probably not well suited to producing jackets. As the economy backed off jackets to start producing microcomputers, the opportunity cost of computers was low, since the resources first shifted, including workers, were likely to be the ones most suited to computer production and least suited to jacket manufacture. Eventually, however, as computers became the dominant product, manufacturing more computers required shifting leather workers to the computer industry. Employing these less suitable resources drives up the opportunity costs of computers.

You may be wondering which point along the PPF is the best for society. Economists have no grounds for stating unequivocally which mixture of goods and services would be ideal. The perfect mixture of goods depends on the tastes and preferences of the members of society. In a capitalist economy, resource allocation is determined largely by individual choices and the workings of private markets. We consider these markets and their operations in the next chapter.

Economic Growth

We have seen that PPFs map out the maximum that an economy can produce: Points to the right of the PPF curve are unattainable. But what if that PPF curve can be shifted to the right? This shift would give economies new maximum frontiers. In fact, we will see that economic growth can be viewed as a shift in the PPF curve outward. In this section, we use the production possibilities model to determine some of the major reasons for economic growth. Understanding these reasons for growth will enable us to suggest some broad economic policies that could lead to expanded growth.

The production possibilities model holds resources and technology constant to derive the PPF. These assumptions suggest that economic growth has two basic determinants: expanding resources and improving technologies. The expansion of resources allows producers to increase their production of all goods and services in an economy. Specific technological improvements, however, often affect only one industry directly. The development of a new color printing process, for instance, will directly affect only the printing industry.

Nevertheless, the ripples from technological improvements can spread out through an entire economy, just like ripples in a pond. Specifically, improvements in technology can lead to new products, improved goods and services, and increased productivity.

Sometimes, technological improvements in one industry allow other industries to increase their production with existing resources. This means producers can produce more output without using added labor or other resources. Alternately, they can get the same production levels as before while using fewer resources than before. This frees up resources in the economy for use in other industries.

When the electric lightbulb was invented, it not only created a new industry (someone had to produce lightbulbs), but it also revolutionized other industries. Factories could stay open longer since they no longer had to rely on the sun for light. Workers could see better, thus improving the quality of their work. The result was that resources operated more efficiently throughout the entire economy.

The modern-day equivalent to the lightbulb might be the cellular phone. Widespread use of these mobile devices enables people all across the world to produce goods and services more efficiently. Insurance agents can file claims instantly from disaster sites, deals can be closed while one is stuck in traffic, and communications have been revolutionized. Thus, this new technology has ultimately expanded time, the most finite of our resources. A similar argument could be made for the Internet. It has profoundly changed how many products are bought, sold, and delivered, and has expanded communications and the flow of information.

Expanding Resources

The PPF represents the constraints on an economy at a specific time. But economies are constantly changing, and so are PPFs. Capital and labor are the principal resources that can be changed through government action. Land and entrepreneurial talent are important factors of production, but neither is easy to change by government policies. The government can make owning a business easier or more profitable by reducing regulations, or by offering low-interest loans or favorable tax treatment to small businesses. However, it is difficult to turn people into risk takers through government policy.

Increasing Labor and Human Capital   A clear increase in population, the number of households, or the size of the labor force shifts the PPF outward, as shown in Figure 3 on the next page. With added labor, the production possibilities available to the economy expand from PPF_0 to PPF_1. Such a labor increase can be caused by higher birthrates, increased immigration, or an increased willingness of people to enter the labor force. This last type of increase has occurred over the past several decades as more women have entered the labor force on a permanent basis. America's high level of immigration (legal and illegal) fuels a strong rate of economic growth.

Rather than simply increasing the number of people working, however, the labor factor can also be increased by improving workers' skills. Economists refer to this as *investment in human capital*. Activities such as education, on-the-job training, and other

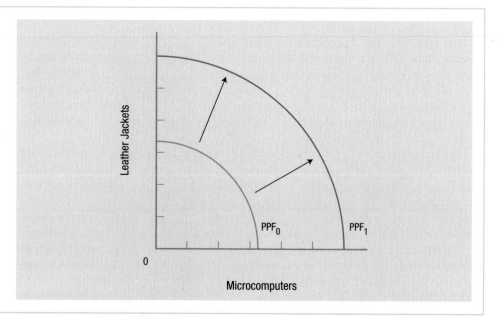

FIGURE 3—Economic Growth by Expanding Resources

A clear increase in population, the number of households, or the size of the labor force shifts the PPF outward. In this figure, a rising supply of labor expands the economy's production possibilities from PPF_0 to PPF_1.

professional training fit into this category. Improving human capital means people are more productive, resulting in higher wages, a higher standard of living, and an expanded PPF for society.

Capital Accumulation Increasing the capital used throughout the economy, usually brought about by investment, similarly shifts the PPF outward, as shown in Figure 3. Additional capital makes each unit of labor more productive and thus results in higher possible production throughout the economy. Adding robotics and computer-controlled machines to production lines, for instance, means each unit of labor produces many more units of output.

The production possibilities model and the economic growth associated with capital accumulation suggest a tradeoff. Figure 4 illustrates the tradeoff all nations face between current consumption and capital accumulation.

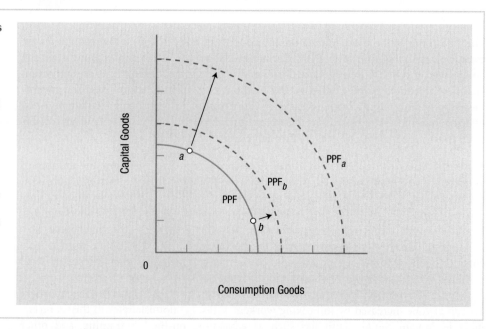

FIGURE 4—Consumption Goods and Capital Goods and the Expansion of the Production Possibilities Frontier

If a nation selects a product mix where the bulk of goods produced are consumption goods, it will initially produce at point *b*. The small investment made in capital goods has the effect of expanding the nation's productive capacity only to PPF_b over the following decade. If the country decides to produce at point *a*, however, devoting more resources to producing capital goods, its productive capacity will expand much more rapidly, pushing the PPF curve out to PPF_a over the following decade.

Let's first assume a nation selects a product mix where the bulk of goods produced are consumption goods—that is, goods that are immediately consumable and have short life spans, such as food and entertainment. This product mix is represented by point *b* in Figure 4. Consuming most of what it produces, a decade later the economy is at PPF_b. Little growth has occurred, since the economy has done little to improve its productive capacity—the present generation has essentially decided to consume rather than to invest in the economy's future.

Contrast this decision to one where the country at first decides to produce at point *a*. In this case, more capital goods such as machinery and tools are produced, while fewer consumption goods are used to satisfy current needs. Selecting this product mix results in the much larger PPF curve a decade later (PPF_a), since the economy steadily built up its productive capacity during those 10 years.

Technological Change

Figure 5 illustrates what happens when an economy experiences a technological change in one of its industries, in this case the microchip industry. As the diagram shows, the economy's potential output of microcomputers expands greatly, though its maximum production of leather jackets remains unchanged. The area between the two curves represents an improvement in the society's standard of living. People can produce and consume more of both goods than before: more microcomputers because of the technological advance, and more jackets because some of the resources once devoted to microcomputer production can be shifted to leather jacket production, even as the economy is turning out more computers than before.

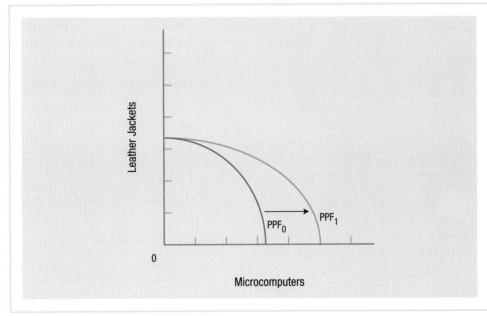

FIGURE 5—Technological Change and Expansion of the Production Possibilities Frontier

In this figure, an economy's potential output of microcomputers has expanded greatly, while its maximum production of leather jackets has remained unchanged. The area between the two curves represents an improvement in the society's standard of living, since more of both goods can be produced and consumed than before. Some of the resources once used for microcomputer production are diverted to leather jackets, even as the number of microcomputers increases.

This example reflects the United States today, where the computer industry is exploding with new technologies. Intel Corporation, the largest microprocessor manufacturer in the world, leads the way. Intel relentlessly develops newer, faster, and more powerful chips, setting a target time of 18 months for the development, testing, and release of each new generation of microprocessors. Consequently, consumers have seen home computers go from clunky conversation pieces to powerful, fast, indispensable machines. Today's microcomputers are more powerful than the mainframe supercomputers of just a few decades ago! And the latest developments in smart phones that allow users to surf the Web and play music, videos, and games do what powerful microcomputers did a decade ago.

Besides new products, technology has dramatically reduced the cost of microprocessor production. These cost reductions have permitted the United States to produce and consume more of other products as our consumption of high-tech items has soared. Our whole PPF has expanded outward.

But technological improvements result not only in smaller and cheaper microchips. An economy's technology also depends on how well its important trade centers are linked together. If a country has mostly dirt paths rather than paved highways, you can imagine how this deficiency would affect its economy: Distribution will be slow, and industries will be slow to react to changes in demand. In such a case, improving the roads might be the best way to stimulate economic growth.

As you can see, there are many ways to stimulate economic growth. A society can expand its output by using more resources, perhaps encouraging more people to enter the workforce or raising educational levels of workers. The government can encourage people to invest more, as opposed to devoting their earnings to immediate consumption. The public sector can spur technological advances by providing incentives to private firms to do research and development or underwrite research investments of its own.

Estimating the Sources of Economic Growth

How important are each of these factors? A recent study by the Organisation for Economic Co-operation and Development (OECD)[1] focused on what has been driving economic growth in 21 nations over the last several decades. The study first looked at contributions to economic growth from the macroeconomic perspective of added resources and technological improvements as we have been discussing in this chapter. It then looked at some benefits from good government policies that stimulate growth, and finally examined the industry and individual firm level for clues to the microeconomic sources of growth. Some of the findings include:

- A 1 percentage point increase in business investment as a percent of gross domestic product (GDP) leads to an increase in per capita GDP of 1.3%.

- An additional one-year increase in average education levels increases per capita GDP by 4 to 7%.

- A 0.1 percentage point increase in research and development as a percent of GDP increases per capita GDP by 1.2%.

- Reducing both the level and variability of inflation by 1 percentage point leads to an increase in per capita GDP of 2.3%.

- A 1 percentage point decrease in the tax burden as a percent of GDP leads to a 0.3% increase in per capita GDP.

- An increase in trade exposure (a combined measure of imports and exports as a percent of GDP) of 10 percentage points increases per capita GDP by 4%.

In less numerical terms, greater investment by business (physical capital), higher levels of education (human capital), high levels of research and development, lower inflation rates, reduced tax burdens, and greater levels of international trade all result in higher standards of living (per capita GDP).

One important point to take away from this discussion is that our simple stylized model of the economy using only two goods gives you a good first framework upon which to judge proposed policies for the economy. While not overly complex, this simple analysis is still quite powerful.

---

[1] *The Sources of Economic Growth in the OECD Countries* (Paris: Organisation for Economic Co-operation and Development), 2003.

Issue: Is There a Moral Dimension to Economic Growth?

As Benjamin M. Friedman has stated, "Why do we care so much about economic growth? When we talk about microeconomic issues in economics, the conversation boils down to efficiency: How can we best organize economic activity—production, buying, selling, consuming—in order to keep the economy as close as possible to the frontier that represents the maximum possible production and satisfaction of the desires of all."

Clearly, economic growth expands the economy's production possibilities frontier and improves our standard of living, but does it improve the quality of life? Benjamin Friedman[2] made a compelling argument that we also care so much about growth because there are moral consequences to

growth. This is the other side of the coin that is rarely discussed.

Looking back at two centuries of historical evidence pertaining to our country and others, Friedman found that when the economy is growing and the general population feels they are getting ahead, they are more likely to protect and enhance their basic moral values. These, he argued, include providing greater opportunity for all; expanding tolerance for people of other races, ethnic groups, and religions; and improving a sense of fairness to those in need. As a result, Americans become more committed to their democratic institutions.

His analysis also brings a warning: When economic growth stagnates for an

Robin Jareaux/Getty Images

extended period, the evidence suggests that "predictable pathologies have flourished in American society in ways that we all regret." Friedman's analysis of the moral implications provides another dimension of economic growth to add to our toolbox.

■ CHECKPOINT

PRODUCTION POSSIBILITIES AND ECONOMIC GROWTH

- A production possibilities frontier (PPF) depicts the different combinations of goods that a fully employed economy can produce, given its available resources and current technology (both assumed fixed in the short run).

- Production levels inside and on the frontier are possible, but production mixes outside the curve are unattainable.

- Because production on the frontier represents the maximum output attainable when all resources are fully employed, reallocating production from one product to another involves *opportunity costs*: The output of one product must be reduced to get the added output of the other. The more of one product that is desired, the higher its opportunity costs because of diminishing returns and the unsuitability of some resources for producing some products.

- The PPF model suggests that economic growth can arise from an expansion in resources or improvements in technology. Economic growth is an outward shift of the PPF curve.

QUESTION: Having abundant resources such as oil or diamonds would seem to be a benefit to an economy, yet some people have considered it a curse. Why would plentiful resources like these be a curse?

Answers to the Checkpoint question can be found at the end of this chapter.

Specialization, Comparative Advantage, and Trade

As we have seen, economics is all about voluntary production and exchange. People and nations do business with one another because all expect to gain from the transactions. Centuries ago, European merchants ventured to the Far East to ply the lucrative spice trades. These days, American consumers buy wines from Italy, cars from Japan, electronics from Korea, and millions of other products from countries around the world.

---

[2] Benjamin M. Friedman, *The Moral Consequences of Economic Growth* (New York: Knopf), 2005.

Many people assume that trade between nations is a zero-sum game—a game in which, for one party to gain, another party must lose. This is how poker games work. If one player walks away from the table a winner, someone else must have lost money. But this is not how voluntary trade works. Voluntary trade is a positive-sum game: Both parties to a transaction score positive gains. After all, who would voluntarily enter into an exchange if he or she did not believe there was some gain from it? To understand how all parties to an exchange (whether individuals or nations) can gain from it, we need to consider the concepts of absolute and comparative advantage developed by David Ricardo roughly 200 years ago.

Absolute and Comparative Advantage

Absolute advantage: One country can produce more of a good than another country.

Figure 6 shows hypothetical production possibilities curves for the United States and Mexico. Both countries are assumed to produce only crude oil and microcomputer chips. Given the PPFs in Figure 6, the United States has an **absolute advantage** over Mexico in

David Ricardo (1772–1823)

David Ricardo's rigorous, dispassionate evaluation of economic principles influenced generations of theorists, including such vastly different thinkers as John Stuart Mill and Karl Marx. The son of Dutch-Jewish immigrants, Ricardo was born in London as the third of 17 children. At age 14 he joined his father's trading business on the London Stock Exchange, but after he married a Quaker and converted to Christianity, his father disowned him. At 21 he borrowed money from friends, started his own brokerage, and within five years had amassed a small fortune.

While vacationing in Bath, England, he chanced on a copy of Adam Smith's *The Wealth of Nations,* and decided to devote his energies to studying economics and writing. He once wrote to his lifelong friend Thomas Malthus (of *Essay on Population* fame) that he was "thankful for the miserable English climate because it kept him at his desk writing." Ricardo and Malthus corresponded on a regular basis, and their exchanges were so important that John Maynard Keynes considered them " . . . the most important literary correspondence in the whole development of political economy."

Later, as a member of the British Parliament, Ricardo was an advocate of sound monetary policies and an outspoken critic of the 1815 Corn Laws, which placed high tariffs on imported grain to protect British landowners. His arguments were sound, but his oration was awful because he had a high-pitched squeal of a voice. His political views would also figure prominently in his economic writings.

Despite a pessimistic streak, Ricardo was an optimist when it came to free trade. His theory of "comparative advantage" suggested that countries would mutually benefit from trade by specializing in export goods they could produce at a lower opportunity cost than another country. His classic example was trade between Britain and Portugal. If Britain specialized in producing cloth and Portugal in exporting wine, each country would gain from a free exchange of goods. Ricardo died in 1823 of an ear infection, leaving an enduring legacy of classical (pre-1930s) economic analysis and his huge estate to his friend Thomas Malthus.

Arco Images Gmbh/Alamy

Sources: E. Ray Canterbery, *A Brief History of Economics* (New Jersey: World Scientific), 2001; Howard Marshall, *The Great Economists: A History of Economic Thought* (New York: Pitman Publishing Corporation), 1967; Steven Pressman, *Fifty Major Economists, 2d ed.,* (New York: Routledge), 2006; John Maynard Keynes, *Essays in Biography* (New York: Norton), 1951.

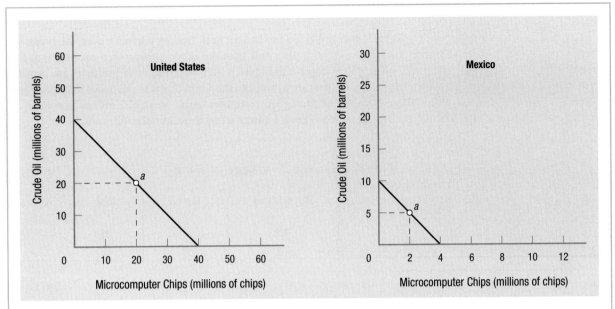

FIGURE 6—Production Possibilities for the United States and Mexico

One country has an absolute advantage if it can produce more of a good than another country. In this case, the United States has an absolute advantage over Mexico in producing both microchips and crude oil—it can produce more of both goods than Mexico can. Even so, Mexico has a comparative advantage over the United States in producing oil, since it can increase its output of oil at a lower opportunity cost than can the United States. This comparative advantage leads to gains for both countries from specialization and trade.

producing both products. An absolute advantage exists when one country can produce more of a good than another country. In this instance, the United States can produce 4 times more oil (40 million vs. 10 million barrels) and 10 times as many microcomputer chips (40 million vs. 4 million microchips) as Mexico. Note that the scales on the axes of the two panels in Figure 6 are different to make them easier to read.

At first glance you might wonder why the United States would even consider trading with Mexico. The United States has so much more productive capacity than Mexico, so why wouldn't it just produce all of its own crude oil and microcomputer chips? The answer lies in comparative advantage.

One country has a **comparative advantage** in producing a good if its opportunity cost to produce that good is lower than the other country's. In Figure 6, Mexico has a comparative advantage over the United States in producing oil. For the United States to produce an additional million barrels of crude oil, the *opportunity cost* is a million microcomputer chips. Each barrel of oil therefore costs the American economy one computer chip.

Contrast this with the situation in Mexico. For every microchip Mexican producers forgo, they are able to produce an additional 2.5 barrels of oil. This means one barrel of oil costs the Mexican economy only 0.4 computer chip. Therefore, Mexico has a comparative advantage in the production of crude oil, since a barrel of oil costs Mexico only 0.4 microchip, but to produce the same barrel of oil costs one microchip in the United States.

Conversely, the United States has a comparative advantage over Mexico in producing computer chips: Producing a microchip in the United States costs one barrel of oil, whereas the same chip in Mexico costs 2.5 barrels of oil. These relative costs suggest that the United States should pour its resources into producing computer chips, while Mexico specializes in crude oil. The two countries can then engage in trade to their mutual benefit.

Comparative advantage: One country has a lower opportunity cost of producing a good than another country.

The Gains from Trade

To see how specialization and trade can benefit both trading partners, even when one has the ability to produce more of both goods than the other, assume each country is at first (before trade) operating at point *a* in Figure 6. At this point, both countries are producing and consuming only their own output; the United States produces and consumes 20 million barrels of oil and 20 million computer chips; Mexico, 5 million barrels of oil and 2 million computer chips. Table 1 summarizes these initial conditions.

TABLE 1	Initial Consumption-Production Pattern		
	United States	**Mexico**	**Total**
Oil	20	5	25
Chips	20	2	22

Now assume Mexico focuses on oil, producing the maximum it can: 10 million barrels. We also assume both countries want to continue consuming 25 million barrels of oil between them. So the United States only needs to produce 15 million barrels of oil since Mexico is now producing 10 million barrels. For the United States, this frees up some resources that can be diverted to producing computer chips. Since each barrel of oil in the United States costs one microchip, reducing oil output by 5 million barrels means that 5 million more microcomputer chips can be produced.

Table 2 shows each country's production after Mexico has begun specializing in oil production.

TABLE 2	Production after Mexico Specializes in Producing Crude Oil		
	United States	**Mexico**	**Total**
Oil	15	10	25
Chips	25	0	25

Notice that the combined production of crude oil has remained constant, but the total output of computer chips has risen by 3 million chips. Assuming the two countries agree to share the added 3 million computer chips between them equally, Mexico will now ship 5 million barrels of oil to the United States in exchange for 3.5 million computer chips. From the 5 million additional computer chips the United States produces, Mexico will receive 2 million (its original production) plus 1.5 million for a total of 3.5 million, leaving 1.5 million additional chips for U.S. consumption. The resulting mix of products consumed in each country is shown in Table 3. Clearly, both countries are better off, having engaged in specialized production and trade.

TABLE 3	Final Consumption Patterns after Trade		
	United States	**Mexico**	**Total**
Oil	20	5	25
Chips	21.5	3.5	25

Issue: Is Trade Really So Important? Neanderthals vs. Homo Sapiens

Neanderthals *(Homo neanderthalensis)* lived 200,000 years before Homo sapiens arrived on the scene. Both species then lived together in roughly the same ranges for another 10,000 years, at which time the Neanderthals died out. Modern evidence suggests that Neanderthals were roughly as intelligent as *Homo sapiens,* stronger, and also capable of speech. Until recently, the generally accepted reason for the Neanderthals' extinction was that *Homo sapiens* had more sophisticated tools, developed modern symbolic thinking, and created a more sophisticated language.

Digging in prehistoric *Homo sapiens'* caves has uncovered such items as paintings, spear points, stone tools made from materials not found in the same location, and seashell jewelry found in inland locations far from the ocean. These discoveries have produced a new theory of why *Homo sapiens* came to dominate the land: They were trading with other colonies of humans. The theory is that trade led to specialization, whereby the best hunters hunted, and the others made weapons, clothes, and other necessities.

To test this theory, several anthropologists created a computer population simulation model that included such variables as rates of fertility and mortality, specialization and trade, hunting ability, and the same number of skilled hunters and craftsmen in each population. They gave *Homo sapiens* an edge in the ability to specialize and trade. As the model ran, *Homo sapiens* had superior hunting success, giving them more meat and driving up fertility and population. The model assumed the number of animals was fixed, so the available meat for the Neanderthals declined, and so did their population. Depending on the model's parameters, the time it took for Neanderthals to die out roughly coincided with that estimated by other anthropologists. Ancient humans may have known the benefits of trade long before David Ricardo developed his theory of absolute and comparative advantage.

Source: "Human Evolution: Homo Economicus?" *The Economist,* April 9, 2005, pp. 67–68; and "Mrs. Adam Smith," *The Economist,* December 9, 2006, p. 85, and Matt Ridley, *The Rational Optimist: How Prosperity Evolves* (New York: HarperCollins) 2010.

The important point to remember here is that even when one country has an absolute advantage over another country, both countries still benefit from trading with one another. In our example, the gains were small, but such gains can grow; as two economies become more equal in size, the benefits of their comparative advantages grow.

Limits on Trade and Globalization

Before leaving the subject of international trade, we should take a moment to note some practical constraints on trade. First, every transaction involves costs, including transportation, communications, and the general costs of doing business. Even so, over the last several decades, transportation and communication costs have been declining all over the world, resulting in growing global trade.

Second, the production possibilities curves for nations are not linear, but rather governed by increasing costs and diminishing returns. Therefore, it is difficult for countries to specialize in producing one product. Complete specialization would be risky, moreover, since the market for a product can always decline, perhaps because the product becomes technologically obsolete. Alternatively, changing weather patterns can wreak havoc on specialized agriculture products, adding further instability to incomes and exports in developing countries.

Finally, though two countries may benefit from trading with one another, expanding this trade may well hurt some industries and individuals within each country. Notably, industries finding themselves at a comparative disadvantage may be forced to scale back production and lay off workers. In such instances, government may need to provide workers with retraining, relocation, and other help to ensure a smooth transition to the new production mix.

When the United States signed the North American Free Trade Agreement (NAFTA) with Canada and Mexico, many people experienced what we have just been discussing. Some American jobs went south to Mexico because of low production costs. By opening up more markets for American products, however, NAFTA did stimulate economic growth, such that retrained workers may end up with new and better jobs.

■ CHECKPOINT

SPECIALIZATION, COMPARATIVE ADVANTAGE, AND TRADE

- An absolute advantage exists when one country can produce more of some good than another.

- A comparative advantage exists if one country has lower opportunity costs of producing a good than another country. Both countries gain from trade if each focuses on producing those goods at which it has a comparative advantage.

- Thus, voluntary trade is a positive-sum game, because both countries benefit from it.

QUESTION: Unlike most people, why do Hollywood stars (and many other rich people) have full-time personal assistants who manage their personal affairs?

Answers to the Checkpoint question can be found at the end of this chapter.

Key Concepts

Production, p. 28
Resources, p. 28
Land, p. 28
Labor, p. 28
Capital, p. 28
Entrepreneurs, p. 29
Production efficiency, p. 29

Allocative efficiency, p. 29
Production possibilities frontier (PPF), p. 30
Opportunity cost, p. 31
Absolute advantage, p. 38
Comparative advantage, p. 39

Chapter Summary

Basic Economic Questions and Production

Every economy must decide what to produce, how to produce it, and who will get the goods produced. How these questions are answered depends on how an economy is organized (capitalist, socialist, or communist).

Production is the process of converting factors of production—land, labor, capital, and entrepreneurial ability—into goods and services. Production efficiency occurs when goods and services are produced at the lowest possible resource cost. Allocative efficiency occurs when the mix of goods and services produced is that desired by society.

Production Possibilities and Economic Growth

The PPF curve shows the different combinations of goods that a fully employed economy can produce, given its available resources and current technology (both assumed to be fixed in the short run). Production levels inside and on the frontier are possible, but production mixes lying outside the curve are unattainable.

Production on the frontier represents the maximum output attainable by the economy when all resources are fully employed. At full employment, reallocating production from one product to another involves opportunity costs: the output of one product that must be reduced to get the added output of the other. As an economy desires more of one product, the opportunity costs for this product rises because of diminishing returns and the unsuitability of some specialized resources to be devoted to producing some products.

The production possibilities model suggests that economic growth can arise from an expansion in resources or from improvements in technology. Expansions in resources expand the production possibilities frontier for all commodities. New technology allows previous output to be produced using fewer resources, thus leaving some resources available for use in other industries.

Economic growth can be enhanced by increasing the quantity or quality of labor available for production. Population growth, caused by higher birthrates or immigration, increases the quantity of labor available. Investments in human capital improve labor's quality. Greater capital accumulation further improves labor's productivity and thus increases growth rates.

Specialization, Comparative Advantage, and Trade

An absolute advantage exists when one country can produce more of some good than another. A country has a comparative advantage if its opportunity costs to produce this good are lower than in the other country. Countries gain from voluntary trade if each focuses on producing those goods at which it enjoys a comparative advantage. Voluntary trade is thus a positive-sum game: Both countries stand to benefit from it.

Questions and Problems

Check Your Understanding

1. When can an economy increase the production of one good without reducing the output of another?

2. Explain the important difference between a straight line PPF and the PPF that is concave (bowed out) to the origin.

3. List the ways an economy can grow, given the discussion in this chapter.

4. Describe how opportunity cost is shown on a PPF.

5. In which of the three basic questions does technology play the greatest role?

6. How would unemployment be shown on the PPF?

Apply the Concepts

7. Describe how a country producing more capital goods rather than consumer goods ends up in the future with a PPF that is larger than a country that produces more consumer goods and fewer capital goods.

8. The United States has an absolute advantage in making many goods, such as short-sleeve cotton golf shirts. Why do Costa Rica and Bangladesh make these shirts and export them to the United States?

9. As individuals, we all know what scarcity means: not enough time (even the rich face a scarcity of time), or insufficient income so we are unable to buy that new car, vacation home, or water-ski boat we want. But for nations as a whole, what does it mean to face scarcity?

10. Why is it that America uses heavy street cleaning machines driven by one person to clean the streets, while China and India use many people with brooms to do the same job?

11. China has experienced levels of economic growth in the last decade that have been 2 to 3 times that of the United States (10% vs. 3 to 4% per year in the United States). Has China's high growth rate eliminated scarcity in China?

12. If specialization and trade as discussed in this chapter lead to a win-win situation where both countries gain, why is there often opposition to trade agreements and globalization?

13. The By the Numbers box at the beginning of this chapter detailed the costs of firing workers in various countries. If the costs of *firing* workers are high, how does this affect the *hiring* of workers?

14. American attitudes about the tradeoff between the environment and economic growth shown in the By the Numbers box at the beginning of the chapter changed

significantly when the economy entered a recession. However, during the recession in 2009, Americans were roughly equally split between their concerns for the environment and economic growth. What would you expect to find in a similar survey in a relatively poor developing nation?

Solving Problems

15. Political commentators often make the argument that growth in another country (most notably China) is detrimental to the economic interests of the United States. Look back at Tables 1 to 3 in the Gains from Trade section of the chapter. Then, assume that Mexico doubles in size, and make those changes to Table 1. Reconstruct Tables 2 and 3 given Mexico's greater capacity. Has the United States benefited by Mexico being able to produce more?

16. The table shows the potential output combinations of oranges and jars of prickly pear jelly (from the flower of the prickly pear cactus) for Florida and Arizona.

    a. Compute the opportunity cost for Florida of oranges in terms of jars of prickly pear jelly. Do the same for prickly pear jelly in terms of oranges.

    b. Compute the opportunity cost for Arizona of oranges in terms of jars of prickly pear jelly. Do the same for prickly pear jelly in terms of oranges.

    c. Would it make sense for Florida to specialize in producing oranges and for Arizona to specialize in producing prickly pear jelly and then trade? Why or why not?

Florida		Arizona	
Oranges	Prickly Pear Jelly	Oranges	Prickly Pear Jelly
0	10	0	500
50	8	20	400
100	6	40	300
150	4	60	200
200	2	80	100
250	0	100	0

17. Complete the following sentences based on the figure below where three different production possibilities frontiers are shown.

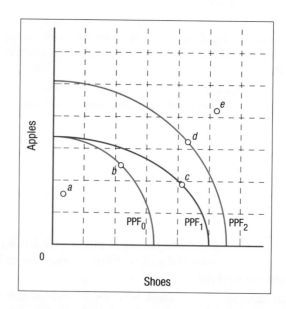

a. If the production possibilities frontier for this nation is PPF_0, then point *a* represents _____.

b. If the production possibilities frontier for this nation is PPF_0, then point *e* represents _____.

c. PPF_1 represents _____.

d. If the initial production possibilities frontier is PPF_0, then PPF_2 represents _____ and is caused by _____.

Answers to Questions in CheckPoints

Check Point: Basic Economic Questions and Production

Typically, entrepreneurs put not only their time and effort into a business but also their money, often pledging private assets as collateral for loans. Should the business fail, they stand to lose more than their jobs, rent from the land, or interest on capital loaned to the firm. Workers can get other jobs, land owners can rent to others, and capital can be used in other enterprises. But the entrepreneur must suffer the loss of personal assets and move on.

Check Point: Production Possibilities and Economic Growth

Abundant resources like oil or diamonds can be a curse because the economy often depends only on these resources for income and develops little else in terms of commerce. Many of the countries in the Middle East and Africa face this situation. Because their major source of income is concentrated in one resource, corruption often results, harming development in other sectors of the economy.

Check Point: Specialization, Comparative Advantage, and Trade

For Hollywood stars and other rich people, the opportunity cost of their time is high. As a result, they hire people at lower cost to do the mundane chores that each of us is accustomed to doing because our time is not as valuable.

Supply and Demand

Illustration Works/Alamy

Imagine you are going to build a house. Your plans are drawn up, the land is purchased, and you are all set to begin construction. What is the first thing you do? Do you immediately start putting up walls or set the painters to work? Of course not! Before you can build any walls, much less start painting, you must lay a foundation. The same is true in economics: Before you can understand more complex economic concepts, you need a foundation. This chapter provides the basic foundation on which all other economic theory rests. This foundation—supply and demand analysis—explains how market economies operate. In the previous chapter on economic growth, we took markets for granted. Here we start examining markets in detail.

In our economy, most goods and services (including labor) are bought and sold through private markets. These products include everything from iPods to airline flights, from haircuts to new homes. Most markets offer consumers a wide variety of choices. The typical Walmart, for instance, features over 500,000 different items, while even a small town has numerous competing choices of hair salons, movie theaters, and shoe stores.

In any given market, prices are determined by "what the market will bear." Which factors determine what the market will bear, and what happens when events that occur in the marketplace cause prices to change? For answers to these questions, economists turn to supply and demand analysis. The basic model of supply and demand presented in this chapter will allow you to determine why product sales rise and fall, what direction prices move in, and how many goods will be offered for sale when certain events happen in the marketplace. Later chapters use this same model to explain complex phenomena such as how personal income is distributed.

This chapter introduces some of the basic economic concepts you need to know to understand how the forces of supply and demand work. These concepts include markets, the law of demand, demand curves, the determinants of demand, the law of supply, supply curves, the determinants of supply, equilibrium, surpluses, and shortages. Lastly, we look at what happens when governments attempt to alter market outcomes by setting limits on prices.

Markets

A **market** is an institution that enables buyers and sellers to interact and transact with one another. A lemonade stand is a market because it allows people to exchange money for a product, in this case lemonade. Ticket scalping, though illegal in many states, similarly represents market activity since it leads to the exchange of money for tickets. The Internet, without a physical location, permits firms and individuals to sell a large number of low-volume niche products and still make money.[1] This includes students who resell their textbooks on Amazon.com and Half.com.

Even though all markets have the same basic component—the transaction—they can differ in a number of ways. Some markets are quite limited because of their geographical location, or because they offer only a few different products for sale. The New York Stock Exchange serves as a market for just a single type of financial instrument, stocks, but it facilitates exchanges worth billions of dollars daily. Compare this to the neighborhood flea market, which is much smaller and may operate only on weekends, but offers everything from food and crafts to T-shirts and electronics. Cement manufacturers are typically restricted to local markets due to high transportation costs, whereas Internet firms can easily do business with customers around the world.

The Price System

When buyers and sellers exchange money for goods and services, accepting some offers and rejecting others, they are also doing something else: They are communicating their individual desires. Much of this communication is accomplished through the prices of items. If buyers sufficiently value a particular item, they will quickly pay its asking price. If they do not buy it, they are indicating they do not believe the item to be worth its asking price.

Prices also give buyers an easy means of comparing goods that can substitute for each other. If margarine falls to half the price of butter, this will suggest to many consumers that margarine is a better deal. Similarly, sellers can determine what goods to sell by comparing their prices. When prices rise for tennis rackets, this tells sporting goods stores that the public wants more tennis rackets, leading these stores to order more. Prices, therefore, contain a huge amount of useful information for both consumers and sellers. For this reason, economists often call our market economy the **price system.**

■ CHECKPOINT

MARKETS

- Markets are institutions that enable buyers and sellers to interact and transact business.

- Markets differ in geographical location, products offered, and size.

- Prices contain a wealth of information for both buyers and sellers.

- Through their purchases, consumers signal their willingness to exchange money for particular products at particular prices. These signals help businesses decide what to produce, and how much of it to produce.

Markets: Institutions that bring buyers and sellers together so they can interact and transact with each other.

Price system: A name given to the market economy because prices provide considerable information to both buyers and sellers.

---

[1] Chris Anderson, *The Long Tail: Why the Future of Business Is Selling Less of More* (New York: Hyperion), 2006.

■ The market economy is also called the price system.

QUESTION: What are the important differences between the markets for financial securities such as the New York Stock Exchange and your local farmer's market?

Answers to the Checkpoint question can be found at the end of this chapter.

Issue: Are There Markets in Everything, Even Marriage?

All else equal, would a woman want to marry a man with greater social status and more resources (wealth)? Of course.

Economic theory suggests the answer is obvious, but proof is difficult to tease from marriage data, and many social scientists scoff at the idea. Two evolutionary psychologists, Thomas Pollet and Daniel Nettle, examined data from the 1910 census and discovered that supply and demand do matter in the marriage market.

In the early part of the last century, the West was relatively unsettled. Because many men moved west, communities often had a scarcity of women. Most of the eastern states had a male/female ratio of one, while in much of the West it was greater than one.

Pollet and Nettle set out to test the proposition that "when men are locally abundant, women will be able to demand a higher 'price' in terms of SES [socio-economic status] for entering a marriage than they can when men are locally scarce."

They found that in states where the ratio of men to women was equal, the marriage rate of high SES and low SES men were roughly the same. In states where men outnumbered the women, nearly twice the percentage of high SES men were married compared to low SES men. Women had the edge and they were pickier.

Pollet and Nettle concluded, "Marriage can be seen as partly involving a trade of female fertility and nurturance for male genes, resources and paternal investment, and, as in any trade, prices are affected by supply and demand." As most economists would expect, there are markets in everything, even marriage.

Sources: Thomas V. Pollet and Daniel Nettle, "Driving a hard bargain: sex ratio and male marriage success in a historical US population," *Biology Letters,* published online, 2007, and "A Buyers' Market," *The Economist,* December 15, 2007, p. 88.

Jupiterimages/Getty Images

Demand

Whenever you purchase a product, you are voting with your money. You are selecting one product out of many and supporting one firm out of many, both of which signal to the business community what sorts of products satisfy your wants as a consumer.

Economists typically focus on wants rather than needs because it is so difficult to determine what we truly need. Theoretically, you could survive on tofu and vitamin pills, living in a lean-to made of cardboard and buying all your clothes from thrift stores. Most people in our society, however, choose not to live in such austere fashion. Rather, they want something more, and in most cases they are willing and able to pay for more. These wants—the desires consumers have for particular goods and services, which they express through their purchases—are known as demands.

The Relationship between Quantity Demanded and Price

Demand refers to the goods and services people are willing and able to buy during a certain period of time at various prices, holding all other relevant factors constant (the *ceteris paribus* condition). Given the current popularity of television, most people would probably love to own a flat-panel HDTV with surround sound and hook it to a digital satellite or cable system that features hundreds of channels. And, indeed, if the products needed for such a setup were priced low enough, virtually everyone owning a television would opt for this system.

Demand: The maximum amount of a product that buyers are willing and able to purchase over some time period at various prices, holding all other relevant factors constant (the *ceteris paribus* condition).

As your television gets bigger and as you upgrade from basic television to cable or digital satellite, the cost of your home entertainment system increases. Yet, as the price of these services increases, the quantity demanded will decrease, since fewer and fewer people will be willing to spend their money on such things.

Thus, in a survey of households with television sets, we would expect to find a few people with virtually no service. A few people would have digital satellite hookups giving them access to sports channels, movie channels, and every other channel imaginable. The vast majority of consumers, however, would fall between these two categories, receiving some, but not all, of the services and channels available, in accord with their tastes and means.

In a market economy, there is a negative relationship between price and quantity demanded. This relationship, in its most basic form, states that as price increases, the quantity demanded falls, and conversely, as prices fall, the quantity demanded increases.

The Law of Demand

Law of demand: Holding all other relevant factors constant, as price increases, quantity demanded falls, and as price decreases, quantity demanded rises.

This principle, that as price increases, quantity demanded falls, and as price decreases, quantity demanded rises—all other factors held constant—is known as the **law of demand.** The law of demand states that the lower a product's price, the more of that product consumers will purchase during a given time period. This straightforward, common-sense notion happens because, as a product's price drops, consumers will substitute the now-cheaper product for other, more expensive products. Conversely, if the product's price rises, consumers will find other, cheaper products to substitute for it.

To illustrate, when videocassette recorders first came on the market 30 years ago, they cost $3,000, and few homes had one. As VCRs became less and less expensive, however, more people bought them, and others found more uses for them. Today, DVD players and digital video recorders (DVRs) are everywhere, and VCRs are essentially consigned to museums. Digital music players have altered the structure of the music business, and digital cameras have essentially replaced film cameras.

Time is an important component in the demand for many products. Consuming many products—watching a movie, eating a pizza, playing tennis—takes some time. Thus, the price of these goods includes not only their money cost, but also the opportunity cost of the time needed to consume them. It follows that, all other things being equal, including the cost of a ticket, we would expect more consumers to attend a two-hour movie than a four-hour movie. The shorter movie simply requires less of a time investment.

The Demand Curve

Demand curve: Demand schedule information translated to a graph.

Several decades ago, computers filling entire air-conditioned rooms laboriously churned out data. Now, inexpensive laptop computers and smart phones can perform even more complex operations in a fraction of the time. This advance in computer technology has led to the widespread use of computers for both business and pleasure. Once offering only Pong, game companies now take millions of players a year into mythical adventures, space battles, military campaigns, and rounds of championship golf. Indeed, games on the three main platforms—Sony's Playstation 3, Microsoft's XBox 360, and Nintendo's Wii—are a driving force behind the development of faster microprocessor technology, because games are voracious users of speed.

The law of demand states that as price decreases, quantity demanded increases. When we translate demand information into a graph, we create a **demand curve.** This demand curve, which slopes down and to the right, graphically illustrates the law of demand.

For example, consider Betty and her demand for computer games. Figure 1 depicts her annual demand in both table (the demand schedule) and graphical (the demand curve) form. Looking at the table and reading down Betty's demand schedule, we can see that Betty is willing to buy more computer games as the price decreases, from zero games at a price of $100 to 20 games at a price of $20. It makes sense that Betty will buy more computer games as the price decreases.

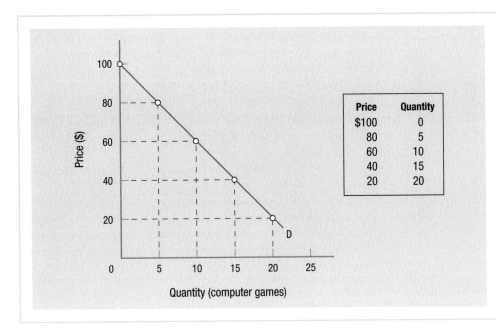

FIGURE 1—Betty's Demand for Computer Games

This figure shows Betty's demand schedule (the table) and her demand curve (the graph) for computer games over a year. Betty will purchase 5 computer games when the price is $80, buy 10 when the price falls to $60, and buy more as prices continue to fall. The demand curve D is Betty's demand curve for computer games.

Price	Quantity
$100	0
80	5
60	10
40	15
20	20

We can take the values from the demand schedule in the table and graph them in a figure, with price as the vertical axis and computer games as the horizontal axis, following the convention in economics of always placing price on the vertical axis and quantity demanded on the horizontal axis. This line is the demand curve. Comparing the table with the graph, we can see that they convey the same information. For instance, find the price of $60 on the vertical axis in the graph and look to the right to the point on the curve; then look down to locate the quantity of 10 computer games. This is the same information conveyed in the table: locating a price of $60 and looking to the right gives you the quantity of 10 computer games demanded.

Both the table and the graph portray the law of demand. As the price decreases, Betty demands more computer games. If the price of each game is $100, Betty will not purchase any games; they are just too expensive. Let the price drop to $40, however, and she will buy 15 games during the year.

Market Demand Curves

Though individual demand curves, like the one showing Betty's demand for computer games, are interesting, market demand curves are far more important to economists, as they can be used to predict changes in product price and quantity. Market demand is the sum of individual demands. To calculate market demand, economists simply add together how many units of a product all consumers will purchase at each price. This process is known as **horizontal summation.**

Figure 2 on the next page shows an example of horizontal summation of individual demand curves to obtain a market demand curve. Two individual demand curves for Abe and Betty, D_a and D_b, are shown. For simplicity, let's assume they represent the entire market, but recognize this process would work for a larger number of people. Note that at a price of $100 a game, Betty will not buy any, though Abe is willing to buy 10 games at $100. Above $100, therefore, the market demand is equal to Abe's demand. At $100 and below, however, we add both Abe's and Betty's demands at each price to obtain market demand. Thus, at $80, individual demand is 15 for Abe and 5 for Betty, so the market demand is equal to 20 (point c). When the price is $40 a game, Abe buys 25 and Betty buys 15, for a total of 40 games (point e). The heavier curve, labeled D_{Mkt}, represents this market demand; it is a horizontal summation of the two individual demand curves.

Horizontal summation: Market demand and supply curves are found by adding together how many units of the product will be purchased or supplied at each price.

FIGURE 2—Market Demand: Horizontal Summation of Individual Demand Curves

Individual demand curves D_a and D_b are horizontally summed to get market demand, D_Mkt. Horizontal summation involves adding together the quantities demanded by each individual at each possible price.

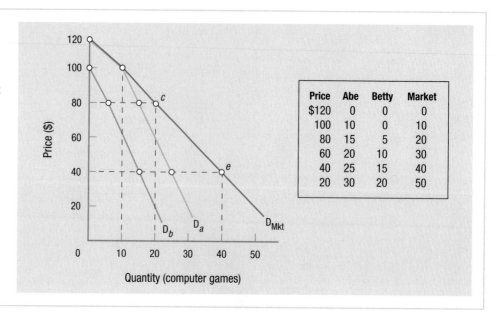

Price	Abe	Betty	Market
$120	0	0	0
100	10	0	10
80	15	5	20
60	20	10	30
40	25	15	40
20	30	20	50

This all sounds simple in theory, but in the real world estimating market demand curves is a tricky business, given that many markets contain millions of consumers. Marketing professionals use sophisticated statistical techniques to estimate the market demand for particular goods and services.

The market demand curve shows the maximum amount of a product consumers are willing and able to purchase during a given time period at various prices, all other relevant factors being held constant. Economists use the term determinants of demand to refer to these other, nonprice factors that get held constant. This is another example of the use of *ceteris paribus:* holding all other relevant factors constant.

Determinants of Demand

Up to this point, we have discussed only how price affects the quantity demanded. When prices fall, consumers purchase more of a product, so quantity demanded rises. When prices rise, consumers purchase less of a product, so quantity demanded falls. But several other factors besides price also affect demand, including what people like, what their income is, and how much related products cost. More specifically, there are five key **determinants of demand:** (1) tastes and preferences, (2) income, (3) prices of related goods, (4) the number of buyers, and (5) expectations regarding future prices, income, and product availability. When one of these determinants change, the *entire* demand curve changes. Let's see why.

Determinants of demand: Nonprice factors that affect demand, including tastes and preferences, income, prices of related goods, number of buyers, and expectations.

Tastes and Preferences

We all have preferences for certain products instead of others, easily perceiving subtle differences in styling and quality. Automobiles, fashions, phones, and music are just a few of the products that are subject to the whims of the consumer.

Remember Crocs, those brightly colored rubber sandals with the little air holes that moms, kids, waitresses, and many others have been favoring for the past several years? They were an instant hit. Initially, demand was D_0 in Figure 3. They then became such a fad that demand jumped to D_1 and for a short while Crocs were hard to find. Eventually Crocs were everywhere. Fads come and go, and now the demand for them has settled back to something like D_2, less than the original level. Notice an important distinction here: More Crocs weren't sold because the *price* was lowered; the entire demand curve shifted rightward when they were hot and more Crocs could be sold at *all* prices. Now that the fad has subsided, fewer can be sold at all prices. It is important to keep in mind that when one of the determinants change, such as tastes and preferences in this case, the *entire* demand curve shifts.

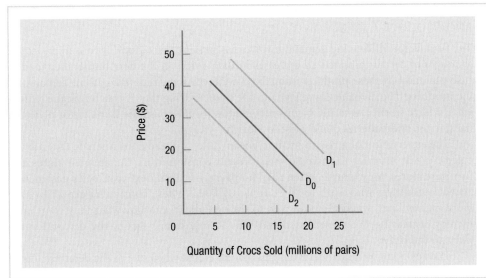

FIGURE 3—Shifts in the Demand Curve

The demand for Crocs originally was D_0. When they became a fad, demand shifted to D_1 as consumers were willing to purchase more at *all* prices. Once the fad cooled off, demand fell (shifted leftward) to D_2 as consumers wanted less at each price. When a determinant such as tastes and preferences changes, the *entire* demand curve shifts.

Income

Income is another important factor influencing consumer demand. Generally speaking, as income rises, demand for most goods will likewise increase. Get a raise, and you are more likely to buy a nice car. Your demand curve will shift to the right (such as from D_0 to D_1 in Figure 3). Products for which demand is positively linked to income—when income rises, demand for the product also rises—are called **normal goods.**

There are also some products for which demand declines as income rises, and the demand curve shifts to the left. Economists call these products **inferior goods.** As your income grows, for instance, your consumption of public transportation will likely fall since you will probably own a car. Similarly, when you graduate from college and your income rises, your consumption of ramen noodles will fall as you begin dining in restaurants.

Normal good: A good for which an increase in income results in rising demand.

Inferior good: A good for which an increase in income results in declining demand.

Prices of Related Goods

The prices of related commodities also affect consumer decisions. You may be an avid concert-goer, but with concert ticket prices often topping $100, if your local movie theater drops its ticket price to $8, you will probably end up seeing more movies than concerts. Movies, concerts, plays, and sporting events are good examples of **substitute goods,** since consumers can substitute one for another depending on their respective prices. When the *price* of concerts rises, your *demand* for movies increases, and vice versa. These are substitute goods.

Movies and popcorn, on the other hand, are examples of **complementary goods.** These are goods that are generally consumed together, such that an increase or decrease in the consumption of one will similarly result in an increase or decrease in the consumption of the other—see fewer movies, and your consumption of popcorn will decline. Other complementary goods include cars and gasoline, hot dogs and hot dog buns, and Windows System 7 and DRAM (dynamic random access memory) chips. Thus, when the *price* of movies increases, your *demand* for popcorn declines (shifts to the left), and vice versa.

Substitute goods: Goods consumers will substitute for one another depending on their relative prices. When the *price* of one good rises and the *demand* for another good increases, they are substitute goods, and vice versa.

Complementary goods: Goods that are typically consumed together. When the *price* of a complementary good rises, the *demand* for the other good declines, and vice versa.

The Number of Buyers

Another factor influencing market demand for a product is the number of potential buyers in the market. Clearly, the more consumers there are who would be likely to buy a particular product, the higher its market demand will be (the demand curve will shift rightward). As our average life span steadily rises, the demands for medical services, rest homes, and retirement communities likewise increase. As more people want smart phones, fewer people want plain-vanilla cell phones, and their demand declines.

Expectations about Future Prices, Incomes, and Product Availability

The final factor influencing demand involves consumer expectations. If consumers expect shortages of certain products or increases in their prices in the near future, they tend to rush out and buy these products immediately, thereby increasing the present demand for the products. The demand curve shifts to the right. During the Florida hurricane season, when a large storm forms and begins moving toward the coast, the demand for plywood, nails, water, and batteries quickly rise in Florida.

The expectation of a rise in income, meanwhile, can lead consumers to take advantage of credit in order to increase their present consumption. Department stores and furniture stores, for example, often run "no payments until next year" sales designed to attract consumers who want to "buy now, pay later." These consumers expect to have more money later, when they can pay, so they go ahead and buy what they want now, thereby increasing the present demand for the sale items. Again, the demand curve shifts to the right.

The key point to remember from this section is that when one of the determinants of demand changes, the *entire* demand curve shifts rightward (an increase in demand) or leftward (a decline in demand). A quick look back at Figure 3 shows that when demand increases, consumers are willing to buy more at all prices, and when demand declines, they will buy less at all prices.

Changes in Demand Versus Changes in Quantity Demanded

When the price of a product rises, consumers simply buy fewer units of that product. This is a movement along an existing demand curve. However, when one or more of the determinants change, the entire demand curve is altered. Now at any given price consumers are willing to purchase more or less depending on the nature of the change. This section focuses on this important distinction between *changes in demand* versus *changes in quantity demanded.*

Changes in demand occur whenever one or more of the determinants of demand change and demand curves shift. When demand changes, the demand curve shifts either to the right or to the left. Let's look at each shift in turn.

Demand increases when the entire demand curve shifts to the right. At all prices, consumers are willing to purchase more of the product in question. Figure 4 shows an increase

Change in demand: Occurs when one or more of the determinants of demand changes, shown as a shift in the entire demand curve.

FIGURE 4—Changes in Demand Versus Changes in Quantity Demanded

A shift in the demand curve from D_0 to D_1 represents an *increase in demand,* and consumers will buy more of the product at each price. A shift from D_0 to D_2 reflects a *decrease in demand.* Movement along D_0 from point *a* to point *c* indicates an *increase in quantity demanded;* this type of movement can only be caused by a change in the price of the product.

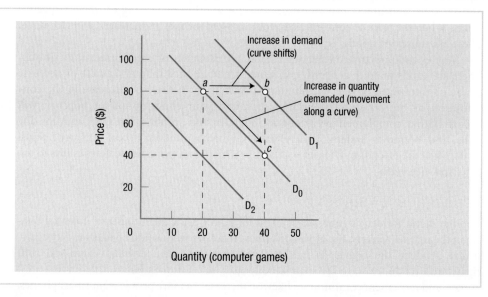

in demand for computer games; the demand curve shifts from D_0 to D_1. Notice that more computer games are purchased at all prices along D_1 as compared to D_0.

Now look at a decrease in demand, when the entire demand curve shifts to the left. At all prices, consumers are willing to purchase less of the product in question. A drop in consumer income is normally associated with a decline in demand (the demand curve shifts to the left). This decrease in demand is shown in Figure 4 as the demand curve shifting from D_0 to D_2.

Whereas a change in demand can be brought about by many different factors, a **change in quantity demanded** can be caused by only one thing: *a change in product price*. This is shown in Figure 4 as a reduction in price from $80 to $40, resulting in sales (quantity demanded) increasing from 20 (point *a*) to 40 (point *c*) games annually. This distinction between a change in demand and a change in quantity demanded is important. Reducing price to increase sales is different from spending a few million dollars on Super Bowl advertising to increase sales at all prices!

These concepts are so important that a quick summary is in order. As Figure 4 illustrates, given the initial demand D_0, increasing sales from 20 to 40 games can occur in either of two ways. First, changing a determinant (say, increasing advertising) could shift the demand curve to D_1 so that 40 games would be sold at $80 (point *b*). Alternatively, 40 games could be sold by reducing the price to $40 (point *c*). Selling more by increasing advertising causes an increase in demand, or a shift in the whole demand curve that brings about a movement from point *a* to point *b*. Simply reducing the price, on the other hand, causes an increase in quantity demanded, or a movement along the existing demand curve, D_0, from point *a* to point *c*.

Change in quantity demanded: Occurs when the price of the product changes, shown as a movement along an existing demand curve.

■ **CHECKPOINT**

DEMAND

- Demand refers to the quantity of products people are willing and able to purchase at various prices during some specific time period, all other relevant factors being held constant.

- Price and quantity demanded have an inverse (negative) relation: As price rises, consumers buy fewer units; as price falls, consumers buy more units. This inverse relation is known as the law of demand. It is depicted as a downward-sloping (from left to right) demand curve.

- To find market demand curves, simply horizontally sum all of the individual demand curves.

- Demand curves shift when one or more of the determinants of demand change.

- The determinants of demand are consumer tastes and preferences, income, prices of substitutes and complements, the number of buyers in a market, and expectations about future prices, incomes, and product availability.

- A shift of a demand curve is a *change in demand*. An increase in demand is a shift to the right. A decrease in demand is a shift to the left.

- A *change in quantity demanded* occurs only when the price of a product changes, leading consumers to adjust their purchases along the existing demand curve.

QUESTION: Sales of hybrid cars are on the rise. The Toyota Prius, while priced above comparable gasoline-only cars, is selling well. Other manufacturers are adding hybrids to their lines. What has been the cause of the rising sales of hybrids? Is this an increase in demand or an increase in quantity demanded?

Answers to the Checkpoint questions can be found at the end of this chapter.

Supply

As mentioned earlier, the analysis of a market economy rests on two foundations: supply and demand. So far, we've covered the demand side of the market. Let's focus now on the decisions businesses make regarding production numbers and sales. These decisions cause variations in product supply.

The Relationship between Quantity Supplied and Price

Supply: The maximum amount of a product that sellers are willing and able to provide for sale over some time period at various prices, holding all other relevant factors constant (the *ceteris paribus* condition).

Supply is the maximum amount of a product that producers are willing and able to offer for sale at various prices, all other relevant factors being held constant. The quantity supplied will vary according to the price of the product.

What explains this relationship? As we saw in the previous chapter, businesses inevitably encounter rising opportunity costs as they attempt to produce more and more of a product. This is due in part to diminishing returns from available resources, and in part to the fact that when producers increase production, they must either have existing workers put in overtime hours (at a higher hourly pay rate) or hire additional workers away from other industries (again at premium pay).

Producing more units, therefore, makes it more expensive for producers to produce each individual unit. These increasing costs give rise to the positive relationship between product price and quantity supplied to the market.

The Law of Supply

Law of supply: Holding all other relevant factors constant, as price increases, quantity supplied will rise, and as price declines, quantity supplied will fall.

Unfortunately for producers, they can rarely charge whatever they would like for their products; they must charge whatever the market will permit. But producers can decide how much of their product to produce and offer for sale. The **law of supply** states that higher prices will lead producers to offer more of their products for sale during a given period. Conversely, if prices fall, producers will offer fewer products to the market. The explanation is simple: The higher the price, the greater the potential for higher profits and thus the greater the incentive for businesses to produce and sell more products. Also, given the rising opportunity costs associated with increasing production, producers need to charge these higher prices to profitably increase the quantity supplied.

The Supply Curve

Supply curve: Supply schedule information translated to a graph.

Just as demand curves graphically display the law of demand, **supply curves** provide a graphical representation of the law of supply. The supply curve shows the maximum amounts of a product a producer will furnish at various prices during a given period of time. While the demand curve slopes down and to the right, the supply curve slopes up and to the right.[2] This illustrates the positive relationship between price and quantity supplied: the higher the price, the greater the quantity supplied.

Market Supply Curves

As with demand, economists are more interested in market supply than in the supplies offered by individual firms. To compute market supply, use the same method used to calculate market demand, horizontally summing the supplies of individual producers. A hypothetical market supply curve for computer games is depicted in Figure 5.

---

[2] There are some exceptions to positively sloping supply curves. But for our purposes, we will ignore them for now.

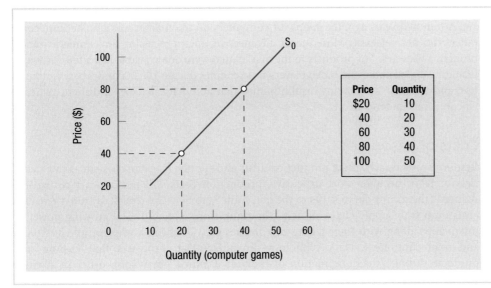

FIGURE 5—Supply of Computer Games

This supply curve graphs the supply schedule and shows the maximum quantity of computer games that producers will offer for sale over some defined period of time. The supply curve is positively sloped, reflecting the law of supply. In other words, as prices rise, quantity supplied increases; as prices fall, quantity supplied falls.

Price	Quantity
$20	10
40	20
60	30
80	40
100	50

Determinants of Supply

Like demand, several nonprice factors help to determine the supply of a product. Specifically, there are six **determinants of supply:** (1) production technology, (2) costs of resources, (3) prices of other commodities, (4) expectations, (5) the number of sellers (producers) in the market, and (6) taxes and subsidies.

Determinants of supply: Nonprice factors that affect supply, including production technology, costs of resources, prices of other commodities, expectations, number of sellers, and taxes and subsidies.

Production Technology

Technology determines how much output can be produced from given quantities of resources. If a factory's equipment is old and can turn out only 50 units of output per hour, then no matter how many other resources are employed, those 50 units are the most the factory can produce in an hour. If the factory is outfitted with newer, more advanced equipment capable of turning out 100 units per hour, the firm can supply more of its product at the same price as before, or even at a lower price. In Figure 6, this would be represented by a shift in the supply curve from S_0 to S_1. At every single price, more would be supplied.

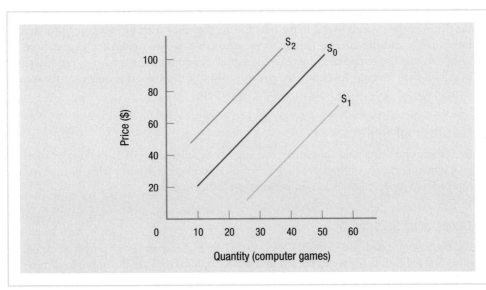

FIGURE 6—Shifts in the Supply Curve

The supply of computer games originally is S_0. If supply shifts to S_1, producers are willing to sell more at *all* prices. If supply falls, supply shifts leftward to S_2. Now firms are only willing to sell less at each price. When a determinant of supply changes, the *entire* supply curve shifts.

Technology further determines the nature of products that can be supplied to the market. A hundred years ago, the supply of computers on the market was zero because computers did not yet exist. More recent advances in microprocessing and miniaturization brought a wide array of products to the market that were not available just a few years ago, including digital audio and video players, auto engines that go 100,000 miles between tune-ups, and constant-monitoring insulin pumps that automatically keep a diabetic patient's glucose levels under control.

Costs of Resources

Resource costs clearly affect production costs and supply. If resources such as raw materials or labor become more expensive, production costs will rise and supply will be reduced (the supply curve shifts to the left, from S_0 to S_2). The reverse is true if resource costs drop (the supply curve shifts to the right, from S_0 to S_1). The growing power of microchips along with their falling cost has resulted in cheap and plentiful electronics and microcomputers. Nanotechnology—manufacturing processes that fashion new products through the combination of individual atoms—may soon usher in a whole new generation of inexpensive products.

On the other hand, if the cost of petroleum goes up, the cost of products using petroleum in their manufacture will go up, leading to the supply being reduced (the supply curve shifts leftward). If labor costs rise because immigration is restricted, this drives up production costs of California vegetables (fewer farm workers) and software in Silicon Valley (fewer software engineers from abroad) and leads to a shift in the supply curve to the left in Figure 6.

Prices of Other Commodities

Most firms have some flexibility in the portfolio of goods they produce. A vegetable farmer, for example, might be able to grow celery, radishes, or some combination of the two. Given this flexibility, a change in the price of one item may influence the quantity of other items brought to market. If the price of celery should rise, for instance, most farmers will start growing more celery. And since they all have a limited amount of land on which to grow vegetables, this reduces the quantity of radishes they can produce. Hence, in this case, the rise in the price of celery may well cause a reduction in the supply of radishes (the supply curve for radishes shifts leftward).

Expectations

The effects of future expectations on market supplies can be complicated, and it often is difficult to generalize about how future supplies will be affected. When producers expect the prices of their goods to rise in the near future, they may react by increasing production immediately, causing current supply to increase (shift to the right). Yet, expectations of price cuts can also temporarily increase the supply of goods on the market as producers try to sell off their inventories before the price cuts hit. In this case, it is only over the longer term that price reductions result in supply reductions.

Number of Sellers

Everything else being held constant, if the number of sellers in a particular market increases, the market supply of their product increases. It is no great mystery why: 10 shoemakers can produce more shoes in a given period than 5 shoemakers.

Taxes and Subsidies

For businesses, taxes and subsidies affect costs. An increase in taxes (property, excise, or other fees) will shift supply to the left and reduce it. Subsidies are the opposite of taxes. If the government subsidizes the production of a product, supply will shift to the right and rise. A luxury tax on powerboats in the 1990s reduced supply (the tax was the equivalent of an increase in production costs), while today's subsidies to ethanol producers are expanding ethanol production.

Changes in Supply Versus Changes in Quantity Supplied

A **change in supply** results from a change in one or more of the determinants of supply; it causes the entire supply curve to shift. An increase in supply of a product, perhaps because advancing technology has made it cheaper to produce, means that more of the commodity will be offered for sale at every price. This causes the supply curve to shift to the right, as illustrated in Figure 7 by the shift from S_0 to S_1. A decrease in supply, conversely, shifts the supply curve to the left, since fewer units of the product are offered at every price. Such a decrease in supply is here represented by the shift from S_0 to S_2.

Change in supply: Occurs when one or more of the determinants of supply change, shown as a shift in the entire supply curve.

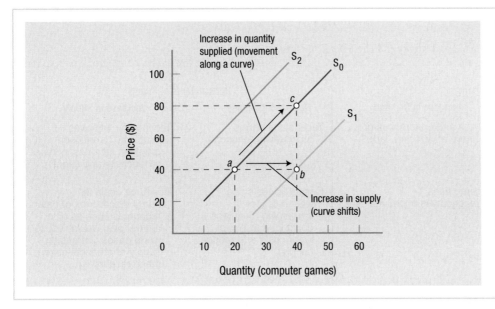

FIGURE 7—Changes in Supply Versus Changes in Quantity Supplied

A shift in the supply curve from S_0 to S_1 represents an *increase in supply,* since businesses are willing to offer more of the product to consumers at *all* prices. A shift from S_0 to S_2 reflects a decrease in supply. A movement along S_0 from point *a* to point *c* represents an *increase in quantity supplied;* it results from an increase in the product's market price from \$40 to \$80.

A change in supply involves a shift of the entire supply curve. In contrast, the supply curve does not move when there is a **change in quantity supplied.** Only a change in the price of a product can cause a change in the quantity supplied; hence, it involves a movement along an existing supply curve rather than a shifting to an entirely different curve. In Figure 7, for instance, an increase in price from \$40 to \$80 results in an increase in quantity supplied from 20 to 40 games, represented by the movement from point *a* to point *c* along S_0.

In summary, a change in supply is represented in Figure 7 by the shift from S_0 to S_1 or S_2, which involves a shift in the entire supply curve. For example, an increase in supply from S_0 to S_1 results in an increase in supply from 20 computer games (point *a*) to 40 (point *b*) provided at a price of \$40. More games are provided at the same price. In contrast, a change in quantity supplied is shown in Figure 7 as a movement along an existing supply curve, S_0, from point *a* to point *c* caused by an increase in the price of the product from \$40 to \$80.

As on the demand side, this distinction between changes in supply and changes in quantity supplied is crucial. It means that when a product's price changes, only quantity supplied changes—the supply curve does not move. A summary of how the determinants affect both supply and demand is shown in Figure 8 on the next page.

Change in quantity supplied: Occurs when the price of the product changes, shown as a movement along an existing supply curve.

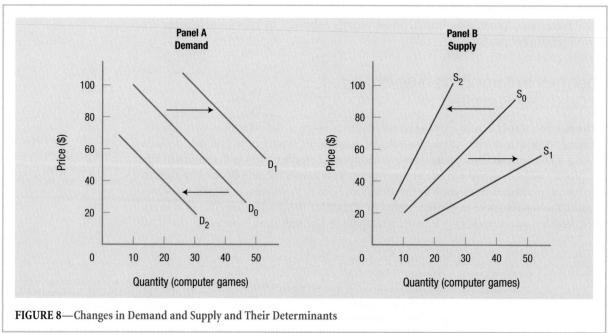

FIGURE 8—Changes in Demand and Supply and Their Determinants

Determinants of Demand		Determinants of Supply	
Decrease in Demand	**Increase in Demand**	**Decrease in Supply**	**Increase in Supply**
Tastes and preferences decline (less advertising, out of fashion).	Tastes and preferences grow (more advertising, fad).	Technology harms productivity (unusual).	Technology improves productivity (production robots in factories increase productivity and supply).
Income falls (economy is in a recession).	Income rises (economy is booming).	Resource costs rise (tough collective bargaining by unions could lead to higher labor costs and reduce supply).	Resource costs fall (large discoveries of natural resources such as oil or natural gas, would reduce world prices, increasing supply of products using these resources).
Price of substitute falls (price of tea falls, coffee demand declines). Price of complement rises (price of gasoline rises, demand for big SUVs drops).	Price of substitute rises (chicken prices rise, demand for beef increases). Price of complement falls (price of DVD players falls, demand for DVD movies increases).	Price of a production substitute rises (cucumber prices rise, reducing the supply of radishes as more cucumbers are planted).	Price of a production substitute falls (price of apples falls, landowners plant grapes instead and eventually the supply of wine rises).
Number of buyers falls.	Number of buyers grows.	Decreasing number of sellers	Rising number of sellers
Expecting future glut; expected surplus in future leads to lower prices so consumers hold off buying now (some consumers wait for after-Christmas sales of unsold—surplus— merchandise).	Expecting future shortages; leads to stocking up now to avoid higher prices in future (predicted gasoline shortages lead to filling of tanks now—an increase in current demand).	Expectation of a rise in future price of product (unsettled world conditions lead to expectations that gold will jump in price, which may lead to a withholding of gold from the market, reducing current supply).	Falling future price expectations for product (if beef prices are expected to fall, producers may sell more cattle now).
		Increase in taxes or reduction in subsidies (increasing taxes on cigarettes or reducing subsidies for ethanol will reduce supplies of both products).	Decrease in taxes or an increase in subsidies (reductions in excise taxes on luxury vehicles and increases in subsidies for education will increase the supply of both).

SUPPLY

- Supply is the quantity of a product producers are willing and able to put on the market at various prices, all other relevant factors being held constant.

- The law of supply reflects the positive relationship between price and quantity supplied: the higher the market price, the more goods supplied, and the lower the market price, the fewer goods supplied.

- As with demand, market supply is arrived at by horizontally summing the individual supplies of all of the firms in the market.

- A change in supply occurs when one or more of the determinants of supply change.

- The determinants of supply are production technology, the cost of resources, prices of other commodities, expectations, the numbers of sellers or producers in the market, and taxes and subsidies.

- A *change in supply* is a shift in the supply curve. A shift to the right reflects an increase in supply, while a shift to the left represents a decrease in supply.

- A *change in quantity supplied* is only caused by a change in the price of the product; it results in a movement along the existing supply curve.

QUESTION: What has been the impact of the iPod, iTunes, and MP3 players in general on high-end stereo equipment production?

Answers to the Checkpoint question can be found at the end of this chapter.

Market Equilibrium

Supply and demand together determine the prices and quantities of goods bought and sold. Neither factor alone is sufficient to determine price and quantity. It is through their interaction that supply and demand do their work, just as two blades of a scissors are required to cut paper.

A market will determine the price at which the quantity of a product demanded is equal to the quantity supplied. At this price, the market is said to be cleared or to be in **equilibrium,** meaning the amount of the product that consumers are willing and able to purchase is matched exactly by the amount that producers are willing and able to sell. This is the **equilibrium price** and the **equilibrium quantity.** The equilibrium price is also called the market-clearing price.

Figure 9 on the next page puts together Figures 2 and 5, showing the market supply and demand for computer games. It illustrates how supply and demand interact to determine equilibrium price and quantity. Clearly, the quantities demanded and supplied equal one another only where the supply and demand curves cross, at point *e*. Alternatively, you can see this in the table that is part of the figure: Quantity demanded and quantity supplied are the same at only one particular point. At $60 a game, sellers are willing to provide exactly the same quantity as consumers would like to purchase. Hence, at this price, the market clears, since buyers and sellers both want to transact the same number of units.

The beauty of a market is that it automatically works to establish the equilibrium price and quantity, without any guidance from anyone. To see how this happens, let us assume that computer games are initially priced at $80, a price above their equilibrium price. As we can see by comparing points *a* and *b*, sellers are willing to supply more games at this price than consumers are willing to buy. Economists characterize such a situation as one of excess supply, or **surplus.** In this case, at $80, sellers supply 40 games to the market (point *b*), yet buyers want to purchase only 20 (point *a*). This leaves an excess of 20 games overhanging the market; these unsold games ultimately become surplus inventories.

Here is where the market kicks in to restore equilibrium. As inventories rise, most firms cut production. Some firms, moreover, start reducing their prices to increase sales.

Equilibrium: Market forces are in balance when the quantities demanded by consumers just equal the quantities supplied by producers.

Equilibrium price: Market equilibrium price is the price that results when quantity demanded is just equal to quantity supplied.

Equilibrium quantity: Market equilibrium quantity is the output that results when quantity demanded is just equal to quantity supplied.

Surplus: Occurs when the price is above market equilibrium, and quantity supplied exceeds quantity demanded.

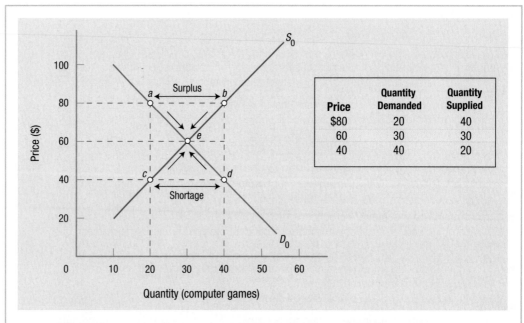

FIGURE 9—Equilibrium Price and Quantity of Computer Games

Market equilibrium is achieved when quantity demanded and quantity supplied are equal. In this graph, that equilibrium occurs at point *e*, at an equilibrium price of $60 and an equilibrium output of 30. If the market price is above equilibrium ($80), a surplus of 20 computer games will result (*b* − *a*), automatically driving the price back down to $60. When the market price is too low ($40), a shortage of 20 computer games will result (*d* − *c*), and businesses will raise their offering prices until equilibrium is again restored.

Shortage: Occurs when the price is below market equilibrium, and quantity demanded exceeds quantity supplied.

Other firms must then cut their own prices to remain competitive. This process continues, with firms cutting their prices and production, until most firms have managed to exhaust their surplus inventories. This happens when prices reach $60 and quantity supplied equals 30, since consumers are once again willing to buy up the entire quantity supplied at this price, and the market is restored to equilibrium.

In general, therefore, when prices are set too high, surpluses result, which drive prices back down to their equilibrium levels. If, conversely, a price is initially set too low, say at $40, a **shortage** results. In this case, buyers want to purchase 40 games (point *d*), but sellers are only providing 20 (point *c*), creating a shortage of 20 games. Because consumers are willing to pay more than $40 to get hold of the few games available on the market, they will start bidding up the price of computer games. Sensing an opportunity to make some money, firms will start raising their prices and increasing production, once again until equilibrium is restored. Hence, in general, excess demand causes firms to raise prices and increase production.

When there is a shortage in a market, economists speak of a tight market or a seller's market. Under these conditions, producers have no difficulty selling off all their output. When a surplus of goods floods the market, this gives rise to a buyer's market, since buyers can buy all the goods they want at attractive prices.

We have now seen how changing prices naturally work to clear up shortages and surpluses, thereby returning markets to equilibrium. Some markets, once disturbed, will return to equilibrium quickly. Examples include the stock, bond, and money markets, where trading is nearly instantaneous and extensive information abounds. Other markets react very slowly. Consider the labor market, for instance. For various psychological reasons, most people have an inflated idea of their worth to both current and future employers. It is only after an extended bout of unemployment, therefore, that many people will face reality and accept a position at a salary lower than their previous job. Similarly, real estate markets can be slow

Alfred Marshall (1842–1924)

British economist Alfred Marshall is considered the father of the modern theory of supply and demand— that price and output are determined by both supply *and* demand. He noted that the two go together like the blades of a scissors that cross at equilibrium.

He assumed that changes in quantity demanded were only affected by changes in price, and that all other factors remained constant. Marshall also is credited with developing the ideas of the laws of demand and supply, and the concepts of consumer surplus and producer surplus—concepts we will study in the next chapter.

As a boy, he suffered from severe headaches, which could only be cured by playing chess. He later swore off chess because "otherwise I would have been tempted to spend all my time on it." When his uncle went to Australia and made a fortune as a farmer, he was able to give Alfred financial support.

With financial help from this uncle, Marshall attended St. John's College, Cambridge, to study mathematics and physics. But after long walks through the poorest sections of several European cities and seeing their horrible conditions, he decided to focus his attention on political economy.

In 1890, he published *Principles of Economics* at the age of 48. In it he introduced many new ideas for the first time, though as Ray Canterbery noted, " . . . without any suggestion that they are novel or remarkable." During his lifetime, the book went through eight editions. In hopes of appealing to the general public, Marshall buried his diagrams in footnotes. And, although he is credited with many economic theories, he would always clarify them with various exceptions and qualifications. He expected future economists to flesh out his ideas.

Above all, Marshall loved teaching and his students. According to John Maynard Keynes, it was impossible to take coherent notes from Marshall's lectures. They were never orderly or systematic since he tried to get students to think *with* him and ultimately think for themselves. At one point near the turn of the twentieth century, essentially all of the leading economists in England had been his students.

More than anyone else, Marshall is given credit for establishing economics as a discipline of study. Keynes, the most influential economist of the last century and Marshall's student, wrote a 70-page, 20,000-word memorial to Marshall, published in the *Economic Journal* 3 months after his death in 1924.

Sources: E. Ray Canterbery, *A Brief History of Economics: Artful Approaches to the Dismal Science* (New Jersey: World Scientific), 2001; Robert Skidelsky, *John Maynard Keynes: Volume Two The Economist as Saviour 1920–1937* (New York: The Penguin Press), 1992; and John Maynard Keynes, *Essays in Biography* (New York: Norton), 1951.

to adjust since sellers will often refuse to accept a price below what they are asking for, until the lack of sales over time convinces sellers to adjust the price downward.

These automatic market adjustments can make some buyers and sellers feel uncomfortable: It seems as if prices and quantities are being set by forces beyond anyone's control. In fact, this phenomenon is precisely what makes market economies function so efficiently. Without anyone needing to be in control, prices and quantities naturally gravitate toward equilibrium levels. Adam Smith was so impressed by the workings of the market that he suggested it is almost as if an "invisible hand" guides the market to equilibrium.

Given the self-correcting nature of the market, long-term shortages or surpluses are almost always the result of government intervention, as we will see later in this chapter. First, however, we turn to a discussion of how the market responds to changes in supply and demand, or to shifts of the supply and demand curves.

Moving to a New Equilibrium: Changes in Supply and Demand

Once a market is in equilibrium and the forces of supply and demand balance one another out, the market will remain there unless an external factor changes. But when the supply curve or demand curve shifts (some determinant changes), equilibrium also shifts, resulting in a new equilibrium price and/or output. The ability to predict new equilibrium points is one of the most useful aspects of supply and demand analysis.

Predicting the New Equilibrium When One Curve Shifts

When only supply or only demand changes, the change in equilibrium price and equilibrium output can be predicted. We begin with changes in supply.

Changes in Supply   Figure 10 shows what happens when supply changes. Equilibrium initially is at point e, with equilibrium price and quantity at P_0 and Q_0, respectively. But let us assume a rise in wages or the bankruptcy of a key business in the market (the number of sellers declines) causes a decrease in supply. When supply declines (the supply curve shifts from S_0 to S_2), equilibrium price rises to P_2, while equilibrium output falls to Q_2 (point a).

FIGURE 10—Equilibrium Price, Output, and Shifts in Supply

When supply alone shifts, the effects on both equilibrium price and output can be predicted. When supply grows (S_0 to S_1), equilibrium price will fall and output will rise. When supply declines (S_0 to S_2), the opposite happens: Equilibrium price will rise and output will fall.

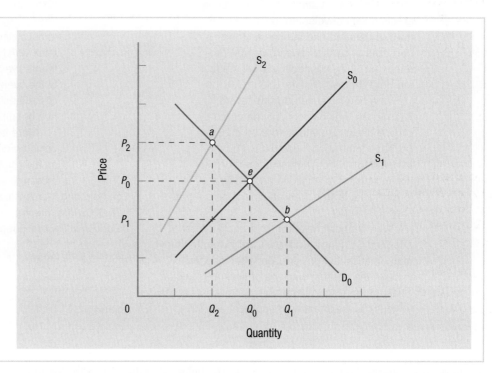

If, on the other hand, supply increases (the supply curve shifts from S_0 to S_1), equilibrium price falls to P_1, while equilibrium output rises to Q_1 (point b). This is what has happened in the electronics industry: Declining production costs have resulted in more electronic products being sold at lower prices.

Changes in Demand   The effects of demand changes are shown in Figure 11. Again, equilibrium is initially at point e, with equilibrium price and quantity at P_0 and Q_0, respectively. But let us assume the economy then enters a recession and incomes sink, or perhaps the price of some complementary good soars; in either case, demand falls. As demand declines (the demand curve shifts from D_0 to D_2), equilibrium price falls to P_2, while equilibrium output falls to Q_2 (point a).

Issue: Two-Buck Chuck: Will People Drink $2 a Bottle Wine?

The great California wines of the 1990s put California vineyards on the map. Demand, prices, and exports grew rapidly. Overplanting of new grape vines was a result. Driving along Interstate 5 or Highway 101 north of Los Angeles, grape vineyards extend as far as the eye can see, and most were planted in the mid- to late 1990s. The 2001 recession reduced the demand for California wine, and a rising dollar made imported wine relatively cheaper. The result was a sharp drop in demand for California wine and a huge surplus of grapes.

Bronco Wine Company President Fred Franzia made an exclusive deal with Trader Joe's (an unusual supermarket that features exotic food and wine products), bought the excess grapes at distressed prices, and with his modern plant produced

inexpensive wine under the Charles Shaw label. Selling for $1.99 a bottle, Two-Buck Chuck, as it is known, is available in chardonnay, merlot, cabernet sauvignon, shiraz, and sauvignon blanc. Consumers have flocked to Trader Joe's and literally haul cases of wine out by the carload. In less than a decade, 400 million bottles have been sold. This is not rotgut: the 2002 shiraz beat out 2,300 other wines to win a double gold medal at the 28th Annual International Eastern Wine Competition in 2004. Still, to many Napa Valley vintners it is known as Two-Buck Upchuck.

Two-Buck Chuck was such a hit that other supermarkets were forced to offer their own discount wines. This good, low-priced wine has had the effect of opening up markets. People who previously avoided

wine because of the cost have begun drinking more. As *The Economist* has noted, the entire industry may benefit because "wine drinkers who start off drinking plonk often graduate to upmarket varieties."[3]

During the same recession just described, the demand for inferior goods (beans and baloney) will rise, as declining incomes force people to switch to cheaper substitutes. For these products, as demand increases (shifting the demand curve from D_0 to D_1), equilibrium price rises to P_1, and equilibrium output grows to Q_1 (point *b*).

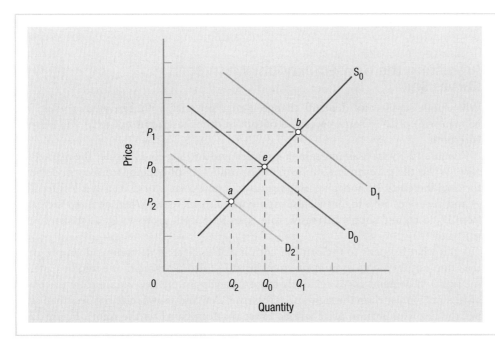

FIGURE 11—Equilibrium Price, Output, and Shifts in Demand

When demand alone changes, the effects on both equilibrium price and output can again be determined. When demand grows (D_0 to D_1), both price and output rise. Conversely, when demand falls (D_0 to D_2), both price and output fall.

---

[3] "California Drinking," *The Economist,* June 7, 2003, p. 56, and Dana Goodyear, "Drink Up: The Rise of Really Cheap Wine", *The New Yorker,* May 18, 2009, pp. 59–65.

Issue: What Happened When the Price of Jumbo Tires Quadrupled?

In mid-2006, as prices for commodities such as copper, coal, oil, zinc, and silver doubled and tripled, the price of one input needed to mine these commodities *quadrupled.* That resource? Supersized tires used on dump trucks and other heavy equipment.

Producing these 4-foot-wide, 12-foot-diameter jumbo tires has always been considered a specialized business, and there have been relatively few manufacturers with limited capacity. Further, these tires require a 24-hour cooling period in the mold, limiting the number that can be produced in a day to two or three.

This leaves the market looking like the accompanying figure. In 2005 jumbo tires were selling for one-fourth their $40,000 cost in 2006. Because the production process is time consuming and the cooling process requires the use of the mold for a day, the quantity of tires available for sale

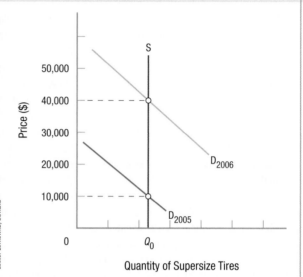

Lester Lefkowitz/CORBIS

is essentially fixed in the short run. Existing firms tried to expand capacity as well as build new factories, but estimates are that this capacity will not come on line for several years.

Because of the shortage of production capacity, mining firms are trying to extend the useful life (roughly 6,000 hours) of these expensive tires by training drivers to

avoid rocks and smoothing the surface of mine roads. Retread companies are also finding they can't meet the demand for these jumbo tires. Commodity prices stayed high until late 2008, when tire prices fell back to normal levels.

Source: Simon Romero, "Big Tires in Short Supply," *The New York Times*, April 20, 2006.

Predicting the New Equilibrium When Both Curves Shift

When both supply and demand change, things get tricky. We can predict what will happen with price in some cases and output in other cases, but not what will happen with both.

Figure 12 portrays an increase in both demand and supply. Consider the market for corn. When the government subsidizes the production of ethanol from corn, demand for corn increases. If bioengineering results in a new corn hybrid that uses less fertilizer and generates 50% higher yields, supply will also increase. When demand increases from D_0 to D_1 and supply increases from S_0 to S_1, output grows to Q_1 as shown in the left panel.

But what happens to the price of corn is not so clear. If demand and supply grow the same, output increases but price remains at P_0 (also captured in the middle panel to the right). If demand grows relatively more than supply, the new equilibrium price will be higher (top panel on the right). Conversely, if demand grows relatively less than supply, the new equilibrium price will be lower (bottom panel on the right). Figure 12 is just one of the four possibilities when both supply and demand change. The other three possibilities are shown in Table 1, and all four possibilities are discussed in detail in the *CourseTutor.*

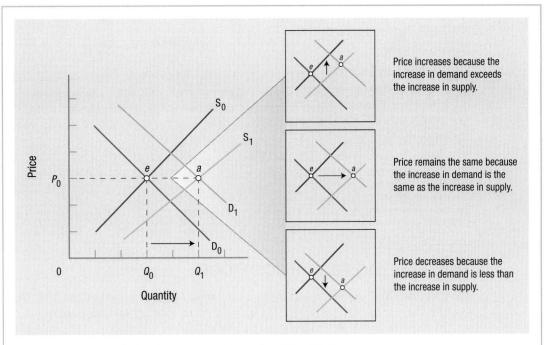

FIGURE 12—Increase in Supply, Increase in Demand, and Equilibrium

When both demand and supply increase, output will clearly rise, but what happens to the new equilibrium price is uncertain. If demand grows relatively more than supply, price will rise, but if supply grows relatively more than demand, price will fall.

TABLE 1	The Effect of Changes in Demand or Supply on Equilibrium Prices and Quantities		

Change in Demand	Change in Supply	Change in Equilibrium Price	Change in Equilibrium Quantity
No change	Increase	Decrease	Increase
No change	Decrease	Increase	Decrease
Increase	No change	Increase	Increase
Decrease	No change	Decrease	Decrease
Increase	Increase	Indeterminate	Increase
Decrease	Decrease	Indeterminate	Decrease
Increase	Decrease	Increase	Indeterminate
Decrease	Increase	Decrease	Indeterminate

■ CHECKPOINT

MARKET EQUILIBRIUM

- Together, supply and demand determine market equilibrium.
- Equilibrium occurs when quantity supplied exactly equals quantity demanded.
- The equilibrium price is also called the market-clearing price.

- When supply and demand change, equilibrium price and output change.

- When only one curve shifts, the resulting changes in equilibrium price and quantity can be predicted.

- When both curves shift, we can predict the change in equilibrium price in some cases or the change in equilibrium quantity in others, but never both. We have to determine the relative magnitudes of the shifts before we can predict both equilibrium price and quantity.

QUESTIONS: As China and India (both with huge populations and rapidly growing economies) continue to develop, what do you think will happen to their demand for energy and specifically oil? What will suppliers of oil do in the face of this demand? Will this have an impact on world energy (oil) prices? What sort of policies or events could alter your forecast about the future price of oil?

Answers to the Checkpoint questions can be found at the end of this chapter.

Price Ceilings and Price Floors

When competitive markets are left to determine equilibrium price and output, they clear. Businesses provide consumers with the quantity of goods they want to purchase at the established prices; there are no shortages or surpluses.

But, there are times when the equilibrium price may not be what many people consider to be a desired or fair price. For political or social reasons—not economic ones—governments will intervene in the market by setting limits on such things as wages, apartment rents, electricity, or agricultural commodities. Government uses price ceilings and price floors to keep prices below or above market equilibrium. But, what happens when government sets prices below or above market equilibrium?

Price Ceilings

Price ceiling: A government-set maximum price that can be charged for a product or service. When the price ceiling is set below equilibrium, it leads to shortages.

When the government sets a **price ceiling,** it is legally mandating the maximum price that can be charged for a product or service. This is a legal maximum; regardless of market forces, price cannot exceed this level.

Figure 13 shows an *effective* price ceiling, or one in which the ceiling price is set below the equilibrium price. In this case, equilibrium price is at P_e, but the government

FIGURE 13—Price Ceiling Below Equilibrium Price Creates Shortages

A price ceiling is a maximum sales price for a product. When the government enacts a price ceiling below equilibrium, it creates shortages. Consumers will demand Q_1 output at a price of P_c, but businesses will supply only Q_2, creating a shortage equal to $Q_1 - Q_2$. The product's price cannot rise to restore equilibrium because of the legal price ceiling.

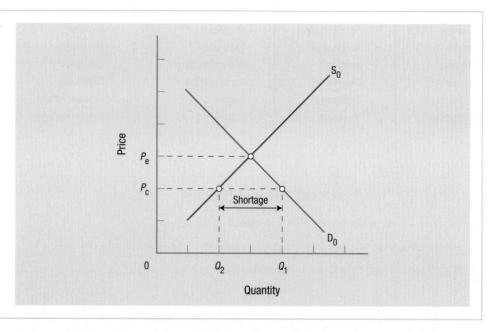

has set a price ceiling at P_c. Quantity supplied at the ceiling price is Q_2, whereas consumers want Q_1, so the result is a shortage of $Q_1 - Q_2$ units of the product. Note that if the price ceiling is set above P_e, the market simply settles at P_e, and the price ceiling has no impact.

Rent controls are a classic example of price ceilings. Many local governments have decided affordable housing is a priority and that tenants need protection from high rental rates (presumably protection from greedy landlords). And in the short run, rent controls work. Landlords cannot easily convert apartment units to alternative uses, so they have little choice but to rent out these units at the lower rates. But as soon as they can, landlords will convert their real estate holdings to condominiums or offices. Other landlords, facing a ceiling on the rents they can charge, will not incur additional upkeep charges and so will let their properties deteriorate. Few landlords, meanwhile, will invest in more rental units. So the shortage we see in Figure 13 will come from a reduced number of rental units due to condo conversion and no new units, while current units are allowed to deteriorate.

Okay, you might say, there will be a shortage of rental units over time, but at least the rents charged will be "fairer." The question is, fairer to whom? The chief beneficiaries are the people already renting. Over time, their rents will be much lower than the equilibrium price. Sufferers include people moving to the area who cannot find a place to rent, or growing families that are trapped in small apartments. When these people do find a potential place, there is a huge incentive for landlords to ask for under-the-table payments, such as a $5,000 payment for keys to the apartment. In New York City, rent control instituted during World War II is still in place: The beneficiary class is not the poor, but people lucky enough to be renters during the early phases of the rent control and who have passed on their apartments to their family. This has led to the gruesome habit of would-be renters reading obituaries to discover renters who died with no obvious heirs. This behavior is a far cry from the normal act of looking for an apartment when markets work freely.

More recently, the federal government has begun placing a form of price ceiling on the Medicare payments to doctors and hospitals. Doctors who accept Medicare patients are not allowed to charge patients more than what is allowed by Medicare for specific procedures. These maximum prices have been getting lower as the Medicare budget has been squeezed. As a result, some doctors no longer accept new Medicare patients, since the fees they can charge will no longer cover their costs. For some patients who are just retiring and joining Medicare, finding a doctor can be difficult. The price ceilings have created a shortage of doctors willing to treat Medicare patients.

The key point to remember here is that price ceilings are intended to keep the price of a product below its market or equilibrium level. The ultimate effect of a price ceiling, however, is that the quantity of the product demanded exceeds the quantity supplied, thereby producing a shortage of the product in the market.

Price Floors

A **price floor** is a government-mandated minimum price that can be charged for a product or service. Regardless of market forces, product price cannot legally fall below this level.

Figure 14 on the next page shows the economic impact of price floors. In this case, the price floor, P_f, is set above equilibrium, P_e, resulting in a surplus of $Q_2 - Q_1$ units. At price P_f, businesses want to supply more of the product (Q_2) than consumers are willing to buy (Q_1), thus generating a surplus. Again, note that if the price floor is set below equilibrium, it has no impact on the market.

For over a half-century, agricultural price supports or price floors have been used to try to smooth out the income of farmers, which often fluctuates wildly due to wide annual variations in crop prices. Government acts as a buyer of last resort, and if surpluses result, the government purchases these commodities. Since these price supports

Price floor: A government-set minimum price that can be charged for a product or service. When the price floor is set above equilibrium, it leads to surpluses.

FIGURE 14—Price Floor Above Equilibrium Price Creates Surpluses

A price floor is the lowest price at which a product can be sold. When the government sets a price floor above equilibrium, it creates surpluses. Businesses try to sell Q_2 at a price of P_f, but consumers are willing to purchase only Q_1 at that price. The result is a market surplus equal to $Q_2 - Q_1$. The price floor prevents the product's price from falling to equilibrium.

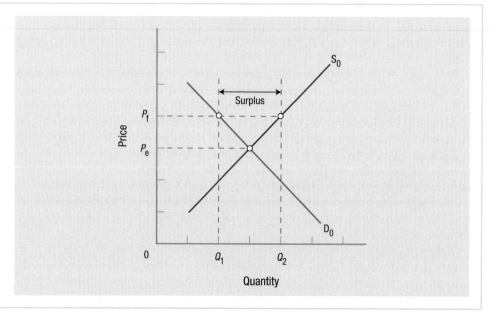

typically are above market equilibrium prices, frequent surpluses have resulted. These surpluses have been stored and earmarked for use in the event of future shortages, but few such shortages have arisen due to improvements in farm technology and rising crop yields. Consumers pay more for agricultural commodities, and surpluses arise and often rot, all in the expectation that the income of farmers will be steady. Despite their questionable economic justification, political pressures have ensured that agricultural price supports and related programs still command a sizable share of the discretionary domestic federal budget.

Another area in which price floors are used is the minimum wage. To the extent that the minimum wage is set above the equilibrium wage, unemployment—a surplus of labor—will result. The groups most affected by this unemployment tend to be low-skilled workers and teenagers, groups that already suffer high unemployment rates. Such people might have been able to find jobs had employers been allowed to pay them the equilibrium wage rate, but these jobs go uncreated when employers are forced to pay the higher minimum wage.

Governments must be careful when setting price ceilings and price floors to avoid creating shortages or surpluses.

■ CHECKPOINT

PRICE CEILINGS AND PRICE FLOORS

- Governments use price floors and price ceilings to intervene in markets.

- A price ceiling is a maximum legal price that can be charged for a product. Price ceilings set below equilibrium result in shortages.

- A price floor is the minimum legal price that can be charged for a product. Price floors set above market equilibrium result in surpluses.

QUESTION: Rent controls are found in cities such as New York and Santa Monica, California, where land prices are at a premium and the city is relatively builtout (very little vacant land remains). Why is rent control not found in cities such as Phoenix, Arizona, or Denver, Colorado?

Answers to the Checkpoint question can be found at the end of the chapter.

Key Concepts

Chapter Summary

Markets

Markets are institutions that enable buyers and sellers to interact and transact business with one another. Markets differ in geographical location, products offered, and size. Prices contain an incredible amount of information for both buyers and sellers. Through their purchases, consumers signal their willingness to exchange money or other valuables for particular products at particular prices. These signals help businesses to decide what to produce and how much of it to produce. Consequently, the market economy is often called the price system.

Demand

Demand refers to the quantity of products people are willing and able to purchase during some specific time period, all other relevant factors being held constant. Price and quantity demanded stand in a negative (inverse) relationship: as price rises, consumers buy fewer units; and as price falls, consumers buy more units. This is known as the law of demand and is depicted in a downward-sloping demand curve.

Market demand curves are found by horizontally summing individual demand curves.

The determinants of demand include (1) consumer tastes and preferences, (2) income, (3) prices of substitutes and complements, (4) the number of buyers in the market, and (5) expectations regarding future prices, incomes, and product availability. Demand changes (the demand curve shifts) when one or more of these determinants change. A shift to the right reflects an increase in demand, whereas a shift to the left represents a decline in demand.

A change in quantity demanded occurs only when the price of a product changes, leading consumers to adjust their purchases by moving along the existing demand curve.

Supply

Supply is the quantity of a product producers are willing and able to put on the market at various prices, all other relevant factors being held constant. The law of supply reflects the positive relationship between price and quantity supplied: The higher the market price, the more goods supplied; and the lower the market price, the fewer goods supplied. It is depicted in an upward-sloping supply curve. Market supply, as with market demand, is arrived at by horizontally summing the individual supplies of all of the firms in the market.

The six determinants of supply are (1) production technology, (2) the costs of resources, (3) prices of other commodities, (4) expectations, (5) the number of sellers or producers in the market, and (6) taxes and subsidies. When one or more of the determinants of supply change, a change in supply results, causing a shift in the supply curve. A shift to the right reflects an increase in supply, whereas a shift to the left represents a decline in supply. A change in quantity supplied is only caused by a change in the price of the product; it results in a movement along the existing supply curve.

Market Equilibrium

Supply and demand together determine market equilibrium. Equilibrium occurs when quantity demanded and quantity supplied are precisely equal: producers are bringing precisely the quantity of some good to market that consumers wish to purchase. The price at which equilibrium is reached is called the equilibrium price, or the market-clearing price.

If prices are set too high, surpluses result, which drive prices back down to equilibrium levels. If prices are set too low, a shortage results, which drives prices up until equilibrium is reached.

When supply and demand change (a shift in the curves), equilibrium price and output change. When only one curve shifts, then both resulting changes in equilibrium price and quantity can be predicted.

When the two curves both shift, the change in equilibrium price can be forecasted in some instances, and the change in equilibrium output in others, but never both.

Price Ceilings and Price Floors

Governments sometimes use price ceilings or price floors to keep prices below or above the market equilibrium.

A price ceiling is the maximum legal price that can be charged for a product. Price ceilings set below equilibrium result in shortages.

A price floor is the minimum legal price that can be charged for a product. Price floors set above market equilibrium result in surpluses.

Questions and Problems

Check Your Understanding

1. Product prices give consumers and businesses a lot of information besides just the price. What are they?

2. As the world population ages, will the demand for cholesterol drugs [increase/decrease/remain the same]? Assume there is a positive relationship between aging and cholesterol levels. Is this change a change in demand or a change in quantity demanded?

3. Describe some of the reasons why supply changes. Improved technology typically results in lower prices for most products. Why do you think this is true? Describe the difference between a change in supply and a change in quantity supplied.

4. Both individual and market demand curves have negative slopes and reflect the law of demand. What is the difference between the two curves?

5. Describe the determinants of demand. Why are they important?

6. Describe a price ceiling. What is the impact of an effective price ceiling? Show this on the figure on the next page. Give an example. Describe a price floor. What

is the impact of an effective price floor? Show this on the figure below. Give an example.

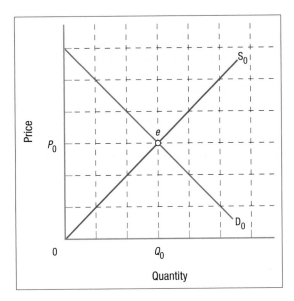

Apply the Concepts

7. Demand for tickets to sports events such as the Super Bowl has increased. Has supply increased? What does the answer to this tell you about the price of these tickets compared to a few years ago?

8. In 2006 rental car companies often charged more to rent a compact car than an SUV or a luxury vehicle. Why do you think rental companies turned their normal pricing structure on its head?

9.

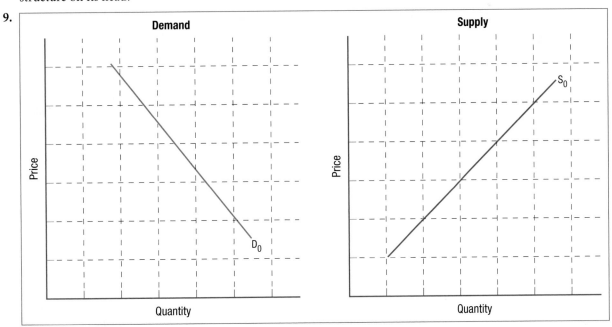

Using the figures above, answer the following questions:

a. On the Demand panel:
- Show an increase in demand and label it D_1.
- Show a decrease in demand and label it D_2.
- Show an increase in quantity demanded.

- ■ Show a decrease in quantity demanded.
- ■ What causes demand to change?
- ■ What causes quantity demanded to change?

b. On the Supply panel:
- ■ Show an increase in supply and label it S_1.
- ■ Show a decrease in supply and label it S_2.
- ■ Show an increase in quantity supplied.
- ■ Show a decrease in quantity supplied.
- ■ What causes supply to change?
- ■ What causes quantity supplied to change?

10. Several medical studies have shown that red wine in moderation is good for the heart. How would such a study affect the public's demand for wine? Would it have an impact on the type of grapes planted in new vineyards?

11. Assume initially that the demand and supply for premium coffees (one-pound bags) are in equilibrium. Now assume Starbucks introduces the world to premium blends, and so demand rises substantially. Describe what will happen in this market as it moves to a new equilibrium. If a hard freeze eliminates Brazil's premium coffee crop, what will happen to the price of premium coffee?

In the News

12. Norrath is a place in the online game EverQuest II. It is a virtual world with roughly 350,000 players "arrayed over worlds that are tethered to dozens of servers." As Rob Walker noted, "EverQuest is filled with half-elves, castles, sword fights and such, and involves a fairly complex internal economy, whose currency is platinum pieces used to buy weapons, food and other goods." This virtual market, however, has led to a real-world market, with real dollars for virtual goods. Players sell weapons, complete characters, and other virtual items on EverQuest's internal market called Station Exchange and on eBay. Common items sell for $10 to $25, while extensive characters or weapons can fetch a thousand dollars or more. (Based on Rob Walker, "The Buying Game: A real market, overseen by a real corporation, selling things that don't really exist," *New York Times Magazine,* October 16, 2005, p. 28.)

    Why would someone buy virtual goods? Does supply and demand play any role in this real market for virtual goods? If there were virtual games similar to EverQuest II where everything is free, would any real markets exist for their virtual goods? How does paying for a virtual product differ from the situation where a buyer could purchase a nice watch for a reasonable price, but decides to buy a luxury brand for 10 to 20 times as much?

13. In December 2005, the *Wall Street Journal* reported that Clark Foam, a major supplier of polyurethane cores (blanks) for hand-shaped surfboards, closed its plant and went out of business (Peter Sanders and Stephanie Kang, "Wipeout for Key Player in Surfboard Industry," *The Wall Street Journal,* December 8, 2005, p. B1). Clark Foam was the Microsoft of surfboard blank makers, and had been supplying foam blanks to surf shops for over 50 years. Polyurethane blanks, while light and sturdy, contain a toxic chemical, toluene diisocyanate (TDI). Over the last two decades the Environmental Protection Agency has increasingly been restricting the use of TDI. Clark Foam's owner Gordon "Grubby" Clark indicated in a letter to customers that he was tired of fighting environmental regulators, lawsuits over injury to employees, and fire regulations. Surf historian and author of *The Encyclopedia of Surfing,* Matt Warshaw said, "It's the equivalent of removing lumber for the housing industry."

    a. If you owned a retail surfboard shop and read this article in the *Wall Street Journal,* would you change the prices on the existing surfboards you have in the shop? Why or why not?

    b. If the demand for surfboards remains constant over the next few years, what would you expect to see happen on the supply side in this industry?

14. Polysilicon is used to produce computer chips and solar photovoltaics. Currently, more polysilicon is used to produce computer chips, but the demand for ultrapure polysilicon for solar panels is rising. According to a 2006 *Business Week* article (John Carey, "What's Raining on Solar's Parade," *Business Week,* February 6, 2006, p. 78), this has created a shortage, and prices have more than doubled between 2004 and 2006.

   a. High oil and energy prices, along with subsidies from U.S. and European governments for solar power, have increased demand, but suppliers are reluctant to build new factories or expand existing facilities, because they fear governments can easily eliminate incentives and at this point they do not know if solar energy is just a fad. Are these legitimate concerns for business?

   b. Given the uncertainty associated with building additional production capacity in the polysilicon industry, what might these manufacturers do to reduce the risk?

15. Nobel Prize winner Gary Becker and Judge Richard Posner ("How to Make the Poor Poorer," *The Wall Street Journal,* January 26, 2007, p. A11) suggested that "unions strongly favor the minimum wage because it reduces competition from low-wage workers (who, partly because most of them work part time, tend not to be unionized) and thus enhances unions' bargaining power." They further argued that "although some workers benefit—those who were paid the old minimum wage but are worth the new higher one to the employers—others are pushed into unemployment, the underground economy or crime. The losers are therefore likely to lose more than the gainers gain; they are also likely to be poorer people." Are both of these statements consistent with the model of price floors discussed in this chapter? Why or why not?

16. Professor Donald Boudreaux wrote (*Wall Street Journal,* August 23, 2006, p. A11) that "there are heaps of bad arguments for raising the minimum wage. Perhaps the worst . . . is that a minimum wage increase is justified if a full-time worker earning the current minimum wage cannot afford to live in a city such as Chicago." He then asked "why settle for enabling workers to live only in the likes of Chicago? Why not raise the minimum wage so that everyone can afford to live in, say, Nantucket, Hyannis Port or Beverly Hills, within walking distance of Rodeo Drive?" Should the minimum wage be a "living wage," so a full-time worker can live comfortably in a given locale? What would be the impact if minimum wages were structured this way?

Solving Problems

17. The table below represents the world supply and demand for natural vanilla in thousands of pounds. A large portion of natural vanilla is grown in Madagascar and comes from orchids that require a lot of time to cultivate. The sequence of events described below actually happened, but the numbers have been altered to make the calculations easier (See James Altucher, "Supply, Demand, and Edible Orchids," *Financial Times,* September 20, 2005, p.12). Assume the original supply and demand curves are represented in the table below.

Price ($/pound)	Quantity Demanded (thousands)	Quantity Supplied (thousands)
0	20	0
10	16	6
20	12	12
30	8	18
40	4	24
50	0	30

a. Graph both the supply (S_0) and demand (D_0) curves. What is the current equilibrium price? Label that point *a*.

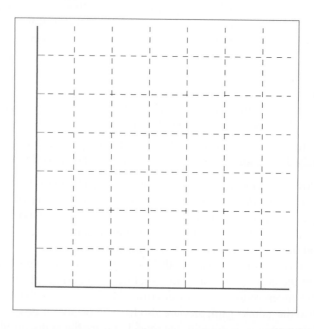

b. Assume that Madagascar is hit by a hurricane (which actually occurred in 2000), and the world's supply of vanilla is reduced by 5/6, or 83%. Label the new supply curve (S_1). What will be the new equilibrium price in the market? Label that point *b*.

c. Now assume that Coca-Cola announces plans to introduce a new "Vanilla Coke," and this increases the demand for natural vanilla by 25%. Label the new demand curve (D_1). What will be the new equilibrium price? Label this new equilibrium point *c*. Remember that the supply of natural vanilla was reduced by the hurricane earlier.

d. Growing the orchids that produce natural vanilla requires a climate with roughly 80% humidity, and the possible grower countries generally fall within 20° north or south of the equator. A doubling of prices encouraged several other countries (e.g., Uganda and Indonesia) to begin growing orchids or up their current production. Within several years, supply was back to normal (S_0), but by then, synthetic vanilla had replaced 80% of the original demand (D_0). Label this new demand curve (D_2). What is the new equilibrium price and output?

18. In late 2006 and early 2007, orange crops in Florida were smaller than expected, and the crop in California was put in a deep freeze by an Arctic cold front. As a result, the production of oranges was severely reduced. In addition, in early 2007, President Bush called for the United States to reduce its gasoline consumption by 20% in the next decade. He proposed an increase in ethanol produced from corn and the stalks and leaves from corn and other grasses. What was the likely impact of these two events on food prices in the United States?

Answers to Questions in CheckPoints

Check Point: Markets

The market for financial securities is a huge, well-organized, and regulated market compared to local farmer's markets. Trillions of dollars change hands each week in the financial markets, and products are standardized.

Check Point: Demand

Rising gasoline prices have caused the demand for hybrids to swell. This is a change in demand.

Check Point: Supply

Since iPods and other MP3 players are substitutes for high-end stereo equipment, production and sales of high-end stereo equipment have declined.

Check Point: Market Equilibrium

Demand for both energy and oil will increase. Suppliers of oil will attempt to move up their supply curve and provide more to the market. Since all of the easy (cheap) oil has been found, costs to add to supplies will rise, and oil prices will gradually rise; in the longer term, alternatives will become more attractive, keeping oil prices from rising too rapidly.

Check Point: Price Ceilings and Price Floors

Cities with a lot of vacant land do not have rents high enough to support activists who try to get people to control rents. Only in cities with little vacant land and high population densities are rents high enough that enough people think it "unfair," resulting in rent controls. If rent controls are introduced where a lot of vacant land exists, the land simply remains vacant because development is stymied.

Market Efficiency, Market Failure, and Government

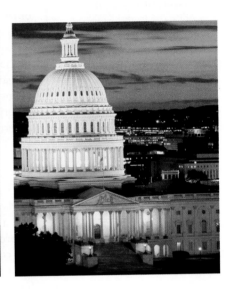

Panoramic Images/Getty Images

Everywhere we look in the world there are markets, from the Tokyo fish markets, where every morning 20,000 flash-frozen tuna weighing 400 to 500 pounds each are auctioned off in a few hours; to Aalsmeer, Holland, where millions of fresh flowers are flown in from all over the world every day, auctioned off, and then shipped to firms in other parts of the world; to Chicago, where billions of dollars of derivative securities and commodities are bought and sold on the futures market daily. Beyond these big markets, moreover, countless smaller markets dot our local landscapes, and many new virtual markets are springing up on the Internet.

In earlier chapters, we saw that every economy faces tradeoffs in the use of its resources to produce various goods and services, as represented graphically by the production possibilities frontier. The last chapter considered how supply and demand work together to determine the quantities of various products sold and the equilibrium prices consumers must pay for them in a market economy. As we saw, Adam Smith's invisible hand works to ensure that, in a market society, consumers get what they want.

Thus far, the markets we have studied have been stylized versions of competitive markets: they have featured many buyers and sellers, a uniform product, consumers and sellers who have complete information about the market, and few barriers to market entry or exit.

In this chapter, we consider some of the complexities inherent to most markets. The typical market does not meet all the criteria of a truly competitive market. That does not mean the supply and demand analysis you just absorbed will not be useful in analyzing economic events. Often, however, you will need to temper your analysis to fit the specific conditions of the markets you study. As we will find, some markets need constraints or rules to ensure that society gets the best results.

This chapter begins by considering the efficiency of the market system. We look at the conditions needed for a market to exist and be efficient. We also present a tool for determining economic efficiency. Efficient markets are rationing devices, ensuring that those who value a product the most are the ones who get it. Prices and profits help to carry out this rationing by serving as important market signals.

Markets rarely live up to our definition of the competitive market ideal. The second section of this chapter discusses markets in light of real-world experience, specifically focusing on market failures, or deviations from conditions of perfect competition. If a market is not competitive, this does not mean it collapses or is no longer a market. It just means that the market fails to contain the mechanisms for allocating resources in the best possible way, from the perspective of the larger society. In this section, we also consider several common solutions to market failures. Some failures require just a minor fix, such as a new regulation or law, but others may require that the government take over and provide products.

In the final section of this chapter, we consider this interplay between markets, market failure, and government intervention during the last century and a half. You will see that the borders between the two have changed over time. Issues like regulating commercial and investment banks, mitigating the impact of climate change, taming globalization, and providing health care all bring markets and government into conflict. The history of the American economy has been one of periodic market failures followed by the growth of government and regulation.

Markets and Efficiency

Markets are efficient mechanisms for allocating resources. Just think how much information a government bureaucrat would need to decide how many plasma HDTVs should be produced, what companies should produce them, and who should get them. When you consider that our country has many millions of people who might want such televisions and several thousand possible suppliers, it becomes clear the likelihood of a lone bureaucrat or agency developing an efficient plan for HDTV production and distribution is extremely small. This was the problem the Soviet Union faced with virtually every good it produced, and it goes a long way toward explaining that nation's economic and political collapse.

The prices and profits characteristic of the market system provide incentives and signals that are nonexistent or seriously flawed in other systems of resource allocation. The old Soviet joke that "They pretend to pay us and we pretend to work" illustrates this problem. But efficient markets do not just spontaneously develop. They need reasonable laws and institutions to ensure their proper functioning.

Efficient Market Requirements

For markets to be efficient, they must have well-structured institutions. John McMillan[1] suggests five institutional requirements for workable markets: (1) information is widely available, or in McMillan's words, "information flows smoothly"; (2) property rights are protected; (3) private contracts are enforced such that "people can be trusted to live up to their promises"; (4) spillovers from other actors are limited, or "side effects of third parties are curtailed"; and (5) competition prevails. Let's briefly discuss each of these requirements.

Accurate Information Is Widely Available

For markets to work efficiently, transactions costs must be kept low. One factor that reduces transactions costs is accurate and readily available information. Negotiations between the parties will be smoother if each party has adequate information about the product.

---

[1] John McMillan, *Reinventing the Bazaar: A Natural History of Markets* (New York: Norton), 2002.

Without good information, one party will not have the confidence needed to value the product, so that party will be reluctant to enter into a transaction. Many products today are highly sophisticated, and consumers need high-quality information in order to make good choices. This is important for buyers and sellers.

Property Rights Are Protected

"Imagine a country where nobody can identify who owns what, addresses cannot be easily verified, people cannot be made to pay their debts, resources cannot be conveniently turned into money, ownership cannot be divided into shares, descriptions of assets are not standardized and cannot be easily compared, and the rules that govern property vary from neighborhood to neighborhood or even from street to street."[2] These are the conditions Hernando de Soto found throughout most of the developing world.

Most of us are accustomed to elaborate title and insurance provisions that govern the transfer of automobiles, real estate, and corporate shares in this country. In many developing nations, however, no such provisions exist. When a government fails to establish and protect **property rights,** more informal economic mechanisms will evolve. Even so, the absence of clear title prevents assets from being used as capital. You cannot borrow against your home, for instance, to purchase the sewing machine needed to start a small tailoring business if your family's long-standing ownership of this home has never been legally documented.

Property rights provide a powerful incentive for the optimal use of resources. With ownership comes the incentive to use resources efficiently, not to waste.

> **Property rights:** The clear delineation of ownership of property backed by government enforcement.

Contract Obligations Are Enforced

A well-functioning legal system makes doing business easier, and it is absolutely essential for large-scale business activity. Without the safeguards of a legal system, firms must rely on discussions with one another to determine whether customers are credit-worthy, or whether a customer's production order is trustworthy.

Still, even when a legal system is operating well, markets require some informal rules to create the general presumption that bargains will be kept. Most civil court systems in developed nations take several years to hear and decide disputes. Lawsuits, moreover, are never cheap.

The more valuable the contract, the more a legal instrument is needed to ensure that it is honored. Business relationships involving small amounts can usually rely on simple honesty. But cheating on a large loan, contract, or shipment might be worth the sacrifice of one's reputation, so something more than a handshake is needed to ensure compliance. Large and complex markets need a well running legal system that enforces contracts and agreements.

There Are No External Costs or Benefits

When you drive your car on a crowded highway, you are inflicting *external costs* on other drivers and the larger society by adding to congestion and pollution. By attending a private college, conversely, you are conferring *external benefits* on the rest of us. You are more likely to become a better citizen, be less likely to commit a crime, and pay a greater share of the tax bill. Thus, we all benefit from your education, even though we do not have to bear the cost of it. These external costs and benefits are called *externalities,* as we will see later in this chapter. Markets operate most efficiently when externalities are minimized.

Competitive Markets Prevail

When a market has many buyers and sellers, no one seller has the ability to raise its price above that of its competitors. To do so would be to lose most of its business. In competitive markets, products are close substitutes, so an increase in price by one firm would simply lead consumers to shift their purchases to other firms.

---

[2] Hernando de Soto, *The Mystery of Capital: Why Capitalism Triumphs in the West and Fails Everywhere Else* (New York: Basic Books), 2000, p. 15.

Competitive markets, moreover, tend to aggregate individual appraisals of value into market information. Without a market, values are determined in one-on-one encounters between buyer and seller. Competitive bargaining between many buyers and sellers gives rise to aggregate market prices and values much like prices are set in an auction. Therefore, competitive markets must be open to entry and exit.

Good information, protection of property, an efficient and fair legal system, the absence of externalities, and competition are all required if society is to get the best from its markets. These elements all work together to make markets efficient, as we will now see.

The Discipline of Markets

Markets impose discipline on consumers and producers. Sellers would like to get away with charging higher prices while producing shoddier goods, thereby earning greater profits. Few manufacturers or service providers turn out terrific goods and services simply to feel good. Rather, their economic survival depends on it.

As for us consumers, we all would like to drive better cars, wear nothing but designer clothes, drink the finest wines, and smoke Cuban cigars. (Well, some of us would like the cigars.) For the superrich, such consumption is not only possible, but commonplace. For the rest of us, the market rations us out of such goods, except on very special occasions.

This is another function of the market: rationing. Given our limited resources, each of us must decide which products are most important to us, since we cannot have unlimited quantities. Everyone chooses based on their tastes, preferences, and limited incomes.

High prices in a market indicate that consumers value a product highly. Higher prices are usually accompanied by higher profits, and these higher profits attract new firms into the market. These new firms increase supply, and this reduces prices. The solution for high prices is high prices. As we saw in the last chapter, however, if something keeps above-market prices from falling, surpluses will accrue. Conversely, if something keeps low prices from rising to their equilibrium level, shortages will result.

Markets can also be useful tools for the government, since markets allocate resources to those individuals or firms that are most efficient. For example, the government uses markets to allocate the radio and cellular spectrum, to supply the nation's electricity, and to reduce pollution. Central planning is difficult for governments, but private firms can use planning effectively, since a firm's management and stockholders have a vested interest in the firm's success. Product and financial markets, moreover, force a discipline on private firms that is absent when governments centrally plan. If a firm fails to innovate, consumers will quit buying its products, financial markets will reduce or call in its loans, and stock markets will decimate its shares.

Consumer and Producer Surplus: A Tool for Measuring Economic Efficiency

Markets determine equilibrium prices and outputs. Both consumers and businesses get extra benefits economists call consumer and producer surplus.

Figure 1 illustrates both in a simple diagram. In both panels, the market determines equilibrium price to be \$6 (point e), at which 6 units of output are sold when S_0 and D_0 are the original curves. Assume that each point on the demand curve represents an individual consumer. Some people value the product highly. For instance, the consumer at point a in panel A thinks the product is worth \$11. This consumer clearly gets a bargain, for although she would be willing to pay \$11 for the product, the market determines that \$6 is the price everyone pays. Economists refer to this excess benefit that these consumers get (\$11 − \$6) as **consumer surplus.** So for the consumer who purchases the first unit of output, consumer surplus is equal to \$5 (\$11 − \$6). For the consumer

Consumer surplus: The difference between market price and what consumers (as individuals or the market) would be willing to pay. It is equal to the area above market price and below the demand curve.

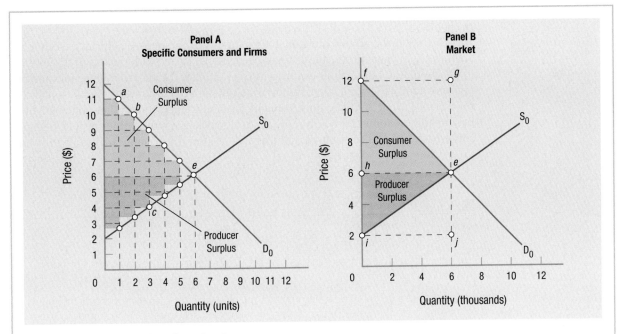

FIGURE 1—Consumer and Producer Surplus

Panel B shows a market consisting of the specific consumers and firms shown in panel A. This market determines equilibrium price to be $6 (point e), and total sales for each firm is 6 units. Consumer surplus is equal to the area under the demand curve but above the equilibrium price of $6. Producer surplus is the area under the equilibrium price but above the supply curve.

purchasing the second unit (point b), consumer surplus is a little less, $4 ($10 − $6). And so on for buyers of the third through fifth units of output. Total consumer surplus for the consumers in panel A is found by adding all of the individual consumer surpluses for each unit purchased. Thus, total consumer surplus in panel A is equal to $5 + $4 + $3 + $2 + $1 = $15.

In a similar way, assume that each point on the supply curve represents a specific firm. Notice at point c that this supplier is willing to provide the third unit to the market at a price of $4. Equilibrium price is $6, so this producer receives a **producer surplus** equal to $2 ($6 − $4). Total producer surplus in panel A is equal to the sum of each firm's producer surplus.

Panel B illustrates consumer and producer surplus for an entire market. For convenience we have simply assumed that the market is 1,000 times larger than that shown in panel A, so the x axis is output in thousands. Whereas in panel A we had discrete individuals and firms, we now have one big market, so consumer surplus is equal to the area under the demand curve above equilibrium price, or the area of the shaded triangle labeled "consumer surplus."

To put a number to the consumer surplus triangle (feh) in panel B, we can compute the value of the rectangle $fgeh$ and divide it in half. Thus, total market consumer surplus in panel B is [($12 − $6) × 6,000] ÷ 2 = ($6 × 6,000) ÷ 2 = $18,000. The shaded triangle labeled "producer surplus" (area hei) is found in the same way by computing the value of the rectangle $heji$ and dividing it in half. Producer surplus is equal to [($6 − $2) × 6,000] ÷ 2 = ($4 × 6,000) ÷ 2 = $12,000.

Markets are efficient from the standpoint that all consumers willing to pay $6 or more got the product from those firms willing to supply it for $6 or less. For demand and supply curves D_0 and S_0, total consumer and producer surplus is maximized. To see why, pick any price other than $6 and *total* consumer and producer surplus is less.

These two concepts are important in helping us to understand the impacts of market shocks and policy changes on consumer and producer well-being. We will use consumer

Producer surplus: The difference between market price and the price at which firms are willing to supply the product. It is equal to the area below market price and above the supply curve.

and producer surplus as a way to evaluate the efficiency of policies throughout the rest of the book.

The vast bulk of economic analysis focuses on questions of efficiency. Economic analysis is good at telling us the costs and benefits associated with various possible courses of action. And this analysis can help us resolve policy disputes that hinge on considerations of equity (or fairness) versus efficiency. If a policy creates considerable unfairness, for instance, while spurring only a small gain in efficiency, some other policy might be better. Still, economists have no more to say about fairness than other people. One person's view of what is fair is just as good as anyone else's. In the end, fairness always comes down to a value judgment.

■ CHECKPOINT

MARKETS AND EFFICIENCY

- Markets are efficient mechanisms for allocating resources. Prices are signals of potential profit.

- For markets to be efficient, information must be widely available, property rights must be protected, private contracts must be enforced, spillovers should be minimal, and competition should prevail.

- Markets impose discipline on producers and consumers.

- Consumer surplus occurs when consumers would have been willing to pay more for a good or service than the going price. Producer surplus occurs when businesses would have been willing to provide products at prices lower than the going price. Together, consumer and producer surplus can be used to understand the effects of public policies.

QUESTION: A *Current Affairs* broadcast by BBC Radio 4 in December 2007 focused on "repugnant markets." The program discussed markets for kidneys, prostitutes, and human cannonballs. For example, many people donate a kidney to a friend or relative, or earmark their kidneys for donation upon death, actions which are considered noble. But a market for kidneys—where people sell one of their kidneys for money—seems to disgust and outrage many of us. Because it is universally illegal to buy or sell kidneys, shortages result, and many people die each year for lack of a donation.

The program also provided the less dramatic example of Manuel Wackenheim, a "professional human missile." He is a dwarf who made his living being "hurled around for public entertainment." When a French government entity banned his performances, he pursued the case in court, eventually to the UN Commission on Human Rights. He argued that the essence of human dignity is "having a job and this is my job." The human cannonball lost. It was just too repugnant an occupation for the Commission.

Assuming that no one is forced to participate in any of these markets, what arguments can you make for and against these repugnant markets?

Answers to the Checkpoint question can be found at the end of this chapter.

Market Failures

For markets to be efficient, they must operate within solid institutional structures. As we saw, these institutional requirements include: accurate information for buyers and sellers, protection of property rights, a legal system that enforces private contracts, an absence of externalities or spillovers, and a fostering of competition. This is a tall order, and many markets do not meet these requirements. When one or more of these conditions are not met, the market is said to fail. Market failure does not mean a market totally collapses or stops existing as a market, but that it fails to provide the socially optimal amount of goods and services. As we will see later, there is one exception: in one particular category of cases, private markets provide no goods whatsoever. In this section, we examine market failures.

Accurate Information Is Not Widely Available: Asymmetric Information

For markets to operate efficiently, accurate information must be widely available. In many markets, one party to a transaction almost always has better information than the other, which is referred to as **asymmetric information.** Many buyers at garage sales have more information about the value of the antiques being sold than their sellers.

More often, however, it is sellers who have the superior knowledge. Let us consider the used car market, which Nobel Prize winner George Akerlof studied many years ago.[3] Would you buy a used car from someone you do not know? If you hesitate, it is because of asymmetric information problems: the seller knows much more about the car than you do. Does the car burn oil? Was it in an accident? Fear of undisclosed information makes you hesitant or may keep you from buying at all.

What happens when sellers have better information than buyers? Buyers cannot differentiate good cars from lemons. Since buyers cannot tell lemons from good cars, they must assume that each car is a lemon.

In this case, the market does not collapse. Instead, dealers will start offering warranties in an attempt to get higher prices for their used cars and to assure buyers that their cars are not lemons. Consumers can then be more confident of getting higher quality used cars from a dealer, since offering a warranty on lemons would be a losing proposition for dealers.

Additionally, car owners can keep scrupulous records of oil changes and repairs, or buyers, trying to reduce their risk, may take used cars to mechanics for inspection before agreeing to purchase them. The lemons problem explains why many high-quality used cars are bought by the friends of the people who sell them: Sometimes only personal trust can overcome asymmetric information.

Asymmetric information: Occurs when one party to a transaction has significantly better information than another party.

Adverse Selection

Adverse selection is a type of asymmetric information that occurs when products of different qualities are sold at the same price. Adverse selection is most apparent in insurance markets. People who purchase health insurance or life insurance know far more about their lifestyles and general states of their health than can an insurance company, even if the insurance company requires a physical.

Insurance rates are determined using averages, but the market includes some people who are higher than average risks and some people who are below average. Who do you think is more likely to purchase insurance? Overwhelmingly, it is those people above the average risk level who buy insurance, while those below the average risk level are more likely to "self-insure." The insurance pool therefore tends to be filled with higher risk individuals, which can lead to payouts exceeding projections and insurance companies losing money. In this case, then, adverse selection skews the insurance pool, giving it a risk level higher than the social average.

How can insurance underwriters deal with this problem? The answer is that they offer policies at different prices to different groups. Health insurance companies, for instance, use deductibles and co-payments to attract low-risk individuals. A deductible means that you must pay the first, say, $1,000 in medical expenses, then the insurance company begins covering a part, or even all, of the remaining costs. Co-payments are small cash payments paid for each visit to the doctor. These policies are attractive to low-risk clients since they have lower monthly premiums. For low-risk people, the likelihood of their needing to cover co-payments or pay their full deductible is low.

Conversely, a policy with a high deductible is not attractive to high-risk individuals, since they can project that the cost of the policy will be too high. They know they will probably have to pay all their monthly premiums, many co-payments, and their full deductible. These people tend to opt for policies with higher premiums but lower deductibles. This ensures that people who are high risk will select policies that accurately reflect their true state of health and lifestyle.

Adverse selection: Occurs when products of different qualities are sold at the same price because of asymmetric information.

---

[3] George Akerlof, "The Market for Lemons: Quality, Uncertainty and the Market Mechanism," *Quarterly Journal of Economics,* 1970, pp. 488–500.

Moral Hazard

Moral hazard: Asymmetric information problem that occurs when an insurance policy or some other arrangement changes the economic incentives and leads to a change in behavior.

Moral hazard occurs when an insurance policy or some other arrangement changes the economic incentives we face, thus leading us to change our behavior, usually in a way that is detrimental to the market. Think about what happens when you get comprehensive coverage, which includes theft insurance, on your car. Does this affect how scrupulously you lock your car doors? Of course it does. The moral hazard occurs because the insurance policy, which compensates you in case of loss, changes your behavior to make loss *more* (not *less*) likely.

Insurance companies place restrictions on individual behavior in some contracts. For example, insurance designed to protect the ability of professional athletes to honor multi-year contracts often prohibits dangerous activities such as skiing, rollerblading, hang gliding, and mountain climbing. In this way they reduce the moral hazard aspects of the policy. Some rental car companies, knowing that you won't check the oil in a rental car, rarely rent cars for more than a month at a time. They want to get their cars back into the shop to ensure all is well.

When high-quality information is not equally available to buyers and sellers, markets must adapt. The less complex the product and the better the information, the more efficient the market will be.

Problems with Property Rights

Property rights provide a powerful incentive to use resources wisely. Incentives to waste are much stronger when property ownership is fuzzy or resources are owned in common. There are two general instances of market failure caused by property right issues: public goods and common property resources.

Public Goods

Most of the goods we deal in are private goods: airline seats, meals at restaurants, songs on iTunes, and bicycles. When we purchase such goods, we consume them, and no one else can benefit from them. To be sure, when you buy an airline ticket, other passengers will be on the same flight, but no one else can sit in your seat for that flight—only you can enjoy its benefits. Thus, private goods are those the buyer consumes, and this precludes anyone else from similarly enjoying them.

Public goods: Goods that, once provided, no one person can be excluded from consuming (nonexclusion), and one person's consumption does not diminish the benefit to others from consuming the good (nonrivalry).

Contrast private goods with **public goods,** which are goods that one person can consume without diminishing what is left for others. My watching PBS does not mean that there is less PBS for you to watch. Economists refer to such a situation as one of *nonrivalry.* Public goods are also *nonexclusive,* meaning that once such a good has been provided for one person, others cannot be excluded from enjoying it. Normally, public goods are both nonrival and nonexclusive, whereas private goods are rival and exclusive.

Free rider: When a public good is provided, consumers cannot be excluded from enjoying the product, so some consume the product without paying.

Public goods give rise to the **free rider** problem. Once a public good has been provided, other consumers cannot be excluded from it, so many people will choose to enjoy the benefit without paying; they will free ride. National Public Radio and PBS are public goods. They exist because they receive donations from individuals, foundations, and governments, but their week-long begging and guilt transference sessions notwithstanding, most listeners and viewers (maybe as high as 90%) still choose to enjoy their services without pledging support.

Other public goods include weather forecasts, national defense, lighthouses, flood control projects, GPS satellites, World Court rulings, mosquito eradication, and immunization. Because these goods are nonrival and nonexclusive, they invariably end up being provided by governments.

This is the one case mentioned above where market failure can lead to no goods at all being provided by private markets. Government must step in. Who would contribute—or contribute adequately—to the costs of providing accurate weather forecasts if your neighbors were free riders? Contributions would soon dry up, and the public good in question would not be provided at all.

Common Property Resources

Another market failure caused by problems with property rights occurs when a good is a **common property resource** or open-access resource. The market failure associated with commonly owned properties is often referred to as "the tragedy of the commons,"[4] where the tendency is for commonly held resources to be overused and overexploited. Because these resources are held in common, individuals have little incentive to use them in a sustainable fashion, so each person races to "get theirs" before others can do the same.

Ocean fisheries are a good example. Fish in the ocean were once in excess supply; there was no need for use of this resource to be restricted. Very often people fished one species until it was exhausted and then moved on to fish another. Since the ocean was so big and fish species so plentiful, no one noticed. As the global demand for fish has risen, improved fishing technologies and boats have allowed fishing boats to increase their hauls and to range around the world. Because many of the world's fisheries are still unregulated, one population after another has been fished out, so much so that it has been estimated that nearly 90% of the ocean's predators are gone. The situation is clearly unsustainable, and indeed, as fish populations have shrunk, so have fishing fleets.

The solution to the problem of common property resources and overexploitation has typically focused on assigning property rights or using government regulation to protect these assets. Nobel Prize winner Elinor Ostrom studied small communities in the developing world and reported that these societies and groups regularly develop and enforce their own rules to prevent overusing their resources. Without formal government in place, the requirements for self-policing were: rules that defined what each party received (implicit property rights), good conflict resolution rules, the acknowledged duty of users to maintain

> **Common property resources:** Resources that are owned by the community at large (parks, ocean fish, and the atmosphere) and therefore tend to be overexploited because individuals have little incentive to use them in a sustainable fashion.

Issue: Tragedy of the "Anticommons"

When the community holds property in common, overuse is often the result. Examples include overfishing, congestion, and the unnecessary use of antibiotics that results in drug-resistant infections. This is the tragedy of the commons.

The opposite is gridlock that occurs when too many people own a given property, often stifling innovation and leading to *underuse*. Spotting overuse is easy, but spotting underuse is more difficult. As Michael Heller[5] tells it, "A few years ago, a drug company executive presented me with an unsettling puzzle. His scientists had found a treatment for Alzheimer's disease, but they couldn't bring it to market unless the company bought access to dozens of patents. Any single patent owner could demand a huge payoff; some blocked the whole deal. This story does not have a happy ending. The drug sits on the shelf though it might have saved millions of lives and earned billions of dollars."

It is difficult to know when we have missed some technological advance because patent rights were held by so many. Heller notes that since airlines were deregulated in 1975, airport congestion has grown because the number of flyers has tripled, but only one new airport (Denver) has been built. In addition, numerous communities and landowners have been able to prevent most runway expansion projects at other congested airports.

Google has faced similar issues in its attempt to develop a database of out-of-print books that would represent a huge online library. Sued by the Author's Guild, Google reached a tentative multimillion-dollar agreement, permitting any author or publisher to "opt-out" of the system. Locating and getting agreement with all copyright holders is complicated by the fact that a copyright lasts for 75 years beyond the death of the author. Locating each heir would have been cost prohibitive and doomed the project from the start. This project will likely be in the courts for years. A smaller firm with fewer resources would have dropped it long ago.

Solutions to gridlock will likely involve legislation that makes it easier to assemble groups of property owners. This may involve forcing patent and copyright holders into pools, in much the same way ASCAP and BMI represent property holders in the music industry. For a fee, radio stations and businesses are permitted to play music, and ASCAP and BMI distribute these revenues to songwriters, musicians, and record labels based on the amount of play. Such a solution may require redefining these property rights.

---

[4] Garrett Hardin, "The Tragedy of the Commons," *Science* 162, 1968, pp. 1243–48.

[5] Michael Heller, *The Gridlock Economy: How Too Much Ownership Wrecks Markets, Stops Innovation, and Costs Lives* (New York: Basic Books), 2008.

the common resource in proportion to their benefits, monitoring and enforcement of the rules by the participants, and users taking part in the rule-making process.

In summary, when property rights are clearly defined, people have an incentive to use resources efficiently. But property rights are not always clearly defined, and this leads to market failure and waste. In the case of public goods, the free rider problem means that these goods may not be provided at all if left to private devices—government needs to step in. With common property resources, there is an incentive for individuals to grab as much as they can. Government must protect these resources.

Contract Enforcement Is Problematical

When an efficient legal system for the enforcement of contracts is lacking, contracts will inherently be small, given that large contracts with complex financial provisions are difficult to enforce informally. Only if the parties to a contract have long histories together and want to continue doing business will an informal system work. Enforcement mechanisms for contracts are essential for widespread business and commercial expansion.

There Are Significant External Costs or Benefits: Externalities

Markets rarely produce the socially optimal output when external costs or benefits are present. The market tends to overproduce goods with external costs, providing them at too low a price. To see why, consider Figure 2, keeping in mind that an **external cost** (or **negative externality**) is some socially undesirable effect of economic activity, such as pollution, overfishing, or traffic congestion.

Demand curve D_P and supply curve S_P represent the private demand and supply for some product. Market equilibrium is at point a. Assume this good's production creates pollution—an external cost. If its producer were forced to clean up its production process, the firm's costs would rise and the supply curve would decrease to $S_{P + Cleanup Costs}$. The result is a new equilibrium at point b with a higher price and lower output.

Output Q_1 is the socially desirable output for this product. But left on its own, this market will produce at Q_0 because consumers and producers of this product will not take

External cost (or negative externality): Occurs when a transaction between two parties has an impact on a third party not involved with the transaction. External costs are negative, such as pollution or congestion. The market provides too much of a product with negative externalities at too low a cost.

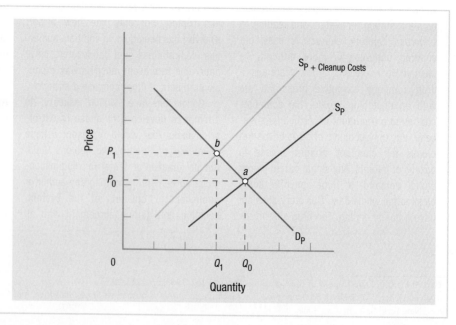

FIGURE 2—Markets with External Costs

Markets tend to overproduce goods with external costs. Demand curve D_P and supply curve S_P represent private demand and supply. Market equilibrium is at point a. If a good's production creates pollution (an external cost) and the producer was forced to clean up the production process, the firm's costs would rise, and the supply curve would decrease to $S_{P + Cleanup Costs}$. The result is the socially optimal equilibrium at point b with a higher price and lower output. Producers and consumers are now paying the full costs associated with the good's production. Markets do not inherently contain mechanisms that force firms or consumers to pay for external costs.

the pollution (and cleanup costs) into consideration. The society as a whole bears the brunt of the pollution. Markets fail because they do not contain mechanisms forcing firms to eliminate external costs. Left unregulated, the firm in this example will produce more of its product than the society wants, pushing the increased costs of this production off onto the larger society as an undesirable externality.

In a similar way, markets tend to provide too little of products that have **external benefits.** College education provides benefits not only to students but to the society as a

External benefits: Positive externalities, such as education and vaccinations. Private markets provide too little at too high a price of goods with external benefits.

Nobel Prize

Paul A. Samuelson

In 1970, Paul Samuelson became the first American to win the Nobel Prize in Economics. One could say that Paul Samuelson literally wrote the book on economics. In 1948, when he was a young professor at the Massachusetts Institute of Technology, the university asked him to write a text for the junior year course in economics. Sixty years later more than 4 million copies of his textbook, *Economics,* have been sold.

Samuelson once described himself as one of the last "generalists" in economics. His interests are wide ranging, and his contributions include everything from the highly technical and mathematical to a popular column for *Newsweek* magazine. He made breakthrough contributions to virtually all areas of economics. Steven Pressman sums up Samuelson's main contributions in macroeconomics and international trade this way: "They have involved explaining how domestic economies work, how they are impacted by engaging in trade with other nations, and how economic policies could be used to improve economic performance."

Born in Gary, Indiana, in 1915, Samuelson attended the University of Chicago as an undergraduate. He received the university's Social Science Medal and was awarded an innovative graduate fellowship that required that he study at another school. He chose Harvard, and while in the graduate program published 11 papers. Over the next several decades he earned every major award open to an economist.

He wanted to remain at Harvard, but was only offered an instructor's position. However, MIT soon made a better offer and, as he describes it, "On a fine October day in 1940 an *enfant terrible emeritus* packed up his pencil and moved three miles down the Charles River, where he lived happily ever after." He often remarked that a pencil was all he needed to

Courtesy The Samuelson Family

theorize. Seven years later, he published his Ph.D. dissertation, the *Foundations of Economic Analysis,* a major contribution to the area of mathematical economics. Robert Lucas, another Nobel winner, declared, "Here was a graduate student in his twenties reorganizing all of economics in four or five chapters right before your eyes . . ."

Harvard made several attempts to lure him back, but he spent his entire career at MIT and is often credited with developing a department as good as or better than Harvard's. Samuelson was an informal advisor to President John F. Kennedy (he turned down an offer to head Kennedy's Council of Economic Advisers). A prolific writer, he averaged one technical paper each month during his active career, and often said "a day spent in committee meetings are for me a day lost." He has written that he "has always been incredibly lucky, throughout his lifetime overpaid and underworked." Quite a modest statement for a man whose *Collected Works* takes up five volumes and includes more than 350 articles. He was an active economist until his death in 2009 at the age of 93. As you read through this book, keep in mind that in virtually every chapter, Paul Samuelson has created or added to the analysis in substantial ways.

Sources: Steven Pressman, *Fifty Major Economists,* 2d ed. (New York: Routledge), 2006; David Warsh, *Knowledge and the Wealth of Nations: A Story of Economic Discovery* (New York: Norton), 2006; Paul Samuelson, "Economics in My Time," in William Breit and Roger Spencer, *Lives of the Laureates: Seven Nobel Economists* (Cambridge, MA: The MIT Press), 1986.

whole. But there is no incentive for an individual to take into consideration this external benefit when deciding to go to college. Government subsidies for higher education address the positive externalities aspect of education.

Externalities lead to market failure. To ensure that products are available at the socially desirable price and output, some government intervention may be required. Regulation or taxation can be used, for instance, to give markets the incentives they need to produce what society wants.

Competitive Markets Do *Not Always* Prevail

In theory, a market left to itself should be competitive. In practice, however, the government often must promote competition in the marketplace if it wants to see the most efficient outcomes. One problem is that one or two firms can dominate some markets, and when this happens, prices rise above what would be the competitive price. We will learn more about this when we examine industrial structure in microeconomics.

In all of these cases of market failure (except in the case of pure public goods), markets do not collapse. Rather, markets do not provide the most efficient distribution of goods and services. They need some ameliorative device, often something provided by government such as laws or incentives, but often provided by private firms and individuals acting on their own behalf (remember used car warranties). The important point to keep in mind is the need for correctives when market failure is present. We will have a lot more to say about these issues in a later chapter.

In this section we have considered market failures and the need for government action. The next section looks at the tension between free markets and government intervention in the United States throughout the last century and a half.

■ **CHECKPOINT**

MARKET FAILURES

- When markets fail, they usually do not totally collapse—they simply fail to provide the socially optimal amount of goods and services.

- Asymmetric information—when one party to a transaction has better information than another—can lead to market failure. Adverse selection occurs when products of different qualities are sold at one price. Moral hazard occurs when an insurance policy or other arrangement changes the economic incentives people face and so leads them to change their behaviors.

- Private goods can be consumed only by the person who purchases them: they are rival and exclusive. Public goods are nonrival and nonexclusive: my consumption does not diminish your consumption, and others cannot be excluded from enjoying it. Public goods give rise to the free rider problem. Public goods may not be provided at all by markets.

- Common property resources are typically subject to overexploitation.

- Markets rarely produce the socially optimal output when externalities (external benefits or costs) are present.

- Noncompetitive markets result in prices higher than what is socially optimal.

QUESTION: Tony Jackson (*Financial Times*, June 29, 2009) offers the following example about markets and market prices: "Suppose I offer to buy a picture from you, knowing (as you do not) that I have a buyer who will pay twice as much. You accept, knowing (as I do not) that the picture is a fake." Will these two parties reach an agreement despite the fact that neither has complete information? Does this simple scenario reflect our day-to-day transactions?

Answers to the Checkpoint questions can be found at the end of this chapter.

Market Failure, Government Intervention, and U.S. Economic History

So far in this chapter and the last one we have seen how markets work and why they are generally efficient, and we have introduced the concepts of producer and consumer surplus. We also looked at the situations in which markets can fail to provide the optimal levels of goods and services to society. But studying economics is not just about acquiring a bunch of terms or theories, it is also about having a sense of how we got here and why the institutions that govern our economy exist. The kind of economy we have today did not happen instantaneously; it has evolved over the last several hundred years in response to specific events. This section briefly highlights the history of our economy and the events that have shaped it.

Throughout the past century and a half, tension has existed between free markets, market failure, and government intervention. Sometimes the market can be creative in solving problems and generating growth, but sometimes markets lead to unbridled excess and cause trouble. In contrast, sometimes government intervention has helped set down the rules of the game and made the economy work more efficiently, and sometimes government intervention has stifled the market and growth. American economic history has witnessed a changing interplay between free markets and government, with the pendulum swinging first one way, then the other.

Industrialization

The era of industrialization was characterized by tremendous growth, with a small role for government. After the Civil War, the U.S. economy went from being a 97-pound weakling to a 250-pound industrial superstar in just a little over three decades. In less than five years (1861–1865), the number of manufacturers in the United States doubled to a quarter of a million and its output tripled. By 1869, the transcontinental railway was complete, giving the West access to eastern markets. In the three decades after the Civil War, railroad track gauge (width) was standardized, bringing the entire country into the system. Rail mileage increased by 6 times and freight tonnage increased by 30 times.

This tremendous growth brought with it some problems. Because rail companies had no local competition, they charged high prices. These high prices gave momentum to the Granger movement, which lobbied for laws favorable to farmers on freight and warehousing charges. Congress agreed, and in 1887 established the Interstate Commerce Commission (ICC) to regulate the railroads.

Other industries, including oil, steel, mining, and agriculture, grew just as rapidly. But as industry developed virtually unchecked and as firms combined into massive industrial giants, Americans became concerned with the "robber barons" who ran these companies. John D. Rockefeller absorbed many firms to create Standard Oil, which by 1890 was just about the only firm refining and distributing kerosene (more important than gasoline at the time). Others, such as Andrew Carnegie and J. P. Morgan, became wealthy by building colossal firms in steel and banking. The benefits of competition were lost as these large firms exploited their market power through high prices to generate huge profits. Ultimately, Congress passed the Sherman Antitrust Act in 1890 to break up these huge firms.

Labor unions were beginning to develop during this period, but the legal system was not supportive of their efforts. Union were mostly guilds of craftsmen until 1870 when the Knights of Labor was formed for all who worked for wages (excluding lawyers and those who sold liquor).[6] By the end of the nineteenth century, Samuel Gompers and the American Federation of Labor had only 500,000 members, but the union would grow dramatically in the first half of the twentieth century. Unions gradually won the right to bargain, and favorable legislation during the Great Depression led to unions representing a third of all workers by 1950.

---

[6] George Tindall and David Shi, *America: A Narrative History* (New York: Norton), 1993, p. 519.

Rise of Consumerism and World War I

The tremendous growth fostered by industrialization raised living standards, which in turn made the consumer more powerful. Henry Ford's Model T made automobiles affordable for a growing number of Americans. In 1908, Ford sold 10,000 cars for a price of $850; ten years later he was selling 1 million at $350 each. Electric appliances were introduced, piggybacking on the electrification of urban areas. By 1920 the automobile industry was the largest industry in America, and ten years later more than 600,000 miles of road had been paved.

The National Bank Act (passed during the Civil War) guided banks for nearly six decades, but financial crises were common and banks went in and out of business much like restaurants today. An attempt by some financiers to corner the copper market caused a deep financial crisis in 1907. It would have been far deeper except J. P. Morgan stepped in, acted like a central banker, and convinced other New York banks to loan cash to the Knickerbocker Trust to stem a bank run. That experience led to the Federal Reserve Act in 1913, which created a central bank to regulate banks and manage the money supply.

In late summer 1914, the assassination of Archduke Franz Ferdinand, heir to the throne of Austria-Hungary, seemed inconsequential, but just over a month later all of Europe was at war. This "War to End All Wars" resulted in more than 10 million casualties. Europe had been the center of Western culture for many centuries, but when the war was over, it was America that became an economic and financial powerhouse and the leader of the free world. The 1919 Treaty of Versailles ended the war by assessing huge reparations on Germany that ultimately led to hyperinflation in the early 1920s and the rise of Hitler during the 1930s.

During the 1920s, Wall Street grew 5 times faster than the economy. The stock market was growing so fast that a poem[7] printed in the *Saturday Evening Post* in the summer of 1929 expressed the speculative fever of the time:

> *Oh, hush thee, my baby, granny's bought some more shares,*
> *Daddy's gone out to play with bulls and the bears,*
> *Mother's buying on tips, and she simply can't lose,*
> *And Baby shall have some expensive new shoes!*

Black Tuesday—the stock market crash—came on October 29, 1929, and within a year nearly 90% of the wealth created by the soaring stock market would be history. America plunged into the Great Depression, forever changing the American economy.

The Great Depression: 1930–1941

We have seen that in the 1920s, the economy boomed as auto sales took off, consumerism began to blossom, and electricity became part of urban life, spurring on the creation of modern appliances. All of this growth encouraged the stock market, which exploded by more than 600%. What happened next had major implications not only for the United States but also the world.

The stock market collapse in late October 1929 created a financial crisis as margin calls went out to investors who had only put 10% down to buy stock and borrowed (margined) the remaining 90%. When stock prices fell, investors had to come up with additional cash to cover their losses or their accounts would be liquidated. Most investors were wiped out. The prevailing view was that the declines in 1929 would be temporary, after which the market would resume its upward trend. For a while, the irrational exuberance continued and investors kept pouring money into their accounts. When the market did not turn around, but instead got worse, investors ran out of money and their accounts (and wealth) evaporated. By the time the stock market bottomed out, losses equaled 87%.

Bankrupt investor Walter Thornton tries to sell his luxury roadster ($1,500 new) for $100 cash on the streets of New York City following the 1929 stock market crash.

---

[7] John Steel Gordon, *An Empire of Wealth: The Epic History of American Economic Power* (New York: HarperCollins Publishers), 2004, p. 314.

Over the next three years, income and output would be cut in half, 25% of workers would become unemployed, and more than 10,000 banks would fail. The nation's economy was in freefall. Was government the cure? Early on, the government exacerbated the problem by enacting policies that many argue turned a difficult recession into a depression.

In 1930, Congress passed the Smoot-Hawley Tariff Act, putting tariffs (charges) on imported goods, which raised their prices by an average of 60%. Despite a letter signed by 1,000 economists asking President Hoover to veto the act, he signed it. In retaliation, other countries raised tariffs on their imported goods (U.S. exports) and world trade collapsed. The Federal Reserve took several actions that led to a decline in prices and tightened credit. As a result of these actions, banks called in loans to maintain their solvency, increasing farm and home foreclosures.

Finally, President Hoover asked Congress to increase taxes to balance the budget. While unemployment took money out of people's hands, the tax increases took money out of the hands of people who still had jobs. This compounded the problems the country faced.

All three of these government actions made a bad situation much worse. Could government action make things better?

Running for president in 1932, candidate Franklin D. Roosevelt promised a "New Deal" for Americans. By March 1933, when Roosevelt was inaugurated, the country was at the bottom of the Depression and bank failures were so catastrophic that the president, in his genius, euphemistically called for a "bank holiday." He closed all banks for four days while he and his staff drafted emergency legislation. The legislation and assistance he proposed permitted most banks to reopen safely. Later that summer, passage of the Glass-Steagall Act created the Federal Deposit Insurance Corporation (FDIC) that protected depositor's funds and separated commercial banking from the more speculative investment banking. Since its passage, bank runs have been rare.

A little known economist and sociologist, Frances Perkins, Roosevelt's secretary of labor and the first female cabinet member in U.S. history, played a crucial role in writing New Deal legislation. She helped develop federal relief programs such as the Civilian Conservation Corps, which provided federal aid to states for unemployment relief that eventually became the system of unemployment compensation we know today. She also helped create the federal minimum wage law; the Fair Labor Standards Act; the National Labor Relations Act, which made it easier to organize a union; and the Social Security Act. As labor secretary for 12 years, she pushed for many of the rights workers take for granted today.

During his first 100 days in office, Roosevelt signed more than a dozen Acts that brought new or additional federal government regulation of such industries as agriculture, banking, electric power, securities trading, home mortgages, and railroads. He also spent billions through the National Recovery Administration (NRA), which ultimately created the Works Progress Administration (WPA) that built more than 100,000 schools, post offices, and other public buildings, a half million miles of roads, 600 airports, and more than 10,000 bridges. The WPA also funded other projects for writers, artists, photographers, actors, and musicians. Many murals you see in post offices today were sponsored by WPA projects during the Depression. Other than the banking Acts that finally stabilized the banking system, the most lasting legacy of the Depression is the Social Security Act of 1935.

World War II 1942–1945

The U.S. buildup of armaments for World War II began right after the Germans invaded France in the summer of 1940. Unemployment was still high at 15% and this slack made the buildup easier. Within a few years, unemployment dropped to just over 1% as *real* (adjusted for inflation) GDP almost doubled in just five years. Virtually all of this additional output was military armaments, but by early 1942, America had left the Great Depression behind. The general consensus is that even though the economy was slowly climbing out of the Depression, war spending greatly accelerated the process. Much of the infrastructure used to build war materiel was quickly turned into civilian production after the war.

Frances Perkins was secretary of labor from 1933 to 1945. As a member of Roosevelt's cabinet, she helped create much of the New Deal labor legislation.

Library of Congress

■ A 1936 WPA poster for the Federal Theatre Project play "Class of 29."

Library of Congress

The Postwar Economy: 1946–1960

World War II resulted in tremendous devastation for much of Europe. Ultimately, the U.S. economy was strengthened. However, most goods and services were in short supply as manufacturing capacity fed the war effort. Labor shortages dramatically changed the working status of both women and African Americans. During the war, taxes were raised to pay some of the war expenses, but selling war bonds raised more money. To keep inflation in check, government controls over wages and prices were implemented, along with rationing. Coupons were issued to limit the amount of sugar, shoes, and gasoline that people could legally buy.

In 1944, delegates from 44 countries met in Bretton Woods, New Hampshire, to create a "new world order" for the postwar economies. Out of this meeting came the International Monetary Fund (IMF) to help promote and finance world trade. Because the American economy was the strongest coming out of the war, American funds provided through the Marshall Plan helped to rebuild postwar Europe.

When the war ended, most people, including many economists, expected the economy to drop back into a depression. They were surprised by the ensuing growth. Pent-up demand from consumers for appliances, new homes, and cars spurred the market. Business investment skyrocketed, and wartime manufacturing capacity was rapidly converted to civilian use.

This economic growth did not go unchecked. The Great Depression and World War II had fundamentally changed our view of economic policy. Congress passed the Employment Act of 1946 that made it the *responsibility of government* to "promote maximum employment, production and purchasing power." The Act established the Council of Economic Advisers (CEA) and the Joint Economic Committee of Congress and required an annual Economic Report of the President. All three exist today.

Before the war, labor unions had grown under the Depression-era Wagner Act, but their bargaining power and wages were heavily limited during the war by the War Labor Board. Union strife came to a head in 1946 with 5,000 strikes involving 5 million workers. The result was the passage of the Taft-Hartley Act in 1947 that made it more difficult for unions to organize workers, outlawed closed shops where union membership was a requirement for work, and permitted employers to actively campaign against an organizing attempt. Taft-Hartley put unions on the defensive and is partly responsible for their decline over the last half century.

In the early 1950s, the United States fought the Korean War to a stalemate. The economy suffered a few recessions, but "creeping inflation" was beginning to be viewed as a long-term problem that might stifle future economic growth. Budget surpluses were seen as the solution, and federal taxes and expenditures were brought into line.

American consumerism and suburbanization expanded after World War II, setting off rapid economic growth and the rise of the middle class. Despite the good times, there was a growing awareness that a large part of America was not sharing in the benefits. The Supreme Court in 1954 concluded that segregation of public schools on the basis of race was unconstitutional, setting in motion the civil rights movement.

Growing Government and Stagflation: 1960–1980

Economists emerged from the Great Depression with a new macroeconomic theory from John Maynard Keynes that justified a crucial role for government in managing the economy. This is called fiscal policy, or using taxing and spending to affect the economy. Using these Keynesian ideas, economists in the early 1960s declared an end to business cycles. If the economy headed into a recession, government could step in and spend more or reduce taxes, thereby stimulating the economy and short-circuiting the recession. Thus, business could always depend on a growing demand for their products and would therefore continue to invest in new factories, creating economic growth. Government would run deficits during an economic downturn and then surpluses when the economy was booming.

President John F. Kennedy adopted the Keynesian approach to economic policy. He cut taxes and expanded government programs designed to grow the economy. Before the Kennedy administration, the emphasis was on balancing the federal budget, which restricted fiscal policy's role. With the new administration (and this carried over to the Johnson years), deficits were less of a concern. Two tax-reduction packages were passed (in 1962 and 1964) even though the budget was in deficit (spending exceeded tax revenues). The focus of the "new economics" was on economic growth through tax rate cuts for individuals and reductions for business using investment tax credits to stimulate new investments in plant and equipment. In the early 1960s, the economy responded to these policies as incomes, investment, and economic growth all rose. As Figure 3 shows, the downside was a "creeping up" of the rate of inflation that was to become a serious problem in the next decade.

FIGURE 3—Unemployment and Inflation, 1947–2009

The economic policies of the 1960's resulted in creeping inflation, while in the 1970s many new government programs, new and costly business regulations along with Vietnam war spending brought on stagflation. Disinflation in the 1980s resulted from tight monetary policy that brought down inflation rates. Stable and low inflation along with lower tax rates and reduced regulation resulted in solid economic growth throughout the period.

President Kennedy's assassination brought Lyndon Johnson to the presidency, who established a host of new "Great Society" and "War on Poverty" government programs and departments, including the following:

- Medicare was created to provide medical care to the elderly, because illness is a principal cause of poverty in older populations. Medicare shifted the cost of their care to the government.

- Medicaid (in cooperation with the states) was created to provide health care to the indigent.

- The Office of Economic Opportunity created new bureaucracies to deal with education, housing, and employment issues.

- The Department of Housing and Urban Development (HUD), a cabinet-level department, was added to promote urban redevelopment.

- The Department of Transportation was established.

- The Open Housing Act prohibited discrimination in the sale or rental of housing.

- The Truth-in-Lending Act added transparency to borrowing.

- The Clear Water Restoration Act dealt with the nation's rivers.

- The Air Quality Act was passed to reduce pollution.

Although many of these "Great Society" government programs were controversial, Figure 4 on the next page shows that the poverty rate was cut in half in less than a decade and has stayed roughly constant over the last 40 years.

FIGURE 4—The Poverty Rate, 1960–1975

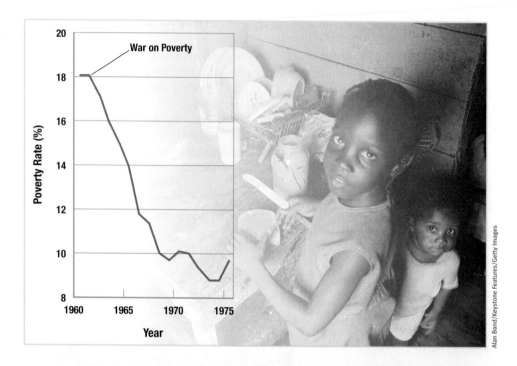

Alan Band/Keystone Features/Getty Images

Two other major events in the 1960s were to have big long-term impacts on our economy: the Civil Rights Act of 1964 and the Vietnam War. The Civil Rights Act opened up the benefits of the economy to all and was a major achievement of President Johnson's administration. The Vietnam War, on the other hand, was controversial, was met with continual antiwar demonstrations, and eventually lost the support of the American people.

But the 1970s would go down in history as a period of *stagflation*: high rates of inflation coupled with high rates of unemployment along with slowing economic growth (see Figure 3). Confidence in the economy declined to such an extent that many economists, for the first time, predicted a lower standard of living for the next generation.

Globalization pressures were advancing as Japan and Western Europe became tough competitors to American business. The Organization of Petroleum Exporting Countries (OPEC) colluded to increase crude oil prices 500% in 1973 and increased them again in the latter part of the decade. Given America's dependence on oil, these price increases resulted in two deep recessions with continued inflation.

In the summer of 1971, President Nixon, in an attempt to deal with a growing problem of rising unemployment and inflation, instituted a 90-day *freeze* on wages, prices, and rents. He followed with wage and price controls later in the year. A regulatory body, the Pay Board, set limits on pay, while a Price Commission set limits on prices and profit increases. Generally viewed as a failure, controls were removed in early 1974. This ended our nation's first and last experiment with peacetime wage and price controls since World War II. Government intervention had gone too far.

The 1970s were also a period of increased government regulation, when the following legislation was passed:

- National Environmental Policy Act (1970)
- Water Quality Improvement Act (1970)
- Occupational Safety and Health Act (1970)
- Supplemental Security Income (added to Social Security in 1972)
- Federal Water Pollution Act (1972)
- Employee Retirement Income Security Act (1974)

Despite all of this new federal governance—or maybe because of it—public opinion was turning. In 1978, the Carter administration substantially deregulated the airline, trucking, and railroad industries. The 1970s ended with the first, and what was considered at the time a successful government bailout of the Chrysler Corporation, but almost 30 years later both Chrysler and General Motors would need federal help to remain in business.

Overall, the 1960s and 1970s were a period of rising government intervention in the economy, both through regulation and higher levels of government spending and taxation. It was also a period of rising inflation accompanied by rising unemployment and slow growth. Not a pretty picture.

To many observers, these events were connected, and economists would spend the next decade untangling the reasons for the stagflation that developed over these two decades. Was government the problem rather than the solution?

Disinflation and Bubbles: 1980 to the Present

When Ronald Reagan took office in 1981, the economy was a mess. Inflation was 14% and rising, unemployment was over 7% and rising, 30-year home mortgage rates were 15%, and real economic growth (adjusted for inflation) was negative, so the economy was declining. Reagan believed intrusive government was the problem. He set out to halt the growth of federal spending, reduce personal and business tax rates, and to repeal burdensome regulations. He saw all of these goals as ways to release the power of markets and get the economy back on track. With the help of the Federal Reserve and especially its chairman, Paul Volcker, inflation began to ease and interest rates began to drop.

We now know that when people and business expect inflation, this can set off an inflationary cycle and these *inflationary expectations* were driving the economy in the early 1980s. To wring these expectations out of the system may require a severe recession, and the recession in the early 1980s was the deepest since the Depression as unemployment reached nearly 11%.

To get economic growth going again, taxes were cut and the deregulation push started by the Carter administration was expanded. This "supply-side" approach, Reagan argued, was needed to provide incentives for business to produce and hire more. Further, reducing personal income tax rates would increase work effort, since families could keep more of what they earned and would be willing to save more. As they saved, interest rates would fall, encouraging business investment in new plant and equipment. This supply-side approach was the opposite of the Keynesian demand-management approach of using government spending to drive (or try to drive) economic growth.

Although President Johnson's War on Poverty cut the poverty rate in half, by 1981 it had produced a political backlash against what many viewed as a welfare state that encouraged dependency rather than encouraging people to escape the cycle of poverty through decent-paying jobs. Social welfare eligibility criteria were tightened, the length of time people could draw benefits shortened, and benefits were reduced. The focus of aid programs shifted to putting people back to work. By the end of the 1980s, "workfare" programs were required of all state welfare systems.

When the air traffic controllers illegally went on strike early in Reagan's presidency, they were fired and the union decertified. Reagan could do this because federal law forbids federal workers from striking. But the unprecedented firing set the tone for labor relations across the country, and unions have not fared well since.

Although Reagan was successful at getting tax rate cuts, he was unable (or unwilling) to persuade Congress to hold down domestic spending in the face of increased military expenditures. As a result, annual federal deficits began an uphill march, roughly doubling to $153 billion during his two terms.

Federal deficits shrank during the 1990s as a technology-fueled boom swelled federal coffers and then turned to surpluses in President Clinton's second term. Clinton continued the restructuring of welfare programs, increased income tax rates on upper-income taxpayers, and pressed for trade legislation, implementing the North American Free Trade Agreement (NAFTA).

In 1999, Congress passed and President Clinton signed the landmark Financial Services Modernization Act that repealed the portion of the 1933 Glass-Steagall Act separating commercial and investment banking. The not-unexpected result was a rapid consolidation of banks, insurance companies, and investment underwriting services into giant conglomerates.

What *was* unexpected was how fast financial firms grew and the level of risk undertaken by commercial banks because of their new investment arms. Many observers attribute part of the severity of the 2008–2009 financial crisis to this Act.

What is most notable about the last quarter-century is the steady reduction in inflation from nearly 14% to about 2% (look back at Figure 3). This feat had as its foundation a policy of purposely putting the economy into a deep recession in the early 1980s to wring out inflation and inflationary expectations. Until just recently, the economy enjoyed steady growth, low inflation, amazingly low unemployment, and just two minor recessions. Much of the credit for this performance is due to a steady hand at the Federal Reserve and a better understanding by economists about inflation dynamics.

How quickly things change! As President Obama took office in January 2009, the economy was in a real mess. Stocks markets plunged, credit markets were frozen, and the nation's biggest banks were on the verge of collapse. General Motors and Chrysler were shells of their former selves, and home mortgage defaults, at unheard of levels, sent home prices falling. Consumer spending dropped, resulting in huge layoffs that pushed unemployment to the highest levels in more than two decades. Many were calling it the "worst recession since the Great Depression."

The reasons for this downturn are complex and are detailed later in this book. But mitigating the impact called for extraordinary measures by both the Federal Reserve and the federal government. The Federal Reserve used every tool available (and then some) to restore credit markets, lowering interest rates to historic levels and injecting massive amounts of liquidity into financial markets. The Obama administration passed a massive stimulus package, running the deficit for fiscal 2009 to nearly $2 trillion, with projections of substantial deficits over the next several years. As Figure 5 illustrates, based on these projections by the Congressional Budget Office, the national debt will nearly double over the near future to

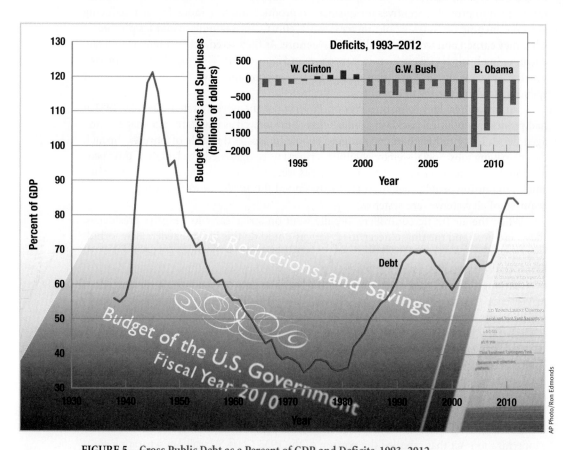

FIGURE 5—Gross Public Debt as a Percent of GDP, and Deficits, 1993–2012

Recent high deficits are pushing the gross public debt to levels not seen since World War II. Note that the 2010–2012 deficits are those projected by the Obama administration.

more than 80% of GDP. Undoubtedly, dealing with these huge deficits and their potential for raising inflation levels will quickly draw the focus of the Obama administration.

The history of our economy has been one of relying mostly on markets to provide and distribute goods and services. But, as we have seen, markets can fail. These failures bring forth a call for another round of government intervention, typically in the form of regulations or new government financing or provision of services. This process has resulted in government (federal, state, and local) growing from a single-digit percentage of GDP in the early 1900s to more than 40% today. We are a capitalist economy with a heavy dose of government.

Since World War II, our economy has endured a long cycle involving rising government intervention and regulation of the economy, accommodative (and sometimes erratic) monetary policy, and rising inflation (1960s and 1970s). This was followed by reductions in government involvement through deregulation, reduced taxes, and steady monetary policy that reduced inflation and kept it down (1980s to 2007). We are now in another period of increased government spending, re-regulation, and greater government involvement in the economy. Whether we will suffer another round of crippling inflation depends on how well we have learned the lessons of the past.

■ CHECKPOINT

MARKET FAILURE, GOVERNMENT INTERVENTION, AND U.S. ECONOMIC HISTORY

■ After the Civil War, the economy grew dramatically. Railroads stretched from coast to coast, and the oil, steel, mining, and agriculture industries flourished.

■ The early 1900s saw the rise of consumerism as automobiles, appliances, and electricity became common in households.

■ The Great Depression brought misery to the country as stock prices fell 90%, unemployment reached 25%, and many thousands of banks failed, wiping out the savings of many families.

■ President Roosevelt's New Deal, including the National Recovery Administration, the Works Progress Administration, and many other additions to the federal government, helped employ people and reduce the impact of the Depression.

■ The buildup for World War II is generally credited with helping the economy pull out of the Depression.

■ The Great Depression changed America's view of the role of government in economic affairs as Congress passed the Employment Act of 1946, making maximum employment, production, and purchasing power the responsibility of the government.

■ The stagflation of the 1970s turned Americans away from government intervention in the economy and back toward markets.

■ The reduction in government regulation seemed to work well because from the early 1980s until just recently, the economy enjoyed relative price stability, low unemployment, and steady growth.

■ The recession of 2008–2009 has Americans debating a bigger role for government in regulating business and stimulating the economy.

QUESTION: Today, many of us pay our bills electronically, use our debit cards, and pay tolls on toll roads with E-ZPass (a little box attached to the windshield). All of these systems clearly make life less hectic and complicated. Economist Amy Finkelstein (*The New York Times*, July 4, 2007, p. B1) examined years of toll records from around the country. What she found was a clear pattern: "After an electronic system is put in place, tolls start rising sharply." Within 10 years, electronic tolls were roughly 30% higher than comparable tollbooth fees. The implication, of course, is that when bills are paid automatically and we don't pay cash or write a check, markets may not work effectively to control prices. What implications does this have for taxes and the possible tradeoff between growth of government versus private activity in our economy?

Answers to the Checkpoint question can be found at the end of this chapter.

Key Concepts

Property rights, p. 81
Consumer surplus, p. 82
Producer surplus, p. 83
Asymmetric information, p. 85
Adverse selection, p. 85
Moral hazard, p. 86

Public goods, p. 86
Free rider, p. 86
Common property resources, p. 87
External cost (or negative externality),
  p. 88
External benefits, p. 89

Chapter Summary

Markets and Efficiency

Markets are efficient mechanisms for allocating resources. The prices and profits characteristic of market systems provide incentives and signals that are nonexistent or seriously flawed in other systems of resource allocation.

For markets to be efficient, they must have well-structured institutions. These include the following requirements: (1) Information is widely available; (2) property rights are protected; (3) private contracts are enforced; (4) spillovers are minimal; and (5) competition prevails.

Markets impose discipline on producers and consumers. Producers would like to charge higher prices and earn greater profits, but their economic survival depends on turning out quality goods at reasonable prices. As consumers, we would all like to engage in frequent extravagant purchases, but given our limited resources, each of us must decide which products are most important to us. As a result, markets are also rationing devices.

Because many consumers are willing to pay more than market equilibrium prices for many goods and services, they receive a consumer surplus. In a similar way, since many businesses would be willing to provide products at prices below equilibrium prices, they receive a producer surplus. The concepts of consumer and producer surplus are helpful when we wish to examine the impacts of public policy.

Market Failures

If markets do not meet the five institutional requirements they will not be efficient. When one or more of these conditions is not met, the market is said to fail. Market failure does not mean that a market totally collapses or fails to exist, but that it fails to provide the socially optimal amount of goods and services.

In some markets, one party to a transaction almost always has better information than the other. In this case, the market is said to fail because of asymmetric information. Asymmetric information can result in the inability of sellers to find buyers for their products, but it usually just involves adjustments in contracting methods. Adverse selection occurs when products of different qualities are sold at one price and involve asymmetric information. Moral hazard occurs when an insurance policy or some other arrangement changes the economic incentives people face, leading people to change their behavior, usually in a way detrimental to the market.

Private goods are those goods that can be consumed only by the individuals who purchase them. Private goods are rival and exclusive. Public goods, in contrast, are nonrival and nonexclusive, meaning my consumption does not diminish your consumption and that once such a good has been provided for one person, others cannot be excluded from enjoying it.

Public goods give rise to the free rider problem. Once a public good has been provided, other consumers cannot be excluded from it, so many people will choose to enjoy the benefit without paying for it: they will free ride. And because of the possibility of free riding, the danger is that no one will pay for the public good, so it will no longer be provided by private markets, even though it is publicly desired. Pure public goods usually require public provision.

Common property resources are owned in common by the community and are subject to the "tragedy of the commons" and overexploitation.

When an efficient legal system for the enforcement of contracts is lacking, contracts will be small because large contracts with complex financial provisions are difficult to enforce informally.

Markets rarely produce the socially optimal output when external costs or benefits are present. The market overproduces goods with external costs, selling them at too low a price. Conversely, markets tend to provide too little of products that have external benefits.

Some markets tend toward noncompetition, so prices go up.

Market Failure, Government Intervention, and U.S. Economic History

After the Civil War, the economy grew dramatically. Railroads stretched from coast to coast, and the oil, steel, mining, and agriculture industries flourished.

The early 1900s saw the rise of consumerism as automobiles, appliances, and electricity became common in households.

The Great Depression brought misery to the country as stock prices fell 90%, unemployment reached 25%, and many thousands of banks failed, wiping out the savings of many families.

President Roosevelt's New Deal, including the National Recovery Administration, the Works Progress Administration, and many other additions to the federal government, helped employ people and reduce the impact of the depression. The buildup for World War II is generally credited with helping the economy pull out of the Depression.

The Great Depression changed America's view of the role of government in economic affairs as Congress passed the Employment Act of 1946, making maximum employment, production, and purchasing power the responsibility of the government.

The stagflation of the 1970s turned Americans away from government intervention in the economy and back toward markets. The reduction in government regulation seemed to work well because from the early 1980s until just recently, the economy enjoyed relative price stability, low unemployment, and steady growth.

The recession of 2008–2009 has Americans debating a bigger role for government in regulating business and stimulating the economy.

Questions and Problems

Check Your Understanding

1. When professors get tenure, essentially guaranteeing them lifetime jobs, does this affect the effort they expend on teaching and research? What concept might be used to explain your answer?

2. Are buying brands (e.g., Coke, Sony, and Dell) a way consumers compensate for asymmetric information? Explain.

3. Describe consumer surplus. Describe producer surplus. Using the graph on the next page show both. Now assume that a new technology reduces the cost of

production. What happens to consumer surplus? Show the impact of the change in the graph.

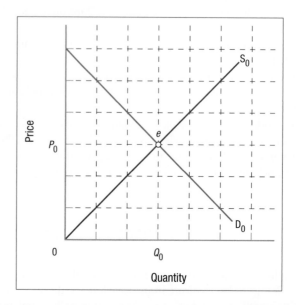

4. Define public goods. What is the free rider problem? Give several examples of public goods.

Apply the Concepts

5. Many observers consider it a market failure when the pharmaceutical industry refuses to do research and development on what are known as neglected diseases: cures for malaria and tuberculosis and vaccines for other diseases in developing countries where the profit potential is small. Further, many drug firms are unwilling to make vaccines for illnesses such as influenza and other biohazards such as anthrax and smallpox. Vaccines are especially prone to large lawsuits because when they are administered, they are administered to millions of people in an emergency, and if there are serious unanticipated side effects, settlement costs can be huge. With anthrax vaccine, ethical considerations prevent exposing someone to anthrax and then injecting the medicine, so these types of vaccines often are used in emergencies without sufficient testing.

a. One of the solutions currently used for neglected diseases is the public–private partnership (PPP). Grants by the Bill & Melinda Gates Foundation currently fund most of the PPPs that are conducted on a "no profit, no loss" basis. The firm's research and development costs are covered, but firms must sell the drugs at cost to developing countries. Why would pharmaceutical firms be willing to spend time on these types of projects?

b. Since lawsuits are an important impediment to research and development of vaccines, what policies could the government institute to solve this problem?

c. Besides the use of the PPP, what other policies might the government introduce to encourage drug firms to do research and development on neglected diseases and orphan diseases (diseases that affect only a few people and thus have extremely limited markets)?

6. "If millions of people are desperate to buy and millions more desperate to sell, the trades will happen, whether we like it or not." This quote by Martin Wolf[8] refers to trades in illicit goods like narcotics, knockoffs (counterfeit goods), slaves, organs, and other goods we generally refer to as "bads." He suggests that the only way to eliminate traffic in these illicit goods is to eliminate their profitability. Do you agree? Why or why not?

7. Academic studies suggest that the amount people tip at restaurants is only slightly related to the quality of service, and that tips are poor measures of how happy people are with the service. Is this another example of market failure? What might account for this situation?

8. The U.S. Department of Labor reports that of the roughly 145 million people employed, just over half (73.9 million) are paid hourly, but less than 3% earn the minimum wage or less; 97% of wage earners earn more. And of those earning the minimum wage or less, 25% are teenagers living at home. If so few people are affected by the minimum wage, why does it often seem to be such a contentious political issue?

9. Adam Smith, in his famous book *The Wealth of Nations,* noted, "Every individual . . . neither intends to promote the public interest, nor knows how much he is promoting it. By preferring the support of domestic to that of foreign industry he intends only his own security; and by directing that industry in such a manner as its produce may be of the greatest value, he intends only his own gain, and he is in this, as in many other cases, led by an invisible hand to promote an end which was no part of his intention." What was he describing and what did it do?

10. What is the purpose of a warranty given by a used-car dealer? Evaluate one used-car warranty that gives your money back if not satisfied in a certain time period, and one that does not give you back your money but lets you put this money toward the purchase of another used car. Which warranty would you prefer?

11. In 2006 Medicare recipients were permitted to sign up for a federally subsidized drug benefit plan. The sign-up phase had a May 15 deadline, and those signing up after that date faced a premium penalty. Does this deadline have anything to do with adverse selection? Explain.

In the News

12. Economist N. Gregory Mankiw is quoted (*The New York Times,* March 18, 2008, p. C9) as suggesting, "If you have flood insurance, you are more likely to build your house on a flood plain, and: if you have fire insurance, you'll be less careful about smoking on the couch." What concept is Professor Mankiw describing?

13. Information would seem to be the ultimate public good. As *The Economist* (February 5, 2005, p. 72) noted, "It is a 'non-rival' good: i.e., your use of it does not interfere with my use. Better still, there are network effects: i.e., the more people who use it, the more useful it is to any individual user. Best of all, the existence of the Internet means that the costs of sharing are remarkably low." Is information a public good? Why then do we have copyright and patent laws to restrict the dissemination of some information?

---

8 Martin Wolf, "The Profit Motive May Be Universal but Virtue Is Not," *Financial Times,* November 16, 2005, p. 13.

Solving Problems

14. Consider the market shown in the figure below.

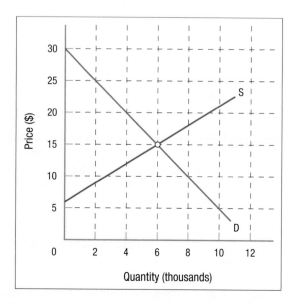

a. Compute the consumer surplus. _____

b. Compute the producer surplus. _____

Now assume that government puts a price floor on this product at $20 a unit.

c. Compute the new consumer surplus. _____

d. Compute the new producer surplus. _____

e. What group would tend to have their advocates or lobbyists support price floors?

Answers to Questions in CheckPoints

Check Point: Markets and Efficiency

Economists generally believe in the benefits of free trade between consenting adults. If trade did not benefit each party, they would not trade. Even in these markets, there is a demand for goods and services. As long as no one is forced to participate and everyone is fully informed, markets will be more efficient (e.g., more kidneys will be available than when relying on donations alone).

These markets are mainly repugnant on moral grounds. Markets for kidneys may result in the poor being targeted, since their opportunities in life are limited, and the equilibrium price for a kidney would be so low as to suggest they might have been exploited. Although illegal, this trade goes on today. The argument against the human cannonball is that his performance was considered demeaning and could bring disrespect and humiliation to other people of restricted growth. Besides the moral argument, prostitution faces health issues and is considered a demeaning occupation by many.

Check Point: Market Failures

Yes, they will probably reach an agreement. Both will go forward on the basis of the information they have at hand. A price will likely be agreed upon, but that price will reflect some uncertainty on the buyer's part. There is always an element of asymmetric information in our transactions, especially those between two individuals who do not know each other and will not likely see each other again. One way most retailers have eliminated this uncertainty for buyers is through warranties and money-back guarantees. The 60-day money-back offer from General Motors was designed to remove the fear of purchasing a car from a company emerging from bankruptcy.

Check Point: Market Failure, Government Intervention, and U.S. Economic History

Only a minority of Americans writes checks to the IRS or state governments on a regular basis. Most have income taxes automatically withdrawn from their paycheck (electronically transferred to the bank) and property taxes are automatically paid as part of their mortgage payments. So most people do not directly feel the pain of writing a large check to pay their bill for government services. Milton Friedman wrote that he came to regret his role in designing the income tax withholding scheme during World War II. "It never occurred to me at the time that I was helping to develop machinery that would make possible a government that I would come to criticize severely as too large, too intrusive, too destructive of freedom" (*The New York Times*, July 4, 2007, p. B1). It seems likely that when consumers (or taxpayers) do not see (or feel) the cost of what they purchase or pay for government services, they may demand more than if they had to directly confront the cost.

Elasticity 5

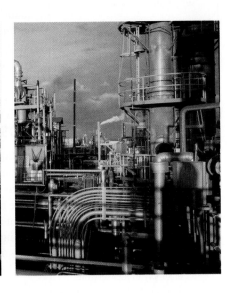

Russ Schelpman/Corbis

In 2008, gasoline prices started to climb. Driven by problems in the Middle East and increased demand from China and India, gasoline prices kept climbing. By the summer, gasoline had reached a price of over $4.00 per gallon, almost three times as high as two years previously.

If you drove a car during this period, what did you do? At first, you probably did nothing but bear with it and pay the higher price. What *could* you do? It is not as if gasoline is the same as chewing gum: A large rise in the price of chewing gum might cause you to give it up. Things are not so easy with gasoline. Maybe you drove a little less. Over time, however, you may have considered alternatives such as buying a smaller car or a hybrid that gets much better gas mileage. Or you may have considered car pooling or public transportation. The drop in sales of large gas-guzzling sport utility vehicles (SUVs) tells us that over time, people responded to the steady rise in gasoline prices by cutting their quantity of gasoline purchased.

Elasticity—the responsiveness of one variable to changes in another—is the term economists use to measure this change. In this gasoline example, we know that the price of gasoline is one variable and the quantity of gasoline demanded is the other variable. The amount of gasoline we buy does not change very much in the short run even though the price might rise. Over the long run, the rise in the price of gasoline has led to some attempts to cut back usage. We can speculate that there will be greater attempts to use less gasoline as prices rise. But how much does the price have to rise before quantity demanded falls significantly? The concept of elasticity lets us measure the relative change in quantity demanded for various changes in the price of gasoline.

Elasticity can be measured for many different items. If the price of cancer-preventing drugs rises, how much will their sales fall? As well as price elasticity, we can look at another elasticity measure, income elasticity, which measures changes in consumer demand in response to changes in consumer income. In a slowing economy, with consumer incomes falling, will the public's purchases of cars and trucks fall off? By how much? When an economy enters a recession, automobile makers want to know how much sales of trucks and cars will decline in response to a fall in consumer income.

Elasticity is a simple economic concept that nonetheless contains a tremendous amount of information about demand for specific products. In the last two chapters, we saw that when prices rise, quantity demanded falls. But how much will quantity demanded fall? If a firm raises its price by 50 cents, will it end up with more in revenue, or will the increase in price lead to a drop in quantity demanded that more than offsets the price increase? If gasoline goes up by 50 cents per gallon, will you still vacation by car? What if the price increase is $2 per gallon?

Knowing a product's price elasticity allows economists to predict the amount by which quantity demanded will drop in response to a price increase, or grow in response to a price decline. Measures of elasticity have a further benefit: By putting changes in a relative (percentage) context, economists can compare the supply and demand curves for different products without worrying about their absolute magnitudes. In essence, the concept of elasticity helps you to put supply and demand concepts to work.

Elasticity of Demand

We know by the law of demand that as prices rise, quantity sold falls. More importantly, *how much* will sales decline? If a small price increase results in *all* of your customers switching to your competitors, it is clearly not a good idea; you are out of business. And if a small price increase still results in a large reduction in quantity sold, then raising prices probably is not a good idea. However, if a large price increase elicits only a small loss in sales, then raising prices may make sense. As we will see, the concept of elasticity and the impact of changing price on a firm's sales revenue help to determine the answer.

Price elasticity of demand (E_d) is a measure of how responsive quantity demanded is to a change in price and is defined as

$$E_d = \frac{\text{Percentage Change in Quantity Demanded}}{\text{Percentage Change in Price}}$$

For example, if prices of strawberries rise by 5% and sales fall by 10%, then the price elasticity of demand for strawberries is

$$E_d = -10 \div 5 = -2$$

Alternately, if a 5% reduction in strawberry prices results in a 10% gain in sales, the price elasticity of demand also is -2 ($E_d = 10 \div -5 = -2$).

Often we are not given percentage changes. Rather, we are given numerical values and have to convert them into percentage changes. For example, to compute a change in price, take the new price (P_{new}) and subtract the old price (P_{old}), then divide this result by the old price (P_{old}). Finally, to put this ratio in percentage terms, multiply by 100. In equation form:

$$\text{Percentage Change} = \frac{(P_{new} - P_{old})}{P_{old}}$$

For example, if the old price of gasoline (P_{old}) was $2.00 a gallon and the new price goes up by $1.00 to $3.00, then the percentage change is

$$\text{Percentage Change} = \frac{\$3.00 - \$2.00}{\$2.00} = \frac{\$1.00}{\$2.00} = 0.50, \text{ or } 50\%$$

Just a reminder: 0.50 times 100 is 50%.

Price elasticity of demand: A measure of the responsiveness of quantity demanded to a change in price, equal to the percentage change in quantity demanded divided by the percentage change in price.

Price Elasticity of Demand as an Absolute Value

The price elasticity of demand is always a negative number. This reflects the fact that the demand curve's slope is negative: As prices increase, quantity demanded falls. Price and quantity demanded stand in an inverse relationship to one another, resulting in a negative value for price elasticity. Economists nevertheless frequently refer to price elasticity of demand in positive terms. They simply use the *absolute value* of the computed price elasticity of demand. Recalling our examples, where $E_d = -2$, we can take the absolute value of -2, written as $|-2|$, and simply refer to E_d as 2. For most comparisons, we can use the absolute value of elasticity and ignore the minus sign.

What does this elasticity value of 2 tell us? Quite simply, that for every 1% increase in price, quantity demanded will decline by 2%. Conversely, for every 1% decline in price, quantity demanded will increase by 2%.

Measuring Elasticity with Percentages

Measuring elasticity in percentage terms rather than specific units enables economists to compare the characteristics of various unrelated products. Comparing price and sales changes for jet airplanes, cars, and hamburgers in dollar amounts would be so complex as to be meaningless. Because a dollar increase in the price for gasoline is different from a dollar increase in the price of a BMW, by using percentage change, we can compare the sensitivity of demand curves of different products. Percentages allow us to compare changes in prices and sales for any two products, no matter how dissimilar they are; a 100% increase is the same percentage change for any product.

We have seen how to compute the elasticity of demand, and we have seen why working with percentage changes is so important. Elasticity is a relative measure giving us a way to compare products with widely different prices and output measures.

Elastic and Inelastic Demand

All products have some price elasticity of demand. When prices go up, quantity demanded will fall. That is the basis of the negative slope of the demand curve. But people are more responsive to changes in the prices of some products than in others. Economists label goods as being *elastic*, *inelastic*, or *unitary elastic*.

Elastic

When the absolute value of the computed price elasticity of demand is greater than 1, economists refer to this as **elastic demand.** An elastic demand curve is one that is responsive to price changes. At the extreme is the *perfectly elastic* demand curve shown in panel A of Figure 1 on the next page. Notice that it is horizontal, showing that the slightest increase in price will result in zero output being sold.

In reality, no branded product—Coca-Cola, Apple iPod, or Toyota Prius—ever has a perfectly elastic demand curve, but for many of us, no other products can perfectly substitute for these products. Still, products with many close substitutes face highly elastic demand curves. One recent study of several brands of bath tissue found the price elasticities of demand for Scott, Kleenex, Charmin, Northern, and other brands ranged from 2.0 to 4.5—highly elastic.[1] Raise the price of Charmin, and watch how quickly sales fall as people switch to Northern or Scott. Canned peaches, nuts and bolts, cereal, and bottled water are all examples of products facing highly elastic demands. If one bottled water company were to raise its price by much, many consumers would simply switch to other brands, since bottled water is nearly identical.

Elastic demand: The absolute value of the price elasticity of demand is greater than 1. Elastic demands are very responsive to changes in price. The percentage change in quantity demanded is greater than the percentage change in price.

---

[1] Lawrence Wu, "Two Methods of Determining Elasticities of Demand and Their Use in Merger Simulation," in Lawrence Wu, *Economics of Antitrust: New Issues, Questions, and Insights* (New York: National Economic Research Associates), 2004, pp. 21–33.

FIGURE 1—Perfectly Elastic, Unitary Elastic, and Perfectly Inelastic Demand Curves

The horizontal demand curve in panel A represents perfectly elastic demand because when price increases, quantity demanded drops to zero. Panel C, on the other hand, illustrates a perfectly inelastic demand curve where quantity demanded is insensitive to changes in price. Panel B shows that if elasticity of demand is unitary, then a 1% increase in price will result in a 1% decrease in quantity demanded. Note that the unitary elastic demand curve is not a straight line.

Inelastic

At the other extreme, what about products that see little change in sales even when prices change dramatically? The opposite of the perfectly elastic demand curve is the curve showing no response to changes in price. Economists call this a *perfectly inelastic* demand curve. An example appears in panel C of Figure 1. This curve is vertical, not horizontal as in panel A. For products with perfectly inelastic demands, quantity demanded does not change when price changes.

What products might be inelastically demanded? Consider products that are immensely important to our lives but have few substitutes—for example, drugs that ameliorate life-threatening illnesses such as heart disease or stroke, and insulin for diabetics. If people who need these products have the money, they will buy them, no matter how high their price. Some products that are relatively, though not perfectly, inelastic include gasoline, tobacco, and most spices. If gasoline prices rise too sharply, some consumers will curtail their driving. Still, it takes a fairly drastic rise in gasoline prices before most people curtail their driving significantly. A doubling of the price of cinnamon will probably not reduce our demand since it is such a small fraction of our overall food budget. Economists define **inelastic demand** as demand curves with elasticity coefficients that are less than 1.

Note that the demand for gasoline is inelastic, but the elasticity for specific brands of gasoline is elastic. Brand preferences for homogeneous commodities such as gasoline are weak, and many different outlets exist for buying gas. If your Shell dealer raises gasoline prices by a significant amount, you probably will go to the Texaco dealer down the street. Giving up using gasoline altogether, on the other hand, is much harder. Over time, public transportation or electric (or hybrid) cars may be possible substitutes for gas-powered cars, but few people will be able to adopt these substitutes in the short run. On the contrary, many people are highly dependent on their gas-powered cars, so gas purchases do not drop substantially when prices rise. Thus, demand for a particular brand of gas (Exxon, Shell) is elastic, while the demand for gasoline as a commodity is inelastic.

Inelastic demand: The absolute value of the price elasticity of demand is less than 1. Inelastic demands are not very responsive to changes in price. The percentage change in quantity demanded is less than the percentage change in price.

Unitary Elasticity

Elastic demand curves have an elasticity coefficient that is greater than 1, while inelastic demand curves have a coefficient of less than 1. That leaves those products with an elasticity coefficient just equal to 1. This condition is called *unit* or **unitary elasticity of demand.** It means the percentage change in quantity demanded is precisely equal to the percentage change in price. Panel B of Figure 1 shows a demand curve where price elasticity equals 1. Note that this demand curve is not a straight line. The reasons for this will become clear in our discussion later on in the chapter.

Unitary elasticity of demand: The absolute value of the price elasticity of demand is equal to 1. The percentage change in quantity demanded is just equal to the percentage change in price.

Determinants of Elasticity

Price elasticity of demand measures how sensitive sales are to price changes. But what determines elasticity itself? The four basic determinants of a product's elasticity of demand are (1) the availability of substitute products, (2) the percentage of income or household budget spent on the product, (3) the time period being examined, and (4) the difference between luxuries and necessities.

Substitutability

The more close substitutes, or possible alternatives, a product has, the easier it is for consumers to switch to a competing product and the more elastic the demand. Beef and chicken are substitutes for many people, as are competing brands of cola such as Coke, Pepsi, and RC Cola. All have relatively elastic demands. Conversely, if a product has few close substitutes, such as insulin for diabetics or tobacco for heavy smokers, its elasticity of demand tends to be lower.

Proportion of Income Spent on a Product

A second determinant of elasticity is the proportion (percentage) of household income spent on a product. In general, the smaller the percent of household income spent on a product, the lower the elasticity of demand. For example, you probably spend little of your income on salt, cinnamon, or other spices. As a result, a hefty increase in the price of salt, say, 25%, would not affect your salt consumption because the impact on your budget would be tiny. But if a product represents a significant part of household spending, elasticity of demand tends to be greater, or more elastic. A 10% increase in your rent, for example, would put a large dent in your budget, significantly reducing your purchasing power for many other products. Such a rent increase would likely lead you to look around earnestly for a cheaper apartment.

Time Period

The third determinant of elasticity is the time period under consideration. When consumers have some time to adjust their consumption patterns, the elasticity of demand becomes more elastic. When they have little time to adjust, the elasticity of demand tends to be more inelastic. Thus, as we saw earlier, when gasoline prices rise suddenly, most consumers cannot immediately change their transportation patterns, so gasoline sales do not drop significantly. However, as gas prices continue to remain high, we see shifts in consumer behavior, to which automakers respond by producing smaller, more fuel-efficient cars.

Luxuries Versus Necessities

Luxuries tend to have demands that are more elastic than do necessities. Necessities like food, electricity, health care, and tobacco for smokers are more important to everyday living, and quantity demanded does not change significantly when prices rise. Luxuries like trips to Hawaii, yachts, and Johnny Walker Blue label scotch, on the other hand, can be

TABLE 1 Selected Estimates of Price Elasticities of Demand

Inelastic		Roughly Unitary Elastic		Elastic	
Salt	0.1	Movies	0.9	Restaurant meals	2.3
Cigarettes	0.24	Private education	1.1	Air travel	2.4
Medical care	0.3	Shoes	0.9	Foreign travel	4.0
Taxi service	0.6	Automobiles	1.2	Furniture	1.5
Gasoline (short run)	0.2	Tires	1.0	Fresh vegetables	2.5
Medical prescriptions	0.3			Commuter rail service (long run)	1.6
Pesticides	0.2–0.5			Shrimp	1.25

Source: Compiled from numerous studies reporting estimates for price elasticity of demand.

postponed or forgotten when prices rise. Table 1 provides a sampling of estimates of elasticities for specific products. Note that as we might expect, medical care and taxi service have relatively inelastic price elasticities of demand, while foreign travel and restaurant meals have relatively elastic demands.

Computing Price Elasticities

When elasticity is computed between two points, the calculated value will differ depending on whether price is increasing or decreasing. For example, in Figure 2, if the price *increases* from $1.00 to $2.00, elasticity is equal to

$$
\begin{aligned}
E_d &= \frac{300 - 500}{500} \div \frac{2.00 - 1.00}{1.00} \\
&= \frac{-200}{500} \div \frac{1.00}{1.00} \\
&= -0.4 \div 1.00 \\
&= |-0.4| \\
&= 0.4
\end{aligned}
$$

FIGURE 2—Computing Elasticity of Demand Using Midpoints

A problem can occur when calculating elasticity over a range of prices. The calculated value can vary depending on whether price is increasing or decreasing. To avoid getting different results when approaching the same analysis from different directions, economists use midpoint price and midpoint quantity.

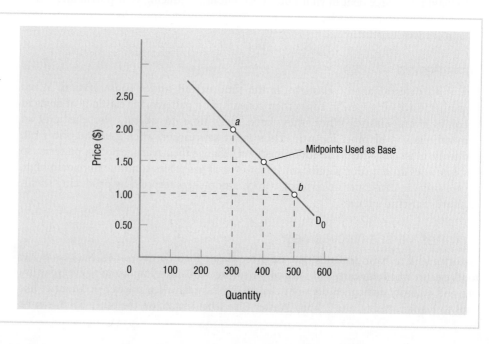

But when price *decreases* from $2.00 to $1.00, elasticity is equal to

$$
\begin{aligned}
E_d &= \frac{500 - 300}{300} \div \frac{1.00 - 2.00}{2.00} \\
&= \frac{200}{300} \div \frac{-1.00}{2.00} \\
&= 0.67 \div -0.5 \\
&= |-1.34| \\
&= 1.34
\end{aligned}
$$

Using Midpoints to Compute Elasticity

To avoid getting different results computing elasticity from different directions, economists compute price elasticity using the midpoints of price $[(P_1 + P_0)/2]$ and the midpoints of quantity demanded $[(Q_1 + Q_0)/2]$ as the base.

Therefore, the *price elasticity of demand* formula (assuming price falls from P_0 to P_1 and quantity demanded rises from Q_0 to Q_1) is

$$
E_d = \frac{Q_1 - Q_0}{(Q_1 + Q_0)/2} \div \frac{P_1 - P_0}{(P_1 + P_0)/2}.
$$

Using the midpoints of price and quantity to compute the relevant percentage changes essentially gives us the average elasticity between point *a* and point *b*. Price elasticity of demand is the difference in quantity over the sum of the two quantities divided by 2, divided by the difference in price over the sum of the two prices divided by 2. In Figure 2, the price elasticity of demand between points *a* and *b* would equal

$$
\begin{aligned}
E_d &= \frac{500 - 300}{(500 + 300)/2} \div \frac{1.00 - 2.00}{(1.00 + 2.00)/2} \\
&= \frac{200}{400} \div \frac{-1.00}{1.50} \\
&= 0.50 \div -0.67 \\
&= |-0.75| \\
&= 0.75
\end{aligned}
$$

Check for yourself to see that this elasticity formula yields the same results whether you compute elasticity for a price increase from $1.00 to $2.00 or for a price decrease from $2.00 to $1.00.

Now that we have seen what price elasticity of demand is and how to calculate it, let's put this knowledge to work by looking at how elasticity affects total revenue.

■ CHECKPOINT

ELASTICITY OF DEMAND

■ Elasticity summarizes how responsive one variable is to a change in another variable.

■ Price elasticity of demand summarizes how responsive quantity demanded is to changes in price.

■ Price elasticity of demand is defined as the percentage change in quantity demanded divided by the percentage change in price.

■ Inelastic demands are relatively unresponsive to changes in price, while quantity demanded is more responsive with elastic demands.

■ Elasticity is determined by a product's substitutability, its proportion of the budget, whether it is a luxury or a necessity, and the time period considered.

■ Economists use midpoints to derive consistent estimates whether price rises or falls.

QUESTION: According to a report from the Federal Trade Commission (FTC), in the first three weeks of August 2003, gas prices in Phoenix, Arizona, jumped from $1.52 to $2.11 a gallon, roughly a 40% increase, due to a ruptured pipeline between Tucson and Phoenix. The pipeline normally brought 30% of Phoenix's fuel from a Texas refinery. During this period, Phoenix gas stations were able to buy gas from West Coast refineries at higher prices. By the end of the month, the rupture was repaired and prices returned to normal. During this three-week period of supply disruption, gasoline sales fell by 8%. What was the approximate price elasticity of demand for gasoline during this period? If the gas stations were unable to get additional gas from the West Coast and supplies fell by the full 30%, how high might have prices risen during that three-week period?

Answers to the Checkpoint questions can be found at the end of this chapter.

Elasticity and Total Revenue

Total revenue: Price times quantity demanded (sold). If demand is elastic and price rises, quantity demanded falls off significantly and total revenue declines, and vice versa. If demand is inelastic and price rises, quantity demanded does not decline much and total revenue rises, and vice versa.

Elasticity is important to firms because elasticity measures the responsiveness of quantity sold to changes in price, which has an impact on the total revenues of the firm. **Total revenue** *TR* is equal to the number of units sold *Q* times the price of each unit *P*, or

$$TR = P \times Q$$

The sensitivity of output sold to price changes greatly influences how much total revenue changes when price changes.

Inelastic Demand

When consumers are so loyal to a product or so few substitutes exist that consumers continue to buy the product even when its price goes up, the product is inelastically demanded. Panel A of Figure 3 shows the impact such a price increase has on total revenue when the demand for a product is inelastic. Price rises from $2.00 to $4.00, and sales decline from

FIGURE 3—Total Revenue and Elasticity of Demand

Given inelastic demand in panel A, when price rises from $2 to $4, revenue rises because the revenue gained from the price hike ($1,000) is greater than the revenue lost from fewer sales ($200). The price hike may have driven off a few customers, but the firm's many remaining customers are paying a much higher price, thus increasing the firm's revenue. When products have elastic demands as shown in panel B, usually because many substitutes are available, firms feel a greater impact from changes in price. A small rise in price causes sales to fall off dramatically.

600 to 500 units. In this case, total revenue *rises*. We know this because the revenue gained from the price hike [(4.00 − 2.00) × 500 = $1,000] is greater than the revenue lost [(2.00 × (600 − 500) = $200]. We can see this by comparing the size of the Revenue Lost area with the Revenue Gained area in the figure. What has happened here? The price hike has driven off only a few customers (a small percent), but the firm's many remaining customers are paying a much higher price (a larger percent), thus driving up the firm's total revenue. This is to be expected: Demand for the firm's product is inelastic, so price increases will be accompanied by smaller declines in sales. The percentage change in quantity (16.7%) is smaller than the percentage change in price (100%).

This may suggest firms would always want the demand for their products to be inelastic. Unfortunately for them, inelastic demand has a flip side. Specifically, if supply increases (due to a technical advance, say), sales will rise only moderately, even as prices fall dramatically. This leads to a drop in total revenue: Consumers indeed buy more of the product at its new lower price, but not enough more to pay the firm for the decline in price.

Elastic Demand

Elastic demand is the opposite of inelastic demand. Firms with elastically demanded products will see their sales change dramatically in response to small price changes. Panel B of Figure 3 shows what happens to total revenue when a firm increases the price of a product with elastic demand. Although price does not increase much, sales fall significantly. Revenue lost greatly exceeds the revenue gained from the price increase, so total revenue falls.

The opposite occurs when prices fall and demand is elastic. The high elasticity of demand faced by restaurants helps explain why so many of them offer "buy one get one free" specials and other discounts. As prices fall to their discounted levels, sales have the potential to expand rapidly, thus increasing revenue.

Unitary Elasticity

We have looked at the impact of changing prices on revenue when demand is elastic and inelastic. When the elasticity of demand is unitary ($E_d = 1$), a 10% increase in price results in a 10% reduction in quantity demanded. As a result, total revenue is unaffected.

Table 2 summarizes the effects price changes have on total revenue for different price elasticities of demand.

TABLE 2	Total Revenue, Price Changes, and Price Elasticity of Demand		
	Elasticity		
Price Change	**Inelastic**	**Elastic**	**Unitary**
Price increases	TR increases	TR decreases	No change in TR
Price decreases	TR decreases	TR increases	No change in TR

Elasticity and Total Revenue Along a Straight-Line Demand Curve

Elasticity varies along a straight-line demand curve. Figure 4 on the next page shows a linear demand curve in panel A and graphs the corresponding total revenue points in panel B. Table 3 on the next page shows the raw data for the figure. In panel A, the elastic part of the curve is that portion above point *e*. Notice that when price falls from $11 to $10, the revenue gained ($100) is much larger than the revenue lost ($10), and thus total revenue rises. This is shown in panel B, where total revenue rises when output grows from 10 to 20 units.

As we move down the demand curve, elasticity will eventually equal 1 (at point *e*) where elasticity is unitary. Price was falling up to this point, while total revenue kept rising

FIGURE 4—Price Elasticity and Total Revenue Along a Straight Line (Linear) Demand Curve

Price elasticity varies along a straight line demand curve. In panel A, the elastic part of the curve lies above point e. Thus, when price falls from $11 to $10, revenue rises, as shown in panel B. As we move down the demand curve, elasticity equals 1 (at point e) where elasticity is unitary. Revenue is maximized at this point. As price continues to fall below $6, demand moves into an inelastic range. When price falls from $3 to $2, revenue declines, as shown in panel B.

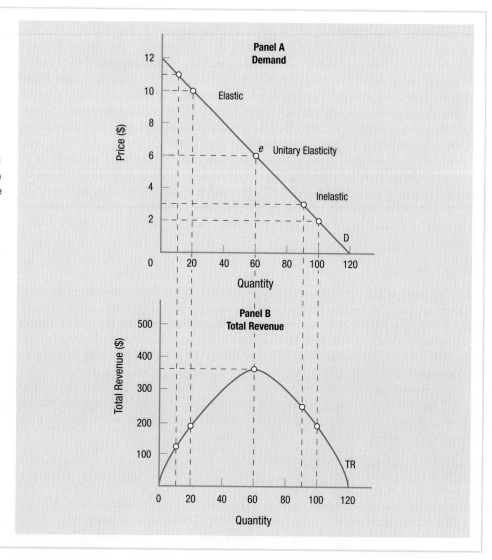

TABLE 3   Data for Demand, Elasticity, and Total Revenue for Figure 4

Price	Quantity	Elasticity	Description	Total Revenue
12	0			0
11	10	23.00	Elastic	110
10	20	7.00	Elastic	200
9	30	3.80	Elastic	270
8	40	2.43	Elastic	320
7	50	1.67	Elastic	350
6	60	1.18	Unitary elastic	360
5	70	0.85	Inelastic	350
4	80	0.60	Inelastic	320
3	90	0.41	Inelastic	270
2	100	0.26	Inelastic	200
1	110	0.14	Inelastic	110
0	120	0.04	Inelastic	0

until the last price reduction just before \$6, where revenue did not change. Revenue is at its maximum at point *e* or a price of \$6 in both panels.

As price continues to fall below \$6, the demand curve moves into an inelastic range because the percentage change in quantity demanded is less than the percentage change in price. Therefore, when price falls from \$3 to \$2, revenue declines. The revenue gained (\$20) is less than the revenue lost (\$90). This decline in revenue is shown in panel B, as total revenue falls as output rises from 90 to 100 units sold.

To summarize, all negatively sloped linear demand curves have an upper portion that is elastic, a midpoint where elasticity is unitary, and a lower part that is inelastic. The logic underlying this fact is straightforward. The slope is constant along the demand curve, so each \$1 change in price leads to a 10-unit change in quantity demanded. Slope is the ratio of *change* in one variable to another. Elasticity is the ratio of the *percentage* change in one variable to another. Thus, when the price of a product is low, a 1-unit change in price is a large percentage change while the percentage change in quantity demanded is small. When the price is high, a 1-unit change in price is a small percentage change but the percentage change in quantity is large.

Other Elasticities of Demand

Besides the price elasticity of demand, two other elasticities of demand are important. The first, *income elasticity of demand,* measures how responsive quantity demanded is to changes in income. Incomes vary as the economy expands and contracts. To plan their future employment and production, many industries want to know how the demand for their products will be affected when the economy changes. How much will airline travel be affected if the economy moves into a recession? What will happen to automobile sales? What will happen to sales of lattes at Starbucks? Each business faces a different situation.

Another type of demand elasticity registers changes that occur when competitors change the prices of their products. This is called *cross elasticity of demand.* If Toyota is planning a price reduction, what impact will this have on the sale of Fords? Ford will want to estimate this to decide whether to ignore Toyota or lower its own automobile prices.

Let's consider these two elasticities of demand more closely, beginning with income elasticity of demand.

Income Elasticity of Demand

The **income elasticity of demand** (E_Y) measures how responsive quantity demanded is to changes in consumer income. We define the income elasticity of demand as

$$E_Y = \frac{\text{Percentage Change in Quantity Demanded}}{\text{Percentage Change in Income}}$$

Depending on the value of the income elasticity of demand, we can classify goods in three ways. First, a **normal good** is one where income elasticity is positive, but less than 1 ($0 < E_Y < 1$). As income rises, quantity demanded rises as well, but not as fast as the rise in income. Most products are normal goods. If your income doubles, you will probably buy more sporting equipment and restaurant meals, but not twice as many.

A second category, *income superior goods* or **luxury goods,** includes products with an income elasticity greater than 1 ($E_Y > 1$). As income rises, quantity demanded grows faster than income. Goods and services such as Mercedes automobiles, caviar, fine wine, and visits to European spas are luxury or income superior goods.

Finally, **inferior goods** are those goods for which income elasticity is negative ($E_Y < 0$). When income rises, the quantity demanded for these goods falls. Inferior goods include potatoes, beans, compact cars, and public transportation. Get yourself a nice raise, and you will probably be taking the bus a lot less. Note that this is an instance where a minus sign conveys important information.

Income elasticity of demand: Measures how responsive quantity demanded is to changes in consumer income.

Normal goods: Goods that have positive income elasticities of less than 1. When consumer income grows, quantity demanded rises for normal goods, but less than the rise in income.

Luxury goods: Goods that have income elasticities greater than 1. When consumer income grows, quantity demanded of luxury goods rises more than the rise in income.

Inferior goods: Goods that have income elasticities that are negative. When consumer income grows, quantity demanded falls for inferior goods.

Understanding how product sales are affected by changing incomes and economic conditions can help firms to diversify their product lines so sales and employment can be stabilized to some extent over the course of the business cycle. For example, firms that produce all three types of goods can try to switch production toward the good that current economic conditions favor: In boom times, production is shifted more toward the making of luxury goods. Ford will produce more Lincoln town cars in boom times, and more compact cars during economic slowdowns.

Cross Elasticity of Demand

Cross elasticity of demand (E_{ab}) measures how responsive the quantity demanded of one good (product a) is to changes in the price of another (product b):

$$E_{ab} = \frac{\text{Percentage Change in Quantity Demanded of Product a}}{\text{Percentage Change in Price of Product b}}$$

Using cross elasticity of demand, we can classify goods in two ways. Products a and b are **substitutes** if their cross elasticity of demand is positive ($E_{ab} > 0$). Common sense tells us that chicken and beef are substitutes. Therefore, if the price of beef rises, people will substitute away from beef and toward chicken, so the quantity demanded for chicken will grow. This illustrates a positive cross elasticity. Similar relationships exist between Toyota and Honda cars, cell phone services provided by AT&T and Sprint, the price of gas and public transportation, and film and digital cameras.

Second, products a and b are **complements** if their cross elasticity of demand is negative ($E_{ab} < 0$). Complementary products are those goods and services that are consumed together, such as gasoline and large SUVs. When the price of gasoline rises, the result is that the quantity demanded for SUVs declines. Other complementary goods include coffee and cream, hamburgers and french fries, and suntan lotion and flip-flops. Finally, two goods are *not related* if a cross elasticity of demand is zero, or near zero.

This is a good place to stop and reflect on what we have discovered so far. We have seen that elasticity measures the responsiveness of one variable to changes in another. Elasticity measures changes in percentage terms so that products of different magnitudes—a bottle of Coca-Cola and an airplane—can be compared. Products that have a price elasticity of demand greater than 1 have elastic demand; products with price elasticity of demand less than 1 have inelastic demand; and products with a price elasticity of demand equal to 1 have unitary elastic demand. We saw that a negatively sloped straight line demand curve has elastic and inelastic ranges, and we also saw that total revenue changes with elastic or inelastic demand. Finally, we saw that as well as price elasticity of demand, we can also look at income elasticity of demand and cross elasticity of demand.

Cross elasticity of demand: Measures how responsive the quantity demanded of one good is to changes in the price of another good. Substitute goods have positive cross elasticities: An increase in the price of one good leads consumers to substitute (buy more) of the other good whose price has not changed. Complementary goods have negative cross elasticities: An increase in the price of a complement leads to a reduction in sales of the other good whose price has not changed.

Substitutes: Goods consumers substitute for one another depending on their relative prices, such as coffee and tea. Substitutes have a positive cross elasticity of demand.

Complements: Goods that are typically consumed together, such as coffee and sugar. Complements have a negative cross elasticity of demand.

■ CHECKPOINT

ELASTICITY AND TOTAL REVENUE

- When demand is inelastic and prices rise, total revenue rises. When demand is inelastic and prices fall, total revenue falls.

- When demand is elastic and prices rise, total revenue falls. When demand is elastic and prices fall, total revenue rises.

- Straight line demand curves have elastic (at higher prices) and inelastic (at lower prices) ranges.

- Income elasticity of demand is a measure of how responsive quantity demanded is to changes in income. This determines whether a good is a luxury, normal, or inferior good.

- Cross elasticity of demand measures how responsive the quantity demanded of one product is to price changes of another. Substitutes have positive cross elasticities while complements have negative ones.

Elasticity of Supply

So far, we have looked at the consumer when we looked at the elasticity of demand. Now let us turn our attention to the producer, and look at elasticity of supply.

Price elasticity of supply (E_s) measures the responsiveness of quantity supplied to changes in the price of the product. Price elasticity of supply is defined as

$$E_s = \frac{\text{Percentage Change in Quantity Supplied}}{\text{Percentage Change in Price}}$$

Note that since the slope of the supply curve is positive, the price elasticity of supply will always be a positive number. Economists classify price elasticity of supply in the same way they classify price elasticity of demand. Classification is based on whether the percentage change in quantity supplied is greater than, less than, or equal to the percentage change in price. When price rises just a little and quantity increases by much more, supply is elastic, and vice versa. The output of many commodities such as gold and seasonal vegetables cannot be quickly increased if their price increases. In summary:

Elastic supply: $E_s > 1$
Inelastic supply: $E_s < 1$
Unitary elastic supply: $E_s = 1$

Looking at the three supply curves in Figure 5 on the next page, we can easily determine which curve is inelastic, which is elastic, and which is unitary elastic. First, note that all three curves go through point a. As we increase the price from P_0 to P_1, we see that the response in quantity supplied is different for all three curves. Consider supply curve S_1 first. When price changes to P_1 (point b), the change in output (Q_0 to Q_1) is the smallest for the three curves. Most important, the percentage change in quantity supplied is smaller than the percentage change in price, so S_1 is an inelastic supply curve.

Contrast this with S_3. In this case, when price rises to P_1 (point d), output climbs from Q_0 all the way to Q_3. Because the percentage change in output is larger than the percentage change in price, S_3 is elastic. And finally, curve S_2 is a unitary elastic curve because the percentage change in output is the same as the percentage change in price.

Here is a simple rule of thumb. When the supply curve is linear, like those shown in Figure 5, you can always determine if the supply curve is elastic, inelastic, or unitary elastic by extending the curve to the axis and applying the following rules:

- Elastic supply curves always cross the price axis, as does curve S_3.
- Inelastic supply curves always cross the quantity axis, as does curve S_1.
- Unitary elastic supply curves always cross through the origin, as does curve S_2.

Time and Price Elasticity of Supply

The primary determinant of price elasticity of supply is time. To adjust output in response to changes in market prices, firms require time. Firms have both variable inputs, such as labor, and fixed inputs, such as plant capacity. To hire more labor, firms must recruit, interview, and hire more workers. This can take as little time as a few hours—a call to a

Price elasticity of supply: A measure of the responsiveness of quantity supplied to changes in price. An elastic supply curve has elasticity greater than 1, whereas inelastic supplies have elasticities less than 1. Time is the most important determinant of the elasticity of supply.

Elastic supply: Price elasticity of supply is greater than 1. The percentage change in quantity supplied is greater than the percentage change in price.

Inelastic supply: Price elasticity of supply is less than 1. The percentage change in quantity supplied is less than the percentage change in price.

Unitary elastic supply: Price elasticity of supply is equal to 1. The percentage change in quantity supplied is equal to the percentage change in price.

FIGURE 5—Price Elasticity of Supply

All three supply curves in this figure run through point *a*, but they respond differently when price changes from P_0 to P_1. Considering supply curve S_1 first, when price changes, the percentage change in quantity supplied is smaller than the percentage change in price, so S_1 is an inelastic supply curve. Curve S_2 is a unitary elastic supply curve, since the percentage change in output is the same as the percentage change in price. For supply curve S_3, the percentage change in output is greater than the percentage change in price, so S_3 is elastic. Elastic linear supply curves cross the price axis, inelastic linear curves cross the quantity axis, and unitary elastic linear curves go through the origin.

temporary agency—or as long as a few months. On the other hand, building another plant or expanding the existing plant to increase output involves considerably more time and resources. In some industries, such as building a new oil refinery or a computer chip plant, it can take as long as a decade, with environmental permits alone often requiring years of study and costing millions of dollars. Economists typically distinguish among three types of time periods: the market period, the short run, and the long run.

The Market Period

Market period: Time period so short that the output and the number of firms are fixed. Agricultural products at harvest time face market periods. Products that unexpectedly become instant hits face market periods (there is a lag between when the firm realizes it has a hit on its hands and when inventory can be replaced).

The **market period** is so short that the output and the number of firms in an industry are fixed; firms simply have no time to change their production levels in response to changes in product price. Consider a raspberry market in the summer. Even if consumers flock to the market, their tastes having shifted in favor of fresh raspberries, farmers can do little to increase the supply of raspberries until the next year. Figure 6 on the next page shows a market period supply curve (S_{MP}) for agricultural products like raspberries. During the market period, the quantity of product available to the market is fixed at Q_0. If demand changes (shifting from D_0 to D_1), the only impact is on the price of the product. In Figure 6, price moves from P_0 (point *e*) to P_1 (point *a*). In summary, if demand grows over the market period, price will rise, and vice versa.

Changes in demand over the market period can be devastating for firms selling perishable goods. If demand falls, cantaloupes cannot be kept until demand grows; they must either be sold at a discount or trashed.

The Short Run

Short run: Time period when plant capacity and the number of firms in the industry cannot change. Firms can employ more people, use overtime with existing employees, or hire part-time employees to produce more, but this is done in an existing plant.

The **short run** is defined as a period of time when plant capacity and the number of firms in the industry cannot change. Firms can, however, change the amount of labor, raw materials, and other variable inputs they employ in the short run to adjust their output to

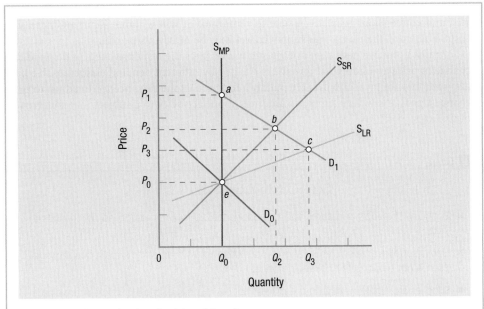

FIGURE 6—Time and Price Elasticity of Supply

During the market period, the quantity of output available to the market is fixed and the only impact will be on the price of the product, which will rise from P_0 to P_1. Over the short run, firms can change the amount of inputs they employ to adjust their output to market changes. Thus, the short-run supply curve (S_{SR}) is more elastic than the market period curve; and price increases are more moderate. In the long run, firms can change their plant capacity and enter or exit an industry. Long-run supply curve S_{LR} is elastic and a rise in demand leads to only a small increase in price.

changes in the market. Note that the short run does not imply a specific number of weeks, months, or years. It simply means a period short enough that firms cannot adjust their plant capacity, but long enough for them to hire more labor to increase their production. A restaurant with an outdoor seating area can hire additional staff and open this area in a relatively short time frame when the weather gets warm, but manufacturing firms usually need more time to hire and train new people for their production lines. Clearly, the time associated with the short run differs depending on the industry.

This also is illustrated in Figure 6. The short-run supply curve, S_{SR}, is more elastic than the market period curve. If demand grows from D_0 to D_1, output expands from Q_0 to Q_2 and price increases to P_2 as equilibrium moves from point e to point b. Because output can expand in the short run in response to rising demand, the price increase is not as drastic as it was in the market period (from P_0 to P_1).

The Long Run

Economists define the **long run** as a period of time long enough for firms to alter their plant capacity and for the number of firms in the industry to change. In the long run, some firms may decide to leave the industry if they think the market will be unfavorable. Alternatively, new firms may enter the market, or existing firms can alter their production capacity. Because all these conceivable changes are possible in the long run, the long-run supply curve is more elastic, as illustrated in Figure 6 by supply curve S_{LR}. In this case, a rise in demand from D_0 to D_1 gives rise to a small increase in the price of the product, while generating a major increase in output, from Q_0 to Q_3 (point c).

In giving long-run supply curve S_{LR} a small but positive slope, we are assuming an industry's costs will increase slightly as it increases its output. Firms must compete with other industries to expand production. Wages and other input prices rise in the industry as firms attempt to draw resources away from their immediate competitors and other industries.

Long run: Time period long enough for firms to alter their plant capacities and for the number of firms in the industry to change. Existing firms can expand or build new plants, or firms can enter or exit the industry.

Some industries may not face added costs as they expand. Fast-food chains, copy centers, and coffee shops seem to be able to reproduce at will without incurring increasing costs. Therefore, their long-run supply curves may be nearly horizontal.

At this point, we have seen how elasticity measures the responsiveness of demand to a change in price and how total revenue is affected by different demand elasticities. We have also seen that supply elasticities are mainly a function of the time needed to adjust to price change signals. Now, let's apply our findings about elasticity to a subject that concerns all of us: taxes.

■ CHECKPOINT

ELASTICITY OF SUPPLY

- Elasticity of supply measures the responsiveness of quantity supplied to changes in price.

- Elastic supplies are very responsive to price changes. With inelastic supply, quantity supplied is not responsive to changing prices.

- Supplies are highly inelastic in the market period, but can expand (become more elastic) in the short run because firms can hire additional resources to raise output levels.

- In the long run, supplies are relatively elastic since firms can enter or exit the industry, and existing firms can expand their plant capacity.

QUESTION: Rank the following industries and businesses in how elastic you think supply is in the long run, from most elastic to least elastic: (a) fast food, (b) nuclear power, (c) crude oil production, (d) Hollywood (movies), (e) computer microchips, (f) grocery stores, (g) airlines, (h) Starbucks.

Answers to the Checkpoint question can be found at the end of this chapter.

Taxes and Elasticity

On average, families pay more than 40% of their income in taxes. These taxes include income, property, estate, sales, and excise taxes. (An excise tax is a sales tax applied to a specific product, such as gasoline or tobacco.) It often seems the government taxes everything! We saw in the last chapter that supply and demand analysis is helpful in analyzing the impact of taxes on markets. In this section we use elasticity to help policymakers determine the impact of these various taxes on individuals, families, and businesses. Again, to simplify the analysis, we will continue to focus on excise taxes.

Economists studying taxes are interested in the **incidence of taxation** and in *shifts* in the tax burden. The incidence of a tax simply refers to who bears its economic burden. Statutes determine what is taxed, who must pay various taxes, and what agencies are responsible for collecting taxes and remitting the revenue collected. Even so, the individuals, firms, or groups who pay a tax may not be the ones bearing its economic burden. As we will see, this burden, or the incidence of a tax, can be shifted onto others. Considering the elasticities of demand and supply will help us determine the incidence of various taxes—who really bears the tax burden—and thus the ultimate impact of various tax policies.

Incidence of taxation: Refers to who bears the economic burden of a tax. The economic entity bearing the burden of a particular tax will depend on the price elasticities of demand and supply.

Elasticity of Demand and Tax Burdens

Let us consider what happens when an excise tax is levied on a product with elastic demand such as strawberries. Panel A of Figure 7 shows the market before an excise tax is imposed. The initial supply curve (S_0) is supply before the tax and demand curve D_0 reflects demand. Originally, the market is in equilibrium at point *e*, where 5,000 baskets are sold for 65 cents each.

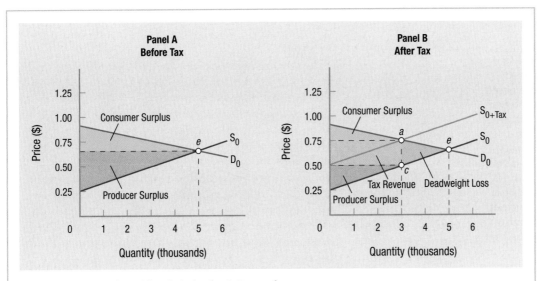

FIGURE 7—Tax Burden with Relatively Elastic Demand

S_0 is the initial supply curve for a product with elastic demand (panel A). When a 25 cent excise tax is placed on the product, the supply curve shifts upward by the amount of the tax, $S_{0+\text{Tax}}$ (panel B. With demand remaining constant at D_0, equilibrium moves to point a (3,000 units). In this case, output falls substantially when the tax is imposed because elastic demand means extreme price sensitivity. As a result, sellers end up bearing most of the burden of this tax, and the deadweight loss is relatively large (area *cae*).

In panel B, we now add a per unit tax—say, $0.25 a basket—paid by the grower. This, in effect, adds 25 cents to the cost for each basket and adds a wedge between what consumers pay and what growers receive. Supply curve S_0 therefore shifts upward by this amount, to $S_{0+\text{Tax}}$. The new supply curve runs parallel to S_0, with the distance the curve has shifted (*ac*) equaling the 25 cent tax per basket.

Assuming demand remains constant at D_0, the new equilibrium is at point *a*, with 3,000 baskets sold for a price of 75 cents each. The firm receives 75 cents per basket, of which it must send 25 cents to the government, keeping 50 cents for itself. Keep in mind that, because this demand is elastic, many consumers are not really willing to pay a higher price for the product; this is why output declines so much and why sellers bear most of the burden of this tax.

Before the tax, both consumer and producer surplus in panel A (discussed in Chapter 4) was substantial. After the tax, the government collects revenue equal to the tax (25 cents) times the number of baskets sold (3,000), or $750 (the blue area), consumer surplus now equals the area above the blue section, and producer surplus equals the area below it. Note that consumers and producers lose surplus equal not only to the revenue gained by the government but also to area *cae*. Economists refer to this area as a **deadweight loss** because this area is lost to society—the government, consumers, and business lose this—because of the tax.

Contrast this situation with the impact of an excise tax when the demand is inelastic (e.g., cigarettes), as in Figure 8 on the next page. Initially, 23,000 packages are sold at $3.00 per package. With a $1.25 tax, supply shifts to $S_{0+\text{Tax}}$, market equilibrium moves to point *g*, price increases from $3.00 to $4.00 per pack, and output declines from 23,000 to 20,000. Inelastic demands are price insensitive, so output hardly declines when this tax is imposed. The $1.25 tax in this case is *gh*, with consumers paying *gi* (a dollar), sellers paying *ih* (25 cents), and a deadweight loss equal to area *hge*. In general, deadweight losses are small when demand is inelastic. A small quantity reduction given a higher price means that nearly all the excise tax is shifted forward to consumers. In this case, consumers pay an additional $1.00 for each unit, but firms end up bearing only a small burden (25 cents).

Deadweight loss: The loss in consumer and producer surplus due to inefficiency because some transactions cannot be made and therefore their value to society is lost.

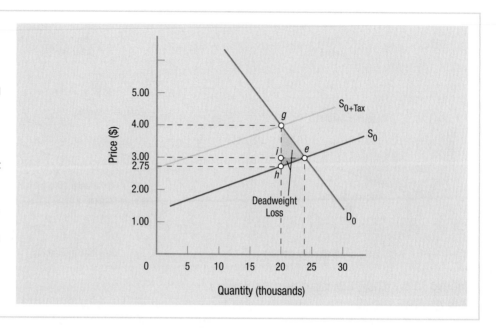

FIGURE 8—Tax Burden with Relatively Inelastic Demand

S_0 is the initial supply curve for a product with inelastic demand. When a $1.25 excise tax is placed on the product, the supply curve shifts upward by the amount of the tax, to S_{0+Tax}. Assuming demand remains constant at D_0, the new equilibrium will be at point g. Because this demand curve is inelastic, consumers are willing to pay a higher price for the product, and bear nearly all the burden of the tax. The deadweight loss (area hge) is relatively small when demand is inelastic.

We can generalize about the effects of elasticity of demand on the tax burden. For a given supply of some product, the greater the price elasticity of demand, the lower the share of the total tax burden shifted to consumers and the greater the share borne by sellers, and vice versa.

This simple analysis shows why proposals to raise excise taxes usually focus on such inelastically demanded commodities such as luxury cars, jewelry, tobacco, gasoline, and alcohol. For products with inelastic demands, the reduction in output is lower when prices rise because of the tax—most smokers keep smoking even when the tobacco tax goes up, and the rich will still buy fancy cars even if they must pay a bit more for them. Therefore, these taxes generate more revenue than would excise taxes on elastically demanded products because the quantity demanded will drop considerably when prices rise on elastically demanded products. Proposals to raise excise taxes are often cloaked in public health and welfare rhetoric, politicians finding it easier to sell the idea of taxes that punish sins or soak the rich. But, if the products in question did not have inelastic demands, the tax revenues generated by such taxes would be small. Because consumers substantially reduce their purchases when demand is elastic, many workers in the industries with such elastically demanded products would become unemployed. As a result, such taxes are rarely ever enacted.

Elasticity of Supply and Tax Burdens

In a similar way, the elasticity of supply is an important determinant of who bears the ultimate burden of taxation. In panel A of Figure 9, demand is held constant at D_0 and equilibrium is initially at point e. Supply curve S_0 is perfectly elastic, or horizontal. When a per unit tax is added to the product, supply shifts vertically to S_{0+Tax} and the new market equilibrium moves to point d, with Q_1 units sold at price P_1. Notice that in this limiting situation of perfectly elastic supply, the full monetary burden of the tax ($P_1 - P_0$) is borne by consumers in the form of higher prices, though industry bears an indirect burden of reduced output and employment. The deadweight loss, area cde, is relatively large with elastically supplied products.

Now consider the case when the supply curve is inelastic, as with S_0 in panel B of Figure 9. When we add the same tax as before to this supply curve, market equilibrium moves to point a. Price increases less than before (P_2 in panel B is lower than P_1 in panel A) and the reduction in output is also less than before ($Q_0 - Q_2$ in panel B is less than $Q_0 - Q_1$ in panel A).

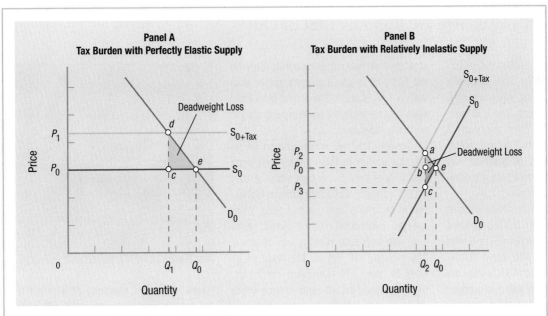

FIGURE 9—Tax Burden and Supply Elasticities

When supply curve S_0 is perfectly elastic as shown in panel A, a per unit excise tax added to the product shifts supply vertically to S_{0+Tax}. In this limiting case of perfectly elastic supply, the full burden of the tax ($P_1 - P_0$) is borne by consumers through higher prices. The deadweight loss is relatively large with elastic supply curves and equal to area *cde*. When supply is inelastic as in panel B, with the same excise tax (*ac* in panel B = *cd* in panel A), price increases are less, and the reduction in output is also less than before. Consumers pay only part of the tax, *ab*, and the deadweight loss to society is equal to area *cae*, less than with the elastic supply shown in panel A.

Consumers pay only part of the tax, *ab*, while sellers must absorb *bc*, and the deadweight loss *cae* is relatively small.

Note what happens in all of these tax cases. Figures 7 to 9 show that whenever a tax is added, the tax moves the market away from its equilibrium point, regardless of whether the tax is borne by consumers, producers, or both. All taxes generate a tax wedge, resulting in a deadweight loss to society. The more elastic the demand or supply, the greater is this deadweight loss. Table 4 summarizes these general results.

These last three chapters have given us the powerful tools of supply and demand analysis. Elasticity is important because it encapsulates the complex relationships among prices, quantity demanded, and total revenues in just two words: elastic and inelastic. When demands are inelastic and some incident marginally reduces supply, policymakers (and

TABLE 4   Summary of Elasticity and Taxes

Elasticity		Tax Burdens			
Demand	**Supply**	**On Consumers**	**On Business**	**Deadweight Loss**	**Figure Where Shown**
Elastic	No change	Lower	Higher	Large	7
Inelastic	No change	Higher	Lower	Small	8
No change	Elastic	Higher	Lower	Large	9A
No change	Inelastic	Lower	Higher	Small	9B

Issue: Hubbert's Peak: Are We Running Out of Oil?

Is the world running out of oil? Ever since the early 1970s, that has been a popular refrain by pundits, environmentalists, and some academics. The U.S. government estimates that there are nearly 3 trillion barrels of oil in the ground worldwide, but some of these oil reserves may require higher prices before they are commercially feasible to pump.

In the mid-1950s, Marion King Hubbert created a model of known U.S. oil reserves and predicted that production in the United States would peak in the early 1970s. Production did peak in 1970, and his model now suggests that world oil production will peak within the next decade. Hubbert's model marks the point where half of the recoverable oil has been pumped out and half remains, so production has peaked. If world economic growth continues, world oil demand will continue to grow, oil production will slow, and the gap between supply and demand will grow, with oil prices correspondingly rising. Several authors suggest that production declines and rapid increases in oil prices will lead to a worldwide recession or even a depression.[2]

There are many reasons to believe that oil prices will continue to be high in the future, but our analysis of markets and elasticity suggests that we are unlikely to run out of oil for a long time, if ever.

First, there is a measurement issue. Controversy surrounds the accurate measurement of world oil reserves. Many experts argue that current estimates understate "proven reserves," and as Daniel Yergin has noted, the reporting system is based on 30-year-old technology and is "roughly analogous to a doctor restricted to making a diagnosis only on the basis of invasive surgery rather than with a CAT scan."[3] The world may have considerably more oil underground than is currently estimated.

Second, there is a substitution issue. We saw earlier in this chapter that price elasticity of demand is dependent in part on the ability to substitute from a higher-priced good to a lower-priced good. What are the substitutes for oil-based gasoline? We might be running out of cheap $30-a-barrel oil, but as the price of oil rises to, say, $60, Canadian tar sands, Brazilian cane-based and switch-grass ethanol, and natural gas and coal converted to liquid become economical. When oil prices reach $80 a barrel, shale and corn-based ethanol become competitive. If prices go higher, biodiesel and other forms of alternative energy become attractive. These are substitutes for oil-based gasoline.

Third, there is an adjustment issue based on time. Over time, the higher price of oil should lead to an increase in supply as newer, more costly technologies such as steam injection permit the recovery of oil still in the ground that earlier technologies couldn't recover.[4] Also over time, consumers will adjust their demands for oil. The short-term elasticity of gasoline is roughly 0.2, making short-term price changes quite responsive to small changes in supplies. The price of crude oil is particularly sensitive in the short run to the political stability of exporting nations (particularly in the Middle East and Africa), natural disasters (hurricanes along the Gulf Coast), and accidents (ruptures in pipelines). In the

Elnur Amikishiyev

longer term, the elasticity of demand is 0.7 to 0.9, and consumers will adjust to rising prices through conservation in its various forms.

Thus, even if we reach Hubbert's peak in the next decade, it will not be like falling off a precipice where prices skyrocket. Prices will rise gradually, especially in the futures markets that reach out five to seven years. This will give us plenty of time to begin adjusting to higher prices and using the alternatives described earlier.

Long before we run out of oil, the world will begin substituting alternative energy sources, and petroleum will be used only for high-valued uses such as manufacturing. The problems of global warming may force this change sooner rather than later. Modern oil companies are becoming less exploration oriented and are focusing more on manufactured oil products. Pure fossil-based fuels will, in the future, need to be blended with other products to reduce their greenhouse emissions. Given all the substitutes for oil, we will never run out. Just what constitutes "oil" will change.

[2] See Kenneth S. Deffeyes, *Hubbert's Peak: The Impending World Oil Shortage* (Princeton: Princeton University Press), 2001. Two other books suggest that Saudi Arabia's major oil fields are hitting their peak; see Paul Roberts, *The End of Oil: On the Edge of a Perilous New World* (New York: Houghton Mifflin), 2004, and Matthew R. Simmons, *Twilight in the Desert: The Coming Saudi Oil Shock and the World Economy* (Hoboken, NJ: John Wiley & Sons), 2005.

[3] Daniel Yergin, "How Much Oil Is Really Down There?" *Wall Street Journal,* April 27, 2006, p. A18.

[4] See "Steady as She Goes: Why the World Is Not About to Run Out of Oil," *Economist,* April 22, 2006, pp. 65–67.

now you) know that price will go up substantially, though consumers will continue to purchase the product. Again, this is what happens when gasoline prices rise—consumers continue to purchase roughly the same amount as before, so oil industry revenue and profits rise substantially in the short run.

If, however, demand is elastic and the same incident reduces supply, prices will rise, but by a smaller amount, and output and employment will fall a lot more. If weather conditions in California and Florida ruin the orange crop, reducing the supply and increasing the price of orange juice, consumers will readily substitute other juices. As a result, output, employment, revenues, and profits will decline in the orange industry.

■ **CHECKPOINT**

TAXES AND ELASTICITY

- When price elasticity of demand is elastic, consumers bear a smaller burden of taxes while more is borne by sellers. When demands are inelastic a higher share of the total tax burden is shifted to consumers.

- When the price elasticity of supply is elastic, buyers bear a larger burden of taxes. Elastic supplies also lead to a larger deadweight loss. When supply is inelastic, more of the tax burden is shifted to sellers, but the deadweight loss is less.

QUESTION: Excise taxes were the principal taxes levied for the first hundred years or so after the Revolutionary War. Today, excise taxes fall mainly on cigarettes, liquor, luxury cars and boats, telephones, gasoline, diesel fuel, aviation fuel, bows and arrows, gas-guzzling vehicles, and vaccines. What do all of these products seem to have in common?

Answers to the Checkpoint question can be found at the end of this chapter.

Key Concepts

Price elasticity of demand, p. 108
Elastic demand, p. 109
Inelastic demand, p. 110
Unitary elasticity of demand, p. 111
Total revenue, p. 114
Income elasticity of demand, p. 117
Normal goods, p. 117
Luxury goods, p. 117
Inferior goods, p. 117
Cross elasticity of demand, p. 118
Substitutes, p. 118

Complements, p. 118
Price elasticity of supply, p. 119
Elastic supply, p. 119
Inelastic supply, p. 119
Unitary elastic supply, p. 119
Market period, p. 120
Short run, p. 120
Long run, p. 121
Incidence of taxation, p. 122
Deadweight loss, p. 123

Chapter Summary

Elasticity of Demand

Price elasticity of demand measures how sensitive the quantity demanded of a product is to price changes. Price elasticity of demand typically is expressed as an absolute value. It is determined by dividing the percentage change in quantity demanded by the percentage change in price. Elasticity measures permit comparisons among diverse products because they are based on percentages.

When the absolute value of the price elasticity of demand is greater than 1, that product has an *elastic* demand. Elastically demanded products have many substitutes and their demand is quite sensitive to price changes. When elasticity is less than 1, demand is *inelastic.* Quantity demanded is not very sensitive to price changes. Necessities such as gasoline, prescription drugs, and tobacco have relatively inelastic demands.

There are four major determinants of elasticity. Elasticity is influenced by the availability of substitute products, the percentage of income spent on the product, the length of time consumers have to adjust, and the difference between luxuries and necessities.

Total revenue is affected by price elasticity of demand. With an inelastically demanded product, quantity demanded is less sensitive to price changes. When prices rise, total revenue rises since quantity demanded falls off less than price increases. When price declines, total revenue falls since quantity sold increases less than price declines.

If a product is elastically demanded, a small price change can lead to large changes in quantity demanded. Thus, when prices fall for an elastically demanded good, sales surge and total revenue rises. However, when price rises, consumers quickly find substitutes and sales plunge, resulting in lower total revenues.

Income elasticity of demand measures how quantity demanded varies with consumer income. Normal goods have a positive income elasticity of demand, but less than 1. Luxury goods have income elasticities greater than 1. Inferior goods have negative income elasticities. As income rises, spending on luxury goods grows faster than income, while spending on inferior goods falls. When income rises, spending on normal goods rises, but at a pace that is less than the increase in income.

Cross elasticity of demand measures how responsive quantity demanded of one good is to changes in the price of another good. If cross elasticity of demand is positive, the two goods are substitutes. If negative, the two goods are complements.

Elasticity of Supply

The price elasticity of supply measures how sensitive the quantity of a product supplied is to changes in price for that product. It is found by taking the percentage change in quantity supplied and dividing it by the percentage change in price (essentially the same formula as that for the price elasticity of demand). The slope of the supply curve is positive, so price elasticity of supply is always positive. An elastic supply curve has a price elasticity of supply greater than 1. Price elasticity is less than 1 for inelastic supply curves, and equal to 1 for unitary elastic supply curves.

The market period, short run, and long run are the three basic time periods economists use to study elasticity. The market period is so short that the output of firms is fixed, or perfectly inelastic. In the short run, companies can change the amount of labor and other variable factors to alter output, but the physical plant and the number of firms in the industry are assumed to be fixed. In the long run, companies have time to build new production facilities, and to enter or exit the industry.

Taxes and Elasticity

Elasticity affects the burden and incidence of taxes. The more elastic the demand, the less a company can shift part of a sales or excise tax to consumers in the form of price increases. This is because consumers can readily substitute for elastically demanded products that rise in price. Elastic demand and supplies generate relatively large deadweight losses for society. An inelastically demanded product, however, can absorb the price increase due to a tax without much impact on quantity demanded. Producers can therefore pass most of the burden for such taxes on to consumers, and the deadweight loss is relatively small. When supply is elastic, the tax burden is higher on consumers, and the deadweight loss is larger. With inelastic supplies, the burden on consumers is less, and the deadweight loss is less.

Questions and Problems

Check Your Understanding

1. When the demand curve is relatively inelastic and the price falls, what happens to revenue? If the demand is relatively elastic and price rises, what happens to revenue?

2. Why is the demand for gasoline relatively inelastic, while the demand for Exxon's gasoline is relatively elastic?

3. Describe cross elasticity of demand. Why do substitutes have positive cross elasticities? Describe income elasticity of demand. What is the difference between normal and inferior goods?

4. Describe the impact of time on price elasticity of supply.

5. Why would the demand for business airline travel be less elastic than the demand for vacation airline travel by retirees?

Apply the Concepts

6. One major rationale for farm price supports is that demand is inelastic and that rapidly improving technology, better crop strains, improved fertilizer, and better farming methods increased supply so significantly that farm incomes were severely depressed. Explain why this rationale would seem to be correct.

7. If the price of chicken rises by 15% and the sales of turkey breasts expand by 10%, what is the cross elasticity of demand for these two products? Are they complements or substitutes?

8. For which of the following pairs of goods and services would the cross elasticity of demand be negative: (a) iPods and songs downloaded from iTunes, (b) digital satellite service and digital video recorders, (c) recreational vehicles and camping tents, (d) bowling and co-ed softball, (e) textbooks and study guides.

9. Consider chip plants: potato and computer. Assume there is a large rise in the demand for computer chips and potato chips.

   a. How responsive to demand is each in the market period?

   b. Describe what a manufacturer of each product might do in the short run to increase production.

   c. How does the long run differ for these products?

10. If one automobile brand has an income elasticity of demand of 1.5 and another has an income elasticity equal to −0.3, what would account for the difference? Give an example of a specific brand for each type of car.

11. Suppose you estimated the cross elasticities of demand for three pairs of products and came up with the following three values: 2.3, 0.1, −1.7. What could you conclude about these three pairs of products? If you wanted to know if two products from two different firms competed with each other in the marketplace, what would you look for?

12. In the 1990s, the government charged Microsoft with being a monopolist (the only seller of operating systems for PCs) with its Windows operating system. Could estimates of cross elasticity of demand help Microsoft defend itself against the charges?

In the News

13. In 2003, London instituted a £5 congestion charge for cars or trucks entering the central city. The levy is said to have reduced congestion by 30% and raised nearly £80 million its first year. London increased the levy to £8 a day, and London's

mayor had this to say: "Congestion charging has achieved its key objective of reducing congestion and has also provided an additional stream of revenue to help the funding of other transport measures within my transport strategy. The charge increase will maintain the benefits currently witnessed in the zone and build upon its success, cutting congestion even further and raising more revenue to be invested in London's transport system." Given what the mayor had to say about the increase in congestion charges and the change in revenue, what must he believe about the elasticity of demand for driving into central London?

14. Alan Greenspan, the former chairman of the Federal Reserve, speaking before the National Petrochemical and Refiners Association in April 2005, made reference to rising oil prices by noting that "higher prices have only brought a modest slowdown in demand for crude oil reflecting a low short-term elasticity of demand. However, the response on the demand side should be more pronounced in the longer term." Is Alan Greenspan correct? Why or why not?

15. Nobel Prize–winning economist, Gary Becker (*Economist,* May 31, 2008) estimated that in the past, "over periods of less than five years, oil *consumption* in the OECD [Organization for Economic Co-operation and Development] dropped by 2–9% when the price doubled. Likewise, oil *production* in countries outside OPEC [Organization of Petroleum Exporting Countries] grew by only 4% every time the price doubled. But over longer periods consumption dropped by 60% and supply rose by 35%." Assume the short-term drop in oil consumption in OECD countries was 5% (not a range of 2 to 9% as Becker estimates). Using these numbers, compute the short- and long-term elasticities of demand and supply of oil. Do your estimates seem roughly consistent with what we have recently seen as oil (and gasoline) prices rose?

Solving Problems

16. Betty's Bakery estimates that they can sell 400 cookies at 60¢ a cookie and will be able to sell 500 if the price drops to 50¢. Using the midpoint formula, what is the elasticity of demand for Betty's cookies? Will total revenue rise or fall if the price of cookies is lowered?

17. Used music CDs rise in price from $7 to $8, and total revenue falls from $700 to $640.

    a. Is the demand curve over this range elastic or inelastic? Why?

    b. Using the midpoint formula, what is the value of the elasticity of demand over this range?

18. Rising world wholesale fair-trade coffee bean prices force the local Dunkin' Donuts franchise to raise its price of coffee from 89 cents to 99 cents a cup. As a result, management notices that donut sales fall from 950 to 850 a day. Shortly after the coffee price spike, the local Cinnabon franchise reduced its price on cinnamon rolls from $1.89 to $1.69. This resulted in a further decline in Dunkin' Donuts donut sales to 750 a day.

    a. What is the cross elasticity of demand for coffee and donuts? Are these two products complements or substitutes?

    b. What is the cross elasticity of demand for Dunkin' Donuts donuts and Cinnabon cinnamon rolls? Are these two products complements or substitutes?

19. Many health plans pay for dental care. If the elasticity of demand for dental care is 0.8, and the health plan increases the price for dental care by 10%, what will be the impact?

20. Your boss, who is the general manager of the Pontiac Rangers, an adequate AA baseball team, has heard that you are taking a principles of economics course

and has asked you to research the demand for summer night games. She has surveyed a sample of 10 people whom she feels accurately represent the potential market. We will assume that they do as well. The results of the survey are presented below:

Number of Night Games Willing to Attend at Various Prices

Name	$5.00	$4.50	$4.00	$3.50	$3.00	$2.50	$2.00
Arvilla	1	2	2	3	3	4	5
Quintha	3	4	5	6	7	7	8
Mary	0	0	1	2	3	5	5
Ray	5	5	5	5	5	6	7
Vern	0	0	0	1	3	3	3
Fran	5	5	5	5	5	5	5
Jerry	2	2	2	2	3	3	3
Richard	5	5	6	6	6	7	8
Whitey	3	6	8	8	8	8	8
Windy	6	6	6	7	7	7	8

a. What ticket price will maximize total revenue for the team?

b. Using the midpoint formula, what is the price elasticity of demand between $2.50 and $2.00?

c. The local bowling alley has extended league play on Wednesday night. Is the cross elasticity of demand positive or negative between night baseball and bowling? If the manager schedules night games on Wednesday, will that affect attendance at the games?

21. J. Crew sells sweaters, pants, and other clothes to college students, among other groups. Many like its clothing, but the company had financial problems nearly a decade ago. In the belief that these problems stemmed from simple merchandising issues—styles, colors, price—J. Crew started to reposition itself in 2003. While some current and potential customers urged the company to lower prices and thereby expand its appeal, in fact prices were raised on many products. For example, a sweater selling for $48 in 2002 sold for $88 at the end of 2003.

a. By raising prices so much, what did J. Crew's management conclude about the price elasticity of demand of its customers?

b. Assume J. Crew sold 100,000 sweaters at the $48.00 price. How many sweaters would they have to sell at the new $88.00 price to have the same total revenue? Assume they sold 80,000 sweaters at the $88.00 price. Using the midpoint formula, what is the price elasticity of demand?

22. Coca-Cola in dispensers located on a golf course sells for $1.25 a can, and golfers buy 1,000 cans. Assume the course raises the price to $1.26 (assume a penny raise is possible) and sales fall to 992 cans.

a. Using the midpoint formula, what is the price elasticity of demand for Coke at these prices?

b. Assume the demand for Coke is a linear line. Would the elasticity of demand be elastic or inelastic at 75 cents a can?

c. At $2.00 a can?

23. For the market shown in the figure below, answer the following questions.

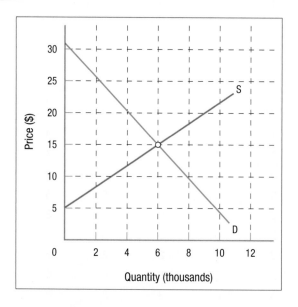

a. Compute the consumer surplus: _____

b. Compute the producer surplus: _____

Now assume that government puts a price ceiling on this product at $10 a unit.

c. Compute the new consumer surplus: _____

d. Compute the new producer surplus: _____

e. What group would tend to have their advocates or lobbyists support price ceilings?

f. How large is the deadweight loss associated with this price ceiling?

Answers to Questions in CheckPoints

Check Point: Elasticity of Demand

If prices in Phoenix rose by 40% and sales fell by 8%, then elasticity is $-0.2 = -0.08/0.40$. Now, if supplies fell by 30% and elasticity is 0.2, then prices could have risen by roughly 150% ($0.30/0.2 = 1.5$) to clear the market.

Check Point: Elasticity and Total Revenue

Store 1 has an elastic demand for its clothes, while store 2 faces an inelastic demand. Look back at Table 2.

Check Point: Elasticity of Supply

There are some close calls in this list, but here is our answer from most to least elastic: Starbucks, fast food, grocery, Hollywood, airlines, microchips, crude oil, nuclear power.

Check Point: Taxes and Elasticity

They all appear to have relatively inelastic demands. This reduces the impact on the industries and leads to higher tax revenues.

Consumer Choice and Demand

AP Photo/Middletown Journal, Pat Auckerman, file

Demand analysis rests on an important assumption: People are rational decision makers. Do people always act rationally? Of course not. A number of economists, called behavioralists, have been studying certain situations where people make irrational decisions. For example, what explains the fact that people often hold on to common stocks long after they rationally recognize that the stocks are dogs and they probably will never make back their losses? It seems that people just do not want to admit—to themselves and others—they have made a stock-picking mistake, and so hold on for years in the vain hope that prices will eventually right themselves.

Important though this work on the irrational is, it does not invalidate the assumption that people choose rationally. If there were a preponderance of irrationality, society would come to a halt because we could not predict anything. In a trivial example, what pedestrian would cross the street even if the light said "walk" if there was a modicum of fear that many drivers would act irrationally and ignore a red light? People *do* miss or ignore red lights, but not often.

So we are left with an underlying assumption of rational decision making that is not bedrock, but is reasonable and powerful nonetheless. We can use it to delve into demand analysis a little more. We know that people determine what price they will pay for various products. How do they make this determination?

We have to choose. We all have a finite quantity of resources at our command. The kinds of products we can purchase are determined, to an extent, by the resources we possess or our income level. For most of us, buying an exotic sports car, a luxury yacht, or a large mansion is simply out of the question—we lack the resources to make such purchases. Making consumer choices, therefore, comes down to buying and enjoying those products that we can, given the fact that we are not Bill Gates or part of his immediate family.

In this chapter, we are going to see what lies behind demand curves by looking at how consumers choose. In the next chapter, we will examine what lies behind supply curves by looking at how producers choose to produce what they do.

There are two major ways to approach consumer choice. We will cover both in this chapter.

The first theory explaining what people choose to buy, given their limited incomes, is known as *utility theory* or *utilitarianism.* This theory holds that rational consumers will allocate their limited incomes so as to maximize their happiness or satisfaction. The clear implication of this theory is that higher incomes should lead to more choices and greater happiness.

Consumer decision making has fascinated economists and philosophers for centuries. Jeremy Bentham (1748–1832), an extraordinary eccentric, argued that every human action is submitted to a "Felicific Calculus"—before acting, we ask ourselves which action would bring the most happiness. That calculus, wrote economic historian Robert Heilbroner,[1] treated "humanity as so many living profit-and-loss calculators, each busily arranging his life to maximize the pleasure of his psychic adding machine."

Bentham's writings were so voluminous that they fill 40 volumes. Still, though Bentham wrote massive draft manuscripts and carried out a correspondence with countless contemporaries, he published little. His influence depended not on publications, but on his personal contacts. Bentham's ideas were so far ahead of their time, moreover, that most of them were not fully developed until well after his death. Forty years after Bentham died, his ideas were rediscovered, refined, and published in *The Theory of Political Economy* by William Stanley Jevons (1835–1882). This work of 1871 marked the beginning of the "marginal revolution."

The second approach, *indifference curve analysis,* is covered in the Appendix to this chapter. Developed by Francis Ysidro Edgeworth, a mathematician who wrote for economists (1845–1926), it added analytical rigor to utility analysis by developing *indifference curves,* which portray combinations of two goods of equal total utility. Edgeworth was a shy man who studied in public libraries because he saw material possessions as a burden. Nevertheless, he brought the precision of mathematics to bear on utility theory and international trade and contributed to statistical analysis by developing the correlation coefficient, which numerically shows the relationship between two variables.

Marginal Utility Analysis

Marginal utility analysis: A theoretical framework underlying consumer decision making. This approach assumes that satisfaction can be measured and that consumers maximize satisfaction when the marginal utilities per dollar are equal for all products and services.

The work of Bentham and Jevons solved the riddles of consumer behavior by developing **marginal utility analysis.** To begin, let's consider more carefully how a limited income puts constraints on our choices.

The Budget Line

As a student, you came to college to improve your life not only intellectually but also financially. As a college graduate, you can expect your lifetime earnings to be triple those of someone with only a high school education. Even once you have achieved these higher earnings, there will be limits on what you can buy. But first, let us return to the present. Assume you have $50 a week to spend on pizza and wall climbing. This is a proxy for a more general choice between food and entertainment. We could use different goods or

---

[1] Robert Heilbroner, *The Worldly Philosophers: The Lives, Times, and Ideas of the Great Economic Thinkers,* 6th ed. (New York: Simon & Schuster), 1986, p. 174.

Jeremy Bentham (1748–1832)

Jeremy Bentham was a social philosopher, legal reformer, and writer who founded the philosophy known as utilitarianism. As an economic theorist, his most valuable contribution was the idea of *utility,* which explained consumer choices in terms of maximizing pleasure and minimizing pain.

Born in 1748, Bentham was the son of a wealthy lawyer. At age 12 he entered Oxford University, then studied for the bar. After hearing Blackstone's famous lectures on English common law, however, Bentham decided not to practice. In 1792, his father died, leaving him a considerable fortune, which allowed him to spend his time writing and thinking. Derided by Karl Marx as the ultimate British eccentric, Bentham dreamed up reform proposals that were both imaginative and remarkably detailed. One of his best-known inventions was the design of a model prison, known as a "Panoptican," which he described as a "mill for grinding rogues honest."

But his primary contribution was analyzing the notion of utility as a driving force in social and economic behavior. Bentham disapproved of notions such as *natural law,* believing that the aim of society and government should be to maximize utility or to promote the "greatest happiness for the greatest number," a phrase Bentham borrowed from a book by Joseph Priestly. In 1789, he published his most famous work, *Introduction to the Principles of Morals,* which laid out his utilitarian philosophy. Bentham believed it was possible to derive a "Felicific Calculus" to compare the various pleasures or pains.

Although modern economists have cast doubt on the notion that utility could be measured or calculated, Bentham had many ideas that were ahead of his time, including the notion of cost-benefit analysis, which logically followed from his utilitarian views on government policies. Bentham also formulated the contemporary notion of marginal utility. After reading this chapter, it will be hard for you to avoid thinking in Bentham's terms about your own consumer choices, and you'll find yourself asking questions like "Do I really get $12 worth of satisfaction out of a Coke and popcorn at the movies, or do I have better alternatives for that money?"

Brand X/SuperStock

more goods, but the principle would still be the same. In our specific example, if pizzas cost $10 each and an hour of wall climbing costs $20, you can climb walls for 2.5 hours or consume 5 pizzas each week, or do some combination of these two. Your options are plotted in Figure 1 on the next page.

This **budget line** (constraint) is a lot like the production possibilities frontier (PPF) discussed in Chapter 2. Though you might prefer to have more of both goods, you are limited to consumption choices lying on the budget line, or inside the budget line if you want to save any part of your $50 weekly budget. As with the PPF curve, however, any points to the right of the line are unattainable for you—they exceed your available income.

In this example, the budget line makes clear that many different combinations of wall climbing and pizzas will exhaust your $50 budget. But which of these possible combinations will you select? That depends on your personal preferences. If you love pizza, you will probably make different choices than if you are a fitness fanatic who rarely consumes fatty foods. Your own preferences determine how much pleasure you can expect to get from the various possible options. Economists call this pleasure the *utility* of an item.

Budget line: Graphically illustrates the possible combinations of two goods that can be purchased with a given income, given the prices of both products.

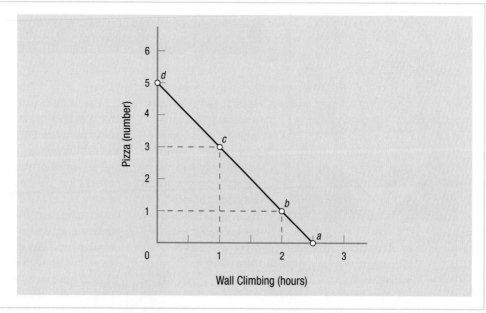

FIGURE 1—The Budget Constraint or Line

When pizzas cost $10 each, wall climbing costs $20 per hour, and you have $50 a week to spend, you could buy 5 pizzas per week, 2.5 hours of wall climbing, or some combination of the two. The budget line makes clear all of the possible purchasing combinations of two products on a particular budget.

Preferences and Utility

Utility: A hypothetical measure of consumer satisfaction.

Utility is a hypothetical measure of consumer satisfaction. It was introduced by early economists attempting to explain how consumers make decisions. The utilitarian theory of consumer behavior assumes, first of all, that utility is something that *can* be measured. It assumes, in other words, that we can quantifiably determine how much utility (satisfaction) you derive from consuming one or more pizzas, and how much utility you derive from spending one or more hours on the climbing wall. Table 1 provides estimates of the utility you derive from both pizzas and wall climbing, measured in *utils*, hypothetical units of satisfaction or utility. Compare columns 1 and 2 with columns 4 and 5.

At first glance, it might seem that if you wanted to maximize your utility, you would simply go wall climbing for 2.5 hours, thereby maximizing your total utility at 270 utils. If you spent a little time with the table, you would notice that combinations give you more total utility. If you went wall climbing for 2 hours and had 1 pizza, your total utility would be 330 utils (260 + 70 = 330), much more than concentrating on one item alone.

Other than trial and error, how do we determine the best combination? Before we can see just which combination of these two goods would actually bring you the most happiness, we need to distinguish between *total utility* and *marginal utility*.

TABLE 1   Total and Marginal Utility from Pizzas and Wall Climbing

Pizza			Wall Climbing		
(1) Quantity	(2) Total Utility	(3) Marginal Utility	(4) Quantity	(5) Total Utility	(6) Marginal Utility
0	0	0	0.0	0	0
1	70	70	0.5	90	90
2	130	60	1.0	170	80
3	180	50	1.5	230	60
4	220	40	2.0	260	30
5	250	30	2.5	270	10

Total and Marginal Utility

Total utility is the total satisfaction that a person receives from consuming a given quantity of goods and services. In Table 1, for example, the total utility received from consuming 3 pizzas is 180 utils, whereas the total utility from 4 pizzas is 220 utils. Marginal utility is something different.

Marginal utility is the satisfaction derived from consuming an *additional* unit of a given product or service. It is determined by taking the difference between the total utility derived from, say, consuming 4 pizzas and consuming 3 pizzas. The total utility derived from 4 pizzas is 220 utils, and that from 3 pizzas is 180 utils. Hence, consuming the fourth pizza yields only an additional 40 utils of satisfaction (220 − 180 = 40 utils).

The marginal utility for both pizza eating and wall climbing is listed in Table 1. Notice that as we move from one quantity of pizza to the next, total utility rises by an amount exactly equal to marginal utility. This is no coincidence. Marginal utility is nothing but the change in total utility obtained from consuming one more pizza (the marginal pizza), so as pizza eating increases by one pizza, total utility will rise by the amount of additional satisfaction derived from consuming that additional pizza. Also note that, for both pizzas and wall climbing, marginal utility declines the more a particular product or activity is consumed.

The Law of Diminishing Marginal Utility

Why does marginal utility decline as the consumption of one product or activity increases? No matter our personal tastes and preferences, we eventually become sated once we have consumed a certain amount of any given commodity. Most of us love ice cream. As youngsters, some of us imagined a world in which meals consisted of nothing but ice cream—no casseroles, no vegetables, just ice cream. To children this might sound heavenly, but as adults, we recognize we would quickly grow sick of ice cream. Human beings simply crave diversity; we quickly tire of the same product or service if we consume it day after day.

This fact of human nature led early economists to formulate the **law of diminishing marginal utility.** This law states that as we consume more of a product, the rate at which our total satisfaction increases with the consumption of each additional unit will decline. And if we continue to consume still more of the product after that, our total satisfaction will eventually begin to decline.

This principle is illustrated by Figure 2 on the next page, which graphs the total utility and marginal utility for pizza eating, as listed in Table 1. Notice that total utility, charted in panel A, rises continually as we move from 1 pizza per week to 5 pizzas. Nevertheless, the rate of this increase declines as more pizzas are consumed. Accordingly, panel B shows that marginal utility declines with more pizzas eaten. On your student budget, you could not afford any more than 5 pizzas a week, but we can imagine that if you were to keep eating pizzas—50 pizzas in a week—your total utility would actually start to drop with each additional pizza. At some point, it simply hurts to stuff any more pizzas down your throat.

It is one thing to grasp the obvious fact that consumers have limited budgets and that the products they can choose among provide them increasing satisfaction but are subject to diminishing marginal utility. It is another thing to figure out exactly how consumers allocate their limited funds so as to maximize their total level of satisfaction or utility. We now turn our attention to how early economists solved the problem of maximizing utility and the analytic methods that flowed out of their work.

Maximizing Utility

Let's take a moment to review everything we need to know to plot the budget line in Figure 1: your total income and the prices of all the products you could purchase. In our example, the weekly budget is $50, pizzas cost $10 apiece, and wall climbing is $20 per hour or $10 per half hour. This is enough information to plot all of the options open to you.

Total utility: The total satisfaction that a person receives from consuming a given amount of goods and services.

Marginal utility: The satisfaction received from consuming an additional unit of a given product or service.

Law of diminishing marginal utility: As we consume more of a given product, the added satisfaction we get from consuming an additional unit declines.

FIGURE 2—Total and Marginal Utility for Pizza

Total utility, charted in panel A, rises continually as we move from 1 pizza per week to 5 pizzas. Nevertheless, the rate of this increase declines as more pizzas are consumed. Accordingly, panel B shows that marginal utility declines with more pizzas eaten.

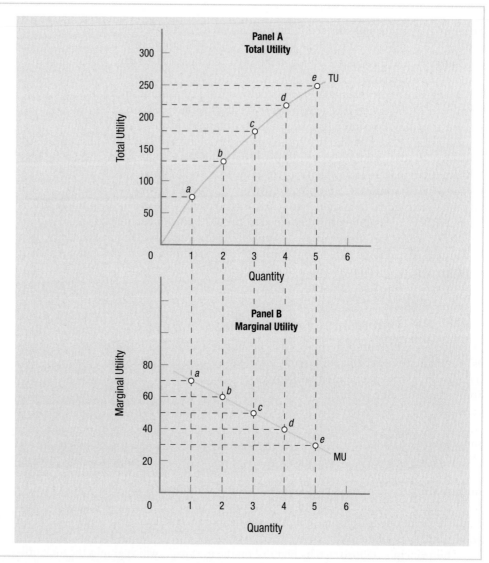

Now, we need to consider the utility we receive from our various levels of consumption of these two products. Take a look at columns (4) and (8) of Table 2. These two columns express the marginal utilities of pizzas and wall climbing, respectively, in terms of marginal utility per dollar; these amounts are computed by dividing the marginal utility of each product by the product's price.

To see the importance of computing marginal utility per dollar, consider the following. Given the figures in columns (4) and (8), and assuming you want to get the most for your money, on which activity would you spend the first $10 of your weekly budget? You can spend the first $10 on a pizza or a half-hour of wall climbing. A pizza returns 70 utils of satisfaction, whereas a half-hour of wall climbing yields 90 utils. Since 90 is greater than 70, clearly the first $10 would be better spent on wall climbing.

Now, for the sake of simplicity, let's keep your spending increments constant. On what will you spend your next $10—pizza or climbing? Look again at the table. Your first pizza still gives you 70 utils, while the second half-hour of wall climbing returns 80 utils. Wall climbing again is the obvious choice. If your total budget had only been $20 per week, you would have been inclined to give up pizzas completely.

TABLE 2	Total and Marginal Utility per Dollar from Pizzas and Wall Climbing						

	Pizza				Wall Climbing		
(1) Quantity (units of pizza)	(2) Total Utility	(3) Marginal Utility	(4) Marginal Utility per Dollar (price = $10)	(5) Quantity (units of wall climbing)	(6) Total Utility	(7) Marginal Utility	(8) Marginal Utility per Dollar (price = $10 per half hour)
0	0	0	0	0.0	0	0	0
1	70	70	7	0.5	90	90	9
2	130	60	6	1.0	170	80	8
3	180	50	5	1.5	230	60	6
4	220	40	4	2.0	260	30	3
5	250	30	3	2.5	270	10	1

Proceeding in the same way, using your third $10 to buy your first pizza will yield an additional 70 utils of satisfaction, whereas using this money to purchase a third half-hour of wall climbing will bring only 60 utils. (Wall climbing is starting to get a bit boring.) Thus, because 70 is greater than 60, with your third $10 you buy your first pizza.

Finally, using the remaining $20 of your budget to buy either additional pizzas or additional half-hours of wall climbing would yield an additional 120 utils of satisfaction. Thus, you split the remaining $20 evenly between these two activities. When the consumption of additional units of two products provides equal satisfaction, economists say consumers are *indifferent* to which product they consume first.

By following this incremental process, therefore, we have determined that you will spend your $50 on 2 pizzas ($20) and 1.5 hours of wall climbing ($30). This results in a total utility of 360 utils (130 for pizza and 230 for wall climbing). *No other combination of pizzas and wall climbing will result in total satisfaction this high,* as you can prove to yourself by trying to spend the $50 differently.

Note also for the last two units of each product consumed, the marginal utilities per dollar were equal at 6. This result is to be expected. Simple logic tells us that if one activity yields more satisfaction per dollar than some other, you will continue to pursue the activity with the higher satisfaction per dollar until some other activity starts yielding more satisfaction. This observation leads to a simple rule for maximizing utility: You should allocate your budget so that the marginal utilities per dollar are equal for the last units of the products consumed. This **utility maximizing rule,** in turn, leads to the following equation, where MU = marginal utility and P = price.

Utility maximizing rule: Utility is maximized where the marginal utility per dollar is equal for all products, or $MU_a/P_a = MU_b/P_b = \ldots = MU_n/P_n$.

$$\frac{MU_{\text{Pizza}}}{P_{\text{Pizza}}} = \frac{MU_{\text{Wall Climbing}}}{P_{\text{Wall Climbing}}}$$

This equation and the analyses described earlier can be generalized to cover numerous goods and services. For all goods and services $a, b, \ldots n$:

$$\frac{MU_a}{P_a} = \frac{MU_b}{P_b} = \cdots = \frac{MU_n}{P_n}$$

The important point to remember is that, according to this theory of consumer behavior, consumers approach every purchase by asking themselves which of all possible additional acts of consumption would bring them the most satisfaction per dollar.

Issue: Tipping and Consumer Behavior

If consumers maximize their utility with a given (limited) budget, why would they ever tip? Consider that tips come at the end of a meal. How can tips affect the quality of service already given?

Many reasons might explain tipping. First, if it is a restaurant you frequent, tips might assure better service in the future. Second, you might consider tips to be rewards for higher-quality service. Third, tipping is a custom and is part of the wages for several dozen occupations.

What would happen if many people refused or neglected to tip? Would various occupations seek to make tipping legally binding? It is likely this would be the result,

if a recent case in New York is any guide. If you have ever gone to a restaurant with a large party, you will notice that menus and bills often state that a set tip will be added for large parties. One large party gave a very small tip after what they considered to be inadequate service. The restaurant sued, claiming that the 18% tip was mandatory. The court's decision for the tipper turned on the phrasing in the menu. This could be viewed as a first shot: If too many people refuse to tip or tip poorly, we can expect legal redress.

We can establish, then, that tipping is a custom that leads to better service, and so is followed even though the tip comes after the service is performed. In this way, it seems to run counter to the idea of people tipping based on a calculation of marginal utility. And how much we tip raises questions about how we calculate marginal utility.

Economists have found only a weak statistical link between quality of service and size of the tip. Tipping also appears to be unrelated to the number of courses in the meal, and whether or not people intend to return to the restaurant. The table

Banana Stock/Jupiter Images

at left shows some of the things that do affect the size of the tip.

Obviously, a waiter or waitress cannot do all of these things and expect to see their tips increase by the sum of all the percentages, but we all have experienced many of these techniques in restaurants. Interestingly, if a waitress draws a smiley face on the bill, her tips go up, but if a waiter does the same, his tips go down. Suggestive selling raises the tip because people tend to tip based on the size of the bill. After having read about this study, you probably will find yourself being a little cynical when some of these techniques are used the next time you dine out.

Source: Based on Raj Persaud, "What's the tipping point?" *Financial Times*, April 9, 2005, p. w3.

Percentage Increase in Tips from Specific Behavior by Wait Staff

Tip Enhancing Action	Change in Tip
Wearing a flower in hair	17%
Introducing yourself by name	53%
Squatting down next to the table	20–25%
Repeat order back to customers	100%
Suggestive selling	23%
Touching customer	22–42%
Using tip trays with credit card insignia	22–25%
Waitress drawing a smiley face on check	18%
Writing "thank you" on the check	13%

See Michael Lynn, *Mega Tips: Scientifically Tested Techniques to Increase Your Tips*, 2004, p. 25. This publication is available free (in PDF format) on the Internet. The author suggests a tip if you find the study helpful.

■ **CHECKPOINT**

MARGINAL UTILITY ANALYSIS

- The budget constraint graphically illustrates the limits on purchases for a given income (budget).

- Utility is a hypothetical measure of consumer satisfaction.

- Total utility is the total satisfaction a person gets from consuming a certain amount of goods.

- Marginal utility is the additional satisfaction a consumer gets from consuming one more unit of the good or service.

- The law of diminishing marginal utility states that as consumption of a specific good increases, the increase in total satisfaction will decline.

- Consumers maximize satisfaction by purchasing goods up to the point where the marginal utility per dollar is equal for all goods.

QUESTIONS: Let's apply the theory of diminishing marginal utility to an all-you-can-eat restaurant meal. First, do you think you will eat more than at a normal restaurant? Why? Second, consider the quality of the food offered at a buffet or an all-you-can-eat restaurant. Recalling what you answered to the first question, what can you predict about the quality of food offered?

Answers to the Checkpoint questions can be found at the end of this chapter.

Using Marginal Utility Analysis

You have seen how the marginal utility analysis of consumer behavior works when we assume that satisfaction or well-being can be measured directly (in utils). We can now use this theory of consumer behavior to derive the demand curve for wall climbing and to examine consumer surplus in a little more depth than when we first introduced this concept in Chapter 4.

Deriving Demand Curves

We know consumers will maximize their utility by spending each dollar of their limited budgets on the goods and services yielding the highest marginal utility per dollar. In our previous example, with pizzas costing $10 each and an hour of wall climbing costing $20, this meant you bought 2 pizzas and 1.5 hours of wall climbing. Would your consumption choices change if these prices changed? Let us consider what happens when the cost of wall climbing rises to $30 per hour.

Now that wall climbing costs $30 per hour or $15 per half hour, column (8) of Table 3 has been altered to reflect this new rate for wall climbing. The first half hour of climbing yields 90 utils and now costs $15, so each dollar yields 6 utils. Now your first $10 will be spent on a pizza ($MU/P = 7$ for pizza versus $MU/P = 6$ for wall climbing).

The next $25 is split between another pizza and a half-hour of wall climbing since $MU/P = 6$ for both. Your final $15 is spent on wall climbing since its marginal utility per dollar (5.33) is higher than for a third pizza (5).

Thus, your final allocation is 2 pizzas and 1 hour of wall climbing. Clearly, consumer choices respond to changes in product prices. With wall climbing at $20 per hour, you consumed 1.5 hours of climbing and 2 pizzas. When the price of wall climbing rose to $30 per

TABLE 3   Total and Marginal Utility per Dollar from Pizzas and Wall Climbing (price of wall climbing increases to $30 per hour or $15 per half hour)

Pizza				Wall Climbing			
(1) Quantity (units of pizza)	(2) Total Utility	(3) Marginal Utility	(4) Marginal Utility per Dollar (price = $10)	(5) Quantity (units of wall climbing)	(6) Total Utility	(7) Marginal Utility	(8) Marginal Utility per Dollar (price = $15 per half hour)
0	0	0	0	0.0	0	0	0.00
1	70	70	7	0.5	90	90	6.00
2	130	60	6	1.0	170	80	5.33
3	180	50	5	1.5	230	60	4.00
4	220	40	4	2.0	260	30	2.00
5	250	30	3	2.5	270	10	0.67

hour you altered your consumption. Now, instead of 1.5 hours and 2 pizzas, you consume 1 hour and 2 pizzas. This new level is shown in the shaded area of Table 3.

Figure 3 plots both your budget constraint and your demand for wall climbing based on the results of Tables 2 and 3. Panel A shows the effect of increasing the price of wall climbing from $20 to $30 per hour. At the increased price of wall climbing, if you were to spend your entire budget on this activity, you could only climb for 1.66 hours ($50/$30 = 1.66). This price increase rotates the budget line leftward, reducing your consumption opportunities, as the figure illustrates.

When the price of wall climbing was $20 per hour, you climbed for 1.5 hours (points *b* in both panels of Figure 3). When the price was increased to $30 per hour, marginal utility analysis led you to reduce your consumption of wall climbing to 1 hour (point *a* in both panels). Connecting these points in panel B of Figure 3 yields the demand curve for wall climbing.

Thus, the marginal utility theory of consumer behavior helps explain both how consumers allocate their income according to their personal preferences and the law of demand. Remember that the law of demand posited an inverse (negative) relationship between price and quantity demanded. This negative relationship is shown in panel B. In addition, this analysis shows why consumers almost always get more than they pay for in terms of the goods and services they buy. This surprising phenomenon that we have seen before is known as **consumer surplus.**

Consumer surplus: The difference between what consumers are willing to pay and what they actually pay for a product in the market.

FIGURE 3—Deriving the Demand for Wall Climbing Using Marginal Utility Analysis

With the price of wall climbing at $20 per hour, you climb for 1.5 hours (point *b* in both panels). When the price increases to $30 per hour, you reduce your consumption of wall climbing to 1 hour (point *a* in both panels). Connecting these points in panel B yields the demand curve for wall climbing.

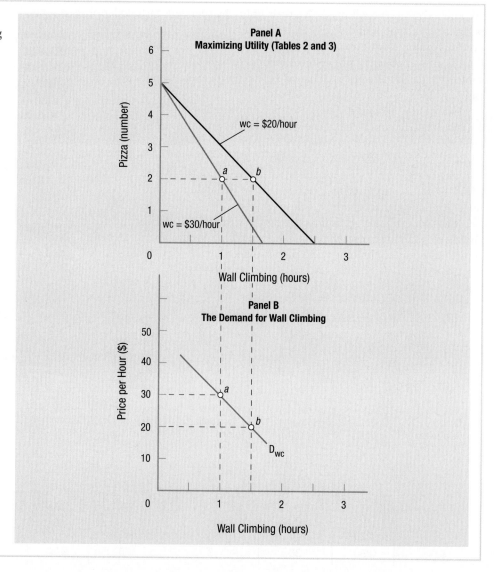

Consumer Surplus

Consumer surplus is another example of the gains that accrue from markets, which we discussed in Chapter 4. Remember, it is the difference between what consumers would be willing to pay for a product and what they must actually pay for the product in the market. Typically, when you purchase something, you can buy all you want of it (within your budget) at the market price. In our initial example, we assumed that the market price of wall climbing was $20 per hour and concluded that you would climb for 1.5 hours per week. When the cost rose to $30 per hour, you reduced your climbing to 1 hour per week. Figure 4 reproduces panel B from Figure 3, highlighting your demand curve for wall climbing for all prices above $20 per hour. Additionally, a supply curve has been superimposed that provides a market equilibrium price of $20 per hour.

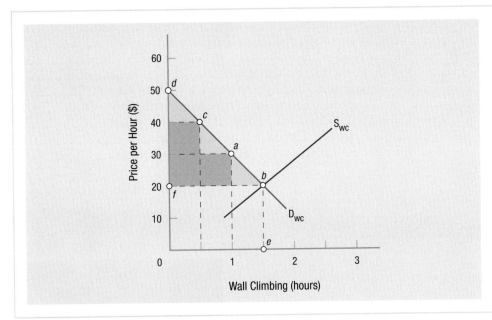

FIGURE 4—Consumer Surplus

Consumer surplus is the difference between what consumers are willing to pay and what they actually pay for a product in the market. When looking at a large market, it is represented by the shaded area *fdb,* the area under the demand curve and above the market price.

Notice that for the first half-hour of climbing, your demand curve shows that you would have been willing to pay $40 per hour (point *c*). Nevertheless, you received that first half-hour for the market price of $20 per hour. That represents a nice gain for you; it is your consumer surplus for the half-hour of climbing. For the next half-hour, you still would have been willing to pay $30 per hour (point *a*), but again you got it for the market price of $20 per hour— not quite as good a deal, but still a nice bargain. Only by the time you are purchasing your third half-hour of climbing must you pay exactly what you would have been willing to pay for this activity, $20 per hour, thus marking the end of your consumer surplus. For this specific instance, your consumer surplus is equal to $30 ($20 + $10 + $0) because we are dealing with a small number of discrete half-hour increments of wall climbing.

The shaded area marked out by triangle *fdb* in Figure 4 represents a more general measure of consumer surplus when we look at large markets.

The total amount spent on climbing in Figure 4 is equal to area 0*fbe.* Total satisfaction from climbing is area 0*dbe.* Consequently, consumer surplus is equal to shaded area *fdb*—that is, area 0*dbe* minus area 0*fbe.* Consumer surplus is a nice "bonus."

Marginal Utility Analysis: A Critique

Marginal utility analysis explains not only how consumers purchase goods and services but also how all household choices are made. We can analyze the decision of whether or not to get a job, for example, by comparing the marginal utility of work versus the marginal utility of leisure. As a college student, you are familiar with having many demands made on your time.

More work means more money but less time for leisure, and vice versa. Marginal utility theory helps us to identify that point where work and leisure (and hopefully study) balance out.

Though marginal utility theory is an elegant and logically consistent theory that helps us understand how consumers behave, it has faced some important criticisms. First and foremost, it assumes that consumers are able to measure the utility they derive from various sorts of consumption. Yet, this is virtually impossible in everyday life—how many utils do you get out of eating a bowl of ice cream? This is not to suggest that marginal utility theory is invalid. It simply requires one very restrictive assumption, namely, that people are able to measure their satisfaction for every purchase. Clearly, this is an assumption that finds little empirical confirmation in everyday life.

Others have argued that it is absurd to think that we could carry out the mental calculus required to compare the ratios of marginal utility to price for all possible goods and services. This is no doubt true, but even if we do not compare all possible goods and services in this way, we do draw some comparisons. After all, we somehow need to be able to distinguish between the desirability of going to a movie or a concert, since we cannot do both at the same time. Marginal utility theory is still a good way of approaching this choice, in a general way.

Recognizing the validity of these criticisms, economists have tried to limit themselves to working with the sorts of data they can collect, in this case purchases by individuals. By formulating hypotheses about what consumers purchase and what this says about their preferences, economists have managed to develop a theory of consumer behavior that does not require that utility be measured. This more modern approach to analyzing consumer behavior reaches the same conclusions as marginal utility theory but requires fewer theoretical restrictions; it is known as *indifference curve analysis* and is discussed in the Appendix to this chapter.

Issue: Are Consumers Really Rational?

Are people really rational utility maximizers? As mentioned at the beginning of this chapter, the challenge comes from behavioral economists. Chief among them are Daniel Kahneman and Richard Thaler.

Let's start with an example. Many companies have retirement plans in which an employee can deduct money tax-free from a paycheck and invest it in a company-sponsored plan where the returns also compound tax-free until retirement. Normally, the various plans are set up with an opt-in feature: When someone is hired, he or she decides whether to set aside any money for the retirement plan (whether to opt in) and how much to contribute. Some companies recently have changed the way employees become part of the retirement plan: Rather than opt in, the companies have automatically enrolled each new employee at a set percentage of pay deducted and employees specifically have to request not to be included (they opt out).

Here is the key: If people are rational utility maximizers, it should make no difference whether they opt in or opt out. The decision should be the same: Should I become part of

this retirement plan and contribute to it? However, Richard Thaler and Cass Sunstein have found that many more people stay with the program if they have to opt out than sign up if they opt in. What accounts for this large difference in behavior for the same decision?

Two explanations have been given for this curious behavior. First, behavioral economists have discovered a "status quo bias," a tendency to go along with a default option. David Laibson claims that the vast majority of U.S. households would save more for retirement if they were rational utility maximizers, and they do not because people have limited rationality, limited self-control, but unbounded optimism.

Thaler and Sunstein suggest a policy prescription for this systematic failure of people to be rational utility maximizers. In a book entitled *Nudge,* they suggest using little nudges to push people in certain preferred directions.

Of course, as soon as companies see the power of the nudge, it is open to abuse. If the default option is set in the wrong way, people can be nudged to do things that might not be in their best interest. In

Ken Bohn/San Diego Zoo/HO/Reuters/Corbis

2008, Frontier Airlines began adding a $10.95 travel insurance charge to all tickets as the default option. Customers had to explicitly opt out of this charge before final purchase. At the same time, Frontier raised fees for changing flights after the time of sale. A Frontier spokesman said: "We believe it's a value to our customers . . . and we think it's in their best interests to buy it." Clearly, there are instances where consumers have biases and act in irrational ways, but it seems unlikely that the bulk of our behavior is irrational.

Sources: Richard Thaler and Cass Sunstein, *Nudge: Improving Decisions about Health, Wealth, and Happiness* (New Haven: Yale University Press), 2008; and Chris Walsh, "Frontier Flier Bolts over Travel Insurance," *Rocky Mountain News,* August 2, 2008, p. 2.

■ **CHECKPOINT**

USING MARGINAL UTILITY ANALYSIS

- Demand curves for products can be derived from marginal utility analysis simply by changing the price of one good and plotting the resulting changes in consumption.

- Consumer surplus is the difference between what you would have been willing to pay for a good and what you actually have to pay.

- Even though marginal utility analysis requires us to measure utility explicitly, it still offers significant insight into how consumers make decisions between products, how consumers react when one product's price changes, and when income drops.

QUESTIONS: Even though convenience stores have significantly higher prices than normal grocery stores such as Safeway, they seem to do well, judging by their numbers. Why are people willing to pay these higher prices? If a Safeway began to operate 24/7, would this affect the sales of a nearby convenience store?

Answers to the Checkpoint questions can be found at the end of this chapter.

Key Concepts

Marginal utility analysis, p. 134
Budget line, p. 135
Utility, p. 136
Total utility, p. 137
Marginal utility, p. 137

Law of diminishing marginal utility, p. 137
Utility maximizing rule, p. 139
Consumer surplus, p. 142

Chapter Summary
Marginal Utility Analysis

The budget line shows the different combinations of goods that can be purchased at a given level of income. Because consumer budgets are limited, consumption decisions often require making tradeoffs—more of one good can be purchased only if less of another is bought.

The utility of a product is a hypothetical measure of how much satisfaction a consumer derives from the product. Though not something that can be measured directly like weight or length, economists estimate the utility of various products at different levels of consumption to understand consumer preference and predict consumer behavior. The standard unit of utility is the *util.*

Total utility is the entire amount of satisfaction a consumer derives from consuming some product; it is equal to the sum of the utility derived from the consumption of each individual unit of this product.

Marginal utility is the amount of utility derived from consuming one more unit of a given product. Note that as a person consumes more units of a product, marginal utility changes—consuming the ninth unit of a product may lead to a different increase in total utility than did consuming the third unit.

The law of diminishing marginal utility states that as more units of any product are consumed, marginal utility declines.

Marginal utility analysis provides a theoretical framework that helps economists understand how consumers make their consumption decisions among different products at varying price levels. It assumes that consumers try to maximize the utility they receive on their limited budgets, by adjusting their spending to the point where the utility derived from the last dollar spent on any product is equal to the utility from the last dollar spent on other products.

Using Marginal Utility Analysis

Consumer surplus is the difference between what consumers are willing to pay for a product and what they must actually pay for the product in the market.

The applicability of marginal utility analysis to the real world is restricted by the fact that it assumes consumers can measure utility accurately and perform complex calculations regarding utility in their heads—both of which are difficult to measure empirically.

Questions and Problems

Check Your Understanding

1. Describe the utility-maximizing condition in words. Explain why it makes sense.

Apply the Concepts

2. Describe the conditions necessary for total utility to be positive but marginal utility is negative. Give an example of such a situation.

3. One luxury goods manufacturer noted that "Our customers do not want to pay less. If we halved the price of all our products, we would double our sales for six months, and then we would sell nothing." Is there something about luxury goods that suggests consumers are irrational? Do luxury goods not follow the law of demand?

4. Advertisements on television both inform consumers and persuade them to purchase products in differing proportion depending on the ad. But today, digital video recorders can be found in 50 to 60 million households, and much of what these households watch is recorded, and the vast bulk of the ads are skipped. If this trend continues, where will consumers find out about new products?

5. Critics of marginal utility analysis argue that it is unrealistic to assume that people make the mental calculus of marginal utility per dollar for large numbers of products. But when you are making a decision to either go to a first-run movie or buy a used DVD of last summer's blockbuster, does this analysis seem so complex? Is it a reasonable representation of your thought process?

In the News

6. A new field called neuroeconomics studies brain activity as people make decisions while trading stocks, gambling, and playing games designed for experiments. The *Wall Street Journal* (April 20, 2006, p. C3) reports that researchers have found that people are particularly afraid of ambiguous risk with unknown odds. Could this simple insight go a long way toward showing why terrorism seems so effective?

7. Harvard economist David Laibson (*Economist*, January 15, 2005, p. 71) has found that "people tend much to prefer, say $100 now to $115 next week, but they are indifferent between $100 a year from now and $115 in a year and a week" Does this seem rational? Using brain scans, he and colleagues found that short-term decisions are governed by the emotional (limbic system) side of the brain, whereas longer-term decisions are governed by the prefrontal cortex, which is associated with reason and calculation. Why might longer-term decisions be more consistent with the consumer choice theories we discussed earlier in this chapter?

8. Richard Layard, in his book *Happiness: Lessons from a New Science*, found that once a country's annual income exceeds $20,000 per capita, there is little relationship between happiness and income. But if you are poor, more money does make you happy. Does this fact suggest that the marginal utility from more income above $20,000 per capita is small?

9. In the summer of 2009, Chrysler announced that beginning with its 2010 models it is dropping the current lifetime powertrain (engine and transmission parts)

warranty and replacing it with a 5-year, 100,000-mile guarantee. The *Wall Street Journal* (August 20, 2009) reported that "Chrysler spokesman Rick Deneau said that the decision was driven by market research that showed customers prefer warranties with a fixed time period." The new five-year warranty will be transferable if the vehicle is sold, while the prior lifetime warranty applied only to the original owner.

Given marginal utility analysis, does it seem reasonable that consumers really prefer a 5-year, 100,000-mile warranty to a lifetime warranty? What customers actually benefit from this new warranty?

Solving Problems

10. Assume a consumer has $20 to spend and for both products the marginal utilities are shown in the table below:

Quantity	MU_A	MU_B
1	20	30
2	10	10
3	5	2

Assume that each product sells for $5 a unit.

a. How many units of each product will the consumer purchase?

b. Assume the price of product B rises to $10 a unit. How will this consumer allocate her budget now?

c. If the prices of both products rise to $10 a unit, what will be the budget allocation?

11. Answer the questions following the table below.

	First-Run Movies			Bottles of Wine	
Quantity	Total Utility	Marginal Utility	Quantity	Total Utility	Marginal Utility
0	0	_____	0	0	_____
1	140	_____	1	180	_____
2	260	_____	2	340	_____
3	360	_____	3	460	_____
4	440	_____	4	510	_____
5	500	_____	5	540	_____

a. Complete the table.

b. Assume that you have $50 a month to devote to entertainment (column labeled First-Run Movies) and wine with dinner (column labeled Bottles of Wine). What will be your equilibrium allocation if the price to see a movie is $10 and a bottle of wine cost $10 as well?

c. A grape glut in California results in Napa Valley wine dropping in price to $5 a bottle, and you view this wine as a perfect substitute for what you were drinking earlier. Now what will be your equilibrium allocation between movies and wine?

d. Given this data, calculate your elasticity of demand for wine over these two prices (see the midpoint equation in Chapter 5).

Answers to Questions in CheckPoints

Check Point: Marginal Utility Analysis

As a general rule, you will eat more because the price for any additional item is zero, so theoretically you eat until the marginal utility is zero. The quality of food, in general, will be lower.

Check Point: Using Marginal Utility Analysis

Convenience stores offer a small set of products at high prices nearer to home and have extended hours of operation. They also provide quicker service in that customers are in and out of the store quickly with what they need. The marginal utility of convenience overcomes the higher prices, so people shop because time is money. A 24/7 Safeway would have an impact on convenience store sales. At off-hours, supermarkets might be as fast as convenience stores, but cheaper.

Appendix: Indifference Curve Analysis

Marginal utility analysis provides a good theoretical glimpse into the consumer decision-making process, yet it requires that utility be measured and that marginal utility per dollar be computed for innumerable possible consumption choices. In reality, measuring utility is impossible, as is mentally computing the marginal utility of thousands of products. To get around these difficulties, economists have developed a modern explanation of consumer decisions that does not require measuring utility. The foundation of this analysis is the indifference curve.

Indifference Curves and Consumer Preferences

If consumers cannot precisely measure the exact satisfaction they receive from specific products, economists reason that people can distinguish between different bundles of goods and decide whether they prefer one bundle to another. This analysis entirely eliminates the idea of consumer satisfaction. It instead assumes that consumers will either be able to choose between any two bundles, or else be *indifferent* to which bundle is chosen. An **indifference curve** shows all points at which consumers' choices are indifferent—points at which consumers express no preference between two products.

To illustrate how an indifference curve works, let us return to our original example of pizzas and wall climbing, now graphed in Figure APX-1. Compare the combination represented by point b (2 pizzas and 1.5 hours of climbing) and the combination at point e (2 pizzas and 0.5 hour of wall climbing). Which would you prefer, assuming you enjoy both of

Indifference curve: Shows all the combinations of two goods where the consumer is indifferent (gets the same level of satisfaction).

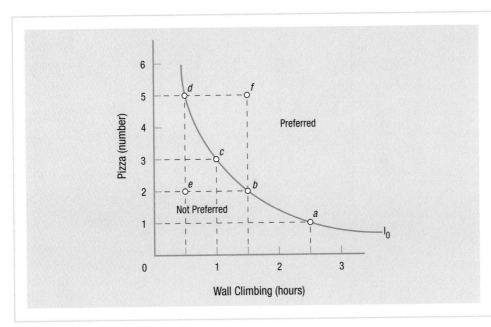

FIGURE APX-1—An Indifference Curve

All of the different possible combinations lying on the indifference curve I_0 represent bundles of goods for which you are indifferent—you would just as soon have any one of these combinations as any other. But compare the combination represented by point b and the combination at point e. Which would you prefer? Point b, of course, because you get more. All points upward and to the right are preferred to all points on indifference curve I_0.

these activities? Clearly, the combination at point *b* is preferable to the combination at point *e* since you get the same amount of pizza but more wall climbing. By the same logic, bundle *f* is preferable to bundle *b* because you get the same amount of climbing, but 3 more pizzas.

These choices have all been easy enough to make. But now assume you are offered bundles *d* and *b*. Bundle *d* contains more pizzas than bundle *b*, but bundle *b* has more climbing time. Given this choice, you may well conclude that you do not care which bundle you get—you are indifferent. In fact, all of the different possible combinations lying on the indifference curve I_0 represent bundles for which you are indifferent, such that you would just as soon have any one of these combinations as any other. And this tells us what an indifference curve is: It identifies all possible combinations of two products that offer consumers the same level of satisfaction or utility. Notice that this mode of analysis does not require us to consider the precise quantity of utility that various bundles yield, but only whether one bundle would be preferable to another.

Properties of Indifference Curves

Indifference curves have negative slopes and are convex to the origin; they bow inward, that is. They have negative slopes because we assume consumers will generally prefer to have more, rather than less, of each product. Yet, to obtain more of one product and maintain the same level of satisfaction, consumers must give up some quantity of the other product. Hence, the negative slope.

Indifference curves are bowed inward toward the origin because of the law of diminishing marginal utility discussed earlier. When you have a lot of pizzas (point *d*), you are willing to give up 2 pizzas to obtain another half-hour of climbing (moving from point *d* to point *c*). But once you have plenty of wall time, yet few pizzas (point *b*), you are unwilling to give up as many pizzas to get more climbing time. This is the law of diminishing marginal utility at work: As we consume more of any particular product, the satisfaction we derive from consuming additional units of this product declines.

Indifference (or Preference) Maps

Indifference map: An infinite set of indifference curves where each curve represents a different level of utility or satisfaction.

An indifference curve is a curve that represents a set of product bundles to which a consumer is indifferent. An **indifference map,** or *preference map*, is an infinite set of indifference curves, each representing a different level of satisfaction. Three possible indifference curves, forming part of a preference map, are shown in Figure APX-2.

FIGURE APX-2—Three Indifference Curves for Pizza and Wall Climbing (An Indifference Map)

An indifference map, or preference map, contains an infinite set of indifference curves, each representing a different level of satisfaction. Three possible indifference curves for pizzas and wall climbing, forming part of a preference map, are shown here.

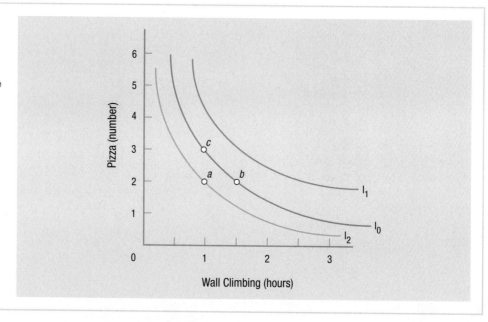

Issue: Auto Advertisements: Utility Versus Indifference Curves

Contrast ads for luxury autos with ads for more prosaic autos such as minivans (denigrated by the trendsetters as the vehicle for "soccer moms"). Why do ads for luxury autos often have few words but instead have images of fancy houses and deserted beaches, while ads for minivans show a passenger door behind the driver's seat, or cup holders, or ways to fold up seats?

The luxury auto ads use an indifference curve approach. For this higher-priced item that often has a status component to it, the ads in effect ask consumers to compare in broad terms the luxury experience with the experience they have with their current

auto. There is no intent to have consumers calculate utility for the various components of the luxury auto—consumers are not asked to calculate the utils received from their current auto's seat with the utils to be received from the high-priced leather seat of the luxury auto.

The less-expensive minivan's ads, in contrast, seem more in line with a marginal utility approach. Individual features are enumerated. Potential customers are pushed into doing at least some mental calculation for each feature. How many utils does one receive from an auto that has cup holders that handle juice boxes as well as cups, since juice boxes are part of a young child's

normal equipment? So, for a less expensive product in the same product category, we see more of a marginal utility approach than an indifference curve approach.

We should be a little cautious in our hypothesis. Soft drinks are inexpensive, yet their ads use an indifference curve approach, probably because the differences between competitors are so small that a marginal utility approach does not make sense. Can you enumerate specific differences between Coca-Cola and Pepsi? Nevertheless, it is useful to look at advertisements for products and use the approaches discussed in this chapter to better understand what advertisers are trying to do.

Indifference curve I_0 is the same curve shown in Figure APX-1. Indifference curve I_1 provides consumers with greater satisfaction than I_0 since it is located farther from the origin. In general, utility rises as curves move outward from the origin, since these curves represent larger quantities of both goods. Conversely, indifference curve I_2 offers consumers less total satisfaction since it is located closer to the origin and represents smaller amounts of both products than I_0.

To confirm the observations just made, compare point *a* on indifference curve I_2 with point *b* on indifference curve I_0. Points *a* and *b* contain the same amount of pizza, but point *b* contains more climbing time. Hence, point *b* offers a higher level of satisfaction than point *a*. An analysis of points *a* and *c* yields a similar conclusion. Since both points *c* and *b* on indifference curve I_0 are preferred to point *a* on I_2, indifference curve I_0 must generally offer higher levels of satisfaction than the points on indifference curve I_2.

This result leads us to one final property of indifference curves: They do not intersect. Since all of the points on any indifference curve represent bundles of goods to which consumers are indifferent, if two indifference curves were to cross, this would mean some of the bundles they represent offered the same level of satisfaction (where the curves meet), but others did not (where the curves do not touch). Yet, this is a logical impossibility, since each indifference curve is defined as a set of bundles offering exactly the same level of satisfaction.

We now turn now to the question of how consumers use such preference maps to optimize their satisfaction within their budget constraints.

Optimal Consumer Choice

Figure APX-3 on the next page superimposes a budget line of $50 per week onto a preference map that assumes pizzas cost $10 each and wall climbing costs $20 per hour. Maximizing your satisfaction on your limited income requires that you purchase some bundle of goods on the highest possible indifference curve. In this example, the best you can do is indicated by point *b*: 2 pizzas and 1.5 hours of wall climbing. Clearly, if you were to pick any other point on the budget line, your satisfaction would be diminished because you would end up on a lower indifference curve (points *a* or *c* in Figure APX-3). It follows that the indifference curve running tangent to the budget line identifies your best option, in this case the indifference curve that just touches the budget line at point *b*.

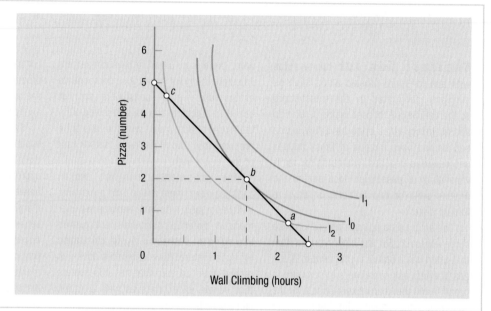

FIGURE APX-3—Optimal Consumer Choice

Maximizing your satisfaction on your limited income requires purchasing some bundle of goods on the highest possible indifference curve. The best you can do in this situation is indicated by point *b*: 2 pizzas and 1.5 hours of wall climbing. Indifference curve I_0 is the highest indifference curve that can be reached with the budget line shown.

Of course, this is the same result we reached earlier using marginal utility analysis, specifically in Table 2. Notice, however, that using indifference curve analysis, we did not have to assume that utility can be measured. We were able to understand how you would allocate your budget between two goods so as to achieve the highest possible level of satisfaction, even without knowing exactly how high that level might be.

Using Indifference Curves

Indifference curves are a useful device to help us understand consumer demand. Economists use indifference curves, for instance, to shed light on the impact of changes in consumer income and product substitution resulting from a change in product price. Indifference curve analysis, moreover, provides some insight into how households determine their supply of labor (this analysis, however, is left to a later chapter). Before we move on to applications of indifference curve analysis, however, we first need to derive a demand curve from an indifference map.

Deriving Demand Curves

We derive the demand curve using indifference curve analysis in much the same way we did using marginal utility analysis. Panel A of Figure APX-4 restates the results of Figure APX-3: When you have a budget of $50 per week, the price of pizza is $10, and climbing is $20 per hour, your optimal choice is found at point *b*. In panel B, we want to plot the demand curve for wall climbing. We know that when wall climbing costs $20 per hour, you will climb for 1.5 hours, so let us indicate this on panel B by marking point *b*.

To fill out the demand curve, let us now increase the price of wall climbing to $30 per hour. This produces a new budget line, *cd*. (Point *d* is located at 1.66 hours because $50/$30 = 1.66 hours of possible wall climbing.) This shift in the budget line yields a new optimal choice at point *a* on indifference curve I_2, now indicating the highest level of satisfaction you can attain. As panel A shows, the ultimate result of this hike in the price of wall climbing to $30 an hour is a reduction in your climbing to 1 hour per week. Transferring this result to panel B, we mark point *a* where price = $30 and climbing hours = 1. Now connecting points *a* and *b* in panel B, we are left with the demand curve for wall climbing.

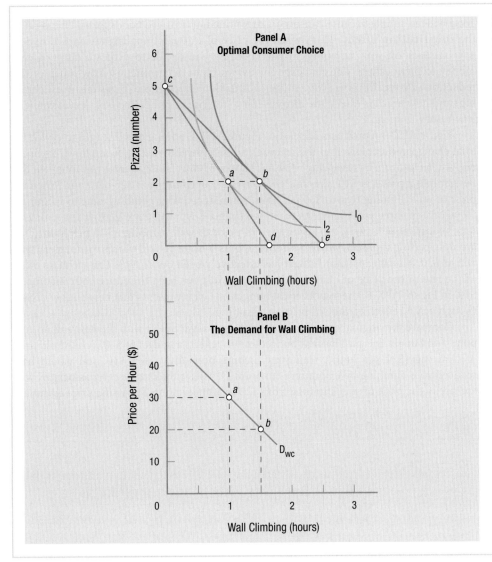

FIGURE APX-4—Deriving the
Demand for Wall Climbing Using
Indifference Curve Analysis

In panel A, when wall climbing
costs $20 per hour, your optimal
choice is found at point *b*. When
the price of wall climbing rises to
$30 per hour, this produces a new
budget line, *cd*, shifting the optimal choice to point *a*. Transferring
points *a* and *b* down to panel B
and connecting the points generates the demand curve for wall
climbing.

Once again, therefore, we arrive at the same conclusion using indifference curve analysis as we did earlier using marginal utility analysis. Both approaches are logical and elegant,
and both approaches tell us something about the thought processes consumers must use as
they make their spending decisions. Indifference curve analysis, however, arrives at its conclusion without requiring that utility be measurable or that consumers perform complex
arithmetic computations.

Income and Substitution Effects

Another way economists use indifference curves is to separate income and substitution
effects when product prices change. First we need to distinguish between these two effects.

When the price of some product you regularly purchase goes up, your spendable
income is thereby essentially reduced. If you always buy a latte a day, for instance, and you
continue to do so even when the price of lattes goes up, you must then reduce your consumption of other goods. This essentially amounts to a reduction in your income. And we
know that when income falls, the consumption of normal goods likewise declines. Hence,
when higher prices essentially reduce consumer incomes, the quantity demanded for normal goods generally falls. Economists call this the **income effect.**

Income effect: When higher prices
essentially reduce consumer income, the
quantity demanded for normal goods falls.

When the price of a particular good rises, meanwhile, the quantity demanded of that good will fall simply because consumers substitute lower priced goods for it. This is called the **substitution effect.** Thus, when the price of wall climbing rises from $20 to $30, you cut back on your climbing, in part, because you decide to dedicate more of your money to pizza eating. The challenge for us now is to determine just how much of this reduction in your climbing is due to the substitution effect (more pizzas mean less climbing) and how much is due to the income effect (the rise in price effectively leaves you with less money to spend).

Figure APX-5 reproduces panel A of Figure APX-4, adding one line (*gh*) to divide the total change in purchases into the income and substitution effects. To see how this line is derived, let us begin by reviewing what has happened thus far. At point *b* you split your $50 budget into 2 pizzas at $10 each and 1.5 hours of wall climbing at $20 per hour. When the price of wall climbing rose to $30 per hour, you reduced your climbing time to 1 hour.

Consider now what happens when we evaluate what you are getting for your *current* allocation of money, but using the *old* price of wall climbing ($20 per hour). You are now getting 2 pizzas, worth $10 apiece, plus 1 hour of wall climbing, formerly valued at $20. This means your budget has effectively been cut to $40. The ultimate effect of the rise in the price of climbing, in other words, has been to reduce your income by $10. In Figure APX-5, the hypothetical budget line *gh* represents this new budget of $40, though again reflecting the old price of climbing.

Compare the original equilibrium point *b* on budget line *ce* with the new equilibrium point *f* on budget line *gh*. This new budget line *gh* reflects a budget of $40 with the old price of climbing ($20 per hour). Had your income previously been $40, you would have reduced your climbing by 15 minutes (to point *f*). This is the *income effect* associated with the rise in the price of wall climbing from $20 to $30 per hour. The rising price essentially

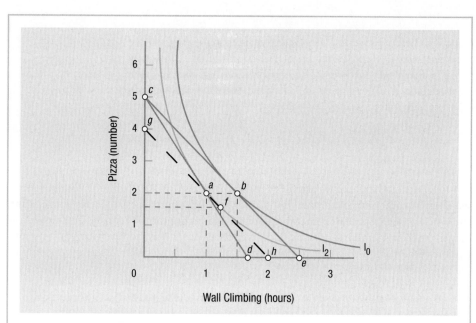

FIGURE APX-5—Income and Substitution Effects

Panel A of Figure APX-4 is reproduced in this figure. The price of climbing having risen to $30 per hour, this effectively reduces your budget to $40 per week, assuming you continue climbing as much as you did before. Line *gh* represents a new budget of $40, though reflecting the old price of climbing. This new budget line *gh* allows us to divide the total change in purchases into the income and substitution effects. Increasing the price of wall climbing from $20 to $30 an hour would mean a reduction in wall climbing (holding income constant at $40) from point *f* to point *a*. This is the substitution effect. The income effect is thus the reduction in consumption from point *b* to point *f*. Adding both effects together yields the total reduction.

reduced your income, and your reduction in wall climbing due to this income reduction alone is 15 minutes.

The change in price is the only thing that differentiates equilibrium point *a* from point *f,* income having been held constant. This difference of 15 minutes between point *f* and point *a* therefore represents a *substitution effect.* It is the effect that comes from changing the price of climbing, while holding income constant.

Combined, the substitution and income effects constitute the entire change in quantity demanded when the price of wall climbing rises by $10 per hour. The income effect (movement from point *b* to point *f*) is a movement from one budget line to another. The substitution effect (movement from point *f* to point *a*) is a movement along the new budget line. Together, they represent the total change in quantity demanded. In this case the income and substitution effects were the same, 15 minutes, but this will not always be the case.

This chapter examined how consumers and households make decisions. Households attempt to maximize their well-being or satisfaction within the constraints of limited incomes. We have seen that the analysis of consumer decisions can be approached in two different ways, using marginal utility analysis or indifference curve analysis.

Marginal utility analysis assumes that consumers can readily measure utility and make complex calculations regarding the utility of various possible consumption choices. Both of these assumptions are empirically rather dubious. This does not, however, invalidate marginal utility analysis; it just makes it difficult to use and test in an empirical context. Indifference curve analysis gives us a more powerful set of analytical tools without these restrictive assumptions.

Issue: Economic Analysis of Terrorism

Since the attack on the World Trade Center on September 11, 2001, combating terrorism has taken center stage in national politics and was an important issue in the 2008 election. Combating terrorism is a complicated, difficult problem that will confront the country for several generations to come. In this brief section, the household indifference curve model outlined in this appendix is applied to this problem. This discussion is based on work by Professors Enders and Sandler. Using the household model, terrorists are treated

Rubberball/Jupiter Images

as rational actors who maximize a set of goals subject to constrained resources.

Terrorist campaigns are not new and extend back to the French Revolution, Russian Revolutions, the IRA campaign in Northern Ireland, and the Palestinian (PLO) struggle against Israel. In essence, as Enders and Sandler note, "Terrorists want to circumvent the normal political channels/procedures and create political change through threats and violence." Terrorism tactics include bombings, assassinations, threats, suicide attacks, and kidnappings all designed to garner support for their cause through extensive media coverage.

Let's apply our household indifference curve model to terrorist activities. Every terrorist organization can achieve its goals using violent terrorist activities *V* and nonviolent political means *N.* The violent means were just

described; the nonviolent means include running candidates for political election and acts of civil disobedience. These activities can be modeled using the indifference curves shown in the figure below. Violent activities can be substituted for nonviolent activities along the indifference curves shown. As long as the goal of more support is reached, terrorists would be indifferent between violent terrorist

continued

activity and nonviolent political activity. The level of the group's utility (or support for their cause) increases for indifference curves moving away from the origin ($I_2 < I_1 < I_0$). From the perspective of terrorist groups, being able to engage in more of both activities is preferable.

Similar to the households we described earlier, terrorist groups do not have unlimited resources (terrorist activities require funding) and face a budget constraint similar to line *ab* shown in the figure. Given the groups' limited resources, if all of their activities are devoted to nonviolent activity, they can engage in $0b$ nonviolent acts, and if all their energies are devoted to terrorism, they can complete $0a$ levels of terrorism. Terrorists maximize their "utility" by engaging in V_0 violent terrorist acts and undertaking N_0 political activities (point *c*). This is the best they can do with their limited resources; any other combination will put them on a lower indifference curve. If terrorists can shift their budget constraint out, they will find themselves on a higher indifference curve, with greater opportunities for both violent and nonviolent activities.

Policy Implications

What can this simple model tell policymakers about how to fight terrorism? Simply, just as terrorist groups want to shift their budget constraints out, governments want to shift the terrorists' budget (or resource) constraints in.

Governments have two general approaches to fighting terrorism, defensive and offensive (proactive). Defensive policies include elaborate airport screening procedures, inspection activities at ports for cargo, and sophisticated protections or barriers at likely targets. Proactive policies include military campaigns against terrorist strongholds, intelligence activities intended to infiltrate terrorist cells, and cooperation with other governments to freeze financial resources and block transfers of funds to potential terrorist cells.

First, let's look at defensive antiterrorist policies. For example, heightening security measures at airports raises the cost of using airplanes to perpetrate vio-

lent terrorist actions. Terrorists have to engage in more elaborate planning, or they might shift resources from targets harder to attack before but now easier because of the relative shift in what is now a hard target or a soft target. If defensive antiterror measures increase the cost (price) of violent acts, the resource constraint rotates from *ab* to *db* in the next figure. There is a rotation of the resource constraint because the cost of violent terrorist activities rises, but there is no change in the cost of nonviolent political activities. The increase in the price of violent activities establishes a new equilibrium at point *e* with a reduction in violence to V_1 and an increase of political activities to N_1.

In a similar way, if government restricts nonviolent political activities, the result is fewer nonviolent activities, but an upsurge in violent terrorist activities. Try this yourself by tilting the original budget line *ab* inward at the bottom so that point *b* moves toward the origin. Then look at the new equilibrium point. This result is consistent with a study by Alan Krueger showing that terrorists tend to come from countries with low levels of civil liberties. He concludes, "When nonviolent means of protest are curtailed, malcontents appear to be more likely to turn to terrorist tactics." Professor Krueger's research also goes a long way to debunk the widely held, often-repeated belief that "instead of being drawn from the ranks of the poor . . . terrorists tend to be drawn from well educated, middle class or high income families."

Alternatively, proactive antiterror measures affect the terrorist resource (or budget) constraint, but in a different way. Proactive intelligence and infiltration of terrorist cells will increase the costs of maintaining a terrorist cell and so rotate the terrorist resource constraint as we saw with defensive antiterrorist meas-

ures, but other proactive measures have a different effect. Military campaigns, freezing of financial assets, and making transfers of purported terrorist funds more difficult reduce the resources available for terrorist activities and nonviolent political activities. This shifts the entire budget constraint in, and a new equilibrium is established at point *f*. Now, com-

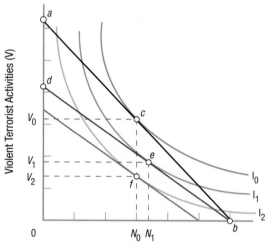

pared to the previous equilibrium at point *e*, terrorism declines to V_2 and in this case nonviolent political activities also decline to N_0.

What comes from this analysis is confirmation of the commonsense notion that both defensive and proactive antiterrorist measures reduce terrorism. What we see a little clearer is the different effects of each type of measure. Using the basic household model to describe terrorist activities, we can conclude that a successful antiterrorist campaign will most likely include both defensive and proactive elements that work in tandem to make terrorist activities more costly and reduce the resources available to terrorist groups.

Sources: Walter Enders and Todd Sandler, *The Political Economy of Terrorism* (New York: Cambridge University Press), 2006. Enders and Sandler, *The Political Economy of Terrorism*, p. 4. Alan Krueger, *What Makes a Terrorist: Economics and the Roots of Terrorism* (Princeton, NJ: Princeton University Press), 2007; and David Wessel, "Princeton Economist Says Lack of Civil Liberties, Not Poverty, Breeds Terrorism," *Wall Street Journal*, July 5, 2007, p. A2.

■ CHECKPOINT

INDIFFERENCE CURVE ANALYSIS

■ Indifference curve analysis does not require utility measurement. All it requires is that consumers can choose between different bundles of goods.

■ An indifference curve shows all the combinations of two goods where the consumer has the same level of satisfaction.

■ Indifference curves have negative slopes, are convex to the origin due to the law of diminishing marginal utility, and indifference curves do not intersect.

■ An indifference map is an infinite set of indifference curves.

■ Consumer equilibrium occurs where the budget line is tangent to the highest indifference curve.

■ When the price of one product rises, not only will your consumption of that product fall (the substitution effect), but also your relative income will be reduced as well, and for normal goods you will consume less (the income effect). The opposite occurs when price falls.

QUESTION: Consumers face a set of goods called "credence goods." These are goods where customers must "take it on faith that the supplier has given them what they need and no more."[2] Examples include surgeons, auto mechanics, and taxis. These experts tell us what medical procedures, repairs, and routes we require to satisfy our needs, and very often we don't know the price until the work is done. If we do not know the price and cannot establish whether we actually need some of these goods, how does this square with our indifference curve analysis?

Answers to the Checkpoint question can be found at the end of this chapter.

Appendix Key Concepts

Indifference curve, p. 149
Indifference map, p. 150

Income effect, p. 153
Substitution effect, p. 154

Appendix Summary
Indifference Curve Analysis

An indifference curve graphically represents all of the combinations of two products that represent the same level of satisfaction to consumers. An indifference curve, in other words, identifies a set of possible consumption combinations that leaves the consumer indifferent.

Like marginal utility analysis, indifference curve analysis helps economists understand how consumers allocate their limited budgets among diverse goods. In fact, indifference curve analysis leads to the same theoretical conclusions as marginal utility analysis. It is subject to less restrictive assumptions, however, in that it does not require that consumers actually measure utility or calculate marginal utility per dollar; instead, consumers can decide which bundles of goods they would prefer to consume under varying circumstances.

The income effect is a change in quantity demanded that comes about as a result of a change in income due to a change in price. When the price of some regularly purchased

[2] "Economic Focus: Sawbones, Cowboys and Cheats," *Economist*, April 15, 2006.

good rises, this leaves consumers with less money to spend buying goods of all sorts. The rise in price, therefore, effectively reduces consumer income, resulting in a drop in demand for most normal goods, often including the good whose price has risen.

When the price of some good rises, quantity demanded for the good will typically fall as consumers begin purchasing cheaper substitute products; this is the substitution effect. Note that when the price of a product rises, quantity demanded for it will typically fall, partially due to the income effect, and partially due to the substitution effect; indifference curve analysis helps us determine how much of this drop in quantity demanded is due to each effect.

Appendix Questions and Problems

Check Your Understanding

1. Indifference curves cannot intersect. Why not?

2. Explain why the following bundles of apples (A) and bananas (B) cannot be on the same indifference curve: (4A, 2B); (1A, 5B); (4A, 3B).

3. Answer the following questions using the figure below:

a. Assume that you have $50 a month to devote to entertainment (First-Run Movies) and wine with dinner (Bottles of Wine). What will be your equilibrium allocation if the price to see a movie or buy a bottle of wine is $10? Graph the equilibrium on the figure and label it point *a*.

b. A grape glut in California results in Napa Valley wine dropping in price to $5 a bottle, and you view this wine as a perfect substitute for what you were drinking earlier. Now what will be your equilibrium allocation between movies and wine? Graph that on the figure and label the new equilibrium as point *b*.

Answers to Appendix Checkpoint Question

CheckPoint: Indifference Curve Analysis

Not very well. They are largely a problem of incomplete information and a challenging problem for consumers. If doctors make more money on complex operations, they will be inclined to prescribe them more often. One study found that doctors elect surgery for themselves less often than nondoctors. As long as consumers are aware of the incentive structure of these transactions, they can build this into the decision calculus, but ultimately, information asymmetries are not adequately represented in this model.

Production and Cost

  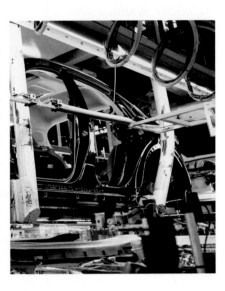

Robert Gilhooly/Alamy

Twenty five years ago, coffee was a commodity product. In the United States, coffee obtained in corporate settings was often dispensed in horrid vending machines: You put your 50 cents in, pressed the button, hoped the paper cup that dropped on the grill would not tip too much the wrong way or even fall out, and waited for the usually tasteless liquid to pour into the paper cup. Coffee brands such as Maxwell House ("good to the last drop") and Folger's advertised on television, but the difference between each was minimal. Not very satisfying, but no great pressure for change, either: How could a new company make any money in such a commodity market?

As you sip your latte or Frappuccino now, it may be hard to imagine a world without Starbucks. Howard Schultz, the key person in the development and growth of Starbucks, was touring the coffee houses in Rome when he wondered why coffee in the United States did not come up to European standards. He thought people would appreciate a superior product that brought with it the coffee-house experience. The number of Starbucks establishments in major cities in the United States shows he was right. So does the almost inconceivable notion of a world without double-shot espressos and lattes.

With entrepreneurs such as Howard Schultz, the idea comes first. They perceive a market need. The next thing that probably goes through their minds is: Can I make a profit out of it? To gauge profits, entrepreneurs have to estimate revenues and costs.

In this chapter, we look at what motivates firms to do what they do—profits. We then look at the production and cost part of the profit equation. In further chapters, we add the revenue part to the production part. In this way, we begin to examine what lies behind supply curves.

Firm: An economic institution that transforms resources (factors of production) into outputs for consumers.

Firms, Profits, and Economic Costs

Firms produce the products and services that you purchase. Most of the business news you see or read concerns giant corporations, but consumers deal most often with small family-owned firms in their neighborhoods. These small firms run the gamut from pizza parlors and CD shops to barber and beauty shops, small garages, and locally owned McDonald's franchises.

As consumers, we take for granted many of the things producers *voluntarily* provide in the market. We all expect businesses to provide us with our morning lattes, fuel for our cars, and up-to-date books for us to read. In fact, it is entrepreneurs in the pursuit of profits who meet all of our needs as consumers.

Firms

A **firm** is an economic institution that transforms inputs, or factors of production, into outputs, or products for consumers. Most firms begin as family enterprises or small partnerships. When successful, these firms can evolve into corporations of considerable size.

In the process of producing goods for consumers, firms must make numerous decisions. First, they have to determine a market need. Then, most broadly, firms must decide what quantity of output to produce, how to produce it, and what inputs to employ. The latter two decisions depend on the production technology the firm selects.

Any given product can typically be produced in a wide variety of ways. Some businesses, like McDonald's franchises and Dunkin' Donuts shops, use considerable amounts of capital equipment, whereas others, such as T-shirt shops and wok eateries, require very little. Even among similar firms, the quality and quantity of resources available often determine what technologies are used. Firms located in areas with an abundance of low-cost labor tend to use low-technology, labor-intensive production methods. In areas where high-skill, high-wage labor is the norm, production is more often done by high-technology, capital-intensive processes.

Entrepreneurs

If a product or service is to be provided to the market, someone must first assume the risk of raising the required capital, assembling workers and raw materials, producing the product, and, finally, offering it for sale. Markets provide incentives and signals, but it is entrepreneurs who provide products and services by taking risks in the hopes of earning profits.

Recent research in neuroscience has shown that "entrepreneurs' brains were more active in the region responsible for taking risky or 'hot' decisions.[1] The research compared entrepreneurs who had founded at least two high-tech firms with senior managers from the private and public sectors. When the decisions were "emotionally neutral," the groups performed the same, but when the decisions were "hot" or risky, the entrepreneurs were more impulsive and more mentally flexible. It is this willingness to take risk to earn profits that distinguishes entrepreneurs from the rest of us.

In the United States, 12% of people ages 18 to 64 classify themselves as entrepreneurs. This means they are running start-up businesses or businesses less than 42 months old. Entrepreneurial rates in Europe are only half the American rate, and Japanese entrepreneurship is less than 2%.[2]

Entrepreneurs can be divided into three basic business structures: sole proprietorships (one owner), partnerships (two or more owners), and corporations (many stockholders). The United States has more than 25 million businesses, over 70% of them sole

---

[1] Andrew Lawrence, et al., "The Innovative Brain," *Nature,* November 13, 2008, pp. 168–69.
[2] *The Economist,* "Enterprising Rising," January 8, 2004, p. 55.

By the *Numbers*

Innovation, Productivity, and Costs Rule Business

To remain in business, firms must innovate not only by improving the products they make but also by controlling their costs. Controlling costs is done by introducing new technologies in production and increasing their productivity. This holds for the service sector as well.

The cost of industrial robots has fallen over 70% since 1990.

Productivity has risen over 50% since 1990.

Christopher Honeywell/Alamy

$9 Billion
Annual revenue needed to support a new semiconductor fabrication plant

9.17 hours
Time spent by the average American on government paperwork

Domestic Content of Autos
Domestic manufacturers	80%
Foreign owned	65%

We've found the key to productivity. It's Fred, down in the shop. He makes the stuff."
From the Wall Street Journal, Permission Cartoon Features Syndicate

Cost Breakdown for an iPod

Retail Price	$299
Costs:	
Hard drive	73
Display module	20
Video processor chip	8
Controller chip	5
Misc. components	34
Assembly	4
Distribution costs	75
Profit for Apple	80

Capacity utilization and employment cost growth have both fallen in recent years. Notice how both fall during recessions (dark bands).

Eric Brown/Alamy

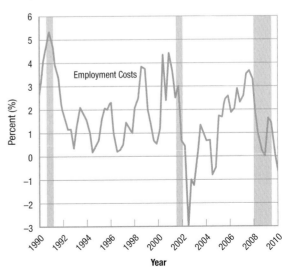

proprietorships or small businesses. Only 20% of American businesses are corporations. Nevertheless, corporations sell nearly 90% of all products and services in the United States. Likewise, around the world, the corporate form of business has become the dominant form. To see why, we must first take a brief look at the advantages and disadvantages of each business structure.

Sole Proprietors

Sole proprietor: A type of business structure composed of a single owner who supervises and manages the business and is subject to unlimited liability.

The **sole proprietor** represents the most basic form of business organization. A proprietorship is composed of one owner, who usually supervises the business operation. Local restaurants, dry cleaning businesses, and auto repair shops are often sole proprietorships. A sole proprietorship is easy to establish and manage, having much less paperwork associated with it than other forms of business organization. But the proprietorship has disadvantages. Single owners are often limited in their ability to raise capital. In many instances, all management responsibilities fall on this single individual. And most important, the personal assets of the owner are subject to unlimited liability. If you as a sole proprietor own a pizza shop and someone slips on your floor, he or she can sue you and take away your house and your life savings if you do not have sufficient insurance.

Partnerships

Partnership: Similar to a sole proprietorship, but involves more than one owner who shares the management of the business. Partnerships are also subject to unlimited liability.

Partnerships are similar to sole proprietorships except that they have more than one owner. Establishing a partnership usually requires signing a legal partnership document. Partnerships find it easier to raise capital and spread around the management responsibilities. Like sole proprietors, however, partners are subject to unlimited liability, not only for their share of the business, but for the entire business. If your partner takes off for Bermuda, you are left to pay all the bills, even those your partner incurred. The death of one partner dissolves a partnership, unless other arrangements have been concluded ahead of time. In any case, the death of a partner often creates problems for the continuity of the business.

Corporations

Corporation: A business structure that has most of the legal rights of individuals, and in addition, the corporation can issue stock to raise capital. Stockholders' liability is limited to the value of their stock.

The **corporation** is today the premier form of business organization in most of the world. Roughly 5,000 American corporations sell nearly $20 trillion worth of goods and services every year. This is an amazing statistic when you consider that the country's nearly 20 million sole proprietorships have sales totaling just over $1 trillion. Clearly, corporations are structured in a way that enhances growth and efficiency.

Corporations possess most of the legal rights of individuals; in addition, they are able to issue stock to raise capital, and most significantly, the liability of individual owners (i.e., stockholders) is limited to the amount they have invested in (or paid for) the stock. This is what distinguishes corporations from the other forms of business organization: the ability to raise large amounts of capital because of limited liability.

Some scholars argue that corporations are the greatest engines of economic prosperity ever known.[3] Daniel Akst wrote, "When I worked for a big company, there was a miracle in the office every couple of weeks, just like clockwork. It happened every payday, when sizable checks were distributed to a small army of employees who also enjoyed health and retirement benefits. Few of us could have made as much on our own, and somehow there was always money left over for the shareholders as well."[4] Without the corporate umbrella, most of the jobs we hold would not exist; most of the products we use would not have been invented; and our standard of living would be a fraction of what it is today.

Business owners of all types are people who react to the profit incentives of the market.

---

[3] John Micklethwait and Adrian Wooldridge, *The Company: A Short History of a Revolutionary Idea* (New York: The Modern Library), 2003.
[4] Daniel Akst, "Where Those Paychecks Come From," *Wall Street Journal*, February 3, 2004.

Issue: Innovation and the Development of the iPod

Your grandmother may have one of those big, heavy radios that were so popular in the 1950s. If you removed the back, you would see a bunch of vacuum tubes. Manufacturers sought to increase the power of each vacuum tube, or get more tubes into the back of each radio. In the early 1960s, Akio Morita of Sony developed the transistor radio, a flimsy-looking yet portable handheld radio that could be taken with you wherever you went. The old-style radio manufacturers pooh-poohed the Sony transistor radio, saying that it was cheap and looked cheap. Maybe more importantly, the manufacturers were bothered aesthetically by the transistor radio: It just was not as ele-

gant as the radio box. Consumers thought otherwise, and the transistor radio was a big hit. And the transistor radio begat the Sony *Walkman.* And the *Walkman* probably had a role in inspiring the creation of the iPod.

The iPod moved consumers away from albums to individual songs. As the iPod, iPhone, and Microsoft's Zune develop, these devices' capabilities are being expanded to carry music, video, cell service, email, PDA functionality, and so on. So when you are walking along listening to your iPod or using your iPhone, consider for a moment how entrepreneurs searching for market needs in the hope of generating profits create these new products for you.

Radius/Jupiter Images

Profits

Entrepreneurs and firms employ resources and turn out products with the goal of making profits. **Profit** is simply the difference between total revenue and total cost.

Total **revenue** is the amount of money a firm receives from the sales of its products. It is equal to the price per unit times the number of units sold ($TR = p \times q$). Note, we use lower case p and q when we are dealing with an individual firm and use upper case when describing a market. *Total cost* includes both out-of-pocket expenses and opportunity costs; we will discuss this concept shortly.

Economists explicitly assume that firms proceed rationally and have the maximization of profits as their primary objective. Alternative behavioral assumptions for firms have been tested, including sales maximization, "satisfactory" profits, and various goals for market share. The biography of Nobel Prize winner Herbert Simon discusses these. Although these more complex assumptions for firm behavior often predict different outcomes, economists have not been persuaded that any of them yield results superior to those of the profit maximization approach. Profit maximization has stood the test of time, and thus we will assume it is the primary economic goal of firms.

Profit: Equal to the difference between total revenue and total cost.

Revenue: Equal to price per unit times quantity sold.

Economic Costs

Economists approach business costs and profits from the opportunity cost perspective discussed in Chapter 2. They separate costs into explicit costs, or out-of-pocket expenses, and implicit costs, or opportunity costs. **Economic costs** are the sum of explicit and implicit costs.

Explicit costs are those expenses paid directly to some other economic entity. These include wages, lease payments, expenditures for raw materials, taxes, utilities, and so on. A company can easily determine its explicit costs by summing all of the checks it has written during the normal course of doing business.

Implicit costs refer to all of the opportunity costs of using resources that belong to the firm. These include depreciation, the depletion of business assets, and the opportunity cost of a firm's capital. In any business, some assets are depleted over time. Machines, cars, and office equipment depreciate with use and time. Finite oil or mineral deposits are depleted as they are mined or pumped. Even though firms do not actually pay any cash as

Economic costs: The sum of explicit (out-of-pocket) and implicit (opportunity) costs.

Explicit costs: Those expenses paid directly to another economic entity, including wages, lease payments, taxes, and utilities.

Implicit costs: The opportunity costs of using resources that belong to the firm, including depreciation, depletion of business assets, and the opportunity cost of the firm's capital employed in the business.

these assets are worn down or used up, these costs nonetheless represent real expenses to the firm.

Another major component of implicit costs is the capital firms have invested. Even small firms incur large implicit costs from their capital investment. Small entrepreneurs, for example, must invest both their own capital and labor into their businesses. Such people could normally be working for someone else, so their "lost salary" must be treated as an implicit cost when determining the true profitability of their businesses. Similarly, any capital invested in a business enterprise could just as well be earning interest in a bank account or returning dividends and capital gains through the purchase of stock in other enterprises. Though not directly paid out as expenses, these forgone earnings nonetheless represent implicit costs for the firm.

Sunk Costs

Sunk costs are costs that have already been incurred and *cannot* be recovered. Examples include previous bets in a poker hand, the tuition you paid this semester, and expenditures on advertising that have run in the media. For example, beyond some point in the term, tuition is a sunk cost. If you drop a course near the beginning of the term and pay by credit hour, you might get a refund for some of the cost of this course. After several weeks in the term, however, most colleges do not provide any refund for dropped courses. Should you *not* drop a course you are doing poorly in and likely will not get better in simply because you paid tuition you cannot get back? Of course not—the tuition is a sunk cost and should be irrelevant to your decision to drop the course or not.

Sunk costs are costs that have been incurred in the past, and you are unable to get them back. These expenses are gone, and future decisions should ignore them. The future benefits from the decision either exceed the future costs or the project is not undertaken, no matter how much has already been spent. The decision to advertise a product in a new magazine depends on the benefits and costs of that advertising, not how much has been spent on television ads in the past. You will hear the phrase that "sunk costs are sunk," meaning ignore them; they are gone.

Economic and Normal Profits

Economists define a *normal rate of return* on the capital invested in a firm as the return just sufficient to keep investors satisfied, and thus just sufficient to keep capital in the business over the long run. The normal rate of return therefore represents the opportunity cost of capital. If a firm's rate of return on capital falls below this rate, investors will put their capital to use elsewhere, and the firm will likely perish; at a minimum, the firm will find it virtually impossible to raise any additional capital. For example, if you could obtain 5% interest in a bank's savings account, why would you invest in a firm that pays less than this rate of return?

Economists include both explicit and implicit costs in their analysis of business profits. They say a firm is earning **economic profits** if it is generating profits in excess of zero once implicit costs are factored in. Economic profits of zero therefore mean a firm is earning just the normal rate of return on its capital, or just enough to cover the opportunity cost of this capital. *Zero economic profits* and **normal profits** thus being equated, anything above zero economic profits represents a true economic profit, and anything below an economic loss. Note that a firm may be earning *accounting profits* as defined by the Internal Revenue Service for tax purposes, yet still be suffering economic losses, since taxable income does not reflect all implicit costs. Table 1 lists some examples of both explicit and implicit costs.

For example, an entrepreneur who opens a small restaurant and earns a $30,000 accounting profit after deducting her out-of-pocket (explicit) costs may or may not have really earned an economic profit. If she could have earned $35,000 a year working

Sunk costs: Those costs that have been incurred and cannot be recovered, including, for example, funds spent on existing technology that have become obsolete and past advertising that has run in the media.

Economic profits: Profits in excess of normal profits. These are profits in excess of both explicit and implicit costs.

Normal profits: The return on capital necessary to keep investors satisfied and keep capital in the business over the long run.

TABLE 1	Examples of Explicit and Implicit Costs
Explicit	**Implicit**
• Salaries	• Earnings that an owner could have made in an alternative job
• Lease payments	• Interest on capital invested in business that could have been made by putting the capital in a bank account
• Cost of goods sold	
• Utilities	
• Insurance	
• Office supplies	

elsewhere, she has suffered a $5,000 economic loss, and we haven't even considered the implicit cost of her capital yet.

Hence, economists designate normal profits as economic profits equal to zero. Normal profits are the profits necessary to keep a firm in business over an extended period of time, or over the long run. This brings us to an important economic distinction, between the short run and the long run.

Short Run Versus Long Run

Although the short and the long run generally differ in their temporal spans, they are *not* defined in terms of time. Rather, economists define these periods by the ability of firms to adjust the quantities of various resources they are employing.

The **short run** is a period of time over which at least one factor of production is fixed, or cannot be changed. For the sake of simplicity, economists typically assume that plant capacity is fixed in the short run. Output from a fixed plant can still vary depending on how much labor the firm employs. Firms can, for instance, hire more people, have existing employees work overtime, or run additional shifts. For discussion purposes, we focus here on labor as the variable factor, but changes in the raw materials used can also result in output changes.

The **long run,** conversely, is a period of time sufficient for a firm to adjust all factors of production, including plant capacity. Since all factors can be altered in the long run, existing firms can even close and leave the industry, and new firms can build new plants and enter the market.

In the short run, therefore, with plant capacity and the number of firms in an industry being fixed, output varies only as a result of changes in employment. In the long run, as plant capacity and other factors are made variable, the industry may grow or shrink as firms enter or leave the business, or some firms alter their plant capacity.

Because all industries are unique, the time required for long-run adjustment varies by industry. Family-owned restaurants, lawn-mowing services, and roofing firms can come and go fairly rapidly. High-capital industries on the other hand, such as the chemical, petroleum, and semiconductor industries, face obstacles to change that require a long time to overcome, whether these be strenuous environmental regulation, immense research and development requirements, or huge capital costs for plant construction. Adding plant capacity in one of these industries can take a decade or more and cost billions of dollars.

The important point to note is that firms seek economic profits and determine profits by first calculating their costs. These costs may differ over the short run versus the long run. Therefore, we look first at production and costs in the short run, then consider costs in the long run.

Short run: A period of time over which at least one factor of production (resource) is fixed, or cannot be changed.

Long run: A period of time sufficient for firms to adjust all factors of production, including plant capacity.

■ CHECKPOINT

FIRMS, PROFITS, AND ECONOMIC COSTS

■ Firms are economic institutions that convert inputs (factors of production) into products and services.

■ Entrepreneurs provide goods and services to markets. Entrepreneurs can be organized into three basic business structures: sole proprietorships, partnerships, and corporations.

■ Corporations are the premier form of business organization because they give owners (shareholders) limited liability, unlike sole proprietorships and partnerships.

■ Profit is the difference between total revenues and costs.

■ Total revenue is price per unit times the number of units sold (TR = $p \times q$).

■ Total cost includes both out-of-pocket and opportunity costs.

■ Explicit costs are those expenses paid directly to some other economic entity, such as taxes, utilities, and the cost of raw materials. Explicit costs can be determined by adding up the checks paid out by a firm.

■ Implicit costs represent the opportunity costs of doing business, including depreciation, depletion, and the firm's capital costs.

■ Economic profits are those in *excess* of a normal rate of return (that return required to keep capital in the firm over a long term).

■ Normal profits are equal to zero economic profits. The firm is earning just enough to keep capital in the firm over the long run.

■ The short run is a period of time where one factor of production (usually plant capacity) is fixed. In the long run all factors can vary and the firm can enter or exit the industry.

QUESTION: Assume for a moment you want to go into business for yourself and you have a good idea. What are the pros and cons of buying an existing business versus starting your own from scratch?

Answers to the Checkpoint question can be found at the end of this chapter.

Production in the Short Run

Production: The process of turning inputs into outputs.

Production is the process of turning inputs into outputs. Most products can be produced using a variety of different technologies. As discussed earlier, these can be either capital-intensive or labor-intensive. Which technology a firm chooses will depend on many things, including ease of implementation and the relative cost of each input into the process.

Again, in the simplified model we are working with, firms can vary their output in the short run only by altering the amount of labor they employ, because plant capacity is fixed in the short run. An individual firm's production possibilities follow the same general pattern as the production function for the entire economy introduced in Chapter 2. Hence, in the short run, output for an existing plant will vary by the amount of labor employed. This output is referred to as *total product*.

Total Product

Imagine you decide to begin manufacturing windsurfing rigs in the unused barn of the farmhouse you rent. (You do not farm the acreage, you just rent the buildings.) Your physical plant is constrained in the short run by the size of the barn. Table 2 lists your firm's total output as you hire more workers.

TABLE 2   Production Data for Windsurfing Sail Firm

(1) L labor	(2) Q (total product)	(3) MP (marginal product)	(4) AP (average product)
0	0	0	—
1	7	7	7.00
2	15	8	7.50
3	25	10	8.33
4	40	15	10.00
5	54	14	10.80
6	65	11	10.83
7	75	10	10.71
8	84	9	10.50
9	90	6	10.00
10	95	5	9.50
11	98	3	8.91
12	100	2	8.33
13	98	−2	7.54
14	95	−3	6.79
15	85	−10	5.67

Panel A of Figure 1 on the next page displays your total product curve for windsurfing equipment, based on the data in columns 1 and 2 of Table 2. Output of rigs varies with the number of people you employ. Output rises from 0 to 40 when four people are working (point *a* in panel A) to a maximum of 100 when 12 people are employed (point *c*). As you continue to hire employees beyond 12, you encounter *negative returns*. Total output actually begins to fall, possibly because your barn has become overly crowded, confusing, hazardous, or noisy. Clearly, hiring any more than 12 employees would be counterproductive, since output falls but costs rise.

Marginal and Average Product

Marginal product (column 3 in Table 2) is the change in output that results from a change in labor input. Marginal product is computed by dividing the change in output (ΔQ) by the change in labor (ΔL). The delta (Δ) symbol is used to denote "change in." Thus, marginal product (MP) is equal to $\Delta Q/\Delta L$; it is the change in output that results from adding additional workers.

Notice that when employment rises from three to four workers, output grows from 25 to 40 rigs. Marginal product is therefore 15 rigs at this point (point *a* in panel B of Figure 1). Contrast this with a change in employment when 12 people are already employed. Adding the 13th employee actually reduces the total output of windsurfing rigs from 100 to 98, so marginal product is −2.

Average product (AP) or output per worker is found by dividing total output by the number of workers employed to produce that output (Q/L). Average product is shown in panel B of Figure 1. When employment is four people and output is 40, for instance, average product is 10 (point *d*).

Increasing and Diminishing Returns

As panel B of Figure 1 shows, when four people are employed, marginal product is 15 (point *a*), exceeding the average product of 10 (point *d*). This portion of the total product curve, where average and marginal products are both rising, is called the **increasing marginal returns**

Marginal product: The change in output that results from a change in labor ($\Delta Q/\Delta L$).

Average product: Output per worker, found by dividing total output by the number of workers employed to produce that output (Q/L).

Increasing marginal returns: A new worker hired adds more to total output than the previous worker hired, so that both average and marginal products are rising.

FIGURE 1—Total Product Curve, Marginal Product, and Average Product

These two panels show the relationship between additional labor and productivity. The top panel shows how increasing labor increases productivity, up to a point. The bottom panel shows marginal and average product. Once you add more than four workers, marginal product starts decreasing. Total product keeps increasing, however, until you hit 12 employees. At that point, marginal product is negative, meaning that each additional employee actually reduces production.

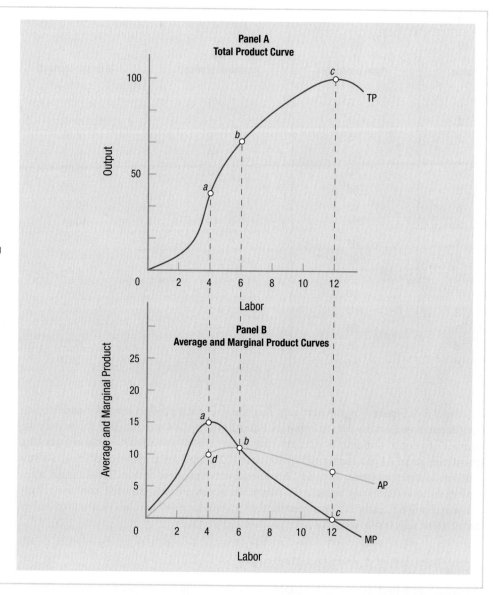

portion of the curve. Each of your first four employees adds more to output than the previous worker hired; thus, in this range, output grows faster as you employ additional labor.

Now note that as you hire your first six employees, average product continues to rise, and the marginal product remains higher than average product. When marginal product exceeds average product—when a new worker adds more to output than the average of the previous workers—hiring an additional worker increases average productivity. This might be because hiring more people allows you to establish more of a production line, say, thus heightening specialization and thereby raising productivity.

Note, however, that after you have employed four people, *marginal productivity* begins to trail off. Between 4 and 12 workers (points *a* to *c*), you face **diminishing marginal returns** since each additional worker adds to total output, but at a diminishing rate. Note that at point *b* (six employees), both marginal and average product are roughly equal and average product is at its maximum (nearly 11 rigs).

Finally, note that once you have hired 12 employees, if you hire any more, this will result in negative marginal returns. Hiring additional people will actually reduce output, so rational firms never operate in this range.

The typical production curves shown in Figure 1 embody the *law of diminishing returns*. Given that your barn size is fixed in the short run, adding more labor will

Diminishing marginal returns: An additional worker adds to total output, but at a diminishing rate.

eventually—in this case, once four people have been hired—result in diminishing marginal returns, each additional worker adding to total production by a smaller and smaller amount.

■ CHECKPOINT
_____

PRODUCTION IN THE SHORT RUN

- Production is the process of turning inputs into outputs.

- Total product is the total output produced by the production process.

- Marginal product (MP) is the change in output that results from a change in labor input and is equal to $\Delta Q/\Delta L$.

- Average product (AP) is output per worker and is equal to Q/L.

- Increasing marginal returns occur when adding a worker adds *more* to output than the previous worker hired.

- Diminishing marginal returns occur when adding a worker adds less to output than the previous worker hired.

- Negative marginal returns occur when adding a worker actually leads to *less* total output than with the previous worker hired.

QUESTIONS: Microsoft has developed, updated, and sold Microsoft Office over the last 30 years, and it accounts for a significant portion of Microsoft revenues. Most users have barely scratched the surface on this product, probably using no more than 10% of the program's features. Has Microsoft reached diminishing returns with this product? Are the free Web-based word processors (e.g., Google Docs and Spreadsheets), which have most of the features people use, a threat to the Microsoft Office franchise?

Answers to the Checkpoint questions can be found at the end of this chapter.

Costs of Production

Production tells only part of the story. We have to calculate how much it costs to produce this output. Let's now bring resource prices, including labor costs, into our analysis to develop the typical cost curves for the firm.

Short-Run Costs

In a very straightforward way, production costs are determined by the productivity of workers. Ignoring all costs except wages, if you, by yourself, were to produce 10 pizzas an hour and you were paid $8 an hour, then each pizza would cost an average of 80 cents to produce—the cost of your labor. Yet, to ignore any other costs would be to neglect a significant portion of business expenses known as *overhead*.

To begin developing the concept of overhead specifically, and production costs more generally, remember that production periods are split into the short run and the long run. In the short run, at least one factor is fixed, whereas in the long run, all factors are variable. This has led economists to define costs as fixed and variable.

Fixed and Variable Costs

Fixed costs, or overhead, are those costs that do not change as a firm's output expands or contracts. Lease or rental payments, administrative overhead, and insurance are examples of fixed costs—they do not rise or fall as a firm alters production to meet market demands. **Variable costs,** on the other hand, do fluctuate as output changes. Labor and material costs are examples of variable costs, since making more products requires hiring more

Fixed costs: Costs that do not change as a firm's output expands or contracts, often called overhead. These include items such as lease payments, administrative expenses, property taxes, and insurance.

Variable costs: Costs that vary with output fluctuations, including expenses such as labor and material costs.

workers and purchasing more raw materials. To keep things simple, let us assume all costs fit into one of these two categories, such that total cost (TC) is equal to total fixed cost (TFC) plus total variable cost (TVC), or

$$TC = TFC + TVC$$

Note that, in the long run, all costs are variable (TFC = 0), since given enough time, a firm can expand or close its plant, and enter or leave an industry.

Average Costs

When a firm produces a product or service, it typically wants a breakdown of how much labor, raw material, plant overhead, and sales costs are imbedded in each unit of the product. Modern accounting systems permit a detailed breakdown of costs for each unit of production. For our purposes, however, that level of detail is not necessary. For us, cost per unit of output (or *average cost*), average fixed cost, and average variable cost is sufficient.

If we divide the previous equation determining TC by total output Q, we get

$$TC/Q = TFC/Q + TVC/Q$$

Economists refer to total fixed costs divided by output (TFC/Q) as **average fixed cost** (AFC). This represents the average amount of overhead for each unit of output. Total variable costs divided by output is known as **average variable cost** (AVC). It represents the labor and raw materials expenses that go into each unit of output. Adding AFC and AVC together results in **average total cost** (ATC), and thus the equation above can be rewritten as

$$ATC = AFC + AVC$$

Hence, average cost per unit (ATC) is the sum of average fixed cost (AFC) and average variable cost (AVC).

Table 3 provides us with more complete production and cost data for your windsurfing business. Note that we have assumed you pay $1,000 per month for rent of the barn, so total fixed costs equal $1,000 (column 5). Wages per worker are assumed to be $11 per hour, or $88 per day, for 20 days a month, and thus $1,760 per month per employee. Note also that, for the sake of simplicity, we have included all material and other variable costs under your labor costs.

Let's go through one row so you can be sure about how we arrived at the numbers in columns 3 to 11. Let's take the row where four workers are hired and therefore 40 windsurfing rigs are produced. Moving right through the table, we see the following. The marginal product of the additional worker as we move from three workers to four is 15 windsurfing rigs because the quantity produced has grown from 25 to 40. Note that this marginal product is more than the third worker produced, but also note that the marginal product peaks with this worker. Since average product is Q/L, average product for four workers is 10.

We now move to columns 5–7. As noted above, you pay $1,000 per month for the barn, and this is your total fixed cost—it does not change with the addition of more workers. Total variable cost does change, rising by $1,760 for each additional worker because this is the wage you need to pay for each worker. For four workers, you pay $1,760 × 4 = $7,040. Total cost is simply total fixed cost plus total variable cost, so when the fourth worker is added, total cost is $1,000 + $7,040 = $8,040.

Now let's move to columns 8–10. Average total cost is total cost divided by quantity produced, so when four workers are hired, $8,040 in total cost is divided by 40 windsurfing rigs produced to equal $201 in ATC. Average variable cost takes the total variable cost of $7,040 for four workers and divides it by 40 windsurfing rigs to equal $176 in AVC. We can calculate average fixed costs in two ways. First, we can take total fixed costs of $1,000 and divide it by 40 windsurfing rigs to equal $25 in AFC. Second, we know that

---

Average fixed cost: Equal to total fixed cost divided by output (TFC/Q).

Average variable cost: Equal to total variable cost divided by output (TVC/Q).

Average total cost: Equal to total cost divided by output (TC/Q). Average total cost is also equal to AFC + AVC.

TABLE 3   Production and Cost Data for Windsurfing Sail Firm

(1) L	(2) Q	(3) MP	(4) AP	(5) TFC	(6) TVC	(7) TC	(8) ATC	(9) AVC	(10) AFC	(11) MC
0	0	—	—	1000	0	1000	—	—	—	—
1	7	7	7	1000	1760	2760	394.29	251.43	142.86	251.43
2	15	8	7.50	1000	3520	4520	301.33	234.67	66.67	220.00
3	25	10	8.33	1000	5280	6280	251.20	211.20	40.00	176.00
4	40	15	10.00	1000	7040	8040	201.00	176.00	25.00	117.33
5	54	14	10.80	1000	8800	9800	181.48	162.96	18.52	125.71
6	65	11	10.83	1000	10560	11560	177.85	162.46	15.38	160.00
7	75	10	10.71	1000	12320	13320	177.60	164.27	13.33	176.00
8	84	9	10.50	1000	14080	15080	179.52	167.62	11.90	195.56
9	90	6	10.00	1000	15840	16840	187.11	176.00	11.11	293.33
10	95	5	9.50	1000	17600	18600	195.79	185.26	10.53	352.00
11	98	3	8.91	1000	19360	20360	207.76	197.55	10.20	586.67
12	100	2	8.33	1000	21120	22120	221.20	211.20	10.00	880.00
13	98	−2	7.54	1000	22880	23880	243.67	233.47	10.20	−880.00
14	95	−3	6.79	1000	24640	25640	269.89	259.37	10.53	−586.70

ATC = AVC + AFC, so if we know that \$201 = \$176 + AFC, we can solve for AFC and obtain \$25 in AFC. Thus, we see that we can calculate average total cost and its components.

Average total cost is an important piece of information for business firms. ATC does not, however, tell us how much costs will rise or fall if output changes. For this, we need to look at marginal cost.

Marginal Cost

Because of increasing and decreasing returns associated with typical production processes, average costs vary with the level of output. Assume for a moment that your firm has orders for, and is producing, 98 windsurfing rigs per month. Now assume you get an order for one more rig. Just how much does this additional windsurfing rig cost to produce? Or, in the language of economics, what is the *marginal cost* of the next rig produced?

Marginal cost is the change in total cost arising from the production of additional units of output. Marginal cost (MC) is equal to the change in total cost (ΔTC) divided by the change in output (ΔQ), or

$$MC = \Delta TC/\Delta Q = \Delta TFC/\Delta Q + \Delta TVC/\Delta Q$$

Note that, for simplicity, we have been discussing changes of one unit of output, but we can calculate MC for a change in output of any amount by plugging in the appropriate value for ΔQ. Note that because fixed costs do not vary with changes in output, ΔTFC/ΔQ = 0, and thus the equation above can be rewritten as

$$MC = \Delta TVC/\Delta Q$$

Let us now examine Table 3 to determine approximately what the marginal cost would be for producing one more rig if you are currently producing 98 rigs.

As Table 3 suggests, at 98 rigs, you are employing 11 people, but producing an additional rig will require hiring a 12th worker. This will actually raise your output by two rigs, to 100—that is, one rig for the new customer and one additional rig for inventory. Paying this new employee's wages increases your costs by \$1,760 per month. And since you produce two additional windsurfing rigs, each rig effectively costs you \$880

Marginal cost: The change in total costs arising from the production of additional units of output (ΔTC/ΔQ). Since fixed costs do not change with output, marginal costs are the change in variable costs associated with additional production (ΔTVC/ΔQ).

($1,760 ÷ 2 = $880). Consequently, the marginal cost to produce these additional rigs is $880 per rig, as shown in column 11 in Table 3. Marginal cost again is the change in variable cost associated with producing one more unit of a product.

Short-Run Cost Curves

Table 3 provides the numerical values for costs. Let us now translate these costs into figures to make their analysis simpler.

Average Fixed Cost (AFC)

The average fixed cost (AFC) for your business is shown in Figure 2. Note that AFC falls continuously as more output is produced; this is because your overhead expenses are getting spread out over more and more units of output. At point a, for instance, when only 25 rigs are produced, AFC is $40, and TFC is equal to area $0fad = $1,000. When output grows to 100, however, TFC remains equal to area $0ebc = $1,000, but AFC drops to $10, since the TFC is being spread over 100 units. (Keep in mind that because AFC = TFC/Q, then TFC = AFC × Q. This will be helpful when we only have graphical analysis to work with.)

FIGURE 2—The Average Fixed Cost Curve

The average fixed cost (AFC) curve always decreases as production increases. This is because, in the short run, total fixed costs do not change, so that increasing production spreads the fixed costs over more units of output.

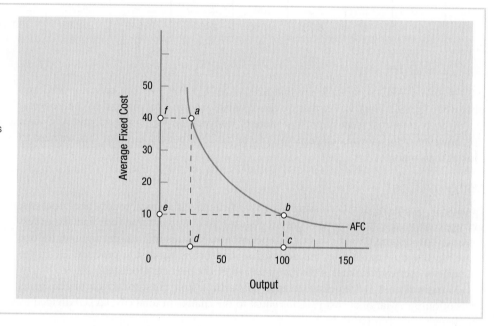

Average Variable Cost (AVC)

Borrowing the data from Table 3, Figure 3 shows the AVC, ATC, and AFC for your hypothetical windsurfing firm. Notice that both the AVC and ATC curves are bowl-shaped. At relatively low levels of output, the curves slope downward, reflecting an increase in returns as average costs drop. As production levels rise, however, diminishing returns set in, and average costs start to climb back up. We get some sense of this by examining Table 3, but the figure makes it far easier to see.

In Figure 3, the average variable cost curve reaches its minimum where 65 rigs are produced (point c). Since AVC = TVC/Q, then TVC = AVC × Q. Thus, at point c, TVC is equal to the rectangular area $0ace$, or $10,560 ($162.46 × 65).

Average Total Cost (ATC)

Average total cost equals average fixed costs plus average variable cost (ATC = AFC + AVC). At an output of 65 rigs in Figure 3, ATC(ed) = AFC(ef) + AVC(ec). (Note that $cd = ef$, since we are adding AFC to AVC to yield ATC.) We know that ATC = TC/Q, so

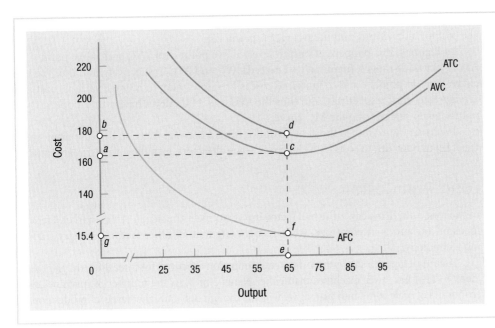

FIGURE 3—Average Total Cost, Average Variable Cost, and Average Fixed Cost

Curves for average total cost and average variable cost have been added to average fixed cost. The bowl shape of these curves demonstrates the law of diminishing returns: Beyond a certain level of output (65 units in this case), average variable costs increase. Total costs are equal to average total costs times output.

TC = ATC $\times$ Q. Hence, when output is 65, ATC = $177.85 and TC = $11,560 ($177.85 $\times$ 65), or the rectangular area 0*bde* in Figure 3.

It is important to note that TC, TFC, and TVC can be found for *any point* on their respective curves by multiplying the average cost at that point by the output produced.

Marginal Cost (MC)

Drawing our discussion of short-run costs to a close, Figure 4 plots the marginal cost curve, adding it to the AVC and ATC curves we have plotted already.

Notice that the marginal cost curve intersects the minimum points of both the AVC and ATC curves. This is not a coincidence. Marginal cost is the cost necessary to produce another unit of a given product. When the cost to produce another unit is *less* than the average of the previous units produced, average costs will *fall*. For the AVC curve in Figure 4, this happens at all output levels below point *c* (65 units); for the ATC curve, it happens at all output

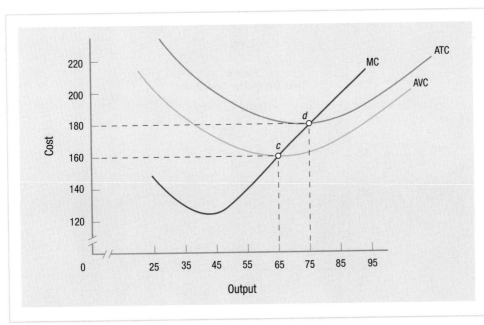

FIGURE 4—Average Total Cost, Average Variable Cost, and Marginal Cost

Marginal costs represent the added cost of producing one more unit of output. Note that the marginal cost curve passes through the minimum points on both the AVC and ATC curves.

levels below point *d* (75 units). But when the cost to produce another unit *exceeds* the average cost for all previous output, average costs will *rise.*

In Figure 4, this happens at output levels above point *c* for AVC and above point *d* for ATC. Over these ranges, marginal cost exceeds AVC and ATC, respectively, and thus the two curves rise. At points *c* and *d,* marginal cost is precisely equal to average variable cost and average total cost, respectively, and thus the AVC and ATC curves have a zero slope at these points, when intersecting the MC curve.

We have now examined short-run costs for firms when one factor, in this case plant size, is fixed. Let us now turn to costs in the long run, when all factors, including plant size, are variable.

Long-Run Costs

In the long run, firms can adjust all factor inputs to meet the needs of the market. Here we focus on variations in plant size, while recognizing that all other factors can vary, including technology.

Panel A of Figure 5 shows three different production functions for three different plant sizes. Plant 1 (TP_1) has fewer machines than either plants 2 or 3. As the number of machines rises, economies of scale come into play, as we will see, though only at higher levels of production.

FIGURE 5—Total Product Curves and Various Short-Run Average Cost Curves

This figure shows the relationship between average total cost and plant size. In panel A, plant 1 (TP_1) has the fewest machines and the least output capacity; plant 3 (TP_3) has the most equipment, or capital, and hence the most capacity. Panel B shows the average total cost curve for each of the three plants. The larger plants have relatively high average total costs at lower levels of output, but much lower average total costs at higher output levels.

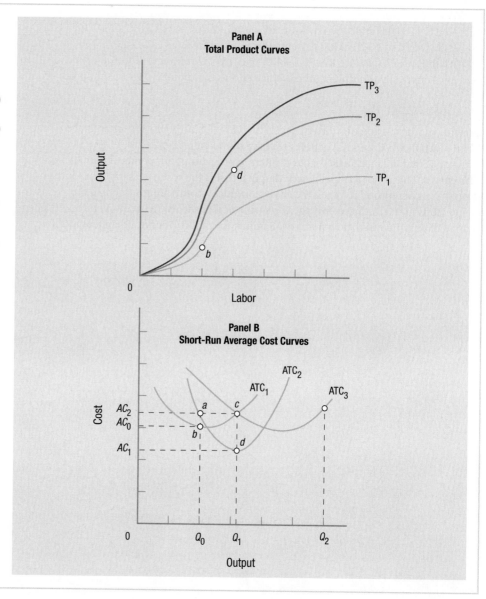

At lower levels of production, the average costs for plants 2 and 3 are quite high, since they have higher fixed costs than plant 1—more expensive machines and more square feet of space to house these machines. This is shown in panel B of Figure 5. For a small output, say Q_0, plant 1 produces for an average cost of AC_0 (point b in panel B). Plant 2, with its additional overhead, can produce Q_0 output, but only for an average cost of AC_2 (point a in panel B).

Once output rises to Q_1, however, plant 2 begins to enjoy the benefits of economies of scale. The additional machines mean that plant 2 can produce Q_1 for AC_1 (point d), whereas the machines in plant 1 get overwhelmed at this level of output, resulting in an average cost of AC_2 (point c). Similarly, if a firm expects market demand eventually to reach Q_2, it would want to build plant 3 because plants 1 and 2 are too small to efficiently accommodate that level of production.

Long-Run Average Total Cost

The **long-run average total cost (LRATC)** curve represents the lowest unit cost at which any specific output can be produced in the long run, when a firm is able to adjust the size of its plant. Figure 6 is equivalent to panel B of Figure 5. In this figure, the LRATC curve is indicated by the green segments of the various short-run cost curves; these are the segments of each curve where output can be produced at the lowest per unit cost (the envelope curve). In short, the concept of LRATC assumes that, in the long run, firms will build plants of the size best fitting the levels of output they wish to produce.

While the LRATC curve in Figure 6 is relatively bumpy, it will tend to smooth out as more plant size options are considered. In some industries, such as agriculture and food service, the options for plant size and production methods are virtually unlimited. In other industries, such as semiconductors, however, sophisticated plants may cost several billion dollars to build and require being run at near capacity to be cost effective.

Long-run average total cost (LRATC): In the long run, firms can adjust their plant sizes so LRATC is the lowest unit cost at which any particular output can be produced in the long run.

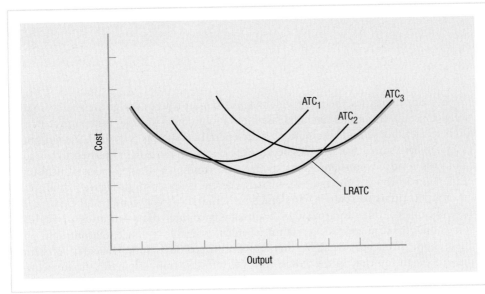

FIGURE 6—The Long-Run Average Total Cost Curve

This figure shows the long-run average total cost (LRATC) for three plants. Firms are free to adjust plant size in the long run, so they can switch from one plant type to the next to minimize their costs at each production level. The heavy envelope curve represents the firm's lowest cost to produce any given output in the long run and represents the LRATC curve.

These huge, sophisticated plants are so complex that Intel Corporation has dedicated teams of engineers that build new plants and operate them exactly as all others. These teams ensure that any new plant is a virtual clone of the firm's other operating facilities. Even small deviations from this standard have proven disastrous in the past.

Economies and Diseconomies of Scale

As a firm's output increases, its LRATC tends to decrease. This is because, as the firm grows in size, **economies of scale** result from such items as specialization of labor and management, better use of capital, and increased possibilities for making several products that utilize complementary production techniques.

Economies of scale: As a firm's output increases, its LRATC tends to decline. This results from specialization of labor and management, and potentially a better use of capital and complementary production techniques.

A larger firm's ability to have workers specialize on particular tasks reduces the costs associated with shifting workers from one task to another. Similarly, management in larger operations can use technologies not available to smaller firms, for instance computers to remotely supervise workers. It is true that today's powerful personal computer networks have begun to narrow the gap in this arena. Larger firms, though, can still afford to purchase larger, more specialized capital equipment, whereas smaller firms must often rely on more labor-intensive methods. This equipment typically requires large production runs to be efficient, and only larger firms with correspondingly large marketing efforts can generate the sales necessary to satisfy these production volume requirements. Finally, larger firms are better able to engage in complementary production and use by-products more effectively.

The area for *economies of scale* is shown in Figure 7 as levels of output below Q_0 (average costs are falling).

FIGURE 7—Economies, Diseconomies, and Constant Returns to Scale

The curve in this figure shows how increasing production affects long-run average total cost (LRATC). Up to Q_0, economies of scale reduce LRATC as production increases. Over the range Q_0 to Q_1, the firm enjoys constant returns to scale, meaning that it can expand without affecting LRATC. Past Q_1, however, diseconomies of scale kick in, such that any further expansion causes an increase in LRATC.

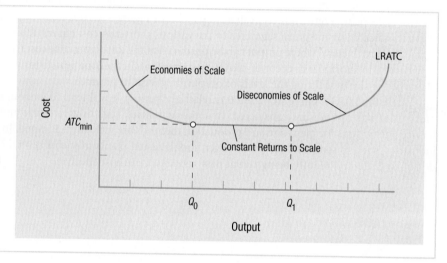

In many industries, there is a wide range of output where average total costs are relatively constant. Examples include fast-food restaurants, upscale restaurants such as Outback Steakhouse, and automotive service operations such as Jiffy Lube. Such businesses tend to have steady average costs because the cost to replicate their business in any community is relatively constant. Constructing and running a Dairy Queen franchise, for example, costs roughly the same no matter where it is operated. In Figure 7, this area of **constant returns to scale** is represented by output levels between Q_0 and Q_1.

As firms continue to grow, they eventually encounter **diseconomies of scale**. At some point, the firm gets so big that management is unable to efficiently control its operations. Some firms become so big that they get bogged down in bureaucracy and cannot make decisions quickly. In the 1980s, IBM fell into this trap—slow to react to changing market conditions for mainframe, mini, and microcomputers, the company was left behind by smaller, sleeker competition. Only through downsizing, reorganizing, refocusing, and a management change did IBM get back on track in the 1990s. Diseconomies of scale—the area where increased output increases costs disproportionately—are shown at outputs above Q_1 in Figure 7.

Economies of Scope

When firms produce a number of products, it is often cheaper for them to produce another product when the production processes are interdependent. These economies are called **economies of scope.** For example, once a company has established a marketing department, it can take on the campaign of a new product at lower costs. It has developed the expertise and contacts necessary to sell the product. Book publishers can introduce a new

Constant returns to scale: A range of output where average total costs are relatively constant. Fast-food restaurants and movie theatres are examples.

Diseconomies of scale: A range of output where average total costs tend to increase. Firms often become so big that management becomes bureaucratic and unable to efficiently control its operations.

Economies of scope: By producing a number of products that are interdependent, firms are able to produce and market these goods at lower costs.

book into the market more quickly and cheaply, and with more success than can a new firm starting in the business.

Some firms generate ideas for products, then send the production overseas. After they have been through this process, they become more efficient. Economists refer to this as *learning by doing*. Economies of scope often play a role in mergers as firms look for other firms with complementary products and skills.

Role of Technology

We know that technology creates products that were the domain of science fiction writers of the past. Dick Tracy's wrist radio, first introduced in the comics of 1940s, has now morphed into the many wireless products we see today.

But we should mention in passing the role technology plays in altering the shape of the LRATC curve. The output level where diseconomies of scale are reached has significantly and continuously expanded since the beginning of the industrial revolution.

Enhanced production techniques, instantaneous global communication, and the use of computers in accounting and cost control are just a few recent examples of ways in which technology has permitted firms to increase their scale beyond what anyone had imagined possible 50 years earlier. Who would have imagined a century ago that one firm could have hundreds of thousands of employees and billions of dollars in annual sales? Today, IBM has more than 400,000 employees and sales of over $80 billion.

What spurs firms and entrepreneurs to develop new technologies and bring new products to market? Three words: profits, profits, and profits. In this chapter, we took a large step in analyzing where profits come from by looking at what firms do, how they measure profits, and how they determine the production and cost side of the profit equation. In the next chapter, we will look at revenues, as well as examine how firms can maximize their profits by adjusting output to market demand.

■ CHECKPOINT

COSTS OF PRODUCTION

- Fixed costs (overhead) are those costs that do not vary with output, including lease payments and insurance. Fixed costs occur in the short run—in the long run, firms can change plant size and even exit an industry.

- Variable costs rise and fall as a firm produces more or less output. These include raw materials, labor, and utilities.

- Total cost equals total fixed cost plus total variable cost (TC = TFC + TVC).

- Average total cost equals total cost divided by output (ATC = TC/Q).

- Average fixed cost is total fixed cost divided by output (AFC = TFC/Q).

- Average variable cost is total variable cost divided by output (AVC = TVC/Q).

- Marginal cost is the change in total cost divided by the change in output (MC = ΔTC/ΔQ).

- Because total fixed cost does not change with output in the short run, then marginal cost is just the change in total variable cost divided by the change in output (MC = ΔTVC/ΔQ).

- The long-run average total cost curve (LRATC) represents the lowest unit cost at which specific output can be produced in the long run. Remember, firms can vary plant size in the long run, so this curve incorporates different plants to achieve the lowest average cost for a given level of output.

- As a firm grows in size, economies of scale result from specialization of labor, better use of capital, and the potential to produce many different products using complementary techniques.

- Diseconomies of scale occur because a firm gets so big that management loses control of its operations, and the firm becomes bogged down in bureaucracy.

- Economics of scope result when firms produce a number of interdependent products, so it is cheaper for them to add another product to the line.

- Modern communications and computers have permitted firms to become huge before diseconomies are reached.

QUESTION: In the late 1990s, Boeing reported that it takes roughly 12 years and $15 billion to bring a new aircraft from the design stage to a test flight. Boeing signed a 20-year exclusive agreement to supply aircraft to Delta, American, and Continental Airlines. The rationale for the agreement was that every time production of the plane doubled, a fifth was cut off the cost of the plane to the commercial airlines.[5] Why would doubling production cut costs per unit by 20%?

Answers to the Checkpoint question can be found at the end of this chapter.

Key Concepts

Firm, p. 160
Sole proprietor, p. 162
Partnership, p. 162
Corporation, p. 162
Profit, p. 163
Revenue, p. 163
Economic costs, p. 163
Explicit costs, p. 163
Implicit costs, p. 163
Sunk costs, p. 164
Economic profits, p. 164
Normal profits, p. 164
Short run, p. 165
Long run, p. 165
Production, p. 166
Marginal product, p. 167

Average product, p. 167
Increasing marginal returns, p. 167
Diminishing marginal returns, p. 168
Fixed costs, p. 169
Variable costs, p. 169
Average fixed cost, p. 170
Average variable cost, p. 170
Average total cost, p. 170
Marginal cost, p. 171
Long-run average total cost (LRATC), p. 175
Economies of scale, p. 175
Constant returns to scale, p. 176
Diseconomies of scale, p. 176
Economies of scope, p. 176

Chapter Summary

Firms, Profits, and Economic Costs

Firms produce the products and services we consume. Firms are economic institutions that transform inputs (factors of production) into outputs (products and services).

Entrepreneurs provide goods and services to the market. Entrepreneurs are organized into three basic business structures: sole proprietorships, partnerships, and corporations.

Corporations are the premier form of business organization in most of the world. Corporations possess most of the legal rights of individuals, and in addition, they are able to issue stock to raise capital. Most significantly, the liability of individual owners (stockholders) is limited to the amount they have invested in the stock, unlike *sole proprietors* and *partnerships*.

---

[5] "Peace in our Time," *Economist*, July 26, 1997.

Profits comprise the difference between total revenue and total costs. Firms are assumed to seek to maximize their profits.

Economic costs are separated into *explicit* (out-of-pocket) and *implicit* (opportunity) costs. Explicit costs are those costs paid to some other entity, including wages, lease expenses, and taxes. Implicit costs include those items for which the firm does not directly pay others, but still incurs a cost, such as the depreciation and depletion of company assets, as well as the cost of the capital the firm employs. Sunk costs are expenses that have been incurred and are not recoverable.

Economists define a *normal return* as that return on capital that keeps investors willing to invest their capital in an industry over the long run. Firms earning just this level of profit are said to be earning normal profits. Firms earning more than this are earning *economic profits,* and firms earning less are taking *economic losses.*

The *short run* is a period of time during which at least one factor of production is fixed, usually plant capacity. Firms can vary output in the short run by hiring more labor or changing other variable factors. In the *long run,* firms are able to vary all factors, including plant size. Moreover, existing firms can leave the industry and new firms can enter.

Production in the Short Run

In the short run, firms can vary the output they produce by varying their labor inputs. The *total product curve* relates labor inputs to outputs. *Marginal product* is the change in output resulting from a change in labor input ($\Delta Q/\Delta L$). Marginal product is thus the change in output associated with hiring one additional worker. *Average product* or output per worker is equal to total output divided by labor input (Q/L).

Typical production functions exhibit both increasing and decreasing returns. When *increasing returns* are present, each additional worker adds more to total output than previous workers. This can occur because of specialization, for instance. All production is eventually subject to the *law of diminishing returns,* whereby additional workers add less and less to total output.

Costs of Production

In the short run, firms have fixed and variable costs. *Fixed costs,* or overhead, are those costs the firm incurs whether it produces anything or not. These costs include administrative overhead, lease payments, and insurance. *Variable costs* are those costs that vary with output, such as wages, utilities, and raw materials costs. Total cost is equal to total fixed cost plus total variable cost ($TC = TFC + TVC$).

Average total cost (ATC) represents cost per unit of total production, or TC/Q. *Average fixed cost* (AFC) is equal to TFC/Q, and *average variable cost* (AVC) is equal to TVC/Q. Consequently, $ATC = AFC + AVC$. *Marginal cost* (MC) is the change in total cost associated with producing one additional unit. Since fixed cost does not change in the short run ($\Delta TFC = 0$), marginal cost is equal to the change in variable costs when one additional unit is produced; hence, $MC = \Delta TVC/\Delta Q$.

In the long run, all factors of production are variable, and firms can enter or leave the industry. The *long-run average total cost* curve (LRATC) represents the lowest unit costs for any specific output level in the long run. *Economies of scale* associated with larger firm size result from such factors as specialization in labor and management. As a firm grows, the average cost of production falls. Eventually, however, a firm encounters *diseconomies of scale* when its size becomes so large that efficient management becomes impossible. At this point, average costs begin to rise. Today, advanced computer and communications technologies have radically increased the size of firms that can be efficiently managed. *Economies of scope* result from the ability of firms producing many interdependent products to add another at substantially lower costs.

Questions and Problems

Check Your Understanding

1. What is the difference between explicit and implicit costs? What is the difference between economic and accounting profits? Are these four concepts related? How?

2. How does the short run differ from the long run? Is the long run the same for all industries? Why or why not?

3. For business, are accounting profits or economic profits more important?

4. Why is the average fixed cost curve not bowl-shaped? Why does it not turn up like the average variable cost and average total cost curves?

5. What is the difference between average total cost and average variable cost?

Apply the Concepts

6. Skype, the Internet phone company, uses peer-to-peer network principles to enable people to make free phone calls over the Internet anywhere in the world. Skype forwards calls through users' computers without having any central infrastructure. Users agree to let their computer's excess capacity be used as transfer nodes. In this way, Skype does not have to invest in more infrastructure as it adds users, and the system is highly robust and scalable. What is the marginal cost to Skype to add another user to its system?

7. List some of the reasons why the long-run average total cost curve has sort of a flat bowl shape. It declines early on, then is rather flat over a portion, and finally slopes upward.

8. The Finger Lakes region in New York State produces wine. The climate favors white wines, but reds have been produced successfully in the past 15 years. Categorize the following costs incurred by one winery as either fixed or variable:

   a. the capital used to buy 60 acres of land on Lake Seneca

   b. the machine used to pick some varieties of grapes at the end of August and the beginning of September

   c. the salary of the chief vintner, who is employed year-round

   d. the wages paid to workers who bind the grape plants, usually in April, and usually over a period of three to four days

   e. the wages paid to the same workers who pick the grapes at the end of August or early September

   f. the costs of the chemicals sprayed on the grapes in July

   g. the wages of the wine expert who blends the wine in August and September, after the grapes have been picked

   h. the cost of the building where wine tastings take place from April to October

   i. the cost of the wine used in the wine tasting

9. Why should sunk costs be ignored for decision making?

10. If marginal cost is less than average total cost, are average total costs rising or falling? Alternatively, if marginal cost is more than average total cost, are average total costs rising or falling? Give an example outside of economics to explain your answer.

11. Describe how marginal cost is related to marginal product.

In the News

12. Economies of scope occur in big organizations with diversified product lines where innovation in one area feeds into others. In his book, *An Army of Davids*, Glenn Reynolds argued that "The balance of advantage—in nearly every aspect of society—

is shifting from big organizations to small ones. Economies of scale and scope matter much less in the information age than in the industrial one" (published by Nelson Current, 2006). Does this statement seem correct?

Solving Problems

13. Using the table below, answer the following questions.

Labor	Output	Marginal Product	Average Product
0	0	_____	_____
1	7	_____	_____
2	15	_____	_____
3	25	_____	_____
4	33	_____	_____
5	40	_____	_____
6	45	_____	_____

a. Complete the table, filling in the answers for marginal and average products.

b. Over how many workers is the firm enjoying increasing returns?

c. At what number of workers do diminishing returns set in?

d. Are negative returns shown in the table?

14. Use the table below to answer the following questions. Assume that fixed costs are $100 and labor is paid $80 per unit (employee).

L	Q	MP	AP	TFC	TVC	TC	ATC	AVC	AFC	MC
0	0	—	—	—	—	—	—	—	—	—
1	7	—	—	—	—	—	—	—	—	—
2	15	—	—	—	—	—	—	—	—	—
3	25	—	—	—	—	—	—	—	—	—
4	40	—	—	—	—	—	—	—	—	—
5	45	—	—	—	—	—	—	—	—	—
6	48	—	—	—	—	—	—	—	—	—
7	50	—	—	—	—	—	—	—	—	—

a. Complete the table.

b. Graph ATC, AVC, AFC, and MC on a piece of paper.

15. After the Enron and other business scandals in the early 2000s, the United States passed the Sarbanes-Oxley Act, adding a number of rules and reporting requirements for U.S. corporations. The business community argues that these reporting requirements are extremely costly and cumbersome with only minimal benefit. Most companies, they argue, were not engaged in illegal or unethical behavior, and they are being punished because of a few. As Jane Sasseen and Joseph Weber (*Business Week*, March 26, 2006) note, one apparent impact of this law was that in 2005, "of the top 25 global initial public offerings (when companies first offer their stock to the general market for purchase), only one was in the United States." This was business lost to the New York Stock Exchange (NYSE) and NASDAQ. Are these kinds of compliance costs established by Sarbanes-Oxley fixed or variable costs? Why would firms care so much about these regulations? Can we expect to see the NYSE and NASDAQ try to buy or merge with other foreign stock exchanges in the near future?

Answers to Questions in CheckPoints

Check Point: Firms, Profits, and Economic Costs

Buying an existing business has several benefits, including that the business has existing customers and a location. In addition, it can generate cash and profits immediately. One downside is that determining a fair price may be difficult and potentially more than you can afford. Starting your own firm is cheaper in the beginning, but it involves doing everything from scratch. It typically takes three to four years for a firm to get a good foothold in the market.

Check Point: Production in the Short Run

Microsoft may well have reached diminishing returns with its Office product. Many firms with a large number of users have been reluctant to upgrade, given the licensing costs and the added training required. The bigger and more complex Office becomes, the more it is best suited for specialized professional jobs, not for the majority of the market. Some have suggested that Microsoft's focus on future products may need to concentrate on ease of use, although its word processor is relatively easy to use even though it has a lot of power. Yes, the Web-based word processors and other open office programs are a threat to the domination of this market by Microsoft.

Check Point: Costs of Production

This immense $15 billion development cost is spread over more planes, and rising volume creates economies. Producing commercial aircraft has huge economies of scale and scope.

Competition

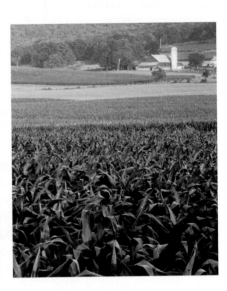

Panoramic Images/Getty Images

In his classic economic treatise, *The Wealth of Nations,* Adam Smith wrote of a "hidden hand" that guides businesses in their pursuit of self-interest, or profits, allowing only the efficient to survive. Some observers have noted similarities between Smith's work, written in 1776, and Charles Darwin's *Origin of Species,* published in 1872. The late biologist and zoologist Stephen Jay Gould wrote that "the theory of natural selection is, in essence, Adam Smith's economics transferred to nature," and that Darwin's account of the struggle for existence and reproductive success is the same "causal scheme applied to nature" as Smith's account of the competitive market.[1] Clearly, the notions of competition and the competitive market have played a prominent role in the history of ideas. In this chapter, we explore some of the implications competition has for markets and consider why the competitive market structure is so central to the thinking of economists. What you learn in this chapter will give you a benchmark to use when we consider other market structures in the following chapters.

Being engaged in stiff competition is the norm for lawn care companies, retail stores, Internet service providers, and restaurants. Large firms such as General Electric or Wal-Mart compete in many different markets, but some smaller firms—for example, the local newspaper or an oral surgeon—have only a few competitors. Firms specializing in standard products such as lumber, fertilizer, and cement tend to face stiff competition, while those focusing on unique services such as stained glass restoration, Web design, or organ transplants tend to have fewer competitors.

---

[1] Stephen Jay Gould, *The Structure of Evolutionary Theory* (Cambridge, MA: Belknap Press of Harvard University Press), 2002, pp. 121–25.

After studying this chapter you should be able to:

☐ Name the primary market structures and describe their characteristics.

☐ Define a competitive market and the assumptions that underlie it.

☐ Distinguish the differences between competitive markets in the short run and the long run.

☐ Analyze the conditions for profit maximization, loss minimization, and plant shutdown for a firm.

☐ Derive the firm's short-run supply curve.

☐ Use the short-run competitive model to determine long-run equilibrium.

☐ Describe why competition is in the public interest.

Market structure analysis: By observing a few industry characteristics such as number of firms in the industry or the level of barriers to entry, economists can use this information to predict pricing and output behavior of the firm in the industry.

To economists, *competition* means more than just competing against one or two other firms. The model of competition in this chapter focuses on an idealized market structure containing so many small businesses that any one firm's behavior is irrelevant to its competitors. Firms in this competitive climate lack discretion over pricing and must perform efficiently merely to survive.

In this and the next two chapters, keep in mind the profitability equation developed in the previous chapter. Profits equal total revenues minus total costs. Total revenues equal price times quantity sold. So keep in mind the three items that determine profitability: price, quantity, and cost. In the next three chapters, we will see how firms try to control each one of these.

Market Structure Analysis

To appreciate intensely competitive markets, we need to look at competition within the full range of possible market structures. Economists use **market structure analysis** to categorize industries based on a few key characteristics. By simply knowing simple industry facts, economists can predict the behavior of firms in that industry in such areas as pricing and sales.

Below are the four factors defining the intensity of competition in an industry and a few questions to give you some sense of the issues behind each one of these factors.

- **Number of firms in the industry:** Is the industry composed of many firms, each with limited or no ability to set the market price, such as local pizza places, or is it dominated by a large firm such as Wal-Mart that can influence price regardless of the number of other firms?

- **Nature of the industry's product:** Are we talking about a homogeneous product such as salt for which no consumer will pay a premium, or are we considering leather handbags (Coach, Gucci) where consumers may think that some firms produce better goods than other firms?

- **Barriers to entry:** Does the industry require low start-up and maintenance costs such as found in a roadside fruit and vegetable stand, or is it a computer-chip business that may require a billion dollars to build a new chip plant?

- **Extent to which individual firms can control prices:** For example, pharmaceutical companies can set prices for new medicines, at least for a set period of time, because of patent protection. Farmers and copper producers have virtually no control and get their prices from world markets.

Possible market structures range from competition, characterized by many firms, to monopoly, where an industry contains only one firm. These market structures will make more sense to you as we consider each one in the chapters ahead. Right now, use this list and the descriptions below as reference points. You can always come back to this point and put the discussion in context.

Primary Market Structures

The primary market structures economists have identified, along with their key characteristics, are as follows:

Competition

- Many buyers and sellers
- Homogeneous (standardized) products
- No barriers to market entry or exit
- No long-run economic profits
- No control over price

Monopolistic Competition

- Many buyers and sellers
- Differentiated products
- No barriers to market entry or exit
- No long-run economic profits
- Some control over price

Oligopoly

- Fewer firms (such as the auto industry)
- Mutually interdependent decisions
- Substantial barriers to market entry
- Potential for long-run economic profits
- Shared market power and considerable control over price

Monopoly

- One firm
- No close substitutes for product
- Nearly insuperable barriers to entry
- Potential for long-run economic profit
- Substantial market power and control over price

Putting off discussion of the other market structures for later chapters, we turn to an extended examination of the requirements for a competitive market. In the remainder of this chapter, we explore short-run pricing and output decisions, and also the importance of entry and exit in the long run. Moreover, we use the conditions of competition to establish a benchmark for efficiency as we turn to evaluate other market structures in the following chapters.

Defining Competitive Markets

The theory of **competition** rests on the following assumptions:

1. Competitive markets have many buyers and sellers, each of them so small that none can individually influence product price.
2. Firms in the industry produce a homogeneous or standardized product.
3. Buyers and sellers have all the information about prices and product quality they need to make informed decisions.
4. Barriers to entry or exit are insignificant in the long run; new firms are free to enter the industry if so doing appears profitable, while firms are free to exit if they anticipate losses.

One implication of these assumptions is that competitive firms are **price takers.** Market prices are determined by market forces beyond the control of individual firms. That is, firms must simply take what they can get for their products. Paper for copy machines, most agricultural products, DRAMs (dynamic random access memory chips), and many other goods are produced in highly competitive markets. The buyers or sellers in these markets are so small that their ability to influence market price is nil. These firms must simply accept whatever price the market determines, leaving them to decide only how much of the product to produce or buy.

Panel A of Figure 1 on the next page portrays the supply and demand for windsurfing sails in a competitive market; the market is in equilibrium at price $200 and industry

Competition: Exists when there are many relatively small buyers and sellers, a standardized product, with good information to both buyers and sellers, and no barriers to entry or exit.

Price taker: Individual firms in competitive markets get their prices from the market since they are so small they cannot influence market price. For this reason, competitive firms are price takers and can produce and sell all the output they produce at market-determined prices.

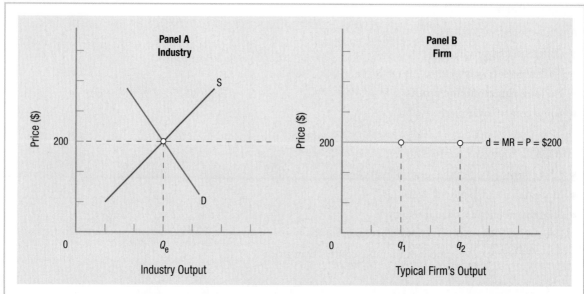

FIGURE 1—The Market for Competitive Products with an Equilibrium Price of $200

Panel A shows a market for standardized windsurfing sails in equilibrium at price $200 and industry output Q_e. This price is determined by the market's many buyers and sellers. Panel B illustrates product demand for an individual seller. The individual firm can sell all it wants to at $200 and has no reason to set its price below that. If it tries to sell at prices higher than $200, it sells nothing. The demand curve for the individual firm is horizontal at $200.

output Q_e. Remember that this product is a standardized sail (similar to two-by-four lumber, crude oil, and DRAMs) and that the market contains many buyers and sellers, who collectively set the product price at $200.

Panel B shows the demand for a seller's products in this market. The firm can sell all it wants at $200 or below. Yet, what firm would set its price below $200 when it can sell everything it produces at $200? Were the firm to set its price above $200, however, it would sell nothing. What consumer, after all, would purchase a standardized sail at a higher price when it can be obtained elsewhere for $200? The individual firm's demand curve is horizontal at $200. The firm can still determine how much of its product to produce and sell, but this is the only choice it has. The firm cannot set its own price, therefore it is a *price taker*.

Recall the profitability equation. Profits equal total revenues minus total costs. Total revenues equal price times quantity sold. In competitive markets, a firm's profitability is based on a given market price, quantity sold, and its costs. So how does it determine how much to sell?

The Short Run and the Long Run (A Reminder)

Before turning to a more detailed examination of how firms decide how much output to produce in a competitive market, we need to recall a distinction introduced in the last chapter between the *short run* and the *long run*.

Again, in the *short run,* one factor of production is fixed, usually the firm's plant size, and firms cannot enter or leave an industry. Thus, in the short run, the number of firms in a market is fixed. Firms may earn economic profits, break even, or suffer losses, but still they cannot exit the industry, nor can new firms enter.

In the *long run,* all factors are variable, and thus the level of profits induce entry or exit. When losses prevail, some firms will leave the industry and invest their capital elsewhere. When economic profits are positive, new firms will enter the industry. The long run is far more dynamic than the short run.

MARKET STRUCTURE ANALYSIS

- Market structure analysis allows economists to categorize industries based on a few characteristics and use this analysis to predict pricing and output behavior.

- The intensity of competition is defined by the number of firms in the industry, the nature of the industry's product, the level of barriers to entry, and how much firms can control prices.

- Market structures range from competition (many buyers and sellers), to monopolistic competition (differentiated product), to oligopoly (only a few firms that are interdependent), to monopoly (a one-firm industry).

- Competition is defined by four attributes: Many buyers and sellers who are so small that none individually can influence price, firms that produce and sell a homogeneous (standardized) product, buyers and sellers who have all the information necessary to make informed decisions, and barriers to entry and exit that are insignificant.

- Firms in competitive markets get the product price from national or global markets. Therefore, competitive firms are price takers.

- In the short run, one factor (usually plant size) is fixed. In the long run, all factors are variable, and firms can enter or leave the industry.

QUESTIONS: Wal-Mart is a huge international firm with over 2,000,000 employees worldwide and sales of many billions of dollars. Where does Wal-Mart fit in our market structure approach? Microsoft? Starbucks? Toyota?

Answers to the Checkpoint questions can be found at the end of this chapter.

Competition: Short-Run Decisions

Figure 1 represents a competitive market with an equilibrium price of $200. This translates into a demand curve for individual firms shown in panel B. Individual firms are price takers in this competitive situation: They can sell as many units of their product as they wish at $200 each.

Marginal Revenue

Economists define **marginal revenue** as the change in total revenue that results from the sale of one added unit of a product. Marginal revenue (MR) is equal to the change in total revenue (ΔTR) divided by the change in quantity sold (Δq); thus,

$$MR = \Delta TR/\Delta q$$

Total revenue (TR), meanwhile, is equal to price per unit (p) times quantity sold (q); thus:

$$TR = p \times q$$

In a competitive market, we know that price will not change. And since marginal revenue is defined as the change in revenue that comes from selling one more unit, in a competitive market, marginal revenue is simply equal to price. The added revenue a competitive firm receives from selling another unit is product price, or $200 in Figure 1. So determining marginal revenue in a competitive market is easy. As we will see in later chapters, this gets more complicated in market structures where firms have some control over price.

Marginal revenue: The change in total revenue from selling an additional unit of output. Since competitive firms are price takers, P = MR for competitive firms.

Profit Maximizing Output

Figure 2 shows the price and marginal cost curve for a firm seeking to maximize its profits. As the price and cost curve show, the firm can sell all it wants at $200 a sail. Our first instinct might be to conclude that the firm will produce all it can, but this is not the case. Given the marginal cost curve shown in Figure 2, if the firm produces 85 units, profit will be less than the maximum possible. This is because revenue from the sale is $200, but the 85th sail costs $210 to produce (point *b*). This means producing this last sail reduces profits by $10.

FIGURE 2—Profit Maximization in the Short Run in Competitive Markets

If the firm produces 85 standardized windsurfing sails, the marginal cost to produce the last sail exceeds the revenue from its sale, thus reducing the firm's profits. For the 84th unit produced, marginal cost and price are both equal to $200, so the firm earns a normal return from producing this unit. Producing only 83 units means relinquishing the normal return that could have been earned from the 84th sail. Hence, the firm maximizes profits at an output of 84 (point *e*) where MC = MR = P = $200.

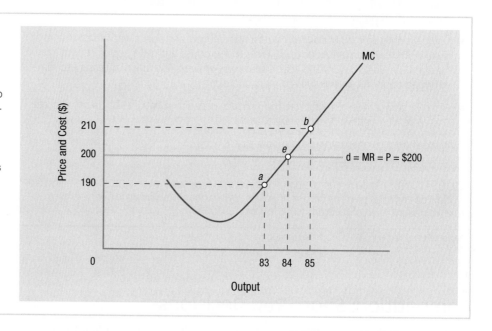

Assume the firm produces 84 sails. The revenue from selling the 84th unit (MR) is $200. This is precisely equal to the added cost (MC) of producing this unit, $200 (point *e*). Therefore, the firm earns zero economic profits by producing and selling the 84th sail. Zero economic profits, or normal profits, mean that the firm is earning a normal return on its capital by selling this 84th sail. If the firm starts producing only 83 sails, however, the additional cost (point a) will be less than the price, and the firm will have to relinquish the normal return associated with the 84th sail. Profits from selling 83 sails will therefore be lower than if 84 sails are sold because the normal return on the 84th sail is lost.

These observations lead us to a **profit maximizing rule:** *A firm maximizes profit by continuing to produce and sell output until marginal revenue equals marginal cost (MR = MC).* As we will see in subsequent chapters, this rule applies to all firms, regardless of market structure.

Profit maximizing rule: Firms maximize profit by producing output where MR = MC. No other level of output produces higher profits.

Economic Profits

Let us return to our example from the previous chapter of your windsurfing sail manufacturing firm. We will assume the market has established a price of $200 for each sail. Your marginal revenue and cost curves are shown in Figure 3. (Incidentally, the MR and MC curves are the same as those shown in Figure 2.) Complete price, production, and cost data are shown in Table 1.

Earlier, we found that profits are maximized when the firm is producing output such that MR = MC, in this case, 84 sails. As Table 1 shows, profit is $1,720 when 84 windsurfing sails are produced and sold at $200 a sail.

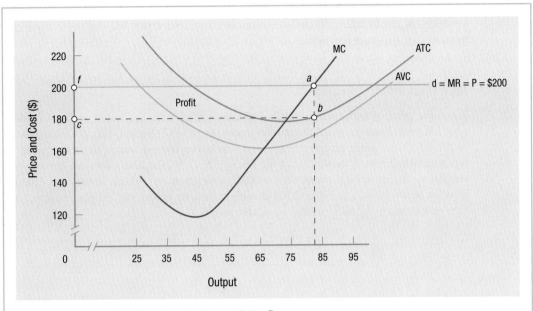

FIGURE 3—Competitive Firm Earning Economic Profits

The marginal revenue and cost curves derived from the data in Table 1 are shown here. As we can see, profits are maximized where MR = MC, or at an output of 84 and a price of $200. Price minus average total cost equals average profit per unit, represented by the distance *ab*. Average profit per unit times the number of units produced equals total profit; this is represented by area *cfab*.

Looking at Figure 3, we see that profits are maximized at point *a*, because this is where MR = MC. (This also can be seen in Table 1, where marginal costs of $195.56 closely approximates marginal revenue of $200.00.) We can also compute the profit in this scenario by multiplying average profit (profit per unit) by output. Average profit equals price minus average total costs (P − ATC). Thus, when 84 sails are produced, average profit is the distance *ab* in Figure 3, or $200 − $179.52 = $20.48. Total profit, or average profit times output, is $20.48 × 84 = $1,720; this is represented in Figure 3 by area *cfab*.

TABLE 1 Production, Cost, and Price for Windsurfing Sail Firm

L	Q	MP	AP	TFC	TVC	TC	ATC	AVC	MC	AFC	P	TR	Profit
0	0	0		1000	0	1000					200.00	0	−1000
1	7	7	7.00	1000	1760	2760	394.29	251.43	251.43	142.86	200.00	1400	−1360
2	15	8	7.50	1000	3520	4520	301.33	234.67	220.00	66.67	200.00	3000	−1520
3	25	10	8.33	1000	5280	6280	251.20	211.20	176.00	40.00	200.00	5000	−1280
4	40	15	10.00	1000	7040	8040	201.00	176.00	117.33	25.00	200.00	8000	−40
5	54	14	10.80	1000	8800	9800	181.48	162.96	125.71	18.52	200.00	10800	1000
6	65	11	10.83	1000	10560	11560	177.85	162.46	160.00	15.38	200.00	13000	1440
7	75	10	10.71	1000	12320	13320	177.60	164.27	176.00	13.33	200.00	15000	1680
8	84	9	10.50	1000	14080	15080	179.52	167.62	195.56	11.90	200.00	16800	1720
9	90	6	10.00	1000	15840	16840	187.11	176.00	293.33	11.11	200.00	18000	1160
10	95	5	9.50	1000	17600	18600	195.79	185.26	352.00	10.53	200.00	19000	400
11	98	3	8.91	1000	19360	20360	207.76	197.55	586.67	10.20	200.00	19600	−760
12	100	2	8.33	1000	21120	22120	221.20	211.20	880.00	10.00	200.00	20000	−2120
13	98	−2	7.54	1000	22880	23880	243.67	233.47	−880.00	10.20	200.00	19600	−4280

Note that there *is* a profit maximizing point. The competitive firm cannot produce and produce—it has to take into consideration its costs. So for the price-taking competitive firm, its cost structure is crucial.

Normal Profits

When the price of windsurfing sails is $200, your firm earns economic profits. Consider what happens, however, when the market price falls to $177.60 a sail. This price happens to be the minimum point on the average total cost curve, corresponding to an output of 75 rigs a month. Figure 4 shows that at the price of $177.60, the firm's demand curve is just tangent to the minimum point on the ATC curve (point *e*), which means the distance between points *a* and *b* in Figure 3 has shrunk to zero. By producing 75 sails a month, your firm earns a normal profit, or zero economic profits.

FIGURE 4—Competitive Firm Earning Normal Profits (Zero Economic Profits)

If the market sets a price of $177.60, the firm's demand curve is tangent to the minimum point on the ATC curve (point *e*). The best the firm can do under these circumstances is to earn normal profits on the sale of 75 windsurfing rigs.

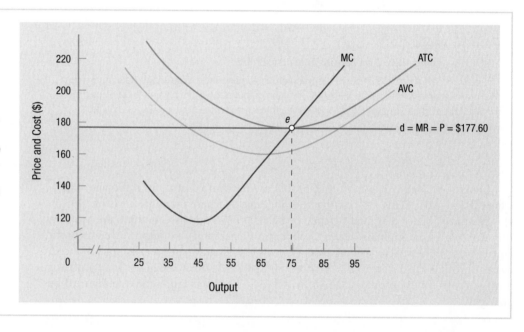

Remember that when a firm earns zero economic profits, it is generating just enough income to keep investor capital in the business. When the typical firm in an industry is earning **normal profits,** there are no pressures for firms to enter or leave the industry. As we will see in a later section, this is an important factor in the long run.

Normal profits: Equal to zero economic profits; where P = ATC.

Loss Minimization and Plant Shutdown

Assume for a moment that an especially calm summer with few winds leads to a decline in the demand for windsurfing equipment. Assume also that, as a consequence, the price of windsurfing sails falls to $170. Figure 5 illustrates the impact on your firm. Market price has fallen below your average total costs of production, but remains above your average variable costs. Profit maximization—or, in this case, *loss minimization*—requires that you produce output at the level where MR = MC. That occurs at point *e*, where output falls somewhere between 65 and 75 units.

For the sake of simplicity, we will assume you cannot hire a partial employee (ignoring the possibility of part-time workers). From Table 1, we know that producing 65 rigs

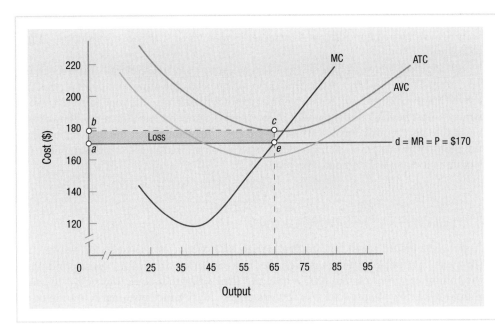

FIGURE 5—Competitive Firm Minimizing Losses

Assume that the price of windsurfing sails falls to $170 a sail. Loss minimization requires an output where MR = MC, in this case at 65 units (point e). Average total cost is $177.85 (point c) so loss per unit is equal to $7.85. Total loss is equal to $7.85 3 65 5 $510.25. Notice that this is less than the fixed costs ($1,000) that would have to be paid even if the plant was closed.

requires six employees. Again referring to Table 1, average total cost at this production level is $177.85, so with a market price of $170, loss per unit is $7.85. The total loss on 65 units is $7.85 × 65 = $510.25, corresponding to area *abce* in Figure 5.

These results may look grim, but consider your alternatives. If you were to produce more or fewer sails, your losses would just mount. You could, for instance, furlough your employees. But you will still have to pay your fixed costs of $1,000, and without revenue, your losses would be $1,000. Therefore, it is better to produce and sell 65 rigs, taking a loss of $510.25, thereby cutting your losses nearly in half.

But what happens if the price of windsurfing sails falls to $162.46? Such a scenario is shown in Figure 6. Your revenue from the sale of sails has fallen to a level just equal to variable costs. If you produce and sell 65 units of output (where MR = MC), you will be able to pay your employees their wages, but have nothing left over to pay your overhead;

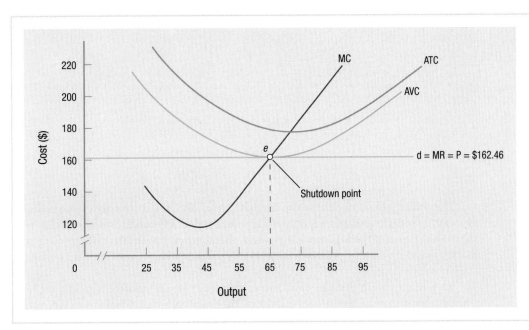

FIGURE 6—Plant Shutdown in a Competitive Industry

When prices fall below $162.46, or below the minimum point of the AVC curve, losses begin to exceed fixed costs. The firm will close if price falls below this minimum point (point e); this is the firm's shutdown point.

thus your loss will be $1,000. Point *e* in Figure 6 represents a **shutdown point,** since your firm will here be indifferent to whether it operates or shuts down—you lose $1,000 either way.

If prices continue to fall below $162.46 a sail, your losses will grow still further, because revenue will not even cover wages. Once prices drop below the minimum point on the AVC curve (point *e* in Figure 6), losses will exceed total fixed costs and your loss minimizing strategy must be to close the plant. It follows that the greatest loss a firm is willing to suffer in the short term is equal to its total fixed costs. Remember that the firm cannot leave the industry at this point, since market participation is fixed in the short run, but it can simply shut down its plant and stop production.

The Short-Run Supply Curve

A glance at Figure 7 will help to summarize what we have learned so far. As we have seen, when a competitive firm is presented with a market price of P_0, corresponding to the minimum point on the AVC curve, the firm will produce output of q_0. If prices should fall below P_0, the firm will shut its doors and produce nothing. If, on the other hand, prices should rise to P_1, the firm will sell q_1 and earn normal profits (zero economic profits). And if prices continue climbing above P_1, say, to P_2, the firm will earn economic profits by selling q_2. In each instance, the firm produces and sells output where MR = MC.

FIGURE 7—The Short-Run Supply Curve for a Competitive Firm

If prices fall below P_0, the firm will shut its doors and produce nothing. For prices between P_0 and P_1, the firm will incur losses, but these losses will be less than fixed costs, so the firm will remain in operation and produce where MR = MC. At a price of P_1, the firm earns a normal return. If price should rise above P_1 (e.g., to P_2), the firm will earn economic profits by selling an output of q_2. The portion of the MC curve above the minimum point on the AVC curve, here darkened, is the firm's short-run supply curve.

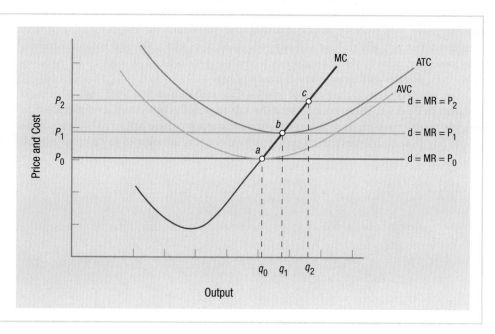

From this quick summary, we can see that a firm's **short-run supply curve** is equivalent to the MC curve above the minimum point on the AVC curve. This curve, shown as the darkened part of the MC curve in Figure 7, shows how much the firm will supply to the market at various prices, keeping in mind that it will supply no output at prices below the shutdown point.

Keep in mind also that the short-run supply curve for an industry is simply the horizontal summation of the supply curves of the industry's individual firms. To obtain industry supply, in other words, we simply add together the output of every firm at various price levels.

Nobel Prize

When he was awarded the Nobel Prize for Economics in 1978, Herbert Simon (1916–2001) was an unusual choice on two fronts. First, he wasn't an economist by trade; he was a professor of computer science and psychology at the time of his award. Second, Simon's major contribution to economics was a direct challenge to one of the basic tenets of economics: firms, in fact, do not always act to maximize profits.

In his book *Administrative Behavior,* Simon approached economics and the behavior of firms from his outsider's perspective. Simon thought real-world experience showed that firms are not always perfectly rational, in possession of perfect information, or striving to maximize profits.

Rather, he proposed, as firms grow larger and larger, the access to perfect information becomes a fiction. As a rule, firms always have to make do with less than perfect information. Furthermore, since firms are run by individuals with both personal and social ties, these individuals' decisions are further altered by their inability to remain perfectly and completely rational in their decision making.

To Simon, the reality is not that firms tilt at the mythical windmill of maximizing profits, but that, as he said in his Nobel Prize acceptance speech, they recognize their limitations and instead try to come up with an "acceptable solution to acute problems." In short, each decision maker in each firm tries to come up with the best solution for his or her problems. By recognizing this approach to decision making, firms can then set realistic goals and make reasonable assessments of their successes or failures.

Simon's views attacked the basic presumption that drives our market structure models and theories. Simon brought data, theories, and knowledge from other disciplines into economics, broadening its scope and applying more realistic conditions actually found in the marketplace. Although the competitive model in this chapter is based on profit maximization (an admitted simplification), its conclusions steer you in the right direction, even though Simon's analysis must always be considered. Today's challenge to profit maximization and rational decisions are coming from behavioral economists.

■ **CHECKPOINT**

COMPETITION: SHORT-RUN DECISIONS

- Marginal revenue is the change in total revenue from selling an additional unit of a product.

- Competitive firms are price takers, getting their price from markets, so they can sell all they want at the going market price. As a result, their marginal revenue is equal to product price and the demand curve facing the competitive firm is a horizontal straight-line demand at market price.

- Competitive firms maximize profit by producing that output where marginal revenue equals marginal cost (MR = MC).

- When price is greater than the minimum point of the average total cost curve, firms earn economic profits.

- When price is just equal to the minimum point of the average total cost curve, firms earn normal profits.

- When price is below the minimum point of the average total cost curve, but above the minimum point of the average variable cost curve, the firm continues to operate, but earns an economic loss.

- When price falls below the minimum point on the average variable cost curve, the firm will shut down and incur a loss equal to total fixed costs.

- The short-run supply curve of the firm is the marginal cost curve above the minimum point on the average variable cost curve.

QUESTION: Describe why profit maximizing output occurs where MR = MC. Does this explain why competitive firms do not sell "all they can produce"?

Answers to the Checkpoint question can be found at the end of this chapter.

Competition: Long-Run Adjustments

We have seen that competitive firms can earn economic profits, normal profits, or losses in the short run because their plant size is fixed, and they cannot exit the industry. We now turn our attention to the long run. In the long run, firms can adjust all factors, even to the point of leaving an industry. And if the industry looks attractive, other firms can enter it in the long run.

Adjusting to Profits and Losses in the Short Run

If firms in the industry are earning short-run economic profits, new firms can be expected to enter the industry in the long run, or existing firms may increase the scale of their operations. Figure 8 illustrates one such possible adjustment path when the firms in an industry are earning short-run economic profits. To simplify the discussion, we will assume there are no economies of scale in the long run.

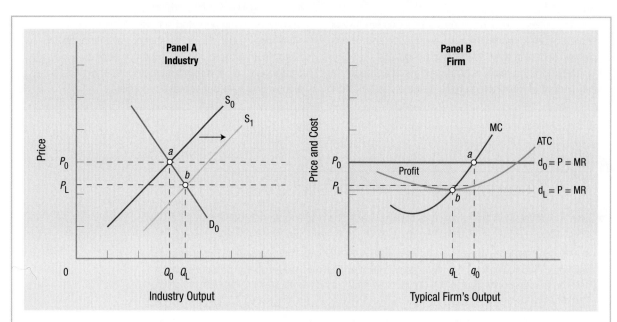

FIGURE 8—Long-Run Adjustment With Short-Run Economic Profits

Panel A shows a market initially in equilibrium at point *a*. Industry supply and demand equal S_0 and D_0, and equilibrium price is P_0. This equilibrium leads to the short-run economic profits shown in the shaded area in panel B. Short-run economic profits lead other firms to enter the industry, thus raising industry output to Q_L in panel A, while forcing prices down to P_L. The output for individual firms declines as the industry moves to long-run equilibrium at point *b* in both panels. In the long run, firms in competitive markets can earn only normal profits, as shown by point *b* in panel B.

In panel A, the market is initially in equilibrium at point *a,* with industry supply and demand equal to S_0 and D_0, and equilibrium price equal to P_0. For the typical firm shown in panel B, this translates into a short-run equilibrium at point *a.* Notice that, at this price, the firm produces output exceeding the minimum point of the ATC curve. The shaded area represents economic profits.

These economic profits (sometimes called supernormal profits) will attract other firms into the industry. Remember that in a competitive market, entry and exit are easy in the long run; so, many firms decide to get in on the action when they see these profits. As a result, industry supply will shift to the right, to S_1, where equilibrium is at point *b,* resulting in a new long-run industry price of P_L. For each firm in the industry, output declines to q_L and is just tangent to the minimum point on the ATC curve. Thus, all firms are now earning normal profits and keeping their investors satisfied. There are no pressures at this point for more firms to enter or exit the industry.

Consider the opposite situation—that is, firms in an industry that are incurring economic losses. Figure 9 depicts such a scenario. In panel A, market supply and demand are S_0 and D_0, with equilibrium price at P_0. In panel B, firms suffer economic losses equal to the shaded area. These losses cause some firms to reevaluate their situations and some decide to leave the industry, thus shifting the industry supply curve to S_1 in panel A, generating a new equilibrium price of P_L. This new price is just tangent to the minimum point of the ATC curve in panel B, expanding output for those individual firms remaining in the industry. Firms in the industry are now earning normal profits, so the pressures to leave the industry dissipate.

Notice that in Figures 8 and 9, the final equilibrium in the long run is the point at which industry price is just tangent to the minimum point on the ATC curve. At this point, there are no net incentives for firms to enter or leave the industry. If industry price rises above this point, the economic profits being earned will induce other firms to enter the industry; the opposite is true if price falls below this point. We will now evaluate this long-run equilibrium.

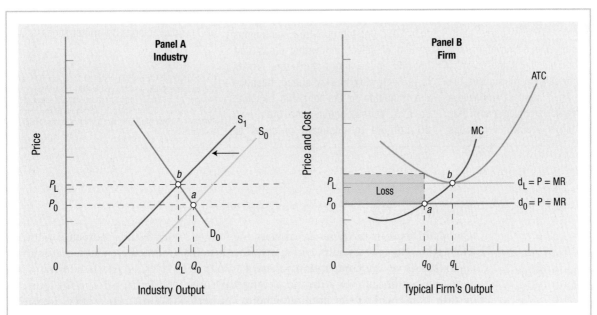

FIGURE 9—Long-Run Adjustment With Short-Run Losses

Panel A shows a market initially in equilibrium at point *a.* Industry supply and demand equal S_0 and D_0, and equilibrium price is P_0. This equilibrium leads to the short-run economic losses shown in the shaded area in panel B, thus inducing some firms to exit the industry. Industry output contracts to Q_L in panel A, raising prices to P_L and expanding output for the individual firms remaining in the industry, as the industry as a whole moves to long-run equilibrium at points *b* in both panels. Again, in the long run, firms in competitive markets will earn normal profits, as shown by point *b* in panel B.

Issue: Can Businesses Survive in an Open-Source World?

Open-source software can be downloaded for free, used for free, and altered by anyone provided that any changes made can also be freely used and altered by anyone else. Open-source systems like Linux and Apache server software are used to run many of the Internet's biggest sites. Other software, including word-processing, spreadsheets, and photo manipulation, is now becoming open source. Because it is digital, the marginal cost of downloading, using, and duplicating this software approaches zero. Making a profit selling open-source software, even with enhanced features, is therefore a difficult process.

But now there is a movement to open-source *hardware*. Ardvino, a simple micro-controller board; Chumby, a device using software to display weather, play music, and so on; and Bug, a modular system that can be used to make many computing devices, are all open-source hardware products and plans that are available for free, which anyone can duplicate, alter if they wish, and sell.

What happens when open-source software is followed by open-source hardware? Cory Doctorow, in his novel *Makers,* imagines a world in which the "system makes it hard to sell anything above the marginal cost of goods unless you have a really innovative idea, which can't stay innovative for long, so you need continuous

invention and reinvention, too." This sounds eerily similar to the battles going on today with smart phones, televisions, video games, ebooks, and other high-tech products. As soon as one company presents a game-changing product (think iPod, iPhone, and iPad), other firms work feverishly to clone it and competition pushes prices and margins down to lower levels. Imagine what would happen if these products were both hardware and software open source.

Makers presents a world where two engineers make three-dimensional (3D) desktop printers that can produce any product consumers want from inexpensive "goop." This is essentially the same way that 3D printers today "print" small parts with overlapping layers of resins to serve as 3D versions of design drawings to check dimensions and fit. In *Makers,* the economy collapses, department stores vanish, and unemployment approaches depression levels of more than 20%. Coming up with a continuous stream of clever innovative ideas that initially make high short-run profits is the only way to stay ahead, because the transition to the long run happens so fast. Worse, people use their own 3D printers to duplicate products or

Courtesy Desktop Factory

designs for virtually nothing (the cost of the goop).

Technology of the kind we are seeing now has the possibility of driving markets to these kinds of levels where marginal cost and profit margins are low. Many companies have thousands of employees that make products from toothbrushes to plastic ware to nearly everything you see at dollar stores. If households had the capability to produce their own products from some cheap substance, many companies we know today would disappear. Cory Doctorow explores what happens when the printers can produce other printers and other open-source machines. Although *Makers* is science fiction, the photo above of Desktop Factory's 3D printer suggests it is not so far-fetched.

Sources: Cory Doctorow, *Makers* (New York: Tom Doherty Associates), 2009; L. Gordon Crovitz, "Technology Is Stranger Than Fiction," *Wall Street Journal,* November 23, 2009, p. A19; and Justin Lahart, "Taking an Open-Source Approach to Hardware," *Wall Street Journal,* November 27, 2009, p. B8.

Competition and the Public Interest

Competitive processes dominate modern life. You and your friends compete for grades, concert tickets, spouses, jobs, and many other benefits. Competitive markets are simply an extension of the competition inherent in our daily lives. Figure 10 illustrates the long-run equilibrium for a firm in a competitive market. Market price in the long run is P_{LR}; it is equal to the minimum point on both the short-run average total cost (SRATC) curve and the long-run average total cost (LRATC) curve. At point *e,* the following is true:

$$P = MR = MC = SRATC_{min} = LRATC_{min}$$

This equation illustrates why competitive markets are the standard (benchmark) by which all other market structures are evaluated. First, competitive markets exhibit

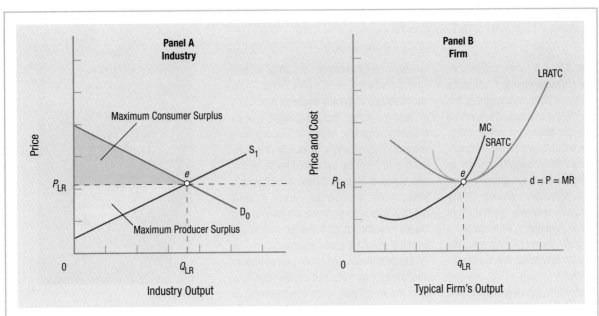

FIGURE 10—Long-Run Equilibrium for the Competitive Firm

Market price in the long run is P_{LR}, corresponding to the minimum point on the SRATC and LRATC curves. At point e, $P = MR = MC = SRATC_{min} = LRATC_{min}$. This is why economists use competitive markets as the benchmark when comparing the performance of other market structures. With competition, consumers get just what they want since price reflects their desires, and they get these products at the lowest possible price ($LRATC_{min}$). Further, as panel A illustrates, consumer and producer surplus is maximized. Any reduction in output reduces the sum of consumer and producer surplus.

productive efficiency. Products are produced and sold to consumers at their lowest possible opportunity cost, the minimum SRATC and LRATC. Given the existing technology, firms cannot produce these products more cheaply. For consumers, this is an excellent situation: They pay no more than minimum production costs plus a profit sufficient to keep producers in business, and consumer surplus shown in panel A is maximized. When we look at monopoly firms in the next chapter, consumers will not get such a good deal.

Second, competitive markets demonstrate **allocative efficiency.** The price consumers pay for a given product is equal not only to the minimum average total cost but also to marginal cost. As panel A illustrates, consumer and producer surplus are maximized. Thus, the last unit purchased in the market is sold for a price equal to the opportunity costs required to produce that unit. Because price represents the value consumers place on a product, and marginal cost represents the opportunity cost to society to produce that product, when these two values are equal, the market is allocatively efficient. This means that the market is allocating the production of various goods according to consumer wants.

The flip side of these observations is that if a market falls out of equilibrium, the public interest will suffer. If, for instance, output falls below equilibrium, marginal cost will be less than price. Therefore, consumers place a higher value on that product than it is costing firms to produce. Society would be better off if more of the product were put on the market. Conversely, if output rises above the equilibrium level, marginal cost will exceed price. This excess output costs firms more to produce than the value placed on it by consumers. We would be better off if those resources were used to produce another commodity more highly valued by society.

Productive efficiency: Goods and services are produced and sold to consumers at their lowest resource (opportunity) cost.

Allocative efficiency: The mix of goods and services produced are just what society desires. The price that consumers pay is equal to marginal cost and is also equal to the least average total cost.

Issue: Globalization and "The Box"

When we think of disruptive technologies that radically changed an entire market, we typically think of computers, the Internet, and cellular phones. Competitors must adapt to the change or wither away. One disruptive technology we take for granted today, but one that changed our world, is "the box"—the standardized shipping container. As Dirk Steenken reported, "Today 60% of the world's deep-sea general cargo is transported in containers, whereas some routes, especially between economically strong and stable countries, are containerized up to 100%."

Before containers, shipping costs added about 25% to the cost of some goods and represented over 10% of U.S. exports. The process was cumbersome; hundreds of longshoremen would remove boxes of all sizes, dimensions, and weight from a ship and load them individually onto trucks (or from trucks to a ship if they were going the other way). This process took a lot of time, was subject to damage and theft, and was costly and inconvenient for business.

In 1955 Malcom McLean, a North Carolina trucking entrepreneur, got the idea to standardize shipping containers. He originally thought he would drive a truck right onto a ship, drop a trailer, and drive off. Realizing that the wheels would consume a lot of space, he soon settled on a standard container that would stack together, but would also load directly onto

a truck trailer. Containers are 20 or 40 feet long, 8 feet wide, and 8 or 8½ feet tall. This standardization greatly reduced the costs of handling cargo. McLean bought a small shipping company, called it Sealand, and converted some ships to handle the containers. In 1956 he converted an oil tanker and shipped 58 containers from Newark, New Jersey, to Houston, Texas. It took roughly a decade of union bargaining and capital investment by firms for containers to catch on, but the rest is history.

Longshoremen and other port operators thought he was nuts, but as the idea took hold, the West Coast longshoremen went on strike to prevent the introduction of containers. They received some concessions, but containerization was inevitable. Containerization was so cost effective that it could not be stopped. It set in motion the long-run adjustments we see in competitive markets. Ports that didn't adjust went out of business, and trucking firms that failed to add containers couldn't compete. The same was true for ocean shipping companies.

Much of what we call globalization today can be traced to "the box." Firms producing products in foreign countries can fill a container, deliver it to a port, and send it directly to the customer or wholesaler in the United States. The efficiency, originally seen by McLean, was that the manufacturer and the ultimate customer would be the only ones to load and unload the container,

Youssouf Cader

keeping the product safer, more secure, and cutting huge chunks off the cost of shipping. Before containers, freight often represented as much as 25% of a product's price. Today, a 40-foot container with 32 tons of cargo shipped from China to the United States costs roughly $5,000, or 7 cents a pound! This efficient, disruptive technology has facilitated the expansion of trade worldwide and increased the competitiveness of many industries.

Sources: Based on Tim Ferguson, "The Real Shipping News," *Wall Street Journal,* April 12, 2006, p. D12; and on Mark Levinson, *The Box* (Princeton, NJ: Princeton University Press), 2006. Dirk Steenken, et al., "Container Terminal Operation and Operations Research," in Hans-Otto Gunther and Kap Hwan Kim, *Container Terminals and Automated Transport Systems* (New York: Springer), 2005. p. 4. Christian Caryl, "The Box Is King," *Newsweek International,* April 10–17, 2006; and Larry Rather, "Shipping Costs Start to Crimp Globalization," *New York Times,* August 3, 2008, p.10.

Long-Run Industry Supply

Economies or diseconomies of scale determine the shape of the long-run average total cost (LRATC) curve for individual firms. A firm that enjoys significant economies of scale will see its LRATC curve slope down for a wide range of output. Firms facing diseconomies of scale will see their average costs rise as output rises. The nature of these economies and diseconomies of scale determines the size of the competitive firm.

Long-run industry supply is related to the degree to which increases and decreases in industry output influence the prices firms must pay for resources. For example, when all firms in an industry expand or new firms enter the market, this new demand for raw materials and labor may push up the price of some inputs. When this happens, it gives rise to an **increasing cost industry** in the long run.

To illustrate, panel A of Figure 11 shows two sets of short-run supply and demand curves. Initially, demand and supply are D_0 and S_0, and equilibrium is at point *a*. Assume demand increases, shifting to D_1. In the short run, price and output will rise to point *b*. As we have seen earlier, economic profits will result and existing firms will

Increasing cost industry: An industry that in the long run, faces higher prices and costs as industry output expands. Industry expansion puts upward pressure on resources (inputs), causing higher costs in the long run.

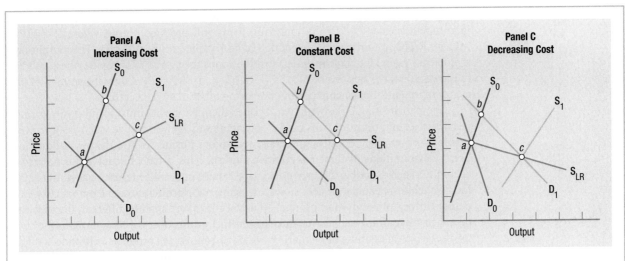

FIGURE 11—Long-Run Industry Supply Curves

Panel A shows an increasing cost industry. Demand and supply are initially D_0 and S_0, with equilibrium at point *a*. When demand increases, price and output rise in the short run to point *b*. As new firms enter the industry, they drive up the cost of resources. Supply increases in the long run to S_1 and the new equilibrium point *c* reflects these higher resource costs. In constant cost industries (panel B), firms can expand in the long run without economies or diseconomies, so costs remain constant in the long run. In decreasing cost industries (panel C), expansion leads to external economies and thus to a long-run equilibrium at point *c*, with lower prices and a higher output than before.

expand or new firms will enter the industry, causing product supply to shift to S_1 in the long run. Note that at the new equilibrium (point *c*), prices are higher than at the initial equilibrium (point *a*). This is caused by the upward pressure on the prices of industry inputs, notably raw materials and labor that resulted from industry expansion. Industry output has expanded, but prices and costs are higher. This is an *increasing cost industry*.

Alternatively, an industry might enjoy economies of scale as it expands, as suggested by panel C of Figure 11. In this case, price and output initially rise as the short-run equilibrium moves to point *b*. Eventually, however, this industry expansion leads to lower prices; perhaps raw materials suppliers enjoy economies of scale as this industry's demand for their product increases. The semiconductor industry seems to fit this profile: As the demand for semiconductors has risen over the past few decades, their price has fallen dramatically. In the long run, therefore, a new equilibrium is established at point *c*, where prices are lower and output is higher than was initially the case. This illustrates what happens in a **decreasing cost industry.**

Finally, some industries seem to expand in the long run without significant change in average cost. These are known as **constant cost industries** and are shown in panel B in Figure 11. Some fast-food restaurants and retail stores like Wal-Mart seem to be able to clone their operations from market to market without a noticeable rise in costs.

Summing Up

This chapter has focused on markets in which there is competition—that is, in which industries contain many sellers and buyers, each so small that they ignore the others' behavior and sell a homogeneous product. Sellers are assumed to maximize the profits they earn through sale of their products, and buyers are assumed to maximize the satisfaction they receive from the products they buy. Further, we assume that buyers and sellers have all the information necessary for informed transactions, and that sellers can sell as much of their products as they want at market equilibrium prices.

Decreasing cost industry: An industry that in the long run, faces lower prices and costs as industry output expands. Some industries enjoy economies of scale as they expand in the long run, typically the result of technological advances.

Constant cost industry: An industry that in the long run, faces roughly the same prices and costs as industry output expands. Some industries can virtually clone their operations in other areas without putting undue pressure on resource prices, resulting in constant operating costs as they expand in the long run.

These assumptions allow us to reach some clear conclusions about how firms operate in competitive markets. In the long run, firms will produce output where $P = MR = MC = LRATC_{min}$ and profits are enough to keep capital in the industry. This output level is efficient because it gives consumers just the goods they want and provides these goods at the lowest possible opportunity costs ($LRATC_{min} = MC = P$). Competitive market efficiency represents the benchmark for comparing other market structures.

Competitive markets as we have described them have what must seem to you like such restrictive assumptions that this model only applies to a few industries such as agriculture, standardized lumber products, minerals, and so on. Businesses you deal with don't look like the assumptions of these competitive markets. This is true, but most businesses you encounter, such as barber shops, salons, bars, restaurants, coffee houses, gas stations, fast-food franchises, cleaners, grocery stores, and shoe and clothing stores, all operate like competitive firms. Although their products (and locations) are slightly different, they basically take their prices from the market and earn normal profits over the long term. In the chapter after next, we examine those markets where consumers see products as branded and different and see how that industry's behavior is different from competitive markets.

Because the competitive market model is so clearly in the public interest and is the benchmark for comparing other market structures, we can ponder the answer to the following question: Do firms seek the competitive market structure? The answer is: Generally, no. Why? Recall the profit equation. In competitive markets, firms are price takers. They can achieve economic profits in the short run but find it almost impossible to have long-run economic profits. And crucially, the only way competitive firms can be profitable at all is to be efficient productively and continually so. There are some firms, such as Intel, that seem to thrive on competitive pressures. But most firms want long-run economic profits without facing such continual pressures to minimize costs. They want some ability to control price. In the next chapter, we will see what firms do to mitigate these competitive pressures.

■ CHECKPOINT

COMPETITION: LONG-RUN ADJUSTMENTS

- When competitive firms are earning short-run economic profits, these profits attract firms into the industry. Supply increases and market price falls until firms are just earning normal profits, and no firms are attracted into the industry.

- The opposite occurs when firms are making losses in the short run. Losses mean some firms will leave the industry. This reduces supply, thus increasing prices until profits return to normal.

- Competitive markets are efficient because $P = MR = MC = SRATC_{min} = LRATC_{min}$.

- Competitive markets are productively efficient because products are produced at their lowest possible opportunity cost.

- Competitive markets are allocatively efficient because $P = MC$, and consumer and producer surplus are at a maximum.

- An industry where prices rise as the industry grows is an increasing cost industry, and increased costs may be caused by rising prices of raw materials or labor as the industry expands.

- Decreasing cost industries see their prices fall as the industry expands, possibly due to huge economies of scale or rapidly improving technology.

- Constant cost industries seem to be able to expand without facing higher or lower prices.

QUESTION: Most of the markets and industries in the world are highly competitive, and presumably most CEOs of businesses know that competition will mean they will only earn normal profits in the long run. Given this analysis, why do they bother to stay in business, since any economic profits will vanish in the long run?

Answers to the Checkpoint question can be found at the end of this chapter.

Key Concepts

Market structure analysis, p. 184
Competition, p. 185
Price taker, p. 185
Marginal revenue, p. 187
Profit maximizing rule, p. 188
Normal profits, p. 190
Shutdown point, p. 192

Short-run supply curve, p. 192
Productive efficiency, p. 197
Allocative efficiency, p. 197
Increasing cost industry, p. 198
Decreasing cost industry, p. 199
Constant cost industry, p. 199

Chapter Summary

Market Structure Analysis

Market structure analysis enables economists to quickly categorize industries by looking at a few key characteristics. Once an industry has been properly categorized, its behavior in such areas as pricing and output can be predicted.

Economists have identified four basic market structures: competition, monopolistic competition, oligopoly, and monopoly. They are defined by the following factors: the number of firms in the industry, the nature of the product produced, the scope of barriers to entry and exit, and the extent to which individual firms can control prices.

The competitive market structure assumes, first, that the market has many buyers and sellers, each so small that they cannot influence product prices. Second, a competitive industry is assumed to produce a homogeneous or standardized product. Third, all buyers and sellers have all relevant information about prices and product quality. Fourth, barriers to entry and exit are assumed to be insignificant.

Competitive firms are price takers; they cannot significantly alter the sales price of their products. Product prices are determined in broad markets.

In the short run, at least one factor of production, usually plant capacity, is fixed. Also in the short run, firms cannot exit an industry, nor can new firms enter. In the long run, all factors of production are variable, with short-run profit levels inducing entry or exit.

Competition: Short-Run Decisions

Total revenue equals price per unit times quantity sold (TR = $p \times q$). Marginal revenue is equal to the change in total revenue that comes from producing an added unit of the product (MR = ΔTR$/\Delta q$). Since, in a competitive market, a firm can sell all it wants at the market price, marginal revenue is equal to market price for the competitive firm.

Firms maximize their profits by selling that level of output at which marginal revenue is just equal to marginal cost (MR = MC). For the competitive firm this translates into MC = MR = P. In the short run, a firm can earn economic profits, normal profits, or economic losses, depending on its product's market price.

If price is above the minimum point on the ATC curve, a firm will earn economic profits in the short run. If price is just equal to the minimum point on the ATC curve, the firm will earn normal profits. If price should fall below the minimum ATC, the firm will earn economic losses. Finally, if the price falls below the minimum point on the AVC curve, the firm will shut down and incur a loss equal to its fixed costs, since firms will not operate if they cannot cover their variable costs.

The short-run supply curve for the competitive firm is the marginal cost curve above the minimum point on the AVC curve.

Competition: Long-Run Adjustments

In the long run, all factors of production are variable, including the ability to exit or enter an industry. When the firms in an industry earn economic profits in the short run, this attracts new firms to the industry, thus reducing product price until firms are earning just normal profits. A corresponding adjustment occurs when the firms in an industry suffer short-term economic losses: Some firms leave the industry, thus raising prices until the remaining firms are again earning normal returns.

Competitive markets serve the public interest by ensuring that firms price their products at their marginal cost, which also equals $LRATC_{min}$. Therefore, just the quantity of products that consumers want is provided at the lowest possible opportunity cost ($LRATC_{min}$). In addition, competitive market equilibrium maximizes consumer and producer surplus.

An industry may be an increasing cost industry, a decreasing cost industry, or a constant cost industry depending on the industry's precise structure, the current state of technology, and the degree of economies and diseconomies of scale.

Questions and Problems

Check Your Understanding

1. Why must price cover average variable costs if the firm is to continue operating?
2. Describe the role that easy entry and exit play in competitive markets over the long run.
3. Why are marginal revenue and price equal for the competitive firm?
4. Why, if competitive firms are earning economic profits in the short run, are they unable to earn them in the long run?
5. Describe the reasons why an industry's costs might increase in the long run. Why might they decrease over the long run?

Apply the Concepts

6. The media reports each quarter on industry profits and losses. Some firms (most notably the airlines) seem to post losses quarter after quarter. Why do they keep operating?
7. Why do competitive firms sell their products only at the market price? Why not try to raise prices to make more profit or lower them to garner market share (more sales)?
8. How is the short-run supply curve for the competitive firm determined?
9. How has the development of the Internet affected small competitive businesses such as used bookstores and antique shops?
10. Of the characteristics that are used to define the four market structures discussed at the beginning of the chapter, which two characteristics intuitively seem to be the most important?
11. Assume a competitive industry is in long-run equilibrium and firms in the industry are earning normal profits. Now assume that production technology improves such that average total costs decline by $5 a unit. Describe the process this industry will go through as it moves to a new long-run equilibrium.
12. When a competitive firm is earning economic profits, is it also maximizing profit per unit? Why or why not?
13. In this chapter we suggested that whenever market price fell below average variable costs that the firm would shut down. At that point revenue is not covering its variable costs and the firm is losing more money than if it just shut down and lost fixed costs. Clearly, shutting the firm is more complicated than that. Under what circumstances might the firm continue to operate even though prices are below average variable costs?

In the News

14. Michelle Slatalla (*New York Times*, February 3, 2005) stated, "The conventional wisdom a few years back was that the Internet would erase price differences among retailers by giving customers instant access to the best deals. Merchants who charged more would be driven out of business." She further quoted Professor Michael Baye, who noted, "The prediction was price-comparison sites would create perfectly competitive environments in which all firms would have to charge the same price." These forecasts for the Internet creating "perfectly competitive" markets were based on the competitive model we have presented in this chapter. Do you think the Internet has helped create more competitive markets or less? Why?

Solving Problems

15. Use the table below to answer the following questions. Assume that fixed costs are $100, and labor is paid $80 per unit (per employee).

L	Q	MP	AP	TFC	TVC	TC	ATC	AVC	AFC	MC
0	0			—	—	—				
1	7	—	—	—	—	—	—	—	—	—
2	15	—	—	—	—	—	—	—	—	—
3	25	—	—	—	—	—	—	—	—	—
4	40	—	—	—	—	—	—	—	—	—
5	45	—	—	—	—	—	—	—	—	—
6	48	—	—	—	—	—	—	—	—	—
7	50	—	—	—	—	—	—	—	—	—

a. Complete the table.

b. Graph ATC, AVC, AFC, and MC in the blank grid below.

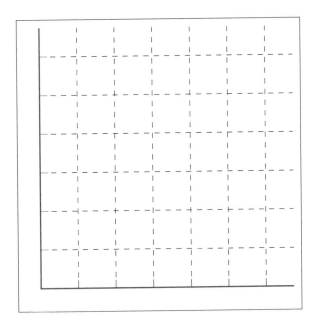

c. Assume the market sets the price at $16 a unit. How much will the firm produce, and what will its profit equal?

d. Assume now that price falls to $10.50. How much will the firm produce, and what will be its profits?

e. Now assume that the price falls to $7.50. Again, how much will the firm produce, and what will be its profits?

16. Use the figure below to answer the following true/false questions:

a. If market price is $25, the firm earns economic profits.

b. If market price is $20, the firm earns economic profit equal to roughly $100.

c. If market price is $9, the firm produces roughly 55 units.

d. If market price is $12.50, the firm produces roughly 70 units and makes an economic loss equal to roughly $175.

e. Total fixed costs for this firm are roughly $100.

f. If market price is $15, the firm sells 80 units and makes a normal profit.

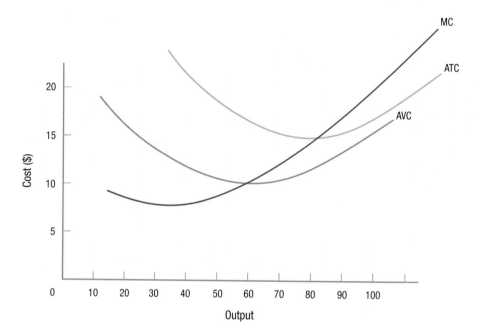

Answers to Questions in CheckPoints

Check Point: Market Structure Analysis

Wal-Mart is clearly a very competitive firm. But does this mean it is a competitor in the market structure sense: In some cases, yes, and probably in others, no. When Wal-Mart opens a store in a rural setting, it takes on a dominant retailing role in the local area and looks more like a monopolist with a large market share. When it opens stores in urban areas, it has a lot of competition, and its market share is small, so it looks more like just another retailer in a competitive environment. If we look at the market internationally, Wal-Mart is just one of many large retailers around the world, so it looks like it fits the competitive market structure in the international market. Microsoft is more toward the monopoly end of the spectrum. Who are its competitors? Starbucks has many competitors but its products are considered somewhat unique by consumers so it is a monopolistic competitor. Toyota and the automobile industry are more oligopolistic, with only a few auto manufacturers of importance in the market.

Check Point: Competition: Short-Run Decisions

Keep in mind that marginal cost is the additional cost to produce another unit of output, and price equals marginal revenue and is the additional revenue from selling one more unit of the product. If MR is greater than MC, the firm earns more revenue than cost by selling that next unit, so the firm will sell up to where MR = MC. At that last unit where MR = MC, the firm is earning a normal profit on that unit (a positive accounting profit). When MC > MR, the firm is spending more to produce that unit than it receives in revenue and is losing money on that last unit, lowering overall profits. Thus, firms will not produce and sell all they can produce: They will produce and sell up to the point where MR = MC.

Check Point: Competition: Long-Run Adjustments

All businesses are looking for the "next new thing" that will generate economic profits and propel them to monopoly status. Even normal profits are not trivial. Remember, normal profits are sufficient to keep investors happy in the long run. When firms do find the right innovation, such as the iPod, Windows operating system, or a blockbuster breakthrough drug, the short-run returns are huge.

Monopoly 9

In the previous chapter, we constructed a model of competitive markets in which many sellers compete against one another for the business of many buyers. This model assumed that different firms sell almost identical products, produce where price equals marginal cost, and face no significant barriers to entry, entering or exiting industries easily.

In this chapter, we turn to the theory of monopoly. Unlike competitive firms, monopolies have pricing power. For example, consider Microsoft's Word program. The marginal cost of printing a CD-ROM with Word on it, putting it in a package, and earning a normal profit on its capital is maybe $15 per package. Yet Microsoft charges more than 10 times this amount. Why?

Monopoly is at the other extreme from the competitive model. Whereas the competitive model is in the public interest, we can guess at the outset that monopolies are not. We will see why monopolies exist and how they act. Then we will see what it means to have monopoly power. After that, we will see what can be done to mitigate the powers of monopolies that must exist, and how the United States tries to prevent monopolies from arising.

Monopoly Markets

The very word *monopoly* almost defines the subject matter: a market in which there is only one seller. Here again, however, economists have attached a more extensive meaning to the word by specifying the types of products sold and the barriers to entry and exit. For economists, a **monopoly** is defined as follows:

■ The market has just one seller—one firm *is* the industry. This contrasts sharply with the competitive market, where many sellers comprise the industry.

> **Monopoly:** A one-firm industry with no close product substitutes and with substantial barriers to entry.

- No close substitutes exist for the monopolist's product. Consequently, buyers cannot easily substitute other products for that sold by the monopolist. If you want anything like the product in question, you must purchase it from the monopolist.

- A monopolistic industry has significant barriers to entry. Though competitive firms can enter or leave industries in the long run, monopoly markets are considered nearly impossible to enter. So monopolists face no competition, even in the long run.

This gives pure monopolists what economists call monopoly power. Unlike competitive firms, which are price takers, monopolists are *price makers.* Their monopoly power, in other words, allows monopolists to adjust their output in ways that give them significant control over product price.

As we will see, nearly every firm has some monopoly power, or some control over price. Your neighborhood dry cleaner, for instance, has some control over price since it is found close to you, and you are probably not going to want to drive 5 miles just to save a few cents. This control over price becomes minor, however, as markets approach more competitive conditions.

Sources of Monopoly Power

Monopoly and monopoly power do not mean the same thing. *Monopoly* is defined as one firm serving a market in which there are no close substitutes and entry is nearly impossible. **Monopoly power** (often referred to as market power) implies that a firm has some control over price. As a market structure approaches monopoly, one firm gains the maximum monopoly power possible for that industry. The key to monopoly power is significant barriers to entry. These barriers can be of several forms.

Economies of Scale

The **economies of scale** in an industry (when average total costs decline) can be so large that demand supports only one firm. Figure 1 illustrates this case. Here the long-run average total cost curve (LRATC) shows extremely large economies of scale. With industry demand at D_0, one firm can earn economic profits by producing between Q_0 and Q_1. If the industry were to contain two firms, however, demand for each would be D_2, and neither firm could remain in business without suffering losses. Economists refer to such cases as *natural monopolies.*

Some contemporary natural monopolies include microprocessors, electric utilities, and local newspapers. Though Intel is not a pure monopolist, it sells most of the world's microprocessors. Opening a production plant for its Core processors costs Intel more than a billion dollars, and it needs over $9 billion in annual sales just to support the plant. In addition, Intel spends billions of dollars each year on research, development, and marketing. The market for microprocessors is huge, but so are the development, production, and marketing scales a firm must attain to be successful. Still, the microprocessor market is so large that Intel does face some competition from another large firm (Advanced Micro Devices, AMD, with annual revenues about one-sixth of Intel's) and from smaller niche firms.

Utilities have traditionally been considered natural monopolists because of the high fixed costs associated with power plants and the inefficiency of several different electric companies stringing their wires throughout a city. Recent technology, however, is slowly changing the utilities industry, as smaller plants, solar units, and wind generators permit a smaller yet efficient scale of operations. Smaller plants can be quickly turned on and off, and the energy from the sun and wind is beginning to be stored and transported to where it is needed in the system.

Control over a Significant Factor of Production

If a firm owns or has control over an important input into the production process, that firm can keep potential rivals out of the market. This was the case with Alcoa Aluminum 50 years ago. The company owned nearly all the world's bauxite ore, one of the key

Monopoly power: A firm with monopoly power has some control over price.

Economies of scale: As the firm expands in size, average total costs decline.

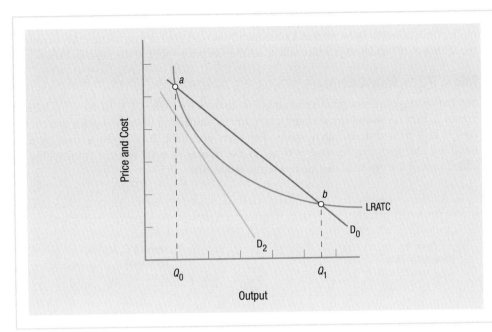

FIGURE 1—Economies of Scale Leading to Monopoly

The economies of scale in an industry can be so large that demand supports only one firm. In the industry portrayed here, one firm could earn economic profits (by producing output between Q_0 and Q_1 when faced with demand curve D_0). If the industry were to contain two firms, however, demand for each would be D_2, and neither firm could remain in business without suffering losses.

ingredients for aluminum production. In the end, the Justice Department moved against Alcoa to break up this monopoly. We discuss policies to combat monopolies later in this chapter.

Government Franchises, Patents, and Copyrights

Some barriers to market entry extend from legal government mandates. A government franchise grants a firm permission to provide specific goods or services, while prohibiting others from doing so, thereby eliminating potential competition. The United States Postal Service, for instance, has an exclusive franchise in the delivery of first-class mail to your mailbox. Similarly, some public utilities and cable companies have been granted special franchises by state or local governments.

Patents are extended to firms and individuals who invent new products and processes. For a limited period, usually 20 years, the patent holder is legally protected from competition in production of the patented product. The basic reason behind the patent system is to give firms and individuals the incentive to invent and innovate. If entrepreneurs had to worry about their ideas being stolen by competitors as soon as they brought new products to the market, fewer new products would be developed. Patents are immensely important to many industries, including pharmaceuticals, computers, and chemicals. Many firms in these industries spend huge sums of money each year on research and development—money they might not spend if they could not protect their investments through patenting.

In a similar vein, copyrights give individuals or firms the exclusive right to produce or reproduce certain types of intellectual property for an extended period. A book, a piece of art, or a piece of software code can all be copyrighted. Copyright protection lay at the heart of the Microsoft legal case of the late 1990s. If Microsoft's Windows operating system had not been protected by copyright, Microsoft would not have enjoyed the monopoly power that sparked the government's lawsuit against it. Some firms guard trade secrets to protect their assets for even longer periods than the limited times provided by patents and copyrights. Only a handful of the top executives at Coca-Cola, for instance, know the secret to blending Coke.

Monopoly Pricing and Output Decisions

We have seen how monopoly power is first attained: barriers to entry. Shortly we will discuss some ways it is maintained. First, however, let us consider monopoly pricing and output decisions. In the previous chapter, we saw that competitive firms maximize profits by producing at a level of output where MR = MC, selling this output at the established market price. The monopolist, however, *is* the market. Consequently, we can predict that the quantity of output the monopolist decides to produce will affect market price—that is, the monopolist's price.

MR < P for Monopoly

For the monopolist, marginal revenue is less than price (MR < P). To see why, look at Figure 2. Panel A shows the demand curve for a competitive firm. At a price of $10, the competitive firm can sell all it wants. For each unit sold, total revenue rises by $10. Recalling that marginal revenue is equal to the change in total revenue from selling an added unit of the product, marginal revenue is also $10.

FIGURE 2—Marginal Revenue for Monopolies and Competitive Firms

Panel A shows the demand curve for a competitive firm. At a price of $10, the competitive firm can sell all it wants. For each unit sold, revenue rises by $10; hence, marginal revenue is $10. Panel B shows the demand curve for a monopolist. Because the monopolist constitutes the entire industry, it faces a downward sloping demand curve (D_0). If the monopolist decides to sell 10 units at $18 each (point *a*), total revenue is $180. Alternatively, if the monopolist wants to sell 11 units, price must be dropped to $17 (point *b*). This raises total revenue to $187 (11 × $17), but marginal revenue falls to $7 ($187–$180, point *c*). Gaining the added $17 in revenue from the sale of the 11th unit requires the monopolist to give up $10 in additional revenue that would have come from selling the previous 10 units for $18 each.

Contrast this with the situation of the monopolist in panel B. Because the monopolist constitutes the entire industry, it faces the downward sloping demand curve (D_0). If the monopolist decides to produce and sell 10 units, they can be sold in the market for $18 each (point *a*), generating total revenue of $180. Alternatively, if the monopolist wants to sell 11 units, their price must be dropped to $17 (point *b*). This raises total revenue to $187 (11 × $17). Notice, however, that marginal revenue, or the revenue gained from selling this added unit, falls to $7 ($187–$180). Gaining the additional $17 in revenue from the sale of the 11th unit requires that the monopolist give up $10 in revenue that would have come from selling the previous 10 units for $18 each. Marginal revenue for the 11th unit is shown as $7 (point *c*) in panel B.

Notice that we are assuming the monopolist cannot sell the 10th unit for $18 and then sell the 11th unit for $17; rather, the monopolist must offer to sell a given quantity to the market for a standard price. We are assuming, in other words, that there is no way for the monopolist to separate the market by specific individuals who are willing to pay different prices for the product. In the next section, we will relax this assumption and discuss *price discrimination.*

In summary, we can see from panel B of Figure 2 that MR < P, and the marginal revenue curve is always plotted below the demand curve for the monopolist. This contrasts with the situation of the competitive firm, for which price and marginal revenue are always the same. We should also note that marginal revenue can be negative. In such an instance, total revenue falls as the monopolist tries to sell more output. However, no profit maximizing monopolist would produce in this range because costs are rising even as total revenue is declining, thus reducing profits.

Equilibrium Price and Output

As noted earlier, product price is determined in a monopoly by how much the monopolist wishes to produce. This contrasts with the competitive firm that can sell all it wishes, but only at the *market-determined price.* Both types of firms wish to make profits. Finding the monopolist's profit maximizing price and output is a little more complicated, however, since competitive firms have only output to consider.

Like competitive firms, the profit maximizing output for the monopolist is found where MR = MC. Turning to Figure 3, we find that marginal revenue equals marginal cost at point *e,* where output is 120 units. Now we must determine how much the monopolist will charge for this output. This is done by looking to the demand curve. An output of 120 units can be sold for a price of $30 (point *a*).

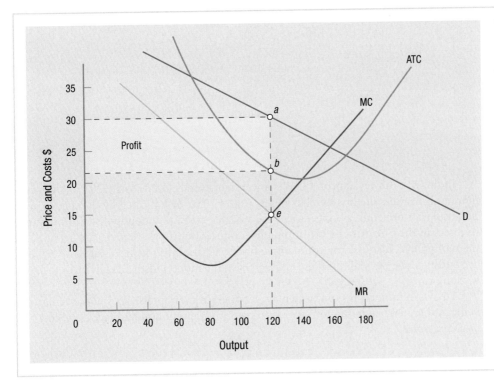

FIGURE 3—Monopolist Earning Economic Profits

Profit maximizing output is found for monopolists, as for competitive firms, at the point where MR = MC. In this figure, marginal revenue equals marginal cost at point *e,* where output is 120 units. These 120 units are sold for $30 each (point *a*). Profit is equal to average profit per unit times units sold: Profit = (P − ATC) × Q = ($30 − $22) × 120 = $8 × 120 = $960. The shaded area represents profit.

Profit for each unit is equal to $8, the difference between price ($30) and average total costs ($22). Profit per unit times output equals total profit ($8 × 120 = $960), as indicated by the shaded area in Figure 3. Following the MR = MC rule, profits are maximized by selling 120 units of the product at $30 each.

In summary, to find the equilibrium level of output and price, first find the point where MR = MC. This point determines the profit maximizing output on the horizontal axis, and by extending a vertical line through the point to the demand curve, it determines price on the vertical axis. The difference between this price and average total costs, multiplied by the number of units sold, equals total profit.

Monopoly Does Not Guarantee Economic Profits

We have seen that competitive firms may or may not be profitable in the short run, but in the long run, they must earn at least normal profits to remain in business. Is the same true for monopolists? Yes. Consider the monopolist in Figure 4. This firm maximizes profits by producing where MR = MC (point *e*) and selling 80 units of output for price $25.

FIGURE 4—Monopolist Firm Making Economic Losses

Like competitive firms, monopolists may or may not be profitable in the short run, but in the long run, they must at least earn normal profits to remain in business. The monopolist shown here maximizes profits (minimizes losses) by producing at point *e*, selling 80 units of output at $25 each. Price is lower than average total costs, so the monopolist suffers the loss indicated by the shaded area. Because price still exceeds average variable cost (AVC), in the short run the monopolist will minimize its losses by continuing to produce.

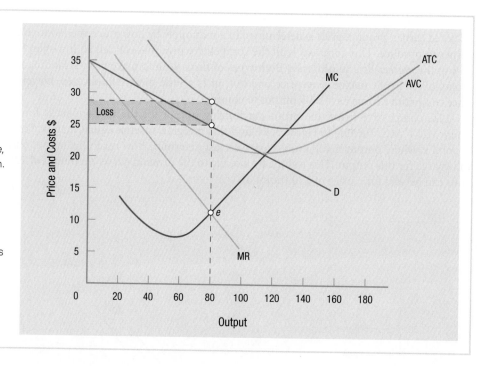

In this case, however, price ($25) is lower than average total costs ($28), and thus the monopolist suffers the loss of $240 (−$3 × 80 = −$240) indicated by the shaded area. Because price nonetheless exceeds average variable costs, the monopolist will minimize its losses in the short run by continuing to produce. But if price should fall below AVC, the monopolist, just like any competitive firm, will minimize its losses at its fixed costs by shutting down its plant. If these losses persist, the monopolist will exit the industry in the long run.

This is an important point to remember. Being a monopolist does not automatically mean there will be monopoly profits to haul in. Even monopolies face *some* cost and price pressures.

Comparing Monopoly and Competition

Would our economy be better off with more or fewer monopolies? This question almost answers itself. Who would want more monopolies—except the few lucky monopolists? The answer is, we want fewer monopolies and more competition. The reasons for this have to do with the losses associated with monopoly markets and monopoly power. As we will discuss in the next two sections, monopoly losses include reduced output at higher prices, deadweight losses, rent-seeking behavior of monopolists, and x-inefficiency losses.

Higher Prices and Lower Output from Monopoly

Imagine for a moment that a competitive industry is monopolized, and the monopolist's marginal cost curve happens to be the same as the competitive industry's supply curve. Figure 5 illustrates such a scenario. The competitive industry produces where MC = P, and thus where price and output are P_C and Q_C (point b). Monopoly price and output, however, as determined as before, are P_M and Q_M (point a).

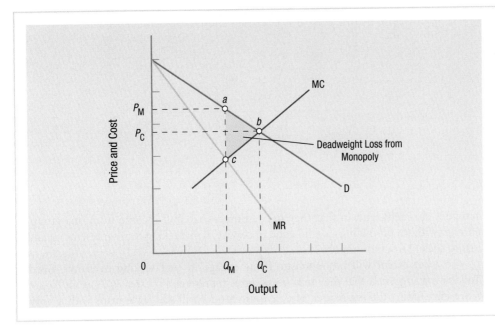

FIGURE 5—Monopoly Inefficiency

This figure shows what would happen if a competitive industry were monopolized and the new monopolist's marginal cost curve was the same as the competitive industry's supply curve. When the industry was competitive, it produced where MC = P, and thus where price and output are P_C and Q_C (point b). Monopoly price and output, however, are P_M and Q_M (point a); output is lower and price is higher than the corresponding values for competitive firms. Shaded area cab represents the deadweight loss suffered from monopoly.

Clearly, monopoly output is lower, and monopoly price is higher, than the corresponding values for competitive industries. Notice that at monopoly output Q_M, consumers value the Q_Mth unit of the product at P_M (point a), even though the cost to produce this last unit of output is considerably less (point c). The *deadweight loss,* otherwise known as the *welfare loss,* from monopoly is shown as the shaded area cab. This area represents the deadweight loss to society from a monopoly market.

Rent Seeking and X-Inefficiency

Monopolies earn economic profits by charging more and producing less than competitive firms. This inefficiency results in a loss of consumer surplus. Figure 6 on the next page resembles Figure 5, except that we are assuming constant-cost conditions. As a result, MC is equal to ATC. Again, the monopolist produces Q_M and sells this output for P_M, while the competitive firm sells Q_C at price P_C. This results in a deadweight loss equal to area cab.

Economic profits in Figure 6 are equal to $P_C P_M ac$. Clearly, this is something monopolists will wish to protect. If entry to the market were eased, this economic profit would soon evaporate, just as it does in competitive markets. How, then, can a monopolist protect itself from potential competition? One way is to spend resources that could have been used to expand its production on efforts to protect its monopoly position.

Economists call this behavior **rent seeking**—behavior directed toward avoiding competition. Firms hire lawyers and other professionals to lobby governments, extend patents, and engage in a host of other activities intended solely to protect their monopoly position. Taxis in New York City, for instance, require licenses; restricting the number of licenses drives up their price and gives license holders a further incentive to restrict the number of new licenses, by lobbying and other means. Many industries spend significant resources lobbying Congress for tariff protection to reduce foreign competition. All these

Rent seeking: Resources expended to protect a monopoly position. These are used for such activities as lobbying, extending patents, and restricting the number of licenses permitted.

FIGURE 6—Rent Seeking and Deadweight Loss in Monopoly

Economic profits are equal to $P_C P_M ac$. To protect these lucrative profits, the typical monopolist will engage in a variety of rent-seeking behaviors—hiring lawyers and other professionals to lobby the government, for instance, or obtaining patents. Some economists argue that monopolistic firms may engage in so much rent-seeking behavior that all monopoly profits are eliminated.

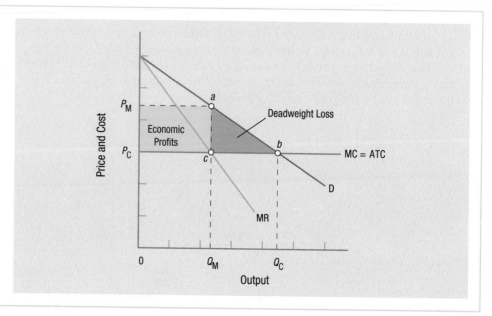

X-inefficiency: Protected from competitive pressures, monopolies do not have to act efficiently. Spending on corporate jets, travel, and other perks of business represent x-inefficiency.

activities are inefficient, in that they use resources and shift income from one group to another without producing a useful good or service. Rent seeking thus represents an added loss to society from monopoly.

To what extent will monopolistic firms engage in rent seeking behavior? Gordon Tullock has suggested that they may go as far as represented by area $P_C P_M ac$ in Figure 6. Since eliminating the entire area of economic profits will still leave firms with a normal return, they may be willing to spend up to this total amount on rent seeking.

Another area where society might lose from monopolies is called **x-inefficiency**. Some economists suggest that because monopolies are protected from competitive pressures, they do not have to operate efficiently. Management can offer itself perks, for instance, without worrying about whether costs are kept at efficient levels. Executive travel in corporate jets, even for private vacations, has been criticized "as a symbol of excess," even though the trip is treated as income for tax purposes (but some companies even pay the taxes for the executives).[1] Deregulation over the last several decades, particularly in the airline and trucking industries, has provided ample evidence of inefficiencies arising when firms are protected from competition by government regulations. Many firms in these industries found it tough sledding when competitive pressures were reintroduced into their industries.

Are there any benefits to monopolies? The answer to this question is, "Possibly yes, though generally no." If the economies associated with an industry are so large that many small competitors would face substantially higher marginal costs than a monopolist, a monopolist would produce and sell more output at a lower price than could competitive firms. Larger firms, moreover, can allocate more resources to research and development than smaller firms, and the possibility of economic profits may be the incentive monopolists require to invest.

Still, economists tend to doubt that monopolies are beneficial enough to outweigh their disadvantages.

In actuality, pure monopolies are rare, in part because of public policy and antitrust laws—more about this later in this chapter—and in part because rapidly changing technologies limit most monopolies to short-run economic profits—witness the battle among Google, Yahoo, and Microsoft for domination of search services, and Sony,

---

[1] See Geraldine Fabrikant, "Executives Take Company Planes as if Their Own," *New York Times*, May 10, 2006, p. C1.

Amazon, Apple, and several other firms to dominate the eBook market. Even so, all firms seek to increase their market or monopoly power and gain some ability to influence price.

We have seen what monopolies are and how they arise. We also saw why a monopolist produces less than the socially optimal quantity at a higher than socially necessary price, and witnessed how monopoly compares unfavorably to the competitive model. Furthermore, we looked at an expensive drawback of monopolies: the amount of resources wasted in maintaining a monopolist's position. In the next section, we look at what monopolists especially would like to do, and how a society might regulate a natural monopoly.

■ CHECKPOINT

MONOPOLY MARKETS

- Monopoly is a market with no close substitutes, high barriers to entry, and one seller; the firm is the industry. Hence, monopolists are price makers.

- Monopoly power can result from economies of scale, control over an important input, or from government franchises, patents, and copyrights.

- For the monopolist, MR < P because the industry's demand is the monopolist's demand.

- Profit is maximized by producing that output where MR = MC and setting the price off the demand curve.

- Being a monopolist does not guarantee economic profits if demand is insufficient to cover costs.

- Monopoly output is lower and price is higher when compared to competition, resulting in a deadweight loss from monopoly.

- Monopolies are subject to rent-seeking behavior directed toward avoiding competition (lobbying and other activities to extend the monopoly).

- Because monopolies are protected from competitive pressures, they often engage in x-inefficiency behavior—extending perks to management and other inefficient activities.

QUESTIONS: Google has 85% of the search business on the Internet and generates a lot of advertising revenue. Microsoft has 90% of the operating system business and 80% or so of the Internet browsers in use. In early 2006, Google, the search monopolist, asked the government to rein in Microsoft's new browser, which has a search box in the upper right hand corner, similar to Firefox and Apple's Safari. The default, of course, is that when you type a search term, you go through Microsoft's search engine. Changing the default is, however, quite easy; Google has the instructions on its Web site. Does Google's effort feel a little like monopolistic rent seeking? Should the government step in, or is this just competition between giants?

Answers to the Checkpoint questions can be found at the end of this chapter.

Monopoly Market Issues

When firms have some monopoly power, they will try to charge different customers different prices. This is called **price discrimination** and it is used to increase their profits. When monopolies must exist, there are policies that can be enacted to mitigate their power. We look at these issues in this section.

Price discrimination: Charging different consumer groups different prices for the same product.

Price Discrimination

When firms with monopoly power price discriminate, they charge different consumers different prices for the same product. For example, senior citizens might pay less for a movie ticket than you do. Remember, unlike monopolies, competitive firms cannot price discriminate because they get their prices from the market (they are price takers). Several conditions are required for successful price discrimination.

- Sellers must have some monopoly (or market) power, or some control over price.
- Sellers must be able to separate the market into different consumer groups based on their elasticities of demand.
- Sellers must be able to prevent arbitrage; that is, it must be impossible or prohibitively expensive for low-price buyers to resell to higher-price buyers.

There are three major types of price discrimination. The first is known as perfect, or first-degree, price discrimination. It involves charging each customer the *maximum price* each is willing to pay. Second-degree price discrimination involves charging different customers different prices based on the *quantities* of the product they purchase. Firms may charge a high price for initial purchases, for instance, and then reduce the price after customers have bought a certain quantity.

The final and most common form of price discrimination is third-degree price discrimination. This occurs when firms *charge different groups of people different prices*. This is an everyday occurrence with airline, bus, and theater tickets.

Perfect Price Discrimination

When perfect price discrimination can be employed, a firm will charge each customer the maximum price each is willing to pay. This type of price discrimination is perhaps best exemplified by the flea market, where sellers and buyers haggle over the price of each product. Figure 7 portrays such a scenario. Every point on the demand curve represents a price. The first few customers—those who value the product most—are charged a high price. The next customers are charged slightly lower prices, the Q_Mth customer is charged P_M (point a), and so on, until the last unit is sold to the Q_Cth customer for P_C (point b). As a result, a perfectly discriminating monopolist earns profits equal to the shaded area $P_C P_T b$.

Figure 7 shows why firms would want to price discriminate. Typical monopoly profits in this case, assuming the monopolist sells Q_M units at price P_M, would be the rectangle area $P_C P_M ac$ (the lighter shaded area). This area is considerably smaller than profit triangle $P_C P_T b$, earned by the perfectly price discriminating monopolist. That is why price discrimination exists—it is profitable. Note also that the *last* unit of the product

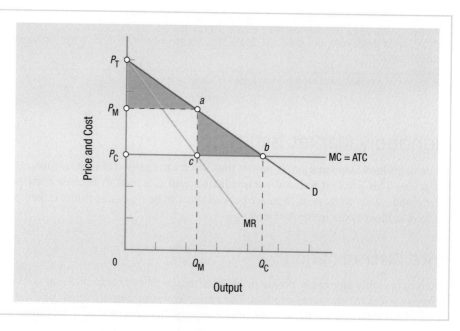

FIGURE 7—Perfect Price Discrimination

With perfect price discrimination, firms charge each customer the maximum price each is willing to pay. Thus, every point on the demand curve in this figure represents a price. The first few customers—those who value the product most—are charged a high price. The next customers are charged a slightly lower price, and so on, until the last unit is sold for P_C (point b). As a result, a perfectly discriminating monopolist earns profits represented by the shaded area $P_C P_T b$. This is considerably more profit than the monopolist would earn by selling Q_M units at price P_M, represented by area $P_C P_M ac$.

sold by this monopolist is priced at P_C, the competitive price. In this limited sense, then, the monopolist who can perfectly price discriminate is as efficient as a competitive firm. Notice that perfectly price discriminating monopolists manage to expropriate the entire consumer surplus.

Second-Degree Price Discrimination

Second-degree price discrimination involves charging consumers for different blocks of consumption. Producers of electric, gas, and water utilities often incorporate block pricing. You pay one rate for the first so many kilowatt-hours of electricity and a lower rate for more, and so on. This block pricing scheme is shown in Figure 8.

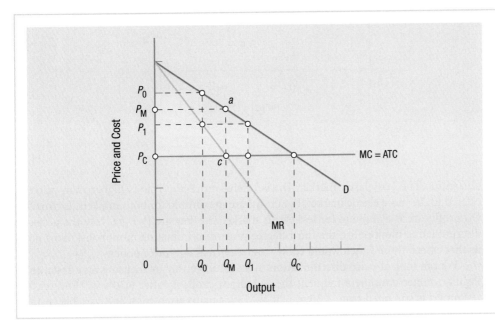

FIGURE 8—Second-Degree Price Discrimination

Second-degree price discrimination involves charging different customers different prices based on the quantities of the product they purchase. A nondiscriminating monopolist would earn economic profits equal to $P_C P_M ac$, but by charging three different prices—P_0, P_1, and P_C—profits increase, as shown by comparing the shaded area with area $P_C P_M ac$.

For the first Q_0 units of the product, consumers are charged P_0; between Q_0 and Q_1, the price falls to P_1; and after that, price is reduced to P_C. This results in profit to the firm equal to the shaded area. The shaded profit area for the discriminating monopolist is greater than that of the monopolist charging just one price P_M (area $P_C P_M ac$): Compare the shaded profit area that does not overlap with this area. The most common price discrimination scheme, however, is third-degree, in which groups of consumers are charged different prices.

Third-Degree Price Discrimination

Third-degree, or imperfect, price discrimination involves charging different groups of people different prices. An obvious example would be the various fares charged for airline flights. Business people have much lower elasticities of demand for flights than do vacationers, so airlines place all sorts of restrictions on their tickets to separate people into distinct categories. Purchasing a ticket several weeks in advance, for instance—which vacationers can usually do, but businesspeople may not be able to—often results in a significantly lower fare. Arbitrage (preventing low-cost buyers from selling to higher-price buyers) is prevented, meanwhile, by rules stipulating that passengers can only travel on tickets purchased in their name. Other examples of third-degree price discrimination include different ticket prices for children, adults, and seniors at movies; student discounts for many services; and even ladies night at clubs.

Third-degree price discrimination is illustrated in Figure 9 on the next page. The two demand curves, D_0 and D_1, represent two segments of a market with different demand

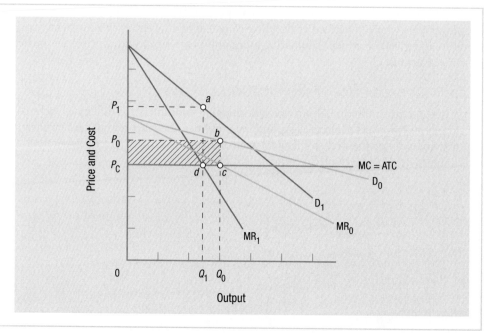

FIGURE 9—Third-Degree Price Discrimination

This figure illustrates third-degree price discrimination. The two demand curves, D_0 and D_1, represent two segments of a market with different demand elasticities. The less elastic market, D_1, is offered price P_1, which is higher than price P_0, offered to the more elastic market, D_0, thus maximizing the profits for both markets.

elasticities. The less elastic market, D_1, is offered price P_1. This is higher than price P_0 offered to the more elastic market, D_0. Profits are maximized for both markets. For market D_0, profits are $P_C P_0 bc$, and for less elastic market D_1, they are $P_C P_1 ad$. Like the perfectly discriminating monopolist, the third-degree price-discriminating monopolist earns profits that exceed those which would come from a normal one-price policy.

We can look at price discrimination in an intuitive way by focusing on a restaurant. Regular dinner customers frequent the restaurant probably after 6:30 P.M. However, the restaurant is still open from 4:30 to 6:30 P.M. and incurs fixed costs and variable costs (if workers start their shifts before the 6:30 rush). It is in the restaurant's interest to offer early bird specials, discounting dinners purchased before 6:30, as long as this policy attracts new customers and does not pull in too many of its later-appearing regular diners. In this way, the restaurant generates profits from two separate groups, while charging two separate prices. As long as the restaurant has some monopoly power—it can offer these two prices without driving its regular customers from higher-priced meals to lower-priced meals—it makes sense for it to act this way. Therefore, we can conclude that firms with some monopoly power will always try to price discriminate.

Regulating the Natural Monopolist

Natural monopoly: Large economies of scale mean that the minimum efficient scale of operations is roughly equal to market demand.

A **natural monopoly** exists when economies of scale are so large that the minimum efficient scale of operation is roughly equal to market demand. In this case, efficient production can only be accomplished if the industry lies in the hands of one firm—a monopolist. Public utilities and water departments are examples. How can policymakers prevent natural monopolists from abusing their positions of market dominance? There are various approaches to dealing with natural monopolies:

> First the firm can be publicly owned . . . , the expectation being that the mechanics of political direction and accountability will be sufficient to meet public interest goals. Secondly, the firm may remain in, or be transferred to, private ownership but be subjected to external constraints in the form of price and quantity regulation . . . thirdly, firms desiring to obtain a monopoly right may be forced to compete for it. . . . As part of their competitive bid, they are required to

stipulate proposed conditions of supply, relating especially to prices and quality; and those conditions then become terms of the license or franchise under which they exercise the monopoly right.[2]

A market representing a natural monopoly is shown in Figure 10. Notice that the average cost and marginal cost curves decline continually because of large economies of scale.

If the monopolist were a purely private firm, it would produce only output Q_M and sell this for price P_M (point *a*). Accordingly, the monopolist would earn economic or monopoly profits, and consumers would be harmed, receiving a lower output at a higher price. This is the major argument for regulation.

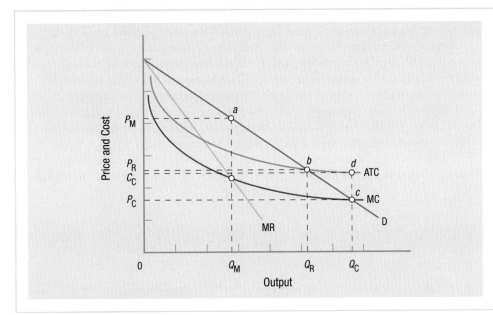

FIGURE 10—Regulating a Natural Monopoly

A natural monopoly exists when economies of scale are so large that the minimum efficient scale of operation is roughly equal to market demand. In this case, efficient production can only be accomplished if the industry lies in the hands of one firm—a monopolist. Yet, if the monopolist is a purely private firm, it will produce only output Q_M, selling it for price P_M (point *a*). This is the principal rationale for regulating natural monopolies to produce output Q_R for a price of P_R (point *b*).

Marginal Cost Pricing Rule

Ideally, regulators would like to invoke the P = MC rule of competitive markets and force the firm to sell Q_C units for a price of P_C. This is the **marginal cost pricing rule** and would be the optimal resource allocation solution. Yet, because price P_C is below the average cost of production for output Q_C, this would force the firm to sustain losses of *cd* per unit, ultimately driving it out of business. The public sector could subsidize the firm by an amount equal to area $P_C C_C dc$; this subsidy allows the firm to supply the socially optimal output at the socially optimal price, while earning a normal return. This approach has not been used often in the United States. However, Amtrak, with its history of heavy subsidies for maintaining rail service, may be the one major exception.

Marginal cost pricing rule: Regulators would prefer to have natural monopolists price where P = MC, but this would result in losses (long term) because ATC > MC. Thus, regulators often must use an average cost pricing rule.

Average Cost Pricing Rule

The more common approach to regulation in the United States has been to insist on an **average cost pricing rule.** Such a rule requires that the monopolist produce and sell output where price equals average total costs. This is illustrated by point *b* in Figure 10, where the demand curve intersects the ATC curve and the firm produces output Q_R and sells it for price P_R. The result is that the firm earns a normal return. Consumers do lose

Average cost pricing rule: Requires a regulated monopolist to produce and sell output where price equals average total costs. This permits the regulated monopolist to earn a normal return on investment over the long term and so remain in business.

[2] A. I. Ogus, *Regulation: Legal Form and Economic Theory* (Oxford: Oxford University Press), 1996, p. 5, cited in J. Lipczynski and J. Wilson, *Industrial Organization: An Analysis of Competitive Markets* (New York: Prentice Hall—Financial Times), 2001.

something, in that they must pay a higher price for less output than they would under idealized competitive conditions. Still, the normal profits keep the firm in business, and the losses to consumers are significantly less than if the firm were left unregulated.

Regulation in Practice

America has a long history of public utility regulation. For most of this history, regulation has been accepted as a lesser of two evils. Monopolists have long been viewed with distrust, but regulators have just as often been portrayed as incompetent and ineffectual, if not lapdogs of the industries they regulate.[3] This is probably unfair: Regulating a large enterprise always presents immense difficulties and tradeoffs.

For one thing, finding a point like *b* in Figure 10 is difficult in practice, given that estimating demand and cost curves is an inexact science, at best, and markets are always changing. In practice, regulators must often turn to *rate of return* or *price cap* regulation.

Rate of return regulation allows a firm to price its product in such a way that it can earn a normal return on capital invested. This leads to added regulations about the acceptable items that can be included in costs and capital expenditures. Can the country club memberships of top executives be counted as capital investments? Predictably, firms always want to include more expenses as legitimate business expenses, and regulators want to include fewer. Regulatory commissions and regulated firms often have large staffs to deal with such issues, and protracted court battles are not uncommon.

Alternatively, regulators can impose **price caps** on regulated firms, which place maximum limits on the prices firms can charge for products. These caps can be adjusted in

Rate of return regulation: Permits product pricing that allows the firm to earn a normal return on capital invested in the firm.

Price caps: Maximum price at which a regulated firm can sell its product. They are often flexible enough to allow for changing cost conditions.

Issue: Re-regulation Pressures

Deregulation began during the Carter administration in the 1980s and then in earnest with the election of Ronald Reagan. Over the years, trucking, airlines, telecommunications, and banking are among those industries that have seen regulations reduced. All of this was done with the aim of removing burdensome regulations from business, thereby stimulating economic activity and reducing prices to consumers.

Under airline regulation, 10 major air carriers controlled 90% of the market. The Civil Aeronautics Board regulated routes and set fares that guaranteed airlines a 12% return on flights that were on average 55% full. Deregulation intended to let new airlines enter and succeed (like Southwest) or fail (150 airlines have failed over the last 30 years). Advocates of deregulation saw success and failure as normal parts of competitive market dynamics.

When you look at freight rates, the price of airline tickets, and the cost of communications (both data and voice), deregulation

looks to be a winner. But all is not well. The mortgage and financial crunch that came to a head in late 2008 capped off an already growing movement to re-regulate utilities, Internet services, student loans, and union organizing rules.

The recent bailout of the financial sector and the political success of Democrats sets the stage for a growing host of new regulations in finance, housing, energy, environmental affairs, and health care.

The re-regulate–deregulate–re-regulate pendulum seems to swing every several decades. The Great Depression ushered in a host of new agencies that covered almost all major industries. This was followed up in the 1960s and 1970s with new bureaucracies to regulate education, the environment, and many other industries. Ronald Reagan's election was partly based on "getting government off our backs," and over the last 30 years market discipline has substituted for government control. The recent financial and credit crunch has resulted in a growing

Stockbyte/Getty Images

chorus for re-regulation and we can expect to see just that. One ironic note, however, is the general consensus to use a market-based emissions trading system (markets) rather than regulation to cap our greenhouse gas emissions. The fight over markets versus government has been around since the country's inception and will continue.

Source: Micheline Maynard, "Did Ending Regulation Help Flyers?," *New York Times*, April 17, 2008, p. C1.

---

[3] See George Stigler, "The Theory of Economic Regulation," *Bell Journal of Economics,* 1971, pp. 3–21.

response to changing cost conditions, including changes in labor costs, productivity, technology, and raw material prices. When a large part of a regulated firm's output is not self-produced but purchased on the open market, price caps can have disastrous results. This was seen in the California energy market, when wholesale prices for energy went through the roof, but price caps prevented private utilities from raising the retail price of electricity; several firms had to file for bankruptcy.

In sum, though regulation imposes costs on the market, these costs are less than the costs of private monopolies. Today, however, the pace of technological change is so rapid that regulation has lost some of its earlier luster and is not used as often. Rather than regulate the few natural monopolies that do arise, government has sought to prevent monopolies and monopolistic practices from arising at all—a topic we cover in the next section.

■ CHECKPOINT

MONOPOLY MARKET ISSUES

- Firms with monopoly power price discriminate to increase profits.

- To price discriminate, firms must have some control over price and must be able to separate the market into different consumer groups based on their elasticity of demand, and sellers must be able to prevent arbitrage.

- With perfect price discrimination the firm can charge each customer a different price and expropriate the entire consumer surplus for itself.

- Second-degree price discrimination involves charging customers different prices for different quantities of the product.

- Third-degree price discrimination (the most common) involves charging different groups of people different prices.

- Regulating monopolies may involve a marginal cost pricing rule (have the monopolist set price equal to marginal cost) or an average cost rule (have the monopolist set price equal to average total cost).

- In practice, regulation often involves setting an acceptable rate of return on capital or setting price caps on charges.

QUESTIONS: Researchers at Yale University and the University of California, Berkeley found that minorities and women pay about $500 more on average for a car than white men when bargaining directly with car dealers. However, when minorities and women used Internet services such as Autobytel.com to purchase a car, the price discrimination disappeared. Is this price discrimination the same as that discussed in this section? Why or why not?

Answers to the Checkpoint questions can be found at the end of this chapter.

Antitrust Policy

Like all antitrust cases, this one must make economic sense.
                              —UNITED STATES V. SYUFY ENTERPRISES

Competition is the market structure that offers consumers the greatest product selection at the lowest prices. Monopolies and firms with substantial monopoly power have the potential to restrict output and increase prices, resulting in significant allocative inefficiencies. The economic model of monopoly forms the basis for the bulk of **antitrust law,** the goal of which is to preserve competition and prevent monopolies and monopoly power from arising.

Antitrust cases can be filed by the Antitrust Division of the Department of Justice, the Federal Trade Commission (FTC), states' attorneys general, or lawyers for private plaintiffs. Currently, there is debate about the extent of efficiency losses that stem from monopoly

Antitrust law: Laws designed to maintain competition and prevent monopolies from developing.

power, and how often antitrust action is needed.[4] Even so, Americans have a visceral sense that monopolies are bad, and historically, antitrust policy has targeted monopolies as threats to economic efficiency.

Brief History of Antitrust Policy

The American economy began to change dramatically after the Civil War. Many people left the farm to seek factory jobs in the cities, and the western territories were opened up as rail lines joined them to the rest of the country. Communications expanded along with transportation, the telephone replacing the telegraph. Markets grew from local to regional in size, and many firms dramatically expanded their size. Unfettered competition led many large firms to engage in brutal practices meant to drive competitors from the market. The largest firms established trusts, which brought many firms under one organizational structure that could set price and output levels, extract concessions from railroads, and act as we would expect monopolies to act. By the end of the century, trusts had become so powerful—and so hated—that Congress passed the first antitrust act, the Sherman Act, in 1890. Antitrust laws and policies, thus, had their origins in trust-busting activity.

Most of the legislators who voted for antitrust laws in the late 1800s and early 1900s were more concerned with equitably distributing income and wealth, and the health of small businesses, than with competition and allocative efficiency. The massive accumulations of wealth by such "robber barons" as John D. Rockefeller (Standard Oil) and Jay Gould (railroads and stock manipulation) sparked resentment and fear. Nobel Prize laureate George Stigler has argued, however, that the economists of the day had little enthusiasm for antitrust policy, viewing all limits placed on business as stifling free enterprise. Today, most economists agree that some antitrust legislation is needed, but that its primary role should be to prevent the allocative inefficiency associated with monopoly behavior.

The Major Antitrust Laws

Several major statutes form the core of the country's antitrust laws. The most important provisions of these laws (as amended) are described in the following sections.

The Sherman Act (1890)

> **Section 1:** *Every contract, combination in the form of trust or otherwise, or conspiracy, in restraint of trade or commerce among the several states, or with foreign nations, is hereby declared to be illegal.*
>
> **Section 2:** *Every person who shall monopolize, or attempt to monopolize, or combine or conspire with any other person or persons, to monopolize any part of the trade or commerce among the several states, or with foreign nations, shall be deemed guilty of a felony.*

Conviction in either section is a felony and carries a fine of up to $10,000,000 for corporations and $350,000 for individuals, and/or a prison sentence of up to 3 years. Section 1 focuses on the "restraint of trade," whereas Section 2 targets "monopolization" and the "attempt to monopolize." Congress purposefully left these terms undefined, thus requiring the courts to flesh them out.

The Clayton Act (1914)

> **Section 2:** *It shall be unlawful for any person engaged in commerce . . . to discriminate in price between different purchasers of commodities of like grade and quality . . . where the effect of such discrimination may be substantially to lessen competition or tend to create a monopoly in any line of commerce, or to injure, destroy, or prevent competition.*

---

[4] See Richard A. Posner, *Antitrust Law,* 2d ed. (Chicago: University of Chicago Press), 2001.

Nobel Prize

George Stigler

Few modern economists have broken ground in so many different areas as George Stigler, described by some admirers as the "ultimate empirical economist." His 1982 Nobel Prize cited seminal work in industrial structure, the functioning of markets, and the causes and effects of public regulation.

Born in 1911 in the Seattle suburb of Renton, Washington, Stigler attended graduate school at the University of Chicago, a center of great intellectual ferment during the late 1930s, with fellow students and Nobel Prize winners Milton Friedman and Paul Samuelson. Professors like Frank Knight and Henry Simons encouraged what he would later describe as "an irreverence toward prevailing ideas bordering on congenital skepticism." Stigler was a professor at the University of Chicago from 1958 until his death in 1991.

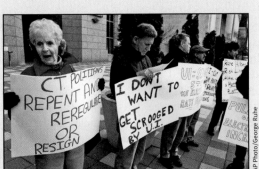

Exploring the relationship between size and efficiency led him to the "Darwinian" conclusion that by observing competition in an industry, he could determine the most efficient sizes for firms, a method he called "the survivor technique." In the 1960s, Stigler studied the impacts of government regulation on the economy, arriving at negative conclusions about its potential value to consumers. He later turned to the causes of regulation, observing that government interventions were often designed to optimize market conditions for producers instead of protecting the public interest. This work opened up a new field known as "regulation economics" and kindled greater interest in the relationship between law and economics.

Stigler considered his work on information theory his greatest contribution to economics. Conventional wisdom suggested that prices for homogeneous industries should be uniform, but in the real world, prices often varied. His research suggested that the variation could be explained by the costs of gathering and diffusing information about goods and prices. The Internet was supposed to bring a convergence of prices for nearly every product because the Internet's low information costs and competition would force firms to quickly meet the lowest seller's price. The fact that there are still widely varying prices for many products suggests that Stigler's insights are still important.

Section 3: *It shall be unlawful for any person engaged in commerce [to] make a sale or contract for sale of goods . . . or other commodities . . . on the condition . . . that the lessee or purchaser thereof shall not use or deal in the goods . . . or other commodities of a competitor or competitors of the seller, where the effect of such lease, sale or contract . . . may be to substantially lessen competition or tend to create a monopoly in any line of commerce.*

Section 7: *That no corporation engaged in commerce shall acquire, directly or indirectly, the whole or any part of the stock or other share capital and no corporation subject to the jurisdiction of the Federal Trade Commission shall acquire the whole or any part of the assets of another corporation engaged also in commerce, where in any line of commerce in any section of the country, the effect of such acquisition may be substantially to lessen competition, or tend to create a monopoly.*

The act goes on to forbid "tying contracts," agreements whereby the sale of one product is contingent upon the purchase of another product. The act further makes it illegal to acquire a competing company's stock and have interlocking directorates, the directors of one company sitting on the boards of competing companies. These practices are deemed illegal if they substantially lessen competition or tend to create a monopoly.

The Federal Trade Commission Act (1914)

> ***Section 5.(a)(1):*** *Unfair methods of competition in or affecting commerce, and unfair or deceptive acts or practices in or affecting commerce, are hereby declared unlawful.*

This act established an independent regulatory body, the Federal Trade Commission (FTC), and gave it the power to enforce the Clayton Act and the Robinson-Patman Act (discussed in the next section). Amended in 1938 by the Wheeler-Lea Amendments to add "unfair or deceptive acts or practices," this FTC Act is the centerpiece of federal consumer protection. The Supreme Court has given the FTC the power to enforce antitrust laws, except the Sherman Act.

Other Antitrust Acts

The Robinson-Patman Act amended the Clayton Act in 1936 to prohibit price discrimination. Passed in the middle of the Depression, this Act was designed to protect mom and pop stores from the growing menace of chain stores and supermarkets. Chain stores have tremendous buying and bargaining power with manufacturers. This bargaining power translates into price discounts that chains can pass on to their customers, putting small businesses at a disadvantage. This same logic is often used today to prevent a Wal-Mart from opening stores in some towns. Today, the federal government rarely enforces these provisions, viewing them as outdated.

The 1950 Celler-Kefauver Antimerger Act closed a merger loophole in the Clayton Act. The original Clayton Act intended to forbid holding companies, and thus it outlawed one company from holding the stock of its competitors. But the Clayton Act did not prohibit anticompetitive mergers through asset acquisition. The Celler-Kefauver Act closed this loophole, and set up elaborate premerger notification requirements for mergers exceeding a certain size.

The intensity of antitrust enforcement has varied with presidential administrations and courts over the past century. Early on the focus was on monopolies and on attempts to monopolize, with actions brought against Standard Oil, American Tobacco, and Alcoa (Aluminum Company of America). Attention then turned to mergers and prenotification issues discussed earlier. More recently, antitrust enforcement has been concentrated on price fixing—conspiracies by firms to agree on industry prices to suppress or eliminate competition. In 2008 the U.S. Justice Department levied fines of $1.27 billion against a dozen airlines, including Air France-KLM, Cathay Pacific, SAS Scandinavian Airlines, British Airways, and Qantas, for fixing cargo rates for international air shipments to and from the United States. To date, this is the largest fine levied against an industry for price fixing.

Although price-fixing cases were of particular interest to the Bush administration, it is merger policy developed in the 1950s that has really stood the test of time. Economists and judges generally agree that the reason for antitrust enforcement is to prevent the inefficiencies associated with significant monopoly power. Premerger notification for approval or challenge by the Justice Department is designed to prevent mergers that have a reasonable likelihood of creating monopoly power. However, the first problem facing the enforcement community involves defining monopoly power. This entails defining the relevant product market and then agreeing on a proper measuring device of monopoly power.

Defining the Relevant Market and Monopoly Power

We have seen that, as an industry moves from competition to monopoly, pricing power rises from zero to total. One of the challenges economists have faced is developing one measure that accurately reflects market power or concentration for all these market structures.

Industries that become more concentrated increase the losses to society. Therefore, any measure of concentration should accurately reflect the ability of firms to increase prices above that point which would prevail under competitive conditions. Such an index would help the Justice Department, for instance, determine when to bring a Sherman Act case against a firm for monopolizing or attempting to monopolize. It could further be used to determine whether two firms should be permitted to merge. Coming up with such a number requires, first, that we define the relevant market, and then that we compute an index number for this market.

Defining the Market

To measure market power and the concentration of a market, we need to determine the limits of the market, geographically and as defined by the product itself.

Some markets can be severely limited geographically, such as concrete, with its extremely high transport costs, and dry cleaning, limited by the unwillingness of consumers to travel far for this service. Other markets are national in scope, like airlines, breakfast cereals, and electronics. Still others extend beyond the borders of a country, with the forces of global competition increasingly reducing domestic market power.

Economists have been unable to reduce the empirical definition of a relevant market to a simple rule. Nearly 50 years ago, George Stigler suggested that "all products or enterprises with large long-run cross-elasticities of supply or demand should be combined into a single industry."[5] This would mean that an industry or market should be regarded as containing those products that are ready substitutes for the main product in the long run. Stigler's suggestion by no means makes delineating a relevant market neat and easy, but at least it gives economists something to work with.

Concentration Ratios

The most widely used measure of industry concentration is the **concentration ratio.** The n-firm concentration ratio is the share of industry sales accounted for by the industry's n largest firms. Typically, four- and eight-firm concentration ratios (CR-4 and CR-8) are reported.

> **Concentration ratio:** The share of industry shipments or sales accounted for by the top four or eight firms.

Though useful in giving a quick snapshot of an industry, concentration ratios express only one piece of the market power distribution picture: the market share enjoyed by the industry's four or eight largest firms. Yet, consider the following two 4-firm concentration ratios. In the first industry, the four largest firms have market shares equal to 65, 10, 5, and 5. This means the concentration ratio is 85; that is, the top four firms control 85% of industry sales. The second industry has market shares equal to 25, 20, 20, 20. This industry's concentration ratio also equals 85. But do the two industries exhibit the same level of monopoly power? Hardly! The second industry, whose top four firms are roughly equal in size, would be expected to be more competitive than the first, where 65% of the market is controlled by one firm.

Without more information about each industry, concentration ratios are not overly informative, except to point out extreme contrasts. If one industry's four-firm concentration ratio is 85, for instance, and another's is 15, the first industry has considerably more monopoly power than the second.

Economists and antitrust enforcers, however, need finer distinctions than concentration ratios permit. For this reason, the profession has developed the Herfindahl-Hirshman index.

Herfindahl-Hirshman Index

The **Herfindahl-Hirshman index (HHI)** is the principal measure of concentration used by the Justice Department to evaluate mergers and judge monopoly power. The HHI is defined by the equation:

> **Herfindahl-Hirshman index (HHI):** A way of measuring industry concentration, equal to the sum of the squares of market shares for all firms in the industry.

$$HHI = (S_1)^2 + (S_2)^2 + (S_3)^2 + \ldots + (S_n)^2,$$

---

[5] George J. Stigler, "Introduction," in National Bureau of Economic Research, *Business Concentration and Price Policy* (Princeton, NJ: Princeton University Press), 1955, p. 4.

where $S_1, S_2, \ldots S_n$ are the percentage market shares of each firm in the industry. Thus, the HHI is the sum of the squares of each market share. In a five-firm industry, for instance, in which each firm enjoys a 20% market share, the HHI is

$$HHI = 20^2 + 20^2 + 20^2 + 20^2 + 20^2$$
$$= 400 + 400 + 400 + 400 + 400$$
$$= 2,000$$

The HHI ranges from roughly zero (a huge number of small firms) to 10,000 (a one-firm monopoly: $100^2 = 10,000$). By squaring market shares, the HHI gives greater weight to those firms with large market shares. Thus, a five-firm industry with market shares equal to 65, 15, 10, 5, 5 would have an HHI equal to

$$HHI = 65^2 + 15^2 + 10^2 + 5^2 + 5^2$$
$$= 4,225 + 225 + 100 + 25 + 25$$
$$= 4,600$$

The HHI is consistent with our intuitive notion of market power. It seems clear that an industry with several competitors of roughly equal size will be more competitive than an industry in which one firm controls a substantial share of the market.

Applying the HHI

In 1976, Congress passed the Hart-Scott-Rodino Act. This Act requires prenotification of large proposed mergers to the FTC and the antitrust division of the Justice Department. Prenotification gives federal agencies a chance to review proposed mergers for anticompetitive impacts. This approach prevents some mergers from taking place that would ultimately have to be challenged by Sherman Act litigation, a far more costly alternative for the government and for the firms involved.

During the prenotification review, the Justice Department or FTC can approve the proposed merger or else negotiate a settlement that introduces restrictions designed to reduce anticompetitive outcomes. Sometimes these agreements involve complex rules and reporting requirements that amount to government regulation. If no agreement is reached, the agencies can challenge the merger in court. When agreements cannot be reached, the merger is usually called off.

The Justice Department and FTC in 1992 issued merger guidelines based on the HHI. These guidelines classify industries as follows:

- HHI < 1,000: Industry is unconcentrated.
- 1,000 < HHI < 1,800: Industry is moderately concentrated.
- HHI > 1,800: Industry is highly concentrated.

Mergers where the resulting HHI is below 1,000 will often be approved. Mergers with postmerger HHIs between 1,000 and 1,800 will be closely evaluated; they are often challenged if the proposed merger raises the HHI by 100 points or more. When the HHI for the industry exceeds 1,800, a postmerger rise in the HHI of 50 points is enough to spark a challenge.

These guidelines have worked well, giving businesses a good idea of when the government will challenge mergers. Most mergers are rapidly approved; the remainder often require only minor adjustments or more information to satisfy government agencies. In the end, only a few proposed mergers are seriously challenged. Clearly, most firms that want to merge will ensure their companies and industries fit in the specified guidelines.

Contestable Markets

Contestable markets: Markets that look monopolistic but where entry costs are so low that the sheer threat of entry keeps prices low.

Sometimes what looks like a monopolist does not act like a monopolist. Markets that are contestable fit this description. **Contestable markets** are those markets with entry costs so low that the sheer threat of entry keeps prices in contestable markets low. Potential competition constrains firm behavior. For example, Microsoft might charge more for its latest version of Windows if Linux was not nipping at its heels.

Many software firms argue, however, that new software innovations are stifled because once a new product has been released, Microsoft can simply clone the product and package it with Windows for free, thus rendering investment in new products unprofitable for smaller companies. It is far easier and cheaper to copy and enhance a software product than to conceive of the idea and bring it to market in the first place. A significant part of the arguments in the original Microsoft legal case revolved around just this issue. Still, the relative ease with which new operating systems can be developed to challenge Windows—witness Linux, Mac OS X, Unix—probably keeps Microsoft from significantly overcharging for Windows.

The Future of Antitrust Policy

American antitrust legislation grew out of economic concentration and the resulting predatory behavior over a century ago. The laws passed to nullify these abuses have resulted in some fascinating legal cases, but in the end, antitrust legislation is rooted in the basic economics and market structure analysis discussed in the last two chapters.

As the United States transitioned from an agrarian to an industrial economy, public policy changed. As our economy today moves from its domestic manufacturing roots to more of a global information and service base, public policy again must adapt.

The Microsoft case was the first real attempt to apply the old antitrust rules to the newly emerging circumstances of the "new economy." The government met with some success in this case, but mostly failure.

The new economy differs from the old economy in many ways. The old economy was grounded in manufacturing and distributing physical goods such as steel, automobiles, appliances, and shoes. These old economy industries enjoyed economies of scale in production, often requiring huge capital requirements and modest rates of innovation.

New economy industries turn these requirements on their heads. Such industries as software, telecommunications infrastructure, and e-commerce operate with modest capital, extremely high rates of innovation, easy entry and exit, and economies of scale in consumption known as **network externalities.**

One phone or Internet connection is worthless; it cannot be used to communicate with anyone. As more people become connected to the network, however, the network becomes more valuable—hence, the term "network externalities." Every firm therefore has a tremendous interest in seeing its innovation adopted as the industry standard, providing the firm with a monopoly in that technology. Witness the recent format war over high-definition optical disc standards eventually won by Blu-ray technology when Sony decided to include a Blu-ray player in its PlayStation video console.

Consumers and the society as a whole may benefit from monopoly standards—how could we exchange computer files if we all used different word-processing programs? But what, then, will keep temporary monopolists from charging excessive prices? To some degree, the answer lies in the contestability of the industry (low capital requirements, easy entry and exit, and rapid innovation). The Linux challenge to Microsoft Windows came from a university student who wrote this operating system as a school project. Often, it is low prices (free, in the case of Linux) that extend markets and create standards. Low prices mean more users, and more users lead to the creation of standards.

Now the Internet itself is presenting a challenge to the dominance of Microsoft Windows and Office. Google introduced its "Chrome" browser, which is designed to run Office-type programs over the Web without loading them physically on each computer. This "cloud" computing has led to inexpensive netbook computers intended to take advantage of Web computing without hard drives for storage. This approach is changing the way software is delivered and used.

Much of what new economy firms produce is intellectual property. In large measure, it is computer code of one form or another. Most of the costs to produce the programs are fixed, already sunk once the product is completed. To produce and distribute the product

Network externalities: Markets in which the network becomes more valuable as more people are connected to the network.

Issue: Oil and Gas—The Rise of Community Monopolies

When we think of monopoly power, we typically think of a large company selling an important product without reasonable substitutes. Rarely would we consider a community of homeowners as a single *seller* or a monopolist. However, rising commodity prices (especially oil and natural gas) in 2008 caused communities of homeowners to band together to bargain with natural gas companies for the drilling rights to their land.

By banding together and presenting a monopoly to the drilling companies, they were able to offer a larger tract of land as well as their use of social pressure to help the companies bring holdouts to the table. Higher gas prices and

new drilling techniques allow companies to drill without disturbing the character of neighborhoods, making areas (suburbs) that were previously undrillable now quite profitable.

By forming these voluntary neighborhood bargaining groups (some as large as 7,000 homeowners), communities have been able to increase their offers from $1,000 to $3,000 an acre with a small (5%) royalty override to more than $20,000 an acre and 25% royalty rates. These neighborhood groups create a bargaining situation where the homeowners have monopoly power and the

power of the oil companies is limited, resulting in a more favorable contract for homeowners.

Source: Ben Casselman, "Homeowners Unite, Get More for Drilling Rights," *Wall Street Journal*, June 6, 2008, p. A4.

costs only a fraction of the product's value; if the Internet is used, distribution costs can approach zero. This means markups and profits are high, which creates a strong incentive to clone successful products. Monopolies, therefore, tend to be transitory in the new economy. The travails of Lotus 123, WordPerfect, Borland, and Netscape all testify to the vulnerability of temporary monopolists in the software industry. All were industry leaders at one point, only to be displaced by some new kid on the block.

Antitrust laws and policy need to be adjusted to new market realities. In our global information and service economy, many of the old rules are irrelevant. One federal judge and economist, Richard Posner, argues that we should repeal all the old antitrust laws, chiefly because of the "gross redundancy of their manifold provisions." He suggests these laws be replaced with a simple statute that prohibits "unreasonably anti-competitive practices."[6]

When a firm's market share approaches monopoly levels, turning to antitrust laws is the obvious response. This and the last chapter looked at the polar opposites of market structures, competition and monopoly. The next chapter looks at the market structures in the middle and also looks at a more modern approach to analyzing firm behavior, game theory.

■ CHECKPOINT

ANTITRUST POLICY

- The Sherman Act (1890) prohibited monopolization and attempts to monopolize.

- The Clayton Act (1914) prohibited price discrimination that lessened competition, prohibited tie-in sales, and prohibited corporate directors from serving on competing boards if this would lessen competition.

- The Federal Trade Commission Act (1914) prohibited unfair or deceptive business practices and established the Federal Trade Commission.

- Defining the relevant market is often difficult, but a focus on cross elasticity of demand is useful.

---

[6] Richard A. Posner, *Antitrust Law,* 2nd ed. (Chicago: University of Chicago Press), 2001, p. 260.

- Concentration ratios measure market concentration by looking at the share of industry sales accounted for by the top n firms.

- The Herfindahl-Hirshman index (HHI) measures concentration by computing the sum of the squares of market shares for all firms in the industry.

- The Justice Department uses the HHI to set premerger guidelines.

- Contestable markets are markets with low entry costs so that the potential threat of entry keeps prices low.

QUESTION: Assume the following table represents the sales figures for the eight largest firms in the auto industry in the United States:

Company	Sales (billions of dollars)
General Motors	2.063
Toyota	1.77
Ford	1.616
Honda	1.151
Chrysler	0.931
Nissan	0.77
Hyundai	0.435
Mazda	0.208
Total	**8.944**

a. Compute the four-firm concentration ratio for the industry.
b. Compute the HHI for the industry.
c. Assuming the industry is represented by these 8 firms, if Toyota and Ford wanted to merge, and you were the head of the Justice Department, would you permit the merger? Why or why not? How about if Hyundai and Mazda wanted to merge?

Answers to the Checkpoint questions can be found at the end of this chapter.

Key Concepts

Monopoly, p. 207
Monopoly power, p. 208
Economies of scale, p. 208
Rent seeking, p. 213
X-inefficiency, p. 214
Price discrimination, p. 215
Natural monopoly, p. 218
Marginal cost pricing rule, p. 219

Average cost pricing rule, p. 219
Rate of return regulation, p. 220
Price caps, p. 220
Antitrust law, p. 221
Concentration ratio, p. 225
Herfindahl-Hirshman index (HHI), p. 225
Contestable markets, p. 226
Network externalities, p. 227

Chapter Summary

Monopoly Markets

A firm can *be* a monopoly; it can *have* monopoly power. For economists, a monopoly is defined by three key characteristics. First, the market has just one seller, thus the monopolistic firm *is* the industry. Second, no close substitutes exist for the monopolist's product, so consumers cannot easily substitute other products for the product sold by the monopolist. Third, significant barriers to entry keep other firms from entering the industry. This means the monopolist faces no competition, even in the long run.

Monopoly power is the degree to which a firm can control the price of its product by adjusting output. Competitive firms are price takers, meaning that they have no monopoly power; the prices for their products are determined by competitive markets. Monopolists, in contrast, are price makers. They enjoy considerable monopoly power and much freedom in deciding what to charge for their products.

The key to monopoly power is significant barriers to entry, which can take several forms. The economies of scale in an industry can be so large that demand will support only one firm. If a firm owns or has control over an important input into the production process, that firm can keep potential rivals out of the market.

Some barriers to market entry extend from the power of government. A government franchise grants a firm permission to provide specific goods or services while prohibiting others from doing so. Patents are extended to firms and individuals that invent new products and processes. For a limited period, the patent holder is legally protected from competition in the production of the patented product. Copyrights give firms or individuals the exclusive right to intellectual products for a long period.

Because the monopolist constitutes the entire industry, it faces a downward sloping demand curve. Product price is determined in a monopoly by how much the monopolist wishes to produce. This contrasts with the competitive firm, which can sell all it wishes, but only at the market determined price.

Like the competitive firm, the monopolist maximizes its profit at output where MR = MC. Because of the monopolist's downward sloping demand curve, however, marginal revenue does not equal price at this point; rather, MR < P. To determine the monopolist's profit maximizing price, extend a vertical line through the point where MR = MC to the demand curve; where this line intersects the demand curve determines the price to be found on the vertical axis. The monopolist's profit equals the difference between this price and average total costs, multiplied by the number of units sold.

Being a monopoly does not guarantee economic profits. If a monopolist's profit maximizing price is lower than average total costs, it will suffer a loss. As long as price exceeds average variable costs, the monopolist will minimize its losses in the short run by continuing to produce. But if price should fall below average variable costs, the monopolist will minimize its losses (equal to its fixed costs) by shutting down. If these losses persist, the monopolist will exit the industry in the long run.

Monopoly output is lower and monopoly price is higher, compared to competitive markets. As a result, monopolies earn economic profits at the expense of consumers: monopoly reduces consumer surplus. The loss to society from monopoly output and pricing is known as deadweight loss, or welfare loss.

To maintain their advantageous position, monopolists often engage in rent-seeking behavior. Rent seeking represents an added loss to society from monopoly because it shifts resources from one group to another without producing a useful good or service.

Some economists argue that monopolies do not have to operate efficiently because they are protected from competitive pressures. This is known as x-inefficiency.

Monopoly Market Issues

When firms with monopoly power price discriminate, they charge different consumers different prices for the same product. The goal is to maximize profits by charging each customer as much as each is willing to pay. Several conditions are required for successful price discrimination: sellers must have some monopoly power, sellers must be able to separate the market into different consumer groups based on their elasticities of demand, and sellers must be able to prevent arbitrage—that is, it must be impossible or prohibitively expensive for low-price buyers to resell to higher-price buyers.

There are three major types of price discrimination. First-degree price discrimination involves charging each customer the maximum price each is willing to pay. Second-degree price discrimination involves charging different customers different prices based on the quantities of the product they purchase. The most common form of price discrimination is third-degree price discrimination: charging different groups of people different prices.

A natural monopoly exists when economies of scale are so large that the minimum efficient scale of operation is roughly equal to market demand. In such cases, policy-makers employ a variety of measures to prevent natural monopolists from abusing their positions of market dominance.

Antitrust Policy

Since 1890, the U.S. Congress has passed a series of major statutes that form the core of the country's antitrust laws. These include the Sherman Act (1890), the Clayton Act (1914), the Federal Trade Commission Act (1914), the Robinson-Patman Act (1936), and the Celler-Kefauver Antimerger Act (1950).

The early antitrust laws were passed with the intention of promoting an equitable distribution of wealth and protecting small businesses against predatory monopolies. The intensity of antitrust enforcement has varied with presidential administrations and courts over the past century. There is general agreement among economists and judges, however, that some antitrust regulation is needed, and that its basic purpose is to prevent the inefficiencies associated with significant monopoly power.

Economists have developed several means of measuring market concentration. The n-firm concentration ratio reports the share of industry sales accounted for by the n largest firms. The Herfindahl-Hirshman index (HHI) is the principal measure of concentration used by the Justice Department to evaluate mergers and judge monopoly power.

Contestable markets are those with entry costs so low that firms can enter or leave the industry rapidly. If a firm is earning economic profits, new firms will enter the market until returns have been driven back down to normal levels. The sheer threat of entry, therefore, keeps prices in contestable markets low, even if the market is now a monopoly.

Questions and Problems

Check Your Understanding

1. Are McDonald's and Starbucks monopolies? Why or why not?
2. Explain why MR < P for the monopolist, but MR = P for competitive firms.
3. What do economists mean when they call monopolies inefficient? What is the deadweight loss of monopoly?

Apply the Concepts

4. Synthetic diamonds are getting better, and starting to give De Beers a lot of competition in the diamond market. What will be De Beers' response?
5. How important is the existence of a significant barrier to entry to maintaining a monopoly? What would be the result if a monopoly market could easily be entered? Why might a monopoly in a high-tech field such as computers, the Internet, and consumer electronics be rather short-lived?
6. The monopoly model we discussed in this chapter suggests that monopolies have little incentive to innovate. In contrast, firms in competitive markets need to keep innovating to continue to exist. Some economists have suggested that if barriers to entry are not large, this is sufficient to keep a monopolist innovating to maintain its monopoly. Does the computer technology industry seem to fit this argument?
7. If cable television services were completely deregulated today, what would happen to the monthly charges?
8. My dentist recently recommended that I have a tooth replaced with a titanium pin inserted in my jaw and capped with a crown. I went to an oral surgeon to have the tooth removed and the pin inserted. The bill for the procedure was $300 to remove

the tooth and $1,500 to insert the titanium pin. Removing the tooth and inserting the pin each took roughly the same amount of time. Since the cost of the pin is negligible and both parts of the procedure took the same time why would the oral surgeon charge 5 times as much to set the pin as to pull the tooth? (Hint: Monopoly power and level of competition underlies the answer.)

In the News

9. According to Peter Marsh (*Financial Times,* September 10, 2005) Swatch, the Swiss watchmaker famous for its inexpensive watches, announced in 2005 that it will no longer supply high-end mechanical movements (parts) to upscale manufacturers. Swatch manufactures and sells roughly 75% of the mechanical movements to such watchmakers as Lacroix, Nardin, and Breitling and has its own brands Omega, Longines, and Breguet. The change did not take place until 2010, but it sent many manufacturers scrambling to replace Swatch as a supplier. Swatch was only earning $3 million from the sale of movements to competitors, who turned them into watches worth several billions of dollars. One manufacturer suggested that "Swatch's decision was driven by its desire to reduce competition." Does this seem correct? Why or why not?

10. In 2006, Maryland passed a law requiring that any company with 10,000 or more employees must spend 8% of its payroll on health care, or must remit the difference to the state. Wal-Mart, the only employer approaching that employment level, was the target of the legislation. George Will's column (*Rocky Mountain News,* January 22, 2006) about this development said, "Maryland's grasping for Wal-Mart's revenues opens a new chapter in the degeneracy of state governments that are eager to spend more money than they have the nerve to collect straightforwardly in taxes. Fortunately, as labor unions and allied rent-seekers in 30 or so other states contemplate mimicking Maryland, Wal-Mart can contemplate an advantage of federalism." What does he mean by "labor unions and allied rent-seekers"? What do they have to gain?

11. Economists Robert Crandall and Clifford Winston (*Wall Street Journal,* March 9, 2006) asked, "Would consumer welfare seriously be threatened if Ford and General Motors merged?" In 1960, together they would have had almost 75% of the automobile and truck market, but today have only a third of the market. How would you answer their question if this was 1960? Today?

12. Being number one in any business attracts a lot of attention. As *The Economist* (December 17, 2005) has noted,

    As soon as a firm climbs above the sharp elbows of its rivals, it starts getting pelted with the eggs of anti-business activities. People who hate big business aim high. So while big, bad Wal-Mart is pilloried, Target has in the past couple of years blithely cut the benefits of its non-union workers. And when was the last time you saw an anti-globalization mob destroy a Burger King outlet?

    Describe some of the benefits of being number two in a large industry. In terms of total revenues (sales), name the number one and two firms in the following industries: major auto manufacturers, semiconductors, major drug manufacturers, banks, and major integrated oil and gas.

13. We often think that government-enforced patents and copyrights are the most frequently used public policies to create (or assist) monopolies. But economist Edward Glaeser (*New York Times,* March 5, 2006) argues that zoning laws and other regulatory hurdles have been a major force in escalating housing prices in many cities. He suggests that zoning and other restrictions on development have made "boutique" cities out of Manhattan, Boston, and San Francisco, where only the skilled and privileged can afford to live. As he notes, "Homeowners have a strong incentive to stop new development, both because it can be an inconvenience and also because, like any monopolist, stopping supply drives up the price of their own homes. Lack of affordable housing isn't a problem to homeowners; that's exactly what they want.

The thing you want most is to make sure that your home is not affordable if you own it." Is Professor Glaeser right in that homeowners are not monopolists, but often act like them to enhance the value of their houses? Would elimination of zoning laws and building codes result in a greater supply of affordable housing?

14. Professor Andrew Zimbalist is quoted (*Wall Street Journal,* November 24, 2007, p. B7) as wondering, "Imagine walking into a department store to buy a pair of slacks and being told by the salesman that in order to buy the pair you like, you would also have to buy a particular shirt, a particular tie and two pairs of socks. Department stores do not attempt such bundling, because the consumer would not stand for it." But this is exactly how the cable and satellite TV industry operates.

   Cable networks are often monopolies in their local markets but typically face direct competition from the two satellite providers (DISH Network and DIRECTV). Does the cable provider's monopoly power explain the various bundling options that cable operators offer? Most networks charge the cable and dish providers a fee per subscriber to carry their programming. Might consumers be better off with an à la carte option where consumers select and pay for just the channels they want? If an à la carte option were offered, what would probably happen to the smaller, less popular channels?

Solving Problems

15. Using the figure for a monopoly firm below, answer the following questions.

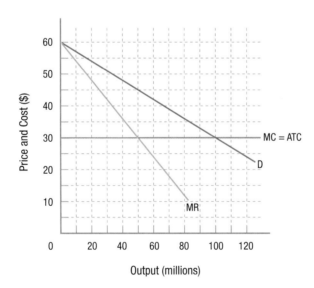

   a. What will be the monopoly price, output, and profit for this firm?
   b. If this monopolist could perfectly price discriminate, what would profit equal?
   c. If this industry was competitive, what would be the price, output, and profit?
   d. How large (in dollars) is the deadweight loss from this monopolist?

16. Using the figure for a natural monopoly firm below, answer the following questions.
   a. Roughly what would be the monopoly price, output, and profit for this unregulated natural monopolist?
   b. Assume that regulators use the competitive P = MC for regulation. Roughly how high would the total subsidy have to be to keep this firm in the industry over the long run?

c. Using P = ATC as the regulatory approach, approximately what would be the price, output, and profits for this monopolist?

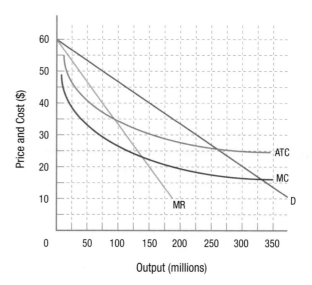

The table below shows data for selected industries. Use this table to answer questions 17–19.

Industry	Number of Companies	CR-4	CR-8	HHI-50 Largest
Dental labs	6,923	12.7	17.8	54.2
Office furniture, mfg.	4,129	24.2	32.4	178.7
Lead pencil and art goods, mfg.	138	58.3	73.1	1,276.1
Aircraft engine and parts, mfg.	296	76.9	82.4	2,527.7
Electric lamp bulb and parts, mfg.	57	88.5	94.1	2,757.6
Household appliance, mfg.	251	62.2	70.8	1,131.9
Household vacuum cleaners, mfg.	29	77.9	96.1	2,096.3
Electronic computer, mfg.	465	75.5	89.2	2,662.4
Pharmaceutical and medicine, mfg.	1,444	34.0	49.1	506.0
Petroleum refineries	88	41.2	63.5	639.7

17. If two firms, one in the CR-4 category and another in the CR-8 category, decided to merge, which of the industries in the table would the Justice Department almost automatically permit?

18. Why do you think that there are so many dental labs and that the concentration is so small?

19. What industries in the table would the Justice Department probably reject if any proposed mergers of two firms in the top eight? In these industries, would the Justice Department be likely to permit two small firms to merge?

Answers to Questions in CheckPoints

Check Point: Monopoly Markets

Yes, this is rent seeking. Google has a huge capital base and cash flow, and could compete with Microsoft in the browser market if it really saw the search box as a threat. The Justice Department announced in May 2006 that it did not feel the search box was a threat to competition.

Check Point: Monopoly Market Issues

No, this is not the same type of price discrimination discussed in this section. This type of discrimination occurs because of information problems, racism, or other factors. The authors conclude that a large part of the price differences between Internet buying and bargaining in the showroom comes from the fact that Internet purchasers have better information. Price discrimination in this section of the chapter is based on consumers with different elasticities of demand, not information problems or racism. Examples include student, senior, and adult pricing in movie theaters.

Check Point: Antitrust Policy

Company	Sales (billions of dollars)	Share of Market	Share Squared
General Motors	2.063	23.07	532.03
Toyota	1.77	19.79	391.64
Ford	1.616	18.07	326.45
Honda	1.151	12.87	165.61
Chrysler	0.931	10.41	108.35
Nissan	0.77	8.61	74.12
Hyundai	0.435	4.86	23.65
Mazda	0.208	2.33	5.41
Totals	**8.944**	**100.00**	**1,627.26**

a. The four-firm concentration ratio is 73.8.

b. The HHI for this industry is 1,627.26.

c. You probably would not permit Ford and Toyota to merge, since that would change the upper mix so significantly. Hyundai and Mazda would not be a problem since combined they would only be 7.19% of the market.

Monopolistic Competition, Oligopoly, and Game Theory 10

Dirk Döring/agefotostock

Pure competition and pure monopoly rarely exist in actual practice. Both models provide the two extremes of market structure and provide direction for public policy when markets approach one or the other. However, the vast majority of markets are somewhere in between the extremes. In this chapter, we focus on the market structures between these polar opposites: monopolistic competition and oligopoly. We look at some of the classic models used to determine imperfectly competitive pricing and output decisions, then turn to the more modern analysis of game theory.

Competitive markets are defined by homogeneous products. This restricted our analysis to products that essentially are commodities: microchips and agricultural products such as wheat, for example. But most of the products we purchase are clearly not homogeneous. Hamburgers from Burger King, McDonald's, Wendy's, and Hardee's are similar, but for many consumers they are quite distinct. The same is true for computers, mobile phones, and cars.

Monopoly analysis required only one firm, and competition required a standardized product, but most of the markets that we encounter have only a few firms offering different products. We are now going to relax these monopoly and competition assumptions and look at markets where many firms offer products that are different (monopolistic competition) and at markets where only a few firms operate (oligopoly). Then we are going to look at game theory as an additional way to understand the behavior of oligopolists.

It is worth taking a moment to remember that most firms begin small in highly competitive environments. Some bring unique products to the market like Facebook, while others add something special to existing markets as is the norm in the restaurant business. Unique products are often exciting at their launch, but they eventually mature, and the firm grows by developing newer versions of older products or introducing new products to begin the cycle anew.

Monopolistic competition: Involves a large number of small firms and is similar to competition, with easy entry and exit, but unlike the competitive model, the firms have differentiated their products. This differentiation is either real or imagined by consumers and involves innovations, advertising, location, or other ways of making one firm's product different from that of its competitors.

Over time, some firms grow through further internal investment, franchising individual operations, or merger with other firms. Only the rare firm begins as a monopolist or even as an oligopolist (typically through a government franchise like local cable TV companies). They emerge as huge, dominant firms in many different ways.

Monopolistic Competition

Until the 1920s, competition and monopoly were the only models of market structure that economists had in their toolbox. During the 1920s, economists began debating the effects of economies of scale on the competitive model. If economies were large relative to the market, one or a few firms would expand and eventually take over the market. Competition could not survive large economies of scale. Firms would then become large enough to affect prices in the market by their supply decisions.

Edward Chamberlin (1899–1967), as a graduate student at Harvard in 1922, decided to write a dissertation on the problems of the competitive model. Chamberlin was a tireless and tenacious person who wanted to alter the way economists thought about market structure. His 1933 book *The Theory of Monopolistic Competition* was not immediately warmly received, but all recognized the originality of his effort. Six months after the publication of Chamberlin's work, a British economist, Joan Robinson (1903–1983), published her *Economics of Imperfect Competition* and stole some of Chamberlin's thunder.

While Chamberlin was famous for this one contribution to economics, Joan Robinson is remembered for a huge variety of work and its radical nature. She was one of the economists who worked alongside John Maynard Keynes during the 1930s when he was developing *The General Theory*. She was responsible for the analysis of price discrimination discussed in the previous chapter, and she was the first woman to be a finalist for the Nobel Prize in Economics. Today, both Chamberlin and Robinson are generally given equal credit for discovering "imperfect" markets.

Monopolistic competition is nearer to the competitive end of the spectrum and is defined by the following:

- A large number of small firms. Like competition, these firms have an insignificantly small market share. They and their competitors cannot appreciably affect the market and, therefore, ignore the reactions of their rivals. They are thus independent of a competitor's reactions.

- Entry and exit is easy.

- Unlike competition, products are different. Each firm produces a product that is different from its competitors or is perceived to be different by consumers. What distinguishes monopolistic competition from competitive markets is product differentiation.

Product Differentiation and the Firm's Demand Curve

Most firms sell products that are differentiated from their competitors. This differentiation can simply take the form of a superior location. Your local dry cleaner, restaurant, grocery, and gas station can have slightly higher prices, and you will not abandon them altogether. Other companies have branded products that give them some ability to increase price without losing all of their customers, as would happen under competition.

Product differentiation gives the firm some (however modest) control over prices. This is illustrated in Figure 1. Demand curve d_c is the competitive demand curve, and d_{mc} is the demand faced by a monopolistic competitor. This is similar to the monopolist's demand, but the demand curve is considerably more elastic. Because a monopolistic competitor is small relative to the market, there are still a lot of substitutes. Thus, any increase in price is accompanied by a substantial decrease in output demanded.

Like a monopolist, the monopolistically competitive firm faces a downward sloping marginal revenue curve, shown in Figure 1 as MR_{mc}.

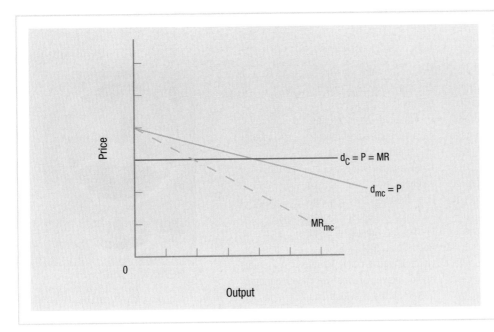

FIGURE 1—Product Differentiation and Demand

Product differentiation means that the firm has some leeway in its pricing policies. Demand curve d_{mc} is the demand curve for a monopolistically competitive firm with modest price-making ability. Marginal revenue curve MR_{mc} also slopes downward, reflecting the weak negative slope of the demand curve.

Product differentiation can be the result of a superior product, a better location, superior service, clever packaging, or advertising. All of these factors are intended to increase demand or reduce the elasticity of demand and generate loyalty to the product or service.

For some products, packaging is paramount; bulk, bagged, and bottled teas seem to fit this mold with their ornate packages and names to fit any mood or occasion. Olive oil—virgin and extra virgin—are sold in bottles and tins covered with pictorial farms, landscapes, animals, and other European scenes. Even wines have succumbed to pictorial animal packaging. Yellow Tail, a good inexpensive Australian wine, has a very attractive label featuring a yellow-tailed rock wallaby that looks like Australian aboriginal art. In five years, Yellow Tail sales in the United States have gone from nothing to over 100 million bottles annually. At least a large chunk of Yellow Tail's success has been due to the unique label, and other vintners have begun adding animals to their bottle labels.

Product differentiation: One firm's product is distinguished from another's through advertising, innovation, location, and so on.

The Role of Advertising

Another important way to differentiate products is through advertising. Economists generally classify advertising in two ways: informational and persuasive. The informational aspects of advertising let consumers know about products and reduce search costs. Advertising is a relatively inexpensive way to let customers know about quality and price of a company's products. It can also enhance competition by making consumers aware of substitute or competitive products. Advertising also has the potential to reduce costs by increasing sales, bringing about economies of scale.

But advertising does have a negative side as well. Because so much of advertising is persuasive, designed to shift buyers among competitors of similar products, the result is that the cost of advertising simply drives up the price of many products. Persuasive ads often have little informational content and may result in consumers purchasing inferior products. With all the advertising we see, a significant portion probably cancels each other out.

Advertising is another area where technology has transformed the medium: Digital video recorders permit ad-skipping and have significantly reduced the impact of TV ads. A lot of advertising dollars are shifting away from conventional media (newspapers, magazines, and television) and moving to the Internet, where consumers can be targeted more inexpensively and efficiently.

All of these ways to differentiate their products gives monopolistically competitive firms some control over price. This means that their profit maximizing decisions will be a little different from competitive firms.

Issue: Do Brands Represent Pricing Power?

What is a brand? All of us know brands through their names and logos. Nike has the swoosh, Intel has a logo and the four-note jingle you hear whenever its processors are advertised, Coca-Cola has a distinctive way of spelling its name. Names and logos are communication devices, but brands are more than this. They are a promise of performance. A branded product or service raises expectations in a consumer's mind. If these expectations are met, consumers pay a price premium. If expectations are not met, the value of the brand falls as consumers seek alternatives.

Brand names start with the company that makes the product or provides the service. In the past, this meant that brand names came from a limited number of sources. Some companies were named after their founders, such as Walt Disney; some companies were named after what they supplied, such as IBM (International Business Machines); and some have also been named by their main product, such as the Coca-Cola Company. Sometimes the company name has a tenuous link with the product but is strong nevertheless, such as the Starbucks name for coffee products:

Master Starbuck was first mate to Captain Ahab in *Moby-Dick* and did drink coffee in the book, but who remembers that?

Whatever their origins, these brands have recognizable brand names, and they command price premiums. According to the *Financial Times,* Google is the most valuable brand, valued at nearly $90 billion, followed by GE (General Electric) at around $70 billion. Eight of the top 10 brands are American, including Microsoft, Coca-Cola, IBM, and Apple. Brands this valuable must convey some considerable pricing power, or what we called monopoly power in the previous chapter. Monopoly power is what companies want.

Toyota is now the highest valued brand in the auto industry at over $35 billion. Toyota has built its business and brand on the basis of an efficient production system, concentration on consistent high quality, a commitment to customer service, and continuous improvement of the product line. The Toyota brand has cachet: At the California plant that until 2009 Toyota shared with General Motors, *identical* cars came off the production line. Some were branded as GM cars, others

Kaplonski/Alamy

Toyotas. When the cars were traded in, the Toyotas had a much higher trade-in value. The Toyota brand conveys quality, which gives Toyota its pricing power. How much will the Toyota brand be tarnished by the gas pedal problem that led to the worldwide recall of over 7 million cars in 2010?

Sources: F. O'Donnell, "Make It a Brand New Year," Life Insurance Marketing and Research Association *MarketFacts* 18:1, January/February, 1999, p. 18; Richard Tomkins, "Branding Consultants Get a Chance to Tell It Like It Is," *Financial Times,* January 30, 2004, p. 14; "The Car Company in Front," *Economist,* January 29, 2005; and John Gapper, "Holding Firm as Downturn Looms," *Financial Times,* April 21, 2008, Special Report, p. 1.

Price and Output under Monopolistic Competition

Profit maximization in the short run for the monopolistically competitive firm is a lot like that for a monopolist, but given the firm's size, profit will tend to be less. Short-run profit maximizing behavior is shown in Figure 2. The firm maximizes profit where $MR = MC$ (point c) by selling output q_0 for a price of P_0. Total profits are the shaded area $C_0 P_0 ab$. All of this should look very familiar from the last chapter. The difference is that the monopolistically competitive demand curve is quite elastic, and economic profits are diminished. The level of profits is dependent on the strength of demand, but in any event will be considerably lower than that of a monopolist.

This does not mean that profits are trivial. Many huge global firms sell their products in even larger global markets, and their profits are significant. They are large firms, but do not have significant monopoly power. Many companies such as Armani, Nike, and Sony are all quite large but relative to their markets face daunting competition.

If firms in the industry are earning economic profits like the firm shown in Figure 2, new firms will want to enter. Since there are no restrictions on entry or exit, new firms will enter, soaking up some industry demand and reducing the demand to each firm in the market. Demand will continue to decline as long as economic profits exist. At equilibrium in the long run, the typical firm in the industry will look like the one shown in Figure 3.

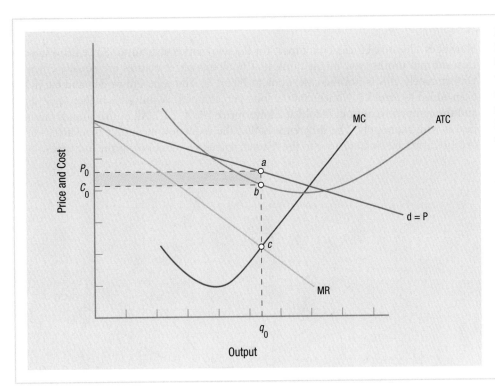

FIGURE 2—Short-Run Equilibrium for Monopolistic Competition

This monopolistically competitive firm will maximize profits in the short run by producing where MR = MC (point *c*). Profits are equal to the shaded area.

Notice that the demand curve is just tangent to the long-run average total cost (LRATC) curve, resulting in the firm earning normal profits in the long run. The firm produces and sells q_L output at a price of P_L (point *a*). Once the typical firm reaches this point, there is no longer any incentive for other firms to enter the industry. Just as the competitive firm does, monopolistically competitive firms earn normal profits in the long run.

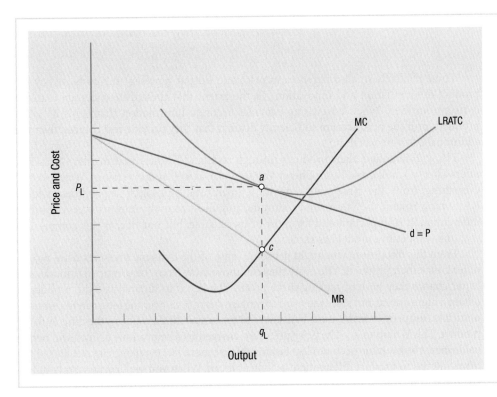

FIGURE 3—Long-Run Equilibrium for Monopolistic Competition

In the long run, easy entry and exit will adjust the demand for each firm so that the demand curve will be tangent (at point *a* in this case) to the long-run average total cost curve. This is long-run equilibrium because existing firms are earning normal profits and there is no incentive for further entry or exit.

Comparing Monopolistic Competition to Competition

How does allocative efficiency compare for the two market structures? Since firms in both earn normal profits, you might think that both market structures are equally efficient. Unfortunately, this is not the case. Look at Figure 4. The competitive demand curve has been added to Figure 3. Notice that the long-run competitive output is higher ($q_c > q_{mc}$), and the competitive output is sold at a lower price ($P_c < P_{mc}$). All of this sounds familiar, just as with monopoly. The difference is that the reduction in output is relatively small because firms are small relative to the market, whereas a monopoly is the industry.

FIGURE 4—Comparing the Long Run for Monopolistically Competitive and Competitive Firms

Long-run equilibrium is at point *b* for competitive firms and at point *a* for monopolistically competitive firms. Equilibrium price is a little higher, and output is a little lower for the monopolistically competitive firm when compared to the competitive firm. These represent the real costs we, as consumers, pay for product differentiation.

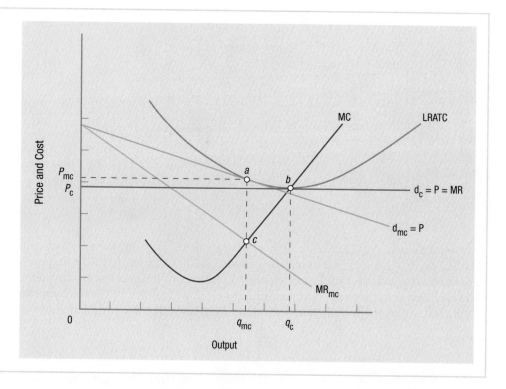

These relatively small differences in price and output represent the costs we pay for product differentiation and innovation. To the extent that these differences are real, the costs are justified. When advertising provides accurate information that helps us select products, or if the products are sufficiently distinct that they provide real choices, then the additional costs are worth it.

Firms differentiate their products through style and features that matter. Coca-Cola offers Cherry, Vanilla, and Black Cherry Vanilla Coke, as well as diet versions. Watches offer everything from the time and date to temperature, stopwatch capabilities, Global Positioning System (GPS) capability, altitude, and, most recently, Internet access. Product differentiation is important and for most of us valuable, but not free, as this comparison with the competitive model has shown.

From this discussion, you might get some sense of the dynamic pressures firms face to differentiate their products. The more they can move away from the competitive model, the better chance they have of making more profit. The key is to differentiate the product to obtain a higher price. But since the price advantage evaporates over the long run for monopolistically competitive firms, these firms have to try to sustain the value in the differentiated product. This is hard to do. The price premium charged by Abercrombie & Fitch will not be paid when Abercrombie becomes less fashionable, or more like everyone else. Yet, it is in the firm's interest to product differentiate as long as it can. When you see firms trying to differentiate their products, ask yourself if the products really are so different after all.

■ CHECKPOINT

MONOPOLISTIC COMPETITION

- Monopolistically competitive firms look like competitive firms (large number of small firms in a market where entry and exit is unrestricted) but have differentiated products.

- Monopolistically competitive firms have very elastic demands.

- Short-run equilibrium output for the monopolistic competitor (like the monopolist) is at an output where MR = MC, but economic profits will be relatively small compared to an industry monopolist because demand is very elastic for the monopolistic competitor.

- In the long run, easy entry and exit result in monopolistically competitive firms earning only normal profits.

- Output is lower and price is higher for monopolistically competitive firms when compared to price and output for competitive firms.

QUESTION: Kelly Crow reports in the *Wall Street Journal* (August 12, 2005) that many of the 40 or so traveling circuses in America have celebrity clowns as their headline acts. These clowns earn high six-figure salaries plus royalties from souvenir sales. Why would circuses emphasize clowns over animal and trapeze acts?

Answers to the Checkpoint question can be found at the end of this chapter.

Oligopoly

Oligopoly markets are those where a large market share is controlled by just a few firms. What constitutes a few firms controlling a large market share is not rigidly defined. Further, these firms can sell either a homogeneous product (e.g., gasoline, sugar) or a differentiated product (e.g., automobiles and pharmaceuticals).

Industries can be composed of a dominant firm with a few smaller firms making up the rest of the industry (e.g., microcomputer operating systems and cell phones), or the industry can be composed of a few similarly sized firms (e.g., automobiles and tobacco). The point of this discussion is that oligopoly models are numerous and varied, and we will explore only a few. Oligopoly models do, however, have several common characteristics.

Oligopoly: A market with just a few firms dominating the industry where (1) each firm recognizes that it must consider its competitors' reactions when making its own decisions (mutual interdependence), and (2) there are significant barriers to entry into the market.

Defining Oligopoly

All oligopoly models share several common assumptions:

- There are only a few dominant firms in the industry.

- Each firm recognizes that it must take into account the behavior of its competitors when it makes decisions. Economists refer to this as **mutual interdependence.**

- There are significant barriers to entry into the market.

Mutual interdependence: When only a few firms constitute an industry, each firm must consider the reactions of its competitors to its decisions.

Since there are only a few firms, the actions of one will affect the ability of the others to successfully sell or price their output. If one firm changes the specifications of its product or increases its advertising budget, this will have an impact on its rivals, and they can be expected to respond in kind. Thus, one firm cannot forecast its change in sales for a new promotion without first making some assumption about the reaction of its rivals. For example, when after 10 years of development Mercedes adds a new driver attention assist system to detect fatigue and advertises this feature, it has to consider whether a competitor such as Lexus will immediately offer this feature as well.

In an industry composed of just a few firms, entry scale is often huge. Plus, with just a few firms, typically brand preferences are quite strong on the part of consumers, and a new firm may need a substantial marketing program just to get a foot in the door. For example, the investment in plant for a new automaker is huge, and the marketing effort also must be large to get people to even consider a new auto brand. Newer car manufacturers like Kia often must resort to long warranties (10 year, 100,000 miles) to entice customers to try its products.

Cartels: Joint Profit Maximization

Cartels are theft—usually by well-dressed thieves.

GRAEME SAMUEL, HEAD OF AUSTRALIA'S ANTITRUST OFFICE

Cartel: An agreement between firms (or countries) in an industry to formally collude on price and output, then agree on the distribution of production.

The first oligopoly model we examine is *collusive* joint profit maximization, or a **cartel** model. Here we assume a few firms collude (combine secretly) to operate like a monopolistic industry, setting the monopoly price and output and sharing the monopoly profits. Cartels are illegal in the United States, though international laws do not ban them. However, this situation may change in the European Union.

As *The Economist* noted, "Just a few years ago, America seemed uniquely obsessed with price-fixing. Today, new measures against cartel behavior (which includes bid-rigging and deals to carve up market share, as well as price-fixing) are being taken from Sweden to South Korea, where the competition body levied its first fine against a foreign firm earlier this year [2002]."[1] Europe, in 2006, fined seven firms for running a cartel in bleaching chemicals.[2] Recently, Europe broke up and fined six firms nearly $500 million for a 20-year-old cartel in zippers.

The most famous cartel operating today is OPEC, the Organization of Petroleum Exporting Countries. OPEC countries meet to establish the price that members can charge and an output level that each individual member can produce, thus carving up shares of the profits. OPEC, formed principally of Middle Eastern countries in the early 1960s, really didn't become effective until 1973. Since then, it has had many successes and some failures.

Issue: Why Did the Government Sponsor an Aluminum Cartel in the 1990s?

What can a CEO of a major American corporation do when foreign firms sell so much aluminum on the world market that the price decline threatens the corporation? Ask the government for help, of course. In the early 1990s, Russia sold more aluminum in world markets. This increase in supply was matched by a fall in demand brought about by slower worldwide economic growth and Russia's reduced production of aircraft. Prices fell by *half*.

Alcoa's CEO, Paul O'Neill, went to the Clinton administration for help. With its approval and the help of government antitrust lawyers, the Overseas Private Investment Corporation (OPIC), and the State Department, an agreement was made limiting aluminum production. In other words, a cartel was formed. With a $250 million equity investment from OPIC, Russian companies were persuaded to reduce their output. Prices rose from roughly 50 cents a pound to nearly 90 cents, and Alcoa's profits rose.

By 1995, worldwide demand for aluminum increased, and problems enforcing the agreement arose; shortly thereafter, the cartel fell apart. Because cartels are normally illegal in the United States, this "aluminum product–overseas investment agreement" was challenged, but dismissed by the courts. Export cartels are permitted in the United States as long as

they do not adversely impact competition in domestic markets.

Source: Based on Joseph E. Stiglitz, *Globalization and Its Discontents* (New York: Norton), 2003, pp. 173–176 and p. 268.

---

[1] See "Cartels: Fixing for a Fight," *Economist*, April 20, 2002, p. 63.

[2] William Echikson, "Europe Fines 7 Chemical Firms $489.8 Million for Bleach Cartel," *Wall Street Journal*, May 4, 2006, p. A2.

Cartels are inherently unstable because of the incentive to cheat by individual members. Even though each firm and the cartel jointly are earning economic profits, they are not being maximized. If all other members of the cartel continue to sell their authorized output, any one firm that can sell additional output for a price above marginal cost can earn additional profits. For oil producing countries, additional production is particularly profitable because a $100 barrel of oil may only cost $10 to $20 to produce. Each firm in the cartel faces these incentives, and if many attempt to sell additional output, the cartel agreement will break down. This analysis has led some economists to lose interest in cartels, since cartels are likely to fail in the long run.

Cartel stability is enhanced with fewer members with similar goals. Further, stability is improved if the cartel is maintained with legal provisions (government protection) and if nonprice competition is not possible. If the firm can give nonprice discounts (enhanced service or some other product as an inducement to purchase), the likelihood of stability is reduced. If their products and cost structures are similar and they are not secretive with each other, stability is enhanced. Finally, if there are significant barriers to entry, the cartel need not worry about new entrants, and the chances improve for the cartel to survive.

The Kinked Demand Curve Model

One early oligopoly model that considered the reactions of other firms is the kinked demand curve model jointly developed by Sweezy, Hall, and Hitch in the late 1930s. These authors noticed that prices tended to be stable for extended periods in oligopolistic industries. It was in an effort to model this price stability that they settled on the idea of a kinked demand curve.

Demand curve d in Figure 5 represents the demand for one firm when all other firms in the industry *do not follow* its price changes. Demand curve D represents demand when all other firms raise or lower prices *in concert*. Demand curve d is relatively more elastic than demand curve D because when the firm raises prices and others do not follow, quantity demanded declines rapidly as customers substitute to the now lower-priced products from competitors. Similarly, when one firm's prices fall and the others ignore this change, demand for the lower-priced products grows rapidly. Hence, demand curve d is relatively elastic.

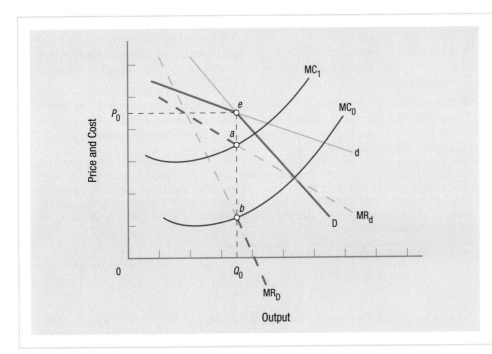

FIGURE 5—The Kinked Demand Curve Model of Oligopoly

The kinked demand curve model of oligopoly shows why oligopoly prices appear stable. The model assumes that if the firm raised its price, competitors will not react and raise their prices, but if the firm lowers prices, other firms will lower theirs in response. These reactions create a "kink" in the firm's demand curve at point *e*, and a discontinuity in the MR curve equal to the distance between points *a* and *b*. This discontinuity permits marginal costs to vary from MC_0 to MC_1 before the firm will change its price.

Kinked demand curve: An oligopoly model that assumes that if a firm
raises its price, competitors will not raise
theirs; but if the firm lowers its price, all
of its competitors will lower their price to
match the reduction. This leads to a kink
in the demand curve and relatively stable
market prices.

Demand curve D, on the other hand, is more like the industry demand. When all firms raise and lower their prices together, demand will be less elastic than demand curve *d*.

The **kinked demand curve** model assumes the following:

- If the firm raises prices for its products, its competitors will not react by raising prices, expecting to see their market share rise.

- If the firm lowers its prices, its competitors will meet the new prices with lower ones of their own to make sure that they do not lose market share.

As a result, the relevant demand curve facing the firm is the darkened portion of demand curves d and D that is kinked at point *e*. The relevant portion of the marginal revenue curve is the darkened dashed curve MR with the discontinuity between points *a* and *b*. Notice, we are just using the relevant portions of MR_d and MR_D. As shown, marginal cost crosses through the discontinuity, resulting in an equilibrium price and output of P_0 and Q_0.

It is, of course, the discontinuity in the MR curve that gives this model its price stability. The marginal cost curve can vary anywhere between points *a* and *b* before the firm will have any incentive to change prices to maximize profits.

Critics of this model suggest that price stability can be explained by other factors, and that the model doesn't explain how prices were initially determined. It explains the existence of the kink but not how it was determined in an oligopoly context. George Stigler argued that the evidence of price stability was weak at best. However, more recent empirical investigations of retailing and others found price declines were more readily followed than price increases in oligopolistic industries.[3]

One clear result of the search for realistic oligopoly models was the realization by economists that the mutual interdependence of firms and their reactions to each other's policies were important. How one firm reacts to a competitor's market strategy determined the nature of competition in the industry. These ideas led to game theory.

■**CHECKPOINT**

OLIGOPOLY

- Oligopolies are markets (a) with only a few firms, (b) where each firm takes into account the reaction of rivals to its policies or firms recognize their mutual interdependence, and (c) where there are significant barriers to entry.

- Cartels result when several firms collude to set market price and output. Cartels typically act like monopolists and share the economic profits that result.

- Cartels are inherently unstable because individual firms can earn higher profits by selling more than their allotted quota. As more firms in the cartel cheat, prices fall, defeating the agreement.

- The observation that prices were stable in oligopolistic industries gave rise to the kinked demand curve model. The model assumes that competitors will follow price reductions but not price increases. This leads to a discontinuity in MR permitting cost to vary substantially before prices are changed.

QUESTION: Alec Guinness, in the 1951 film *The Man in the White Suit*, invents cloth that shrugs off dirt and doesn't wear out. Rather than treated as a hero, Guinness is attacked by the textile oligopoly and labor unions because "if the cloth is indestructible, how will the industry survive?" Name a recent invention that has had a large disruptive influence on oligopolies.

Answers to the Checkpoint question can be found at the end of this chapter.

[3] See A. Kashyap, "Sticky Prices: New Evidence from Retail Catalogs," *Quarterly Journal of Economics*, 1995, pp. 245–274; and S. Domberger, and D. Fiebig, "The Distribution of Price Changes in Oligopoly," *Journal of Industrial Economics*, 1993, pp. 295–313.

Game Theory

If you say why not bomb them tomorrow, I say why not today? If you say today at 5 o'clock, I say why not one o'clock?

—JOHN VON NEUMANN

Game theory developed from analysis of imperfect competition. The earliest analysis was done by French economist Antoine Cournot (pronounced core-no), in which he examined pricing principles for a duopolist (two firms). He analyzed how one firm would react to output changes from its rival. His analysis led to reaction curves (or functions) for each firm representing the best strategy that each firm could adopt given the behavior of the other firm. This model of mutual interdependence was the precursor to game theory.

Modern game theory owes its origins to John von Neumann (1903–1957), who published a paper titled "Theory of Parlor Games" in 1928 and subsequently published (in 1944) the *Theory of Games and Economic Behavior* with Oskar Morganstern. Born in Hungary at the turn of the century, von Neumann was a brilliant mathematician who was able to divide two 8-digit numbers in his head and by his senior year in high school was

Game theory: An approach to analyzing oligopoly behavior using mathematics and simulation by making different assumptions about the players, time involved, level of information, strategies, and other aspects of the game.

Antoine Augustin Cournot (1801–1877)

Antoine Cournot is one of the great unsung heroes of microeconomics. He was the first economist to derive a demand curve. He pioneered the use of mathematics in analyzing market structures, prices, and equilibrium. Throughout his career, however, Cournot was bitterly disappointed by the lack of appreciation of his work. It was only near the end of his life that other economists began to notice the importance of what he had written.

Born in 1801 in Gray, a small town in central France, Cournot completed his math degree at the Sorbonne in 1823. Cournot spent the next 10 years assisting a French official prepare his memoirs. In his free time, he earned a doctorate in science and began publishing articles on mathematics. His work brought him to the attention of the mathematician Simeon-Denis Poisson. With the help of Poisson, he obtained an appointment as a pro-

fessor at Lyon and later an administrative position at the Academy of Grenoble. In 1838, he was appointed Inspector General of Education in Paris.

That same year he published his most important work, *Researches into the Mathematical Principles of the Theory of Wealth*, which introduced differential calculus to economic analysis. He was the first to describe the downward slope of a demand curve, suggesting that the quantity demanded of a good such as wine depended on the price of that good. In other words, increasing the price of wine would reduce the quantity demanded. Cournot demonstrated that the equilibrium price was reached at the point where demand and supply were equal.

Cournot made other surprising discoveries, which he described in his book. He explained how, under conditions of monopoly, sellers could maximize profits by producing output where marginal costs equaled marginal revenue. The economist Alfred Marshall later adapted this notion in his *Principles of Economics* in 1890. Cournot also explored the dynamics of duopolies, and his ideas were later used by John Nash in his Nobel Prize–winning work on game theory.

Corbis Premium RF/Alamy

considered a professional mathematician.[4] Von Neumann worked on the Manhattan Project during the Second World War, and it has been suggested that he probably was the model for Dr. Strangelove in Stanley Kubrick's 1963 film *Dr. Strangelove, Or How I Learned to Stop Worrying and Love the Bomb*.[5]

Modern game theory has developed into a sophisticated mathematical and simulation science. Five people have been awarded the Nobel Prize in Economics for their work in game theory. To get a feel for the potential richness that game theory offers, let's look at some of the types of games economists use to model oligopolistic market behavior.

Types of Games

Games can be simple or complicated depending on the various characteristics of the market they represent. As you will see by the following breakdown, we can have nearly as many games as we have different markets. Game theory characteristics include the following:

- **Cooperation:** *Cooperative* games permit players to collude on prices, output, or other variables, much as OPEC does in setting output quotas for each producer. *Noncooperative* games are the opposite in that they prevent player communication and collusion.

- **Players:** Simple games involve only two players, but many modern simulation games involve multiplayer environments.

- **Time:** In *static* games, all players choose their strategies at the same time. *Dynamic* games involve sequential decision making; for example, one firm sets a price, and the other responds to this price.

- **Information:** Players could have *complete (perfect)* information about the game or they could have *incomplete (imperfect)* information. Exact payoffs may be unknown or subject to uncertainty. Firms often have good information about their own costs but may not have equal information about their competitor's costs. *Asymmetric* information is also possible (in the case of used cars—sellers usually have better information than buyers).

- **Strategies:** Many games have *discrete* strategies where players choose from a few choices such as "advertise or do not advertise," "confess or do not confess," "enter the industry or not." *Continuous* strategies typify business-constant-pricing decisions where firms often have a large number of prices and products that are subjected to various (and sometimes random) events.

- **Repetition:** Whether the game is a *one-off* decision or will be *repeated* introduces another level of complexity. In a one-off game (as in the Prisoner's Dilemma, described later) players only have to consider the payoffs (impacts) on that one decision. In repeated games, players can react to the other player's past strategies. In one round where one player makes a choice that harms the other player, that harmed player can be expected to change strategies in the future.

- **Profit-Loss:** In a *zero-sum* game (poker, duels, and most sporting events), each winner is essentially paired with a loser. If the game is a *non-zero-sum* game, both players can stand to benefit.

These characteristics permit simple and complex games covering nearly all economic situations and reflect the importance of game theory's analytic method in modern economics. In the remainder of this chapter, we focus on several simple games and apply the general analysis to price discounting and advertising, then take a brief look at the strategies introduced with repeated games. The Prisoner's Dilemma is our first widely applicable game.

---

[4]Steven Pressman, *Fifty Major Economists* (New York: Routledge), 1999, pp. 124–128.
[5]See William Poundstone, *Prisoner's Dilemma* (New York: Doubleday), 1992, p. 5.

The Prisoner's Dilemma

In *noncooperative* games, each player imagines how his opponent intends to play the game, then uses this information to help formulate his own strategy. However, it is impossible for players to communicate or collaborate in making their decisions or strategies. The classic static, noncooperative game is the **Prisoner's Dilemma.**

Two criminal suspects (Chris and Matthew) are apprehended for robbery. They are separated, put in solitary confinement, and are unable to speak to each other. Each prisoner is offered the same bargain: Testify against your partner and you will go free while your partner will go to prison for three years. If neither confesses, the state likely will convict them both on lesser charges resulting in a one-year sentence. Finally, if both confess, they each will go to prison for two years.

The dilemma facing each prisoner is shown in Table 1. The payoff table is arranged so that Matthew's payoff (time in prison) is the first number, and Chris's payoff is the second number. Thus, a payoff of 3,0 represents three years in prison for Matthew while Chris goes free.

Prisoner's Dilemma: A noncooperative game where players cannot communicate or collaborate in making their decisions about whether to confess or not, which results in inferior outcomes for both players. Many oligopoly decisions can be framed as a Prisoner's Dilemma.

TABLE 1	The Prisoner's Dilemma	
	Chris	
Matthew	Do not confess	Confess
Do not confess	1,1	3,0
Confess	0,3	2,2

The prisoners must make a decision, but each cannot find out what the other has done, and both decisions are irrevocable. Each prisoner is only concerned with his own welfare—minimizing his time in prison. Is there a unique solution?

Consider Matthew's situation, shown as the *first* payoff in each cell. Suppose Chris *confesses*. Matthew is better off confessing since two years in prison is better than three. This is read vertically in the "Confess" column of the payoff table. Now suppose that Chris *does not confess*. Matthew is still better off confessing since going free is preferred to one year in prison. Thus, from Matthew's perspective, no matter which strategy Chris selects, Matthew is better off confessing because his sentence is reduced by a year in both cases.

Similarly, no matter what Matthew does, Chris is better off confessing. The logical result is that both will confess despite the fact that both would be better off if neither did: 1 year served in prison versus two.

Von Neumann referred to this strategy and its outcome as a *minimax* solution; both prisoners are minimizing their maximum prison sentences. They are minimizing their worst outcome in this instance. Notice that this is not the best outcome for both prisoners. They would be better off not confessing, but neither could trust the other to not confess given the structure of the payoffs. It is important to note that this result (confess, confess) is due to the structure of the payoffs, not the absolute levels.

The Prisoner's Dilemma is not simply an idle game dreamed up by mathematicians and economists. Robert Harris[6] noted that

> In robberies where murders occur, for example, there is often more than one criminal involved and thus more than one person who may be eligible for the death penalty. But for a prosecutor, "what's important is that you score one touchdown," in the form of a death sentence, said Franklin R. Zimring, University of California, Berkeley, law professor and a capital punishment expert.
>
> Frequently, a race ensues in which the robbers try to be the first to point the finger at an accomplice and make a deal with the prosecutor to testify in return for leniency.
>
> Sometimes, Zimring said, it never becomes clear whether the person who got leniency or the person on trial for his life actually pulled the trigger.

---

[6] R. A. Harris, *Los Angeles Times*, January 29, 1990, cited in William Poundstone, *Prisoner's Dilemma* (New York: Doubleday), 1992, p. 119.

John von Neumann (1903–1957)

The economist Nicholas Kaldor once described fellow Hungarian John von Neumann as "the nearest thing to a genius" he had ever encountered. In addition to being one of the leading mathematicians of his day, von Neumann made important contributions to quantum physics and helped develop the first computer. Von Neumann is best known, however, as the originator of game theory, which has many important uses in economics.

Born in Budapest in 1903, von Neumann was a math prodigy with a photographic memory. He entertained his parents' dinner guests by reciting pages from the phone book by memory. By the age of 8, he had learned calculus. During his final year in high school, he was publishing professional mathematical papers.

According to Tim Harford, von Neumann was "asked to assist with the design of a new supercomputer required to solve a new and important mathematical problem, which was beyond the capabilities of existing supercomputers. He asked to have the problem explained to him, solved it in

Photo courtesy of National Nuclear Security Administration/Nevada Site Office

moments with pen and paper, and turned down the request."

In 1944, von Neumann and Oskar Morganstern published the *Theory of Games and Economic Behavior*, a seminal work that has inspired a generation of mathematicians and economists, including Kenneth Arrow, Gerard Debreu, and John Nash.

In game theory, individuals compete with one another without knowing what strategies the other will employ. Many economic interactions involve similar dynamics between groups and individuals. For example, von Neumann and Morganstern wrote about situations in which players would form coalitions to gain advantage over players, which is comparable to markets in which two firms in an oligopolistic industry combine to overcome other competitors. Other analogies might be the decision for individuals to form a union or for industry groups to form lobbying organizations to push for favorable legislation from government.

During World War II, von Neumann helped the U.S. military develop the first computer and later worked on the Manhattan Project with Robert Oppenheimer. A strong supporter of the nuclear weapons program, he served as an advisor to President Truman and was appointed to the Atomic Energy Commission by President Eisenhower. Von Neumann died in 1957.

Source: Tim Harford, *The Undercover Economist* (Oxford: Oxford University Press), 2006, p. 156.

Nash Equilibrium

John von Neumann's focus was on two-person zero-sum games and was the initial building blocks for game theory. In a zero-sum game, the amount won equals the amount lost, as in a poker game where one person's winnings have to come at the expense of another person, or other people. While zero-sum games are realistic for poker, they are not as fruitful for strategic business interactions. It is not always the case that where one firm gains, another must lose. Other possibilities include mutually beneficial or mutually destructive strategies. Sometimes the most interesting economic games are complex multiperson, non-zero-sum games.

In 28 lines (a one-page paper), John Nash (of *A Beautiful Mind* fame) was able to prove that an *n*-person game where each player chooses his optimal strategy, given that all other players have done the same, has a solution. Nash assumed that each player would imagine what all other players would select as their best strategy. Then each player would select a strategy that represented his best strategy given the other players' intended strategies. Nash was able to show that given these conditions, equilibrium (a **Nash equilibrium**) would always exist for any *n*-person non-zero-sum game.

This is a very important result. Economists could now develop realistic (and often complex) games or models of market interactions and know that a solution for the game existed.

Nash equilibrium: An important proof that an *n*-person game where each player chooses his optimal strategy, given that all other players have done the same, has a solution. This was important because economists now knew that even complex models (or games) had an equilibrium, or solution.

One-Off Games: Applying Game Theory

In this section, we examine some examples of how game theory can be used to model oligopoly decisions. First we look at static games where the decisions are made simultaneously, then we take a brief look at dynamic games where decisions are make sequentially.

Static Games

Static games involve simultaneous decisions, and we will focus on those with perfect information and certain payoffs. In addition, these games are one-off and are not repeated.

Static games: One-off games (not repeated) where decisions by the players are made simultaneously and are irreversible.

Price Discounting: Dairy Queen and Foster's Freeze   The game shown in Table 2 is a straightforward extension of the Prisoner's Dilemma applied to business. This example could represent dueling advertising campaigns, decisions about research and development expenditures, or price changes. The game in Table 2 represents the decision to lower price facing two oligopolists.

TABLE 2   Payoff Matrix for Price Change Game

	Foster's Freeze's Price	
Dairy Queen's Price	$3	$2
$3	$100,000,$100,000	$60,000,$150,000
$2	$150,000,$60,000	$75,000,$75,000

We assume that the two firms Dairy Queen and Foster's Freeze are currently charging $3 for banana splits and face roughly the same costs and demand curves. Now assume that both are thinking about reducing price to gain market share.

Notice that both are currently making $100,000 profit on this product. If only one firm lowers its price, that firm will earn $50,000 in added profit because sales rise. Some of this increase in sales comes from those of the other firm and some comes from the added quantity demanded at the lower price. Both firms, of course, can see that each firm can gain by lowering price. But if both firms lower their price, each will see its profits fall (to $75,000). What is the new equilibrium point? Both firms will lower price, anticipating that the other will lower the price as well. This strategy maximizes their minimum profit (they each make at least $75,000). If their competitor lowers price, they cannot do better.

Advertising: Lowe's and Home Depot   Firms, politicians, special interest groups, and, it often seems, *everyone* advertises. The decision to advertise or not can be put in the Prisoner's Dilemma game theory framework as well.

Advertising costs money, but firms hope to garner market share and greater profits. However, if their competitors advertise as well, little is gained unless the impact of all the advertising is to grow the entire market sufficiently to compensate for the higher costs. Two home improvement big-box operations—Lowe's and Home Depot—face this dilemma.

Table 3 on the next page presents hypothetical numbers for the advertising decisions that Lowe's and Home Depot must make. If neither firm advertises, both will earn

TABLE 3   Payoff Matrix for Advertising by Lowe's and Home Depot

Lowe's	Home Depot	
	Don't advertise	Advertise
Don't advertise	$100,000,$100,000	$50,000,$120,000
Advertise	$120,000,$50,000	$80,000,$80,000

$100,000 in profit. If either Lowe's or Home Depot decides to spend the $30,000 required to advertise, it will take $50,000 in business away from the other, and its net profit will be $120,000, leaving $50,000 for the other. If both advertise, the market grows a little, but each firm's costs have risen, and profits drop to $80,000 for both firms. If the decision must be made simultaneously without either firm having information about the decision of the other, the equilibrium is that both will advertise, and both will earn $80,000 in profits.

Dynamic Games

The static analysis above inherently assumes that pricing and advertising decisions are irreversible, occur simultaneously, and occur before the other knows what has happened. But most markets are dynamic, and firms are constantly trying new prices and other sales techniques to increase profits. This reality has led to the development of **dynamic games.**

Dynamic games: Sequential or repeated games where the players can adjust their actions based on the decisions of other players in the past.

Price Discounting Reconsidered   Another way to look at the pricing outcome in Table 2 is to assume that each firm knows these payoffs and will respond as soon as the other firm lowers its price. This makes the decision process a sequential process. Each firm waits for the other firm to alter price, then it follows suit. Since each firm has perfect knowledge and knows what each payoff is, a new equilibrium is reached; neither firm lowers prices for its banana splits, and profits remain at $100,000. Neither firm would be inclined to lower price since profits would drop for both firms. This outcome is similar to the kinked demand curve model discussed earlier.

Advertising: Another Look   Once the game becomes dynamic and sequential, the outcome between Lowe's and Home Depot shown in Table 3 will be that neither firm advertises, and profits for each firm remain at $100,000. You have probably noticed that Lowe's and Home Depot tend to locate near each other, and both firms tend to advertise only at specific times of the year mostly in spring and fall. Both tend to focus on competing on the basis of service and somewhat on price. Both have come to the conclusion that spending huge amounts on advertising does not pay, given the nature of the competition.

Predatory Pricing

Predatory pricing involves offering sufficiently low prices to consumers in the short run to eliminate competitors, so that eventually prices can be increased in the longer run once the competitors are gone. Firms with monopoly power in a market can use price wars or threaten their use to keep firms from entering the market. Such was the case involving American Airlines and several low-cost carriers at Dallas-Fort Worth Airport (DFW) in the mid-1990s.[7]

    American Airlines is the dominant air carrier at DFW, and several low-cost carriers (Vanguard, Western Pacific, and SunJet) entered the market. As the court noted:

Predatory pricing: Selling below cost to consumers in the short run, hoping to eliminate competitors so that prices can be raised in the longer run to earn economic profits.

---

[7] *U.S. v. AMR et al.,* 140 F. Supp. 2d (2001).

During this period, these low-cost carriers created a new market dynamic, charging markedly lower fares on certain routes. For a certain period (of differing length in each market) consumers of air travel on these routes enjoyed lower prices. The number of passengers also substantially increased. American responded to the low-cost carriers by reducing some of its own fares and increasing the number of flights serving the routes. In each instance, the low-fare carrier failed to establish itself as a durable market presence, and so eventually moved its operations or ceased its separate existence entirely. After the low-fare carrier ceased operations, American generally resumed its prior marketing strategy, and in certain markets reduced the number of flights and raised its prices, roughly to levels comparable to those prior to the period of low-fare competition.[8]

Table 4 captures the essence of the case using hypothetical data.

TABLE 4   Payoff Matrix for American Airlines and Low-Cost Carriers

Low-Cost Carriers (potential entrants)	American Airlines (incumbent)	
	Normal	Price war
Enter	$100,000,$100,000	−$100,000,−$100,000
Do not enter	$0,$400,000	$0,$400,000

Without the entry of the low-cost carriers, American earns $400,000 in profit. When they enter, American has a choice: continue to operate as normal and not slash prices (Normal column), or compete vigorously by lowering prices and offering more flights (Price War column). Normal activity results in profits to both parties of $100,000, whereas engaging in a price war brings losses of $100,000 to both, which ultimately the newly formed, lower-capitalized carriers probably cannot sustain. Once the low-cost carriers are gone, prices and routes can return to their original states.

This case raises an interesting issue: Was American just dropping fares to meet competition, or was it actually engaging in predatory behavior? Standard economic theory suggests that predatory behavior is unprofitable and unlikely. The argument goes like this: Suffering large losses to remove competition and then making it up through monopoly pricing is not likely to be profitable in the long run. Once the competitors are removed and high prices return, these same high prices provide a strong incentive for new firms to enter, and the monopoly is stuck continually lowering prices to maintain its monopoly. Modern game theory has challenged this view.

Table 4 and the American Airlines episode illustrate the new thinking by game theorists on predatory pricing. One possibility is that the profits from the monopoly are sufficient to offset the bouts of price wars required to maintain the monopoly. Second, this is a potentially repeatable game, and American (at least at DFW) has effectively shown that it stands ready to defend its turf. This *commitment* to lower prices (Price Wars) is a warning to other airlines that are considering whether to enter the market. Repeated games permit firms to demonstrate their strategic decisions, thereby creating a *reputation* for fierce competitive behavior, thus influencing the decisions of others. Ultimately, American won this case and also won on further appeal in 2003. The courts were not convinced that American did anything except match the prices of its competitors: In the words of the court, American engaged "only in bare, but not brass knuckle competition."

---

[8] *U.S. v. AMR*, p. 1141.

This case makes it clear that when the game is repeatable, the strategic matrix expands substantially. We now turn to some of the strategies that game theorists look at for repeated games.

Repeated Game Strategies

Games can be endlessly (infinitely) repeated or repeated for a specific number of rounds. In either case, repeating opens the game to different types of strategies that are unavailable for the one-off game. These strategies can take into account the past behavior of rivals and can be more nuanced than one-off or limited sequential decisions. This section briefly explores these new strategies and some of their implications for understanding oligopoly behavior.

One possibility is simply to cooperate or defect from the beginning. These simple strategies, however, leave you at the mercy of your opponent, or lead to unfavorable outcomes where both firms earn less or suffer losses. A more robust set of strategies are **trigger strategies:** action is taken contingent on your opponent's past decisions. These strategies are described in the following sections.

> **Trigger strategies:** Action is taken contingent on your opponent's past decisions.

Grim Trigger

Let's start by considering an industry that is earning oligopoly profits. Suppose that all of a sudden, one firm lowers its price, maybe because it is in financial trouble and wants to increase sales right away. Under the grim trigger rule, the other firms lower their prices—but they do not stop there. They permanently lower their prices, making the financial condition of the original firm who reduced prices even more severe.

The grim trigger rule, thus, is this: Any decision by your opponent to defect (choose an unfavorable outcome) is met by a permanent retaliatory decision forever. This is a harsh decision rule. Its negative aspect is that it is subject to misreading. For example, has your competition lowered its price in an attempt to gain market share at your expense, or has the market softened for the product in general? This strategy can quickly lead to the unfavorable Prisoner's Dilemma result. To avoid this problem, researchers have developed the trembling hand trigger strategy.

Trembling Hand Trigger

This strategy simply allows for one mistake by your opponent before you retaliate forever. This gives your opponent a chance to make a mistake and reduces misreads that are a problem for the grim trigger strategy. This approach can be extended to accept two nonsequential defects, and so on, but they can be exploited by clever opponents who figure out they can get away with a few "mistakes" before their opponent retaliates.

Tit-for-Tat

This is a simple strategy that repeats the prior move of competitors. If one firm lowers its price, its rivals follow suit one time. If the same firm offers rebates or special offers, rivals do exactly the same in the next time period. This strategy has the efficient qualities that it rewards cooperation and punishes defection. It also offers forgiveness for defectors, so it avoids the misreading problems of the grim and trembling hand triggers. **Tit-for-tat strategies** also have been extended to include forgiveness of a single defection on a random basis.

> **Tit-for-tat strategies:** Simple strategies that repeat the prior move of competitors. If your opponent lowers price, you do the same. This approach has the efficient quality that it rewards cooperation and punishes unfavorable strategies (defections).

This short list of strategies illustrates the richness of repeated games. Strategies tend to be more successful if they are relatively simple and easy to understand by competitors, tend to foster cooperation, have some credible punishment to reduce defections, and provide for forgiveness to avoid the costly mistakes associated with misreading opponents.[9]

Game theory took a long time to enter the profession, but it is now firmly entrenched. Its usefulness is in bringing forth insights for not only human behavior, but for oligopolistic market behavior, that is mutually interdependent.

---

[9] Nick Wilkinson, *Managerial Economics: A Problem Solving Approach* (Cambridge: Cambridge University Press), 2005, p. 373.

Issue: Can We Use Game Theory to Predict the Future?

Professor Bruce Bueno de Mesquita of New York University thinks so. He has developed a game theory simulation program that he uses to predict the outcome of future negotiations as well as to suggest strategies to alter the likely outcome of negotiations.

His model quantifies the following four pieces of information using the opinions of participants and experts:

1. Catalog every individual or group with a meaningful stake or interest in the outcome (*stakeholders*).

2. Estimate what each of the stakeholders wants (*position*).

3. Approximate how important the issue is to each of these individuals or groups (*salience*).

4. Estimate how influential each of the players are relative to each other (*influence*).

First, he determines a numerical scale of outcomes and then assigns a numerical estimate for position, salience, and influence to each of the stakeholders.

As an example, most corporate firms face a large array of laws and regulations that pose potential legal tangles. Litigation is costly, time consuming, and typically involves threats of huge fines and/or criminal charges. Professor Bueno de Mesquita detailed a case of a firm embroiled in litigation with the Justice Department. The outcomes in this case were given numerical values and ranged from multiple severe felonies (100), to one severe felony (75), to several lesser felonies (60), to multiple

misdemeanors (25), to just one misdemeanor (0). He then consulted participants and experts to estimate position, salience, and influence (using the same 100-point scale) for each stakeholder and created a table like the one below.

This table represents only a sample of the stakeholders and outcomes Professor Bueno de Mesquita considered. He included nearly 50 stakeholders and 8 categories of outcomes. Using just this data, the initial run of the simulation suggested that a settlement would give a result around 80, one severe felony and several lesser felonies. This turned out to be what the executives and their lawyers feared would happen.

The firm did not consider this a fair outcome because they felt it was not obvious that they were responsible for the injuries, nor did they intend any harm to the victims. What could be done? By altering the firm's numbers and running the simulation over several times, a better outcome was suggested by the model. First, the attorney for one executive had to harden his initial set-

tlement offer and demand misdemeanors only. Similarly, the company's directors who were eager to settle had to harden their initial demands to misdemeanors only. One thing that is clear in these types of negotiations is that whether criminal charges are warranted or not, they tend to encourage defendants to settle whether guilty or not.

By adopting the new negotiation strategy, the firm was able to achieve a settlement of one lesser felony and several misdemeanors (40 on the scale). This was roughly the outcome predicted when the modified positions were run through the game theory simulation.

Professor Bueno de Mesquita's model has been used to predict the results of such wide-ranging issues as Middle East peace negotiations, Securities and Exchange Commission investigations into fraud, and Environmental Protection Agency investigations of potential chemical harm when a firm suddenly introduces a "new and improved" version of a successful product where a significant chemical is absent in the new version. A declassified CIA study finds that his model "hit the bull's-eye about twice as often as the government's experts" who provided the data. While not useful for all types of predictions, his approach is highly useful for many negotiations.

Sources: Bruce Bueno de Mesquita, *The Predictioneer's Game: Using the Logic of Brazen Self-Interest to See and Shape the Future* (New York: Random House), 2009; and Nicholas Thompson, "Forecast: Self-Serving," *New York Times Magazine* November 8, 2009, p. 30.

Stakeholder	Position	Salience	Influence
Affected individuals (plaintiffs)	90	80	15.71
Union	85	80	5.61
Senior executives (defendants)	25	80	7.26
Corporate council	25	75	3.63
Dept. of Justice attorney	100	85	11.16
OHSA representative	25	65	16.43

Summary of Market Structures

In this and the previous two chapters, we have studied the four major market structures: competition, monopolistic competition, oligopoly, and monopoly. As we move through this list, market power becomes greater, and the ability of the firm to earn economic profits in the long run grows.

Table 5 summarizes the important distinctions between these four market structures. Keep in mind that market structure analysis allows you to look at the overall characteristics of the market and predict the pricing and profit behavior of the firms. The outcomes for competition and monopolistic competition are particularly attractive for consumers because firms price their products equal to average total costs and earn just enough to keep them in the business over the long haul.

TABLE 5	Summary of Market Structures			
	Competition	**Monopolistic Competition**	**Oligopoly**	**Monopoly**
Number of Firms	Many	Many	Few	One
Product	Homogeneous	Differentiated	Homogeneous or differentiated	Unique
Barriers to Entry or Exit?	No	No	Yes	Yes
Strategic Interdependence?	No	No	Yes	Not applicable
Long-Run Price Decision	P = ATC	P = ATC	P > ATC	P > ATC
Long-Run Profits	Zero	Zero	Usually economic	Economic
Key Summary Characteristic	Price taker	Product differentiation	Mutual interdependence	One-firm industry

In contrast, the outcomes for oligopolistic and monopolistic industries are not as favorable to consumers. Concentrated markets have considerable market power, which shows up in pricing and output decisions. However, keep in mind that markets with market power (oligopolies) often involve giants competing with giants. Even though there is a mutual interdependence in their decisions, and they may not always compete vigorously over prices, they often are innovative because of some competitive pressures. We see this today especially in the electronics and automobile markets.

Only the Paranoid Survive is the title of a book by a former president of Intel Corporation, Andy Grove. His point is that you must keep ahead of the competition in innovation and technology if you want to remain in business. The last couple of years saw many large firms (Enron, WorldCom, Kmart, Lehman Brothers, and the Italian company Parmalat) fail or go bankrupt, costing their stockholders billions. Without the government bailouts during 2008–2009, many more large firms would have failed. Bigness does not make firms immune to market pressures.

■ CHECKPOINT

GAME THEORY

- Game theory uses sophisticated mathematical analysis to model oligopolistic mutual interdependence.

- Game theory characteristics include (a) degrees of cooperation, (b) number of players, (c) simultaneous or sequential decision making, (d) information completeness, (e) discrete or continuous strategies, (f) one-off or repeated games, and (g) zero-sum or non-zero-sum games.

- The Prisoner's Dilemma is a static noncooperative game where players minimize their maximum prison time by both confessing, a strategy that neither would have taken had they been able to communicate with one another.

- Nash equilibrium analysis showed that a solution exists for n-person games if each player chooses his optimal strategy, given that all other players have done the same.

- Games that are repeated lead to more nuanced trigger strategies, including grim trigger, trembling hand trigger, and tit-for-tat.

QUESTION: Game theory and sophisticated mathematical modeling can be used to develop PokerBots and chess software that consistently beat chess champions and will eventually probably beat poker champions. What might keep this same analysis from being used to beat the stock market?

Answers to the Checkpoint question can be found at the end of this chapter.

Key Concepts

Monopolistic competition, p. 238
Product differentiation, p. 239
Oligopoly, p. 243
Mutual interdependence, p. 243
Cartel, p. 244
Kinked demand curve, p. 246
Game theory, p. 247

Prisoner's Dilemma, p. 249
Nash equilibrium, p. 251
Static games, p. 251
Dynamic games, p. 252
Predatory pricing, p. 252
Trigger strategies, p. 254
Tit-for-tat strategies, p. 254

Chapter Summary
Monopolistic Competition

Monopolistic competition assumes nearly the same characteristics as the competitive model, including the following:

- There are a large number of small firms with insignificant market share.
- There are no barriers to entry and exit.
- Unlike competition, the products sold by monopolistically competitive firms are similar, but differentiated. Product differentiation is the key to this market structure.

Although product differences are often modest, each firm nonetheless faces a downward sloping demand curve with an associated marginal revenue curve. This demand curve is, however, highly elastic.

Pricing and output behavior in the short run for the monopolistically competitive firm look a lot like that for a weak monopolist. Profit is maximized by selling an output where MR = MC.

In the long run, entry and exit of other firms will eliminate short-run profits or losses. If short-run profits exist, entry will reduce individual demand curves until the demand curve is just tangent to the average total cost curve. If short-run losses are the rule, exit will expand the demand curve of remaining firms until, again, the demand curve is tangent to the long-run average total cost (LRATC) curve.

At long-run equilibrium, P = ATC, and the firm earns normal profits. This output level is not, however, equal to the minimum point on the LRATC curve—it is lower than output needed to minimize costs. This is the cost to consumers from product differentiation. Costs of advertising, rapid innovation, and "me too" copying are all included in the price of the products we purchase.

Oligopoly

Oligopoly industries are those in which the market is controlled by just a few firms. What constitutes a few firms is not precisely defined. Oligopoly products can be the same or differentiated, and barriers to entry are usually substantial.

Because there are only a few firms, decisions by one firm are dependent on what other firms in the industry decide to do. Economists refer to this as mutual interdependence. This is the key characteristic of oligopolies.

Cartels are illegal in the United States, but they are permitted in other parts of the world. Firms in cartels collude and agree to set monopoly prices and share the market according to some formula. Cartels are inherently unstable because cheating is profitable.

The kinked demand curve model of oligopoly answers the question of why oligopoly prices appear stable. The model assumes that if the firm raises its price, competitors will not react and raise theirs, but if the firm lowers its price, other firms will lower theirs in response. These reactions by competitors create a "kink" in the firm's demand curve and a discontinuity in the MR curve. This discontinuity permits marginal costs to vary considerably before the firm will change its pricing structure.

Game Theory

Modern game theory owes its origins to the mathematician John von Neumann.

The Prisoner's Dilemma is a static, noncooperative game in which each player must anticipate whether the other is going to confess or not. Both players would be better off not confessing, but each will confess in the end. Both players end up minimizing their worst outcome (minimax solution).

John Nash showed that there is a solution in an *n*-person game if each player chooses his optimal strategy, given that all other players have done the same. This was an important result that allowed economists to develop realistic but complex games of market interactions, because they knew a solution existed.

Dynamic games allow for sequential decision making. This often changes the equilibrium outcome. When games are repeated, a host of new (more complex) strategies are introduced. They include trigger strategies such as grim trigger, trembling hand trigger, and tit-for-tat.

Questions and Problems
Check Your Understanding

1. How do monopolistic competitive markets differ from competitive markets? If monopolistically competitive firms are making economic profits in the short run, what happens in the long run?

2. Describe the assumption underlying the kinked demand curve model. Describe why marginal cost can vary, but price remains constant.

3. How many firms constitute an oligopoly? What else characterizes oligopoly markets?

4. When economists speak of "mutual interdependence" in oligopoly markets, what do they mean? Why is mutual interdependence such an important element of oligopoly markets?

5. What makes the strategies so different for repeated games than for one-off games?

6. Why is it difficult for cartels to effectively maintain high prices over the longer term?

Apply the Concepts

7. Google has a huge share of the search activity on the Internet, as well as the online advertising revenue it generates. Microsoft had roughly the same percentage for operating system sales on microcomputers when the government filed its antitrust suit. Why hasn't the government filed a similar suit against Google?

8. Holding the industry constant, why does a monopolist earn more profits than a firm in an oligopolistic setting? Why does the oligopolist earn more than a monopolistic competitor?

9. "Monopolistic competition has a little of monopoly and a little of competition, hence its name." Do you agree? Why or why not?

10. We saw in the last chapter that the HHI (Herfindahl-Hirshman index) is used by the Department of Justice to measure industry concentration. Since domestically we have virtually no monopolies, some would argue that the HHI is really used to measure the degree of oligopoly. However, the HHI represents domestic concentration, and many of the products we purchase are made globally and sold in the United States by foreign firms. Has global competition made these HHI estimates less meaningful? Are old-line American oligopolies (autos, steel, and airlines) more like monopolistic competitors today? Why or why not?

11. In both competitive and monopolistically competitive markets, firms earn normal profits in the long run. What enables oligopoly firms to have the opportunity to earn economic profits in the long run?

12. As new firms enter a monopolistically competitive market, what happens to the average total cost curve for existing firms? What happens to the individual firm demand curve? What happens to individual firm profits?

13. The 1982 Export Trading Company Act and the 1918 Webb-Pomerene Act permit export cartels in the United States. Export cartels are groups of firms that can legally collude, set prices, and share marketing and distribution of their products in foreign countries. These cartels must register with the government, and their activities cannot affect domestic competition. Economic theory suggests that cartels are entities that exist to maximize monopoly profits for members. Given this, why would the United States permit these cartels to exist?

14. When trying to get tickets to a Broadway show recently, my wife may have had a chance to see game theory in action. Tickets for shows 6 months away went on sale online at 6:00 in the morning and she was there at 6:02. Every time she requested seats in a good area, she was informed they were unavailable, but others in much worse locations were available. No matter what day or which show, less attractive alternatives were suggested. Can you think of a game theory explanation that might suggest why this was happening?

15. Why does the U.S. Department of Justice successfully sue a cartel of leading foreign producers of LCD flat screens for price fixing in 2008, but not go after the OPEC (Organization of Petroleum Exporting Countries) cartel?

In the News

16. As we have seen, cartels face a difficult time holding their group together. According to *The Economist* (March 31, 2007, p. 84), "Co-ordinating a price is one thing; sticking to it is another. Companies face the same dilemma that has undone countless hypothetical prisoners in economics textbooks." How is the incentive structure that leads to cheating in a cartel similar to that of the Prisoner's Dilemma?

17. John Gapper titled his article "Little Laptops Snap at the Oligopoly" (*Financial Times,* June 16, 2009, p. 9), and makes the point that netbooks (small, light, cheap laptop computers) are putting competitive pressure on the "three-way alliance among Microsoft, Intel and Dell." He is suggesting that these three firms constitute an oligopoly. Do you agree that Microsoft, Intel, and Dell Computer constitute an oligopoly? Why or why not?

Answers to Questions in CheckPoints

Check Point: Monopolistic Competition

Clowns are unique; their acts are copyrighted and protected, and this is one way to differentiate your circus from others. Celebrity clowns draw crowds, especially youngsters, and are cheaper than buying, keeping, training, and insuring animals (not to mention the hassles from animal rights groups).

Check Point: Oligopoly

The most recent example is the Internet. Barriers to entry in a large number of well-established industries (big and small) are affected. It is clearly changing the software, music, publishing, and entertainment industries. In a similar way, sequencing of DNA is another innovation that is rapidly changing the pharmaceutical industry.

Check Point: Game Theory

Game theory is best used with a relatively small number of decision makers. Chess has a finite (but huge) number of moves, and computers can search for the optimal play. Poker involves a limited number of opponents. Games give insights into human behavior that can be used as inputs into stock market decisions. But when the number of participants, stocks, and economic variables are considered, the computing power required to solve the stock market problem probably prevents its use in real time.

Theory of Input Markets

11

Illustration Works/Alamy

The role model for indignant managers is the film director Alfred Hitchcock. When asked by anxious movie stars what their "motivation" was in a scene, his answer was blunt. "Your salary," he would say.

—Stefan Stern[1]

Hardly a day goes by without media reference to some celebrity's income or some CEO's astronomical salary laden with stock options. Rock stars and professional athletes command seven-figure salaries (that's millions of dollars), while your economics instructor labors away for a five-figure pittance that barely covers the costs of living. Meanwhile, shortages in nursing and elementary education seem to persist year after year, and we see numerous wage discrimination cases going to litigation. How are all these developments to be explained? Labor markets are complex institutions, and as usual, understanding the issues connected with them will require some simplification.

Input markets, also called factor markets, are extremely important to our economy. To this point in the book, we have focused on product markets, mentioning input markets only incidentally. Sitting behind the production of goods and services, however, are workers, machinery, and manufacturing plants. Few firms can operate without employees or capital. Similarly, few households could survive without the income that work provides.

The analysis of input markets in this chapter focuses on the labor and capital markets, while briefly touching on land rents and entrepreneurial profits. The first two sections look

---

[1] Stefan Stern, "The Meaning of Life at Work and Other Employee Perks," *Financial Times*, March 11, 2008, p. 16.

at competitive labor markets where the participants—firms and employees—are price takers. We examine some imperfections in the labor market and look for differences in outcomes. We then turn to the role that capital markets play in the economy. The chapter closes with a brief examination of land and entrepreneurship, the source of rents and profits. In the following chapter, we will return to the labor market and take a closer look at several pressing labor issues, including human capital, economic discrimination, and the economics of labor unions.

Competitive labor markets are similar to competitive product markets. First, we assume that firms operate in competitive industries with many buyers and sellers, a homogeneous product, and easy entry and exit to the industry. As you will recall, moreover, the firms in competitive industries are price takers. Each firm is so small that it has no perceptible impact on industry price; all firms can do is adjust their output in response to changes in industry price.

A second assumption of competitive labor markets, inhumane as it may sound, is that workers are considered homogeneous, and labor is treated as a homogeneous commodity. One unit of labor is a perfect substitute for another in the competitive market, and no potential employees are "special." More precisely, all employees are regarded as equally productive, such that firms have no preference for one employee over another.

Third, a competitive labor market assumes that information in the industry is widely available and accurate. Everyone knows what the going wage rate is, so well-informed decisions about how much labor to supply are made by workers, and firms can wisely decide how many workers to hire.

A firm's demand for labor is a derived demand; it is derived from consumer demand for the firm's product and the productivity of labor. The labor supply, on the other hand, is determined by the individual preferences of potential workers for work or leisure. Like all competitive markets, supply and demand interact to determine equilibrium wages and employment. Much of this analysis you have seen before, but we now apply these analytical techniques to labor markets. We begin by looking at how the decisions by individuals to participate in labor markets generate the supply of labor.

Competitive Labor Supply

When you decide to work, you are giving up leisure, understood broadly as nonwork activity, in exchange for the income that work brings. Economists assume people prefer leisure activities to work. This may not be entirely true, since work can be a source of personal satisfaction and a network of social connections, as well as provide many other benefits. For our discussion, however, we follow the practice of economists in simply dividing individual or household time into work and leisure. Note that the term *leisure* encompasses all activities that do not involve paid work, including caring for children, doing household chores, and activities that are truly leisurely.

Individual Labor Supply

Supply of labor: The amount of time an individual is willing to work at various wage rates.

The **supply of labor** represents the time an individual is willing to work—the labor the individual is willing to supply—at various wage rates. On a given day, the most a person can work is 24 hours, though clearly such a schedule could not be sustained for long, given that we all need rest and sleep. For high wages, you would probably be willing to work horrendous hours for a short time, whereas if wages were low enough, you might not be willing to work at all. Between these two extremes lies the normal supply of labor curve for most of us.

Panel A of Figure 1 shows a typical labor supply curve for individuals. This individual is willing to supply l_1 hours of work a day when the wage is W_1. What happens if the wage rate increases? Assume that wages increase to W_2: This individual now is willing to increase hours spent working from l_1 to l_2 (point b), reducing her hours of leisure.

Karl Marx (1818–1883)

"Working men of all countries unite!" With this exhortation, Karl Marx ended his seminal *Communist Manifesto,* neatly summing up both his philosophy and his view of the world. The solution was revolution by the proletariat—the working class that was the hero of all Marx believed and proposed.

Karl Marx was born in Germany in 1818. He spent much of his adult life, however, in England, where he died in 1883. By the time of his death, Marx and Friedrich Engels had crafted the essence of communism—the last ideology to seriously challenge capitalism in the 20th century. In

their two major works, *The Communist Manifesto* (1848) and *Das Kapital* (1867), Marx and Engels offered a severe critique of capitalism and extolled the virtues of proletariat rebellion and the utopia of a stateless world order.

To preserve their privileges, the ruling class had always striven to oppress the underclasses. Marx saw a struggle between the bourgeoisie (or property owners) and the proletariat (or workers). Modern states were merely a way to repress workers for the benefit of the bourgeoisie.

This exploitation—the essence of capitalism—not only kept the bourgeoisie in power, but it also alienated the proletariat from its own labor, which to Marx was the true essence of all economic value. The only prescription to cure the monopolistic and monopsonistic exploitation of labor was proletariat revolution.

Substitution Effect

When wages rise, people tend to substitute work for leisure since the opportunity cost of leisure grows. This is known as the **substitution effect.** The substitution effect for labor supply is always positive; it leads to more hours of work when the wage rate increases.

Note that this effect is similar to the substitution effect consumers experience when the price of a product declines. When the price of one product falls, consumers substitute that

> **Substitution effect:** Higher wages mean that the value of work has increased, and the opportunity costs of leisure are higher, so work is substituted for leisure.

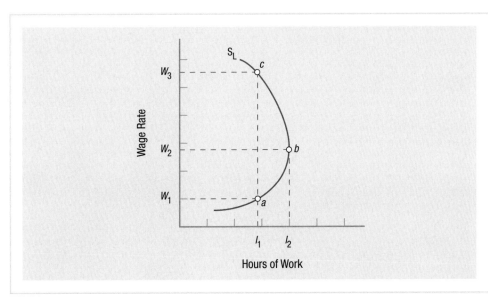

FIGURE 1—Individual Supply of Labor

When wages are W_1, this individual will work l_1 hours, but when the wage rate rises to W_2, her willingness to work rises to l_2. Over these two wage rates she is substituting work for leisure. Once the wage rises above W_2, the income effect begins to dominate, since she now has sufficient income that leisure is now more important and her labor supply curve is backward bending.

product for others. The substitution effect for consumer products, however, is negative (price falls and consumption rises), while it is always positive for labor (wages rise and the supply of labor increases).

Income Effect

When wages rise, if you continue to work the same hours as before, your income will rise. When wage rates are very high, however, the income from working a few hours may be enough to support the lifestyle you wish. Higher wages may permit you to work fewer hours, but also enjoy a higher standard of living. This **income effect** on labor supply is normally negative—higher wages and income lead to fewer hours worked. As a result, the supply curve for *individuals* in Figure 1 is *backward bending*: At wages above W_2, workers increasingly elect to substitute leisure for the income that comes from additional work.

Once again, this is similar to the income effect consumers experience when the price of a common product drops. The falling price of this product permits consumers to purchase the same quantity as before and still have some added income left over to spend on other products. Higher wages mean a higher income, and with a higher income leisure looks more attractive.

The labor supply curve for individuals shows that, at wages below W_2, people will substitute work for leisure; income is more important than leisure at these wage levels. When wages are above W_2, workers will do the opposite, substituting leisure for work; they have enough income so leisure is more important.

When the labor supply curve is positively sloped, as it is below W_2 in Figure 1, the substitution effect is stronger than the income effect; thus, higher wages lead to more hours worked. Conversely, when the supply of labor curve bends backward, as it does above W_2, the income effect overpowers the substitution effect. In this case, higher wages mean fewer hours worked.

Backward bending labor supply curves have been observed empirically in developed and developing countries. Still, it takes rather high income levels before the income effect begins to overpower the substitution effect. People like to have incomes well beyond what is required to satisfy their basic needs before they select more leisure over work as wages rise.

Market Labor Supply Curves

The labor supply for any occupation or industry is upward sloping; higher wages for a job mean more inquiries and job applications. Thus, although an individual's labor supply curve may be backward bending, market labor supply curves are normally positively sloped as shown in Figure 2. Note that this is true for all other inputs to the production process,

FIGURE 2—Market Labor Supplies

Market labor supplies are positively related to the wage rate. Increasing wages in one industry attract labor from other industries (a movement from point *d* to point *e* as the wage rises from W_1 to W_2). In contrast, market labor supply curves *shift* in response to demographic changes, changes in the nonwage benefits of jobs, wages paid in other occupations, and nonwage income.

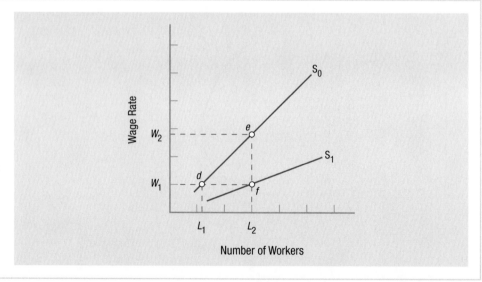

including raw materials such as copper, steel, and silicon, as well as for capital and land: Higher prices mean higher quantities supplied.

Changes in wage rates change the quantity of labor supplied. For example, increasing wages in one industry attract labor from other industries. This is a movement along the market labor supply curve, shown as a movement along S_0 from points d to e as wages (input prices) rise from W_1 to W_2.

Factors That Change Labor Supply

But what factors will cause the entire market labor supply curve to shift from, say, S_0 to S_1 in Figure 2 so that L_2 workers are willing to work for a wage of W_1 (point f)? These include demographic changes, nonwage benefits of jobs, wages paid in other occupations, and nonwage income.

Demographic Changes

Changes in population, immigration patterns, and labor force participation rates (the percentage of individuals in a group who enter the labor force) all change labor supplies by altering the number of qualified people available for work. Over the past three decades, labor force participation rates among women have steadily risen, continually adding workers to the expanding American labor force; dual-earner households are increasingly the norm. Today, both parents work in two-thirds of all married-couple households with children. Other demographic changes have shifted the labor supply curve by modifying the labor–leisure preferences among workers. Health improvements, for example, have lengthened the typical working life.

Nonmoney Aspects of Jobs

Changes in the nonwage benefits of an occupation will similarly shift the supply of labor in that market. If employers can manage to increase the pleasantness, safety, or status of a job, labor supply will increase. Other nonmoney perks also help. The airline industry, for example, has greatly increased the number of people willing to work in mundane positions by allowing employees (and in some instances their immediate families) to fly anywhere for free on a standby basis.

Wages in Alternative Jobs

When worker skills in one industry are readily transferable to other jobs or industries, the wages paid in those other markets will affect wage rates and the labor supply in the first industry. For example, Web and computer programming skills are useful in all industries, and their wages in one industry affect all industries. Because at least some of the skills that all workers possess will benefit other employers, all labor markets have some influence over each other. Rising wages in growth industries will shrink the supply of labor available to firms in other industries.

Nonwage Income

Changes in income from sources other than working (such as income from a trust) will change the supply of labor. As nonwage income rises, hours of work supplied declines. If you have enough income from nonwork sources, after all, the retirement urge will set in no matter what your age. Maybe this is where the term "idle rich" came from.

The key thing to remember here is that market labor supply curves are normally positively sloped, even though an individual's labor supply curve may be backward bending. In the next section, we put this together with the other blade in the scissors: the demand for labor in competitive labor markets.

Issue: Digital Bedouins and the World of Work

Some people suggest we are becoming "digital Bedouins," or nomads. Cell phones, Wi-Fi laptops, and Internet-connected smart phones (such as Blackberry and iPhone) are changing the way we work, where we live, and how we communicate with friends and family. As the table below shows, the impact of mobile technology is far greater for the young than those over 50.

Over half of the world's population subscribes to a mobile phone network. A growing number of people now use their smart phones and laptops as an office.

Firms are jettisoning cubicles and other office space for more in-demand mobile space and encouraging employees to work at home or on the road with only periodic get-togethers with colleagues.

MoveOn.org is an example of a purely nomadic organization. MoveOn has several dozen staffers, thousands of consultants, and several million volunteers, and a company rule that "no *two* people anywhere may share a physical office." This prevents organizational cliques. Through the use of instant messaging, they know who is available to help make a decision. Since MoveOn is an advocacy group, this process may be sufficient, and it clearly minimizes administrative expenses.

But working at home or on the move also has its drawbacks. When people work together in physical offices, the interaction helps to cement

Josef Niedermeier/Photolibrary

relationships. Also, work presumably ends when you leave the office. Being a nomad has the potential to be isolating and, unless you have discipline, all-consuming.

Nomads are also changing how buildings are designed, how cities and parks are developed, and where many young people choose to live. Soon, entire cities will be Wi-Fied with WiMax or some other technology, and buildings will have specific areas for mobile computing. The world is changing to serve a new generation of digital Bedouins.

Source: Based on "Nomads at Last: A Special Report on Mobile Telecoms," *Economist*, April 12, 2008.

Mobile Phone or PDA Use by Age Group

Activity	Age 18–29	Age 50–64
Send or receive text messages	85%	38%
Play a game	47	13
Play music	38	5
Access the Internet	31	10
Send or receive instant messages	26	11
Watch a video	19	4

■ CHECKPOINT

COMPETITIVE LABOR SUPPLY

- Competitive labor markets assume that firms operate in competitive product markets and purchase homogeneous labor, and that information is widely available and accurate.
- The supply of labor represents the time an individual is willing to work.
- The substitution effect occurs when wages rise, as people tend to substitute work for leisure because the opportunity cost of leisure is higher or vice versa when wages fall.
- When wages rise and you continue to work the same number of hours, your income rises. When wages rise high enough, an income effect occurs in which leisure is traded for income, and the supply of labor curve for individuals is backward bending.
- Industry or occupation labor supply curves are upward sloping.
- The labor supply curve shifts with demographic changes, changes in the nonwage aspects of an occupation, changes in the wages of alternative jobs, and changes in nonwage income.

QUESTIONS: Assume that you take a job with flexible hours, but initially your salary is based on a 40-hour week. Your salary begins at $15 an hour, or $30,000 a year. Assuming your salary rises, at what salary (hourly wage) would you begin to work fewer than 40 hours a week (remember, the job permits flexible hours)? If your rich aunt dies and leaves you $500,000, would this alter the wage rate where you cut your work hours? Do you think this wage rate will be the same when you are 35 and have two children?

Answers to the Checkpoint questions can be found at the end of this chapter.

Competitive Labor Demand

The competitive firm's **demand for labor** is derived from the demand for the firm's product and the productive capabilities of a unit of labor.

Demand for labor: Demand for labor is derived from the demand for the firm's product and the productivity of labor.

Marginal Revenue Product

Assume a firm wants to hire an additional worker, and that worker is able to produce 15 units of the firm's product. Further, assume that the product sells for $10 a unit, and labor is the only input cost (such as blackberry picking in Oregon), with this cost including a normal return on the investment. The last worker hired is therefore worth $150 to the firm ($15 \times $10 = $150). If the cost of hiring this worker is $150 or less (remember, a normal profit is included in the wage), then the firm will hire this person. If the wage rate for labor exceeds $150, a competitive firm will not hire this marginal worker.

To see how this works in greater detail, look at Table 1. The production function here is similar to the one used earlier in the chapter on production. Column 1 (L) is labor input, Column 2 (Q) is total output, and Column 3 (MPP_L) is the **marginal physical product of labor.** This last value is the additional output a firm receives from employing an added unit of labor ($MPP_L = \Delta Q \div \Delta L$). For example, adding a fourth worker raises output from 25 to 40 units, so the marginal physical product of labor for this additional worker is 15 units.

Marginal physical product of labor: The additional output a firm receives from employing an added unit of labor ($MPP_L = \Delta Q \div \Delta L$).

TABLE 1   Competitive Labor Market

(1) L	(2) Q	(3) MPP_L	(4) P	(5) $MRP_L = VMP_L$	(6) W
—	0	—	10	—	100
1	7	7	10	70	100
2	15	8	10	80	100
3	25	10	10	100	100
4	40	15	10	150	100
5	54	14	10	140	100
6	65	11	10	110	100
7	75	10	10	100	100
8	84	9	10	90	100
9	90	6	10	60	100
10	95	5	10	50	100

In this example, the firm is operating in a competitive market, so it can sell all the output it produces at the prevailing market price of $10. The value of another worker to the firm, called the **marginal revenue product** (MRP_L), is equal to the marginal physical product of labor times marginal revenue:

Marginal revenue product: The value of another worker to the firm is equal to the marginal physical product of labor (MPP_L) times marginal revenue (MR).

$$MRP_L = MPP_L \times MR$$

In our example, adding a fourth worker leads to a marginal revenue product of $150; we multiply the marginal physical product of labor of 15 units by the marginal revenue—or price in this competitive market—of $10 per unit.

Column 5 contains the firm's MRP_L. Additional workers add this value to the firm. Thus, the marginal revenue product curve is the firm's demand for labor, which is graphed in Figure 3 on the next page. Note how the marginal revenue product reaches a maximum at four workers, as shown in column 5 of the table and in the figure.

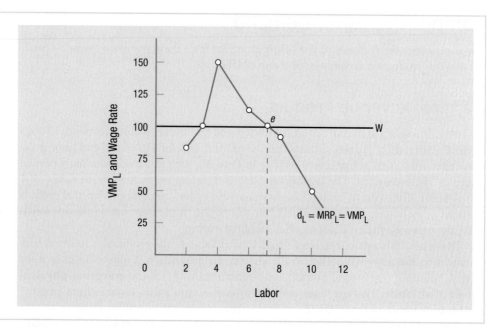

FIGURE 3—The Competitive Firm's Demand for Labor

This figure reflects the data from columns 5 and 6 from Table 1. In this example, the firm is operating in a competitive market, so it can sell all the output it produces at the prevailing market price. The value of the additional worker to the firm, the value of the marginal product (VMP_L), is equal to the marginal physical product of labor times price (or marginal revenue in this case). VMP_L is the competitive firm's demand for labor. If wages are equal to $100, the firm will hire seven workers (point e).

Value of the Marginal Product

Value of the marginal product: The value of the marginal product of labor (VMP_L) is equal to price multiplied by the marginal physical product of labor, or $P \times MPP_L$.

Competitive firms are price takers for whom marginal revenue is equal to the price of the product ($MR = P$). The **value of the marginal product** is defined as $VMP_L = MPP_L \times P$. For the fourth worker in Table 1, the value of the marginal product of labor is 15 units times $10, or $150. This is the same as the marginal revenue product of labor we just calculated. In the competitive case, $MR = P$, hence $VMP_L = MRP_L$. The distinction between VMP and MRP is of little importance here, but when we look at imperfect labor markets, these two will differ because marginal revenue will not equal price and the difference will have policy implications.

Competitive firms hire labor from competitive labor markets. Because each firm is too small to affect the larger market, it can hire all the labor it wants at the market-determined wage. Remember, we are assuming labor is a homogeneous commodity, and one unit of labor is the same as all others.

Table 1 and Figure 3 assume that the going wage for labor (W) is $100. For our firm, this results in seven workers being hired at $100 (point e), since this is the employment level at which $W = VMP_L$. Note that $W = VMP_L$ at three workers as well, but since the value of the marginal product is greater than the wage rate for workers four to six, the firm would hire seven workers, not three, to maximize its gains. The value to the firm of hiring the seventh worker is just equal to what the firm must pay this worker. Profits are maximized for the competitive firm when workers are hired out to the point where $VMP_L = W$.

However, if market wages were to fall to $90, the firm would hire an eighth worker to maximize profits, since with eight employees, VMP_L is also equal to $90.

Factors That Change Labor Demand

The demand for labor is derived from product demand and labor productivity—how much people will pay for the product and how much each unit of labor can produce. It follows that changes in labor demand can arise from changes in either product demand or labor productivity. Because most production also requires other inputs, changes in the price of these other inputs also change the demand for labor.

Change in Product Demand

A decline in the demand for a firm's product will lead to lower market prices reducing VMP_L, and vice versa. As VMP_L for all workers declines, labor demand will shift to the left. Anything that changes the price of the product in competitive markets will shift the firm's demand for labor.

Changes in Productivity

Changes in worker productivity (usually increases) can come about from improving technology or because a firm uses more capital or land along with its workforce. As MPP_L rises, the demand for the marginal worker rises, and thus the firm is willing to pay higher wages for a workforce of the same size, or else to expand its workforce at the same wage rate. As more capital is employed—say, an excavation company shifts from shovels to back loaders—the demand for labor will rise. To be sure, the number of workers hired for a job may decline with mechanization, but the workers running the digging equipment, since they are more productive, will earn higher wages. This is why capital-intensive industries often employ fewer workers than other industries, but their workers are usually high-skill, high-wage employees.

Changes in the Prices of Other Inputs

An increase in the price of capital will drive up the demand for labor. More expensive capital means that labor will be substituted for capital in new projects, thus increasing the demand for labor.

    More labor will be hired when wages fall, but how much more? The answer depends on the elasticity of demand for labor.

Elasticity of Demand for Labor

The **elasticity of demand for labor** (E_L) is the percentage change in the quantity of labor demanded (Q_L) divided by the percentage change in the wage rate (W). This elasticity is found the same way we calculated the price elasticity of demand for products, except that we substitute the wage rate for the price of the product:

$$E_L = \frac{\%\Delta Q_L}{\%\Delta W}$$

    The elasticity of demand for labor measures how responsive the quantity of labor demanded is to changes in wages. An inelastic demand for labor is one where the absolute value of the elasticity is less than 1. Conversely, an elastic curve's computed elasticity is greater than 1.

    The time firms have to adjust to changing wages will affect elasticity. In the short run, when labor is the only truly variable factor of production, elasticity of demand for labor is more inelastic. In the long run, when all production factors can be adjusted, elasticity of demand for labor tends to be more elastic.

Factors That Affect the Elasticity of Demand for Labor

Although time affects elasticity, three other factors also affect the elasticity of demand for labor: elasticity of product demand, ease of substituting other inputs, and labor's share of the production costs. Let's briefly consider each of these.

Elasticity of Demand for the Product

The more elastic the price elasticity of demand for a product, the greater the elasticity of demand for labor. Higher wages result in higher product prices, and the more easily consumers can substitute away from the firm's product, the greater the number of workers who will become unemployed. An elastic demand for labor means that employment is more responsive to wage rates. The opposite is true for products with inelastic demands.

Elasticity of demand for labor: The percentage change in the quantity of labor demanded divided by the percentage change in the wage rate.

Ease of Input Substitutability   The more difficult it is to substitute capital for labor, the more inelastic the demand for labor will be. At this point, computers cannot yet substitute for pilots in commercial airplanes, which results in an inelastic demand for pilots. As a result, pilots have been able to secure high wages from airlines through their union representatives. The easier it is to substitute capital for labor, the less bargaining power workers have, and labor demand tends to be more elastic.

Labor's Share of Total Production Costs   The share of total costs associated with labor is another factor determining the elasticity of demand for labor. If labor's share of total costs is small, the demand for labor will tend to be rather inelastic. In the example of airline pilots above, the percentage of costs going to pilot wages is small, perhaps 10%. Thus, a 20% increase in pilot wages, though a major raise, would increase ticket prices by only 2%. The resulting change in the demand for air travel would be small, and thus its effect on the demand for pilot labor is small. The opposite is true when labor's share of costs is large.

Competitive Labor Market Equilibrium

Generalized market equilibrium in competitive labor markets requires that we take into account the industry supply and demand for labor. The market supply for labor (S_L) is the horizontal sum of the individual labor supply curves in the market.

The market demand for labor, however, is not simply a summation of the demand for labor by all the firms in the market. When wages fall, for instance, this affects all firms—all want to hire more labor and produce more output. This added production reduces market prices for their output and negatively affects the demand for labor. For our purposes it is enough to be aware that market demands for labor are not simply the horizontal summation of individual firm demands.

Turning to Figure 4, we have put both sides of the market together. In panel A, the competitive labor market determines equilibrium wage ($100 per day) and employment (300 workers) based on market supply and demand. Individual firms, in light of their own situation, hire 6 workers where this equilibrium wage is equal to marginal

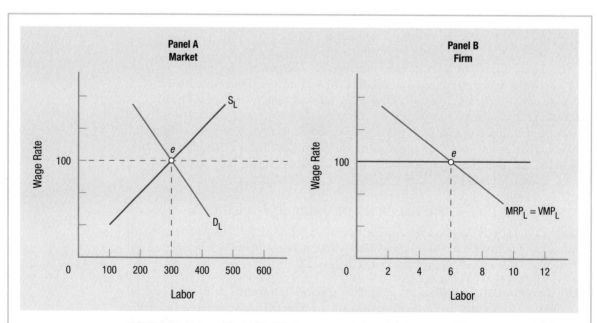

FIGURE 4—Competitive Labor Markets

In panel A, the competitive labor market determines equilibrium wages ($100 per day) and employment (300 workers). Individual firms hire six workers, where this equilibrium wage is equal to marginal revenue product (MRP_L), point *e* in panel B.

revenue product (MRP$_L$), point *e* in panel B. Much like the product markets we discussed in earlier chapters, the invisible hand of the marketplace sets wages and in the end determines employment.

■ CHECKPOINT

COMPETITIVE LABOR DEMAND

- The firm's demand for labor is a derived demand—derived from consumer demand for the product and the productivity of labor.

- Marginal revenue product is equal to the marginal physical product of labor times marginal revenue.

- Value of the marginal product is equal to marginal physical product of labor times the price of the product.

- Since MR = P for the competitive firm, VMP$_L$ = MRP$_L$.

- The demand for labor is equal to the value of the marginal product of labor for competitive firms.

- The demand for labor curve will change if there is a change in the demand for the product, if there is a change in labor productivity, or if there is a change in the price of other inputs.

- The elasticity of demand for labor is equal to the percentage change in quantity of labor demanded divided by the percentage change in the wage rate.

- The elasticity of demand for labor will be *more* elastic the greater the elasticity of demand for the product, the easier it is to substitute other factors for labor, and the larger the share of total production costs attributed to labor.

- Market equilibrium occurs where market labor demand and supply intersect.

QUESTIONS: Individuals are different in terms of ability, attitude, and willingness to work. Given this fact, does it make sense to assume labor is homogeneous? Does this model better fit firms such as Wal-Mart that hire 800+ employees at each store at roughly standardized wages than, say, firms such as Google that look for high-skilled computer geeks?

Answers to the Checkpoint questions can be found at the end of this chapter.

Imperfect Labor Markets and Other Input Markets

The previous two sections focused on conditions in competitive product and input markets. In this section, we are going to relax our assumptions and look at imperfect labor markets. We also will consider the three other inputs in some depth: capital, land, and entrepreneurship.

Imperfect Labor Markets

In the world as we know it, markets are not perfectly competitive. Product markets and labor markets contain *monopolistic* and *oligopolistic* elements. In many product markets, a few firms control the bulk of market share. They may not be monopolies, but they do have some monopoly power, through brand loyalty if nothing else.

Similarly, in most communities, there is only one government hiring firefighters and police officers. When the market contains only one buyer of a resource, economists refer to this lone buyer as a *monopsonist. Monopsony power,* meanwhile, is the control over input supply that the monopsonist enjoys. Before we look at the impact of **monopsony** on the labor market, let us first consider monopoly power in the product market.

Monopsony: A labor market with one employer.

Monopoly Power in Product Markets

As we know, firms that enjoy monopoly power in product markets are price makers, not price takers. Because P > MR, it follows that $VMP_L > MRP_L$. Figure 5 shows why. The firm depicted has monopoly power in the product market, but buys inputs in a competitive environment.

As Figure 5 shows, a competitive firm would equate wage and value of the marginal product (VMP_L), hiring L_C workers and paying the going wage of W_0 (point c). The firm with monopoly power, however, will equate wage and marginal revenue product (MRP_L), thus hiring L_0 workers, though again paying the prevailing wage W_0 (point a). So, although both firms hire workers at the same wage, the firm with monopoly power hires fewer workers.

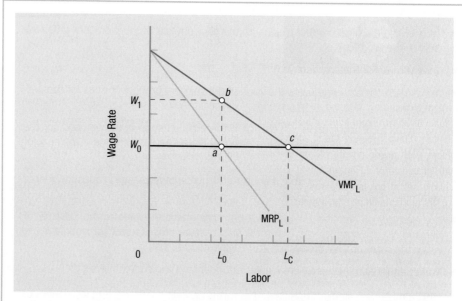

FIGURE 5—Monopoly Firm in Product Market Employing Labor from a Competitive Market

Firms with monopoly power in product markets are price makers. Because P > MR, it follows that $VMP_L > MRP_L$. A competitive firm would equate wages and value of the marginal product (VMP_L), hiring L_C workers and paying the going wage of W_0 (point c). A firm with monopoly power, however, will equate wages and marginal revenue product (MRP_L), thus hiring L_0 workers, though again paying the prevailing wage W_0 (point a). Hence, although both firms hire workers at the same wage, the firm with monopoly power hires fewer workers. Also, the value of the marginal product (VMP_L) of workers in the monopolistic firm is much higher than what they are paid; their value to the firm is W_1 (point b), though they are only paid W_0 (point a). This difference is called monopolistic exploitation of labor.

This means the value of the marginal product (VMP_L) of workers in the monopolistic firm is much higher than what they are paid. Their value to the firm (point b) is W_1, though they are only paid W_0. This difference is referred to as **monopolistic exploitation of labor**. The term is loaded, but what economists mean by it is simply that workers get paid less than the value of their marginal product when working for a monopolist. This is, as you might expect, a source of monopoly profits.

Monopsony

A monopsony is a market with one buyer or employer. The Postal Service, for instance, is the sole employer of mail carriers in this country, just as the armed forces are the only employer of military personnel. Single-employer towns used to dot the American landscape, and some occupations still face monopsony power regularly. Nurses and teachers, for example, often have only a few hospitals or local school districts where they can work.

Monopolistic exploitation of labor: When a firm has monopoly power in the product market, marginal revenue is less than price (MR < P) and the firm hires labor up to the point where MRP_L = wage. Because MRP_L is less than the VMP_L, workers are paid less than the value of their marginal product, and this difference is called monopolistic exploitation of labor.

Since a monopsonist is the only buyer of some input, it will face a positively sloped supply curve for that input, such as supply curve S_L in Figure 6. This firm could hire 14 workers for $10 (point a), or it could increase wages to $11 and hire 15 workers (point b). Since the supply of labor is no longer flat, however, as it was in the competitive market, adding one more worker will cost the firm more than simply the new worker's higher wage. But just how much more?

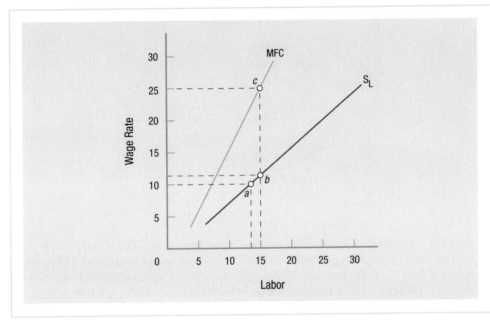

FIGURE 6—Marginal Factor Cost

This monopsonistic firm faces a positively sloped supply curve, S_L. The firm could hire 14 workers for $10 an hour (point a), or it could increase wages to $11 an hour and hire 15 workers (point b). Since the supply curve is positively sloped, however, adding one more worker will cost the firm more than simply the cost of a new worker. To hire an added worker requires a higher wage, and all current employees also must be paid the higher wage. Therefore, the total wage bill rises by more than just the added wages of the last worker hired. The marginal factor cost curve reflects these rising costs.

Marginal factor cost (MFC) is the added cost associated with hiring one more unit of labor. In Figure 6, assume that 14 workers earn $10 an hour (point a), and hiring the 15th worker requires paying $11 an hour (point b). Assume that you decide to go ahead and hire a 15th worker. When you employed 14 workers, total hourly wages were $140 ($10 × 14). But when 15 workers are employed at $11 an hour, all workers must be paid the higher hourly wage, and thus the total wage bill rises to $165 ($11 × 15). The total wage bill has risen by $25 an hour, not just the $11 hourly wage the 15th worker demanded. The marginal factor cost of hiring the 15th worker, in other words, is $25. This is shown as point c. Because the supply of labor curve is positively sloped, the MFC curve will always lie above the S_L curve.

How does being a monopsonist in the labor market affect the hiring of a firm that is competitive in the product market? The monopsonist shown in Figure 7 on the next page is a competitor in the product market and has a demand for labor equal to its VMP_L. This firm faces the supply of labor, S_L. It will hire at the level where $MFC = VMP_L$ (point a), thus hiring L_0 workers at wage W_1 (point b). Note that these L_0 workers, though paid W_1, are actually worth W_0. Economists refer to this disparity as the **monopsonistic exploitation of labor.** Again, the term is loaded, but to economists it simply describes a situation in which labor is paid less than the value of its marginal product.

Note that the wages paid in the monopsony situation (W_1) are less than those paid under competitive conditions (W_C), and that monopsony employment (L_0) is similarly lower than competitive hiring (L_C). As was the case with monopoly power, monopsony power leads to results that are less than ideal when compared to competitive markets.

To draw together what we have just discussed, Figure 8 on the next page portrays a firm with both monopoly and monopsony power. The firm's equilibrium hiring will be at the point where $MFC = MRP_L$ (point a), and thus the firm will hire L_0 workers, though at

Marginal factor cost (MFC): The added cost associated with hiring one more unit of labor. For competitive firms, it is equal to the wage; but for monopsonists, it is higher than the new wage (W) because all existing workers must be paid this higher new wage, making MFC > W.

Monopsonistic exploitation of labor: Because monopsonists hire less labor than competitive firms, and workers are paid less than the value of their marginal products, this difference is referred to as monopsonistic exploitation of labor.

FIGURE 7—Competitive Firm in the Product Market That Is a Monopsonist in the Input Market

The monopsonist in this figure is a competitor in the product market and has a demand for labor equal to its VMP_L, while facing supply of labor, S_L. The firm will hire at the level where $MFC = VMP_L$ (point a), hiring L_0 workers at wage W_1 (point b). Note that these L_0 workers, though paid W_1, are worth W_0. This is called the monopsonistic exploitation of labor. Note also that the wages paid in this monopsony situation (W_1) are less than those paid under competitive conditions (W_C), and that monopsony employment (L_0) is lower than competitive employment (L_C).

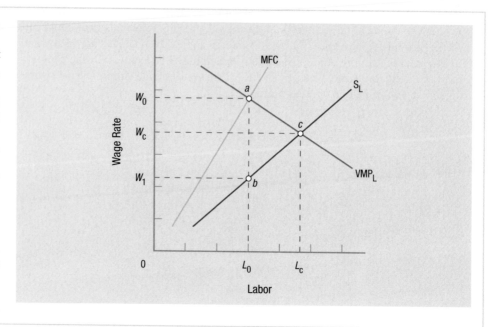

wage W_0. Note that this is the lowest wage and employment level shown in the graph. If the firm only had monopsony power, it would hire L_1 workers (point b) at a wage of W_1, which is higher than W_0. If the firm only had monopoly power, it would also hire L_1 workers for wage W_1 (point c). Both of these employment levels and wage rates are less than the competitive outcome of L_C and W_C (point d).

The key lesson to remember here is that competitive input (factor) markets are the most efficient, since inputs in these markets are paid precisely the value of their marginal products, and the highest employment results. This translates into the lowest prices for consumers at the highest output, assuming efficient production. Thus, just as competition is good for product markets, so too is it good for labor and other input markets.

FIGURE 8—Monopolist Firm in the Product Market That Is a Monopsonist in the Input Market

This firm has both monopoly and monopsony power. The firm's equilibrium hiring will be at the point where $MFC = MRP_L$ (point a), and thus the firm will hire L_0 workers, though at wage W_0. Note that this is the lowest wage and employment level shown in the graph. If the firm only had monopsony power, it would hire L_1 workers (point b) at a wage of W_1. If the firm only had monopoly power, it would also hire L_1 workers for wage W_1 (point c). Both of these employment levels and wage rates are less than the competitive outcome of L_C and W_C (point d).

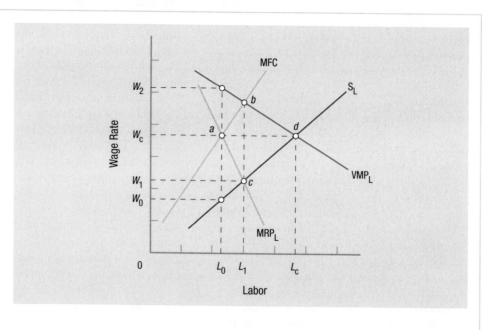

Issue: Are Minimum Wage Laws Good Public Policy?

In 2007, Congress passed a whopping 40% increase in the minimum wage: Between 2007 and 2009, it shot up from $5.15 to $7.25. Passed while the economy was booming, this rapid rise in the minimum wage has many people concerned about its impact during the subsequent recession. As the figure below shows, the real minimum wage (adjusted for inflation) was around $4.00 per hour until the mid-1980s. After that, the real minimum wage fell to around the $3.00 an hour range.

The first minimum wage laws were passed in New Zealand and Australia in the 1890s, adopted in England in the early 1900s, and became part of the Fair Labor Standards Act in the United States in 1938.

- Balancing the bargaining power between employers and workers to help ensure workers are paid a "fair" wage.
- Raising the incomes of low-income families and reducing poverty.
- Reducing wage inequality in the marketplace.

How well minimum wage laws stack up on these goals will give us a way to determine their effectiveness.

Like any other public policy, minimum wage laws involve tradeoffs. As we saw in Chapter 3, if labor markets are competitive, establishing a wage floor (the minimum workers can be paid) will lead to

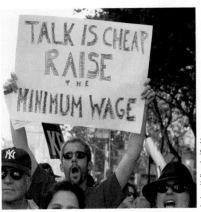

Andrew Holbrooke/Corbis

$8 per hour (point *e* in panel B). When the government imposes a minimum wage of $7.25 an hour, the cost of an additional worker is now just $7.25 an hour, so the firm's supply of labor (the marginal factor cost) is the darkened horizontal line at $7.25 per hour as far out as 26,000 workers; then continues as the remainder of the supply of labor curve, S_L. In this case, the firm now hires 15,000 workers at the minimum wage (point *a*).

Whether employment rises or falls has been the subject of numerous studies and some controversy. David Neumark and William Wascher, in their book *Minimum Wages*, examined over 40 studies of the impact of minimum wages on low-wage workers, and they concluded that "our overall sense of the literature is that the preponderance of evidence supports the view that minimum wages reduce the employment of low-wage workers." For roughly every 10% increase in the minimum wage, employment of minimum wage workers falls by roughly 2%, which is more similar to the explanation in panel A.

But the low-wage workers who remain employed gain a 10% pay raise. Neumark and Wascher looked at the other goals of minimum wage legislation and concluded, "The research on the distribution effects of

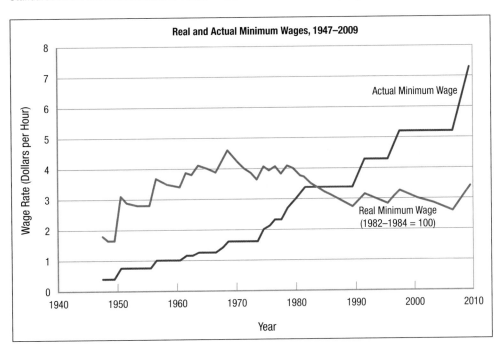

Because minimum wage laws have a 100-year history, the question of whether they are good public policy would seem to be moot. But recent research raises questions about the benefits and costs of laws mandating minimum wages.

These laws were originally passed to prevent "sweatshops" from employing women and young people at substandard wages. Minimum wage workers tend to be young, female, part-time workers who are not very well educated. As a result, minimum wage laws have other goals, including:

lower employment. At the other extreme, if the employer is a monopsonist and the minimum wage is set above the monopsony wage, employment will rise.

These two extremes are shown in the figure on the next page. In the competitive market in panel A, initial equilibrium is at point *e*, with 20,000 people hired. Employment falls from 20,000 to 15,000 (point *a*) when the minimum wage is set at $7.25.

In the monopsony case, initially wages are set by the firm at $4.00 an hour and 13,000 workers are hired at a MFC of around

(continued)

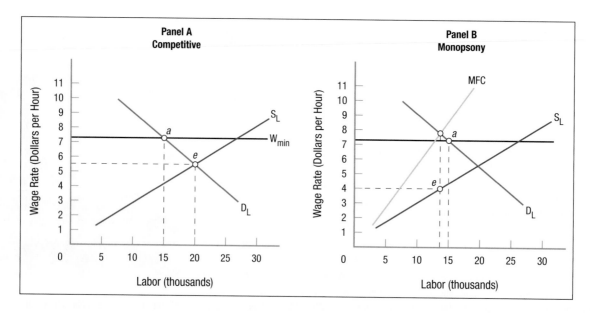

minimum wages, though far less extensive [than research on employment changes], finds virtually no evidence that minimum wages reduce the proportion of families with income near or below the poverty line, and some of it indicates that minimum wages adversely affect low-income families. Finally minimum wages appear to inhibit skill acquisition by reducing education attainment and perhaps training, resulting in lower adult wages and earnings."

If minimum wage laws cause loss of employment for low-wage people, have virtually no impact on poverty and the distribution of income, and may act as a disincentive for acquiring human capital, why do they continue to exist? The short answer is that they are popular. Surveys consistently show that over three-quarters of Americans support minimum wage laws and nearly every time state voters are given the chance to raise their state minimums above federal minimums, they approve the measures. Liberal advocacy groups and labor unions support minimum wages and people generally want to help low-income workers and their families. Finally, since the number of people earning minimum wages is small, roughly 1 to 2% of the workforce, the impact of raising minimum wages is trivial for most family budgets. These laws are so popular that even if people were aware of their potential to reduce employment and the other negative effects, they might still be supported.

Labor markets for minimum wage workers are generally quite competitive and it would be a mistake for policymakers to use the monopsony model in panel B, to suggest the impacts of minimum wage legislation on employment of minimum wage workers.

Sources: Based on David Neumark and William Wascher, *Minimum Wages* (Cambridge, MA: The MIT Press), 2008; and Guillaume Rocheteau and Murat Tasci, "The Minimum Wage and the Labor Market," *Economic Commentary*, Federal Reserve Bank of Cleveland, May 1, 2007.

Capital Markets

Capital: All manufactured products that are used to produce goods and services.

Capital includes all manufactured products that are used to produce goods and services. *Capital markets* are those markets in which firms obtain financial resources to purchase capital goods. Financial resources come from the savings of households and other firms. Suppliers of funds and the demanders of these funds interact through what is called the *loanable funds market.* As with competitive labor markets, in which the market determines wages, each individual firm determines how many workers to employ, and the loanable funds market determines interest rates, leaving individual firms to calculate how much they should borrow.

Through their interactions in the loanable funds market, suppliers and demanders determine the interest rates to be charged for funds. Individual firms then evaluate their investment opportunities to determine their own investment levels. Figure 9 shows how this process works. The demand and supply of loanable funds is shown in panel A, where equilibrium interest rates equal i_0. Note that the demand for loanable funds looks just like a normal demand curve. Its downward slope shows that, as the price of funds declines—as interest rates go down—the quantity of funds demanded rises. The supply of funds is positively sloped since individuals will be willing to supply more funds to the market when their price (interest rate) is higher.

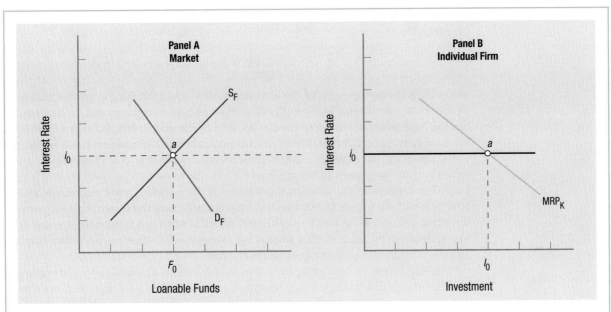

FIGURE 9—Loanable Funds Market and Individual Firm Investment

Panel A shows the market demand and supply of loanable funds, with equilibrium interest rates equal to i_0. Individual firms like the one shown in panel B will take this rate of interest, or cost of capital, and determine how much to invest. Firms make their best investments first, and then continue investing (to I_0) until the cost of capital (i_0) is equal to the MRP$_K$.

Investment

Once the market has determined an equilibrium rate of interest, an individual firm like the one shown in panel B will take this rate of interest, or cost of capital, and determine how much to invest. The marginal revenue product of capital (MRP$_K$) is downward sloping, showing that the returns a firm earns on its investments diminish as more capital is invested. Firms make their best investments first, and then continue investing until the cost of capital (i_0) is equal to the MRP$_K$. This admittedly simplifies the investment process, but it is a good general model of investment decisions. Next, we turn to two more precise ways in which investment is determined, the present value approach and the rate of return approach.

Present Value Approach

When a firm considers upgrading its information system or purchasing a new piece of equipment, a building, or a manufacturing plant, it must evaluate the returns it can expect over time. Firms invest money today, but earn returns over years. To compare investments having different income streams and different levels of required investment, firms look at the *net* **present value** of the investment.

One hundred dollars *a year from now* is worth *less* than one hundred dollars *today*. This is illustrated by the fact that you could put less than a hundred dollars in the bank today, earn interest on this money over the next year, and still end up with one hundred dollars at year's end. Yet, just how much less than one hundred dollars would you be willing to take for one hundred dollars a year from today? To answer this question, let us begin by looking at the simplest form of financial assets, annuities.

An annuity is a financial instrument that pays the bearer a certain dollar amount forever. Assume that the market rate of interest is 5%, and you are offered an annuity that pays you or the holder of the annuity $1,000 a year indefinitely. How much would you be willing to pay for this annuity? If you want to follow the market in earning 5% a year, then the simple question you must ask is this: On what amount of money

Present value: The value of an investment (future stream of income) today. The higher the discount rate, the lower the present value today, and vice versa.

does $1,000 a year forever represent a 5% return? The answer is found through the simple formula:

$$PV = X/i$$

where PV is the present value of the investment (what you are willing to pay for the annuity today), X is the annual income ($1,000 in this case), and i is the market interest rate. In this case, you would be willing to pay $20,000 for this annuity, since $20,000 = $1,000/0.05. We have thus reduced an infinite stream of income to the finite amount you would pay today. You would pay $20,000, and the annuity would give you $1,000 a year, for an annual return on your investment of 5%.

What happens to the value of this annuity if the market interest rate should rise to 10%? You will still receive $1,000 a year, but if you want to sell the annuity to someone else, the buyer will only be willing to pay $10,000 for it ($10,000 = $1,000/0.10). Interest rates having doubled, the value of your annuity has been halved. Higher interest rates mean that income in future years is not worth as much today.

Valuing future income today by this process is known as *discounting*. This principle applies not only to annuities, but computing for years less than perpetuity requires a more complex formula. For example, assume that someone agrees to pay you $500 in two years, and that the going interest rate is 5%. What would you be willing to pay today for this future payment of $500? The answer is found using the following formula:

$$PV = X/(1 + i)^n$$

Again, PV is the present value of the future payment, X is the future payment of $500, i is the interest rate (5%), and n is the number of years into the future before the payment is made. In this case the calculations are

$$
\begin{aligned}
PV &= \$500/(1 + 0.05)^2 \\
&= \$500/[(1.05)(1.05)] \\
&= \$500/1.1025 \\
&= \$453.51
\end{aligned}
$$

Hence, you would be willing to pay only $453.51 for this $500 payment coming two years in the future. Again, the higher the interest or discount rate, the lower your price.

When only one future payment is at stake, computing the present value of that payment is fairly simple. When future streams of income are involved, however, things get more complicated. We must compute the present value of each individual future payment. The general formula looks nearly the same as before:

$$PV = \Sigma \, X_n/(1 + i)^n$$

Here, the Greek letter Σ (sigma) stands for "sum of," and X_n is the individual payment received at year n. Assume, then, that you are going to receive $500, $800, and $1,200 over the next three years, and that the interest rate is still 5%. The present value of this income stream is therefore

$$
\begin{aligned}
PV &= \$500/(1.05)^1 + \$800/(1.05)^2 + \$1,200/(1.05)^3 \\
&= \$500/(1.05) + \$800/(1.1025) + \$1,200/(1.1576) \\
&= \$476.19 + \$725.62 + \$1,036.63 \\
&= \$2,238.44
\end{aligned}
$$

Given the complexity of such computations, economists often use computers to solve for present value, especially when the annual income stream is complicated. When the annual income is constant, tables of discount factors are also available. In any case, the point to note is that payments to be made in the future are worth a lower dollar amount today.

Firms often use present value analysis to determine if potential investments are worthwhile. Assume a machine will yield a stream of income exceeding operating costs over a given period. The present value of this income is then compared to the cost of the machine. The machine's *net present value* (NPV) is equal to the difference between the present value of the income stream and the cost of the machine. If NPV is positive, the firm will invest; if it is negative, the firm will decline to invest.

When interest rates are high, firms will find fewer investment opportunities where NPV is positive since the higher discount rate reduces the value of the income streams for investments. As interest rates fall, more investment is undertaken by firms.

Rate of Return Approach

An alternative approach to determining whether an investment is worthwhile involves computing the investment's rate of return. This rate of return is also known as a firm's *marginal efficiency of capital,* or its *internal* **rate of return.**

Computing an investment's rate of return requires using essentially the same present value formula for income streams introduced above with a slight modification: You have to explicitly consider the cost of capital in the calculation. This new formula is

$$PV = [\Sigma\, X_n/(1 + i)^n] - C$$

where C represents the cost of capital. The question we must ask is: At what rate of interest (i) will the investment just break even? You would compute the present value of the income streams, then subtract the cost of the capital investment, and finally find the rate of interest (i) where the present value equals zero. This discount rate is the rate of return on the investment.

The calculated rate of return can be compared to the firm's required rate of return on investments to determine whether the investment is worthwhile. The firm might require, say, a 20% yield on all projects, in which case investments yielding returns of less than 20% are deemed not worthwhile. Risk in investment projects is usually managed by adding a risk premium to the required rate of return for risky projects. This risk premium can vary by project type or with the business cycle. Some investments, such as drilling for oil or researching innovative new drugs, are risky and require high rates of return if they are to be undertaken.

Rate of return: Uses the present value formula, but subtracts costs, then finds the interest rate (discount rate) at which this investment would break even.

Land

For economists, the term *land* includes both land in the usual sense and other natural resources that are inelastically supplied. **Rent,** sometimes called *economic rent,* is any return or income that flows to land as a factor of production. This is a different meaning than when we speak of the rent on an apartment. Land is unique among the factors of production because of its inelasticity of supply.

In some instances, the supply of land is perfectly inelastic. Finding an empty lot on which to build in San Francisco is virtually impossible. The land available to San Franciscans is fixed by the terrain; it cannot be added to nor moved from one place to another.

Figure 10 on the next page shows how rent is determined when the available supply of land is fixed. In this example, the number of acres of usable land is fixed at L_0 (or supply S_0). If the demand for land is D_0, the economic rent will be r_0 (point *a*). When demand rises to D_1, rent increases to r_1 (point *b*). Notice that because the supply of land in this example is perfectly inelastic, rent depends entirely on demand. If demand were to fall, rent would fall as well.

In a strict sense, land is not perfectly fixed in supply. Land can be improved. Land that is arid, like the deserts of Arizona, can be improved through irrigation. Jungles can be cleared, swamps can be drained, and mountains can be terraced, making land that was once worthless productive. Still, even if the supply of land is not perfectly inelastic, it is quite inelastic when compared to other production inputs.

The supply inflexibility in land led Henry George (1839–1897) to propose a single tax on land to finance government needs. In his 1879 book *Progress and Poverty,* George argued that

Rent: The return to land as a factor of production. Sometimes called economic rent.

FIGURE 10—Determination of Rent

This figure shows how rent is determined when the available supply of land is fixed. The acres of usable land are fixed at L_0 (supply S_0). If the demand for land is D_0, the economic rent is r_0 (point *a*). When demand rises to D_1, rent increases to r_1 (point *b*). Notice that because the supply of land in this example is perfectly inelastic, rent depends entirely on demand. If demand were to fall, rent would fall as well.

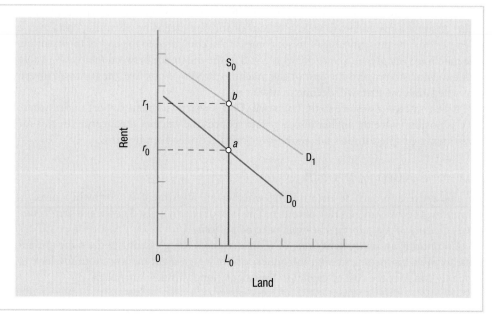

increases in rents and land values were the result of speculation, population growth, and public improvements in the community's infrastructure (raising demand to D_1 in Figure 10). Since landholders apparently do nothing to earn these rental increases, George thought they could and should be taxed away. His approach became known as the single-tax movement, since he thought all government spending could be financed from the revenue of this tax.

It should be added that George proposed to tax only the pure ground rent of land, not the improvements made on land. Thus, his tax is also sometimes called a "site tax." Although such a tax would probably not cover all government spending today, some economists are sympathetic to the concept. Nobel Prize winner Milton Friedman has noted, "In my opinion, the least bad tax is the property tax on the unimproved value of land, the Henry George argument of many, many years ago."[2]

As a final note, land will theoretically continue to earn rent forever. To quickly approximate the value of a piece of land, we can use our annuity formula ($PV = X/i$). Given a 5% rate of interest, a parcel of land earning $10,000 a year in rent will be worth $200,000 ($200,000 = $10,000/0.05). To apply to the real world, this simple approximation would require a few qualifications. Even so, it gives us a first approximation of how land is valued.

Entrepreneurship

Profits are the rewards entrepreneurs receive for (1) combining land, labor, and capital to produce goods and services and (2) assuming the risks associated with producing these goods and services. Entrepreneurs must combine and manage all the inputs of production; make day-to-day production, finance, and marketing decisions; innovate constantly if they hope to remain in business over the long run; and simultaneously bear the risks of failure and bankruptcy.

As we saw at the turn of the century—just a few years ago in 2000, not 1900—large firms that have become household names can implode within months. Enron, Arthur Anderson, and more recently Lehman Brothers, General Motors, and Chrysler come to mind. Even for large firms, business is risky. Bankruptcy or business failure, meanwhile, can be exceedingly painful for business owners, stockholders, employees, and communities. Still, a free economy requires such failures. If firms were guaranteed never to fail, perhaps

---

[2] Mark Blaug, *Great Economists before Keynes: An Introduction to the Lives & Works of One Hundred Great Economists of the Past* (Atlantic Highlands, NJ: Humanities Press International), 1986, p. 86.

through government subsidies (bailouts), they would have little incentive to be efficient or innovate, or to worry about what consumers want from them.

When a firm earns economic profits—profits exceeding normal profits—this is a signal to other firms and entrepreneurs that consumers want more of the good or service the profitable firm provides, and that they are willing to pay for it. Profit signals shift resources from areas of lower demand to the products and services consumers desire more highly.

By far, the largest part of national income—roughly 70%—goes to labor, the smallest goes to rental income, and the remainder is split between interest and profits. Labor is thus the most important factor of production, and labor issues are often paramount for policymakers. The next chapter will look into some specific labor issues, including investment in human capital, economic discrimination, and labor unions.

■ CHECKPOINT

IMPERFECT LABOR MARKETS AND OTHER INPUT MARKETS

- When a firm is a monopolist in the product market and hires labor from competitive markets, the firm will hire labor where the marginal revenue product is equal to the competitive wage.

- Monopolistic exploitation results because the monopolist pays less than the value of the marginal product of labor.

- Monopsony is a market with one employer. A monopsonist who sells its product in a competitive market hires labor where the value of the marginal product is equal to the marginal factor cost.

- Monopsonistic exploitation occurs when the monopsonist pays labor less than the value of its marginal product.

- Capital markets are markets in which firms get financial resources to purchase capital goods.

- Firms will use either the net present value approach or the rate of return approach to compare investments with different income streams.

- Land includes both land and natural resources and is inelastically supplied. Returns on land are called rents (or economic rent).

- Because land is inelastically supplied, the rent on land is determined by demand.

- Entrepreneurs earn profits for combining other inputs to produce products and for assuming the risks of producing goods and services.

QUESTIONS: Are public schools in rural areas a monopsony? Do they set wages in a way that is different from how wages are set in large urban areas?

Answers to the Checkpoint questions can be found at the end of this chapter.

Key Concepts

Supply of labor, p. 262
Substitution effect, p. 263
Income effect, p. 264
Demand for labor, p. 267
Marginal physical product of labor,
  p. 267

Marginal revenue product, p. 267
Value of the marginal product, p. 268
Elasticity of demand for labor, p. 269
Monopsony, p. 271
Monopolistic exploitation of labor,
  p. 272

Chapter Summary

Competitive Labor Supply

Competitive labor markets comprise firms that are price takers; these firms compete with other firms in the wider market for labor. Labor is assumed to be a homogeneous input; one unit of labor is just as productive as all others. Information about prices and wages is assumed to be widely available, and supply and demand interact to determine the equilibrium wage for the industry. Each firm then decides how much labor to purchase at the going wage rate.

The supply of labor is the time an individual is willing to work (the labor the person is willing to supply) at various wage rates. The supply of labor is positively sloped, since at higher wages, workers will substitute work for leisure. When wages rise high enough, however, the income effect may swamp the substitution effect. Workers may elect more leisure over greater income, resulting in a backward-bending supply of labor curve.

Changes in wage rates will change the quantity of labor supplied, or cause movements along the market supply of labor curve. Demographic changes and changes in the non-money aspects of a job, the wages for alternative jobs, and nonwage income will all shift the supply of labor curve. Such a shift might be precipitated, for instance, by a change in the labor force participation rates, a reduction in the riskiness of a job, or a change in nonwage incomes of workers.

Competitive Labor Demand

The demand for labor is a derived demand; it is derived from the productive capabilities of labor and the demand for the good or service produced. The demand for labor is equivalent to the marginal revenue product (MRP_L) curve. Marginal revenue product is equal to marginal physical product of labor times the product's marginal revenue.

Because competitive firms are price takers, marginal revenue is equal to price. So the competitive firm's demand for labor is equal to what economists call the value of the marginal product (VMP_L). The value of the marginal product is equal to marginal physical product times price.

Since the demand for labor is a derived demand, changes in labor demand will come about because of changes in labor productivity or changes in product demand. Anything that changes the price of a firm's product will change its labor demand.

The elasticity of demand for labor is the percentage change in the quantity of labor demanded divided by the percentage change in the wage rate. Elasticity of demand for labor is determined by the elasticity of demand for the product, the ease of input substitutability, and the size of labor's share in production costs.

Competitive labor markets determine an equilibrium wage, then individual firms must look at their own needs and hire employees up to the point where equilibrium wage is equal to marginal revenue product (or, equivalently for competitive markets, equal to the value of the marginal product of labor).

Imperfect Labor Markets and Other Input Markets

If wages are determined in a competitive market, a firm will hire labor until $MRP_L = W$. But if the firm enjoys some monopoly power in the product market, marginal revenue product will be less than the value of the marginal product because $MR < P$. The difference between the value of the marginal product and marginal revenue product is known as monopolistic exploitation of labor.

A monopsony is a market with a single buyer or employer. Marginal factor cost (MFC) is the added cost associated with hiring one more unit of labor. For the monopsonist, the MFC curve lies above the supply of labor curve because the firm must increase the wages of all workers to attract added labor. If the monopsonist purchases labor from a competitive market, it hires labor up to the point where MRP = MFC > W. At this point, the value of labor's marginal product exceeds the wage rate; economists refer to this as monopsonistic exploitation of labor.

Capital includes all manufactured goods that are used to produce other goods and services. Capital markets are those markets where financial resources are available for the purchase of capital goods. The loanable funds market determines equilibrium interest rates for these funds. Firms look at their potential investment projects and borrow money to invest when the rate of return on a project is greater than or equal to the market interest rate.

Two approaches are used to determine whether investments are potentially profitable. The present value approach discounts projected future streams of income to determine their present value. This is then compared to the cost of the investment to determine whether the investment will be profitable. The rate of return approach uses the same present value formula, but looks for the rate of return, or discount rate, where the potential income stream and investment costs will be just equal.

Land, to the economist, means land and other natural resources that are nearly fixed in supply, or inelastically supplied. Because the supply of land is fixed, the rent on land is determined by demand.

Profits are rewards to entrepreneurs for combining the other inputs of production—land, labor, and capital—in ways that produce goods and services and for assuming the risks associated with production. Economic profits are profits that exceed normal levels. They act as signals to other entrepreneurs and firms that consumers want more of the profitable product. These signals produce shifts in resources toward those goods that consumers want.

Questions and Problems

Check Your Understanding

1. How do the income and substitution effects related to labor supply differ?

2. Why does a monopolist in the product market hire fewer workers than if the industry is competitive?

3. If the interest rate is 6% and you are offered a bond that will pay you $2,000 in two years, but no interest between now and then, what would you be willing to pay for this bond today?

4. What factors will increase the demand for labor?

5. Why are individual supply curves of labor potentially backward bending, but market and industry supply curves are always positively sloped?

Apply the Concepts

6. As the baby boomer generation—those born between 1946 and 1964—begins retiring in earnest in the near future, wealthy economies like the United States and Europe will need to replace these skilled workers. These workers are an immense storehouse of knowledge and specialized skills that are not easily replaced. This is particularly acute in the engineering fields where college enrollments are falling (*Economist*, March 4, 2006). Would it make sense for America, as *The Economist* (November 5, 2005, p. 86) noted, to "no longer welcome the tired and the huddled; [but] to compete ever more fiercely for the bright and the qualified"? What could companies do to encourage these older workers to remain on the job?

7. Adam Smith, in the *Wealth of Nations,* noted that, "The wages of labour vary with the ease or hardship, the cleanliness or dirtiness, the honourableness or dishonourableness of the employment." He is referring to the nonwage or "amenities" aspect of employment. By making the "job" more enjoyable, cleaner, or more honorable, or adding more amenities, employers should be able to pay lower wages, since the positive attributes compensate for higher wages. If so, why don't all employers offer amenities to lower their wage bill?

8. Fifty years ago, married women age 35 to 44 worked for pay only 10 hours per week on average; today they work over 26 hours on average. During the same period, the workweek for married men of the same age has been relatively constant, between 42 and 44 hours. Can you think of reasons why women's working hours have nearly tripled in the last half century?

9. Since 1970 the number of dual-earning households as a percent of total U.S. households has grown from 39% to nearly 65% today. Do you think there is a relationship between this growth in dual-earning households and the rapid growth in restaurants?

10. How do times of growth in the general economy encourage capital investments? How do recessions discourage capital investments? What happens to the cost of capital in boom times when the economy is growing? What happens in recessionary times?

11. Why do college professors who usually spend five to seven years in graduate school and play such an important role in shaping our society make so much less than a Hollywood producer such as Jerry Bruckheimer, who most people don't even know (he has produced over 40 films and a dozen TV shows)?

12. Since all college professors mostly teach classes and do research, why are they not all paid the same wage?

13. We often hear that America needs cheap unskilled foreign workers to do the jobs that Americans will not do. But Professor Barry Chiswick (*New York Times,* June 3, 2006, p. A23) suggested, "If the number of low-skilled foreign workers were to fall, wages would increase. Low-skilled American workers and their families would benefit, and society as a whole would gain from a reduction in income inequality." Is Professor Chiswick's argument consistent with the competitive labor market described in this chapter? Why or why not?

14. In 2008, IBM paid $65 million to settle a lawsuit regarding overtime pay (*Wall Street Journal,* January 24, 2008, p. B6). Salaried ($80,000 per year) technicians who installed and repaired computers averaged 45 hours a week, 5 hours over the Fair Labor Standards Act that requires hourly employees be paid time-and-a-half for hours over 40. As part of its program to reclassify employees who were previously incorrectly classified as "exempt" salaried employees, IBM announced that over 7,000 employees would have their base pay cut by 15%, but with overtime their overall compensation should remain roughly the same. Does this action by IBM seem consistent with W = MRP = VMP for competitive markets discussed in this chapter?

15. Some employees feel locked into their jobs because employer benefits like health insurance are not transferrable to other companies. This "job lock" phenomenon is especially severe with health insurance coverage for employees if someone in their family has a severe preexisting condition that prevents them from getting private health insurance at reasonable rates. What are the impacts of this type of inflexibility on labor markets? What would be the impact if some form of health care reform eliminated the potential loss of health insurance for workers?

In the News

16. Tightened visa rules since 9/11 have reduced the number of high-skill legal immigrants. Stiffer security rules and insufficient personnel have substantially increased the waiting time (and certainty) of visas. Spencer Ante (*Business Week,* November, 2004, pp. 90–94) quotes Nobel Prize winner Gary Becker: "We benefit enormously from high-skilled immigration . . . we have to try to maintain that." He further suggests that the United States should "give the highest priority to people with high skills and allow large numbers to come in, maybe unlimited numbers." Do you agree with Becker? If so, what might be some of the obstacles to implementing such a policy? If not, why not?

17. "Where labour is scarce and expensive, businesses have an incentive to invest in labour-saving technology, which boosts productivity growth by enabling fewer workers to produce more" (Michael Lind, *Financial Times,* June 9, 2006, p. 13). Do you agree with this statement? Why or why not? Would bringing in a large number of unskilled workers improve productivity and living standards?

Solving Problems

18. The figure below shows the supply of labor, marginal factor costs, and the demand for labor for a firm that is large enough that it is essentially a monopsonist in the community where it operates. Assume that all workers are paid the same wage and that they work 2,000 hours per year (40 hours a week for 50 weeks).

a. What is the total wage bill (total wages paid by the firm) for this monopsonistic firm?

b. If the firm was actually hiring from a competitive labor market, what would be the total wage bill for the firm?

c. What is the total value of the monopsonistic exploitation of labor by this firm?

d. Is the firm a competitor or a monopolist in the product market?

Answers to Questions in CheckPoints

Check Point: Competitive Labor Supply

Each person will have a different wage where their supply of labor curve bends backward. Getting a large inheritance will generate substantial nonwage income and typically lead to fewer hours worked. Having a family will probably raise the income required before you will cut your hours.

Check Point: Competitive Labor Demand

For many jobs, firms have standardized procedures that each employee follows. Therefore, the difference in productivity between individuals is relatively narrow. While homogeneous labor is a simplification, taking in everyone's difference would make analysis impractical. No, the model explains both since markets exist for each broad category of workers.

Check Point: Imperfect Labor Markets and Other Input Markets

Yes, they are monopsonists when it comes to hiring teachers. Generally, there is only one school district in rural areas. They probably act more like monopsonists when setting wages when compared to their urban counterparts, which have competition for teachers from other districts and private schools.

Labor Market Issues 12

imagebroker/Alamy

Why are some people paid more than others? Is there a relationship between your earnings and your education? Does discrimination explain wage differences between groups? Why are there different wages for different occupations? What role will unions play in the 21st-century economy?

To get a better sense of what this chapter covers, let us pause for a moment on the last question: What role will unions play in the 21st century? Many of us already have some familiarity with unions, which are legal associations of employees that bargain with employers over terms and conditions of work. Unions use strikes and the threat of strikes to achieve their goals. You may have heard of craft unions such as the Teamsters, which represents truck drivers, or industry unions, such as the UAW (United Auto Workers), which represents auto workers.

One of the fastest growing labor groups is made up of part-time and independent contract workers. They freelance in graphic design, in Web design services and programming, as nannies, and in many other areas. Pay and terms of work are typically set by individual negotiation. This group clearly could use a union, since they are rarely provided benefits beyond the agreed-upon compensation.

But how could a union serve such a diverse group of people in terms of skills, compensation, locations, industries, and working conditions? Sara Horowitz asked herself that question and decided that a union could provide self-employed workers with similar services that full-time employees take for granted. She formed the Freelancers Union in New York and provides her members with health insurance, 401(k)-type retirement plans,

Investment in human capital: Investments such as education and on-the-job training that improve the productivity of human labor.

redress for employer or client nonpayment, and other benefits.[1] This union does not strike like traditional unions, but the union has grown to 13,000 members and is an advocacy organization for freelance workers.

Labor markets in the 21st century are changing dramatically. Adjustments are being made: flexible hours, job sharing, working at home instead of in a centralized office, and more part-timers and freelancers in the market. In this chapter, we will address these labor market issues, and more.

Investment in Human Capital

Let us first consider the role education and on-the-job-training (OJT) play in determining wage levels in labor markets. Workers, students, and firms all invest in themselves or their employees to increase productivity. This is called **investment in human capital.** Workers invest by accepting lower wages while they undertake apprenticeships. Students invest by paying for tuition and books, and by forgoing job opportunities, to learn new skills. Firms invest in their workers through OJT and in-house training programs that involve workers being paid to attend classes. These investments entail costs in the current period that are borne in the interest of raising future productivity. They can be analyzed using the investment analysis we developed in the last chapter.[2]

Education and Earnings

One of the surest ways to advance in the job world and increase your income is by investing in education. The old saying, "To get ahead, get an education," still holds true. Table 1 shows the age/earnings profiles for all Americans between 25 and 64 for 2006. It provides strong evidence that education and earnings are related.

Average earnings for those without a high school education peaked at $25,688 a year, while those completing high school peaked at $37,173, a 44% increase. Getting a college degree bumped peak earnings up to $66,061, over a 150% rise. Going on to get a professional degree moved the peak all the way up to $133,151, over a 100% increase over a bachelor's degree alone. These figures represent average earnings. It is easy to see that earnings in all age groups were much higher for those with higher levels of education.

Table 1 suggests that education is a good investment. But like any investment, future earnings must be balanced against the cost of obtaining that education. The costs of education must be borne today, but the earnings benefits do not arrive until later. Evaluating educational decisions therefore requires that we use some of the tools developed in the last chapter when we studied investment in the capital markets.

TABLE 1	Average Earnings by Highest Degree Earned, 2006				
Age Grouping	No HS Diploma	HS Diploma	Some College	College Degree	Professional
25–34	$21,153	$28,448	$31,026	$48,724	$78,119
35–44	24,333	35,083	40,943	63,335	133,151
45–54	25,438	37,173	43,027	66,061	131,011
55–64	25,688	34,845	40,968	60,393	123,759

Source: U.S. Census Bureau, *Statistical Abstract of the United States, 2009* (Washington, DC: U.S. Government Printing Office), 2009, Table 224.

---

[1] "Face Value: Freelancers of the World Unite," *Economist,* November 11, 2006, p. 76; and see the Freelancers Union Web site at www.freelancersunion.org.
[2] Gary S. Becker, *Human Capital,* 2nd ed. (New York: National Bureau of Economic Research), 1975. Becker won the Nobel Prize in 1992 for this and other work in economics.

Education as Investment

To keep our analysis simple, we will focus on the decision to attend college for four years. The basic approach outlined in this section will nonetheless apply to other investments in education or training.

Figure 1 presents a stylized graph showing the benefits and costs of a college education. For simplicity, we will assume students go to college at age 18. If an individual chooses not to go to college, the high school earnings path applies: On leaving high school, the person enters the labor market immediately, and earnings begin rising along the path labeled "High School." Note that the earnings are positive throughout the individual's working life.

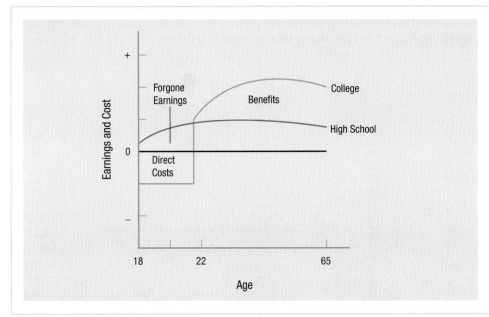

FIGURE 1—Benefits and Costs of a College Education

If an individual chooses not to go to college at age 18, he or she enters the labor market on leaving high school, and earnings rise and fall along the path labeled "High School." The college student incurs the direct costs of education, such as tuition and books, and the forgone earnings of not immediately entering the job market. The benefits of the college education show up as the difference in earnings from ages 22 to 65.

A college student immediately incurs costs in two forms. First, tuition, books, and other fees must be paid. These direct costs exclude living expenses, such as food and rent, since these must be paid whether you work or go to college. Tuition varies substantially depending on whether you attend a private or public university.

Second, students give up earnings as they devote full time to their studies (and to the occasional party). These costs can be substantial when compared to the direct costs of an education at a state-supported institution, since the average earnings for high school graduates range between $15,000 and $20,000 a year.

The benefits from a college degree show up as the difference in earnings from ages 22 to 65. If the return on a college degree is to be positive, this area must offset the direct costs of college and the forgone earnings. We must also keep in mind that a large part of the income high school and college graduates earn will not come until well into the future. For college graduates, this is especially important, since they will not see income for at least four years. How can we tell if this sacrifice is worth it? The fact that the median earnings of college graduates in 2007 exceeded that of high school graduates by over 80% suggests a college education is worth it.[3]

An alternate way to decide which of the two career paths is best is by computing the rate of return on a college degree. If the annual return on a college education over the course of one's working life is 10% a year, the earnings of the college graduate in middle

---

[3]U.S. Census Bureau, *Statistical Abstract of the United States, 2010* (Washington D.C.: U.S. Government Printing Office), 2010.

age will exceed those of the high school graduate by enough to generate a 10% return. A lower return would mean that the difference in earnings is smaller, while a higher return suggests the difference in earnings is greater. An extensive study[4] of rates of return to higher education in nearly 100 countries put the average return at nearly 20%. That is, college graduates around the world earn on average nearly 20% more per year over the course of their working lifetime than high school graduates, taking into consideration all of the costs of going to college.

Equilibrium Levels of Human Capital

Each of us must decide how much to invest in ourselves. This decision, like so many in economics, ultimately depends on supply and demand, in this case, the supply of, and demand for, funds to be used for human capital investment. A hypothetical market for human capital is shown in Figure 2. In this scenario, "price" is the percentage rate of return on human capital investments and the interest cost of borrowing funds.

FIGURE 2—Equilibrium Levels of Investment in Human Capital

This graph portrays a hypothetical market for human capital; the percentage rates of return and the interest costs of borrowing funds are shown on the vertical axis. With demand D_0 and supply S_0, equilibrium will be at point e. If the supply of funds is reduced (S_1), interest rates and the cost of investment increase, resulting in less investment. Reduced demand for education (D_1) similarly reduces human capital investment.

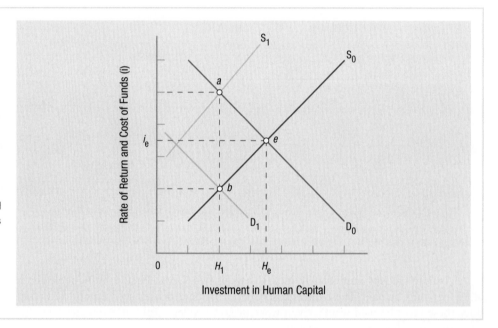

The demand for human capital investment slopes down and to the right, reflecting the diminishing returns of more education and that more time in school leaves you less time to earn back its costs. Students pursuing a Ph.D. or a medical degree are often well into their thirties before they can begin paying back their student loans. As a result, they require higher salaries to bring their rates of return up above those of college-educated workers.

The supply of investable funds, meanwhile, is positively sloped, since students will use the lowest-cost funds first—mom and dad paying for college—then turn to government-subsidized funds, and finally use private market funds, if needed.

With demand (D_0) and supply (S_0), equilibrium in this market is at point e. Human capital investment is equal to H_e, with the rate of return equaling the interest rate (i_e). Notice that reducing the supply of funds, or shifting the supply curve to S_1, will increase interest rates and the cost of investment. This results in lower investments in education.

---

[4] G. Psacharopoulos and H. Patrinos, "Returns to Investment in Education: A Further Update," *Education Economics*, 2004.

Similarly, anything reducing the demand for funds, or shifting the demand curve to D_1, will result in reduced human capital investment. Let us briefly consider some of the factors that might cause these curves to shift.

The most important factor determining the supply of investable funds for students consists of family resources. Students from well-off families can draw on a pool of inexpensive funds, but students from poorer families must scratch together funds that are often expensive. At the aggregate level, reductions in federally subsidized low-interest student loans will result in a shift in the supply curve to S_1, meaning lower investments in human capital (H_1). Conversely, the GI Bills enacted after World War II and the Vietnam War greatly increased college enrollments and the stock of human capital in America.

The demand for human capital is influenced by an individual's abilities and learning capacity: the more able the person, the larger the expected benefits of human capital investment.

Discrimination in the labor market also plays an important role in determining whether an investment in education is worthwhile or not, since expected earnings are affected by wage or occupational discrimination. Assume D_0 represents the demand for human capital investment for individuals facing no discrimination in the labor market. If these same people were to face a reduced wage in the market from wage discrimination, their demand for education would fall to D_1, reflecting the reduced return on investment in human capital. A similar decline in demand would result if the choice of jobs is limited by occupational discrimination. We look at discrimination more closely in the next section.

Implications of Human Capital Theory

Individuals are more productive because of their investment in human capital, and thus they are capable of earning more during their working lives. Because younger people have longer earning horizons, they are more likely to invest in human capital and education. As workers get older and gain labor market experience and higher wages, their opportunity costs for attending college grow larger, while their potential postcollege earning period shrinks. This explains why most students in college classrooms are young.

The greater the market earnings differential between high school and college graduates, the more people will attend college, since a higher earnings differential raises the return on college educations. Similarly, reductions in the cost of education lead to greater educational investment.

Last, the more an individual discounts the future—the higher i is in present value formulas—the less investment in human capital we would expect. If your discount rate is high, this means you value the present highly but do not place as much value on future outcomes. People with high discount rates often are not willing to pursue doctoral or medical degrees because the time between the beginning of the training process and the point when earnings begin is simply too long.

Human Capital as Screening or Signaling

Human capital theorists see investments in human capital as improving the productivity of individuals. This higher productivity then translates into higher wages. There is another view why higher educational levels lead to higher wages: Higher education acts as a **screening/signaling** device for employers.

Economists who advocate this view concede that some education will undoubtedly lead to higher productivity. But these economists argue that higher education is largely an indicator to employers that the college graduate is trainable, has discipline, and is intelligent. In their view, the job market is one big competition where entry-level workers compete for on-the-job training. As a result, earning a college degree does little more than give the college graduate a leg up in this competition.

Screening/signaling: The argument that higher education simply lets employers know that the prospective employee is intelligent and trainable and has the discipline to potentially be a good employee.

One implication of this view is the controversial suggestion that the social benefits for more public spending on education may be low. If college educations do not enhance productivity but simply trigger competitive pursuits for resume items, then the return to public funds will be low. In the words of *The Economist,*

> *How can more education fail to make a country more prosperous? A first crucial point is that education is a "positional good": that is, getting yourself tagged for high wages is not just about being educated, it is also about being better educated than the next man. To some extent, education is a race: if everybody runs faster, that may be good in itself, but it does not mean that more people can finish in the top 10%. In that sense, much of the extra effort may be wasted. In weighing the social benefits of higher spending on education against the cost, this needs to be borne in mind.*[5]

Still, it is doubtful that screening is the only purpose served by higher education. If it were, the high costs of college education and the higher wages employers must pay college graduates would create tremendous incentives for workers and employers to develop an alternative, less expensive screening device.

On-the-Job Training

On-the-job training: Training typically done by employers, ranging from suggestions at work to sophisticated seminars.

On-the-job training (OJT) can take many different forms. Often training amounts to nothing more than receiving instructions from a supervisor on how to help customers, operate a machine, or retrieve items from inventory. Sometimes this training takes place in a more formal setting away from the job, almost like a college course.

Today, spending on OJT approaches $80 billion a year, including training costs and the wages paid to employees during training. The costs of OJT are usually borne by employers, but workers may bear some of the costs through reduced wages throughout the training period. Firms benefit from OJT by gaining more productive workers, and workers gain by becoming more versatile, and thus more competitive, in labor markets.

General Versus Specific Training

Nobel Prize winner Gary Becker was one of the pioneers of human capital theory. In his book, *Human Capital,* he outlined two distinct forms of OJT: general training and specific training.

General training: Training that improves a worker's productivity in all firms.

General training improves productivity in all firms. Learning to use computers, word processors, and spreadsheets, for example, raises your productivity no matter where you work. The same is true for a college education, as well as for the apprenticeships electricians, plumbers, and carpenters undertake.

Specific training: Training that improves a worker's productivity in a specific firm.

Specific training, in contrast, increases a worker's productivity only within the particular firm. Firm-specific training might cover the way a firm handles such issues as order flow, inventory control and purchasing, or familiarization of workers with the firm's specific products.

Firms usually will not provide general training. Since productivity is increased equally for all firms, workers must acquire these skills at their own expense. Firms will provide specific training, however, if the returns from this investment compare favorably to other investment alternatives.

Because investing in OJT is just one of many investments a firm can undertake, the rate of return to OJT must equal or exceed those of other investments if it is to be worthwhile. On-the-job investments entail present costs meant to yield future benefits. These

---

[5] "Economic Focus: The Education Shibboleth," *The Economist,* June 8, 2002, p. 73. See Alison Wolf, *Does Education Matter? Myths About Education and Economic Growth,* (London: Penguin Books), 2002.

Nobel Prize

The 1992 winner of the Nobel Prize in Economic Sciences, Gary Becker, applied the theory of "rational choice" to areas of human behavior not ordinarily associated with economic analysis and research. Through his academic work and columns in *Business Week* magazine, he has offered provocative insights on a broad array of subjects, including family relations, racial discrimination, and the criminal justice system.

Born in Pottsville, a coal-mining community in eastern Pennsylvania, Becker completed his undergraduate degree in three years at Princeton University. He then entered the University of Chicago, where he studied under economist Milton Friedman.

In 1957, he published his dissertation, *The Economics of Discrimination,* an analysis of the effects of racial prejudice on earnings and employment among minorities. The book was favorably reviewed in journals but failed to make an impact on mainstream economics. The support of Friedman and other economists at the University of Chicago, however, encouraged Becker to continue along this line of research. Becker taught for several years at Chicago and then Columbia. In 1970, he rejoined the faculty at Chicago and befriended George Stigler, collaborating with him on two influential papers. His work with Stigler rekindled an interest

in the relationship between economics and politics. In the 1980s, he wrote two papers that analyzed the impact of special interest groups on the political process.

In 1981, he published his book, *A Treatise on the Family,* viewing the family as a "small factory." According to his theory, rising wages led to changes in the family, including more women working outside the home instead of "specializing" in child care and housework. He also traced the declining rate of fertility to a rational choice of having fewer children and investing more in education for the individual child.

On questions of crime and punishment, Becker suggested that most criminals react in predictable ways to the costs and benefits of illegal activity. His empirical studies indicated that the probability of being caught and punished was a greater deterrent than the harsh nature of the punishment. On the question of race, Becker viewed discrimination as a "tax wedge" between social and private returns, concluding that prejudice tends to be economically detrimental to all parties concerned.

---

investments can be analyzed just like those involving college education that we looked at earlier. Figure 3 on the next page shows the benefits and costs of OJT.

Wages and productivity (marginal revenue product, or MRP) are shown on the vertical axis. For simplicity, individuals without training are assumed to have productivity (MRP) and earn wages equal to W_0 throughout their working careers. Further, we will assume that workers are provided training at the beginning of their careers, which improves their productivity in that firm for the remainder of their working lives. The heavy line labeled "With Training" reflects this increased productivity.

If OJT is general training, workers will be expected to accept reduced wages during the training period, and then earn wages equal to W_2 once the training is completed. In Figure 3, the area below W_0 and above W_1 represents the costs workers bear during the training period. Historically, this is how apprenticeship programs in the trades have operated. Today, professional internships provide college students with OJT at reduced wages over the summer. Hiring summer interns is a good way for firms to get an extended look at potential employees. The internships provide students, meanwhile, with

FIGURE 3—Benefits and Costs of On-the-Job Training

Individuals without training are assumed to earn wages W_0 throughout their working careers. Trained workers have an increased productivity for the remainder of their working lives, as shown by the heavy line labeled "With Training." If OJT is general, workers will get reduced wages during the training period, then earning wages equal to W_2 once the training is completed. If the training is specific, the firm will often absorb the cost, keeping wages at W_0 throughout the training process, then raising wages to somewhere between W_2 and W_0.

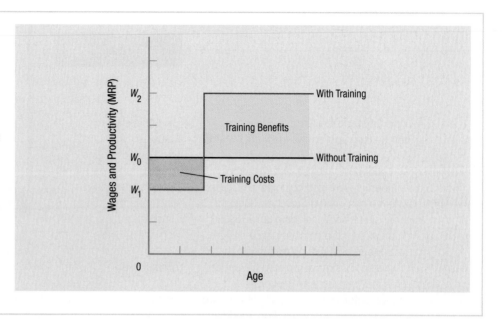

a look at several different firms and industries before graduating and entering the job market.

Specific training is usually handled differently. Because this training increases productivity only within the firm providing the training, the firm will usually absorb the cost of this training, keeping wages at W_0 throughout the training process. Once workers have completed the training, their productivity rises to W_2. The firm will not, however, raise their pay all the way to W_2, since then it would not recoup the training costs. Instead, the firm will share the benefits of specific training with the newly trained workers, raising their pay to somewhere between W_2 and W_0. Paying these workers something more than W_0 will reduce turnover, since the workers could expect to earn only W_0 if they went to another firm, given that specific training only increases productivity in the firm providing the training.

As we have seen, investments in human capital go a long way toward explaining why people are paid different wages. Education and earnings are closely related. Human capital theorists believe that this is because education and productivity are closely related. Other economists question whether more education translates into higher productivity; they view education as little more than a screening device for employers. In any case, the investment in human capital is just one of the reasons for wage differentials. Economic discrimination is another, as we will see next.

■ CHECKPOINT

INVESTMENT IN HUMAN CAPITAL

- Investment in human capital includes all investments in human beings such as education and on-the-job training.

- There is a positive relationship between education and earnings.

- The rate of return to education is computed by comparing the streams of income of two levels of education.

- The greater the wage differential between two levels of education, the more people will pursue that next level of education.

- The higher the rate of return to education, the more people will attain that level.

- Higher education may just be a screening or signaling device telling potential employers that this individual is trainable, has discipline, and is smart.

- Firms will provide specific training (training that enhances productivity in the firm only) but usually will not provide general training (training that enhances productivity in all firms).

QUESTIONS: If the United States decided, as part of an immigration reform package, to restrict immigration only to those with college degrees, and thus decided to allow only 500,000 foreigners a year to enter, what would happen to the rate of return on college education? Alternatively, if, as part of a reform package, 500,000 low-skilled people were permitted to enter the United States, what would happen to the rate of return on college education?

Answers to the Checkpoint questions can be found at the end of this chapter.

Economic Discrimination

Economic discrimination takes place whenever workers of equal ability and productivity are paid different wages or are otherwise discriminated against in the workplace because of their race, color, religion, gender, age, national origin, or disability. This can mean that one group is paid lower wages than another for doing the same job, or that members of different groups are segregated into occupations that pay different wages.

Economic theories of discrimination generally take one of two approaches. The first, developed by Gary Becker, rests on the notion that bias is articulated in the *discriminatory tastes* of employers, workers, and consumers. The second approach, the *segmented markets approach,* maintains that labor markets are divided into segments based on race, gender, or some other category. This approach is often referred to as the *job crowding hypothesis,* or the *dual labor market hypothesis.*

> **Economic discrimination:** When workers of equal ability are paid different wages or in any other way discriminated against because of race, color, religion, gender, age, national origin, or disability.

Becker's Theory of Economic Discrimination

Gary Becker's main contribution to economics is that he vastly broadened the issues that economists study. This was no small feat. Before Becker's influence, economists focused almost exclusively on the production and exchange of material goods and services. One early example shows the difficulties Becker faced in broadening this focus.

In 1955, Becker was asked to speak at Harvard about his dissertation on the economics of discrimination. Becker noted that his audience was perplexed. "They thought I would discuss price discrimination"—that is, the analysis of why businesses charge different prices for the same goods. "No one conceived that an economist would talk about race discrimination in those days."[6]

Published in 1957, *The Economics of Discrimination* was not warmly received by the profession. Not until the mid-1960s, when the civil rights movement gained momentum, did the book get the recognition it deserved. Surprisingly enough, Becker challenged the conventional view that discrimination benefits the person who discriminates. Let's see why he thought the conventional wisdom was wrong.

Becker argued that employers who discriminate against women will lose market share and profit opportunities, both because they do not hire the best employees available, and because they must pay mostly high-wage male employees. Nondiscriminating firms, in contrast, will have lower labor costs, having more low-wage women on the payroll. Nondiscriminating firms will attract the most productive managers and employees, many of whom will likely be women. Profits for the nondiscriminating firm should therefore be higher. Becker concluded that the cost of wage differentials and the pressures of the marketplace should drive discrimination down to zero in the long run.

[6] Peter Passell, "New Nobel Laureate Takes Economics Far Afield," *New York Times*, October 14, 1992, p. D1.

In practice, we know that wage discrimination still exists. Why might competition fail to erase wage differentials? For one thing, the adjustment costs of firing unproductive workers, giving them severance pay, then recruiting and training new workers can be extremely high, especially considering the protections unions and the legal system offer workers. Second, women may be less mobile than men when it comes to work. They may be less willing to move to accommodate employer preferences, and thus be forced to accept lower wage positions. Third, if women continue to choose occupations with more flexible career paths that do not heavily penalize extended absences from the labor market, wage differentials between men and women may always exist. Note, however, that such differentials could also be caused by discrimination that precedes labor market entry, as when social norms direct girls toward lower-wage occupations such as elementary education or social work.

Segmented Labor Markets

Segmented labor markets: Labor markets split into separate parts. This leads to different wages paid to different sectors even though both markets are highly competitive.

Economists who advocate **segmented labor market** theories argue that discrimination does not arise due to a lack of competitive labor markets, but rather because these markets, though competitive, are segmented into a variety of constituent parts. And these different parts, while interacting, are noncompeting sectors. Segmented labor market theories have been developed along several different lines.

- The *dual labor market hypothesis* splits the labor market into primary and secondary sectors. As Doeringer and Piore wrote, "Jobs in the primary market possess several of the following characteristics: high wages, good working conditions, job stability, chances of advancement, equity and due process in the administration of work rules. Jobs in the secondary market, in contrast, tend to have low wages and fringe benefits, poor working conditions, high labor turnover, little chance of advancement, and often arbitrary and capricious supervision."[7]

- The *job crowding hypothesis* breaks occupations into predominately male and female jobs. In 1922, Edgeworth recognized this problem when he wrote, "The pressure of male trade unions appears to be largely responsible for that crowding of women into a comparatively few occupations, which is universally recognized as a main factor in the depression of their wages. Such crowding is prima facie a flagrant violation of that free competition which results in maximum production in . . . equal pay for equal work."[8]

- The *insider-outsider theory* maintains that workers are segregated into those who belong to unions and those who are unemployed or non-union workers. Alternatively, economists have recognized that large firms use internal promotion and job security to inspire loyalty to the firm. Company customs, norms, and policies provide loyal workers with clear advancement paths. The preference given to promotion from within can be a good recruiting vehicle for a firm, but it can also become an indirect method of segregating the labor market.

These hypotheses all predict that separate job markets will emerge for different groups. Figure 4 shows how segregated markets can lead to significant wage differentials, such as those we see for men and women.

In a world without discrimination, equilibrium wages for everyone would be W_e, with total employment at $M_0 + F_0$. If some form of discrimination in male-dominated jobs is present, labor supply to that segment will decline to S_1, wages will rise to W_1, and hiring will fall to M_1 (point a). Those women who are excluded from jobs in this sector will have to move to jobs available in the female-dominated sector, thus increasing the supply of

---

[7] P. Doeringer and M. Piore, *Internal Labour Markets and Manpower Analysis* (1971), p. 165, cited in Stephen Smith, *Labour Economics* (New York: Routledge), 1994, p. 104.

[8] F. Y. Edgeworth, "Equal Pay to Men and Women for Equal Work" (1922), p. 439, cited in Stephen Smith, *Labour Economics* (New York: Routledge), 1994, p. 102.

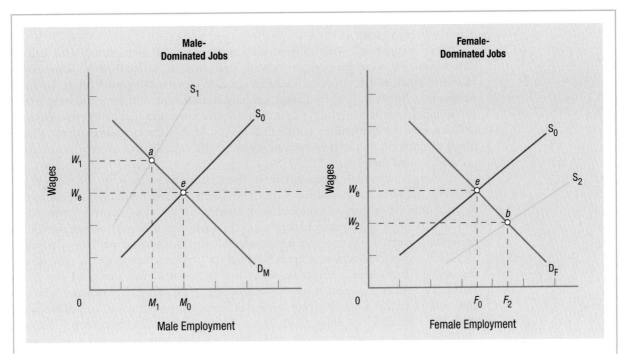

FIGURE 4—Job Crowding and a Dual Labor Market

Segregated markets can lead to significant wage differentials between men and women. Absent discrimination, equilibrium wages will be W_e for everyone, with total employment at $M_0 + F_0$. If, however, there is some form of discrimination in male-dominated jobs, the supply of labor to that segment will decline to S_1, wages will rise to W_1, and employment will fall to M_1 (point a). Those women who are excluded from jobs in this sector will have to move to available jobs in the female-dominated sector, thus increasing the labor supplied for these jobs to S_2, raising employment to F_2, but reducing wages to W_2 (point b). The result is a wage differential equal to $W_1 - W_2$.

labor there to S_2 and reducing wages to W_2, employment climbing to F_2 (point *b*). The result is a wage differential equal to $W_1 - W_2$.

Notice that once such a wage differential is established, the firms in competitive markets have no real incentive to eliminate the gap. Men and women are both being paid their marginal revenue products, so no profits are gained by substituting workers.

Wage differentials can arise for a variety of reasons. Some people may simply prefer one occupation to another. If such preferences have their roots in specific social groups, groupwide wage differentials can be expected to arise. Wages will vary between occupations, moreover, because of differences in their attractiveness, difficulty, riskiness, social status, and the human capital investments required.

Markets may naturally gravitate toward different equilibrium wage levels for different occupations. Two occupations may require the same skills and effort, for instance, but be valued differently by consumers. Finally, government policies that promote or restrict entry into occupations or professions affect wages. Licensing requirements for everything from hair styling to surgery today create wage differentials in over 700 different occupations.

Occupational segregation may also arise from disparate degrees of labor force attachment. Female labor force participation is often interrupted when women take a break from working to have children. Skills and other forms of human capital depreciate during these interruptions, which influences the occupational choices of women and employer decisions concerning which employees to offer specific training. For women who anticipate spells out of the labor force, jobs that mostly involve general training—nursing, teaching, retail sales, and secretarial or administrative work—may look attractive. These occupations do not require climbing long career ladders, so women can leave their jobs, later returning or finding a new employer, with little loss in salary or benefits. The downside to these occupations, however, is that most of them do not pay high wages.

Some occupational wage differentials are the result of socialization: Our culture stereotypes some occupations as "men's work" and others as "women's work." Some of this may be rational; men, for instance, are better suited to jobs involving heavy lifting. For most occupations, however, gender differences should be irrelevant. Still, lingering wage differentials today may be the result of past discriminatory practices that barred women from entering some occupations or professional schools. At one time or another, firms, educational institutions, and unions have all restricted the entry of women into high-paying occupations and professions.

Do wage differentials necessarily mean that discrimination exists in the market? Job crowding and wage differentials could just reflect different levels of human capital investment or different professional choices. Many women, for instance, may truly prefer occupations that are complementary to parenting. These will tend to be jobs without significant career ladders and that do not require considerable specific training, mobility, or travel.

Table 2 shows the average salary differential for women with college and professional degrees who had career interruptions of at least 18 months. This survey of over 6,000 Harvard graduates and another based on University of Chicago MBAs between 1990 and 2006 confirmed that career interruptions and differences in weekly hours worked explained the bulk of the earnings differentials. The authors note that, "Mothers seem to actively choose jobs that are family friendly and avoid jobs with long hours and greater career advancement opportunities." They also found that, "Mothers with high-earning spouses reduce their labor supply much more [than] mothers with lower earning spouses . . ."

TABLE 2 *Financial Cost to Women from an 18-Month Career Interruption*

MBA	−41%
J.D.	−29
Ph.D.	−29
B.A. only	−25
M.D.	−16
Other/master's	−13

Sources: Claudia Goldin and Lawrence Katz, "Transitions: Career and Family Life Cycles of the Educational Elite," *American Economic Review: Papers & Proceedings*, 2008, pp. 363–369; Marianne Bertrand, Claudia Goldin, and Lawrence Katz, "Dynamics of the Gender Gap for Young Professionals in the Financial and Corporate Sectors," unpublished working paper, January 2009; and David Leonhardt, "Careers That Work for Families," *New York Times*, May 27, 2009, p. B1.

Although initially both men and women were paid the same, women were working and earning considerably less than their male counterparts 10 years later. Balancing careers and family responsibilities for today's dual-earner households continues to be a challenge for both families and employers.

Public Policy to Combat Discrimination

For the first half of the last century, the inequities associated with various forms of discrimination were simply accepted as a part of life in the United States. Gradually, however, a groundswell developed to end racial segregation and other forms of discrimination, culminating in passage of the Civil Rights Act in 1964. In what follows, we briefly outline the major acts and public policies that have been implemented with the goal of ending discrimination. Because of these policies, discrimination, wage differentials, and segmented labor markets have declined markedly over the past four decades.

The Equal Pay Act of 1963

Equal Pay Act of 1963 amended the Fair Labor Standards Act of 1938; it requires that men and women receive equal pay for equal work. Equal work is defined as work performed under similar circumstances requiring equal effort, skill, and responsibility. Some argue that the Equal Pay Act was a hollow victory because occupational segregation forced women into specific occupations, causing them to earn less than men for essentially comparable work.

Civil Rights Act of 1964

Title VII of the Civil Rights Act of 1964 makes it unlawful to "refuse to hire or to discharge any individual, or otherwise to discriminate against any individual with respect to his compensation, terms, conditions, or privileges of employment, because of such individual's race, color, religion, sex, or national origin." The act also created the Equal Employment Opportunity Commission (EEOC) to administer the Act.

To date, most of the litigation brought under this statute has focused on the meaning of the phrase *to discriminate*. Amendments to the statute and court cases have ruled that, to show discrimination, a plaintiff must show that an employment practice inflicts a "disparate" or unequal impact on members of a minority group, as compared to its impact on others. Once this has been demonstrated, the burden shifts to the defendant (the employer) to show that its employment practices—seniority rules, prehiring examinations or other screening devices, weight or height requirements—are related to employee performance or are otherwise a matter of "business necessity." Plaintiffs may sue for a full range of remedies, including back pay, reinstatement, court costs, attorney's fees, and punitive damages.

Executive Order 11246—Affirmative Action

In 1965, President Lyndon Johnson issued Executive Order 11246. This order established the Office of Federal Contract Compliance Programs (OFCCP) in the Department of Labor. A key provision of this order required that firms doing at least $50,000 in business with the federal government submit an affirmative action program that includes a detailed analysis of their labor force.

Affirmative action programs have been controversial from the outset. Critics see such programs as "enforced quotas," whereas supporters see them as a way of breaking down discriminatory hiring barriers.

In the summer of 2003, the U.S. Supreme Court ruled in the University of Michigan case (*Gratz v. Bollinger*) that adding a large specific numerical adjustment for minority group status to university admission criteria was unacceptable. The undergraduate admissions program automatically added 20 points (out of a total of 100) to minority candidates for admission. The Law School at Michigan, on the other hand, simply took race into account in a nuanced approach to improving diversity of the class. The Supreme Court found this approach acceptable (*Grutter v. Bollinger*).

Age and Disabilities Acts

Two other acts were designed to reduce discrimination based on age and physical or mental disabilities. The Age Discrimination in Employment Act of 1967 protects workers over age 40 from discrimination based on age. The Americans With Disabilities Act of 1990 prohibits discrimination against people with a physical or mental disability who could still perform a job with reasonable accommodation by an employer. What constitutes "reasonable accommodation" has been a point of contention in many recent court cases.

■ CHECKPOINT

ECONOMIC DISCRIMINATION

- Economic discrimination occurs whenever workers of equal ability and productivity are paid different wages or otherwise discriminated against because of their race, color, religion, gender, age, national origin, or disability.

- Becker's analysis of discrimination assumed that employers had a taste for discrimination, and he showed that both parties were harmed by discrimination.

- Segmented labor markets assume that separate markets lead to wage differentials that represent discrimination.

- Public policy to eliminate discrimination has included the Equal Pay Act of 1963, Civil Rights Act of 1964, Executive Order 11246 (Affirmative Action), Age Discrimination in Employment Act of 1967, and Americans With Disabilities Act of 1990.

QUESTION: The Civil Rights Act of 1964 made defendants liable for the plaintiffs attorney's fees if they lost the case, but it did not have the same provision for plaintiffs if they lost the case. Why do you think Congress wrote this part of the law this way? (Hint: Who did Congress assume would be plaintiffs and who would be defendants under the Civil Rights Act?)

Answers to the Checkpoint question can be found at the end of this chapter.

Labor Unions and Collective Bargaining

A friend who had been working for a large construction company for eight years as an engineer and project coordinator recently staged a one-man strike. He had been training new employees on various aspects of cost estimating and job specification, and he noticed that these new people were being hired at salaries approaching his own. He requested a raise several times, but was essentially ignored. Exasperated, he refused to go to work one day, informing his boss that he would not return without a raise. He did not quit; he simply staged a walkout and refused to return until given a raise. He was out for 2 weeks before his supervisor called and asked him how much he wanted. They settled on a raise of over 20%.

This story is unique in that one-person strikes are rarely successful; more often they are career busters. In most instances, individual employees have little control over wages or job conditions, essentially being at the mercy of employers and the market. This is the primary reason that unions exist: Collective action is more powerful than the action of one individual. As individuals, we can easily be replaced (except, apparently, my friend above). To replace an entire workforce, on the other hand, imposes serious costs to an employer. This section looks at the role unions play in our economy, their history, and their effects.

Types of Unions

Labor unions are legal associations of employees that bargain with employers over terms and conditions of work, including wages, benefits, and working conditions. They use strikes and threats of strikes, as well as other tactics, to try to achieve their goals. Elections determine union representatives who negotiate on the workers' behalf, and employers are legally required to "bargain in good faith" with the union.

Unions are usually defined by industry, or by craft or occupation. A *craft* union represents members of a specific craft or occupation, such as air traffic controllers (PATCO), truck drivers (Teamsters), and teachers (AFT). An *industrial* union represents all workers employed in a specific industry. Examples include auto workers (UAW) and public employees (AFSCME).

Benefits and Costs of Union Membership

Without a union, each individual employee would have to bargain with management for his or her own wages, benefits, and working conditions. Unions bring collective power to this bargaining arrangement. The source of this power is ultimately the willingness of the union to strike if no agreement is reached during negotiations. Collective bargaining often leads to a more equitable pay schedule than individual negotiation. It also provides workers with greater job security by protecting them against arbitrary or vindictive decisions by management.

Management's unilateral authority is curbed by the union contract, specifically through restrictions on job assignments and restrictions that severely limit the ability of management to fire employees without good cause and due process. These rules are subject to an elaborate grievance procedure laid out in the union contract's work rules.

Union membership, like everything else, has its price. First, union members must pay monthly dues. Then, if negotiations break down and a strike is called, wages are lost and the possibility exists, however remote, that management will refuse to settle with the union and replace the entire workforce. Finally, union workers must give up some individual flexibility since their work rules are more rigid.

Brief History of American Unionism

Labor unions date from the late 18th century in England. In this country, public attitudes toward unions were highly unfavorable until the Great Depression. In the early part of the 20th century, employers could easily secure legal injunctions against union organization by arguing that unions behaved like monopolies, in violation of antitrust laws. Employers often required employees to sign enforceable *yellow dog contracts,* in which they agreed not to join a union as a condition of employment.

Figure 5 shows union membership as a percentage of total employment since 1930. Going into the 1930s, unions represented just over 7% of workers because of public attitudes and legal restrictions. With the onset of the Depression, attitudes about collective bargaining began to change. In 1932, Congress passed the Norris-LaGuardia Act, which outlawed yellow dog contracts and prohibited injunctions against union organizing. Then, in 1935, Congress passed a sweeping reform by enacting the Wagner Act, or the National Labor Relations Act (NLRA). It prohibited a variety of unfair labor practices by employers,

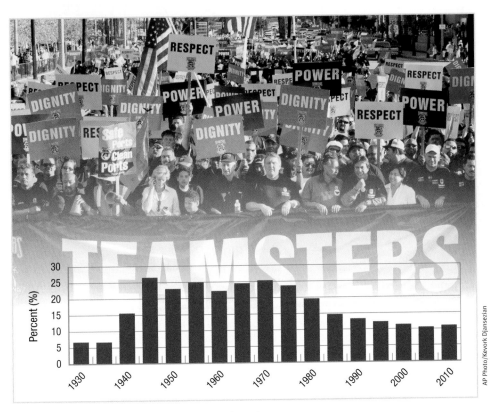

FIGURE 5—Union Membership as a Percent of Employment

Union membership grew dramatically from the mid-1930s until after World War II. Following the war, over one-quarter of American workers were unionized. Union membership has fallen because benefits obtained by unions for union members spread throughout the wider workforce, making the benefits of joining a union less valuable. Also, the changing economy led to faster growth in the more difficult-to-unionize service sector.

including firing employees for engaging in union activities. The Act also required employers to "bargain in good faith" with those unions that had won recognition through a majority vote of the firm's workers.

The NLRA also established the National Labor Relations Board (NLRB) to oversee union certification elections. These elections were to be held to determine which union, if any, would represent employees. The NLRB was also given the power to investigate complaints by labor and management about elections and the bargaining process.

As Figure 5 illustrates, union membership grew dramatically from the mid-1930s until after World War II. Following the war, union membership covered over one-quarter of American workers. It was concentrated in a few major industries.

Figure 6 shows work stoppages, or strikes, since 1950. In 1946 a rash of strikes turned public opinion against the unions; many people felt unions had become too powerful. Because of this swing in popular opinion, in 1947 Congress passed the Taft-Hartley Act, which prohibits some unfair labor practices by unions. Unions could no longer coerce or discriminate against workers who chose not to join the union, and unions were required to

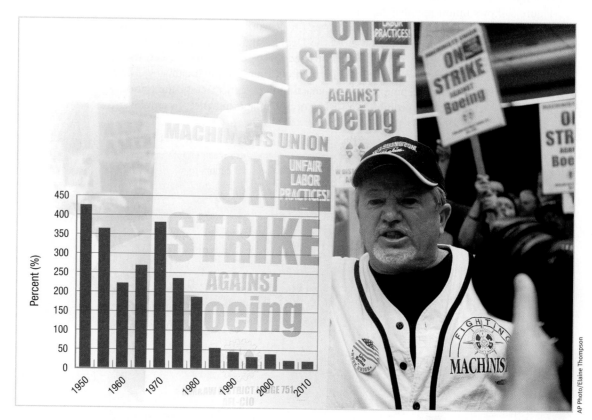

FIGURE 6—Work Stoppages (Strikes)

This figure shows work stoppages, or strikes, since 1950. In 1946, numerous strikes turned public opinion against the unions. In 1947, Congress reacted by passing the Taft-Hartley Act, seeking a balance between unions and management. After this, the use of work stoppages by unions gradually began to decline.

Secondary boycott: Occurs when unions clash with one firm and put pressure on a neutral, second firm to enlist the help of the second firm to obtain the union's objectives with the original firm.

Closed shop: Workers must belong to the union before they can be hired.

bargain in good faith, just like employers. With the passage of this Act, the prolabor aspects of the 1935 Wagner Act were balanced.

Taft-Hartley changed the collective bargaining landscape dramatically by ending secondary boycotts and closed shops, and establishing procedures for decertification elections. A **secondary boycott** occurs when unions clash with one firm—the primary firm—but put pressure on neutral secondary firms by getting their union members to refuse to process the products of the primary firm. A **closed shop** is a workplace where workers are required to be union members before they can be hired.

A **union shop** is one where nonunion hires must join the union within a specified period, usually 30 days. In an **agency shop,** employees are not required to join the union, but they must pay union dues to compensate the union for its services. The Taft-Hartley Act outlawed closed shops outright, while permitting states to pass *right-to-work statutes* that prohibit union shops. Today, over 20 states have **right-to-work laws.**

Near the end of the 1950s, union corruption had become a serious issue, as various union leaders were accused of taking kickbacks, committing pension fund fraud, and engaging in a variety of other illegal activities. In response to these problems, Congress in 1959 passed the Labor Management Reporting and Disclosure Act, or the Landrum-Griffin Act. This Act protects union members from their leaders by promoting union democracy and requiring financial transparency.

Until 1962, all collective bargaining statutes focused on the private sector; public employees were prohibited from organizing. In 1962, however, President Kennedy signed Executive Order 10988, giving federal workers the right to bargain collectively. Still, public employees are not permitted to strike. Rather, when an impasse is reached, both sides must submit to binding arbitration in which a neutral arbitrator resolves the dispute.

Union shop: Nonunion hires must join the union within a specified period of time.

Agency shop: Employees are not required to join the union, but must pay dues to compensate the union for its services.

Right-to-work laws: Laws created by the Taft-Hartley Act that permitted states to outlaw union shops.

Issue: Why Are Unions Pushing for Pledge Card Organizing?

As if declining membership wasn't enough trouble for labor, in the summer of 2005 several big unions broke away from the AFL-CIO in a disagreement over whether extensive political involvement or a focus on organizing new members was the best long-run strategy for the union movement. The breakaway unions, essentially led by the Service Employees International Union (SEIU), want to emphasize organizing new members and they are fighting with new strategies.

Under the National Labor Relations Act, the union creation process starts with pledge cards. Either employees of a non-union firm contact a union or a union contacts employees of a firm and offers to represent them. Interest in a union is revealed by employees signing pledge cards. Nothing official occurs until employee "interest" in a union is shown by obtaining pledge cards from 30% of employees. A petition is then filed with the NLRB, and a secret ballot is held. This often results in a heavily contested brawl with employers, and unions typically win fewer than half of the elections. As a result, unions employ new strategies and tactics that emphasize "pledge card check recognition," neutrality agreements, public relations, and advertising to win new members.

Pledge cards are the size of index cards, which workers sign to indicate that they would like to have a union represent them. Before organizing begins, unions approach employers for voluntary recognition if more than 50% of workers sign pledge cards. If employers insist on following NLRB election certification rules, the union tries to get employers to sign neutrality agreements whereby employers are restricted from actively campaigning against union recognition.

Now, why would an employer want to voluntarily recognize a union or agree to remain neutral during the election campaign? Here's where the second half of the union's new tactics, the "corporate campaign," comes into play. Firms who refuse the unions' overtures will face public relations and advertising campaigns to harm their corporate image as well as grassroots community opposition to new facilities, mergers, or requests for regulatory relief.

These tactics have proven quite successful. When unions get neutrality agreements signed, the organizational success rate climbs to 45%; when card check agreements are added, the union success rate exceeds 75% of their attempts to organize. In 2006, janitors at the University of Miami staged walkouts, sit-ins, and hunger strikes to get the university service contractor to agree to pledge card recognition if the union got 60% of the workers to sign cards, thus

Anderson Ross/Jupiter Images

avoiding a secret ballot election. Some students supported the janitors. During the walkout, the service contractor increased wage rates by one-third at the request of the university. Media attention was directed at university president Donna Shalala, President Clinton's former Secretary of Health and Human Services, who tried to remain neutral. In the end, the service contractor agreed to the union's demands.

These strategies are effective. With labor union membership such a small fraction of the workforce, unions are using these new tactics to increase membership and influence.

Sources: See "Unions Favor Card Check Recognition in Organizing," *National Law Journal,* January 10, 2005; and Timothy Aeppel, "Not-So-Big Labor Enlists New Methods for Greater Leverage," *Wall Street Journal,* August 29, 2005, p. A2.

Why has union membership declined as a percentage of wage and salary workers since World War II? The answer lies partly with the changes in labor laws just discussed, the country's changing economy—notably, a larger service sector that is hard to organize—and ironically, the very success of labor at pushing its agenda through Congress and the courts. In addition, management has become more aggressive and sophisticated in defeating certification elections along with the rising labor force participation of women who historically have been difficult to organize.

Before unionization, employees were *hired at will*, which meant they could be fired "for a good reason, a bad reason, or no reason at all." Unions and their supporters pressed Congress and the courts for work safety legislation, minimum wage laws, Social Security, antidiscrimination statutes, restrictions on firing employees, laws that put restrictions on plant closures, and many other statutes and rules that protect workers.

Each of these successes resulted in union membership being a little less valuable. Over this same period, the service sector has become a bigger share of our economy. This sector has always been difficult for labor to organize, and as a result, union membership may continue to shrink as a percentage of the workforce.

Union Versus Nonunion Wage Differentials

Why join a union? The primary benefit to unionization should be higher wages, given the union's collective bargaining power. The general theoretical argument for union–nonunion wage differentials is illustrated in Figure 7.

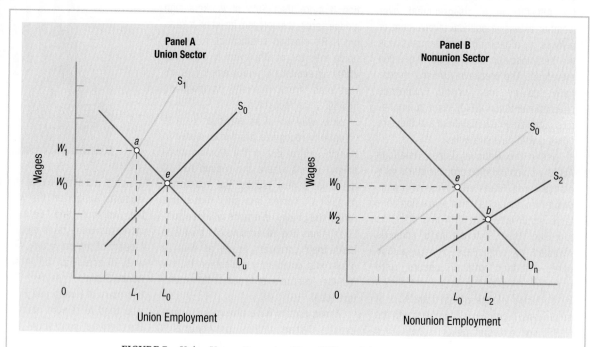

FIGURE 7—Union Versus Nonunion Wage Differentials

This figure illustrates the argument for union–nonunion wage differentials. Unions increase wages in their sectors by restricting entry into union jobs. Assuming the markets for unionized and nonunionized jobs begin at equilibrium, at point e in both panels, union and nonunion wages are initially W_0. If the union successfully restricts supply to S_1 in panel A, union wages will rise to W_1, but employment will fall to L_1 (point a). Those workers released will have no choice but to move to the nonunion sector represented in panel B, thus increasing its supply to S_2. Equilibrium in the nonunion sector thus moves to point b, where more workers (L_2) are employed at a lower wage (W_2). The result is a wage differential equal to $W_1 - W_2$.

This figure shows how unions are able to increase the wages in their sectors by restricting entry into union jobs. The markets for both unionized and nonunion labor begin at equilibrium, at point e in both panels of Figure 7. Thus, union and nonunion wages are initially equal, at W_0. If the union successfully restricts supply to S_1 in panel A, union wages will rise to W_1, but employment will fall to L_1 (point a). Those workers who are released have no choice but to move over to the nonunion sector represented in panel B, thus shifting its supply to S_2. Equilibrium in the nonunion sector moves to point b, where more workers (L_2) are employed at lower wages (W_2). The resulting wage differential, $W_1 - W_2$, is caused by successful collective bargaining in the union sector. Notice that this analysis is substantially the same as that for discrimination in the segmented labor force described in Figure 4 earlier.

Unions also have several ways of negotiating higher wages without losing members to unemployment. They can engage in activities that increase demand for their firm or industry's products, reduce the elasticity of demand for the product, or increase union productivity. One approach, advertisements encouraging consumers to buy the union label, fell flat.

More successful activities have included featherbedding, or forcing companies to hire redundant personnel. Examples include the firemen kept on trains long after diesels had replaced coal-burning steam engines, and the backup orchestras required by union contracts in New York City. This approach works in industries with significant pricing power, and in which labor costs are a small fraction of total costs. Under such conditions, it is simply not worth it for a firm to fight union demands for a few extra positions.

Union–nonunion wage differentials vary by the union, occupation, industry, and historical period. In general, average union wages are 10% to 20% higher than the average nonunion wage. Union wage effects are most pronounced among blue-collar workers and service employees. These differentials suggest that unionization may tend to reduce the inequities inherent in labor markets.

Evolving Labor Markets and Issues

Labor markets, like all other markets, change with time and the wishes of their participants. Over the last three decades, the entry of women into the labor force has been a major factor spurring economic growth. Over this same period, two-earner families increased so that today over half of all families with small children are two-earner households.

These demographic changes have shifted the focus of labor politics from union bargaining to issues such as telecommuting, family leave policies, affirmative action, and the question of how much employers should pay for medical benefits. As Social Security begins to look more fragile and the baby boomers begin flooding the retirement ranks, employer retirement packages will undoubtedly receive even more attention.

Immigration, legal and illegal, has caught the attention of labor economists. The United States, unlike Europe, has relatively open borders. Some argue that we need new immigrants to do the work that most Americans are unwilling to do. Other economists suggest that, in the absence of such inflows, salaries in these low-skill occupations would be high enough to attract the needed labor. In any case, immigrants are doing what they have done for centuries: entering the economy at lower skill levels and hoping that circumstances will be better for their children.

This great tide of immigrants into low-skilled, low-wage jobs, together with the growth of high-skilled, high-wage, high-tech jobs and the rise in dual-earner households, has resulted in growing income inequality. Executive pay scales compared to average salaries have exploded in the last decade. These pressures have renewed the debate surrounding income distribution and the welfare system. We discuss these issues in more detail in a later chapter.

■ CHECKPOINT

LABOR UNIONS AND COLLECTIVE BARGAINING

- Unions are typically organized around a craft or an industry.

- Unions and the managers of firms must bargain "in good faith."

- Secondary boycotts occur when unions put pressure on a neutral second firm to not process the products of the intended target. They were outlawed by the Taft-Hartley Act.

- In a closed shop, only union members are hired. In a union shop, nonunion workers can be hired, but they must join the union within a specified period. An agency shop permits both union and nonunion workers, but the nonunion workers must pay union dues.

- Union wage differentials are between 10% and 20% higher.

QUESTION: Union negotiations always seem to run up against a "strike deadline." Are there incentives for both sides to put off a settlement until the very last moment?

Answers to the Checkpoint question can be found at the end of this chapter.

Key Concepts

Investment in human capital, p. 288
Screening/signaling, p. 291
On-the-job training, p. 292
General training, p. 292
Specific training, p. 292
Economic discrimination, p. 295

Segmented labor markets, p. 296
Secondary boycott, p. 302
Closed shop, p. 302
Union shop, p. 303
Agency shop, p. 303
Right-to-work laws, p. 303

Chapter Summary

Investment in Human Capital

Workers invest in themselves by going to school or learning a trade. Firms invest in workers through OJT or in-house training for employees. The value of these activities can be analyzed using investment analysis.

Investments in education involve the direct costs of education and forgone earnings. The benefits of such investments are then spread over the individual's working life.

Anything that reduces the availability of funds will reduce investments in human capital. The demand for human capital, meanwhile, is influenced by an individual's abilities and learning capacity. Human capital improves an individual's productivity, thereby resulting in higher lifetime earnings. Productivity thus links education and earnings.

Some economists suggest that investments in human capital do little more than serve as screening or signaling devices for employers. With this view, a college degree is merely a proxy for trainability, discipline, good work habits, and intelligence.

On-the-job training falls into two categories: general and specific training. General training improves productivity at all firms, while specific training improves productivity only at one specific firm. Firms rarely provide general training, but firms will provide specific training if the returns are high enough.

Economic Discrimination

Economic discrimination occurs whenever workers of equal ability and productivity are paid different wages or otherwise discriminated against in the workplace because of their race, color, religion, gender, age, national origin, or disability. Lower wages, segregation into different occupations, and restrictions on entry into professions are all examples of economic discrimination.

Gary Becker concluded that employers who discriminate lose profit opportunities, so competitive pressures should end this discrimination. Competitive forces, however, may not be enough to end discrimination because of the significant costs associated with hiring and firing and otherwise restructuring a firm's workforce. Some workers, moreover, are less mobile than others. If this is true of a group of workers, such as women, this could lead to wage differences that are not clearly discriminatory.

Another approach to analyzing economic discrimination in labor markets rests on the existence of segmented markets. Various forces can segment workers from different groups into different, noncompeting sectors of the labor market. The labor market can be split into primary and secondary markets (the dual labor market hypothesis); it can be broken into predominantly male and female jobs (the job crowding hypothesis); or it can be split into union and nonunion or unemployed workers (insider-outsider theory).

Labor Unions and Collective Bargaining

Labor unions are legal associations of employees formed to bargain collectively with employers over the terms and conditions of employment.

Collective bargaining provides workers with increased job security, a more structured work environment, and potentially higher wages. In return, monthly dues must be paid to the union, flexibility on the job is often restricted, and infrequently strikes are required, resulting in a loss of wages and possible job loss.

Questions and Problems

Check Your Understanding

1. Would unions be more likely to successfully organize firms in highly competitive markets or firms with monopsony power? Why or why not?

2. Why are colleges filled with young people rather than middle-aged individuals? If interest rates rose to over 10%, would this have any impact on the number of people attending college or its composition?

3. Why would it be so difficult to unionize part-time and contract employees (independent contractors)?

4. When there is discrimination in the labor market, who loses? Why? Why is it harder to discriminate when both labor and product markets are competitive?

Apply the Concepts

5. When a company uses resources to train staff or subsidize tuition for employees, it is clearly investing in human capital. However, this investment is treated as current spending (cost of selling or producing goods) rather than investment. Should these activities be treated as investments and be reflected in the investment statistics of the economy?

6. Why do we all work Monday through Friday? Why not stagger the workweek and reduce highway congestion and pollution?

7. Americans work on average 400 hours more (roughly 10 weeks) each year than German or French workers. What might be some of the reasons for this?

8. Has globalization made it more difficult for unions to negotiate higher wages? Why or why not?

9. We saw in the previous chapter that wage rates rose when productivity rose. Unions now face serious foreign competition that restricts its ability to simply use its bargaining strength to increase wages. What can unions do to increase the productivity of its members to make it easier to bargain for higher wages?

10. Does it seem reasonable that a certain portion of the benefits of a college education is essentially a way to show prospective employers that you are reasonably intelligent, trainable, and have a certain degree of discipline?

11. Some politicians during any election campaign offer proposals to make college more affordable by increasing subsidies through higher Pell grants and subsidizing reduced rate loans. If these policies come to pass, and college becomes less expensive, more people will attend college. What will this do to the rate of return on a college education?

12. If unions can raise wages 10% to 20%, as suggested by empirical studies, why doesn't everyone join a union?

13. The airline pilots union has been very successful in negotiating six-figure salaries for pilots. The unions representing flight attendants have not been nearly as successful. What probably accounts for the difference?

14. Why do we permit price discrimination with different ticket prices at movies based on age, or ladies' nights at bars (when women get in free or get cheaper drinks) or insurance where women sometimes pay more (health) or less (automobile), but we do not permit discrimination in wage rates?

15. It is often suggested that American businesses are at a competitive disadvantage because other countries supply health care to workers via the central government while big American companies have to pay for their employees' health insurance. If labor markets are essentially national and workers are paid wages and benefits, explain why American companies might only gain a short-term advantage if the government implemented a national health care alternative to health care insurance being part of the wage package. (Hint: If health care was provided nationally and workers had to buy insurance from the government or pay higher taxes, would they expect to get higher wages?)

In the News

16. Two decades ago, General Motors was the top automobile firm in the United States, and as such a strong company, its profits seemed secure. During negotiations with the United Auto Workers (UAW), GM gave workers wage and benefit packages that were unsustainable, including the "job bank" that gave laid-off employees full pay until they were brought back. General Motors filed for bankruptcy in June 2009. As reported by the *New York Times* (January 25, 2010), "G.M. sold its good assets to a new government-owned company," and "The federal government will hold nearly 61 percent of the new company, with the Canadian government, a health care trust for the United Autoworkers union and bondholders owning the balance." How does this new ownership structure change the bargaining process for the UAW?

17. *The Economist,* March 4, 2006, reported that "a woman with middling skills who has a baby at age 24 loses $981,000 in lifetime earning compared with one who remains childless." If the woman waits a few years before having a baby, the figure is lower, but still large. What are the reasons that having children reduces women's earnings so much?

Answers to Questions in CheckPoints

Check Point: Investment in Human Capital

Letting in a large number of college-educated immigrants would drive the rate of return on college down as wages of college graduates would not grow very rapidly. The opposite would occur when unskilled immigrants enter, holding down the wages of those without college educations, leading to a growing gap between those with college degrees, increasing the rate of return to a college degree.

Check Point: Economic Discrimination

Congress felt that most people who were discriminated against were unlikely to be able to afford an attorney. This provision encourages lawyers to take on these cases knowing that if they prevail, they will be paid.

Check Point: Labor Unions and Collective Bargaining

Both sides work hard to get the best bargain for their constituents. There are incentives to continue negotiations up to the last moment to get the most and to appear to be driving a hard bargain. Strikes involve costs, and both sides use the threat of imposing these costs as a bargaining chip.

Public Goods, Externalities, and Environmental Economics

Tim Foley Illustration

We humans are about as subtle as the asteroid that wiped out the dinosaurs. . . . The damage we do is increasing. In the next 20 years, the population will increase by 1.5 billion. These people will need food, water and electricity, but already our soils are vanishing, fisheries are being killed off, wells are drying up, and the burning of fossil fuels is endangering the lives of millions. We are heading for cataclysm.

APRIL 2001 GLOBAL SUPPLEMENT FROM *NEW SCIENTIST*

Psychologically, the population explosion first sunk in on a stinking hot night in Delhi. The streets were alive with people. People eating, people washing themselves, people sleeping, people working, arguing and screaming. People reaching their hands in through taxi windows to beg. People sitting, people pissing. People hanging off buses. People driving animals through the streets. People, people, people.

PAUL EHRLICH, *THE POPULATION BOMB,* 1968

This is my long-run forecast in brief: The material conditions of life will continue to get better for most people, in most countries, most of the time, indefinitely. Within a century or two, all nations and most of humanity will be at or above today's western living standards. I also speculate, however, that many people will continue to think and say that the conditions of life are getting worse.

JULIAN SIMON (1932–1998)

At its most basic, all environmental policy involves a rearrangement of property rights.

CHARLES PEARSON, *ECONOMICS AND THE GLOBAL ENVIRONMENT,* 2000

311

As the quotes above illustrate, people have radically different ideas about how well we live and what impact human existence is having on the globe. Many environmentalists and others see the Earth as wasting away as human beings exhaust its natural resources, foul its air and water, and decimate animal species. Others optimistically regard advancing technologies, newfound efficiencies, and rising standards of living as signs that people are taking ever better care of the planet.

In 1980, Julian Simon offered the following bet:

> This is a public offer to stake $10,000, in separate transactions of $1,000 or $100 each, on my belief that mineral resources (or food or other commodities) will not rise in price in future years adjusted for inflation. You choose any mineral or other raw material (including grain and fossil fuels) that is not government controlled, and the date of settlement.

The bet was an open offer, but Simon aimed it at environmental activist Paul Ehrlich, author of *The Population Bomb*. Ehrlich and two other Stanford University colleagues accepted the bet in October 1980, selecting copper, chrome, nickel, tin, and tungsten for a 10-year period. Ehrlich noted that he would "accept Simon's astonishing offer before other greedy people jumped in," since the "lure of easy money can be irresistible."[1]

Ten years later, in October 1990, Ehrlich sent Simon a check for $576.07. The real value (adjusted for inflation) of the basket of minerals had gone down over the decade by $576.07. New sources of supply had been discovered, the tin cartel collapsed during the intervening period, and other minerals had become substitutes for some in the original five. Not only had the value of the five resources declined, the price of each one of the metals had fallen. Simon offered the same bet again, but Ehrlich declined.

Are there lessons to be drawn from this bet? Surely one is that forecasting economic and market conditions far into the future is difficult, at best. Another is that overly pessimistic predictions about growth and the environment almost always turn out to be wrong.[2] It is true that the Earth is finite in size, and the natural resources it contains are limited. Even so, economic growth is often accompanied by increasing efficiencies in resource use. Rising incomes and standards of living, moreover, are typically accompanied by falling population growth rates. Were it not for immigration, population would be declining in the United States today.

Many trends involving living standards and the environment are moving in the right direction, yet that does not mean all is well. Clearly, we still have many environmental problems that must be addressed, including global climate change, species extinction, overharvesting of fisheries, and overcrowding of our highways and parks at the national level.

Environmental economics is a discipline that applies the principles and methods of economics to the study of the environment and natural resources. This marriage of economics and the environment may seem like a stretch to some, but economists must already deal with the environment regularly; environmental and natural resources are frequently inputs into economic production, and at times are economic products or services. Resources such as coal, iron, and oil, for instance, are extracted from the Earth and moved directly into the production process. National parks and the restrictions on their use, meanwhile, show that the natural environment is itself a product that has value to us.

Public Goods

We saw in Chapter 4 that markets do not always provide the socially optimal amount of a good at the socially optimal price. Either too much or too little of the good is produced, or it is offered at too high or too low a price. Before we dive into our discussion of how

---

[1] Bjorn Lomborg, *The Skeptical Environmentalist: Measuring the Real State of the World* (Cambridge: Cambridge University Press), 2001, p. 137.

[2] Both Simon's book *The Ultimate Resource 2* and Lomborg's book *The Skeptical Environmentalist* provide numerous examples.

By the *Numbers*

The Environment and Sustainability

Having a sustainable economy will likely require a focus on energy other than fossil fuels, finding better methods to recycle waste, and developing methods to manage the natural environment.

Hybrid car sales have been rising since 2000 and are slated to grow even faster in the near future.

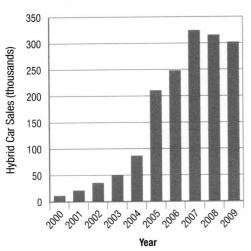

80,000 European fishing boats are fishing out Atlantic cod using advanced technology that makes finding and catching fish easier.

Jeff Rotman/Alamy

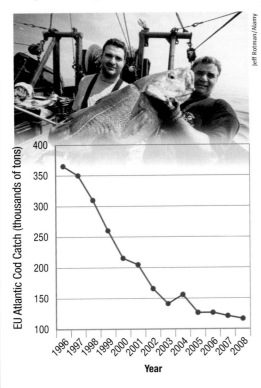

120 million
Number of electric bicycles in China

342%
Increase in wind energy generated in the United States between 2004 and 2009

$39
Annual savings from replacing five 60-watt bulbs with compact fluorescents

1.5 (0.2)
Acres of arable land per person in the United States (and China)

40¢
Gasoline tax in the United States

$4.25
Gasoline tax in Britain

Millions of tons of solid waste fill landfills, while some is recovered and recycled. To be sustainable, the United States must recover more in the future.

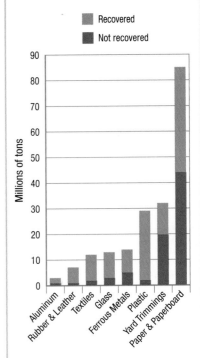

Top 10 States in Wind Capacity (megawatts)

Texas	8,361
Iowa	3,043
California	2,787
Minnesota	1,805
Washington	1,575
Oregon	1,408
New York	1,264
Colorado	1,068
Kansas	1,014
Illinois	915

Panoramic Images/Getty Images

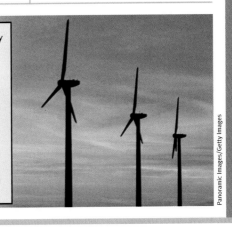

market failures can lead to environmental problems, let us first briefly review the concepts of consumer and producer surplus. These two concepts are often used to measure the impact environmental policies have on social welfare.

A Brief Refresher on Producer and Consumer Surplus

Recall that demand curves represent, in dollar terms, the utility consumers receive from a given product. Supply curves represent the marginal cost to producers of producing goods and services; a supply curve similarly represents the opportunity cost to society of producing and distributing a given product. Figure 1 depicts a market for a product that has no environmental impacts. The supply curve thus represents the full marginal cost to society of producing this product.

Consumer Surplus

Equilibrium in Figure 1 is found at point *e,* where 6,000 units are sold for $30 each. The area under the demand curve and above equilibrium price is **consumer surplus** and is equal to $90,000 [(($60 − $30) × 6,000)/2]. When we look at changes in environmental policy, monitoring changes in consumer surplus will help us measure the gains or losses to consumers from policy changes.

Producer Surplus

The area below equilibrium price and above the marginal cost (supply) curve is **producer surplus,** the revenue firms get over the costs they would willingly bear to supply the product. It is equal to the triangle shown in Figure 1 and is equal to $60,000 [(($30 − $10) × 6,000)/2].

Social Welfare

Social welfare is equal to consumer surplus plus producer surplus. This is the value produced over what would be required for the product to be brought to market; it is equal to $150,000 in Figure 1. This is often referred to as the net welfare resulting from the production and consumption of this product. An activity or policy that increases net welfare is considered efficient.

Markets provide us with most of the products and services we consume. Under competitive conditions, as we have seen, markets will provide consumers with what they want

Consumer surplus: The difference between what consumers (as individuals or the market) would be willing to pay and the market price. It is equal to the area above market price and below the demand curve.

Producer surplus: The difference between market price and the price at which firms would be willing to supply the product. It is equal to the area below market price and above the supply curve.

Social welfare: The sum of consumer and producer surplus.

FIGURE 1—Consumer and Producer Surplus

The product in this market has no environmental impacts. Supply represents the full marginal costs to society of producing this product. The area under the demand curve but above the equilibrium price of $30 is consumer surplus. The area above the marginal cost curve and below equilibrium price is producer surplus. Total social welfare is equal to consumer surplus plus producer surplus.

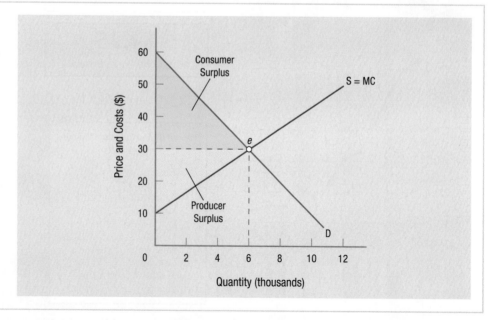

at the lowest possible opportunity costs. In what follows, we examine some of the reasons why a competitive market allocation may not always be the best solution for society. These reasons all fall under the heading of **market failures,** and they underpin our environmental laws and regulations.

As noted earlier, market failure occurs when a market does not provide the socially optimal amount of a good at the socially optimal price. Either too much or too little of the good is produced, or it is offered at too high or too low a price. There are three main causes of market failure: The product or service in question is a *public good,* the good is a *common property resource,* or the production or consumption of the product or service creates *externalities.*

> **Market failures:** When markets are not competitive or involve public goods, externalities, or common property resources, markets will fail to provide the optimal level of output, and will provide output at too high or low a price.

What Are Public Goods?

Pure **public goods** are nonrival in consumption, and exhibit nonexcludability. **Nonrivalry** means that the consumption of a good or service by one person does not reduce the utility of that good or service to others. **Nonexcludability** means that it is not feasible to exclude some consumers from using the good or service once it has been provided.

By way of contrast, a can of Coke is a rival product. When you drink a can of Coke, no one else can drink that same can. Airline flights exhibit excludability—when a flight is full, no one else is allowed to board the plane. But consider a lighthouse. Once it is built and in operation, all ships can see the lighthouse and use the light to avoid obstacles. One captain's use of the lighthouse does not prevent another from using it, nor can a ship realistically be excluded from using the lighthouse's services. Hence, the lighthouse is a public good. Other examples of public goods include national defense, accumulated knowledge, standards such as a national currency, protection of property rights, vaccinations, mosquito spraying, and clean air. Table 1 provides a taxonomy of private and public goods.

> **Public goods:** Goods that, once provided, no one person can be excluded from consuming (i.e., nonexclusion), and one person's consumption does not diminish the benefit to others from consuming the good (i.e., nonrivalry).

> **Nonrivalry:** The consumption of a good or service by one person does not reduce the utility of that good or service to others.

> **Nonexcludability:** Once a good or service is provided, it is not feasible to exclude others from enjoying that good or service.

TABLE 1   Taxonomy of Private and Public Goods

	Property Rights	
Characteristics of Goods	**Exclusive**	**Nonexclusive**
Rival	Pure private good ■ Airline seat ■ Ice cream bar	Common property resource ■ Ocean fishery ■ Highways
Nonrival	Public good with exclusion ■ Cable TV ■ National park	Pure public good ■ National defense ■ Law enforcement

Since consumers cannot be excluded from a public good once it is provided, they have little incentive to pay for the good in question. Instead, most will essentially be free riders. Think of the lighthouse again. If you have a ship and cannot be excluded from the benefits the lighthouse provides, why should you contribute anything to its upkeep? But if everyone took this position, there would be no support for the lighthouse, and it would go out of business. With free riders, private producers cannot hope to sell many units of a good, and so they have no incentive to produce it. Private markets will therefore fail to provide public goods, even if the goods are things everyone would like to see produced. This is why the government must get involved in the provision of products and services that have significant public good characteristics.

The Demand for Public Goods

Assessing the public's demand for public goods is clearly different from that of private goods where we found market demand by horizontally summing private demands. But the fact that once a public good is supplied, no one can be excluded from consuming it, and

FIGURE 2—Demand for Public Goods: Vertical Summation of Individual Demand Curves

For public goods, exclusion is not possible, individuals can consume the good simultaneously, and market demand is found by summing vertically. Market demand for public goods is really a willingness to pay curve since the government will have to provide the good and levy taxes to pay the cost. The total demand for the public good is shown by the heavy line labeled $D_{Public\ Goods}$ and is the vertical summation of individual demands.

one person's consumption does not affect another's, plays a crucial role. Figure 2 provides a solution to finding the demand for public goods.

Figure 2 shows demand for a public good by two different consumers. Individual A wants none when the price is $40 and is willing and able to buy 40 units when the price approaches zero. Individual B wants none when price is $60 and only is willing to buy 30 units when the price nears zero. Because each consumer can consume any given amount of a public good at the same time, the total demand for a public good is found by summing the individual demands *vertically*. To see why, consider when both individuals demand 20 units. This is the point where the two demand curves cross, and both are willing to pay $20 for 20 units. Thus, total demand for 20 units is $40. The total demand for the public good in Figure 2 is shown by the heavy line labeled $D_{Public\ Goods}$ and is the vertical summation of individual demands.

Notice how this differs from our discussion of market demand curves for private goods. There others could be excluded from consuming any good we bought, so demands were horizontally summed. In contrast, with public goods, exclusion is not possible, so we both can consume the good simultaneously, and market demand is found by summing vertically. Market demand for public goods is really a *willingness to pay curve*, because the government will have to provide the good and levy taxes to pay the cost.

Optimal Provision of Public Goods

Providing the optimal amount of public goods is easy in theory and is illustrated in Figure 2. The supply of public goods is equal to the marginal cost curve (S = MC) shown in the figure. Just like the competitive market equilibrium we covered earlier, optimal allocation is where MC = P, and in this instance, it is 20 units of the good at a total price of $40 (point *e*). In this example, the taxes are split equally between individuals A and B. Determining how much tax each person should (or would be willing to) pay is hampered by the fact that once the public good is provided, no one can be excluded, so individuals will be unwilling to reveal their true preferences for the good because it might mean they would have to pay a higher tax.

In reality, providing public goods involves the political process. This means that politicians, bureaucrats, special interest groups, and many others generate the decisions on how much of any particular public good to provide. The typical provision process uses some form of **cost-benefit analysis** (CBA). Since the demand for a public good represents the benefits to society and the supply curve represents society's costs, equating marginal benefits and marginal costs yields the optimal amount. But estimating the demand (benefits)

Cost-benefit analysis: A methodology for decision making that looks at the discounted value of the costs and benefits of a given project.

from public goods and their costs can be a complex process. Since people cannot be excluded from the good, once provided, people have little incentive to reveal their true preferences. Cost-benefit analysis was developed to help policymakers bridge this gap. The following section is a brief overview of CBA to give you an idea of the issues involved.

Cost-Benefit Analysis

Cost-benefit methodology was introduced into the Flood Control Act of 1936 and eventually grew more sophisticated; by 1960, it became an important element of the decision-making process of the Office of Management and Budget (OMB). The OMB's circular A-94 provides a straightforward summary of what CBA is designed to accomplish:

> The standard criterion for deciding whether a government program can be justified on economic principles is net present value—the discounted monetized value of expected net benefits (i.e., benefits minus costs). Net present value is computed by assigning monetary values to benefits and costs, discounting future benefits and costs using an appropriate discount rate, and subtracting the sum total of discounted costs from the sum total of discounted benefits. Discounting benefits and costs transforms gains and losses occurring in different time periods to a common unit of measurement. Programs with positive net present value increase social resources and are generally preferred. Programs with negative net present value should generally be avoided. Although net present value is not always computable (and it does not usually reflect effects on income distribution), efforts to measure it can produce useful insights even when the monetary values of some benefits or costs cannot be determined.

Cost-benefit analysis provides a rational model for policy decisions, forces a focus on alternatives (opportunity costs), draws conclusions about the optimal *scale* of projects, makes the intergenerational aspects explicit through discounting, and takes into account the explicit preferences of individuals. The explicit steps of a CBA are:[3]

- Specify the set of alternative projects.
- Decide whose benefits and costs count (the standing question).
- Catalogue the impacts and select measurement indicators.
- Predict the impacts quantitatively over the life of the project.
- Monetize (attach dollar values to) all impacts.
- Discount benefits and costs to obtain present values.
- Compute the net present value of each alternative.
- Perform sensitivity analysis (change some variables to see impacts).

One of the major difficulties with CBA for big public projects and environmental programs is measuring nonmarket or intangible aspects of projects. Economists have developed several different approaches to measuring these intangibles.[4] Some environmental goods have a bundle of characteristics, and some of them resemble market traded goods, so determining values in this way provides an estimate. Another approach looks at the travel costs people incur to recreational sites. The operating assumption is that these costs infer something about the value of parks and other recreational sites. Another approach is to look to the funds and effort people expend to avert harm. If you live by an airport and install double-pane glass to reduce noise, or purchase safety equipment (helmets, car seats, or bigger automobiles) to avoid injury from auto accidents, you are providing some evidence of the value (cost) of the harm.

---

[3] Anthony E. Boardman et al., *Cost-Benefit Analysis: Concepts and Practice* (Upper Saddle River, NJ: Pearson-Prentice Hall), 2006, p. 8.
[4] Organisation for Economic Co-operation and Development, *Cost-Benefit Analysis and the Environment* (OECD), 2006.

A more controversial method is contingent valuation. This method uses direct surveys to determine the value of such environmental qualities as species and forest preservation, biodiversity, and water quality projects. Those surveyed are provided an open-ended willingness-to-pay question or an iterative bidding questionnaire. The open-ended approach might ask how much you would pay (in increased taxes) to keep the Preble's meadow jumping mouse from going extinct. The iterative approach provides an initial value: If you agree with that number, then the number is iteratively increased until you say no; if you initially answer no, the number is reduced until you express willingness to pay. The numbers are then aggregated by the population to get total values.

Cost-benefit analysis, then, is a rational approach to valuing some things that are hard to put a price on, because people have no incentive to reveal their willingness to pay. This is what makes the decision to provide public goods so difficult.

Common Property Resources

Tragedy of the commons: Resources that are owned by the community at large (e.g., parks, ocean fish, and the atmosphere) and therefore tend to be overexploited because individuals have little incentive to use them in a sustainable fashion.

Commonly held resources are subject to nonexclusion but are rival in consumption. The market failure associated with commonly owned resources is often referred to as "the **tragedy of the commons.**"[5] The tragedy here is the tendency for commonly held resources to be overused and overexploited. Because the resource is held in common, individuals race to "get theirs" before others can grab it all.

One example of commonly held resources giving rise to problems involves oil fields. Oil reservoirs often span the surface property of many landowners. Because oil reservoirs are regarded as common property, each surface owner has an incentive to drill as many wells as possible and to pump out oil as rapidly as possible. Having too many wells pumping too quickly, however, reduces the oil field's water and gas pressure, thus reducing the total recoverable oil from the reservoir. Each owner's decision to drill a well therefore imposes an external cost on the other owners of land over the reservoir. At one point, this problem grew so severe that it resulted in passage of the 1935 Connolly "Hot Oil" Act. This Act restricted drilling, regulated the number and location of oil wells, and capped pumping rates.[6]

Road congestion is another illustration of the tragedy of the commons. Figure 3 shows a market for usage of a road that is fully used and is right at the tipping point

FIGURE 3—Road Congestion

Assume this road is fully used and is right at the tipping point before becoming congested. Demand for driving on this road is D_0, and the marginal cost of using the road—gas, time, and auto expenses—is MC_0. Equilibrium is at point e, with Q_0 miles a day being driven. Consumer surplus is area P_0ae for the typical driver. When a new driver begins using the road, this increases the marginal cost of driving to MC_1 for everyone, since the tipping point has been passed, and the road is now congested. Consumer surplus shrinks because of overuse of this common good.

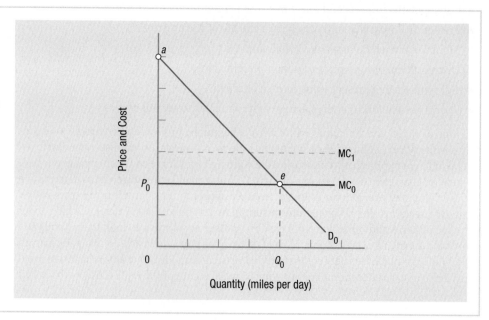

[5] Garrett Hardin, "The Tragedy of the Commons," *Science* 162, 1968, pp. 1243–1248.
[6] Daniel Yergin, *The Prize* (New York: Simon & Schuster), 1991.

Issue: Tragedy of the Commons: The Perfect Fish

Ocean fisheries are another good example of the problem of common property resources. Fish in the ocean were once in excess supply; there was no need to restrict the use of this resource. As the global demand for fish has risen, improved fishing technologies have allowed fishing boats to increase their hauls. Because many of the world's fisheries are still unregulated, one population after another has been fished out. Each fishing fleet grabbed as much as they could, and there was no incentive to hold back. The situation is clearly unsustainable, and indeed, as fish populations have shrunk, so have fishing fleets.

The Patagonian toothfish, as it is known, lives up to 50 years and can weigh over 200 pounds. This big, ugly, gray-black fish lives in the cold deep waters of the Southern Ocean near Antarctica, and in the 1990s, it became the signature dish of top restaurants in the United States, Japan, and Europe. It became so popular that during the mid-1990s, the annual catch was estimated at 100,000 metric tons.

How did such an ugly fish with such an unappetizing name become so popular? In the late 1970s, Lee Lantz, a Los Angeles fish merchant, visited the docks in Valparaiso, Chile, and spotted a toothfish. He bought a sample and cooked it, but the oily flesh had little taste. Most

fish have bladders that they inflate to adjust their buoyancy, reducing the energy it takes to move up and down in the water. Toothfish do not have bladders, but use oil (lighter than water) secreted to create buoyancy. Also, Patagonian toothfish are predators, waiting in ambush for prey. Thus, they do not need a lot of blood rushing through their system. As a result, toothfish meat is oily and white like cod. It is this oiliness—along with the fact that it absorbed any spice—that made the toothfish a hit with restaurants. No matter what you do, you can't overcook it, and this made it popular with busy restauranteurs and chefs.

As the reputation of the toothfish spread, so did the take in the ocean. Because this fish is found in the Southern Ocean, where it is cold and where few venture, it was highly susceptible to poaching. A full hold of toothfish could bring a million dollars wholesale!

Soon it became clear to many that the species was being seriously overharvested, and chefs began to notice that the filets were getting smaller. The tragedy of the commons was playing out again. So the chefs from the best restaurants organized a boycott campaign called "Take a Pass on Chilean Sea Bass." (The Patagonian toothfish was renamed Chilean sea bass by Lee Lantz in 1977.)

Rodez/Getty Images

Today, limits are set on the catch, and Chilean sea bass is coming back from the brink of extinction. But as G. Bruce Knecht reported in his book *Hooked,* keeping pirates from poaching the toothfish is a dangerous job for the Australian Customs patrols. The toothfish's problem is that it is the perfect fish.

Source: G. Bruce Knecht, *Hooked: Pirates, Poaching, and the Perfect Fish* (Emmaus, PA: Rodale), 2006.

---

before becoming congested. In Figure 3, demand for driving on this road is D_0, and the marginal cost to use the road—gas, time, and auto expenses—is initially MC_0. Equilibrium is at point *e*, with Q_0 miles per day driven. Consumer surplus is area P_0ae for the typical driver.

Now assume a new driver begins using the road. This increases the marginal costs of driving to MC_1 for everyone, since the tipping point has been passed, and the road is now congested. Consumer surplus shrinks because of overuse of the commons. Note that the new driver did not take these external costs into consideration; the driver assumed that MC would be equal to MC_0, not MC_1.

Possible solutions to common property resource problems can involve establishing private property rights, using government policy to restrict access to the resource, or informal organizations that restrict each user's benefits from the resource. Reduced congestion, for example, could be achieved by raising the tax on gasoline, subsidizing bus or rapid transit travel, or privatizing roads and allowing the owners to charge tolls.

Nobel Prize

Elinor Ostrom

When economists talk about common property (or pool) resources, they typically discuss the tragedy of the commons and suggest a solution that involves privatization or central government takeover and management of the resource. Elinor Ostrom was awarded the 2009 Nobel Prize in Economics for challenging this conventional wisdom. The Nobel committee noted that her studies of *user-managed* "fish stocks, pastures, woods, lakes, and groundwater basins" led to the conclusion that the outcomes often do not lead to the "tragedy" forecasted by conventional theory.

Born in 1933 at the depth of the Great Depression and growing up during World War II when her family and others had a victory garden, she began to see how people could cooperate to solve a resource issue. In high school while on the debate team, she concluded that "debate was a fabulous thing to learn . . . especially for appreciating that there are at least two positions to every issue." Completing her doctorate in political science in 1965, her dissertation looked at a case where saltwater was seeping into western Los Angeles' water basin. A group of individuals formed a water association to solve the problem by creating rules and injected water along the coast. Without the efforts of this group, the water basin would have been irreparably harmed. This experience led her to look at other common resource problems from a new perspective.

She used field studies and thousands of case studies by other social scientists along with game theory to determine how these informal organizations evolved and what conditions make them successful. The game that consistently reflected her case studies was a repeated *n*-person prisoner's dilemma where participants are permitted to punish other players for uncooperative behavior.

Her work has determined the requirements for sustainable user-managed common pool property, including (a) rules must clearly define entitlement to the resource, (b) adequate conflict resolution measures must exist, (c) an individual's duty to maintain the resource must be in proportion to their benefits, (d) monitoring and sanctioning must be by users or accountable to users, (e) sanctions should be graduated—mild for a first violation and stricter as violations are repeated, (f) governance and decision processes must be democratic, and (g) self-organization is recognized by outside authorities. When these institutional conditions are met, user management of common pool resources typically is successful.

Professor Ostrom's insights and research have opened up a third policy alternative to prevent the tragedy of the commons. Her work will be particularly important as nations begin working together to reduce the potential harm from global climate change, maybe our biggest common resource problem to date.

Luciano Leon/Alamy

 CHECKPOINT

PUBLIC GOODS

- Social welfare is equal to consumer plus producer surplus.

- Pure public goods are nonrival in consumption, and once the good is provided, no one can be excluded from using it.

- The demand for public goods is found by vertically summing individual demand curves.

- Optimal provision of public goods is found where the marginal benefit of public goods (demand) is equal to the marginal cost of provision.

- Determining the optimal provision of public goods is easy in theory, but difficult in practice. Cost-benefit analysis (CBA) helps policymakers allocate scarce public funds to competing projects.

- Common property resources have the characteristics of nonexcludability but are rival. This typically leads to overuse and overexploitation.

QUESTIONS: In the June 1, 2006, issue of the *New York Times,* the Humane Society ran a full-page ad with a picture of a baby harp seal and the headline, "Did You Know That Over 300,000 Baby Seals Were Killed in Canada This Year for Their Fur?" Below the picture, it reads, "Over 1,000 U.S. Restaurants, Grocers and Seafood Distributors Do and They're Doing Something to End It." The ad then asks you to join them and 256,000 individuals who are boycotting Canadian seafood until commercial seal hunting ends. Is this essentially the equivalent of a secondary boycott that labor unions once used but was subsequently outlawed by the Taft-Hartley Act? Does this boycott seem fair to Canadian fishermen who do not hunt seals? How does this boycott differ from the one by restaurants to save the Chilean Sea Bass?

Answers to the Checkpoint questions can be found at the end of this chapter.

Externalities

Externalities, often called *spillovers,* arise when two parties engage in a transaction, yet some third party uninvolved in the transaction either benefits or is harmed. If the market exchange imposes costs on others, it is called a *negative externality* or an *external cost.* If a third party benefits, this is a *positive externality* or an *external benefit.* Negative externalities include air and water pollution, littering, and chemical runoff that affect fish stocks. Some examples of activities that generate positive externalities are education, beehives next to apple orchards, and quieter lawn equipment.

Both producers and consumers can create externalities and can feel the effects of them. The matrix in Table 2 identifies the origin and impact of some common external effects. The effects are negative unless otherwise noted.

Externalities: The impact on third parties of some transaction between others where the third parties are not involved. An external cost (or negative externality) harms the third parties, whereas external benefits (positive externalities) result in gains to them.

TABLE 2   Externalities by Origin and Impact

Origin of Externality	Impact Victims and Beneficiaries of Externality	
	Consumers	**Producers**
Consumers	■ Auto air pollution ■ Littering ■ Park congestion ■ Smoking ■ Private schools and colleges (beneficial)	■ Private auto use that adds to road congestion, slowing down commercial traffic
Producers	■ Factory air pollution on wilderness hikers ■ Clear cutting of forest trees ■ Agricultural pesticide runoff affecting trout fishing	■ Honey bees and apple orchards (beneficial) ■ Commercial pollution that harms commercial fishing

Negative Externalities

Again, when a market transaction harms people not involved in the transaction, negative externalities exist. Pollution of all sorts is the classic example. Firms and consumers rarely consider the impact their production or consumption will have on others. For simplicity, we focus on the pollution caused by production. Figure 4 shows a typical market.

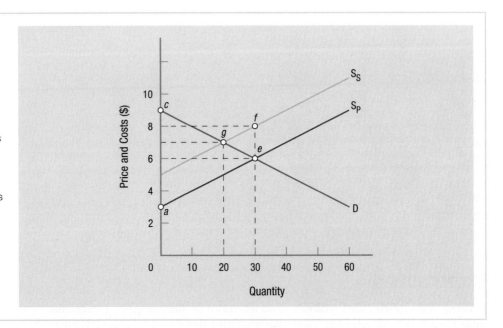

FIGURE 4—The Negative Externality Case

Supply curve S_P represents the manufacturer's supply when only its private costs are considered, ignoring the external costs imposed on others through pollution. Market equilibrium is 30 units sold at $6 each (point e). If each unit of production results in $2 in pollution costs, then supply curve S_S represents the true social costs to manufacture the product. Socially optimal output is 20 units sold at $7 each (point g).

Supply curve S_P represents the manufacturer's supply curve when only its private costs are considered (the subscript P stands for private). This supply curve ignores the external costs imposed on others from the pollution generated during production. These external costs might include toxic wastes dumped into lakes or streams, smokestack soot, or the clear cutting associated with timber harvests. Ignoring these costs, market equilibrium is at point e, where the product is priced at $6 and 30 units are sold. Total consumer surplus plus producer surplus is equal to $90 $[(($9 - $3) \times 30)/2]$ or area ace.

Now let's assume that for every unit of the product produced, pollution costs (or effluent) equal to $2 is generated. Thus, at an output level of 30 units (point e), $60 in pollution costs (or negative externalities) is generated. Subtracting this $60 in pollution from total consumer and producer surplus results in $30 of real social benefit from this output.

This means the true marginal cost of producing the product, including pollution costs, is equal to supply curve S_S (the subscript S stands for social). This new supply curve incorporates both the private and social costs of production, thus shifting supply upward by an amount equal to ef, or $2. Equilibrium moves to point g, where 20 units of the product are sold at $7. This is the socially optimal production for this product given the pollution it creates.

So why is it better for society than when 30 units were produced? First, notice that when output is 20, the cost of the last unit produced—including the cost of pollution—is $7 (point g). This is just equal to the value society attributes to the product. Hence, consumers get just what they want when all costs are considered. Second, notice that consumer and producer surplus at an output of 20 units is $40 $[(($9 - $5) \times 20)/2]$. More important, it is now higher than the $30 of consumer and producer surplus minus the pollution costs when output was 30 units (point e).

Each unit of output produced beyond 20 costs more—taking both private and social costs into account—than its value to consumers.

Imagine a situation in which external costs exceed the consumer and producer surplus from consuming the good. Such a situation might arise when an extremely toxic substance is a by-product of production. Society is better off not permitting production of this good.

What has this analysis shown? First, when negative externalities are present, an unregulated market will produce too much of a good at too low a price. Second, optimal pollution levels are not zero, except in the case just mentioned of extremely toxic agents. In Figure 4, the socially optimal production is 20 units with total pollution costs of $40. Pollution reduction as a good has no price. Even so, we can infer a price, known as a shadow price, equal to the marginal damages—$2 in this case. As we will see later, prices for the "rights to pollute" will provide us with better approximations of the costs of pollution.

The Coase Theorem

Ronald Coase was awarded the Nobel Prize in Economics for his seminal paper, "The Problem of Social Cost." Coase has written few articles—less than a dozen—but, as economist Robert Cooter noted, though "most economists maximize the amount they write, Coase maximized the amount others wrote about his work."[7] Indeed, Coase's paper on social cost is one of the most cited works in economics.

Reducing output to the optimal level results in gains to "victims" because pollution is reduced. The reduction in output, however, causes losses to producers. The presence of losses and gains to two distinct parties, Coase argued, introduces the possibility of bargaining, provided the parties are awarded the property rights necessary for negotiation.

The **Coase theorem** states that if transaction costs are minimal (near zero), the resulting bargain or allocation of resources will be efficient—output will decline to the optimal level—regardless of the initial allocation of property rights. The socially optimal level of production will be reached, that is, no matter whether polluters are given the right to pollute or victims are given the right to be free of pollution.

Even so, the distribution of benefits or income will be different in these two cases. If victims, for example, are assigned the property rights, their income will grow, but if polluters are assigned these rights, the income of victims will decline.

As Coase noted, for these efficient results to be achieved, transaction costs must approach zero. This means it must be possible for polluters and victims to accurately determine their collective interests, then negotiate and enforce an agreement. In many situations, however, this is simply not feasible. In cases involving air pollution, for instance, polluters and victims are so widely dispersed that negotiating is impracticable. In other cases, individuals may be both victims and polluters, making it difficult for an agreement to be reached and enforced.

Another problem associated with assigning rights to one party or another might be called *environmental mugging*. Polluters might at first threaten to pollute more than they anticipate, for instance, simply to increase their bargaining leverage and, ultimately, their income. Victims, in like manner, might assert exaggerated environmental concerns, again simply to bid up their compensation. Alternatively, if negotiations should prove unfruitful, polluters might start lobbying for legal relief, thus devoting their money to rent-seeking behaviors rather than buying pollution-abatement equipment.

Although the private negotiations Coase proposed have their limitations, his insights proved to be a turning point in environmental policy. Coase challenged the prevailing practice of assuming victims had a right to be pollution-free. His analysis stressed that a clear assignment of rights and responsibilities by the law might not be needed. No matter how property rights were assigned, if information was good and transaction costs were low, efficiency would result. Given the costs of pollution, affected parties have an incentive to work out efficient agreements.

This idea was so radical when Coase published "The Problem of Social Cost" in 1960 that another Nobel Prize winner, George Stigler, wondered "how so fine an economist

Coase theorem: If transaction costs are minimal (near zero), a bargain struck between beneficiaries and victims of externalities will be efficient from a resource allocation perspective. As a result, the socially optimal level of production will be reached.

[7] Peter Passell, "Economics Nobel to a Basic Thinker," *New York Times*, October 16, 1991, p. D6.

Nobel Prize

University of Chicago professor Ronald Coase won the Nobel Prize in Economic Sciences in 1991 for "his discovery and clarification of the significance of transaction costs and property rights" in the institutional structure and functioning of the economy. According to his analysis, traditional microeconomic theory was incomplete because it neglected the costs of executing contracts and managing firms. To Coase, these "transaction costs" were the principal reason that firms existed. Economic actors found it cost efficient to create a more complex organization to minimize transaction costs.

Coase also analyzed the economy in terms of the *rights* to use goods and factors (inputs) of production rather than the actual goods and factors themselves. These "property rights" could be defined in different ways according to contracts and rules within organizations. Coase introduced the concept of property rights as an important element of economic analysis. His work stimulated interest in the intersection between economics and legal theory for which the University of Chicago is well known.

Born in 1910 in Willesden, a suburb of London, Coase attended the London School of Economics (LSE), where he earned a Bachelor of Commerce degree in 1932. During 1931–1932 he was awarded the Sir Ernest Cassel Traveling Scholarship by the University of London to research industrial organization in the United States. During that year he traveled throughout America to visit business and industrial plants.

From the fall of 1932 to 1939, he taught at the Dundee School of Economics, the University of Liverpool, and the London School of Economics. Returning to LSE after the war, he earned a Doctor of Science degree in economics in 1951. Coase later cited his first seminar in economics with the commerce professor Arnold Plant as a life-changing experience. "What Plant did was to introduce me to Adam Smith's hidden hand," he wrote. "He made me aware of how a competitive economic system could be coordinated by the pricing system."

Becoming disillusioned with the future of British socialism and taking "a liking for life in America," he migrated to the United States in 1951 and taught at the University of Buffalo. Coase's 1960 article on "The Problem of Social Cost" questioned whether governments could efficiently allocate resources for social purposes through taxes and subsidies. He argued that arbitrarily assigning property rights and using markets to reach a solution was usually better than costly government regulation. This was instantly controversial and led to a lengthy exchange of papers in economics journals.

In 1964, Coase joined the faculty at the University of Chicago and became editor of the *Journal of Law and Economics*. The journal was an important catalyst in developing the economic interpretation of legal issues.

could make such an obvious mistake." Coase was later invited to the University of Chicago to discuss his ideas; Stigler described what transpired:

> We strongly objected to this heresy. Milton Friedman did most of the talking, as usual. He also did much of the thinking, as usual. In the course of two hours of argument the vote went from twenty against and one for Coase to twenty-one for Coase. What an exhilarating event! I lamented afterward that we had not had the clairvoyance to tape it.

The Coase theorem has changed the way economists look at many issues, not just environmental problems. In cases where the costs of negotiation are negligible and the number of parties involved is small, economists and jurists have begun to look more closely at legal rules assigning liability.

Positive Externalities

When private market transactions generate benefits for others, a situation opposite to that just described results. Figure 5 illustrates a positive externality. Market supply curve S and private demand curve D_P represent the market for private college education. Equilibrium is at point e, with Q_e students enrolling. Society would clearly benefit, however, if more people earned college educations: Tax revenues would rise, crime rates would fall, and a better-informed electorate might produce a better-operating democracy.

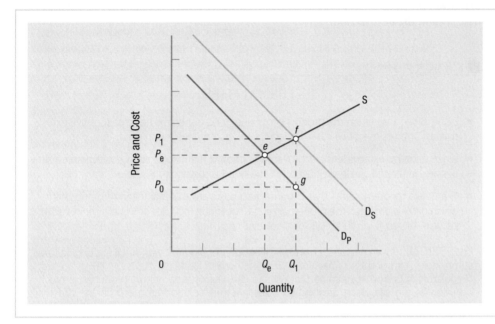

FIGURE 5—The Positive Externality Case

Market supply curve S and private demand curve D_P represent the market for private college education. Equilibrium is at point e, and students enrolled are Q_e. Society would benefit, however, if more people would go to college. Social demand curve D_S represents the private demand for college education plus the external benefits that flow from it. Socially optimal enrollment would be Q_1 (point f).

Taking these considerations into account, social demand curve D_S is the private demand for college education plus the external benefits that flow from it. Socially optimal enrollment would be Q_1 (point f). How can society tweak the market so that more students will attend college? Students will demand Q_1 levels of enrollment only if its price is P_0 (point g). The public must therefore subsidize private education by fg to draw its price down to P_0.

The U.S. government recognizes that private education benefits society at large when it provides low-interest student loans, grants, and scholarships to students attending private colleges and universities.

Limitations

Some caveats about our analysis of externalities need to be noted. First, producer and consumer surpluses are good measures of society's welfare if all incomes are weighted equally or the distribution of income is optimal. When income is unequally distributed, gross unfairness created throughout society swamps any improvements from efficiency. Thus, measures of efficiency like consumer and producer surplus can become unconvincing for public policy. Since no one can agree on the correct distribution of income, economists generally ignore this question and focus on efficiency.

Second, the discussion has focused on the pollution that arises from production, not consumption. The results applied to congestion and littering, however, would be substantially the same.

Third, the examples presented here have assumed, moreover, that pollution has no cumulative effects. And, indeed, smaller amounts of pollution effluence may just flow into the ocean, for instance, with no lasting effects. But the same will not hold true for sustained higher pollution levels.

Fourth, for convenience, we have assumed we can assign specific amounts to the damages resulting from pollution. In practice, this is not always easy to do.

Fifth, we have assumed pollution can be reduced only by reducing output, but in real markets, there are other ways to reduce pollution.

Despite these limitations, the analysis presented here helps us focus our attention on ways of reducing the harm done to society by negative externalities.

In summary, the market failures associated with public goods, externalities, and commonly held resources all lead to overuse of resources and environmental degradation. To address these problems, collective or government action is required. Solutions range from privatization—assigning property rights—to government regulations or prohibitions, described in the next section.

■ CHECKPOINT

EXTERNALITIES

- Externalities arise when the production of one good generates benefits (positive externalities) or costs (negative externalities) for others not involved in the transaction.

- When negative externalities exist, overproduction is the result. When positive externalities are generated, underproduction of the good is the norm.

- The Coase theorem states that if transaction costs are minimal (near zero), no matter which party is provided the property rights to pollution (polluter or victim), the resulting bargain will result in the socially optimal level of pollution.

QUESTION: Lawn mowers, chainsaws, and other equipment with small gas engines are surprisingly high-polluting machines. *The Economist* (June 9, 2007, p. 36) reported, "Regulators in California estimate that using a chain-saw for two hours produces as much pollution as ten cars each driving 250 miles." As one solution to the problem, the Los Angeles air quality management district offered residents a $400 electric lawn mower for $100 if they traded in an old gas burning mower. Describe and show graphically why the Los Angeles air quality district is making this offer.

Answers to the Checkpoint question can be found at the end of this chapter.

Environmental Policy

We have seen that market failure can lead to excessive amounts of products that pollute or generate other negative externalities. This section looks at the broad approaches to environmental policy available to the government, focusing on emissions. First, we look briefly at government failure. Government policies can fail to improve such situations if the incentives of politicians and policymakers are not aligned with the public interest. Balanced public policies must take intergenerational effects into account. Then, we look at the actual policies used by government regulators to reduce pollution, ranging from direct intervention and control to the use of various market instruments to reduce emissions. Policymakers also occasionally use publicity and moral suasion to encourage polluters to voluntarily reduce emissions.

Government Failure

Market failure is one reason unregulated markets may produce inequitable or inefficient results. Government policies, however, do not always make things better. The terrible environmental record the Eastern Bloc countries accumulated during the Soviet era illustrates that, in environmental policy as elsewhere, governments—like markets—can fail.

Government failure occurs when (1) public policies do not bring about an optimal allocation of resources and/or (2) the incentives of politicians and government bureaucrats are not in line with the public interest. As Nobel Prize winner George Stigler has argued,

Government failure: The result when the incentives of politicians and government bureaucrats do not align with the public interest.

economic regulation often benefits the group being regulated at the expense of the larger public. Government failures are often more acute in nondemocratic societies. Yet, even in the United States, public policy formation involves a struggle among interest groups, lobbyists, politicians, large corporate interests, and the public at large. The sausage calling itself "public policy" that results from this tug-of-war is often not pretty.

Government failure may result from the practical inability of policymakers to gather enough information to set good policies. Water pollution, for instance, is well understood, resulting in fairly obvious regulatory policies, but the same is not true for issues like global climate change. Even if we all agree that the Earth is getting warmer and humans are partly to blame, controversy remains about the adequacy of public policy to address this problem. Though calls for government action—"there ought to be a law"—are often justified, we do well to maintain a healthy skepticism about the ability of the public sector to solve our problems.

Intergenerational Questions

Should politicians consider the interests of voters whose great-grandparents have not yet been born? Environmental issues raise complex questions involving how resources are to be allocated across generations. Some resources, such as sunlight, are continual and renewable. Others, like forests, fisheries, and the soil are exhaustible yet renewable, though they can be exhausted if overexploited. And some resources are nonrenewable, such as oil and coal. These resources are finite and cannot be renewed, but their available stock can be expanded through exploration or the use of new technologies that allow greater extraction or more efficient use.

When we develop environmental policies, we need to consider and evaluate different possible futures. Discounting was discussed earlier, but Figure 6 is a reminder of the effects discount rates have on the present value of a fixed payment that will come due at some date in the future. For environmental policies, the discount rate we choose is crucially important.

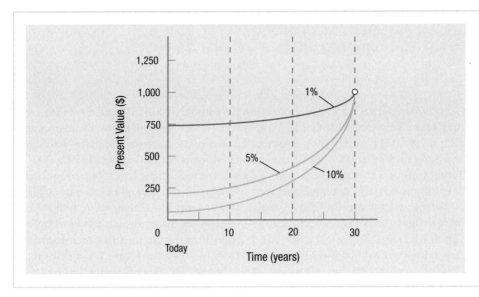

FIGURE 6—Present Value of $1,000 to Be Paid in 30 Years Discounted at 1%, 5%, and 10%

This figure is a reminder of the effects discount rates have on the present value of a fixed payment that will come due at a future date. A higher discount rate means the value today of a future payoff will be lower. The higher the discount rate we choose, the lower the value we place on the environmental damage to be suffered by future generations. The lower our discount rate, the more we are willing to protect the health of the future environment.

A higher discount rate means the value today of a future payoff will be less. At a 10% discount, a payment of $1,000 in 30 years is worth only $42 today, whereas discounting the same $1,000 at 1% yields a present value of $748. The higher the discount rate we choose, the lower the value we place on the environmental damage to be suffered by future generations. The lower our discount rate, conversely, the more we are willing to protect the health of the future environment. As always, crafting good public policies requires striking a balance between the two.

Socially Efficient Levels of Pollution

We have already seen that some pollution is acceptable to society. To require that no one pollute, period, would bring most economic activity as we know it to a halt. Yet, pollution damages our environment. The harmful effects of pollution range from direct threats to our health coming from air and water pollution to reductions in species from deforestation.

In general terms, the more pollution we create, the greater the harm to the environment. The damages that come from pollution are a cost we incur for living: To be alive is to generate some pollution. Our focus is on marginal damage, which resembles the marginal cost curves we have studied earlier. The marginal damage (MD) curve in Figure 7 shows the change in damages that come from a given change in emission levels. Notice that as emissions levels rise, the added damages rise.

FIGURE 7—Marginal Damages and Marginal Abatement Costs

The marginal damage curve (MD) shows the *change* in damages that come from a given *change* in emission levels. The horizontal axis measures pollution. Note that E_0 is the maximum pollution that can occur without environmental cleanup. The vertical axis measures the environmental costs of this pollution. Marginal abatement costs curve (MAC) begins at zero at E_0, then rises as emission levels are reduced (moving leftward from E_0). Socially optimal pollution is E_S, at a cost to society of C_e (point *e*).

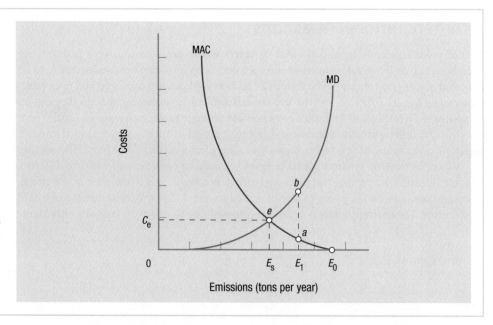

The horizontal axis of Figure 7 measures the tons of pollution emitted into the environment (tons per year). Note that E_0 represents the maximum pollution (no environmental cleanup at all). The vertical axis measures the environmental costs in dollars. These costs represent a dollar value for various environmental losses, including the physical costs of pollution (asthma attacks and other lung diseases), the aesthetic losses (visual impact of clear cutting), and the losses associated with species reduction (we all miss the dodo bird).

Abatement costs are the costs associated with reducing emissions. A utility plant dumping effluent into a river can treat the effluent before discharge, but this costs money. In Figure 7 marginal abatement costs (MAC) begin at zero at E_0, then rise as emission levels are reduced (moving leftward from E_0). The MAC curve in Figure 7 is a generalized abatement cost function, but in practice, the costs vary for different sources of pollution and the technologies available for reducing them. Chemical plants face different problems than utilities that release hot water into rivers. Cooling the water before release clearly requires a different technology—and is much easier—than eliminating toxic chemicals from effluent flow.

The socially optimal level of pollution in Figure 7 is E_S, at a cost to society of C_e (point *e*). To see why this is so, assume we are at pollution level E_1. The cost to reduce another unit of emissions is equal to point *a* (measuring on the vertical axis), while the damage that would result from this pollution is shown at point *b*. Since $b > a$, society is better off if emissions are reduced. Once we begin reducing emissions below E_S, however, abatement costs overtake marginal damages, or the costs of cleanup begin to outweigh the benefits.

The total damage from pollution in Figure 7 is represented by the area beneath the marginal damages curve and to the left of E_S. Total abatement costs, meanwhile, are equal to the area beneath the marginal abatement costs curve and to the right of E_S. Combined, these two costs represent the total social costs from emissions. We turn now to consider how environmental policy can ensure that emissions approach this optimal level.

Overview of Environmental Policies

Over the years, many types of environmental policies have been developed in response to different problems, covering the spectrum from centralized control to decentralized economic incentives. To be effective, all environmental policies must be efficient, fair, and enforceable, and they must provide incentives for improvement in the environment.

As a general rule, the more centralized an environmental policy, the more likely it represents a **command and control** philosophy. This means a centralized agency sets the rules for emissions, including levels of effluents allowed, usable technologies, and enforcement procedures. Command and control policies usually set standards of conduct that are enforced by the legal and regulatory system. Abatement costs at this point become compliance costs of meeting the standards. Standards are popular because they are simple, they treat all firms in an industry the same way, and they prevent competing firms from polluting.

At the other end of the spectrum are **market-based policies,** which use charges, taxes, subsidies, deposit-refund systems, or tradable emission permits to achieve the same ends. Examples of this approach include water effluent charges, user charges for water and wastewater management, glass and plastic bottle refund systems, and tradable permits for ozone reduction. We begin with a brief look at command and control policies, contrasting them with abatement taxes, then look at the case for tradable emission permits.

Command and Control Policies

Policymakers determine the pollution control or abatement that is best, then introduce the most efficient policies to achieve those ends. Figure 8 shows the supply and demand for pollution abatement. Demand curve $D_A = MB_A$ represents society's demand for abatement; it is a reflection of the marginal damage curve we looked at earlier. Note that the demand curve for abatement is negatively sloped because the *marginal benefit* from abatement declines as the environment becomes cleaner. The gains from an ever cleaner environment eventually become smaller and smaller because of the law of diminishing returns.

Command and control policies: Environmental policies that set standards and issue regulations, which are then enforced by the legal and regulatory system.

Market-based policies: Environmental policies that use charges, taxes, subsidies, deposit-refund systems, or tradable emission permits to achieve environmental ends.

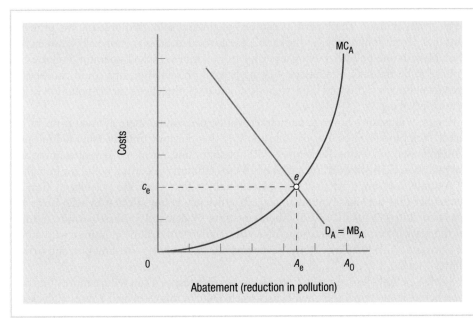

FIGURE 8—Marginal Cost of Abatement and Abatement Demand

Demand curve D_A represents society's demand for abatement. The marginal benefit from abatement (MB_A) declines as the environment becomes cleaner, since the gains from an ever cleaner environment become smaller and smaller (diminishing returns). The marginal costs of abatement are the costs of reducing pollution. These costs rise with abatement efforts and become high as zero pollution A_0 is approached (again, because of the law of diminishing returns, or increasing costs). Optimal abatement is A_e, costing c_e. This means optimal pollution, $A_0 - A_e$, is greater than zero.

The marginal costs of abatement are the costs of cleaning up pollution. These costs rise with abatement efforts and become high as zero pollution, A_0, is approached. Optimal abatement comes at A_e, costing c_e. This means optimal pollution, $A_0 - A_e$, is greater than zero. Command and control policies could set A_e as the abatement requirement and then set the right standards to meet this requirement. Aiming for abatement higher than A_e would be inefficient, since marginal costs would exceed benefits.

Setting abatement requirements (or standards) equal to A_e in Figure 8 is a classic example of command and control policies. Alternatively, policymakers could enact an effluent tax equal to c_e per unit of pollution. Firms would adopt pollution controls up to A_e, because the costs to reduce pollution to this point are less than the tax. Firms would emit only $A_0 - A_e$ pollution.

Again, command and control policies that set rigid standards for polluters have long been a favorite of policymakers. Yet, this approach can lead to inefficiencies, since different industries may emit the same (or equivalently dangerous) substances but face different technical problems and costs in reducing their pollution. To minimize the cost of reducing pollution, each source of pollution needs to be reduced to the point where the marginal cost of abatement is equal for all sources.

Market-Based Policies

Economists have increasingly begun to argue that market-oriented, or indirect, approaches to environmental policy are more efficient than command and control policies. One of the most popular and effective of these indirect approaches is marketable or tradable permits.

Marketable or Tradable Permits   Economists first proposed marketable or tradable permits when environmental laws were first being debated and enacted in the 1960s and 1970s. Environmental regulators essentially ignored this suggestion until the 1990s.

Today, tradable permits are used to reduce water effluents in the Fox River in Wisconsin, Tar-Pamlico River in North Carolina, and Dillon Reservoir in Colorado. One of the most successful uses of marketable permits for air pollution has reduced the sulfur dioxide (SO_2) emissions in the Midwest that create acid rain in the East. Originally, the cost of this cleanup was expected to be significant, and the price of permits did start out fairly high. As the cleanup has progressed, however, technical advances have steadily reduced abatement costs, causing the price of the permits to decline sharply. This success with SO_2 has spawned the use of similar permits in Europe, where opposition to marketable permits historically was strong.

Marketable permits require that a regulatory body set a maximum allowable quantity of effluents allowed, typically called the "cap," and issue permits granting the "right" to pollute a certain amount. These permits can be bought and sold, thus creating the property rights that permit transactions of the sort Coase advocated. Sales are normally between two polluters, with one polluter buying a permit from a more efficient operator. Polluters do not have to be the only purchasers: victims or environmental groups could conceivably purchase pollution rights and hold them off the market, thereby reducing pollution below the established cap.

Figure 9 illustrates how such a market works. We assume there are two firms in the market, each producing 10 tons of pollution, and that the government wishes to limit pollution to a total of 10 tons. Remember, without restrictions, firms do zero abatement and total pollution is 20 tons. Setting a goal of 10 tons amounts to cutting pollution in half.

Assume, for simplicity, that the government at first gives the permits to firm X. (Remember that the Coase theorem suggests efficiency is not affected by who owns the rights to pollute.) Demand curve D_Y represents firm Y's demand for these permits. Assume that the market for permits is competitive, thus equilibrium will be at point e with a permit price equal to $300. Firm Y buys seven permits and pollutes that amount, and firm X pollutes 3 tons.

Firm X pollutes less and sells 7 permits to firm Y because it can reduce more of its pollution before its marginal abatement costs reach $300. In this case, firm Y faces high cleanup costs that reach $300 a ton at 3 tons. Thus, it buys 7 tons of abatement from firm X.

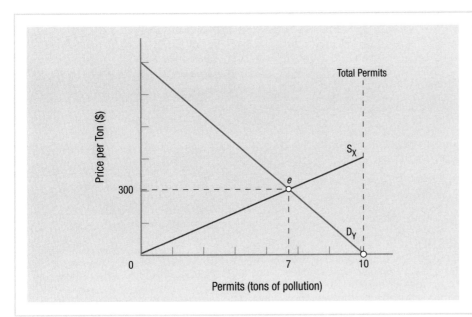

FIGURE 9—Tradable Permits

This figure illustrates how a market for tradable pollution permits works. Again, assume there are only two firms (X and Y) in the market and the government wishes to limit total pollution to 10 tons. Without restrictions, both firms do zero abatement and pollution is 20 tons. Setting a goal of 10 tons therefore amounts to cutting pollution in half. Assume the government gives the permits to firm X. Demand curve D_Y represents firm Y's demand for these permits. Given a competitive market for permits, equilibrium will be at point e with a permit price equal to $300. Firm Y buys seven permits and pollutes that amount, and firm X emits 3 tons of pollution.

Firm X in this example ends up with the revenue from permit sales, while firm Y's income declines by the same amount ($2,100). Auctioning off the permits produces the same result, but the government gets the revenue.

Keep in mind that regulators could have set a $300 per ton tax on effluents and achieved the same result. One advantage of permits over taxes is that no knowledge of marginal abatement costs is needed to ensure that the tax rate is optimal. The market price of permits will adjust to variances in abatement costs; all the regulator must determine is how much to reduce pollution levels. If reducing pollution by a certain amount, regardless of the cost, is the goal, permits will achieve this goal.

Other Market-Based Policies   We have looked at two of the most frequently used market-based policies, taxes/charges and marketable permits. Emission taxes and charges have been used for water effluents, waste management, pesticide packaging, batteries, tires, and other products and processes. User charges are the most common way to finance wastewater treatment facilities.

Federal subsidies, the flip side of taxes or charges, are used when local communities do not have the resources for pollution control. Marketable permits have been most successful in programs to reduce air pollution, as well as those targeting acid rain and ozone reduction. Deposit-refund systems have been used mainly for recyclable products such as cans, bottles, tires, and batteries.

Over the years, most environmental policies have been of the command and control variety. The 1969 Clean Air Act focused on specific forms of air pollution—particulates, carbon dioxide (CO_2), and so forth—and established air quality standards. Standards were set for vehicles and stationary sources of pollution including power plants and factories.

Today, economic or market-based approaches to environmental policy are considered more efficient than command and control policies. Most environmental agencies, however, in this country and abroad, have not used these tools until recently.

One reason for this is probably that many people in the regulatory and environmental communities resist viewing environmental resources as commodities to be subjected to market forces of supply and demand. It is market failures, after all, that led to environmental decay in the first place; why would we want to put the environment on the market? Many pollutants, moreover, are frequently mixed together and their individual impacts are difficult to determine. Consequently, setting the right tax rate or issuing the right number of allowable permits is difficult. Finally, some policymakers balk at giving corporations the right to pollute, even for a limited amount of pollution.

ENVIRONMENTAL POLICY

- Government failure can occur when politicians and government do not have the right incentives to bring about an optimal allocation of resources.

- The discount rate chosen for environmental policies determines the intergenerational impact of policy.

- The socially optimal level of pollution occurs where the marginal damage is equal to the marginal abatement costs.

- Policymakers determine the optimal pollution levels and then often use command and control policies to set the most efficient regulations or levels of abatement.

- Tradable permits use market forces to bring pollution within limits set by regulators.

QUESTION: In the 1960s, the Environmental Protection Agency (EPA) initially focused on pollution, principally air and water. In a similar way, the Bureau of Land Management initially honed in on multiple-use of public lands with an emphasis on timber harvests. Today both agencies have a much broader focus that looks at maintaining an ecological balance, and their activities extend beyond pollution and timber to species and habitat protection. Is this just another example of bureaucratic mission creep?

Answers to the Checkpoint question can be found at the end of this chapter.

Economic Aspects of Climate Change

Global warming may turn out to be the mother of all market failures.[8] There is a growing scientific consensus that "without big changes in emission rates, global warming from the buildup of greenhouse gases is likely to lead to substantial, and largely irreversible, transformations of climate, ecosystems and coastlines later this century."[9] The economics surrounding this issue are complex and require almost all of the tools of microeconomics we have studied, and then some.

A sense of urgency surrounds climate change because the state of climate science has advanced to the point where scientists can now put probability estimates on certain impacts of warming, some of which are catastrophic. Current levels of greenhouse gases are roughly 430 parts per million (ppm). This compares to 280 ppm before the Industrial Revolution. If the annual levels of emissions remain constant at today's levels across the world, levels of greenhouse gases will rise to 550 ppm by 2050. And if emissions increase, the level of greenhouse gases will be greater than 550 ppm.

What will happen as greenhouse gases increase and lead to global warming? Table 3 estimates these effects. The top part of the table shows a range of greenhouse gases from 400 ppm to 800 ppm, with predicted effects on temperature below it. The bottom panel estimates the impacts likely to arise with each increase in temperature. The estimated effects of a difference of just 1 or 2 degrees raise serious concerns.

Unique Timing Aspects

Global climate change is essentially a huge global negative externality. But what makes analysis and decision making so difficult is the long time horizon that must be considered. Most cost-benefit studies do not look out 50 to 100 years and beyond. This extended time horizon adds a host of difficulties and uncertainties.

[8] Nicholas Stern, *The Economics of Climate Change* (Cambridge: Cambridge University Press), 2007. This section draws heavily from this study, also known as the "Stern Review."
[9] Andrew C. Revkin, "Yelling 'Fire' on a Hot Planet," *New York Times,* April 23, 2006, p. wk1.

TABLE 3   Greenhouse Gases, Likely Temperature Changes, and Estimated Impacts

	Greenhouse Gases (ppm)				
	400	**450**	**550**	**700**	**800**
	Eventual Temperature Change (relative to preindustrial)				
	1°C	**2°C**	**3°C**	**4°C**	**5°C**
Food	Rising crop yields in high-latitude developed countries	Rising number of people at risk from hunger	Falling crop yields in developing regions	Major decline in crop yields in all regions	?
Water	Small mountain glaciers disappear	Over a 30% drop in runoff in South Africa and the Mediterranean	Large numbers of people suffer water shortages	Billions of people affected by water shortages	Sea level rise threatens major cities, including New York, Hong Kong, and London
Ecosystems	Ocean coral reef systems damaged	Many ecosystems unable to maintain their current form	Part of Amazon rain forest begins to collapse	20% to 50% species extinction possible	?
Extreme Weather Events	Rising levels of storms, fires, droughts, floods, and heat waves →				
		Rising hurricane intensity →			
Major Irreversible Impacts	Risk of weakening the natural carbon absorption system →				
		Rising risk of large-scale shifts in climate system →			

Source: *Stern Review*

Air or water pollution is something that we can see on the horizon, can be measured, is typically localized, and can be altered in a short period of time by some of the approaches discussed earlier. Global warming, in contrast, is not something we can generally see; it is cumulative (this year's CO_2 adds to that from the past to raise concentrations in the future); and once it reaches a certain level, it may lead to extreme consequences that cannot be reversed.

Cleaning up pollution problems typically involves finding that level of abatement where the marginal costs of abatement equal the marginal benefits from abatement and either taxing, assigning (or auctioning) marketable permits, or using command and control policies to require the optimal level of abatement. However, reducing global warming gases is not a onetime change, but a cumulative process across many years. As a result, the abatement process is dynamic, and the marginal benefits of abatement depend on the future stock of emissions. To find the optimal abatement in any one period (say, the current period) requires that we look at the optimum path of abatement across many years and assume in the future that abatement will be set optimally for all future periods.

Because of the cumulative nature of greenhouse gases, our short-run decisions will have immense impacts in the long run (50 to 100 years out). Small changes in emissions today will have little impact immediately or even for the current generation, but will have sizable effects many decades out. This aspect of the problem seriously complicates any policymaking and economic analysis.

Public Good Aspects

To further compound the problem, global climate change is a public good. Greenhouse gas emissions "are the purest example of a negative public good; nobody can have less of them because someone else has more; and nobody can be excluded from their malign consequences or the efforts of others to ameliorate them."[10] One of the solutions is technical innovation that reduces our output of CO_2. But knowledge and technology have large public good aspects, so private firms will find it difficult to collect the full returns on their innovation investments that reduce greenhouse gases. Other firms and countries will to some extent be free riders on private innovation, so society (and the world) may get less than the socially optimal level of innovation. This will mean that a substantial amount of climate change research and development will have to be financed by governments. Since the governments of developed nations have more resources than the governments of less-developed nations, the burden will fall on them.

Equity Aspects

Why should I do anything for posterity? What has posterity ever done for me?

GROUCHO MARX

Much of what we do today will have little immediate impact on our lives. The impacts will show up in the latter half of the century. So any action taken today principally benefits our great-grandchildren. Groucho Marx's joke not withstanding, this fact makes it more difficult to get a political consensus to act.

Also, rich countries will have to make the biggest sacrifices, yet they will not get the biggest benefits from efforts to reduce the impacts of global warming. Let us say that the United States reduces its dependence on carbon. What about China and India? They may decide that growth is worth more than a cleaner environment. At that point, the United States would have to be willing to pay China and India large sums to get them to decarbonize their economies. How well will that sell to American voters? Probably not well, but it may be what is ultimately necessary. After all, the developed world is responsible for three-quarters or more of all greenhouse gasses emitted since the Industrial Revolution began.

People in developing countries living along bodies of water will face floods if current climate forecasts come to pass. These are some of the world's poorest people, and adapting to flooding will be extremely difficult given their hopelessly limited resources. In addition, developing nations rely heavily on agriculture, one industry that will be hardest hit as the warming of the Earth inevitably leads to famines.

The long time horizon for policymaking and global climate change puts a different light on the discounting process typically used in cost-benefit analysis. When you use any reasonable discount rate (3% to 5%) on benefits 75 to 100 years into the future, they become miniscule numbers today. Nicholas Stern argued that "there is no compelling reason to value the welfare of future generations much below our own."[11] As a result, the Stern Review adopts a discount rate near zero.

Finding a Solution

Since climate change is global, it will take a concerted international effort and cooperation. According to the Stern Review, it will take cooperation "in creating price signals and markets for carbon, spurring technology research, development and deployment, and promoting adaptation, particularly in developing countries."[12]

---

[10] Martin Wolf, "Curbs on Emissions Will Take a Change of Political Climate," *Financial Times,* November 8, 2006, p. 15.

[11] Martin Wolf, "After the Arguments, the Figures Still Justify Swift Climate Action," *Financial Times,* November 15, 2006, p. 15.

[12] Stern Review, p. i.

A temperature rise of 3°C to 4°C will likely lead to serious consequences for food and water shortages in developing nations, and increase the rate of species extinction and possibly more extreme weather events (see Table 3). If the temperature increase is large, the events become catastrophic. Since there is a positive probability that these extreme events will occur, we should invest in ways to reduce the risks of this happening. Consider it a form of insurance.

Many economists, including Nicholas Stern, argue that using smaller levels of resources now will result in lower spending in the future. The Stern Review estimates that the costs of stabilizing greenhouse gases at 550 ppm will cost roughly 1% of world gross domestic product (GDP) if we begin soon.

This will require a transition to a low-carbon economy that will only be accomplished by establishing a worldwide price for carbon that includes its external costs. This can be done using carbon taxes or tradable permits. Permits for acceptable levels of carbon emissions could be auctioned and then traded on open markets on exchanges such at the EU-ETS (Emissions Trading Scheme) and the US-CCX (Chicago Climate Exchange). Europe's system has been plagued by national governments issuing too many permits (for free and to specific industries), so the resulting market price for carbon offsets was a fraction of what was needed to provide the right incentives to reduce emissions. Firms bought permits at these cheap prices rather than attempting to reduce their emissions. There is the problem of having too many permits: Prices are too low. For carbon markets to operate effectively and provide the right incentives to reduce emissions, "countries need independent agencies to issue the permits, just as there are independent central banks to issue money."

Robert Socolow of Princeton University has suggested that much of the technology needed to reduce our carbon footprint is available today.[13] He and several colleagues suggest that we could use techniques such as the following to keep our carbon emissions constant over the next 50 years:

- Use more efficient vehicles and reduce use.
- Build more efficient buildings.
- Capture CO_2 at power plants.
- Use nuclear power.
- Exchange biomass fuels for fossil fuels.
- Use wind and solar power.
- Reduce deforestation.

Each of these has the capacity to reduce CO_2 emissions by 1 billion tons per year by 2057. The wedges shown in Figure 10 on the next page would prevent our CO_2 emissions from doubling over the next 50 years.

Clearly, undertaking some policies to reduce our carbon footprint as a nation represents an insurance policy on the future. All of the activities suggested in Figure 10 are sufficiently flexible such that as new climate change information becomes available, we can adjust our policies. And making some moves now will reduce the potential costs in the future.

To that end, the Obama administration tried to put carbon dioxide emissions on the political agenda. Unfortunately, the recession made it harder to get people's attention on this issue. Furthermore, questions arose about the initial grant of permits in any cap-and-trade program. Do large established companies with huge capital resources get permits? What about smaller, possibly more innovative alternative energy companies? Do permits get auctioned off, and does this then favor the richer, more established companies? Political issues combine with economic issues to make this a thorny problem for the future.

---

[13] Robert Socolow et al., "Solving the Climate Problem: Technologies Available to Curb CO_2 Emissions," *Environment*, December 2004, p. 8–19.

FIGURE 10—Stabilization Wedges

This figure, based on the work of Robert Socolow and colleagues, shows the contribution to reduction in carbon emissions that seven wedges can make. Each approach can reduce our carbon footprint by 1 billion tons per year by 2057. Adopting these changes will stabilize our carbon emissions to roughly 7 or 8 billion tons per year.

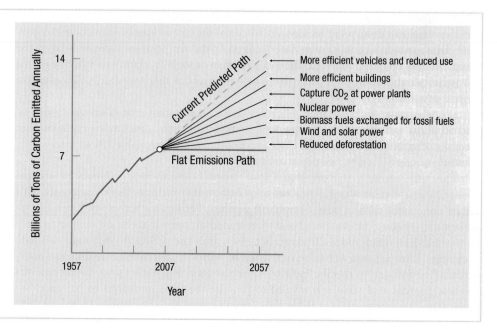

CHECKPOINT

ECONOMIC ASPECTS OF CLIMATE CHANGE

- Global climate change is essentially a huge negative externality with an extremely long time horizon.

- The public goods aspects of climate change make it a truly global problem.

- Balancing the current generation's costs and benefits against the potential harm to future generations raises difficult economic issues.

- Actions taken today to reduce a potential future calamity are a form of insurance.

QUESTION: Professor Wilfred Beckerman, writing in the *Financial Times* (April 22, 2009, p. 10) puts the most difficult aspect presented by climate change policy into perspective when he writes, "How much certain sacrifice is one prepared to impose on people living today, most of whom are desperately poor, in the interests of future generations who, as it happens, are projected to be much richer?" He cites two studies about peoples' attitudes toward discounting the future that showed one group (Washington, DC, and Maryland) would "trade 45 lives in 100 years time against one life today" and another similar study from Sweden showed that they were willing to trade off 243 lives. Just how important to the global climate change policymaking issue is the discount rate used for the potential harm to future generations?

Answers to the Checkpoint question can be found at the end of the chapter.

Key Concepts

Consumer surplus, p. 314
Producer surplus, p. 314
Social welfare, p. 314
Market failures, p. 315
Public goods, p. 315
Nonrivalry, p. 315
Nonexcludability, p. 315

Cost-benefit analysis, p. 316
Tragedy of the commons, p. 318
Externalities, p. 321
Coase theorem, p. 323
Government failure, p. 326
Command and control policies, p. 329
Market-based policies, p. 329

Chapter Summary

Public Goods

Consumer surplus is the difference between what people are willing to pay for a product and what they actually pay for it. Producer surplus is the difference between the revenues firms earn from a product and the costs they would be willing to bear to supply it.

Market failure occurs whenever a market does not provide the socially optimal quantity of a product at the socially optimal price. Market failure can occur because of public goods, externalities, or common property resources.

Public goods exhibit both nonrivalry in consumption and nonexcludability. Nonrivalry means that one person's consumption of a good does not reduce the availability of that good to others. Nonexcludability means that once a product has been provided, no consumers can be excluded from consuming the product. Candy bars are a rival and exclusive product; clean air is nonrival and nonexclusive.

Because common property resources are owned by the community, individuals tend to overuse and overexploit them, as has happened with ocean fishing. Solutions to such problems involve either direct government regulation or establishing private property rights.

Externalities

Externalities, or spillovers, arise when a transaction benefits or harms parties not involved in the transaction. Pollution and littering are examples of negative externalities, or external costs. Positive externalities, or external benefits, include education and vaccinations.

The Coase theorem suggests that if transaction costs are near zero, how property rights are allocated (to pollute or to be free from pollution) will not affect the efficiency of the ultimate allocation of resources. The resulting bargain between the parties will lead to an optimal allocation of resources. Benefits, however, will be distributed differently, depending on the original assignment of property rights.

Environmental Policy

Sometimes government policies do not make things better. Government failures occur when the incentives of policymakers and bureaucrats do not coincide with the public interest. Government regulators are often captured by the industries they regulate, resulting in regulations that benefit the industry rather than consumers.

When developing environmental policies, policymakers must consider and evaluate different possible futures. This intergenerational aspect of environmental issues depends on the discount rate chosen. The higher the discount rate, the lower the value we place on events farther into the future, which can result in significant burdens being placed on future generations. Conversely, if we select a low discount rate, the current generation may be overburdened in paying for benefits to be enjoyed by future generations.

Some pollution is acceptable to society. Optimal pollution levels are found where marginal abatement costs equal the marginal benefits. These costs and benefits vary for different types of pollution, industries, and regions of the country.

Environmental policy in the United States has been based on command and control policies that set standards for polluters, which are systematically enforced through inspections and reports. Another option is to enact effluent taxes that lead to optimal pollution levels.

More recently, market-based policies have been recognized as being more efficient than command and control policies. First, the government determines a permissible pollution level; then firms are allocated permits to pollute, which they may buy, sell, and trade.

Economic Aspects of Climate Change

Global climate change is a huge global externality accompanied by public goods aspects and extremely long time horizons. These issues complicate the solution, and the fact that the developed countries will have to bear the brunt of containing the impacts from climate change—but will get few of the benefits—introduces equity issues into the policymaking equation. The solution to this problem must include global carbon pricing that is credible and covers the full costs of carbon-based products.

Questions and Problems

Check Your Understanding

1. What makes public goods so different from private goods?

2. Put the following list of goods and services in order of mostly public goods in nature to mostly private: National Public Radio, a slice of pizza, cable TV, music down-loaded from iTunes, your economics class, a seat in a sports bar for Monday Night Football, summer spraying for mosquitoes, the Coast Guard, a ski patrol on Aspen mountain, and an Oklahoma toll road.

3. Assume that you are convinced that if something isn't done now, global warming is going to create extensive problems and damage at the end of this century. If you were preparing a CBA of the impacts and had a 100-year horizon for your projections, would you use a 3% or an 8% discount rate?

4. What is the tragedy of the commons? How can it be solved?

5. When trying to estimate the external benefits of a college education, what kinds of specific benefits would you include?

6. How might the government use market forces to encourage recycling?

Applying the Concepts

7. As a way to increase the funds for wildlife conservation, why don't we just auction off (say, on eBay) the right to name a new species when it is discovered? Why not do the same for existing species?

8. We can estimate the emissions caused in one year from automobile use. What can you do to offset these emissions? Buy a *green tag*. These voluntary purchases are akin to carbon offsets traded in Europe. For a small fee, individuals can purchase carbon offsets for their cars or SUVs, or companies can use them as a way to purchase wind power for their stores. Organizations selling the green tag (both for-profit and non-profit) provide a decal; most of the fee collected is provided to alternative energy producers as a subsidy, which then can lower their prices to the market to encourage use. Is this a public good being sold privately? Why would someone or a business buy a tag when they can free ride?

9. One's home (or apartment) is typically thought of as one's castle. But not so in the condominiums with homeowners associations (HOAs) in Jefferson County, Colorado. In an older four-unit condo, the HOA voted 3–1 to adopt a no-smoking rule (inside the individual condos) after smokers bought one of the units and smoke permeated the walls of the structure. In 2006, a district judge ruled that the HOA's adoption of no-smoking rules were reasonable restrictions on ownership rights, stating that the rules were designed to prevent the odor of cigarettes from penetrating the walls of neighboring condos.

    Since there are a small number of people involved (3 nonsmoking units, 1 smoking), you would think that transaction costs would be minimal. Why do you think the homeowners could not work out an agreement (à la Coase) and ended up in court? According to the Coase theorem, would it have made any difference if the judge had ruled against the HOA?

10. Internalizing the cost of negative externalities means that we try to set policies that require each product to include the full costs of its negative spillovers in its price. How do such policies affect product price and industry output and employment? Are these kinds of policies easy to implement in practice? How has globalization of production affected our ability to control pollution?

11. Garbage dumps are a particular source of a potent global-warming gas, the methane that bubbles up as the garbage decomposes. Does it make sense for companies in the European Union (EU) to help Brazilian garbage dumps reduce their releases of methane as a way of meeting their Kyoto obligations?

12. The Presidio, previously a military base in San Francisco, is now a national park. It sits in the middle of San Francisco on some of the most valuable real estate in the United States. Congress, when it created the park, required that it rehabilitate the aging buildings and be self-sufficient within a decade or so, or the land would be sold off to developers. The park appears to be well on its way to self-sufficiency by leasing the land to private firms—Lucas Films has built a large digital animation studio, and other firms have undertaken similar projects. These projects all must maintain the general character of the park and generate rent that will cover the park's expenses in the future. Would this privatization approach work with most of America's other national parks? Why or why not?

13. Nobel Prize winner Simon Kuznets once suggested that poor nations tend to pollute more as they grow—until they reach a certain level of income per capita—after which they pollute less. Does this observation by Kuznets seem reasonable? Why or why not?

In the News

14. Environmental regulation is undergoing change as many companies seek to be part of the regulatory process and get ahead of regulation. *The New York Times* (May 17, 2006, p. 10) reported that

> The Environmental Protection Agency has long been concerned about the possible toxicity of perfluorooctanoic acid (usually called PFOA), a chemical in waterproof clothing and nonstick cookware. Regulating the substance could take years, said Susan B. Hazen, acting assistant administrator for the agency's Office of Prevention, Pesticides and Toxic Substances. So last year, the agency called together a group of chemical companies and environmentalists to discuss how to control PFOA's. Each company voluntarily curtailed its use of the substance. "Everyone set aside their parochial interests, and we reached agreement in a few months," Ms. Hazen said.

Does knowing that regulations are inevitable make it easier for companies to get on board early? What is the benefit to companies from adapting their production to reduce toxic waste and pollution?

15. Some environmentalists suggest that the airline industry is contributing greatly to global warming. This is because aircraft emit greenhouse gases at high altitudes, and these gases have several times the impact of the same gases emitted at ground level. Air travel alone could account for roughly 5% of our total impact on climate change. Aside from restricting air travel, there doesn't appear to be much that can be done about it. Other nonfossil fuels are not technically or safely possible, and the other small fixes (towing aircraft to the runway, filling all seats in the plane, etc.) don't really reduce fuel consumption enough. Could this just be a situation where society is better off with more pollution? In general, when are we better off with more pollution?

Answers to Questions in CheckPoints

Check Point: Public Goods

Yes, it is a secondary boycott, designed to get the Canadian seafood industry to put pressure on the government to eliminate the hunts. No, it does not seem fair. Chilean sea bass was one product that chefs focused on. Since most sea bass was sold to restaurants, the boycott was successful. Also, the price of sea bass rose as supply declined (as the result of overfishing), making it easier for restaurants to substitute other fish.

Check Point: Externalities

The social benefits from homeowners using electric lawn mowers are shown in the figure below as D_S, while the private benefits are much less (shown as D_P). Fewer electric mowers are sold (Q_P) than is socially desirable (Q_S), so the Los Angeles air quality district is subsidizing electric mowers by \$300 to encourage their use.

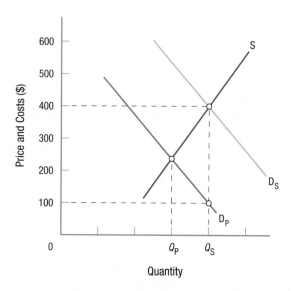

Check Point: Environmental Policy

In the last 50 or so years, as the United States has become richer, environmental issues and our willingness to pay have grown. Simultaneously, science has developed new insights, changing approaches to managing natural environments. Also, when the EPA was formed, pollution was a high-priority item because many streams and cities were fouled. Yes, the EPA probably has suffered mission creep, but it probably reflects the public's desire for a cleaner environment as the U.S. economy has become more prosperous.

Check Point: Economic Aspects of Climate Change

The discount rate used to determine the costs and benefits for global climate policymaking is quite important. If set too high, the benefits to future generations will look trivial in today's dollars. But if set too low, future harm, no matter how trivial when discounted to today, will be huge because of the time span involved. Ultimately, how much we are willing to do today depends crucially on the sacrifice the developed nations of the world (including China and India) are willing to make on behalf of future generations. Perhaps Professor Beckerman said it best when he argued, "But perhaps the whole of this debate is irrelevant. We are confronted with a minute but totally unquantifiable risk of some unquantifiable catastrophe in the distant future. There is no algorithm in cost-benefit analysis that can make this judgment for us. We must each make up our own minds on the basis of our own intuitions and sensibilities."

Poverty and Income Distribution 14

Ross Pictures/Corbis

Income inequality and poverty are among the most contentious issues facing economists and other social scientists today. Many people have trouble accepting that baseball pitchers earn millions, while teachers earn only thousands (and just a few at that) and many others eke out wages that just barely permit subsistence.

Is it fair that some people earn so much when others have so little? Questions of fairness are normative questions. They can only be answered through individual value judgments; economics has no right or wrong answers to offer in this area. Still, economists can contribute *something* to our discussions of economic fairness. What might this be?

Earlier, we saw that when input and product markets are competitive, wages are determined by worker productivity and the market value of output produced. The supply of people willing and able to work and the demand for labor sets the prevailing wages. Many of us are willing to play professional baseball, but few are called, and those who do reach "The Show" are so much more skilled than the rest of us that they command huge contracts.

The teaching profession, in contrast, requires far fewer specific skills and less training. Besides, hundreds of thousands of positions are always available. The result is that teacher salaries are much closer to what average folks earn. Clearly, teachers perform a valuable service, arguably more valuable than the service performed by professional baseball players. Still, there is no real shortage of people willing and able to teach at prevailing wages. But there is a real shortage of people able to throw a 95 mph fastball.

It must also be remembered that our economy contains people whose skill levels and discipline are so low that their income-earning possibilities are dismal. High school dropouts, transients, and many other people with all variety of problems are of little

Income: A flow measure reflecting the funds received by individuals or households over a period of time, usually a week, month, or year.

Wealth: A stock measure of an individual's or family's assets, net of liabilities, at a given point in time.

Functional distribution of income: The distribution of income for resources or factors of production (land, labor, capital, and entrepreneurial ability).

economic value in a market economy. Society has various safety net programs designed to provide these people with basic services to help them become more self-sufficient.

Economic analysis gives us some insight into why income inequality exists. We have already seen how monopoly, monopsony, unions, and discrimination can potentially skew income distribution. Even when public policy focuses on reducing these market imperfections, inequalities persist.

This chapter looks at income inequality, its trends, its causes, and how it is measured. We then take a brief historical look at income inequality and the policies designed to reduce it. Next, we turn our attention to poverty, focusing on how poverty is traditionally measured, and the U.S. Census Bureau's new approach to measuring poverty. Finally, we look at current poverty trends and the causes of poverty. Throughout this chapter, we use economics to provide a framework for analyzing income distribution, poverty, and the public policies used to combat poverty and to change the distribution of income.

The Distribution of Income and Wealth

Income is a *flow,* **wealth** is a *stock.* Income measures the receipts of funds by individuals or households over time, usually a week, month, or year. Income is a *flow of funds* measure. Wealth, in contrast, measures a family's assets and net liabilities at a given point in time. You may earn a certain income in 2011, but your net wealth is measured on a specific day, say, December 31, 2011. Many people were wealthy on January 1, 2000, but after twice suffering the ravages of a falling stock market, they were considerably less wealthy on July 1, 2003.

You can be wealthy with low income if you do not work and your assets are in low-yielding certificates of deposit. Alternately, you can have little wealth, yet a high income, like a rookie professional ball player who earns a seven-figure salary but has not yet accumulated assets.

Life Cycle Effects

Family and individual incomes vary significantly over the course of people's lives. Young people just starting their careers and their families often earn only modest incomes. Over their working careers, they become more experienced and their salaries increase, with income peaking roughly between the ages of 45 and 55. At some point between ages 45 and 60, family size begins to decline as the kids grow up and leave home. Somewhere approaching 60, income also begins declining, though household saving rises as the family prepares for retirement. Incomes decline with retirement, but then again, so do family responsibilities.

One result of this economic life cycle is that a society that is growing older can expect to see changes in income distribution as greater numbers of households fall into lower income brackets. The life cycle also has implications for the economic effects of immigration. Newcomers to the United States are often unskilled, so when the country admits more immigrants, it can expect more low-income households. The children of immigrants, however, move up the income distribution ladder.

The Distribution of Income

Income distribution can be considered from several different perspectives. First, we can look at the **functional distribution of income,** which splits income among the inputs (factors) of production. The functional distribution for the United States between 1929 and 2009 is shown in Table 1.

Labor's share of national income rose from 1929 to become relatively stable from the 1970s onward, but falling slightly each decade. The share of income going to small businesses, called "proprietor's income," has declined over this period. Rental income has grown recently to where it was in 1970. The share accruing to corporate profits has hovered around 10%.

As Table 1 illustrates, the biggest fluctuations in income share have been associated with income from interest. It declined into the 1960s, then rose again in the last decade.

TABLE 1 Functional Distribution of Income (absolute dollars in billions, numbers in parentheses are percentages)

Year	Wages	Proprietor's Income	Rent	Corporate Profits	Net Interest
1929	51.1 (60.3)	14.9 (17.6)	4.9 (5.8)	9.2 (10.8)	4.7 (5.5)
1940	52.1 (65.4)	12.9 (16.2)	2.7 (3.4)	8.7 (10.9)	3.3 (4.1)
1950	154.8 (65.5)	38.4 (16.3)	7.1 (3.0)	33.7 (14.3)	2.3 (1.0)
1960	296.4 (69.4)	51.9 (12.1)	16.2 (3.8)	52.3 (12.2)	10.7 (2.5)
1970	617.2 (73.7)	79.8 (9.5)	20.3 (2.4)	81.6 (9.7)	38.4 (4.6)
1980	1651.7 (73.6)	177.6 (7.9)	31.3 (1.4)	198.5 (8.8)	183.9 (8.2)
1990	3351.7 (72.2)	381.0 (8.2)	49.1 (1.1)	408.6 (8.8)	452.4 (9.7)
2000	5715.2 (71.6)	715.0 (9.0)	141.6 (1.8)	876.4 (11.0)	532.7 (6.7)
2009	7727.8 (70.1)	1028.0 (9.3)	262.0 (2.4)	1226.5 (11.1)	784.4 (7.1)

Source: Bureau of Economic Analysis.

Personal or Family Distribution of Income

When most people use the term "the distribution of income," they typically mean **personal or family distribution of income.** This distributional measure is concerned with how much income, in percentage terms, goes to specific segments of the population.

To analyze personal and family income distribution, the Census Bureau essentially arrays households from the lowest incomes to the highest. It then splits these households into quintiles, or fifths, from the lowest 20% of households to the highest 20%. After totaling and averaging household incomes for each quintile, the Census Bureau computes the percentage of income flowing to each quintile.

Today, the United States contains just over 100 million households. So the 20 million households with the lowest incomes compose the bottom quintile, and the 20 million households with the highest incomes compose the upper quintile.

Table 2 shows the official income distribution estimates for the United States since 1970. These estimates are based "solely on *money income before taxes* and do not include the value of employment based fringe benefits nor of government-provided noncash benefits such as food stamps, Medicaid and public or subsidized housing."[1]

Personal or family distribution of income: The distribution of income to individuals or family groups (typically quintiles, or fifths, of the population).

TABLE 2 Share of Aggregate Income Received by Each Household Quintile: 1970–2008 and the Gini Coefficient

Year	Lowest	Second	Third	Fourth	Highest	Gini Coefficient
1970	4.1	10.8	17.4	24.5	43.3	0.394
1975	4.4	10.5	17.1	24.8	43.2	0.397
1980	4.3	10.3	16.9	24.9	43.7	0.403
1985	4.0	9.7	16.3	24.6	45.3	0.419
1990	3.9	9.6	15.9	24.0	46.6	0.428
1995	3.7	9.1	15.2	23.3	48.7	0.450
2000	3.6	8.9	14.9	23.0	49.6	0.462
2008	3.4	8.7	14.8	23.4	49.7	0.463

Source: U.S. Census Bureau, Current Population Reports, P60-236, *Income, Poverty, and Health Insurance in the United States: 2008* (Washington, DC: U.S. Government Printing Office), 2009.

[1] U.S. Census Bureau, *Money Income in the United States: 2004–05*, p. 2.

Note that if the income distribution were perfectly equal, all quintiles would receive 20% of aggregate income. A quick look at these income distributions over the past three decades suggests that our distribution of income has been growing more unequal. Keep in mind that these numbers ignore taxes and transfers (direct payment to households such as welfare and food stamps).

Compressing distribution data into quintiles allows us to see how distribution has evolved. Economists have developed two primary measures that allow comparisons to be drawn with ease across time and between countries. These measures are Lorenz curves and the Gini coefficient.

Lorenz Curves

Lorenz curves: A graphical method of showing the income distribution by cumulating families of various income levels on the horizontal axis and relating this to their cumulative share of total income on the vertical axis.

Lorenz curves cumulate families of various income levels on the horizontal axis, relating this to their cumulated share of total income on the vertical axis. Figure 1, for simplicity, shows a two-person economy. Assume that both people earn 50% of the total income, or that income is divided evenly. Point *a* in Figure 1 marks out this point, resulting in equal distribution curve 0*ac*.

The second curve in Figure 1 shows a two-person economy where the low-income person earns 25% of the total income and the upper income person receives 75% (point *b*). This graph is skewed to the right (curve 0*bc*), indicating an unequal distribution. If this two-person income distribution were as unequal as possible (0% and 100%), the Lorenz curve would be equal to curve 0*dc*.

FIGURE 1—Lorenz Curves (two-person economy)

If both people in this two-person economy earn 50% of the total income, income will be distributed perfectly equally, shown by the equal distribution curve 0*ac*. Curve 0*bc* represents the same economy in which the low-income person earns 25% of the total income and the upper-income person earns 75%. This curve is skewed to the right, indicating an unequal distribution. The most extreme distribution between these two individuals (0% and 100%) is represented by the Lorenz curve 0*dc*.

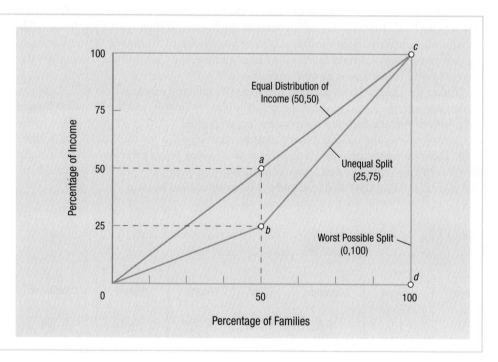

Figure 2 and its accompanying table offer more realistic Lorenz curves for income and wealth data for the United States. The quintile income distribution in the second column of the table is cumulated in the third column and plotted in Figure 2. (To *cumulate* a quintile means to add its percentage of income to the percentages earned by all lower quintiles.)

In Figure 2, for instance, the share of income received by the lowest fifth is 3.5%; it is plotted as point *a*. Next, the lowest two quintiles are summed (3.5 + 8.7 = 12.2) and plotted as point *b*. The process continues until all quintiles have been plotted to create the Lorenz curve.

Figure 2 also plots the Lorenz curve for wealth; it shows how wealth is much more unequally distributed than income. The wealthiest 20% of Americans control over 80% of wealth, even though they earn only half of all income.

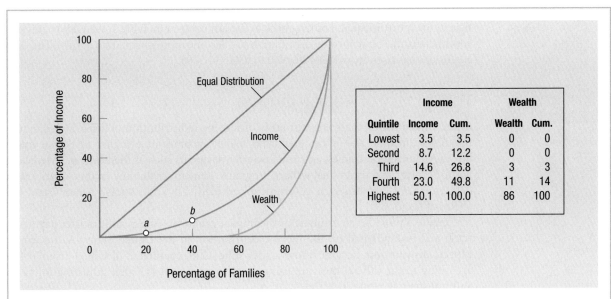

FIGURE 2—Lorenz Curves

The graph shows the most recent Lorenz curves for income and wealth in the United States. The quintile distribution of income, found in the second column of the accompanying table, is cumulated in the third column and then plotted as a Lorenz curve. Notice how wealth is much more unequally distributed than income.

Gini Coefficient

Lorenz curves give us a good graphical summation of income distributions, but they can be inconvenient to use when comparing distributions between different countries or across time. Economists would like one number that represents an economy's income inequality. The **Gini coefficient** provides such a number.

The Gini coefficient provides a precise method of measuring the position of the Lorenz curve. It is defined as the ratio of the area between the Lorenz curve and the equal distribution line, in the numerator, and the total area below the equal distribution line, in the denominator. In Figure 3, the Gini coefficient is the ratio of area *A* to area (*A* + *B*).

If the distribution were equal, area *A* would disappear (equal zero), so the Gini coefficient would be zero. If the distribution were as unequal as possible, with one individual or household earning all national income, area *B* would disappear, so the Gini coefficient would be 1.

Gini coefficient: A precise method of measuring the position of the Lorenz curve, defined as the area between the Lorenz curve and the equal distribution line divided by the total area below the equal distribution line.

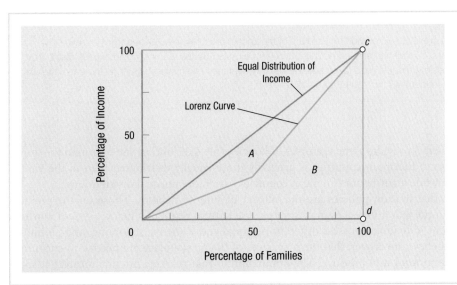

FIGURE 3—The Gini Coefficient

The Gini coefficient is a precise method of measuring the position of the Lorenz curve. It is defined as the ratio of the area between the Lorenz curve and the equal distribution line, and the total area below the equal distribution line. Thus, the Gini coefficient is equal to the ratio between area *A* and area (*A* + *B*). If distribution were equal, area *A* would be zero, and the Gini coefficient would equal zero. If distribution were as unequal as possible, area *B* would disappear, so the Gini coefficient would be 1.

As a rule, the lower the coefficient, the more equal the distribution; the higher the coefficient, the more unequal. Looking back at the last column in Table 2, the Gini coefficient confirms that the basic income distribution has become more unequal since 1970. The Gini coefficient has risen from 0.394 in 1970 to 0.463 in 2008.

The Impact of Redistribution

In the United States, there is a vast array of income redistribution policies, including the progressive income tax (a tax that taxes higher incomes at a higher rate than lower incomes), housing subsidies, and other transfer payments such as Medicaid and Medicare, Social Security, and traditional welfare programs. Remember that the income distribution data in Table 2 *excluded* such government-provided cash and noncash benefits, and the effects of taxation.

Figure 4 provides an estimate of the impact progressive taxes and transfer payments (cash and in-kind) had on the income distribution in the United States. As we would expect, distribution became more equal: The Gini coefficient declined from 0.463 according to the official measure using gross income to 0.412 after adjusting for taxes and transfer payments.

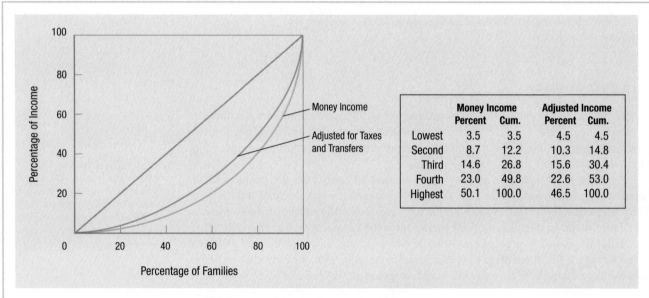

	Money Income		Adjusted Income	
	Percent	Cum.	Percent	Cum.
Lowest	3.5	3.5	4.5	4.5
Second	8.7	12.2	10.3	14.8
Third	14.6	26.8	15.6	30.4
Fourth	23.0	49.8	22.6	53.0
Highest	50.1	100.0	46.5	100.0

FIGURE 4—Lorenz Curves for the United States: Money Income and Income Adjusted for Taxes and Transfer Payments

These Lorenz curves provide an estimate of the impact progressive taxes and transfer payments (cash and in-kind) had on income distribution in the United States. As one would expect, distribution becomes more equal once taxes and transfer payments are taken into account. In this case, the Gini coefficient declined from 0.463 to 0.412.

Table 3 provides some examples of how income distribution varies around the world. Income in European countries is generally more equally distributed than in the United States, while many South American countries have more unequal distributions.

Redistribution policies are the subject of intense debates. Those on the political right argue that differences in income are the natural result of a market system in which different individuals possess different personal endowments, schooling, and ambition. They believe, moreover, that the incentives of the marketplace are needed to encourage people to work and produce. The opportunities that markets provide mean that some

TABLE 3	Gini Coefficients for Various Countries, 2007
Country	**Gini Coefficient**
Australia	0.352
Bolivia	0.582
Brazil	0.550
Canada	0.326
Chile	0.520
China	0.415
Denmark	0.247
France	0.327
Israel	0.392
Italy	0.360
Japan	0.249
Mexico	0.481
New Zealand	0.362
South Africa	0.578
Spain	0.347
Sweden	0.250
United Kingdom	0.360
United States	0.408

Source: World Bank, *World Development Indicators* (Washington, DC: World Bank), 2009.

people will be winners and others will lose. These analysts are unconcerned about the distribution of income unless it becomes so unequal that it discourages incentives and reduces efficiency.

Those on the political left argue that public policy should ultimately be guided by human needs. They see personal wealth as being the product of community effort as much as individual effort, and therefore they favor greater government taxation of income and wealth. By and large, European nations have found this argument more compelling than has the United States. This is reflected in the breadth of European social welfare policies. Because there is no correct answer (except possibly keeping distribution away from the extremes), this debate continues.

Causes of Income Inequality

Many factors contribute to income inequality in our society. First, as just mentioned, people are born into different circumstances with differing natural abilities. Families take varying interest in the well-being of their children, with some kids receiving immense inputs of family time and capital, while others receive little. These family choices largely fall outside the realm of public policy.

Human Capital

The guarantee of a free public education through high school and huge subsidies to public colleges and universities for all Americans are designed to even out some of the economic differences among families. Still, public education does not eliminate the disparities. Some parents plan their children's educations long before they are born, while other parents ignore education altogether.

Table 4 on the next page provides evidence of the impact investments in education have on earnings. Those without high school diplomas earned the least, roughly a third less than high school graduates. A college degree resulted in mean earnings nearly 3 times higher than what individuals without high school diplomas earned.

TABLE 4	Mean Earnings by Highest Degree Earned, 2006			
	Mean Earnings by Highest Degree			
	No High School Diploma	**High School Graduate**	**College Graduate**	**Professional**
All Persons	$20,873	$31,071	$56,788	$116,214
Male	24,072	37,356	69,818	132,991
Female	15,352	23,236	43,302	86,010
White	21,464	32,083	57,932	117,718
Black	17,823	26,368	47,903	101,374
Hispanic	20,581	27,508	45,371	82,627

Source: U.S. Census Bureau, Current Population Survey, *2009 Statistical Abstract of the United States,* Table 224.

The U.S. economy has become more technologically complex. Manufacturing jobs have dwindled, reducing the demand for these workers, reducing their real wages. Several decades ago, people with low education levels could find highly productive work in manufacturing, with good wages and benefits. Globalization and increased capital mobility, however, have caused many of these jobs to migrate to lower-wage countries. The result: Real wages have declined for Americans in many manufacturing occupations.

Our economy is increasingly oriented toward service industries, making investments in human capital more important than ever. The service industry spans more than just burger flipping, maid service, and landscaping. The United States is still the world leader in the design and development of new products, basic scientific research and development, and other professional services. All these industries and occupations have one thing in common: the need for highly skilled and highly educated employees.

Other Factors

In an earlier chapter, we saw that economic discrimination (dual labor markets or segmented markets) leads to an income distribution skewed against those subject to discrimination. Reduced wages then reduce an individual's incentive to invest in human capital since the returns are lower, perpetuating a vicious circle.

Table 5 outlines some characteristics of households occupying two different income quintiles. By comparing the lowest quintile with the highest, we can see some of the reasons for income inequality. As the Census Bureau summarizes these differences, "High-income households tended to be family households that included two or more earners, lived in the suburbs of a large city, and had a working householder between 35 and 54 years old. In contrast, low-income households tended to be in a city with an elderly householder who lived alone and did not work."

The rise in two-earner households over the last two decades accounts for a large part of the growing inequality in income. Note in Table 5 that only 5.8% of the lowest-quintile households had two earners, while 76.4% of the highest quintile did. Also, only 3% of top quintile householders did not work, but 58.6% of those in the bottom quintile were not working.

It is hardly surprising that households with two people working should tend to have higher incomes than households with only one person or none working. In most households, whether one or two people work represents a choice. Today, clearly more couples are opting for two incomes. This is significant, given that rising income inequality is often cited as evidence that the United States needs to change its public policies to reduce inequalities. Yet, if the rise in inequality is due largely to changes in household attitudes toward work and income, with more couples choosing dual-career households, changes in public policy may not be needed. Rising inequality may simply be a reflection of the changing personal choices of many households.

This overview of income distribution and inequality provides a broad foundation for the remainder of the chapter, which focuses on poverty, its causes, and possible cures.

TABLE 5	Distribution of Households by Selected Characteristics within Income Quintiles, 2008	
Characteristic	**Lowest Quintile**	**Highest Quintile**
Type of Residence		
Inside metropolitan area	79.4%	90.2%
Inside central city	39.5	29.3
Outside central city	39.8	60.8
Outside metropolitan area	20.6	9.9
Type of Household		
Family households	40.5	87.4
Married-couple families	18.1	79.3
Nonfamily households	59.5	12.6
Householder living alone	59.5	12.6
Age of Householder		
15 to 34 years	22.1	15.0
35 to 54 years	26.8	53.6
55 to 64 years	14.7	21.3
65 years or older	36.4	10.0
Number of Earners		
No earners	58.6	3.0
One earner	35.6	20.6
Two or more earners	5.8	76.4
Work Experience of Householder		
Worked	35.5	88.4
Worked full-time, year-round	21.5	78.8
Worked part-time or part year	14.0	9.6
Did not work	64.5	11.6

Source: U.S. Census Bureau, Current Population Reports, P60-236, *Income, Poverty, and Health Insurance Coverage in the United States: 2008* (Washington, DC: U.S. Government Printing Office), 2009.

■ CHECKPOINT

THE DISTRIBUTION OF INCOME AND WEALTH

- The functional distribution of income splits income among factors of production.

- The family or personal distribution of income typically splits income into quintiles.

- Lorenz curves cumulate families of various income levels on the horizontal axis and their cumulative share of income on the vertical axis.

- The Gini coefficient is the ratio of the area between the Lorenz curve and the equal distribution line to the total area below the equal distribution line. It is used to compare income distribution across time and between countries.

- Income redistribution activities such as progressive taxes, Medicare, Medicaid, and other transfer and welfare programs reduce the Gini coefficient and reduce the inequality in the distribution of income.

- Income inequality is caused by a number of factors, including individual investment in human capital, natural abilities, and discrimination.

Poverty

Thus far, we have examined income distribution in general terms, looking at the spectrum from the top to the bottom. This section focuses on the bottom of the income spectrum—those who live in poverty. First, we look at poverty thresholds and how they are defined. Then we turn to the incidence of poverty and its trends. Last, we take a brief look at some experimental measures of poverty, considering their impact on measured rates of poverty.

Measuring Poverty

Poverty thresholds: Income levels for various household sizes, below which people are considered to be living in poverty.

Poverty thresholds were developed by Mollie Orshansky in the 1960s. They were based on the Agriculture Department's Economy Food Plan, the least expensive plan by which a family could feed itself. The Agriculture Department first surveyed the food-buying patterns of low-income households, using these data to determine the cost of a nutritionally balanced food plan on a low-income budget. Orshansky then extrapolated these costs to determine the cost of maintaining such a food plan for households of various compositions. Finally, to determine the official poverty threshold, Orshansky multiplied the cost of the food plan, adjusted for family size, by 3. This multiplier was based on an earlier household survey that had shown the average family of three or more spends roughly a third of its income on food.[2]

Since the 1960s, the poverty thresholds have been updated every year for changes in inflation using the consumer price index (CPI). Table 6 shows the poverty thresholds for 2008. If a family's income is less than the threshold, every person in the household is considered poor. Official thresholds do not vary geographically. "Income" includes all money income before taxes, including cash benefits, but not capital gains or noncash benefits such as public housing, food stamps, and Medicaid. Later, we will briefly look at some new alternative measures that do adjust for these factors.

TABLE 6   Average Poverty Thresholds, 2008

One person	$10,991
Two people	14,051
Three people	17,163
Four people	22,025
Five people	26,049
Six people	29,456
Seven people	33,529
Eight people	37,220
Nine people	44,346

Source: U.S. Census Bureau, Current Population Reports, P60-236, *Income, Poverty, and Health Insurance in the United States: 2008* (Washington, DC: U.S. Government Printing Office), 2009.

[2] See Constance F. Citro and Robert T. Michael, *Measuring Poverty: A New Approach* (Washington DC: National Academy Press), 1995, p. 13 and Chap. 2 for more detail on how thresholds are measured.

Issue: Why Do We Use an Outdated Measure of Poverty?

Why does the United States still define poverty as 3 times the cost of a *1963* low-income food budget adjusted for inflation? You might think that government policymakers could design a measure that reflects a family's well-being by looking at more than just money income based on some old formula nearly a half-century old.

Based on this measure, poverty rates have fluctuated between 10% and 15% over the four decades. But in that time, antipoverty programs were generously increased to include reduced tax burdens on the poor, as well as the expansion of food stamp and housing programs, the earned income tax credit, and Medicare, Medicaid, and other programs that have undoubtedly helped the poor. But the measure doesn't reflect this success and as a result provides little guidance to solving poverty. As Professor Rebecca Blank at the University of Michigan observes, "In a very fundamental way, our poverty statistics failed us and made it easy to claim that public spending on the poor had little effect."

Why has the Census Bureau failed to update our poverty measure in the same way that employment, unemployment, consumer prices, national income accounts, and many other economic statistics have been improved? The answer is straightforward and surprising. Through a historical accident, the Executive Office of the President is in charge of the measure. The decision resides at the Office of Management and Budget (OMB), and the president must ultimately approve any change. To date, no White House has been willing to approve any change. If a change in measurement results in falling poverty rates, some will claim manipulation. If a

Aurora Photos/Alamy

change results in higher poverty rates, the administration risks being seen as a failure on this front. Ultimately, we will probably not see improvement until Congress gives the Census Bureau responsibility for the statistic.

Source: Rebecca Blank, "Presidential Address: How to Improve Poverty Measurement in the United States," *Journal of Policy Analysis and Management,* 2008, pp. 233–254.

The Incidence of Poverty

Poverty rates for the United States since 1960 are shown in Figure 5 on the next page. Poverty fell rapidly between 1960 and 1975 but has remained roughly stable ever since, fluctuating with the business cycle: rising around recessions (the shaded vertical bars) and falling when times are good.

Poverty rates vary considerably along racial and ethnic lines. Figure 6 on the next page charts the poverty rate since 1970. Over most of this time, the poverty rate for blacks and Hispanics was roughly twice the rate for whites. Both of these minority groups benefited, however, from the strong economic growth of the 1990s, their poverty rates dropping from around 30% at the beginning of the decade to below 25% today. White poverty remained fairly steady over the 1990s, fluctuating between 10% and 11%.

These data suggest that robust economic growth is a major force for reducing poverty. The expression "a rising tide floats all boats" would appear to have something to it.

Table 7 on page 353 shows other characteristics that contribute to poverty. Single parent households have 2 to 5 times the poverty rate of married couples. Not surprisingly, working part-time or not working at all leads to higher poverty rates. And, as we saw in Figure 6, black and Hispanic poverty rates are roughly twice that of whites.

Depth of Poverty

It is one thing to say that a certain percentage of the population is poor. It is another to determine just how poor they are. The poverty threshold for a family of four today is over $22,000. If most poor families have incomes approaching this threshold, we could be confident poverty was just a transitory stage—one phase of the life cycle—and that many people who are poor today would have higher incomes tomorrow.

FIGURE 5—Poverty Rates in the United States, 1960–2008

Poverty fell rapidly between 1960 and 1975 but has remained roughly stable ever since.

Source: U.S. Census Bureau, Current Population Reports, P60-236, *Income, Poverty, and Health Insurance in the United States: 2008* (Washington, DC: U.S. Government Printing Office), 2009.

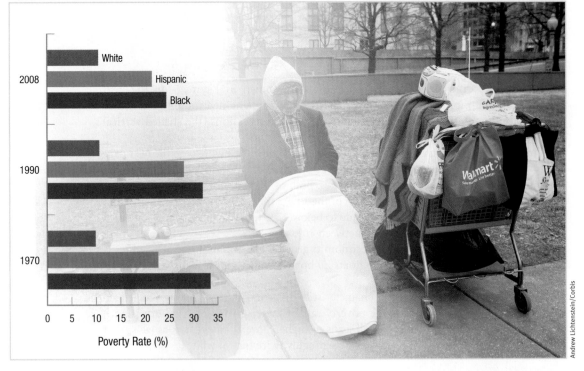

FIGURE 6—Poverty Rates by Race and Ethnic Origin, 1970–2008

Poverty rates vary considerably along racial and ethnic lines. Over most of this period, the poverty rate for blacks and Hispanics was roughly twice the rate for whites. Both of these minority groups benefited, however, from the strong economic growth of the 1990s, their poverty rates dropping from around 30% at the beginning of the decade to below 25% today. White poverty remained fairly steady over the 1990s, fluctuating between 10% and 11%.

Source: U.S. Census Bureau, Current Population Reports, P60-236, *Income, Poverty, and Health Insurance in the United States: 2008* (Washington, DC: U.S. Government Printing Office), 2009.

These results are not merely hypothetical. This is the story of free trade, which has been played out time and again: Some sectors of the economy win, and some lose. American consumers have been happy to purchase Japanese cameras such as Minolta and Nikon, given their high quality and low prices. American camera makers such as Kodak and Polaroid have not been so pleased, nor have their employees. These firms, watching their prices, sales, and employment decline, have had to adapt to the competition from abroad.

Similarly, the ranks of American textile workers have been decimated over the past two decades as domestic clothing producers have increasingly become nothing but designers and marketers of clothes, shifting their production overseas to countries where wages are lower. American-made clothing is now essentially a thing of the past.

To be sure, American consumers have enjoyed a substantial drop in the price of clothing, because labor forms a significant part of the cost of clothing production. Still, being able to purchase inexpensive T-shirts made in China is small consolation for the unemployed textile worker in North Carolina.

The undoubted pain suffered by the losers from trade often is translated into pressure put on politicians to restrict trade in one way or another. The pain is often felt more strongly than the "happiness" felt by those who benefit from trade.

How Trade Is Restricted

Trade restrictions can range from subsidies provided to domestic firms to protect them against lower-priced imports to embargoes in which the government bans any trade with a country. Between these two extremes are more intermediate policies, such as exchange controls that limit the amount of foreign currency available to importers or citizens who travel abroad. Regulation, licensing, and government purchasing policies are all frequently used to promote or ensure the purchase of domestic products. The main reason for these trade restrictions is simple: The industry and its employees actually feel the pain and lobby extensively for protection, while the huge benefits of lower prices are diffused among millions of customers whose benefits are each so small that fighting against a trade barrier isn't worth their time.

The most common forms of trade restrictions are tariffs and quotas. Panel A of Figure 5 on the next page shows the average U.S. tariff rates since 1900. Some economists have suggested that the tariff wars that erupted in the 1920s and culminated in the passage of the Smoot-Hawley Act in 1930 were an important factor underlying the severity of the Great Depression. Panel B shows the impact of higher tariffs on worldwide imports from 1930 to 1933. The higher tariffs reduced trade, leading to a reduction in income, output, and employment, and added fuel to the worldwide depression. Since the 1930s, the United States has played a leading role in trade liberalization, with average tariff rates declining to a current rate of roughly 2%.

Effects of Tariffs and Quotas

What exactly are the effects of tariffs and quotas? **Tariffs** are often ad valorem taxes. This means the product is taxed by a certain percentage of its price as it crosses the border. Other tariffs are unit taxes: A fixed tax per unit of the product is assessed at the border. Tariffs are designed to generate revenues and to drive a wedge between the domestic price of a product and its price on the world market. The effects of a tariff are shown in Figure 6 on page 371.

Domestic supply and demand for the product are shown in Figure 6 as S and D. Assume that the product's world price of $400 is lower than its domestic price of $600. Domestic quantity demanded (4,000 units) will consequently exceed domestic quantity supplied (2,000 units) at the world price of $400. Imports to this country will therefore be 2,000 units.

Now assume that the firms and workers in the industry hurt by the lower world price lobby for a tariff and are successful. The country imposes a tariff of $100 on this product. The results are clear. The product's price in this country rises to $500 and imports fall to 1,000 units

Tariff: A tax on imported products. When a country taxes imported products, it drives a wedge between the product's domestic price and its price on the world market.

FIGURE 5—Average U.S. Tariff Rates, 1900–2004, and the Downward Spiral of World Imports, 1930–1933

Tariffs and quotas are the most common forms of trade restrictions. Panel A shows that tariff rates in the United States peaked during the Great Depression. For the last several decades, tariffs have stayed at roughly a rate of 2%. When tariffs jumped with the passage of the Smoot-Hawley Act in 1930, world imports spiraled downward as shown in panel B. As trade between nations declined, incomes, output, and employment also fell worldwide. In panel B, total monthly imports in millions of U.S. dollars for 75 countries is shown spiraling downward from $2,738 million in January 1930 to $1,057 million in March 1933.

Source: Charles Kindleberger, *The World Depression 1929–1939* (Berkeley: University of California Press), 1986, p. 170.

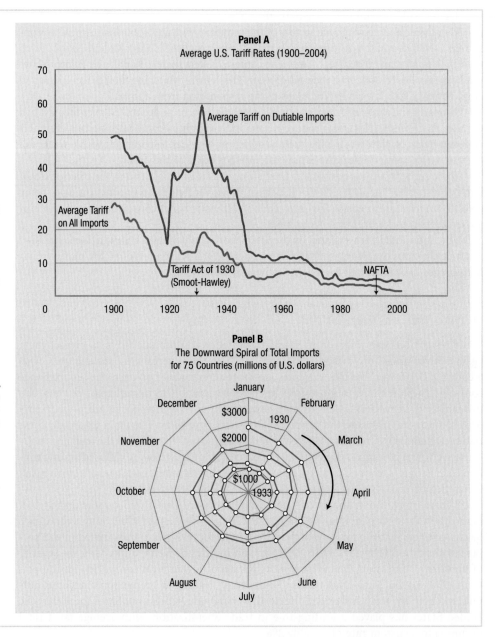

Panel A
Average U.S. Tariff Rates (1900–2004)

Average Tariff on Dutiable Imports

Average Tariff on All Imports

Tariff Act of 1930 (Smoot-Hawley)

NAFTA

Panel B
The Downward Spiral of Total Imports for 75 Countries (millions of U.S. dollars)

(3,500–2,500). Domestic consumers consume less of the product at higher prices. Even so, the domestic industry is happy, since its prices and output have risen. The government, meanwhile, collects revenues equal to $100,000 ($100 × 1,000), the shaded area in Figure 6. These revenues can be significant: In the 1800s, tariffs were the federal government's dominant form of revenue. It is only in the last century that the federal government has come to rely more on other sources of revenue, including taxes on income, sales, and property.

Figure 7 shows the effects of a **quota.** They are similar to what we saw in Figure 6, except that the government restricts the quantity of imports into the country to 1,000 units. Imports fall to the quota level, and consumers again lose, because they must pay higher prices for less output. Producers and their employees gain as prices and employment in the domestic industry rise. For a quota, however, the government does not collect revenue. Then who gets this revenue? The foreign exporting company gets it in the form of higher prices for its products. This explains why governments prefer tariffs over quotas.

The United States imposed quotas on Japanese automobiles in the 1980s. The primary effect of these quotas was initially to dramatically raise the minimum standard

Quota: A government-set limit on the quantity of imports into a country.

FIGURE 6—Effects of a Tariff

What are the effects of a typical tariff? Supply and demand curves S and D represent domestic supply and demand. Assume the product's world price of $400 is lower than its domestic price. Imports will therefore be 2,000 units. If the country imposes a tariff of $100 on this product, the domestic price rises to $500, and imports fall to 1,000 units. Domestic consumers now consume less of the product at higher prices. However, the domestic industry is happy since its prices and output have risen. Also, the government collects revenues equal to the shaded area.

equipment and price for some Japanese cars and to increase ultimately the number of Japanese cars made in American factories. If a firm is limited in the number of vehicles it can sell, why not sell higher-priced ones where the profit margins are higher? The Toyota Land Cruiser, for instance, was originally a bare-bones SUV selling for under $15,000. With quotas, this vehicle became a $60,000 luxury behemoth with all the extras standard.

One problem with tariffs and quotas is that when they are imposed, large numbers of consumers pay just a small amount more for the targeted products. Few consumers are willing to spend time and effort lobbying Congress to end or forestall these trade barriers from being introduced. Producers, however, are often few in number, and they stand to gain tremendously from such trade barriers. It is no wonder that such firms have large lobbying budgets and provide campaign contributions to congressional candidates.

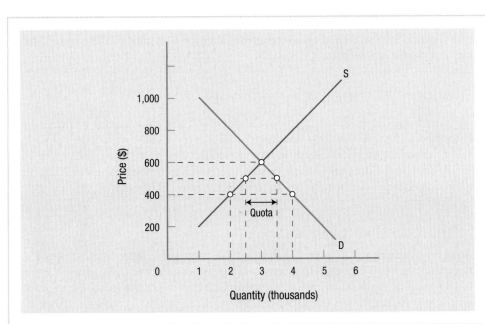

FIGURE 7—Effects of a Quota

What are the effects of a quota? They are similar to the effects of a tariff, except that the government restricts the quantity of imports into the country to 1,000 units. Imports fall to the quota level, and again consumers lose as they must pay higher prices for less output. Producers and their employees gain as prices and employment in the domestic industry rise. With a quota, however, the government does not collect revenues.

■ **CHECKPOINT**

THE TERMS OF TRADE

- The terms of trade are determined by the ratio of the price of exported goods to the price of imported goods.

- The terms of trade are set by the markets in each country and by exports and imports that eventually equalize the prices.

- Trade leads to winners and losers in each country and in each market.

- Trade restrictions vary from subsidies to domestic firms to government bans on the import of foreign products.

- Tariffs are taxes on imports that protect domestic producers and generate revenue for the government.

- Quotas represent restrictions on the volume of particular imports that can come into a country. Quotas do not generate revenue for governments and are infrequently used.

QUESTION: When the government imposes a quota on foreign trucks, who benefits and who loses?

Answers to the Checkpoint question can be found at the end of this chapter.

Arguments Against Free Trade

"If goods do not cross borders, soldiers will."

FRÉDÉRIC BASTIAT

We have seen the benefits of trade, and have looked at how trade undoubtedly benefits some and harms others. Those who are harmed by trade often seek to restrict trade, primarily in the form of tariffs and quotas. Because trade leads to some loss, those who are harmed by trade have made arguments against free trade.

The arguments against free trade fall into two camps. Traditional economic arguments include protection for infant industries, protection against dumping, low foreign wages, and support for industries judged vital for national defense. More recent arguments focus on globalization (social and economic) concerns that embody political-economy characteristics. These include domestic employment concerns, environmental concerns, and the impact of globalization on working conditions in developing nations. In what follows, we take a critical look at each of these arguments, showing that most of these arguments do not have a solid empirical basis.

Traditional Economic Arguments

Arguments against trade are not new. Despite the huge gains from trade, distortions (subsidies and trade barriers) continue because changing current policies will hurt those dependent on subsidies and trade restrictions, and these firms and workers will show their displeasure at the voting booth. All of these traditional economic arguments against free trade seem reasonable on their face, but on closer examination, they look less attractive.

Infant Industry Argument

Infant Industry: An industry so underdeveloped that protection is needed for it to become competitive on the world stage or to ensure its survival.

An **infant industry,** it is argued, is one that is too underdeveloped to achieve comparative advantage or perhaps even to survive in the global environment. Such an industry may be too small or undercapitalized, or its management and workers may be too inexperienced, to compete. Unless the industry's government provides it with some protection through tariffs, quotas, or subsidies, it might not survive in the face of foreign competition.

In theory, once the infant industry has been given this protection, it should be able to grow, acquiring the necessary capital and expertise needed to compete internationally. Germany and the United States used high tariffs to protect their infant manufacturing sectors in the 1800s, and Japan continued to maintain import restrictions up until the 1970s.

Though the infant industry argument sounds reasonable, it has several limitations. First, protecting an industry must be done in a way that makes the industry internationally competitive. Many countries coddle their firms, and these producers never seem to develop into "mature," internationally viable firms. Once protection is provided (typically a protective tariff), it is difficult to remove after an industry has matured. The industry and its workers continue to convince policymakers of the need for continued protection.

Second, infant industry protection often tends to focus on capital manufacturing. Countries with huge labor supplies would do better to develop their labor-intensive industries first, letting more capital-intensive industries develop over time. Every country, after all, should seek to exploit its comparative advantages, but it is difficult to determine which industries have a chance of developing a comparative advantage in the future and should be temporarily protected.

Third, many industries seem to be able to develop without protections, so countries may be wasting their resources and reducing their incomes by imposing protection measures.

Clearly, the infant industry argument is not valid for advanced economies such as the United States, much of Europe, and Japan. The evidence for developing nations shows some benefits but is mixed for the reasons noted above.

Antidumping

Dumping means that goods are sold at lower prices (often *below cost*) abroad than in their home market. This is typically a result of government subsidies.

In the same way that price discrimination improves profits, firms can price discriminate between their home markets and foreign markets. Let's assume that costs of production are $100 a unit for all firms (domestic and foreign). A state subsidy of $30 a unit, for example, reduces domestic costs to $70 a unit and permits the firm to sell its product in world markets at these lower prices. These state subsidies give these firms a cost advantage in foreign markets.

Firms can use dumping as a form of predatory pricing, using higher prices in their domestic markets to support unrealistically low prices in foreign markets. The goal of predatory pricing is to drive foreign competitors out of business. When this occurs, the firm doing the dumping then comes back and imposes higher prices. In the long run, these higher prices thereby offset the company's short-term losses.

Dumping violates American trade laws. If the federal government determines that a foreign firm is dumping products onto the American market, it can impose antidumping tariffs on the offending products. The government, however, must distinguish among dumping, legitimate price discrimination, and legitimate instances of lower cost production arising from comparative advantage.

Dumping: Selling goods abroad at lower prices than in home markets, and often below cost.

Low Foreign Wages

Some advocates of trade barriers maintain that domestic firms and their workers need to be protected from displacement by cheap foreign labor. Without this protection, it is argued, foreign manufacturers that pay their workers pennies an hour will flood the market with low-cost products. As we have already seen, this argument has something to it: Workers in advanced economies can be displaced by low-wage foreign workers. This is what has happened in the American textile industry.

Once a handful of American clothing manufacturers began moving their production facilities overseas, thereby undercutting domestic producers, other manufacturers were forced to follow them. American consumers have benefited from lower clothing prices, but many displaced textile workers are still trying to get retrained and adapt to work in other industries. More recently, many manufacturing jobs have drifted overseas, and high-technology firms today are shifting some help desk facilities and computer programming to foreign shores.

On balance, however, the benefits of lower-priced goods considerably exceed the costs of lost employment. The federal government has resisted imposing protection measures for the sake of protecting jobs, instead funding programs that help displaced workers transition to new lines of work.

National Defense Argument

In times of national crisis or war, the United States must be able to rely on key domestic industries, such as oil, steel, and the defense industry. Some have argued that these industries may require some protection even during peacetime to ensure that they are already well established when a crisis strikes and importing key products may be impossible. Within limits, this argument is sound. Still, the United States has the capacity to produce such a wide variety of products that protections for specific industries would seem to be unjustified and unnecessary.

So what are we to make of these traditional arguments? Although they all seem reasonable, they all have deficiencies. Infant industries may be helped in the short run, but protections are often extended well beyond what is necessary, resulting in inefficient firms that are vulnerable on world markets. Dumping is clearly a potential problem, but distinguishing real cases of dumping and comparative advantage has often proven difficult in practice. Low foreign wages are often the only comparative advantage a developing nation has to offer the world economy, and typically, the benefits to consumers vastly outweigh the loss to a particular industry. Maintaining (protecting) industries for national defense has merit and may be appropriate for some countries, but for a country as huge and diversified as the United States, it is probably unnecessary.

Recent Globalization Concerns

Expanded trade and globalization have provided the world's producers and consumers with many benefits. Some observers, however, have voiced concerns about globalization and its effects on domestic employment, the global environment, and working conditions in developing nations. Let's look at each one of these globalization concerns.

Trade and Domestic Employment

Some critics argue that increased trade and globalization spell job losses for domestic workers. We have seen that this can be true. Some firms, unable to compete with imports, will be forced to lay off workers or even close their doors. Even so, increased trade usually allows firms that are exporters to expand their operations and hire new workers. These will be firms in industries with comparative advantages. For the United States, these industries tend to be those that require a highly skilled workforce, resulting in higher wages for American workers.

Clearly, those industries that are adding workers and those that are losing jobs are different industries. For workers who lose their jobs, switching industries can be difficult and time consuming, and often it requires new investments in human capital. American trade policy recognizes this problem, and the Trade Adjustment Assistance (TAA) program provides workers with job search assistance, job training, and some relocation allowances. In some industries sensitive to trade liberalization, including textiles and agriculture, trade policies are designed to proceed gradually, thus giving these industries and their workers some extra time to adjust.

Possible employment losses in some noncompetitive industries do not seem to provide enough justification for restricting trade. By imposing trade restrictions such as tariffs or quotas in one industry, employment opportunities in many other industries may be reduced. Open, competitive trade encourages producers to focus their production on those areas in which the country stands at a comparative advantage. Free trade puts competitive pressure on domestic firms, forcing them to be more productive and competitive, boosting the flow of information and technology across borders, and widening the availability of inputs for producers. At the end of the day, consumers benefit from these efficiencies, having more goods to choose from and enjoying a higher standard of living.

Trade and the Environment

Concerns about globalization, trade, and the environment usually take one of two forms. Some people are concerned that expanded trade and globalization will lead to increased environmental degradation as companies take advantage of lax environmental laws abroad, particularly in the developing world. Others worry that attempts by the government to strengthen environmental laws will be challenged by trading partners as disguised protectionism.

Domestic environmental regulations usually target a product or process that creates pollution or other environmental problems. One concern in establishing environmental regulations, however, is that they not unfairly discriminate against the products of another country. This is usually not a serious problem. Nearly all trade agreements, including the World Trade Organization Agreements and the NAFTA, have provisions permitting countries to enforce measures "necessary to protect human, animal or plant life or health" or to conserve exhaustible natural resources. Nothing in our trade agreements prevents the United States from implementing environmental regulations as long as they do not unreasonably discriminate against our trading partners.

Will free trade come at the expense of the environment? Every action involves a trade-off. Clearly, there can be cases where the benefits of trade accruing to large numbers of people result in harm to a more concentrated group. In 1995, however, President Clinton's Council of Economic Advisers concluded:

> There are also complementarities between good trade policies and good environmental policies. Agricultural protection in industrialized countries is a case in point. The protection of developed-country agriculture leads to more intensive farming, often of lands that are of marginal use, causing unnecessary soil erosion, loss of biological diversity, and the excessive use of pesticides and chemicals. Liberalizing trade in agriculture and lowering agriculture production subsidies can lead to a pattern of world farming that causes less environmental damage.
>
> Also, high trade barriers to labor-intensive imports, such as clothing, from developing countries lead these countries instead to export products that are intensive in natural resources, causing environmental damage. In addition, high-value-added natural resource-based products such as wood or paper products often face high tariff barriers, whereas the raw natural resource itself does not; this forces developing countries to rely on exports of unprocessed natural resources while denying them the revenue gains from the downstream products.[1]

We have seen that trade raises incomes in developed and developing countries. And environmental protection is an income elastic good: As incomes rise, the demand for environmental protections rises faster. Studies suggest that once a country's per capita income exceeds roughly $5,000, its environmental protection efforts begin to improve.

In poor, developing nations, environmental protection will not at first be a priority. Critics of globalization are concerned that because environmental and labor standards in many developing nations are well below those of the developed countries, there will be pressure to adopt these lower standards in rich nations due to trade and foreign direct investment. But as Bhagwati and Hudec argue, there has been no systematic "race to the bottom" and many corporations often have the highest environmental and labor standards in the developing world.[2] Also, it is worth noting that over time, as incomes rise, environmental protection takes on added importance even in poorer nations. On balance, trade probably benefits the environment over the longer term, as incomes grow in developing nations and environmental protections take on greater importance.

---

[1] *Economic Report of the President* (Washington, DC: U.S. Government Printing Office), 1995, p. 242.

[2] Jagdish Bhagwati and Robert Hudec (eds.), *Fair Trade and Harmonization, Vol. 1: Economic Analysis* (Cambridge, MA: MIT Press), 1996.

Trade and Its Effect on Working Conditions in Developing Nations

Some antiglobalization activists argue that for the United States to trade with developing countries where wages are low and working conditions are deplorable simply exploits workers in these developing countries. Clearly, such trade does hurt American workers in low-wage, low-skilled occupations who simply cannot compete with the even lower-wage

Issue: Is Outsourcing Just Another Form of Trade?

Lawrence Summers, President Obama's top economist, once argued that developed countries should consider moving "dirty" industries offshore to less developed countries (LDCs). Those countries have lower opportunity costs because pollution costs depend primarily on forgone earnings. He also suggested that developed nations should ship their solid waste to LDCs. He was roundly criticized for being "perfectly logical but totally insane." But what he suggested is just the logical extension of the generally agreed upon gains from comparative advantage and trade.

Professor N. Gregory Mankiw, who at the time headed President G.W. Bush's Council of Economic Advisers, suggested that outsourcing was only "the latest manifestation of the gains from trade that economists have talked about at least since Adam Smith. . . . More things are tradable than were tradable in the past, and that's a good thing."

These two highly respected economists seem to have few reservations about extending the benefits of comparative advantage and trade to seemingly unpopular sectors. For some time now, the popular media has blamed globalization and outsourcing for most of the United States's economic troubles. But are those critics correct?

Outsourcing became a hot topic right after the 2001 recession. The recovery was sluggish and job creation was anemic. Outsourcing, plant closings, and the shipping of production or services to low-cost areas has been going on in the United States for years. Manufacturing has been moving from north to south for a half-century. Nearly all new auto plants (both foreign and domestic) have been built in the South. Trade in products has been accepted throughout history, and manufacturing has been drifting offshore for several decades. But technological

progress in computers, communications, and the Internet has made the process easier, sparking an intense debate about shipping jobs overseas.

Most of the arguments against outsourcing were based on anecdotal evidence—a plant closing here, a closing there, and so on. But in the mid-2000s, the Bureau of Labor Statistics developed a survey to quantify the levels of both outsourcing and insourcing (the flow of jobs to the United States by firms from other countries) and discovered that the *net* effect was that roughly 2 million jobs (around 1% of total jobs) were being outsourced over those insourced. Further studies by several economists found that rising employment by U.S. multinational firms at their foreign subsidiaries led to more employment in the United States as well.

As we have seen, there are both winners and losers in trade. But in general, economists found that there is a net increase in income to U.S. residents from outsourcing. When all impacts are considered, including savings to consumers from lower product costs, imports of U.S. goods by foreigners, profits to U.S. affiliates, and the value of labor reemployed, a dollar spent on outsourcing resulted in over a dollar of increased income to U.S. residents.

Clearly, those who lose their jobs to outsourcing suffer. But our policy approach should not be to curtail outsourcing, but rather to help displaced workers receive assistance and training to move to jobs in high demand. Also, when a firm saves money through outsourcing, it can redirect those savings to other activities, such as product design or research and development, activities that strengthen the firm in the long run.

However, outsourcing is not without its inherent problems. It requires good commu-

Andrew Holbrooke/Corbis

nication and coordination with the foreign firm. NCR outsourced the production of bank ATMs in 2007 to cut costs. But ATMs are complex and company engineers often had to fly around the world to solve production and design problems, leading to delays that frustrated customers. Two years later, because of these problems, NCR moved production for domestic sales to a new plant in Georgia, just two hours from its corporate headquarters and its research campus.

The issue of outsourcing became a heated political debate in the jobless recovery of the mid-2000s. In response, the Bureau of Labor Statistics undertook its effort to actually measure the impact of outsourcing and insourcing. Once economists had hard numbers, the issue didn't feel so damaging to the economy (just specific workers in specific industries) and the profile of the issue seems to have faded. Outsourcing is just another example of the net benefits to trade, but policymakers should not lose sight of the harm to individuals and policy should be directed to retraining and getting them back on their feet.

Sources: N. Gregory Mankiw and Phillip Swagel, "The Politics and Economics of Offshore Outsourcing," *AEI Working Paper #122,* December 7, 2005; Peter Engardio, "Why NCR Said 'Let's Go Back Home'," *Business Week,* August 24, 2009; and W. Michael Cox, Richard Alm, and Justyna Dymerska, "Labor Market Globalization in the Recession and Beyond," *Economic Letter,* Federal Reserve Bank of Dallas, December 2009.

workers overseas. But it is not clear that workers in developing countries would be helped if the United States were to cut off its trade with those countries that refuse to improve their wages or working conditions.

Restricting trade with countries that do not raise their wages to levels we think acceptable or bring working conditions up to our standards would probably do more harm than good. Low wages reflect, among other factors, the low investments in human capital, low productivity, and low living standards characteristic of developing nations. Blocking trade with these nations may deprive them of their key chance to grow and to improve in those areas where we would like to see change.

Liberalized trade policies, economic freedom, and a legal system that respects property rights and foreign capital investment probably provide the best recipe for rapid development, economic growth, environmental protection, and improved wages and working conditions.

In summary, trade does result in job losses in some industries, but the gain to consumers and the competitive pressures that trade puts on domestic companies is beneficial to the economy as a whole. Trade raises incomes in developing nations, resulting in a growing demand for more environmentally friendly production processes. Trade is not the reason for low environmental standards in developing countries; they result from low incomes, low standards of living, and poor governmental policies. Trade brings about higher levels of income and ultimately better working conditions.

■ **CHECKPOINT**

ARGUMENTS AGAINST FREE TRADE

- The infant industries argument claims that some industries are so underdeveloped that they need protection to survive in a global competitive environment.

- Dumping involves selling products at different prices in domestic and foreign markets, often with the help of subsidies from the government. This is a form of predatory pricing to gain market share in the foreign market.

- Some suggest that domestic workers need to be protected from the low wages in foreign countries. This puts the smaller aggregate loss to small groups ahead of the greater general gains from trade. Also, for many countries, a low wage is their primary comparative advantage.

- Some argue that select industries need protection to ensure they will exist for national defense reasons.

- Clearly, globalization has meant that some U.S. workers have lost jobs to foreign competition, and some advocates would restrict trade on these grounds alone. But, on net, trade has led to higher overall employment. The U.S. government recognizes these issues and has instituted a Trade Adjustment Assistance (TAA) program to help workers who lose their jobs transition to new employment.

- Concern about the environment is often a factor in trade negotiations. Those concerned about globalization want to ensure that firms do not move production to countries with lax environmental laws, while others are concerned that environmental regulation not be used to justify protectionism. Trade ultimately raises income and environmental awareness in developing nations.

- Some antiglobalization activists consider shifting production to countries with low wages as exploitation and demand that wages be increased in other countries. Globalization has typically resulted in higher wages in developing nations, but not up to the standards of developed nations.

QUESTION: "The biggest gains in exports, imports, employment, and wages all occurred during the 1990s which was one of our greatest periods of economic growth. Thus it is clear that trade benefits both consumers and the economy." Evaluate this statement.

Answers to the Checkpoint question can be found at the end of this chapter.

Key Concepts

Absolute advantage, p. 364
Comparative advantage, p. 364
Terms of trade, p. 367
Tariff, p. 369

Quota, p. 370
Infant industry, p. 372
Dumping, p. 373

Chapter Summary

The Gains from Trade

Worldwide foreign trade has quadrupled over the past 25 years. Improved communications and transportation technologies have worked together to promote global economic integration. Most governments around the world have reduced trade barriers in recent years.

Free trade has not always been popular. In 1929–1930, many countries attempted to protect their domestic industries by imposing trade restrictions that discouraged imports. In 1930, the United States enacted the Smoot-Hawley tariffs, which imposed an average tax of 60% on imported goods. This hurt industries around the world and has been credited with adding to the depth of the global depression.

In a zero-sum game such as poker, for one party to gain, the other party must lose. Voluntary exchange and trade is a positive-sum game, meaning that both parties to a transaction can gain. These gains arise because of comparative advantage.

One country has an absolute advantage over another if it can produce more of some good than the other country. A country has a comparative advantage over another if its opportunity cost to produce some good is lower than the other country's. Even when one country has an absolute advantage over another, both stand to benefit from trade if each focuses its production on the goods or industries with a comparative advantage.

The Terms of Trade

The terms of trade determine the prices of imports and exports. When countries trade many commodities, the terms of trade are defined as the average price of exports divided by the average price of imports.

When two countries begin trading, the price charged for one good may be different in the two countries. As market forces lead each country to focus its production on the goods and industries at which it has a comparative advantage, that good's price will tend to equalize in the two countries, moving to an equilibrium level somewhere between the two original prices.

Though beneficial to both countries, trade produces winners and losers. Losers often seek trade restrictions.

The most common forms of trade restrictions are tariffs and quotas. A tariff is a tax on imports.

Tariffs generate revenues while driving a wedge between a product's domestic price and its price on the world market. When a tariff is imposed on a product, its price will rise. This benefits domestic producers, increasing their sales and the price they can charge, but the resulting price increase hurts domestic consumers. The government collects the tariff revenues.

Quotas restrict the quantity of imports into a country. Quotas have much the same effect as tariffs, except that they do not generate revenues for the government.

Arguments Against Free Trade

Despite the many benefits of free trade, arguments continue for restricting trade. One is that infant industries exist and require some protection to survive. The problem is determining when these industries mature.

Some American trade laws target dumping, which occurs when a foreign firm sells its goods below cost in the United States or at a price below what it charges in its domestic market. If the federal government determines that a foreign firm is dumping products onto the American market, it can impose antidumping tariffs on the offending products.

Some advocates of trade barriers maintain that domestic firms and their workers need to be protected from displacement by cheap foreign labor. Most economists estimate that the benefits of lower-priced imported goods exceed the costs of lost employment. The federal government has resisted imposing measures to protect jobs, instead funding programs that help displaced workers transition to new lines of work.

In times of national crisis or war, the United States must be able to rely on key domestic industries such as oil, steel, and the defense industry. Some argue that these industries require some protection even during peacetime to ensure that they exist when a crisis strikes and importing resources may be difficult.

Some critics argue that increased trade and globalization spell job losses for domestic workers. Increased trade, however, allows firms that are exporters to expand their operations and hire new workers. For workers who lose their jobs, switching industries can be difficult and time consuming, and often requires new investments in human capital. American trade policy recognizes this problem. The Trade Adjustment Assistance (TAA) program provides workers with job search assistance, job training, and some relocation allowances.

Concerns about globalization, trade, and environmental degradation are countered by the rising income brought on by trade, which in turn increases the demand for environmental protections.

Some antiglobalization activists argue that for the United States to trade with developing countries where wages are low and working conditions are deplorable simply exploits workers in these developing countries. But restricting trade with these countries would probably do more harm than good. Low wages reflect low investments in human capital, low productivity, and low living standards characteristic of developing nations. Blocking trade with these nations may deprive them of their only chance to grow and thus improve in these areas.

Questions and Problems

Check Your Understanding

1. What is the difference between absolute and comparative advantage? Why would Michelle Wie, who is better than you at both golf and laundry, still hire you to do her wash?

2. Who are the beneficiaries from a large U.S. tariff on French and German wine? Who are the losers?

Apply the Concepts

3. Brandeis University professor Stephen Cecchetti has argued that "if people understood the benefits of free trade as well as they do the rules of a favorite sport, there would be solid support for trade liberalization." Do you agree with Professor Cecchetti? Why or why not?

4. South Korean film production companies have been protected for half a century by policies enacted to protect an infant industry. But beginning in July 2006, the days that local films *must* be shown by any movie house was reduced to 73 from 146. South Korean film celebrities and the industry are fighting the changes even though local films command half the box office. Why would a country enact special protection for the local film industry? Who would be the major competitor threatening the South Korean film industry? If films made by the local industry must be shown 146 days a year, does the local industry have much incentive to develop good films and be competitive with the rest of the world?

5. Expanding trade in general benefits both countries, or they would not willingly engage in trade. But we also know that consumers and society often gain while particular industries or workers lose. Since society and consumers gain, why don't the many gainers compensate the few losers for their loss?

6. Some activist groups are calling for "fair trade laws" in which other countries would be required to meet or approach our environmental standards and provide wage and working conditions approaching those of developed nations in order to be able to trade with us. Is this just another form of rent seeking by industries and unions for protection from overseas competition?

7. Is outsourcing another example of the benefits of trade, in this case, trade between two companies? Many of the opponents of outsourcing are fans of the "open source" software movement that farms programming out to "volunteer" programmers or firms around the world. These individuals or firms must give their changes to the software to the open source community (run by a few people) and cannot sell the software, but can charge for services such as a help desk, technical improvements, or other services. Does the open source concept seem like trade between individuals?

8. Why is there free trade between states in the United States but not necessarily between countries?

9. Several decades ago, at the behest of the United Auto Workers (UAW) union and General Motors, Ford, and Chrysler, quotas were placed on the importation of Japanese cars to protect American auto manufacturers. Why didn't these quotas work? Would additional trade restrictions benefit American auto workers in the UAW? Would they benefit American consumers?

10. Remittances from developed countries are over $200 billion each year. These funds are sent to their home countries by migrants in developed nations. Is this similar to the gains from trade discussed in this chapter, or are these workers just taking jobs that workers in developed countries would be paid more to do in the absence of the migrants?

11. Why might protectionist trade barriers not save American jobs or benefit the economy?

12. Suppose Brazil developed a secret process that effectively quadrupled its output of coffee from its coffee plantations. This secret process enabled it to significantly undercut the prices of U.S. domestic producers. Would domestic producers receive a sympathetic ear to calls for protection from Brazil's lower-cost coffee? How is this case different from that of protection against cheap foreign labor?

13. Three economists estimated the benefits of trade to the American economy since 1950.[3] Looking at the benefits from comparative advantage, economies of scale, diffusion of production technology, and many other factors, they estimated that trade accounted for roughly 20% of the gains in GDP per person. With such gains from trade to the average household, why would so many people seem to be against trade and globalization?

In the News

14. Economist Steven Landsburg (*New York Times* January 16, 2008, p. A23) makes the point that "bullying and protectionism have a lot in common. They both use force (either directly or through the power of the law) to enrich someone else at your involuntary expense. If you're forced to pay $20 an hour to an American for goods you could have bought from a Mexican for $5 an hour, you're being extorted." He also argues, "Surely we have fellow citizens who are hurt by those [trade] agreements, at least in the limited sense that they'd be better off in a world where trade

---

[3] Scott C. Bradford, Paul L. E. Grieco, and Gary Clyde Hufbauer, "The Payoff to America from Global Integration," in C. Fred Bergsten and the Institute for International Economics, *The United States and the World Economy* (Washington, DC: Institute for International Economics, 2005), Chap. 2.

flourishes, except in this one instance. What do we owe those fellow citizens?" The United States has programs to educate and retrain workers displaced from free trade agreements. Do we even owe them that? Why?

15. *The Economist* (November 21, 2009) suggests that in a highly globalized world where production is easily moved to other countries, there is an inherent tension between our desire to reduce carbon emissions to stem global climate change and our commitment to free trade. Do you agree? Why or why not?

Solving Problems

16. The figure below shows the production possibilities frontiers (PPFs) for Italy and India for their domestic production of olives and tea. Without trade, assume that each is consuming olives and tea at point *a*.

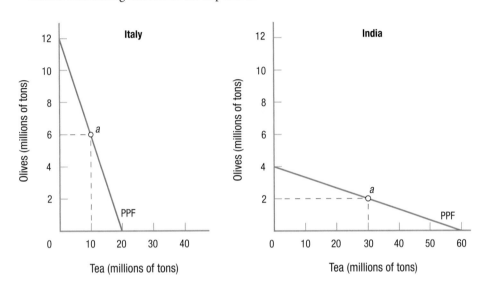

a. If Italy and India were to consider specialization and trade, what commodity would each specialize in? What is India's opportunity cost for tea and olives? What is Italy's opportunity cost for tea and olives?

b. Assume the two countries agree to specialize entirely in one product (the one in which each country has a comparative advantage), and agree to split the total output between them. Complete the table below. Are both countries better off after trade?

Country and Product		Before Specialization	After Specialization	After Trade
Italy	Olives	6 million tons	_____	_____
	Tea	10 million tons	_____	_____
India	Olives	2 million tons	_____	_____
	Tea	30 million tons	_____	_____

17. The figure on the next page shows the annual domestic demand and supply for 2GB compact flash cards for digital cameras.

a. Assume the worldwide price of these 2GB cards is $10. What percent of United States sales would be imported?

b. Assume the U.S. government puts a $5 tariff per card on imports. How many 2GB flash cards would be imported into the United States?

c. Given the tariff in question b, how much revenue would the government collect from this tariff?

d. Given the tariff in question b, how much more sales revenue would domestic companies enjoy as a result of the tariff?

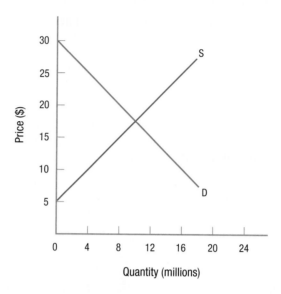

18. Most of the developed countries (Canada, Australia, the United States, Switzerland and Hong Kong) in the By-The-Numbers graph at the beginning of the chapter have relatively low tariff barriers while much the developing world still has high tariffs on imports. What reasons might account for why these countries continue to have high tariffs?

Answers to Questions in CheckPoints

Check Point: The Gains From Trade

Yes, in general, nations would not trade unless they benefit. However, as we have seen, even though nations as a whole gain, specific groups—industries and their workers who do not have a comparative advantage—lose.

Check Point: The Terms of Trade

When a quota is imposed, the first beneficiary is the domestic industry. Competition from foreign competition is limited. If the market is important enough (as we saw with automobiles), the foreign companies build new plants in the United States and compete as if they are domestic firms. A second beneficiary is foreign competitors in that they can increase the price or complexity of their products and increase their margins. Losers are consumers and, to some extent, the government, because a tariff could have accomplished the same reduction in imports and the government would have collected some revenue.

Check Point: Arguments Against Free Trade

Clearly the 1990s were a period of high growth in both trade and employment. The 1990s were also a time of heavy investment by businesses in technology and communications. Some industries and their employees were losers from trade, but the economy and other industries were clearly winners. Production employment has been on a steady decline over the last half-century as services have become more important. When the most recent recession led to lost jobs and unemployment rose, more attention was focused on trade and outsourcing as a source of those lost jobs.

Glossary

Absolute advantage One country can produce more of a good than another country.

Adverse selection Occurs when products of different qualities are sold at the same price because of asymmetric information.

Agency shop Employees are not required to join the union, but must pay dues to compensate the union for its services.

Allocative efficiency The mix of goods and services produced is just what the society desires. The price that consumers pay is equal to marginal cost and is also equal to the least average total cost.

Antitrust law Laws designed to maintain competition and prevent monopolies from developing.

Asymmetric information Occurs when one party to a transaction has significantly better information than another party.

Average cost pricing rule Requires a regulated monopolist to produce and sell output where price equals average total costs. This permits the regulated monopolist to earn a normal return on investment over the long term and so remain in business.

Average fixed cost Equal to total fixed cost divided by output (TFC/Q).

Average product Output per worker, found by dividing total output by the number of workers employed to produce that output (Q/L).

Average total cost Equal to total cost divided by output (TC/Q). Average total cost is also equal to AFC + AVC.

Average variable cost Equal to total variable cost divided by output (TVC/Q).

Budget line Graphically illustrates the possible combinations of two goods that can be purchased with a given income, given the prices of both products.

Capital Includes manufactured products such as welding machines, computers, and cellular phones that are used to produce other goods and services. The payment to capital is referred to as interest.

Cartel An agreement between firms (or countries) in an industry to formally collude on price and output, then agree on the distribution of production.

Ceteris paribus Assumption used in economics (and other disciplines as well), where other relevant factors or variables are held constant.

Change in demand Occurs when one or more of the determinants of demand changes, shown as a shift in the entire demand curve.

Change in quantity demanded Occurs when the price of the product changes, shown as a movement along an existing demand curve.

Change in quantity supplied Occurs when the price of the product changes, shown as a movement along an existing supply curve.

Change in supply Occurs when one or more of the determinants of supply change, shown as a shift in the entire supply curve.

Closed shop Workers must belong to the union before they can be hired.

Coase theorem If transaction costs are minimal (near zero), a bargain struck between beneficiaries and victims of externalities will be efficient from a resource allocation perspective. As a result, the socially optimal level of production will be reached.

Command and control policies Environmental policies that set standards and issue regulations, which are then enforced by the legal and regulatory system.

Common property resources Resources that are owned by the community at large (parks, ocean fish, and the atmosphere) and therefore tend to be overexploited because individuals have little incentive to use them in a sustainable fashion.

Comparative advantage One country has a lower opportunity cost of producing a good than another country.

Competition Exists when there are many relatively small buyers and sellers, a standardized product, with good information to both buyers and sellers, and no barriers to entry or exit.

Complementary goods Goods that are typically consumed together. When the *price* of a complementary good rises, the *demand* for the other good declines, and vice versa.

Complements Goods that are typically consumed together, such as coffee and sugar. Complements have a negative cross elasticity of demand.

Concentration ratio The share of industry shipments or sales accounted for by the top four or eight firms.

Constant cost industry An industry that in the long run faces roughly the same prices and costs as industry output expands. Some industries can virtually clone their operations in other areas without putting undue pressure on resource prices, resulting in constant operating costs as they expand in the long run.

Constant returns to scale A range of output where average total costs are relatively constant. Fast-food restaurants and movie theatres are examples.

Consumer surplus The difference between market price and what consumers (as individuals or the market) would be willing to pay. It is equal to the area above market price and below the demand curve.

Contestable markets Markets that look monopolistic but have entry costs so low that the sheer threat of entry keeps prices low.

Corporation A business structure that has most of the legal rights of individuals, and in addition, the corporation can issue stock to raise capital. Stockholders' liability is limited to the value of their stock.

Cost-benefit analysis A methodology for decision making that looks at the discounted value of the costs and benefits of a given project.

Cross elasticity of demand Measures how responsive the quantity demanded of one good is to changes in the price of another good. Substitute goods have positive cross elasticities: An increase in the price of one good leads consumers to substitute (buy more) of the other good whose price has not changed. Complementary goods have negative cross elasticities: An increase in the price of a complement leads to a reduction in sales of the other good whose price has not changed.

Deadweight loss The loss in consumer and producer surplus due to inefficiency because some transactions cannot be made and therefore their value to society is lost.

Decreasing cost industry An industry that in the long run faces lower prices and costs as industry output expands. Some industries enjoy economies of scale as they expand in the long run, typically the result of technological advances.

Demand The maximum amount of a product that buyers are willing and able to purchase over some time period at various prices, holding all other relevant factors constant (the *ceteris paribus* condition).

Demand curve Demand schedule information translated to a graph.

Demand for labor Demand for labor is derived from the demand for the firm's product and the productivity of labor.

Determinants of demand Nonprice factors that affect demand, including tastes and preferences, income, prices of related goods, number of buyers, and expectations.

Determinants of supply Nonprice factors that affect supply, including production technology, costs of resources, prices of other commodities, expectations, number of sellers, and taxes and subsidies.

Diminishing marginal returns An additional worker adds to total output, but at a diminishing rate.

Diseconomies of scale A range of output where average total costs tend to increase. Firms often become so big that management becomes bureaucratic and unable to efficiently control its operations.

Dumping Selling goods abroad at lower prices than in home markets, and often below cost.

Dynamic games Sequential or repeated games where the players can adjust their actions based on the decisions of other players in the past.

Economic costs The sum of explicit (out-of-pocket) and implicit (opportunity) costs.

Economic discrimination When workers of equal ability are paid different wages or in any other way discriminated against because of race, color, religion, gender, age, national origin, or disability.

Economic profits Profits in excess of normal profits. These are profits in excess of both explicit and implicit costs.

Economies of scale As a firm's output increases, its LRATC tends to decline. This results from specialization of labor and management, and potentially a better use of capital and complementary production techniques.

Economies of scope By producing a number of products that are interdependent, firms are able to produce and market these goods at lower costs.

Efficiency How well resources are used and allocated. Do people get the goods and services they want at the lowest possible resource cost? This is the chief focus of efficiency.

Elastic demand The absolute value of the price elasticity of demand is greater than 1. Elastic demands are very responsive to changes in price. The percentage change in quantity demanded is greater than the percentage change in price.

Elastic supply Price elasticity of supply is greater than 1. The percentage change in quantity supplied is greater than the percentage change in price.

Elasticity of demand for labor The percentage change in the quantity of labor demanded divided by the percentage change in the wage rate.

Entrepreneurs Entrepreneurs combine land, labor, and capital to produce goods and services. They absorb the risk of being in business, including the risk of bankruptcy and other liabilities associated with doing business. Entrepreneurs receive profits for this effort.

Equilibrium Market forces are in balance when the quantities demanded by consumers just equal the quantities supplied by producers.

Equilibrium price Market equilibrium price is the price that results when quantity demanded is just equal to quantity supplied.

Equilibrium quantity Market equilibrium quantity is the output that results when quantity demanded is just equal to quantity supplied.

Equity The fairness of various issues and policies.

Explicit costs Those expenses paid directly to another economic entity, including wages, lease payments, taxes, and utilities.

External benefits Positive externalities, such as education and vaccinations. Private markets provide too little at too high a price of goods with external benefits.

External cost (or negative externality) Occurs when a transaction between two parties has an impact on a third party not involved with the transaction. External costs are negative, such as pollution or congestion. The market provides too much of a product with negative externalities at too low a cost.

Externalities The impact on third parties of some transaction between others where the third parties are not involved. An external cost (or negative externality) harms the third parties, whereas external benefits (positive externalities) result in gains to them.

Firm An economic institution that transforms resources (factors of production) into outputs for consumers.

Fixed costs Costs that do not change as a firm's output expands or contracts, often called overhead. These include items such as lease payments, administrative expenses, property taxes, and insurance.

Free rider When a public good is provided, consumers cannot be excluded from enjoying the product, so some consume the product without paying.

Functional distribution of income The distribution of income for resources or factors of production (land, labor, capital, and entrepreneurial ability).

Game theory An approach to analyzing oligopoly behavior using mathematics and simulation by making different assumptions about the players, time involved, level of information, strategies, and other aspects of the game.

General training Training that improves a worker's productivity in all firms.

Gini coefficient A precise method of measuring the position of the Lorenz curve, defined as the area between the Lorenz curve and the equal distribution line divided by the total area below the equal distribution line.

Government failure The result when the incentives of politicians and government bureaucrats do not align with the public interest.

Herfindahl-Hirshman index (HHI) A way of measuring industry concentration, equal to the sum of the squares of market shares for all firms in the industry.

Horizontal summation Market demand and supply curves are found by adding together how many units of the product will be purchased or supplied at each price.

Implicit costs The opportunity costs of using resources that belong to the firm, including depreciation, depletion of business assets, and the opportunity cost of the firm's capital employed in the business.

Incidence of taxation Refers to who bears the economic burden of a tax. The economic entity bearing the burden of a particular tax will depend on the price elasticities of demand and supply.

Income A flow measure reflecting the funds received by individuals or households over a period of time, usually a week, month, or year.

Income deficit The difference between the poverty threshold and a family's income.

Income effect When higher prices essentially reduce consumer income, the quantity demanded for normal goods falls.

Income effect, labor Higher wages mean you can maintain the same standard of living by working fewer hours. The impact on labor supply is generally negative.

Income elasticity of demand Measures how responsive quantity demanded is to changes in consumer income.

Increasing cost industry An industry that in the long run faces higher prices and costs as industry output expands. Industry expansion puts upward pressure on resources (inputs), causing higher costs in the long run.

Increasing marginal returns A new worker hired adds more to total output than the previous worker hired, so that both average and marginal products are rising.

Indifference curve Shows all the combinations of two goods where the consumer is indifferent (gets the same level of satisfaction).

Indifference map An infinite set of indifference curves where each curve represents a different level of utility or satisfaction.

Inelastic demand The absolute value of the price elasticity of demand is less than 1. Inelastic demands are not very responsive to changes in price. The percentage change in quantity demanded is less than the percentage change in price.

Inelastic supply Price elasticity of supply is less than 1. The percentage change in quantity supplied is less than the percentage change in price.

Infant industry An industry so underdeveloped that protection is needed for it to become competitive on the world stage or to ensure its survival.

Inferior goods Goods that have income elasticities that are negative. When consumer income grows, quantity demanded falls for inferior goods.

Investment in human capital Investments such as education and on-the-job training that improve the productivity of human labor.

Kinked demand curve An oligopoly model that assumes that if a firm raises its price, competitors will not raise theirs; but if the firm lowers its price, all of its competitors will lower their price to match the reduction. This leads to a kink in the demand curve and relatively stable market prices.

Labor Includes the mental and physical talents of individuals who produce goods and services. The payment to labor is called wages.

Land Includes natural resources such as mineral deposits, oil, natural gas, water, and land in the usual sense of the word. The payment to land as a resource is called rent.

Law of demand Holding all other relevant factors constant, as price increases, quantity demanded falls, and as price decreases, quantity demanded rises.

Law of diminishing marginal utility As we consume more of a given product, the added satisfaction we get from consuming an additional unit declines.

Law of supply Holding all other relevant factors constant, as price increases, quantity supplied will rise, and as price declines, quantity supplied will fall.

Long run Time period long enough for firms to alter their plant capacities and for the number of firms in the industry to change. Existing firms can expand or build new plants, or firms can enter or exit the industry.

Long-run average total cost (LRATC) In the long run, firms can adjust their plant sizes so LRATC is the lowest unit cost at which any particular output can be produced in the long run.

Lorenz curves A graphical method of showing the income distribution by cumulating families of various income levels on the horizontal axis and relating this to their cumulative share of total income on the vertical axis.

Luxury goods Goods that have income elasticities greater than 1. When consumer income grows, quantity demanded of luxury goods rises more than the rise in income.

Macroeconomics The broader issues in the economy such as inflation, unemployment, and national output of goods and services.

Marginal cost The change in total costs arising from the production of additional units of output ($\Delta TC/\Delta Q$). Since fixed costs do not change with output, marginal costs are the change in variable costs associated with additional production ($\Delta TVC/\Delta Q$).

Marginal cost pricing rule Regulators would prefer to have natural monopolists price where $P = MC$, but this would result in losses (long term)

Marginal cost pricing rule (*continued*) because ATC > MC. Thus, regulators often must use an average cost pricing rule.

Marginal factor cost (MFC) The added cost associated with hiring one more unit of labor. For competitive firms, it is equal to the wage; but for monopsonists, it is higher than the new wage (W) because all existing workers must be paid this higher new wage, making MFC > W.

Marginal physical product of labor The additional output a firm receives from employing an added unit of labor ($MPP_L = \Delta Q \div \Delta L$).

Marginal product The change in output that results from a change in labor ($\Delta Q / \Delta L$).

Marginal revenue The change in total revenue from selling an additional unit of output. Since competitive firms are price takers, P = MR for competitive firms.

Marginal revenue product The value of another worker to the firm is equal to the marginal physical product of labor (MPP_L) times marginal revenue (MR).

Marginal utility The satisfaction received from consuming an additional unit of a given product or service.

Marginal utility analysis A theoretical framework underlying consumer decision making. This approach assumes that satisfaction can be measured and that consumers maximize satisfaction when the marginal utilities per dollar are equal for all products and services.

Market failures When markets are not competitive or involve public goods, externalities, or common property resources, markets will fail to provide the optimal level of output, and will provide output at too high or low a price.

Market period Time period so short that the output and the number of firms are fixed. Agricultural products at harvest time face market periods. Products that unexpectedly become instant hits face market periods (there is a lag between when the firm realizes it has a hit on its hands and when inventory can be replaced).

Market structure analysis By observing a few industry characteristics such as number of firms in the industry or the level of barriers to entry, economists can use this information to predict pricing and output behavior of the firm in the industry.

Market-based policies Environmental policies that use charges, taxes, subsidies, deposit-refund systems, or tradable emission permits to achieve environmental ends.

Markets Institutions that bring buyers and sellers together so they can interact and transact with each other.

Microeconomics The decision making by individuals, businesses, industries, and governments.

Monopolistic competition Involves a large number of small firms and is similar to competition, with easy entry and exit, but unlike the competitive model, the firms have differentiated their products. This differentiation is either real or imagined by consumers and involves innovations, advertising, location, or other ways of making one firm's product different from that of its competitors.

Monopolistic exploitation of labor When a firm has monopoly power in the product market, marginal revenue is less than price (MR < P) and the firm hires labor up to the point where MRP_L = wage. Because MRP_L is less than the VMP_L, workers are paid less than the value of their marginal product, and this difference is called monopolistic exploitation of labor.

Monopoly A one-firm industry with no close product substitutes and with substantial barriers to entry.

Monopoly power A firm with monopoly power has some control over price.

Monopsonistic exploitation of labor Because monopsonists hire less labor than competitive firms, and workers are paid less than the value of their marginal products, this difference is referred to as monopsonistic exploitation of labor.

Monopsony A labor market with one employer.

Moral hazard Asymmetric information problem that occurs when an insurance policy or some other arrangement changes the economic incentives and leads to a change in behavior.

Mutual interdependence When only a few firms constitute an industry, each firm must consider the reactions of its competitors to its decisions.

Nash equilibrium An important proof that an *n*-person game where each player chooses his optimal strategy, given that all other players have done the same, has a solution. This was important because economists now knew that even complex models (or games) had an equilibrium, or solution.

Natural monopoly Large economies of scale mean that the minimum efficient scale of operations is roughly equal to market demand.

Network externalities Markets in which the network becomes more valuable as more people are connected to the network.

Nonexcludability Once a good or service is provided, it is not feasible to exclude others from enjoying that good or service.

Nonrivalry The consumption of a good or service by one person does not reduce the utility of that good or service to others.

Normal goods Goods that have positive income elasticities of less than 1. When consumer income grows, quantity demanded rises for normal goods, but less than the rise in income.

Normal profits Equal to zero economic profits; where P = ATC. The return on capital necessary to keep investors satisfied and keep capital in the business over the long run.

Oligopoly A market with just a few firms dominating the industry where (1) each firm recognizes that it must consider its competitors' reactions when making its own decisions (mutual interdependence), and (2) there are significant barriers to entry into the market.

On-the-job training Training typically done by employers, ranging from suggestions at work to sophisticated seminars.

Opportunity cost The cost paid for one product in terms of the output (or consumption) of another product that must be forgone. The next best alternative; what you give up to do something or purchase something.

For example, to watch a movie at a theater, there is not just the monetary cost of the tickets and refreshments, but the time involved in watching the movie. You could have been doing something else (knitting, golfing, hiking, or studying economics).

Partnership Similar to a sole proprietorship, but involves more than one owner who shares the management of the business. Partnerships are also subject to unlimited liability.

Personal or family distribution of income The distribution of income to individuals or family groups (typically quintiles, or fifths, of the population).

Poverty thresholds Income levels for various household sizes, below which people are considered to be living in poverty.

Predatory pricing Selling below cost to consumers in the short run, hoping to eliminate competitors so that prices can be raised in the longer run to earn economic profits.

Present value The value of an investment (future stream of income) today. The higher the discount rate, the lower the present value today, and vice versa.

Price caps Maximum price at which a regulated firm can sell its product. They are often flexible enough to allow for changing cost conditions.

Price ceiling A government-set maximum price that can be charged for a product or service. When the price ceiling is set below equilibrium, it leads to shortages.

Price discrimination Charging different consumer groups different prices for the same product.

Price elasticity of demand A measure of the responsiveness of quantity demanded to a change in price, equal to the percentage change in quantity demanded divided by the percentage change in price.

Price elasticity of supply A measure of the responsiveness of quantity supplied to changes in price. An elastic supply curve has elasticity greater than 1, whereas inelastic supplies have elasticities less than 1. Time is the most important determinant of the elasticity of supply.

Price floor A government-set minimum price that can be charged for a product or service. When the price floor is set above equilibrium, it leads to surpluses.

Price system A name given to the market economy because prices provide considerable information to both buyers and sellers.

Price taker Individual firms in competitive markets get their prices from the market since they are so small they cannot influence market price. For this reason, competitive firms are price takers and can produce and sell all the output they produce at market-determined prices.

Prisoner's Dilemma A noncooperative game where players cannot communicate or collaborate in making their decisions about whether to confess or not, which results in inferior outcomes for both players. Many oligopoly decisions can be framed as a Prisoner's Dilemma.

Producer surplus The difference between market price and the price at which firms are willing to supply the product. It is equal to the area below market price and above the supply curve.

Product differentiation One firm's product is distinguished from another's through advertising, innovation, and location, and so on.

Production The process of converting resources (factors of production)—land, labor, capital, and entrepreneurial ability—into goods and services. Also can be considered the process of turning inputs into outputs.

Production efficiency Goods and services are produced at their lowest resource (opportunity) cost.

Production possibilities frontier (PPF) Shows the combinations of two goods that are possible for a society to produce at full employment. Points on or inside the PPF are feasible, and those outside of the frontier are unattainable.

Productive efficiency Goods and services are produced and sold to consumers at their lowest resource (opportunity) cost.

Profit Equal to the difference between total revenue and total cost.

Profit maximizing rule Firms maximize profit by producing output where $MR = MC$. No other level of output produces higher profits.

Property rights The clear delineation of ownership of property backed by government enforcement.

Public goods Goods that, once provided, no one person can be excluded from consuming (nonexclusion), and one person's consumption does not diminish the benefit to others from consuming the good (nonrivalry).

Quota A government-set limit on the quantity of imports into a country.

Rate of return Uses the present value formula, but subtracts costs, then finds the interest rate (discount rate) at which this investment would break even.

Rate of return regulation Permits product pricing that allows the firm to earn a normal return on capital invested in the firm.

Ratio of income to poverty The ratio of family income to the poverty threshold. Families with ratios below 0.5 are considered severely poor, families with ratios between 0.5 and 1.0 are considered poor, and those families with ratios between 1.0 and 1.25 are considered near poor.

Rent The return to land as a factor of production. Sometimes called economic rent.

Rent seeking Resources expended to protect a monopoly position. These are used for such activities as lobbying, extending patents, and restricting the number of licenses permitted.

Resources Productive resources include land (land and natural resources), labor (mental and physical talents of people), capital (manufactured products used to produce other products), and entrepreneurial ability (the combining of the other factors to produce products and assume the risk of the business).

Revenue Equal to price per unit times quantity sold.

Right-to-work laws Laws created by the Taft-Hartley Act that permitted states to outlaw union shops.

Scarcity Our unlimited wants clash with limited resources, leading to scarcity. Everyone faces scarcity (rich and poor) because, at a minimum, our time is limited on earth. Economics

Scarcity *(continued)*
focuses on the allocation of scarce resources to satisfy unlimited wants.

Screening/signaling The argument that higher education simply lets employers know that the prospective employee is intelligent and trainable and has the discipline potentially to be a good employee.

Secondary boycott Occurs when unions clash with one firm and put pressure on a neutral, second firm to enlist the help of the second firm to obtain the union's objectives with the original firm.

Segmented labor markets Labor markets split into separate parts. This leads to different wages paid to different sectors even though both markets are highly competitive.

Short run Time period when plant capacity and the number of firms in the industry cannot change. Firms can employ more people, use overtime with existing employees, or hire part-time employees to produce more, but this is done in an existing plant.

Short-run supply curve The marginal cost curve above the minimum point on the average variable cost curve.

Shortage Occurs when the price is below market equilibrium, and quantity demanded exceeds quantity supplied.

Shutdown point When price in the short run falls below the minimum point on the AVC curve, the firm will minimize losses by closing its doors and stopping production. Since P < AVC, the firm's variable costs are not covered, so by shutting the plant, losses are reduced to fixed costs only.

Social welfare The sum of consumer and producer surplus.

Sole proprietor A type of business structure composed of a single owner who supervises and manages the business and is subject to unlimited liability.

Specific training Training that improves a worker's productivity in a specific firm.

Static games One-off games (not repeated) where decisions by the players are made simultaneously and are irreversible.

Substitute goods Goods consumers will substitute for one another depending on their relative prices. When the *price* of one good rises and the *demand* for another good increases, they are substitute goods, and vice versa.

Substitutes Goods consumers substitute for one another depending on their relative prices, such as coffee and tea. Substitutes have a positive cross elasticity of demand.

Substitution effect When the price of one good rises, consumers will substitute other goods for that good, so the quantity demanded for the higher priced good falls.

Substitution effect, labor Higher wages mean that the value of work has increased, and the opportunity costs of leisure are higher, so work is substituted for leisure.

Sunk costs Those costs that have been incurred and cannot be recovered, including, for example, funds spent on existing technology that have become obsolete and past advertising that has run in the media.

Supply The maximum amount of a product that sellers are willing and able to provide for sale over some time period at various prices, holding all other relevant factors constant (the *ceteris paribus* condition).

Supply curve Supply schedule information translated to a graph.

Supply of labor The amount of time an individual is willing to work at various wage rates.

Surplus Occurs when the price is above market equilibrium, and quantity supplied exceeds quantity demanded.

Tariff A tax on imported products. When a country taxes imported products, it drives a wedge between the product's domestic price and its price on the world market.

Terms of trade The ratio of the price of exported goods to the price of imported goods (P_x/P_m).

Tit-for-tat strategies Simple strategies that repeat the prior move of competitors. If your opponent lowers price, you do the same. This approach has the efficient quality that it rewards cooperation and punishes unfavorable strategies (defections).

Total revenue Price times quantity demanded (sold). If demand is elastic and price rises, quantity demanded falls off significantly and total revenue declines, and vice versa. If demand is inelastic and price rises, quantity demanded does not decline much and total revenue rises, and vice versa.

Total utility The total satisfaction that a person receives from consuming a given amount of goods and services.

Tragedy of the commons Resources that are owned by the community at large (e.g., parks, ocean fish, and the atmosphere) and therefore tend to be overexploited because individuals have little incentive to use them in a sustainable fashion.

Trigger strategies Action is taken contingent on your opponent's past decisions.

Union shop Non-union hires must join the union within a specified period of time.

Unitary elastic supply Price elasticity of supply is equal to 1. The percentage change in quantity supplied is equal to the percentage change in price.

Unitary elasticity of demand The absolute value of the price elasticity of demand is equal to 1. The percentage change in quantity demanded is just equal to the percentage change in price.

Utility A hypothetical measure of consumer satisfaction.

Utility maximizing rule Utility is maximized where the marginal utility per dollar is equal for all products, or $MU_a/P_a = MU_b/P_b = \ldots = MU_n/P_n$.

Value of the marginal product The value of the marginal product of labor (VMP_L) is equal to price multiplied by the marginal physical product of labor, or $P \times MPP_L$.

Variable costs Costs that vary with output fluctuations, including expenses such as labor and material costs.

Wealth A stock measure of an individual's or family's assets, net of liabilities, at a given point in time.

X-inefficiency Protected from competitive pressures, monopolies do not have to act efficiently. Spending on corporate jets, travel, and other perks of business represent x-inefficiency.

Index

The following pages consist of

Gerald R. Stone's
Course Tutor
for
Chapter 3
Supply and Demand

The *CourseTutor* is a comprehensive learning tool for students. Gerald Stone created and wrote the CourseTutor as an integrated resource for students using his textbook.

The complete CourseTutor can be packaged for no additional charge with *CoreEconomics, CoreMicroeconomics,* or *CoreMacroeconomics.*

Please contact your local Worth representative for ordering instructions.
Or email us at salessupport@worthpub.com.
Visit us at www.wortheconomics.com.

Supply and Demand 3

Illustration Works/Alamy

Most Economic Issues Involve Supply and Demand in Some Way

Supply and demand form the foundation of economics. You will use these concepts throughout the remainder of the semester. To understand how market economies operate, you will need to have a firm grasp of supply and demand analysis. Nearly every economic problem you confront will be clarified in some way by this analysis.

This Is What You Need to Know	STEP 1

After studying this chapter you should be able to

- Describe the nature and purposes of markets.
- Describe the nature of demand, demand curves, and the law of demand.
- Describe the determinants of demand and be able to forecast how a change in one or more of these determinants will change demand.
- Describe the difference between a change in demand and a change in quantity demanded.
- Describe the nature of supply, supply curves, and the law of supply.
- Describe the determinants of supply and be able to forecast how a change in one or more of these determinants will change supply.
- Describe the difference between a change in supply and a change in quantity supplied.
- Determine market equilibrium price and output.

■ Determine and predict how price and output will change given changes to supply and demand in the market.

■ Understand the impacts of government intervention in markets.

STEP 2

Review the Key Terms

Markets: Institutions that bring buyers and sellers together so they can interact and transact with each other.

Price system: A name given to the market economy because prices provide considerable information to both buyers and sellers.

Demand: The maximum amount of a product that buyers are willing and able to purchase over some time period at various prices, holding all other relevant factors constant (the *ceteris paribus* condition).

Law of demand: Holding all other relevant factors constant, as price increases, quantity demanded falls, and as price decreases, quantity demanded rises.

Demand curve: Demand schedule information translated to a graph.

Horizontal summation: Market demand and supply curves are found by adding together how many units of the product will be purchased or supplied at each price.

Determinants of demand: Nonprice factors that affect demand, including tastes and preferences, income, prices of related goods, number of buyers, and expectations.

Normal good: A good for which an increase in income results in rising demand.

Inferior good: A good for which an increase in income results in declining demand.

Substitute goods: Goods consumers will substitute for one another depending on their relative prices.

Complementary goods: Goods that are typically consumed together.

Change in demand: Occurs when one or more of the determinants of demand changes, shown as a shift in the entire demand curve.

Change in quantity demanded: Occurs when the price of the product changes, shown as a movement along an existing demand curve.

Supply: The maximum amount of a product that sellers are willing and able to provide for sale over some time period at various prices, holding all other relevant factors constant (the *ceteris paribus* condition).

Law of supply: Holding all other relevant factors constant, as price increases, quantity supplied will rise, and as price declines, quantity supplied will fall.

Supply curve: Supply schedule information translated to a graph.

Determinants of supply: Nonprice factors that affect supply, including production technology, costs of resources, prices of other commodities, expectations, number of sellers, and taxes and subsidies.

Change in supply: Occurs when one or more of the determinants of supply change, shown as a shift in the entire supply curve.

Change in quantity supplied: Occurs when the price of the product changes, shown as a movement along an existing supply curve.

Equilibrium: Market forces are in balance when the quantities demanded by consumers just equal the quantities supplied by producers.

Equilibrium price: Market equilibrium price is the price that results when quantity demanded is just equal to quantity supplied.

Equilibrium quantity: Market equilibrium quantity is the output that results when quantity demanded is just equal to quantity supplied.

Surplus: Occurs when the price is above market equilibrium, and quantity supplied exceeds quantity demanded.

Shortage: Occurs when the price is below market equilibrium, and quantity demanded exceeds quantity supplied.

Price ceiling: A government-set maximum price that can be charged for a product or service. When the price ceiling is set below equilibrium, it leads to shortages.

Price floor: A government-set minimum price that can be charged for a product or service. When the price floor is set above equilibrium, it leads to surpluses.

Work Through the Chapter Tutorials	STEP 3

Demand

Frequently Asked Questions

Q: What are markets, and why are they important?

A: Markets are institutions that enable buyers and sellers to interact and transact business with one another. Through their purchases, consumers signal their willingness to buy particular products at particular prices. These signals help businesses to decide what and how much to produce.

Q: What is demand, and how are price and quantity demanded related?

A: *Demand* refers to the quantity of products people are willing and able to purchase at various prices during some specific time period, all other relevant factors held constant. The *demand curve* shown in Figure 1 depicts the relationship between price and quantity demanded. Price and quantity demanded are negatively (inversely) related: As prices rise, consumers buy less, and vice versa. This inverse relation is known as the *law of demand*.

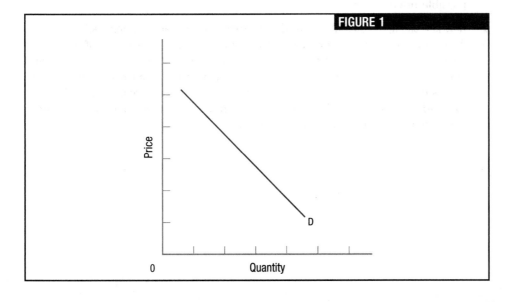

FIGURE 1

Q: What are the determinants of demand?

A: The *determinants of demand* include the following:

- Consumer tastes and preferences
- Income
- Prices of substitutes and complements
- The number of buyers in the market
- Expectations regarding future prices, incomes, and product availability

Q: What causes the demand curve to shift?

A: *Demand changes (shifts)* when one or more of these determinants change. In Figure 2 a new popular ad campaign for Nalgene bottles would shift demand from D_0 to D_1. Alternatively, the ease of making digital copies could reduce the demand for music CDs, as shown by the demand curve declining from D_0 to D_2.

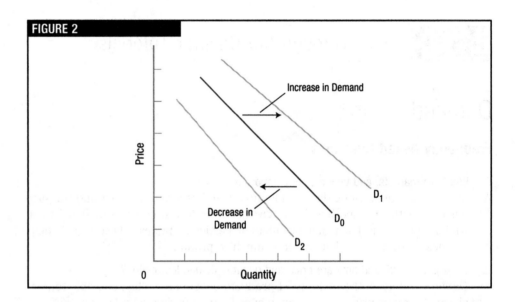

FIGURE 2

Q: How are market demand curves determined?

A: *Market demand curves* are found by horizontally summing individual demand curves. We simply add the total quantities demanded by all consumers for each possible price.

Q: How is a change in quantity demanded different from a change in demand?

A: A *change in quantity demanded* occurs only when the *price* of a product changes, leading consumers to adjust their purchases along an existing demand curve. This is shown in Figure 3 as a movement from point a to point b. Note in this case that a reduced price of P_2 was required to increase sales. Contrast this with the movement from point a to point c (an increase in demand), where much more is sold at the same price, P_0.

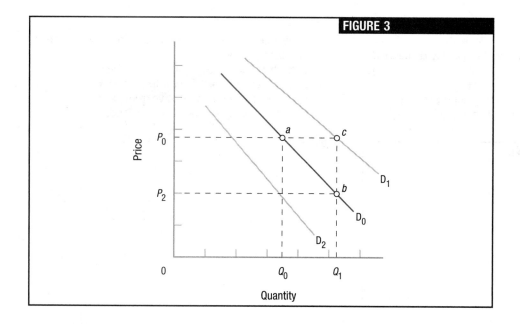

FIGURE 3

Demand Quick Check

Circle the Correct Answer

1. (T/F) The major benefit of markets is that they bring sellers and buyers together to transact business.
2. (T/F) The law of demand states that demand increases (demand curves shift to the right) when income increases.
3. (T/F) All markets have roughly the same number of buyers and sellers.
4. (T/F) Demand curves always have positive slopes reflecting the law of demand.
5. Which of the following is *not* a determinant of demand for orange juice?
   a. consumer after-tax income
   b. price of tomato juice
   c. medical research on the benefits of orange juice
   d. agricultural subsides (government payments) to farmers to grow more oranges
6. Which of the following will cause an increase in the demand for steel?
   a. Price of automobile tires increases because of a shortage of rubber from Malaysia.
   b. Concrete steel reinforcing rods are replaced by aluminum to reduce rust along the Atlantic seaboard.
   c. Gasoline prices are reduced by 50% because OPEC countries (the Middle East oil cartel) break into a quarrel and all countries expand production.
   d. McDonald's increases its production of hamburgers and fries to meet demand when a medical study concludes that fries are healthy alternatives to vegetables.
7. Which of the following is *not* a determinant of demand for MP3 players?
   a. the price of television sets
   b. consumer income
   c. the quality of music available in MP3 format
   d. the quantity of music available in MP3 format
8. An increase in demand means that
   a. the demand curve shifts upward and to the left.
   b. the demand curve shifts downward and to the right.
   c. more goods are purchased at the same price.
   d. fewer sellers are willing to sell the good.

9. The essence of a sale is (see Figure 4)
    a. reducing price to increase the quantity demanded.
    b. an attempt by sellers to increase consumer satis-faction.
    c. a movement from point *a* to point *c* in the figure.
    d. a shift in the demand curve from D_0 to D_1 in the figure.

10. A decrease in quantity demanded in Figure 4 can be characterized by
    a. a shift in the demand curve from D_0 to D_1.
    b. a movement from point *a* to point *c*.
    c. a shift in the demand curve from D_0 to D_2.
    d. a movement from point *b* to point *a*.

Score: ____

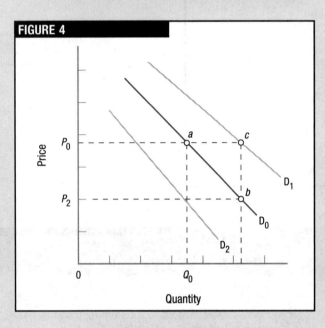

FIGURE 4

If You Got 9 or 10 Correct

You have the concepts of demand, changes in demand, and changes in quantity demanded under control. Keep in mind that a change in one or more of the determinants of demand *shifts* the demand curve and is a *change in demand*, while a *change in quantity demanded* is caused by a change in the price of the product and is a movement *along* an existing demand curve. Go on to the next section, Supply.

If You Didn't Get at Least 9 Correct

Keep in mind that it may take more than a cursory reading of the text to capture these concepts. To be able to use the analysis presented, it may take some time and effort. But given the importance of demand and supply analysis to the study of economics, give it a little more time than usual. Take a moment and go back and review the section on demand.

Keep in Mind

■ Demand refers to
  ☐ the amount of a product . . .
  ☐ that people are willing and able to buy . . .
  ☐ at various prices . . .
  ☐ over some time period . . .
  ☐ holding all other relevant factors constant.
■ The other relevant factors are the determinants of demand:
  ☐ tastes and preferences
  ☐ income

- prices of substitutes and complements
- number of buyers in the market
- expectations of future prices, income, and product availability
- When a determinant changes, the demand curve shifts.
- A change in one or more of the determinants *shifts* the demand curve and is a *change in demand*, while a *change in quantity demanded* is caused by a change in the product's *price* and is a movement *along* an existing demand curve.

Now that you have reread the section, take a crack at the problem below. Once you have answered the questions yourself, follow along as the solution to the problem takes you through getting from individual demands to a market demand curve. ∎

Solved Problem: Market Demands from Individual Demands

Use the table below, assuming the market consists only of the three people given. First, fill in the table by determining the market demand curve. Next, use the grid to construct the individual demand curves. Finally,

Quantity Demanded						
Price	Lisa	Mildred	Nan	Market	50%	200%
$100	0	1	1	_____	_____	_____
80	1	2	3	_____	_____	_____
60	2	3	5	_____	_____	_____
40	3	4	7	_____	_____	_____
20	4	5	9	_____	_____	_____

construct the market demand curve. Now assume some event reduces the market demand by one-half (50%). Complete the table and show the new demand curve on the graph. Next, assume that just the opposite occurs and the market doubles (200%). Again, complete the table and show the new market demand on the graph.

Solution-Discussion

The market demand curve is the horizontal summation of individual demands. When the price is $100, adding up the quantities demanded by each of the three individuals gives 2 (Mildred and Nan each are willing and able to buy one apiece, and Lisa wants none). When the price is $60, Lisa buys 2 (point *a*); Mildred, 3 (point *b*); and Nan, 5 (point *c*). Adding all three quantities demanded equals 10 (point *d*) on the market demand curve. Doing the same for all five prices yields the market demand as shown. All four curves are plotted in Figure 5. Next, when demand drops by 50%, it equals half of the total of the original market demand, which in this instance is just equal to Nan's demand. When demand doubles (200%), all values double; demand shifts outward by twice the original demand curve and is shown as $D_{200\%}$.

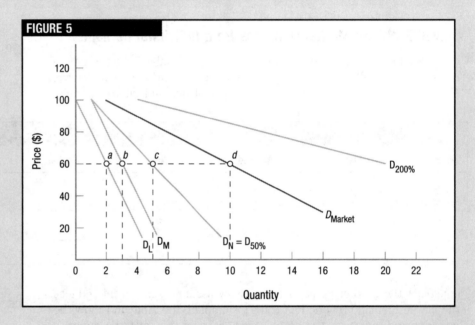

FIGURE 5

Quantity Demanded						
Price	Lisa	Mildred	Nan	Market	50%	200%
$100	0	1	1	2	1	4
80	1	2	3	6	3	12
60	2	3	5	10	5	20
40	3	4	7	14	7	28
20	4	5	9	18	9	36

Ideally, you now see the logic behind demand. If you are not comfortable with this section on demand, reread the Frequently Asked Questions, then retake the quick quiz above. Because the supply section is quite similar in structure to demand, you will in all likelihood begin to see the pattern. Good luck with supply.

Supply

Frequently Asked Questions

Q: **What is supply, and how are price and quantity supplied related?**

A: *Supply* represents the quantity of a product producers are willing and able to put on the market at various prices, when all other relevant factors are held constant. The *law of supply* reflects the positive relationship between price and quantity supplied: As the supply curve in Figure 6 shows, the higher the market price, the more goods supplied, and vice versa. *Market supply*, as with market demand, is arrived at by horizontally summing the individual supplies of all firms.

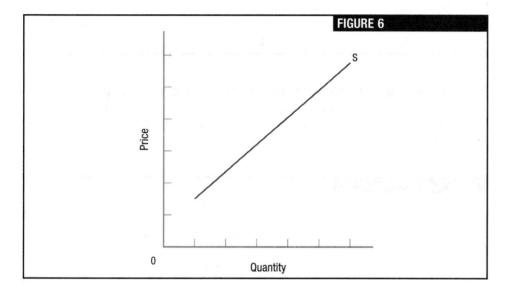

FIGURE 6

Q: **What are the determinants of supply?**

A: The *determinants of supply* are the following:
- production technology
- the cost of resource inputs
- prices of other commodities
- expectations
- number of sellers or producers in the market
- taxes and subsidies

Q: **How is a change in supply defined?**

A: A *change in supply* results when one or more of the determinants of supply change. A shift to the right, as shown in Figure 7 on the next page, reflects an increase in supply (from S_0 to S_1), whereas a shift to the left (from S_0 to S_2) represents a decrease in supply.

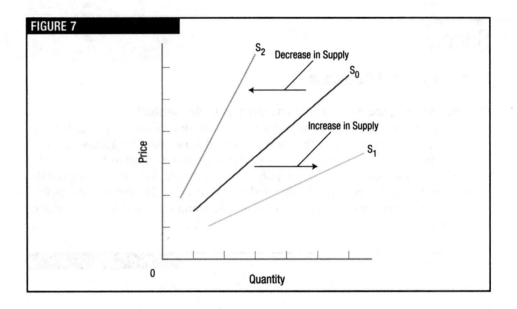

FIGURE 7

Q: How does a change in quantity supplied differ from a change in supply?

A: A *change in quantity supplied* is only caused by a change in the *price* of the product; it is a movement along an existing supply curve. A reduction in price results in a reduction of quantity supplied. This is shown in Figure 8 as a

FIGURE 8

movement from point b to point a, on supply curve S_0. A price increase leads to an increase in quantity supplied. This is shown as the reverse movement from point a to point b.

Contrast this with the movement from point a to point c (an increase in supply) where much more is sold, even though the price is held to P_0.

Supply Quick Check

Circle the Correct Answer

1. (T/F) The law of supply states that higher prices will lead producers to offer less of their product for sale during a given period.
2. (T/F) A supply curve always slopes up and to the right to show that quantity supplied increases with price.
3. (T/F) If producers expect higher prices, that usually leads to an increase in supply.
4. Which of the following is *not* a determinant of supply?
   a. costs of resources
   b. consumer tastes and preferences
   c. production technology
   d. the number of sellers (producers) in the market
5. A decrease in supply will cause the supply curve to shift
   a. up and to the left.
   b. up and to the right.
   c. down and to the left.
   d. down and to the right.
6. When the price of a product increases from P_0 to P_1 in Figure 9,
   a. quantity supplied decreases from S_0 to S_2.
   b. quantity supplied increases from Q_0 to Q_1.
   c. supply decreases to S_2.
   d. supply increases to S_1.

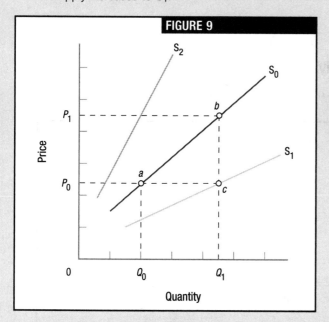

FIGURE 9

7. The prices of other commodities affect supply because
   a. producers will switch to produce a more profitable commodity.
   b. consumers will buy more of a cheaper commodity.
   c. consumers will switch to complementary goods.

d. producers will increase their price to keep pace with other commodities.

8. A change in supply of HDTV sets
   a. results from a change in consumer tastes and preferences.
   b. results from a price change.
   c. results in a change in the amount of HDTVs offered at every price.
   d. leads to a corresponding change in demand for HDTV sets.
   e. results from an improved picture aspect ratio.
9. Determinants of supply affect
   a. the entire supply curve.
   b. the quantity supplied only.
   c. the number of consumers who want the product.
   d. the quantity demanded.
10. Which of the following is correct concerning the market for baseball gloves shown in Figure 10?
    a. If glove manufacturers raise the price of their gloves from P_0 to P_1, quantity supplied decreases from S_0 to S_2.
    b. Excess livestock production leads to falling leather prices, so quantity supplied increases from Q_0 to Q_1.
    c. Excess livestock production leads to falling leather prices, resulting in supply decreasing to S_2.
    d. Excess livestock production leads to falling leather prices, so supply increases to S_1.

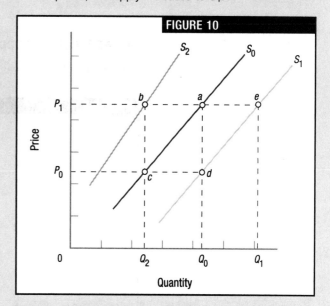

FIGURE 10

Score: ____

If You Got 9 or 10 Correct

You have mastered the concepts of supply, changes in supply, and changes in quantity supplied. You obviously noticed how closely the concepts of supply and demand structurally parallel each other. Keep in mind that a change in one or more of the determinants of supply *shifts* the supply curve and is a *change in supply*, while a *change in quantity supplied* is caused by a change in the product's price and is a movement *along* an existing supply curve. Go on to the next section, Market Equilibrium.

If You Didn't Get at Least 9 Correct

You probably didn't do well on the previous section either. Both demand and supply follow the same general principles for different sides of the market. Demand focuses on consumers' decisions and what they wish and are able and willing to purchase, while supply looks at business decisions to supply goods, but in a quite similar way.

Keep in Mind

Changes in demand and changes in supply are defined in a similar fashion: They are caused by a change in one (or more) of the determinants. Similarly, a change in quantity demanded or a change in quantity supplied are both caused by just a change in the price of that product. A change in quantity demanded or supplied means a movement from one point on the curve to another. In contrast, a change in demand or supply means that the market now faces an entirely new demand or supply curve.

Before you move on, work through the solved problem below. ■

Solved Problem: Supply

Use Figure 11 to answer the questions that follow.

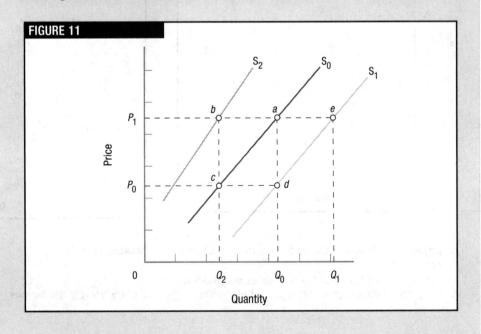

FIGURE 11

a. Assume the market is initially at point a on S_0. A decline in quantity supplied would be represented by what point? _____

b. If the market was initially at point a and production technology underwent substantial improvement, which curve would represent the resulting increase in supply? _____

c. Assume the market is initially at point d. An increase in quantity supplied would be represented by which point? _____

d. If supply is initially S_0, which curve represents a decline in supply?

_____

e. A move from point a to point c represents a _____.

f. A movement from point c to point b represents a _____.

Solution-Discussion

a. A decline in quantity supplied is a movement along an existing supply curve, so quantity supplied declines from point a to point c, and this is caused by a reduction in price from P_1 to P_0.

b. Supply curve S_1 would represent an improvement in technology increasing supplies to the market.

c. An increase in quantity supplied is caused by a change in price from point d to point e.

d. Supply curve S_2 represents a decrease in supply. Increases in input costs, for example, will shift the supply curve to the left.

e. A decrease in quantity supplied, because it is a movement along an existing supply curve.

f. A decrease in supply, since the curve has shifted to the left. Note that on supply curve S_2, less is provided to the market at each price.

Now that you have worked through this solved problem, see if you can complete the following exercise before you go on to the next section on market equilibrium. This short exercise asks you to create both demand and supply curves and explain some of their features.

Exercise for You to Complete

1. Using the blank grid on the next page, draw the axis lines and label the vertical axis "price" and the horizontal axis "quantity."

2. Draw a demand curve on this graph and label it D_0. Pick any point on the demand curve and label it point a. Pick another point on the demand curve with a lower price and label it point b.

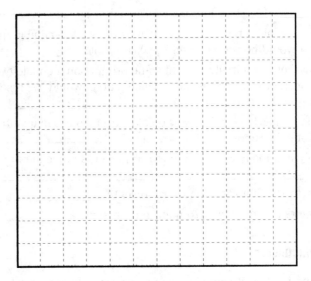

3. Explain how points *a* and *b* illustrate the law of demand. _____

_____

_____

4. When price rises from point *b* to point *a* and quantity demanded drops, economists refer to this as a(n) _____.

5. Recessions tend to put a damper on demand. Draw a new demand curve that represents a decrease in demand and label it D_1. How is this different from what you described in question 4?

_____

_____

6. Again, using the blank grid below, draw the axis lines and label the vertical axis "price" and the horizontal axis "quantity."

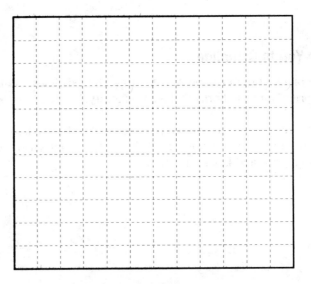

7. Draw a supply curve on this graph and label it S_0. Pick any point on the supply curve and label it point c. Pick another point on the supply curve with a higher price and label it point d.

8. Explain how points c and d illustrate the law of supply.

_____

_____

9. When price rises from point c to point d and quantity supplied grows, economists refer to this as a(n) _____.

10. When the cost of microcomputer chips falls, it increases supply. Draw a new supply curve in the graph reflecting this increase. How is this different from what you described in question 9?

_____

_____

Answers

(3) When the price of a product is reduced from point a to point b, quantity demanded increases. This is the law of demand. (4) Decrease in quantity demanded. (5) Shifting to a new curve is a decrease in demand: At all prices, consumers want to buy less of the product. (8) When the price of a product is increased from point c to point d, quantity supplied increases. This is the law of supply. (9) Increase in quantity supplied. (10) Shifting to a new curve (the supply curve shifts rightward) is an increase in supply: At all prices, firms are willing to provide more of the product to the market.

Keep in mind that supply and demand form the foundation of most of what you will study this semester. At this point, you may want to reread both of these sections in the text, then rework the previous two sections again. The next section on equilibrium brings the concepts of supply and demand together, and the level of complexity grows. Spend a little extra time here; it will pay dividends throughout the remainder of the course.

Market Equilibrium

Frequently Asked Questions

Q: What is market equilibrium?

A: Supply and demand together determine *market equilibrium*. Equilibrium occurs when quantity demanded and quantity supplied are equal. Equilibrium is shown in Figure 12 on the next page as point e. This means that producers offer for sale precisely the quantity that consumers are willing to purchase at that price. Equilibrium price, P_0, is that price where the market clears the equilibrium quantity of Q_0. If price temporarily gets above market equilibrium, inventories accumulate as consumers buy less than suppliers want to provide, so the market price drops to equilibrium. If price is temporarily below equilibrium, buyers want more than sellers are willing to sell, so prices begin rising toward equilibrium at point e.

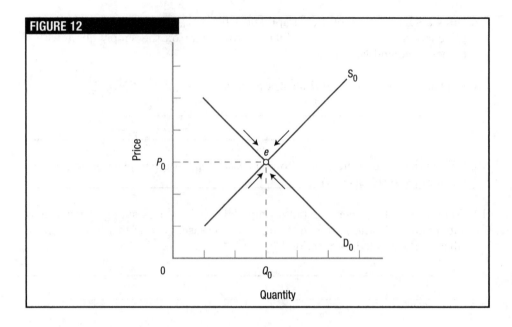

FIGURE 12

Q: When supply or demand change, what can be predicted?

A: When supply and demand change (a shift in the curves), equilibrium price and
output change. When only *one* curve shifts, both resulting changes in equilibrium price and quantity can be predicted. For example, in Figure 13, if demand
increases from D_0 to D_1, both equilibrium output and price will rise as equilibrium moves from point e to point c.

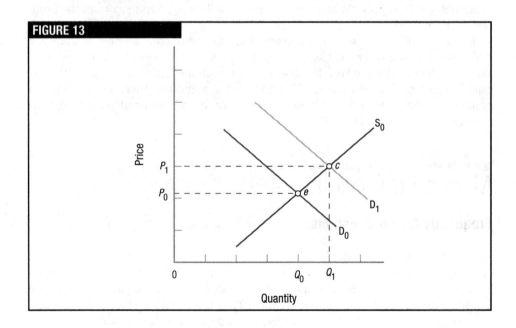

FIGURE 13

Q: When supply and demand both change, what can be predicted?

A: When *both* curves shift, the change in equilibrium price can be forecast in some
instances, and the change in equilibrium output in others, but in no case can
both be forecast without more information. For example, when demand rises
and supply falls, the equilibrium price will rise to P_2 (point b in Figure 14),
but the change in equilibrium output is uncertain. Whether output will rise or
fall depends on the relative size of the shifts between demand and supply.

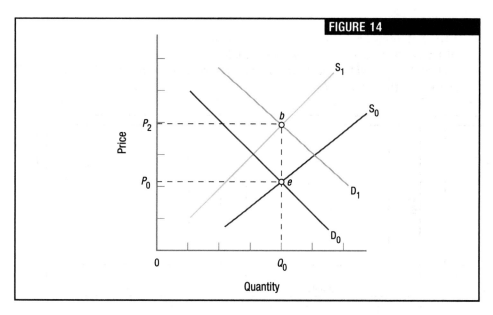

FIGURE 14

Alternatively, when demand rises and supply rises (people want more and more is available), equilibrium output will rise, but the change in equilibrium price is indeterminate without knowing about the relative size of the shifts between demand and supply.

Solved Problem: When Both Supply and Demand Curves Shift

1. Consider a scenario in which consumer demand for influenza vaccine increases because of a more severe than normal winter flu epidemic, while drug manufacturers are using new DNA techniques that permit them to produce vaccines more quickly and cheaply.

   Graph the three possible price and output scenarios for the flu vaccine market in the grids below.

   a. What will happen to the price of vaccines? (rise, fall, uncertain)

   _____

   b. What will happen to the output of vaccines? (rise, fall, uncertain)

   _____

2. Now consider what happens in the cellular phone market if cell phone use is shown to have serious detrimental health effects if used more than 10 minutes a day. At the same time, microchip production confronts the

end of Moore's Law (the speed of microchips doubles every 18 months at lower costs) and costs rise substantially.

Graph the three possible price and output scenarios for the cell phone market in the grids below.

  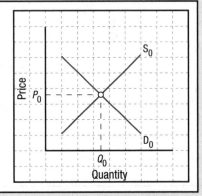

    a. What will happen to the price of cell phones? (rise, fall, uncertain)

           _____

    b. What will happen to the output of cell phones? (rise, fall, uncertain) _____

3. Now consider the market for Toyota's vehicles if China offers high prices for steel and absorbs most of the world's output for its own development efforts, increasing the price of steel. Toyota, however, develops a plug-in hybrid that averages over 100 miles per gallon, goes 100 miles on a charge, and sells for under $20,000.

Graph the three possible price and output scenarios for Toyota cars in the grids below.

    a. What will happen to the price of Toyota cars? (rise, fall, uncertain)

           _____

    b. What will happen to the output of Toyota cars? (rise, fall, uncertain) _____

4. Finally, let's look at the market for tape recorders and their decline in the digital age. However, costs to manufacture these devices have also fallen given changing production technology.

Graph the three possible price and output scenarios for the tape recorder market in the grids below.

a. What will happen to the price of tape recorders? (rise, fall, uncertain) _____

b. What will happen to the output of tape recorders? (rise, fall, uncertain) _____

Solution-Discussion

1. See Figure 15 below. In this situation both demand and supply increase and output will rise. What will happen to equilibrium price is uncertain. If demand and supply increase at the same rate, the price will remain the same (panel B). If the change in demand is larger than the change in supply, the price will rise (panel A), and the price will drop when supply increases more than demand (panel C).

FIGURE 15

2. See Figure 16 on the next page. In this situation both demand and supply for cell phones decline and output will fall. Again, what will happen to equilibrium price is uncertain. If demand and supply decline at the same rate, the price will remain the same (panel B). If the drop in demand is larger than the drop in supply, the price will fall (panel A), but if supply drops more than demand, price will rise (panel C).

FIGURE 16

3. See Figure 17 below. In this situation the supply of Toyotas declines because a input into production costs more, but the development of the plug-in hybrid results in an increase in demand. In this case, price will clearly rise, but what happens to equilibrium output is uncertain. If demand and supply change at the same rate, output will remain the same (panel B). If the increase in demand is larger than the drop in supply, output will rise (panel A), and if supply drops more than the increase in demand, output will fall (panel C).

FIGURE 17

4. See Figure 18. In this situation the supply of tape recorders increases due to technology, but the demand declines given the digital alternatives. In this case, price will fall, but again, what happens to equilibrium output is uncertain. If demand and supply change at the same rate, output will remain the same (panel B). If the drop in demand is larger than the increase in supply, output will fall (panel A), and if supply increases more than the decrease in demand, output will rise (panel C).

FIGURE 18

Panel A
Change in Demand > Change in Supply

Panel B
Change in Demand = Change in Supply

Panel C
Change in Demand < Change in Supply

Market Equilibrium Quick Check

Circle the Correct Answer

1. (T/F) Markets clear at the equilibrium price.
2. (T/F) A product's equilibrium price found where the demand curve intersects the supply curve.
3. At equilibrium
   a. producers store surpluses for times of shortage.
   b. producers offer the exact amount of a product consumers want.
   c. producers switch to substitution products.
   d. consumers switch to complementary products.

Use Figure 19 to answer questions 4, 5, and 6. For questions 4 and 5, begin each question with market supply and demand equal to S_0 and D_0, respectively, with the market in equilibrium at point e. If demand or supply changes, assume it shifts to either D_1 or S_1.

4. If supply decreases and demand increases, what is the new equilibrium output?
5. The economic boom of the late 1990s caused incomes to rise dramatically in California. Assume the figure represents the housing market in San Jose, California. What is the new equilibrium price for housing?
6. (T/F) The movement from point a to point c in the figure is caused by an increase in both demand and supply.
7. Which of the following is *not* how markets adjust to shocks and disturbances?
   a. almost instantaneously
   b. after a period of adjustment
   c. only with government intervention
   d. differently

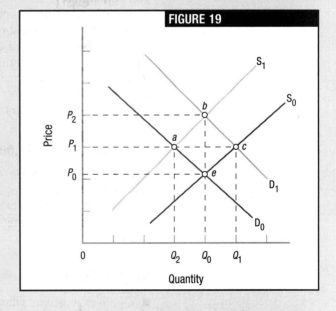

FIGURE 19

Use Figure 20 on the next page to answer questions 8, 9, and 10. For questions 8 and 9, begin each question with market supply and demand equal to S_0 and D_0, respectively, with the market in equilibrium at point e.

8. If supply increases and demand decreases, what is the new equilibrium price? _____
9. Nextel walkie-talkies are shown to increase worker productivity in auto glass delivery. This reduces costs to auto glass repair shops. Assume the figure represents the auto glass repair business. What is the impact on

FIGURE 20

equilibrium price for auto glass repairs? _____

_____

10. Describe what causes this market in the figure to move from point *a* to point *c*. _____

_____

Score: ____

If You Got 9 or 10 Correct

You seem to have the concepts of demand, supply, changes in supply and demand, and market equilibrium well in hand. Keep in mind that supply and demand together determine market equilibrium. If supply *or* demand change, you can predict the change in *both* price and quantity sold. If both of the supply *and* demand curves shift, *either* price or quantity sold can be predicted, but not both; one will be indeterminate without information on the relative size of the shifts between demand and supply. This is a little tricky, but you seem to have mastered it. Take a moment to review the section Hints, Tips, and Reminders.

If You Didn't Get at Least 9 Correct

Don't panic. This is some of the most difficult material in the chapter and the book. It often takes students several attempts at this material to really master it. But keep in mind that it is probably the most important material in the book. Five years from now when you are moving up in your career, this is one of the three to four things you will remember from this course.

Keep in Mind

- Equilibrium occurs where quantity supplied equals quantity demanded.
- When supply or demand (one or the other curve) shifts, you can determine the change in *both* price and quantity sold. The table below summarizes the predicted changes from an initial equilibrium when either the supply or demand curve shifts.

Change in Demand or Supply	Change in Price	Change in Quantity Sold
Demand increases	Increase	Increase
Demand decreases	Decrease	Decrease
Supply increases	Decrease	Increase
Supply decreases	Increase	Decrease

- When both curves shift, you can only predict the change in either price or quantity sold, but not both. The table below summarizes which variable (price or quantity sold) is predictable given that both curves have shifted.

Change in Demand	Change in Supply	Change in Price	Change in Quantity Sold
Increase	Increase	Indeterminate	Increase
Decrease	Decrease	Indeterminate	Decrease
Increase	Decrease	Increase	Indeterminate
Decrease	Increase	Decrease	Indeterminate

Before you move on, take some time to work through the solved problem below. Also, when you read the daily newspaper or the *Wall Street Journal*, look for articles where you can apply the concepts of supply and demand. You will find that there are several each week. This solved problem takes you through all that you have studied in this chapter. Pay particular attention to the description of the solution. ■

Solved Problem

The monthly supply and demand data for MP3 players is outlined in the table below.

Price	Quantity Demanded	Quantity Supplied	New Supply
$130	600	1,200	_____
120	700	1,100	_____
110	800	1,000	_____
100	900	900	_____
90	1,000	800	_____
80	1,100	700	_____
70	1,200	600	_____

Use the grid and data in the table to answer the following questions.

a. Graph the curves in the grid above. Label the curves S_0 and D_0.

b. Equilibrium price is equal to _____.

c. Equilibrium output is equal to _____.

d. Assume initially that the price of MP3 players was set at $120. Would there be a shortage or surplus in this market? _____ How large would the shortage or surplus be? _____

Describe the kind of pressures that would exist in this market to move the price toward equilibrium. _____

_____

e. Now, assume, as is so often the case in these types of markets, that technological improvements in electronics manufacturing mean that supply increases by 25%. List the new supply values for each price in the last column of the table. Plot the new supply curve and label it S_1.

f. What is the new equilibrium price? _____

g. What is the new equilibrium output? _____

Solution-Discussion

a.

FIGURE 21

b. $100. At $100, quantity supplied (900) is equal to quantity demanded (900).

c. 900

d. Surplus, 400. Excess inventories lead to sales and other actions that would reduce prices.

e. See Figure 21. At every price, quantity supplied has increased by 25% (see table below).

Price	Quantity Demanded	Quantity Supplied	New Supply
$130	600	1,200	1,500
120	700	1,100	1,375
110	800	1,000	1,250
100	900	900	1,125
90	1,000	800	1,000
80	1,100	700	875
70	1,200	600	750

f. $90

g. 1,000

As a final exercise, check to see what the new equilibrium price and output would be if demand now increased by 40%. This answer is that price rises to nearly $110, and output grows to around 1,200. Simple numerical problems like this provide the kind of insight you need when the questions get complicated. Always draw the original supply and demand curves and then work out the shifts (always the hard part), and the answers will be clear.

Price Ceilings and Price Floors

Frequently Asked Questions

Q: **When does government use price ceilings and price floors?**

A: When competitive markets are left to determine equilibrium price and output, they clear; that is, businesses provide consumers with the quantity of goods they want to purchase at the established prices. Nevertheless, the equilibrium price may not be what many people consider fair. The government may then use price ceilings or price floors to keep prices below or above the market equilibrium.

Q: **What are price ceilings, and what can happen with them?**

A: A price ceiling is the *maximum* legal price that can be charged for a product. Price ceilings set below market equilibrium result in shortages. In Figure 22, a price ceiling set at P_1 when the equilibrium price is P_e will result in shortage $Q_2 - Q_1$.

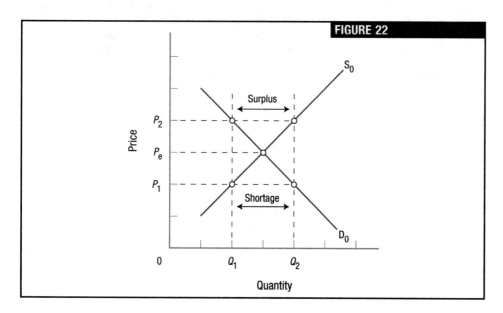

FIGURE 22

Q: **What are price floors, and what can happen with them?**

A: A price floor is the *minimum* legal price that can be charged for a product. Price floors set above market equilibrium result in surpluses. In Figure 22, a price floor set at P_2 when the equilibrium price is P_e will result in surplus $Q_2 - Q_1$.

Q: **Why do taxes cause a deadweight loss?**

A: Taxes drive a wedge between what consumers pay for a product and what business receives. They raise the price of products and reduce the quantity sold. The result is that some transactions that would have occurred in the absence of taxation do not, and this means that some consumer and producer surplus are lost to society.

Price Ceilings and Price Floors Quick Check

Circle the Correct Answer

1. (T/F) Governments use price ceilings or price floors when markets do not clear.
2. (T/F) When price ceilings are set above the equilibrium price, shortages occur.
3. (T/F) Governments will use price ceilings when markets do not work.
4. If the government sets a price floor above an equilibrium price, this means
   a. shortages will occur.
   b. surpluses will occur.
   c. nothing will happen.
   d. the market will quickly return to equilibrium.
5. If the government sets a price ceiling below an equilibrium price, this means
   a. shortages will occur.
   b. surpluses will occur.
   c. nothing will happen.
   d. the market will quickly return to equilibrium.
6. If the government sets a price floor below an equilibrium price, this means
   a. shortages will occur.
   b. surpluses will occur.
   c. nothing will happen.
   d. the market will quickly return to equilibrium.
7. New York City politicians believe that private parking rates in Manhattan are too high, so they institute price ceilings below the current price. What happens to private parking spaces?
   a. Shortages occur.
   b. Surpluses occur.
   c. Nothing.
   d. The market adjusts quickly back to equilibrium.
8. Hospital orderlies convince the local government that they are being paid poorly for the work they do. The government decides to set a minimum wage that all hospitals must pay. After much discussion, the minimum wage is set $2.00 below the current wage. What happens to the number of hospital orderlies?
   a. There are fewer orderlies than wanted by hospitals.
   b. There are more orderlies than wanted by hospitals.
   c. Nothing.
   d. Dislocation happens at first, and then the market returns to equilibrium.
9. Now consider that the government sets the minimum wage at $2.00 above the current wage. What happens?
   a. There are fewer orderlies than wanted by hospitals.
   b. There are more orderlies than wanted by hospitals.
   c. Nothing.
   d. Dislocation happens at first, and then the market returns to equilibrium.
10. Some consumers convince state politicians that electricity is priced too high. They claim that families are being hurt by greedy utilities. The politicians then set a price ceiling at the current equilibrium price. Suddenly, the weather turns brutally hot in June, and people run their air conditioners much more. What happens?
   a. There is a surplus of electricity because the greedy utilities provide more in the hopes of making money from the situation.
   b. There is a shortage of electricity because utilities cannot meet the increased demand because of the price ceiling. There may be brownouts.
   c. Equilibrium is maintained because increased demand is a signal for utilities to increase supply.
   d. There are shortages at first because the utilities face an information problem of figuring out what demand is going to be, but this is solved quickly.

Score: ____

Answers: 1. F; 2. F; 3. F; 4. b; 5. a; 6. c; 7. a; 8. c; 9. b; 10. b

If You Got 9 or 10 Correct

You picked up the concepts of price ceilings, price floors, and the impact of taxes on consumer and producer surplus and the resulting deadweight loss. Even so, you might find it useful to take a quick look at the section titled Hints, Tips, and Reminders.

If You Didn't Get at Least 9 Correct

You need to review this material slowly because the principles are straightforward:

- Start by looking again at Figure 22. Put your pencil above and then below the equilibrium price, and ask yourself what happens when the government institutes a price ceiling or a price floor. Remember that price ceilings are the highest price a firm can charge, and price floors are the lowest price a firm can charge or pay.
- Go back to the text and review the two Figures 13 and 14; they separate price ceilings from price floors. This may help you see why shortages and surpluses can result.

Key Point to Remember

Effective price ceilings and floors have an impact on markets. An effective price ceiling is the maximum price that can be charged, but if it is set below the equilibrium price, it will cause shortages. An effective price floor is the minimum price that can be charged or paid, but if it is set above equilibrium, it will cause surpluses.

Some of the questions in this section were a little difficult. Go back and reason out why you missed a question. Then take some time to work through the Hints, Tips, and Reminders section below. You will find some suggestions that will make studying this chapter easier. ■

Consider These Hints, Tips, and Reminders   STEP 4

1. Reminder: A change in one or more of the determinants of demand shifts the demand curve and is a change in demand, while a change in quantity demanded is caused by a change in the product's price and is a movement along an existing demand curve.

2. Reminder: A change in one or more of the determinants of supply shifts the supply curve and is a change in supply, while a change in quantity supplied is caused by a change in the product's price and is a movement along an existing supply curve.

3. Reminder: Supply and demand together determine market equilibrium. If supply or demand (one curve) changes (shifts), you can predict the change in both price and quantity sold. If both curves change (shift), either price or quantity sold can be predicted, not both; one variable will be indeterminate without more information on the relative size of the shifts between demand and supply.

4. The core graph on the next page shows market equilibrium along with a surplus and shortage. Shortages (surpluses) result when the price is temporarily below (above) equilibrium price.

5. One of the areas where students tend to falter is drawing graphs and working through changes in supply and demand in markets. One good approach to this issue is to always draw a graph when you are confronted with a question or

Core Graph: Market Equilibrium

Key Points

When price is temporarily *above* equilibrium, there is a surplus since quantity supplied exceeds quantity demanded.

When supply and demand intersect and quantity demanded equals quantity supplied, the market is in equilibrium.

When price is temporarily *below* equilibrium, there is a shortage since quantity demanded exceeds quantity supplied.

problem involving supply and demand. To begin your analysis, start with a graph like that for the video cell phone market shown here.

Use the subscript 0 for the original position. Begin with equilibrium labeled "e"; then ask "Is only price changing?" If so, you know that you are moving along an original supply or demand curve. If the answer is no, then ask "Do the facts of the question mean that a determinant is changing?" Note that the question could be such that nothing relevant is changing (this can be tricky). So, if a determinant is changing, is the impact on supply or demand? Figure out which, then shift the curve in the graph. Draw in the dot for the new equilibrium point, and make your conclusions. It may seem a little complex at first, but once you do it a few times, it will become commonplace.

6. To help you see the correct direction for shifts in supply and demand caused by changing determinants, exaggerate the change! For example, if you are looking at the demand for high-mileage hybrid cars, and gasoline prices rise, assume that gas prices jump by $5.00 a gallon. In this way it becomes obvious that demand for hybrid cars increases. By exaggerating the degree of change, the shift in the curve jumps out at you.

7. Here is another trap to avoid. When the price of a good rises (or falls), students (and commentators) often are heard to say that demand has fallen (risen) when they should be saying that quantity demanded has fallen (risen). The terminology is precise for a reason. Moving along an existing curve and selling more when price falls (a sale is in progress) is much different from selling more at the previous price because demand has risen (the entire demand curve shifts to the right). This also applies to supplies.

8. Here is one final trap to avoid. Supply and demand both increase when the curves shift to the right and decline when they shift to the left. Don't be tempted to think that an upward shift in the supply curve is an increase (as it is for demand) and that a shift downward in the supply curve is a decline (again this is true for demand). Thinking this way will lead to errors when you are faced with changes in the supply curve. Note that an upward shift in supply is a decrease in supply, and vice versa! Think of an increase as a shift to the right and a decrease as a shift to the left.

Do the Homework for Chapter 3
Supply and Demand

STEP 5

Instructor _____ Time _____ Student _____

Use the answer key below to record your answers to these homework questions.

1. _____   6. _____   11. _____   16. _____
2. _____   7. _____   12. _____   17. _____
3. _____   8. _____   13. _____   18. _____
4. _____   9. _____   14. _____   19. _____
5. _____   10. _____   15. _____   20. _____

Use these paragraphs and Figure HW-1 to answer question 1.

On December 8, 2007, *The Economist* reported that, adjusted for inflation, food prices had risen by 75% between 2005 and 2007. Without stopping, the prices of food and other commodities (oil, aluminum, steel, etc.) continued rising at a quicker pace for most of 2008. Much of these higher prices have been driven by growth and development of the emerging markets of India and China. Higher incomes result in changing diets and a higher demand for manufactured goods. Questions 1–6 explore many of the specific changes that took place in particular markets in the first half of 2008 and then the changes that the recession of 2008–2009 imposed on these same markets.

For example, worldwide, roughly 90% of rice grown is consumed in the home country. One exception is Australia, which exports most of the rice it grows. But the *New York Times,* April 17, 2008, reported that Australia has faced a serious drought since 2000.

Rice is a very water-intensive crop and the extended drought resulted in a reduction of rice exports from 1.7 million metric tons in 2000 to less than 100,000 metric tons in 2008. Most of Australia's rice lands have now been converted to wine grapes, requiring far less water.

1. Use Figure HW-1 to visualize the impact of these developments in Australia on both the rice and wine markets.

   What would you expect happened to
   I. the price of rice? ((a) rise, (b) fall, (c) no change)
   II. the price of wine? ((a) rise, (b) fall, (c) no change)
   III. the quantity of rice produced? ((a) rise, (b) fall, (c) no change)
   IV. the quantity of wine produced? ((a) rise, (b) fall, (c) no change)

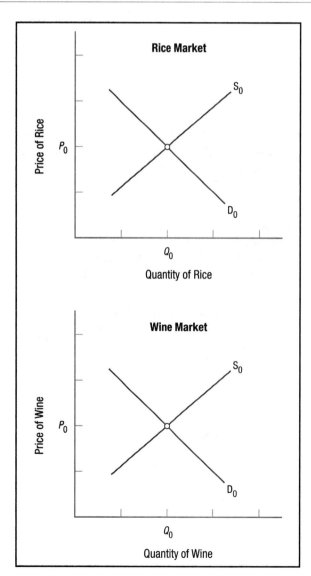

HW-1

2. Researchers are looking to genetically modify rice seeds so they bloom earlier in the day (to counter the effects of global warming) and do not need as much water. Assume these new varieties of rice are capable of producing current yields in adverse conditions. What will be the impact on
   I. the price of rice? ((a) rise, (b) fall, (c) no change)
   II. the price of wine grapes? ((a) rise, (b) fall, (c) no change)
   III. the quantity of rice produced? ((a) rise, (b) fall, (c) no change)
   IV. the quantity of wine grapes produced ((a) rise, (b) fall, (c) no change)

3. The drought in Australia is being felt across Europe. Europe has been "confronted by plummeting prices due to overproduction and competition from well-marketed and moderately priced New World wines," and prices have fallen by a quarter (*New York Times*, August 4, 2007).

Europe subsidizes wine production and this has contributed to the glut of grapes. Which of the following policy changes could help European wineries by reducing the amount of grapes and wine in the marketplace resulting in higher average prices for European wine? (Write down the letters of all that apply.)
a. Increase subsidies to wineries
b. Lower tariffs on imported wine
c. Increase excise taxes on European wine
d. Exempt European wines for VAT taxes (VAT taxes act like sales taxes)
e. Raise tariffs on Australian and American wines
f. Institute an advertising program that encourages Europeans to drink more domestically produced wine
g. Pay wineries to destroy grape vines
h. Institute an advertising campaign in the United States encouraging Americans to drink more French wine
i. Begin a grape ethanol program in Europe

Use this paragraph and Figure HW-2 to answer questions 4 and 5.

Congress passed an energy bill in 2005 and then updated it in 2007. The net effect was to heavily subsidize the building and expansion of corn-based ethanol plants and to mandate a rising percent of gasoline be composed of ethanol. Use Figure HW-2 to answer the following questions.

4. Assume these congressional changes result in a doubling of demand for corn in 2010. Assume initially that supply remains the same. What will be the new equilibrium price and output in the market?
   I. Price   II. Output

5. Given this new demand, farmers convert to genetically modified seed that triples output. What will be the new equilibrium price and output in this market?
   I. Price   II. Output

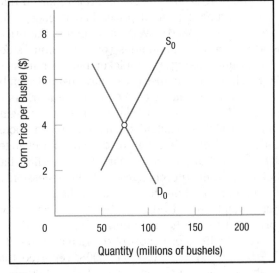

HW-2

---

6. The price of gasoline rose to $4 a gallon in the summer of 2008. What will be the impact on the following markets if the financial crisis of 2008–2009 and the worldwide recession lasts for two to three years?
   I. The price of gasoline ((a) rise, (b) fall, (c) no change)
   II. The number of new ethanol plants built ((a) rise, (b) fall, (c) no change)
   III. The price of farmland ((a) rise, (b) fall, (c) no change)

IV. The number of BMWs sold ((a) rise, (b) fall, (c) no change)

7. Market demand curves are
   a. the average demand faced by business.
   b. the horizontal sum of individual demand curves.
   c. not a very useful concept; individual demands are most important.
   d. easily estimated for nearly all products and services.

Use Figure HW-3 to answer questions 8 and 9.

8. Assume the market is initially at point c with Q_1 sold at a price of P_0. An increase in quantity demanded would be represented by which of the following?
   a. a movement to point a
   b. a shift in the demand curve to D_1
   c. a movement to point b
   d. a shift in the demand curve to D_2

9. Assume the market is initially at point c with Q_1 sold at a price of P_0. An increase in demand would be represented by which of the following?
   a. a movement from point a to point c
   b. a shift in the demand curve to D_1
   c. a movement to point b
   d. a shift in the demand curve to D_2

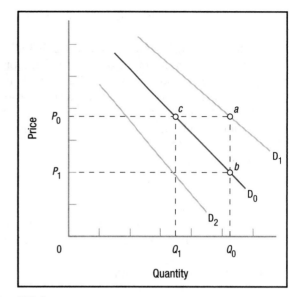

HW-3

10. The law of supply suggests that
    a. more will be demanded as the price falls.
    b. higher prices lead to greater quantity supplied.
    c. more advertising leads to consumers buying more.
    d. as prices rise, consumers find other (cheaper) products to buy.

Use Figure HW-4 to answer questions 11 and 12.

11. Assume the market is initially at point a. An increase in quantity supplied would be represented by a
    a. movement to point d.
    b. movement to point c.
    c. movement to point b.
    d. shift in the supply curve to S_2.

12. Assume the market is initially at point a. An increase in supply would be represented by a
    a. movement to point d.
    b. movement to point c.
    c. movement to point b.
    d. shift in the supply curve to S_2.

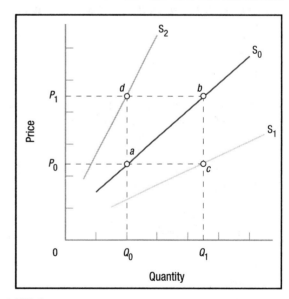

HW-4

13. Determinants of supply affect
    a. the quantity supplied.
    b. how much consumers demand.
    c. the entire supply curve.
    d. the quantity demanded.

14. A change in supply results from
    a. a change in one of the determinants of demand.
    b. a change in the price of the product.
    c. a shift in the demand curve.
    d. a change in one of the determinants of supply.

Use Figure HW-5 to answer questions 15 and 16.

15. Assume the market for cell phones is initially in equilibrium at point b with Q_0 units sold at a price of P_2. Now assume that the Surgeon General releases a report that says that extensive use of cellular phones has a negative impact on hearing. The new equilibrium
    a. will be at point e.
    b. will be at point c.
    c. will be at point a.
    d. will not change.

16. Assume the market for cell phones is initially in equilibrium at point c with Q_2 units sold at a price of P_1. Now assume that the industry develops a new method of producing phones that halves the cost. The new equilibrium
    a. will be at point e.
    b. will be at point b.
    c. will be at point a.
    d. will not change.

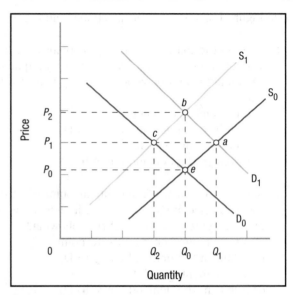

HW-5

Use Figure HW-6 to answer questions 17–20. In each case assume that the market begins in equilibrium at point e.

17. How much will consumers purchase if the government placed a price floor of $8 on this market?
    a. 300
    b. 200
    c. 400
    d. none

18. What will be the impact if the government places a price floor of $4 on this market?
    a. a shortage equal to 200
    b. no impact at all
    c. equilibrium price would fall to $4
    d. a surplus equal to 200

19. How much will consumers purchase if the government places a price ceiling of $6 on this market?
    a. 300
    b. 400
    c. 200
    d. none

20. What would be the impact if the government placed a price ceiling of $4 on this market?
    a. a shortage equal to 200
    b. no impact at all
    c. a shortage equal to 300
    d. a surplus equal to 200

HW-6

Use the ExamPrep to Get Ready for Exams   STEP 6

This sheet (front and back) is designed to help you prepare for your exams. The chapter has been boiled down to its key concepts. You are asked to answer questions, define terms, draw graphs, and, if you wish, add summaries of class notes.

Markets

Describe markets and their role:

Demand

Describe a demand curve:

Describe the law of demand:

Describe how we calculate market demand:

List the determinants of demand:

1. _____   2. _____
3. _____   4. _____

Define a change in quantity demanded:

Define a change in demand:

Now in Figure EP-1, draw a demand curve, show a change in quantity demanded, and show a change in demand.

EP-1

Supply

Describe a supply curve:

Describe the law of supply:

Describe how we calculate market supply:

List the determinants of supply:

1. _____   2. _____
3. _____   4. _____

Define a change in quantity supplied:

Define a change in supply:

Now in Figure EP-2, draw a supply curve, show a change in quantity supplied, and show a change in supply.

EP-2

Market Equilibrium

Define market equilibrium:

Show market equilibrium in Figure EP-3.

Now draw a shortage in the figure. What causes a shortage?

Now draw a surplus in the figure. What causes a surplus?

EP-3

Predicting a New Market Equilibrium

When Only One Curve Shifts

Complete Figures EP-4 and EP-5
and the tables below (indicate
whether equilibrium price and
output increase or decrease).
Start with an initial equilibrium
where D_0 and S_0 cross at point e.
In Figure EP-4 only shift demand,
and in Figure EP-5 only shift supply.

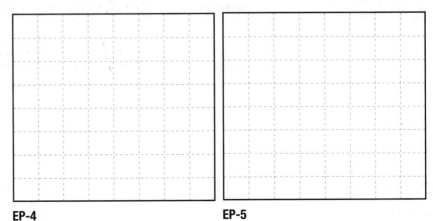

EP-4   EP-5

Only Demand Changes	Price	Quantity
Demand increases to D_1		
Demand decreases to D_2		

Only Supply Changes	Price	Quantity
Supply increases to S_1		
Supply decreases to S_2		

When Both Curves Shift

Complete Figures EP-6 and EP-7
and the tables below (indicate
whether equilibrium price and
output increase or decrease). Start
with an initial equilibrium where
D_0 and S_0 cross at point e. In
Figure EP-6, show supply increasing,
and have demand first increase and
then decrease. In Figure EP-7,
show supply decreasing, and have
demand first increase and then
decrease.

EP-6   EP-7

Supply Increases	Price	Quantity
Demand decreases to D_1		
Demand decreases to D_2		

Supply Decreases	Price	Quantity
Demand increases to D_1		
Demand decreases to D_2		

Price Ceilings and Price Floors

Use Figure EP-8 to describe price ceilings and floors. Begin with
initial supply and demand curves labeled S_0 and D_0.

Price Ceilings

Draw a price ceiling below equilibrium price. What are the implications
for the market?
List some examples of price ceilings:

Price Floors

Draw a price floor above the initial equilibrium price. What are the
implications for the market?
List some examples of price floors:

EP-8

Additional Study Help Chapterwide Practice Questions

Matching

Match the description with the corresponding term.

___ 1. Markets
___ 2. Demand
___ 3. Supply
___ 4. Substitutes
___ 5. Complements
___ 6. Equilibrium
___ 7. Shortage
___ 8. Surplus

a. The amount of output that businesses are willing to produce and offer at various prices.
b. A balance between supply and demand where producers make exactly the amount of product that consumers want to buy.
c. An excess of a product caused by supply exceeding demand.
d. Institutions that bring buyers and sellers together to make transactions.
e. The amounts of a good or service that consumers are willing and able to buy at various prices.
f. Products that are used together.
g. Too little of a product is available in the market at current prices.
h. A competing product that consumers will switch to if the price of the original product rises.

Fill-In

Circle the word(s) in parentheses that complete the sentence.

1. Markets are institutions that permit (buyers and sellers, government and consumers) _____ to transact with each other, and the market is often referred to as (capitalism, socialism, the price system) _____.

2. Demand refers to the goods and services that people (want, are willing and able) _____ to buy during some period of time. A negative relationship exists between price and (demand, quantity demanded) _____. This is known as the law of demand, which states that as price increases, (demand, quantity demanded) _____ falls, and vice versa.

3. Market demand curves are the (horizontal, vertical) _____ summation of individual demand curves. Market demands will change if one or more of the determinants change. These include tastes and preferences, income, (costs of resources, prices of related goods) _____, and expectations regarding future prices, income, the number of buyers and product availability.

4. When income rises and demand for a given product rises, that product is a(n) (normal, inferior) _____ good. But if demand declines when income grows, the product is a(n) (normal, inferior) _____ good.

5. Movies and sporting events are (substitute, complementary) _____ goods, while coffee and cinnamon rolls are (substitute, complementary) _____ goods.

6. A change in price will result in a change in (demand, quantity demanded) _____, while a change in income will cause a change in (demand, quantity demanded) _____. When Taco Bell drops the price of its burritos to 50 cents, the demand for McDonald's hamburgers will (rise, fall) _____ because these two products are generally considered (substitutes, complements) _____. But when McDonald's raises the price of its hamburgers by 50 cents, its sales will fall because demand (falls, rises, remains constant) _____.

7. The law of supply states that there is a (direct, inverse) _____ relationship between price and quantity supplied. A change in price will result in a change in (supply, quantity supplied) _____, while a change in resource costs will cause a change in (supply, quantity supplied) _____. When General Motors finds that the price of steel has risen by 10%, its supply curve for Chevy Trucks will (shift to the right, shift to the left, not change) _____.

8. Market equilibrium results when quantity supplied equals quantity demanded. If price is set temporarily above equilibrium, a (surplus, shortage) _____ results, but if the price is set below equilibrium, a (surplus, shortage) _____ results.

9. When either the supply or demand curve shifts (one curve only), you are able to predict the new (price, quantity sold, both price and quantity sold) _____. If demand increases, equilibrium price will (rise, fall) _____, and equilibrium output will (rise, fall) _____. If supply increases, equilibrium price will (rise, fall)

_____, and equilibrium output will (rise, fall) _____.

10. When both the supply and demand curves shift, you are able to predict the new (price, quantity sold, either price or quantity sold but not both) _____. If demand increases and supply falls, equilibrium price will (rise, fall, be indeterminate) _____, and equilibrium output will (rise, fall, be indeterminate) _____. If both supply and demand increase, equilibrium price will (rise, fall, be indeterminate) _____, and equilibrium output will (rise, fall, be indeterminate) _____.

True-False

Circle the correct answer.

T / F   1. All markets offer a wide variety of products for sale.

T / F   2. You can only buy products in markets. Services are traded through a different mechanism.

T / F   3. The most basic component of markets is transactions.

T / F   4. According to the law of demand, quantity demanded is inversely related to price changes.

T / F   5. A demand curve always slopes up and to the right to show that quantity demanded increases with price.

T / F   6. When prices rise, demand decreases.

T / F   7. Demand refers to the goods and services people are willing and able to buy during a certain period of time.

T / F   8. According to the law of demand, all other factors held constant, as price increases, quantity demanded falls.

T / F   9. A supply curve shows the maximum amount of a good or service that businesses will offer at various prices.

T / F   10. If producers expect higher prices, that *usually* leads to an increase in supply.

T / F   11. A change in product price leads to a change in supply.

T / F   12. Signing a new union contract with substantial increases in wages and benefits typically will result in an increase in supply.

T / F   13. An improvement in technology only results in an increase in quantity supplied.

T / F   14. A product's equilibrium price is fully determined by the demand for that product.

T / F   15. A cleared market is a market in equilibrium.

T / F   16. The equilibrium price is also called the market clearing price.

T / F   17. All other relevant factors held constant, an increase in supply will lead to an increase in output and a decrease in price.

T / F   18. All other relevant factors held constant, if supply and demand both rise, price will necessarily rise.

T / F   19. If both the supply curve and the demand curve for a product change, you can't calculate either the new price or the new quantity produced.

T / F   20. When supply and demand move in opposite directions, it is easy to predict a change in output.

T / F   21. To be effective, a price floor must be set below the equilibrium price.

T / F   22. Price ceilings typically give rise to product shortages.

T / F   23. Price ceilings and floors are meant to achieve socially beneficial results, but they often have unintended detrimental consequences.

T / F   24. A raise in the minimum wage typically reduces unemployment among lower-skilled workers.

Multiple Choice

Circle the correct answer.

1. All markets
   a. offer the same basics products.
   b. bring buyers and sellers together to transact business.
   c. are the same size.
   d. offer either products or services, but not both.

2. How do markets best help buyers and sellers to communicate?
   a. by providing a place for buyers and sellers to interact online
   b. by providing information about the quality and quantity of government goods and services
   c. through price
   d. by providing technology for communication

3. Quantity demanded changes as a result of a change in
   a. demand.
   b. supply.
   c. product quality.
   d. product price.

4. The law of demand states that
   a. quantity demanded rises as price falls.
   b. quantity demanded rises as price rises.
   c. demand rises as price rises.
   d. demand falls as price falls.

5. A demand curve always slopes
   a. up and to the right.
   b. down and to the right.
   c. consistent with the corresponding supply curve.
   d. parallel to the corresponding supply curve.

6. Which of the following is a determinant of demand?
   a. production technology
   b. resource input cost
   c. income
   d. number of sellers

7. Substitute goods are
   a. goods that are consumed together.
   b. goods whose quantity demanded does not fluctuate with price changes.
   c. related goods that consumers will turn to when prices rise.
   d. related goods that consumers will turn to when prices fall.

8. An increase in the number of buyers
   a. decreases demand.
   b. increases demand.
   c. decreases quantity demanded.
   d. increases quantity demanded.

9. Market demand curves are
   a. the horizontal sum of individual demand curves.
   b. the vertical sum of individual demand curves.
   c. the statistical average of individual demand curves.
   d. a graph of business demand for resources and employees.

10. An increase in demand means
    a. consumers will pay the same price for more output.
    b. consumers will buy more output at every price.
    c. consumers will only buy more output at the current price.
    d. consumers will only pay more for the current output.

11. Change in quantity demanded is caused by
    a. a change in consumer tastes.
    b. an increase in buyers.
    c. a change in income levels.
    d. a change in price.

12. Which statement best describes the law of demand?
    a. The higher the price of the product, the more of the product is likely to be produced.
    b. The lower a product's price, the more of that product consumers will purchase during a given time period.
    c. The greater the need, the greater the demand.
    d. Demand is related to many different factors.

13. Use Figure MC-1 to answer the questions that follow.

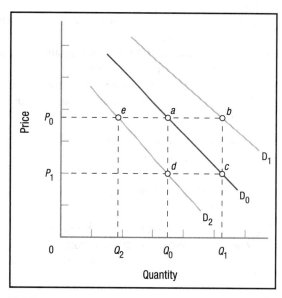

MC-1

a. Assume the market is initially at point a on D_0. An increase in quantity demanded would be represented by what point? _____
b. If the market was initially at point a and consumer income increased, an increase in demand would be represented by _____.
c. Assume the market is initially at point d. A decrease in quantity demanded would be represented by which point? _____
d. If demand is initially D_0, which curve represents a decline in demand? _____
e. A movement from point a to point d represents a(n) _____.

f. A movement from point *c* to point *b* represents a(n) _____ .

14. Supply is
    a. dependent on consumer demand.
    b. the minimum amount of output producers will offer at a given price.
    c. the maximum amount of output producers will offer at various prices.
    d. an unimportant aspect of markets.

15. When the price of a product increases,
    a. quantity supplied decreases.
    b. quantity supplied increases.
    c. supply decreases.
    d. supply increases.

16. The idea that higher prices will lead to higher quantity supplied is part of
    a. the law of quantity supplied.
    b. the law of quantity demanded.
    c. the law of demand.
    d. the law of supply.

17. A supply curve shows
    a. the minimum amount of output businesses will make at various prices.
    b. the maximum amount of output businesses will offer for sale at various prices.
    c. the value consumers place on a good or service.
    d. the cost of the inputs required to sell a good or service.

18. Determinants of supply affect
    a. the entire supply curve.
    b. the quantity supplied.
    c. the number of consumers.
    d. the quantity demanded.

19. Improvements in production technology
    a. generally increase production cost.
    b. often allow for the creation of new products.
    c. have no effect on supply.
    d. generally decrease demand.

20. The prices of other commodities affect supply because
    a. when possible, producers will switch to produce a more profitable commodity.
    b. consumers will buy more of a cheaper commodity.
    c. consumers will switch to complementary goods.
    d. producers will increase their price to keep pace with other commodities.

21. An increase in the number of sellers of a product
    a. increases product price.
    b. has no long-term effect on supply.
    c. increases supply.
    d. decreases supply.

22. A change in supply
    a. results from a change of one of the determinants of demand.
    b. results in a price change.
    c. results in a change in the amount of product offered at every price level.
    d. leads to a corresponding change in demand.

23. A change in the price of a product causes a change in
    a. quantity supplied.
    b. supply.
    c. input cost.
    d. expectations.

24. When a market clears,
    a. producers bring more of a product to market than consumers are willing to purchase at the market price.
    b. producers bring less of a product to market than consumers would be willing to purchase at the market price.
    c. producers bring precisely the amount of a product to market that consumers wish to purchase at the market price.
    d. the price of a particular good is higher than the market will bear.

25. If there is a *surplus* of sports cars on the market, which of the following statements will *not* be true?
    a. Producer inventories of sports cars are rising.
    b. The market price of sports cars lies below their equilibrium price.
    c. Producers are bringing more sports cars to market than consumers are willing to purchase at the market price.
    d. The market price of sport cars exceeds their equilibrium price.

26. When the real estate market is in a "seller's market," which of the following can occur?
    a. Homebuyers can expect to find a wide selection of relatively inexpensive homes.
    b. There is a surplus of homes on the market.
    c. All real estate transactions take place in realtors' offices.
    d. There is a shortage of homes on the market.

27. All other relevant factors held constant, if there is a decrease in demand,
    a. price and output will drop.
    b. price will drop, but output will rise.
    c. price and output will rise.
    d. price will rise, but output will drop.

28. All other relevant factors held constant, if supply and demand both decrease,
    a. output will rise, but price will fall.
    b. output will fall, with the effect on price being indeterminate.

c. output will rise, with the effect on price being indeterminate.

d. price will rise, with the effect on output being indeterminate.

29. At equilibrium,
    a. producers store surpluses for times of shortage.
    b. producers offer the exact amount of a product consumers want.
    c. producers switch to substitution products.
    d. consumers switch to complementary products.

30. All markets respond to disturbances in equilibrium
    a. instantly.
    b. after a long period of adjustment.
    c. only when government intervenes.
    d. differently.

31. A cleared market is one that
    a. has a surplus.
    b. has a shortage.
    c. has an artificial price limit.
    d. is in equilibrium.

32. The market response to a surplus is
    a. increased demand.
    b. decreased demand.
    c. increased prices.
    d. decreased prices.

33. Equilibrium prices are
    a. *not* determined by the forces of supply and demand.
    b. easily determined by businesses.
    c. set by the government.
    d. the natural outcome of market forces.

34. If demand increases,
    a. equilibrium price and output increase.
    b. equilibrium price and output decrease.
    c. equilibrium price increases, and output decreases.
    d. equilibrium price decreases, and output increases.

35. Which of the following is an example of a price ceiling?
    a. the minimum wage
    b. agricultural price supports
    c. rent controls
    d. unemployment insurance

36. Which of the following is an example of a price floor?
    a. rent controls
    b. caps on the Medicare payments made to doctors and hospitals
    c. a private company running a sale on its products
    d. agricultural price supports

37. A price ceiling set above a product's equilibrium price will generally result in
    a. a product shortage.
    b. a product surplus.

c. the product being sold at its equilibrium price and clearing the market.

d. none of the above.

38. A price floor set above a product's equilibrium price will generally result in
    a. a product shortage.
    b. a product surplus.
    c. the product being sold at its equilibrium price and clearing the market.
    d. none of the above.

39. A price ceiling set below a product's equilibrium price will generally result in
    a. a product shortage.
    b. a product surplus.
    c. the product being sold at its equilibrium price and clearing the market.
    d. none of the above.

Use Figure MC-2 to answer Questions 40–43. Equilibrium occurs at price P_e.

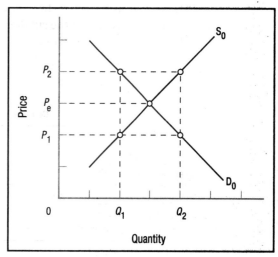

MC-2

40. What happens if the government sets a price ceiling at price P_2?
    a. Nothing.
    b. There will be a surplus of $Q_2 - Q_1$.
    c. There will be a shortage of $Q_2 - Q_1$.
    d. The market will settle back to equilibrium in a short period of time.

41. What happens if the government sets a price ceiling at price P_1?
    a. Nothing.
    b. There will be a surplus of $Q_2 - Q_1$.
    c. There will be a shortage of $Q_2 - Q_1$.
    d. The market will settle back to equilibrium in a short period of time.

42. What happens if the government sets a price floor at price P_2?
   a. Nothing.
   b. There will be a surplus of $Q_2 - Q_1$.
   c. There will be a shortage of $Q_2 - Q_1$.
   d. The market will settle back to equilibrium in a short period of time.

43. What happens if the government sets a price floor at price P_1?
   a. Nothing.
   b. There will be a surplus of $Q_2 - Q_1$.
   c. There will be a shortage of $Q_2 - Q_1$.
   d. The market will settle back to equilibrium in a short period of time.

1. What is the essence of markets?

2. Explain how the laws of demand and supply differ.

3. Prices of related goods or other commodities are determinants for both demand and supply. How do they differ?

Essay-Problem

Answer in the space provided.

Some of the questions below can be challenging. Don't get discouraged if your answers are not always the same as those we suggest. Use these sample answers as another way to assess your progress but, more important, to discover and learn some of the subtleties surrounding markets and supply and demand.

In the table below, use the spaces provided to answer whether, in the market specified, demand, supply, equilibrium quantity, and equilibrium price increases ($\uparrow$), decreases ($\downarrow$), remains the same (NC), or is indeterminate (?). In the Comment-Discussion column briefly state the reasons for your answer.

Market Changes	Demand	Supply	Equilibrium Quantity	Equilibrium Price	Comment-Discussion
4. Assume there is a freeze in Florida that ruins its orange crop this year. What happens in the market for tomato juice?					
5. gain, assume there is a freeze in Florida that ruins its orange crop this year. Now what happens in the market for orange juice?					
6. Again, assume there is a freeze in Florida that ruins its orange crop this year. In addition, an extended drought in California significantly reduces the tomato crop. Now what happens in the market for tomato juice?					
7. Hard bargaining by southern California grocery unions results in higher wages and expanded health benefits for all workers in all stores. What will be the impact on the grocery market?					
8. Growth hormones are scientifically shown to increase vigor and quality of life without significant side effects. Advances in chip design make manufacturing these hormones nearly costless. What happens in the market for mountain bikes?					

Market Changes	Demand	Supply	Equilibrium Quantity	Equilibrium Price	Comment-Discussion
9. Growth hormones are scientifically shown to increase vigor and quality of life without significant side effects. Advances in chip design make manufacturing these hormones nearly costless. What happens in the market for televisions?					
10. The Federal Reserve, becoming concerned with inflation, raises interest rates too high, accidentally driving the economy into a deep recession. At the same time, improved technology drives the costs of memory chips lower and lower. What happens in the MP3 player market?					

What's Next

You now have a good understanding of how markets work using supply and demand analysis. We have assumed throughout this chapter that markets have large numbers of buyers and sellers and are highly competitive. In addition, we assumed that both buyers and sellers had good information about prices and the products themselves.

In the next chapter, we look at some of the imperfections in markets and how our competitive market supply and demand analysis must be adjusted to account for these problems. For example, sometimes sellers have better information than buyers (used cars), and they use this knowledge to gain an edge on buyers. These issues do not, however, negate the usefulness of the analysis. Just be aware that the conclusions may have to be modified.

Answers to Chapterwide Practice Questions

Matching

1. d	3. a	5. f	7. g
2. e	4. h	6. b	8. c

Fill-In

1. buyers and sellers, the price system
2. are willing and able, quantity demanded, quantity demanded
3. horizontal, prices of related goods
4. normal, inferior
5. substitute, complementary
6. quantity demanded, demand, fall, substitutes, remains constant
7. direct, quantity supplied, supply, shift to the left
8. surplus, shortage
9. both price and quantity sold, rise, rise, fall, rise
10. either price or quantity sold but not both, rise, be indeterminate, be indeterminate, rise

True-False

1. F	7. T	13. F	19. F
2. F	8. T	14. F	20. F
3. T	9. T	15. T	21. F
4. T	10. T	16. T	22. T
5. F	11. F	17. T	23. T
6. F	12. F	18. F	24. F

Multiple Choice

1. b	13. b. D_1	20. a	33. d
2. c	13. c. e	21. c	34. a
3. d	13. d. D_2	22. c	35. c
4. a	13. e. decrease in	23. a	36. d
5. b	demand	24. c	37. c
6. c	13. f. increase in	25. b	38. b
7. c	demand	26. d	39. a
8. b	14. c	27. a	40. a
9. a	15. b	28. b	41. c
10. b	16. d	29. b	42. b
11. d	17. b	30. d	43. a
12. b	18. a	31. d	
13. a. c	19. b	32. d	

Essay-Problem

1. They bring buyers and sellers together.
2. Demand curves are negatively sloped while supply curves are positively sloped, and the two laws reflect these differences.
3. Price of related goods for demand refers to prices of substitutes or complements in consumption. The price of hamburger affects the demand for chicken. On the supply side, the prices of related commodities refer to substitutes in production. If firms can produce either of two commodities, and the market price of one rises, firms will produce more of that product and its supply will rise. This is an important distinction that you should analyze carefully when looking at changes to demand and supply caused by changes in determinants.

Market Changes	Demand	Supply	Equilibrium Quantity	Equilibrium Price	Comment-Discussion
4. Assume there is a freeze in Florida that ruins its orange crop this year. What happens in the market for tomato juice?	↑	NC	↑	↑	Demand for a substitute rises.
5. Again, assume there is a freeze in Florida that ruins its orange crop this year. Now what happens in the market for orange juice?	NC	↓	↓	↑	Supply of orange juice declines due to freeze.

Market Changes	Demand	Supply	Equilibrium Quantity	Equilibrium Price	Comment-Discussion
6. Again, assume there is a freeze in Florida that ruins its orange crop this year. In addition, an extended drought in California significantly reduces the tomato crop. Now what happens in the market for tomato juice?	↑	↓	?	↑	Demand for substitute rises (tomato juice), drought reduces the supply of tomato juice. Price rises, but impact on output sold is indeterminate.
7. Hard bargaining by southern California grocery unions results in higher wages and expanded health benefits for all workers in all stores. What will be the impact on the grocery market?	NC	↓	↓	↑	Input costs (labor) rise, so supply declines.
8. Growth hormones are scientifically shown to increase vigor and quality of life without significant side effects. Advances in chip design make manufacturing these hormones nearly costless. What happens in the market for mountain bikes?	↑	NC	↑	↑	More healthy people will engage in mountain biking.
9. Growth hormones are scientifically shown to increase vigor and quality of life without significant side effects. Advances in chip design make manufacturing these hormones nearly costless. What happens in the market for televisions?	NC	NC	NC	NC	No impact. Television demand is unaffected by health issues.
10. The Federal Reserve, becoming concerned with inflation, raises interest rates too high, accidentally driving the economy into a deep recession. At the same time, improved technology drives the costs of memory chips lower and lower. What happens in the MP3 player market?	↓	↑	?	↓	The recession lowers income and demand, while technology reduces cost, increasing supply.